Pharmaceutical Prices in the 21st Century

Zaheer-Ud-Din Babar
Editor

Pharmaceutical Prices in the 21st Century

Adis

Editor
Zaheer-Ud-Din Babar
Faculty of Medical and Health Sciences
University of Auckland
Auckland
New Zealand

ISBN 978-3-319-12168-0 ISBN 978-3-319-12169-7 (eBook)
DOI 10.1007/978-3-319-12169-7
Springer Cham Heidelberg New York Dordrecht London

Library of Congress Control Number: 2014958090

Printed on acid-free paper

Springer is part of Springer Science+Business Media (www.springer.com)

To my parents

Preface

Drug prices impact the population in general; however, the issues related to prices are changing fast in an economically diverse environment where the face of health is changing and technological development is exponential. In low- and middle-income countries, the price of medicine is the single most important factor determining availability and affordability. In high-income countries, where medicine reimbursement systems are often in place, the price may have less impact on affordability for consumers; however, drug prices are important for governments, for insurance companies, and for drug buying agencies.

This book provides a detailed account of international drug pricing issues through country level case studies from around the globe. Countries range from the United States (USA) to United Arab Emirates (UAE) and from European Union to Canada, Turkey, Ethiopia, India, Egypt, and China, to name a few. Coverage is diverse with a mix of high-, middle-, and low-income economies being represented. The book reports on countries with stable and supportive medicine reimbursement systems such as Australia, New Zealand, and Canada to countries that are much more market driven such as the USA and Malaysia.

In addition to a focus on global difference, this book also covers the range of medicine pricing mechanisms including policies based on cost-plus pricing, value-based pricing, pricing, and innovation in pharmaceutical industry and the countries where compulsory pharmacoeconomic analysis is used for drug reimbursement.

We expect this book to be well used and beneficial to a wide stakeholder group including funders and planners, policy makers, pharmaceutical industry, academic institutions, governments, and students of pharmacy, medicine, economics, public policy, public health, and law.

Auckland, New Zealand   Zaheer-Ud-Din Babar
October 2014

Contents

Chapter 1
Pharmaceutical Pricing Policies in Australia

Agnes Isabelle Vitry, Loc Thai, and Elizabeth E. Roughead

Abstract This chapter presents the health care system in Australia, the regulation and funding of medicines, the medicine supply chain, and the successive medicine pricing policies that have been implemented over the last two decades. We include an analysis of the impact of these policies on prices of pharmaceuticals in Australia compared to prices in other similar countries.

The Pharmaceutical Benefits Scheme (PBS) is the Australian public insurance program that provides subsidised prescription medicines to all Australian residents. The Scheme is also the process by which medicine prices are regulated. Reference pricing and value based pricing have been the cornerstones of the pricing of subsidised pharmaceuticals since the introduction of mandatory economic evaluation in 1993. In the 1990s, Australian medicine prices were found to be competitive compared to similar countries. Since 2000 there has been a change in the structure of the medicine market driven by a large increase in the number of generic medicines as a result of the end of patent protection of commonly used branded medicines. A number of pricing reforms were implemented successively in 2005, 2007, 2010 and 2014 with the objective to align PBS prices for generic medicines with pharmacy purchase prices. The price reforms included a series of mandatory price reductions and the introduction of price disclosure cycles, the latter which require manufacturers of generic medicines to provide information about their market prices to pharmacists so that PBS-listed medicines prices can be adjusted in line with the market price.

Overall, these policies have been effective in decreasing medicines prices and pharmaceutical expenditure. However, there are still higher prices of generic medicines compared to some countries such as New Zealand and the United Kingdom. The high prices for new medicines requested by the pharmaceutical industry may now represent the most pressing challenge faced by the Australian PBS and will require further development of pricing agreements.

A.I. Vitry (✉) • L. Thai • E.E. Roughead
Quality Use of Medicines and Pharmacy Research Centre, School of Pharmacy and Medical Sciences, University of South Australia, Adelaide, SA 5001, Australia
e-mail: agnes.vitry@unisa.edu.au; loc.thai@mymail.unisa.edu.au; Libby.Roughead@unisa.edu.au

Z.-U.-D. Babar (ed.), *Pharmaceutical Prices in the 21st Century*,
DOI 10.1007/978-3-319-12169-7_1

1.1 Introduction

This chapter presents the health care system in Australia, the regulation and funding of medicines, the medicine supply chain, and the successive medicine pricing policies that have been implemented over the last two decades. We include an analysis of the impact of these policies on prices of pharmaceuticals in Australia compared to prices in other similar countries.

1.2 The Australian Health Care System

Australia is the world's sixth largest country with a population in 2014 of 23 million. Most Australians enjoy high-quality health-care. In 2010, life expectancy at birth was 81.8 years, the fifth highest among countries of the Organisation for Economic Co-operation and Development (Organisation for Economic Co-operation and Development (OECD) 2013). However, the life expectancy for the Indigenous population (330,000 people) is around 10 years lower than non-Indigenous Australians (Australian Institute of Health and Welfare 2012).

The health-care system comprises a complex mix of public and private funding. Australia is a federation of six states and two territories. Constitutionally, health care is the responsibility of the states. However, much of the funding is supplied by the Commonwealth (federal) government. There is interdependence and overlap of health policy and health-care service responsibilities between the Commonwealth government and the states. State governments administer public hospitals, which comprise the largest single component of health care expenditure. But the majority of the funding for the public hospital system comes from the federal government through an agreement with each state and territory that stipulates provision to all Australians of 'timely access to quality health services based on their needs, not ability to pay, regardless of where they live in the country' (Council of Australian Governments 2012). State governments are also responsible for community and public health services. Doctors, pharmacists, dentists and other health professionals in private practice provide the vast bulk of medical and pharmacy services. There is also a private hospital sector comprising both for-profit or not-for-profit non-government organisations (Willis et al. 2012).

Total health spending in 2011–2012 accounted for 9.5 % of GDP, positioning Australia close to the median within the OECD group of countries. In 2011, Australia spent a similar proportion of GDP on health as Spain and the United Kingdom, a higher proportion than Sweden, Norway and Ireland, and a lower proportion than New Zealand, Canada and France (Australian Institute of Health and Welfare 2013). As typical for highly developed economies, health-care expenditure is predominantly public, accounting for more than two-thirds of total health spending (World Health Organization 2014). In Australia, the Commonwealth contributes about two-thirds of the public funding for health care, with other levels of government the remaining third. Slightly less than half of the population pay for some level of private health insurance, which also attracts subsidy by taxpayers. Private insurance schemes contribute about 8 % of funding for the health-care system, and various accident compensation schemes contribute another 5 % (Australian Institute of Health and Welfare 2013). Out-of-pocket expenditures accounted for 17 % of the total health expenditure (Australian Institute of Health and Welfare 2013).

Notwithstanding federalism, it is the Commonwealth government that sets the direction in most areas of health policy (Fenna 2012). The Commonwealth directly operates two national subsidy schemes under the umbrella of Medicare. The first, the Medicare Benefits Scheme (MBS) subsidises payments for services provided by private doctors, optometrists and, in some circumstances, other health professionals. The second national subsidy scheme under Medicare is the Pharmaceutical Benefits Scheme (PBS) (with the Repatriation Pharmaceutical Benefits Scheme (RPBS)) as further explained below.

1.3 Regulation and Funding of Medicines

The National Medicines Policy provides the overarching framework for the regulation and funding of medicines in Australia (Australian Government, Department of Health 2014d). The overall aim of the National Medicines Policy is to meet medication and related service needs so that optimal health outcomes and economic objectives are achieved. The National Medicines Policy has four central objectives: medicines meeting standards of safety, quality and efficacy, timely access to necessary medicines at a cost the Australian community and the individual can afford, quality use of medicines and the maintenance of a viable and responsible medicines industry. Australia has also developed a National Strategy for Quality Use of medicines with the objective to make the best possible use of medicines to improve health outcomes for all Australians (Australian Government, Department of Health 2014i).

Responsibility for most aspects of regulation in the pharmaceutical sector rests with the Commonwealth. The Therapeutic Goods Administration (TGA), an agency under the Department of Health, has responsibility for regulating the medicines that are marketed in Australia and has the remit to ensure acceptable quality, safety and efficacy of medicines (Australian Government, Department of Industry 2014). The Advisory Committee on Prescription Medicines assesses scientific data on the efficacy, safety and quality of new medicines or new indications. Where medicines meet the standards, they are then included in the Australian Register of Therapeutic Goods (Australian Government, Department of Health 2014b). The TGA licenses pharmaceutical manufacturers. All production processes must comply with the principles of Good Manufacturing Practice (Australian Government, Department of Health 2014a).

1.3.1 The Australian Pharmaceutical Benefits Scheme

The PBS is designed to provide timely and affordable access to necessary and lifesaving medicines at an affordable price that both the individual and community can afford. Medicine subsidisation first started in Australia with the establishment of the Repatriation Pharmaceutical Benefits Scheme in 1919, a scheme which provided pharmaceuticals free of charge to veterans. In 1944, the Pharmaceutical Benefits Act passed authorizing provision of pharmaceuticals free of charge to all residents of Australia. However, the scheme itself was not established until 1948, when a list of 139 life-saving and disease preventing drugs were provided free of charge. In 2012–2013, the PBS subsidised around 750 medicines available in more than 1,970 forms and marketed as more than 4,500 differently branded items (Australian Government, Department of Health and Ageing 2013a). In 2012–2013, 197 million prescriptions were subsidised under the PBS (Australian Government, Department of Health and Ageing 2013a). Prescriptions for PBS subsidised medicines can be written by medical practitioners and, with restricted formularies, by nurse practitioners, dentists, optometrists, and surgical podiatrists. Prescriptions for PBS subsidised medicines can only be dispensed by approved community pharmacies and hospitals. There is a specific formulary (section 100) for highly specialised drugs, with supply restricted to public and private hospitals. In the majority of states, PBS-listed medicines are funded for outpatients and for patients on discharge from hospital. Special arrangements also exist for indigenous groups (Australian Government, Department of Health 2014a), as well as palliative care patients (Australian Government, Department of Health 2014e) and funding of human growth hormone (Australian Government, Department of Health 2014f). There are non-PBS funding programs for Herceptin (trastuzumab) (Australian Government, Department of Health, Medicare 2014c) and life-saving drugs (Australian Government, Department of Health 2014c).

The centralised features of the program make it possible to generate detailed statistics on subsidised prescriptions. In 2012–2013, PBS government expenditure was \$9 billion[1] representing 83 % of the total cost of PBS prescriptions. The remaining cost is met by patient contributions (PBS Information Management Section and Pharmaceutical Policy Branch 2013). The majority of government expenditure on PBS prescriptions supports concessional cardholders (\$5.5 billion, 78.5 % of the total). Concession cardholders include aged and disability pensioners, unemployment and sickness beneficiaries and low income earners. There is less precise and reliable data on private and non-subsidised PBS prescriptions, including PBS items priced below the level of the co-payments. The collection of under co-payment prescription data started in April 2012 (Australian Government, Department of Health 2014j). During the first full financial year of the collection (July 2012 to June 2013), approximately 62 million under co-payment prescriptions representing 22.7 % of total PBS/RPBS prescriptions were processed.

[1] All prices are expressed in Australian dollars in this chapter.

1.3.2 Contribution of Patients

The cost to both general and concessional consumers of PBS-listed medicines is subsidised if prescribed for approved conditions and the product is priced above the level of the co-payment. In 2014 the general co-payment was $36.90 for general beneficiaries and $6.00 for concessional patients. Safety net thresholds provide protection against very high costs within a calendar year. The safety net thresholds apply at the family level, not the individual, and were $1,421.20 for general beneficiaries and $360 for concessional patients in 2014. Co-payments and safety net thresholds are adjusted annually in line with the consumer price index (Australian Government, Department of Health 2014). Once general patients reach the general safety net threshold, the patient contribution to the total cost of prescription medicines is at the level of the concessional co-payment. Once concession card holders reach the concessional safety net threshold, they receive all remaining prescriptions free of charge. Additionally, special patient contributions may apply when a manufacturer and the government cannot agree about the price of a product listed on the PBS. These result from the Brand Premium policy (extra payment paid for brands with higher prices than the lowest priced brand) and the Therapeutic Group Premium Policy (extra payment for brands of a medicine within a therapeutic group that attracts a therapeutic group premium) (Australian Government, Department of Health 2014b; Pharmaceutical Benefits Pricing Authority 2013).

1.3.3 Medicines Supply Chain

Patients have access to medicines through community pharmacies and hospitals, either as inpatients or outpatients. The medicines supply chain comprises three principal participants: manufacturers (originators and generics), wholesalers and pharmacists.

The Australian pharmaceutical industry comprises over 40 originator companies (mostly subsidiaries of multi-national companies), and around 10 generic companies (Medicines Australia 2010). Medicines Australia is the peak body for originator companies. The Generic Medicines Industry Association (GMiA) is the representative body of generic medicine suppliers.

Wholesalers are eligible to receive government funding from the Community Service Obligation (CSO) funding pool if they agree to comply with a number of service standards including the supply, when requested, of the full range of PBS medicines within 24 h. There are currently three national Community Service Obligation distributors (Australian Pharmaceutical Industries, Sigma and Symbion) and several state-based distributors.

1.3.3.1 Community Pharmacies

There are 5,350 community pharmacies across Australia. Pharmacy ownership is governed by state and territory legislation, which largely restricts community pharmacy ownership to registered pharmacists. The majority of community pharmacies in Australia are owned by pharmacists, with a small number being owned by not-for-profit entities. Location rules restrict the opening of a new pharmacy in areas of less than a 1.5 km radius from an existing pharmacy (Australian Government, Department of Health 2014g). The Pharmacy Guild of Australia represents the interests of the majority of community pharmacy owners. Of those community pharmacies owned by pharmacists, over three thousand are part of a banner group or franchise, whilst others not affiliated with any group are classified as independent pharmacies. Some of the banner groups operate as retail brands of the three major pharmaceutical wholesalers. The two largest banner groups are currently Priceline Pharmacies, which is a subsidiary of the API wholesaler, and Chemist Warehouse (Feros 2011). Most pharmacy income is derived from dispensing of PBS-subsidised medicines, with the remaining income derived from private prescriptions, sale of over-the-counter medicines and other retail goods such as beauty and health products (Beecroft 2007).

In addition to dispensing prescription medicines to patients, community pharmacies deliver a range of professional services including the provision of medicines information, clinical interventions, medication management services and preventative care services. Every 5 years, a Community Pharmacy Agreement (CPA) is negotiated and agreed between the Australian government and the Pharmacy Guild of Australia. The Fifth Community Pharmacy Agreement operates for the 5 year period between 1 July 2010 and 30 June 2015 (Commonwealth of Australia and Pharmacy Guild of Australia 2010; Pharmacy Guild of Australia 2014a). Originally these agreements addressed pharmacy remuneration and location rules but have expanded in scope to provide for more professional pharmacy services. The Fifth Community Pharmacy Agreement provides a total of $15.4 billion of funding over 5 years including $13.8 billion (90 %) for pharmacy remuneration (pharmacy fees, pharmacy and wholesale mark-up), $386 million for rural support programs, Aboriginal and Torres Strait Islander programs, medication management programs, $277 million for electronic reporting of controlled dugs, supply from medicines from a medication chart in residential aged care, continued dispensing of PBS medicines in defined circumstances, clinical interventions, and dose administration aids, and $949 million for the Community Service Obligation funding pool.

The dispensed price of each PBS medicine is made up of the ex-manufacturer price (i.e. an amount that recognises the cost of the medicine from the manufacturer), a wholesaler margin (i.e. a percentage or flat fee that recognises the wholesaler's role in storing and distributing medicines to pharmacy (currently 7.52 % wholesaler mark-up for drugs costing less than $1,000)), a pharmacy mark-up (i.e. a percentage or flat fee[2] that recognises the pharmacy's role in storing medicines and making them available for consumers); and a dispensing fee (i.e. a fee that recognises the pharmacist's professional role in dispensing medicines to consumers that are adjusted on 1 July each year in line with the Consumer Price Index ($6.76 dispensing fee September 2014)) (Australian Government et al. 2014d). Dispensing fees are adjusted on 1 July each year. Other pharmacy fees include the fee for extemporaneous preparation and fee for supply of dangerous drug. Almost all the prescription dispensing and payment processes are made in real-time using the electronic PBS online platform (Pharmacy Guild of Australia 2014b).

Medication management programs funded by under the Fifth Community Pharmacy Agreement include the Home Medicine Review program. Under this program medication reviews are conducted, in collaboration with a patient's general medical practitioner, by an accredited pharmacist in the patient's home. There is also the Residential Medication Management Program for medications reviews conducted for residents of aged care facilities, as well as MedsChecks and Diabetes Medschecks which are in-pharmacy medicine reviews.

The Aboriginal and Torres Strait Islander programs aim to improve access to quality, community pharmacy services by Aboriginal and Torres Strait Islander people by strengthening the Aboriginal and Torres Strait Islander pharmacy workforce, as well as providing allowances to approved pharmacies which deliver PBS medicines and quality use of medicines services to participating Aboriginal health services (Pharmacy Guild of Australia 2014a). Under the provisions of section 100 of the *National Health Act 1953*, clients of participating Aboriginal health services are able to receive medicines without the need for a normal PBS prescription form and without charge (Australian Government and Department of Health 2014a).

1.4 Listing and Pricing of Medicines on the PBS

Following marketing approval by the TGA, pharmaceutical companies apply for PBS listing, which is normally necessary for sales to be commercially viable. Since 2011, parallel TGA and PBAC processes have been introduced (The Commonwealth of Australia 2011). Applications for listing are evaluated by the Pharmaceutical Benefits Advisory Committee (PBAC), an independent expert body, and its sub-committees, for comparative efficacy, safety and cost-effectiveness. Where the application is judged to have met the criteria for listing, the PBAC makes a recommendation to the Minister for Health. The final decision to list new medicines on the PBS is made by the Minister for Health.

---

[2]
- For drugs between $0 and $30 the mark-up is 15 %.
- For drugs between $30 and $45 the mark-up is a flat fee of $4.50.
- For drugs between $45 and $180 the mark-up is 10 %.
- For drugs between $180 and $450 the mark-up is $18.
- For drugs between $450 and $1,750 the mark-up is 4 %.
- For drugs over $1,750 the flat fee is $70.00.

Since 1 March 1988, the PBAC has been required by law to take cost-effectiveness into account. Listing of new medicines may be recommended on the basis of cost-minimisation (reference pricing), where medicines are considered to be of similar safety and efficacy as existing listed medicines and so priced at the same price. New medicines may be also recommended if they offer an acceptable incremental cost effectiveness ratio (ICER) compared to existing therapy. There is no fixed ICER threshold, as factors other than the ICER are taken into account. However, it has been shown that medicines are unlikely to be listed when the ICER is above $75,000 per Quality-Adjusted Life Year (QALY) (Chim et al. 2010). The financial impact on the medicine budget has also shown to be an important determinant of PBAC listing decisions (Mauskopf et al. 2013). Medicines listed on the PBS can fall into three broad categories: 'unrestricted benefits' for medicines with no restrictions on therapeutic use, 'restricted benefits' for medicines that can only be prescribed for specific therapeutic uses, and 'authority required benefits' for medicines that require prior approval from the Department of Human Services. Prescribing restrictions may limit use to indications for which the medicine has been deemed effective or cost-effective and may include rules for initiation or continuation of treatment.

Until recently, a positive PBAC recommendation was followed by price negotiations with the supplier through the Pharmaceutical Benefits Pricing Authority (PBPA), an independent non-statutory body established in 1988, which included representatives from Medicines Australia and the Generic Medicines Industry Association. The PBPA considered a range of factors such as PBAC's comments on clinical and cost effectiveness of the medicine, the prices of alternative brands of the medicine, comparative prices of medicines in the same Anatomical Therapeutic Classification (ATC) Group, cost information, prescription volumes, economies of scale and other factors including expiry dates, storage requirements, product stability, special manufacturing requirements, and prices of medicines in comparable countries (Pharmaceutical Benefits Pricing Authority 2013).

The PBPA was terminated on 1 April 2014 and pricing negotiations were integrated into the PBAC evaluation process (Australian Government and Department of Health 2014k). The implications of this change are unclear at the time of writing. Although there is no capped budget for the PBS, any medicine the PBAC recommends for listing that is expected to cost more than $20 million per year in any of the first 4 years after listing must be approved by Cabinet (The Hon Peter Dutton MP 2013).

The Drug Utilisation Sub Committee (DUSC) of the PBAC assesses estimates of projected usage and financial cost for medicines (Australian Government and Health 2014a). It also collects and analyses data on actual use (including in comparison with different countries), and provides advice to PBAC. The PBAC also undertakes post-market reviews to assess medicines utilisation and strengthen medicine pricing management through better targeting of medicines and avoidance of preventable wastage or inappropriate prescribing (Australian Government, Department of Health 2014b). These reviews may result in changes to the prescribing rules or to medicine prices. For example, a review undertaken for the biological disease modifying antirheumatic drugs in 2009 resulted in a revision of the eligibility criteria and price reductions (Pharmaceutical Benefits Advisory Committee 2009). A review of the medicines for Alzheimer's disease in 2013 found that they were being used in a much broader population and for longer periods of time than originally agreed as cost-effective (Pharmaceutical Benefits Advisory Committee 2013a). It resulted in a termination of the continuation rules and a 40 % decrease in the medicine prices.

1.4.1 Reference Pricing and Value Based Pricing

Reference pricing and value based pricing have been the cornerstones of the Australian pricing policy since they were introduced in 1993. Reference pricing is used where medicines are considered to be of similar safety and efficacy for pricing purposes and are recommended by the PBAC based on a cost-minimisation assessment. Reference pricing of branded medicines resulted in highly competitive prices for medicines on the PBS in Australia at first. A study undertaken by the Australian Productivity Commission compared the prices for a basket of 150 widely used PBS medicines with seven other countries: Canada, France, Spain, Sweden, New Zealand, the United Kingdom (UK) and the United States of America (USA) in June 2000 (Australian Productivity Commission 2001). It showed that Australian medicine prices were between 51 and 61 % of the price paid by comparator countries, excluding New Zealand and Spain. The largest price differences were observed for 'me-too' pharmaceuticals and for generic pharmaceuticals. Prices for innovative medicines were similar to those in the other countries.

Since 2001, the prescription medicines market has changed due to a large increase in the number of generic medicines available as a result of expiry of patent protection for commonly used branded medicines. Several studies in the subsequent years showed prices of medicines in Australia were higher compared with similar countries as generics prices approximated those of the originator brands (Australian Government and Department of Health and Ageing 2005; Spinks and Richardson 2011). A study comparing the prices of nine medicines between Australia, the UK and New Zealand showed that all nine medicines on the PBS were more expensive than in both the UK and New Zealand (Australian Government, Department of Health and Ageing 2005). In August 2005, the government introduced a statutory 12.5 % price reduction when the first generic of a medicine was listed on the PBS (Australian Government and Department of Health and Ageing 2005). This policy led to decreases in the prices of generic medicines. However, generics prices still remained higher than in similar countries. A 2007 study comparing the prices of 34 medicines (including 11 generics) between Australia and New Zealand showed that the prices of ten medicines were more expensive in Australia than in New Zealand, a total cost difference which amounted to $460 million for the 2007 year (Spinks and Richardson 2011). Rather than competing on price to the government, generics suppliers engaged in competitive discounting of price, often

50 % or more, to pharmacists. This resulted in the government reimbursing pharmacists at prices well above the prices actually paid (Lofgren 2009; Bulfone 2009).

1.4.2 2007 PBS Reforms

In August 2007, major PBS reforms were undertaken by the government. The main objective of the reforms was to align government payments for generic medicines to pharmacy purchase prices. The 2007 PBS reforms package comprised a range of inter-connected measures including changes to the pricing of PBS listed medicines, and changes to the pharmacy and pharmaceutical wholesaler compensation arrangements (mostly increases to mark-up and dispensing fees and to the Community Service Obligation funding pool). In addition, a generic medicines awareness campaign was implemented. The new pricing policies consisted of three major components: the establishment of two formularies for PBS medicines, known as F1 and F2 formularies, statutory price reductions and the introduction of price disclosure.

Formulary one (F1) medicines are those for which only a single brand is listed, in most cases because of a patent. Formulary two (F2) contains multiple brand medicines and single brand medicines which are interchangeable with multiple brand medicines at the patient level. A transitional pricing arrangement applied to F2 listed medicines with two sub-formularies being created, F2A, containing all medicines that were not subject to high levels of discounting to pharmacies, and F2T, containing all the medicines which were subject to high levels of discounting to pharmacists. The F2A and F2T formularies were merged on 1 January 2011 to form the single F2 formulary (Australian Government, Department of Health and Ageing 2010). Different pricing mechanisms are applicable to each formulary. While value based pricing is used for setting prices for medicines in the F1 formulary, the prices for most medicines in the F2 formulary are based on market competition between multiple suppliers. The prices of F2 medicines were subjected to mandatory price reductions of 2 % per year for 3 years for F2A listed products and a one-off 25 % mandatory price reduction for F2T listed products followed by annual price reductions resulting from compulsory price disclosure from August 2007 for F2A listed medicines and January 2011 for F2T listed medicines. Medicines listed in F1 become F2 listed when a new brand of the same product is listed.

The price disclosure reforms required that manufacturers provide to the Department of Health information about the actual selling price (ex-manufacturer). Based upon this information, a weighted, one-year average, disclosed price (WADP) is calculated. The PBS price is then reduced to the level of the WADP if the current ex-manufacturer price is greater than 10 % of the WADP.

The preliminary impact of 2007 PBS reforms was assessed by the government in 2010 (Australian Government, Department of Health and Ageing 2010). Price reductions of 25 % for 450 PBS items on F2T and of 2 % for 449 PBS items on

F2A resulted in estimated savings of $274 million to the government in 2008–2009. Seven of a total of 38 drugs subjected to the first round of price disclosure reforms had price reductions ranging from 14.6 to 71.8 % (Australian Government, Department of Health and Ageing 2010). In recognition that these reforms would impact on community pharmacy profitability, the government also funded structural adjustment packages to community pharmacists and wholesalers. In the initial year, the costs of implementing the reforms were more costly than the savings, mostly because of the structural adjustment packages. However, savings in the longer term were anticipated (Australian Government, Department of Health and Ageing 2010).

1.4.3 2010 Memorandum of Understanding

In December 2010 the government introduced a second raft of reforms agreed to with Medicines Australia through a Memorandum of Understanding (Australian Government, Department of Health 2010). The first component was further price reductions in October 2010 for medicines listed on the F2 formulary (additional 2 % reduction for F2A medicines and 5 % reduction for F2T medicines). The second component was an increase in the price reductions from 12.5 to 16 % for first-time listed generic medicines from April 2011. The third component was an expansion of the price disclosure policy to encompass all F2 medicines with price disclosure cycles reduced from 24 to 18 months, known as Expanded and Accelerated Price Disclosure (EAPD).

As a result of the first EAPD cycle in April 2012, 237 PBS listed products across 75 molecules had their price reduced, with reductions ranging from 10 to 83 % (Australian Government and Department of Health and Ageing 2012b). The second EAPD cycle in April 2013 delivered price reductions ranging from 10 to 87 % for 62 molecules in total (Australian Government, Department of Health and Ageing 2013b).

Overall, the pricing reforms resulted in a $72.5 million, $301.8 million and $661.3 million in savings in PBS expenditure in 2010–2011, 2011–2012 and 2012–2013 respectively (Australian Government and Department of Health and Ageing 2011, 2012a, 2013a). Overall, 160 medicines had price reductions following price disclosures between April 2012 and August 2014 with an average price reduction of 42 % (range 10–98 %) (Medicines Australia 2014).

1.4.4 2014 Policy Changes

The latest development in pricing policy includes a Simplified Price Disclosure (SPD) policy that will be implemented from October 2014 (Australian Government, Department of Health 2014h). Simplified Price Disclosure streamlines price disclosure processes and allows PBS prices to be adjusted to market prices more quickly. Price disclosure cycles are reduced from 18 to 12 months and data collection is reduced from 12 to 6 months per cycle.

1.4.5 Generic Medicines Market

Increasing the utilisation of generic medicines has been shown to decrease total pharmaceutical expenditure (Godman et al. 2014). In Australia, the utilisation of generic medicines had been low compared to other European countries and the US (Simoens and De Coster 2006; Clarke and Fitzgerald 2010) but is rising rapidly. A number of policies have been developed to enhance generic utilisation in many countries, mainly through demand-side initiatives such as financial incentives for prescribers, pharmacists, and consumers, prescribing restrictions, prescribing targets or education. In Australia, there is a brand price premium policy to encourage generic medicine use. Consumers may have to pay a brand price premium if they want to use the branded product. In 2012–2013, the weighted average brand premium was $2.41 and 13.2 million prescriptions (20 % of prescription of PBS-subsidised medicines which include brands with a brand premium) were dispensed with a brand premium (Pharmaceutical Benefits Pricing Authority 2013). There are also incentive payments to community pharmacies ($1.68 per generic prescription from 1 August 2014). Generic medicines awareness campaigns have been rolled out by NPS MedicineWise, an Australian organisation funded by the federal government. NPS MedicineWise has run several educational campaigns on generic medicines directed to the public and health professionals since 2008. In 2010, NPS was allocated $10.4 million over for 4 years to continue and develop these campaigns. There are no restrictive policies on the use of patented medicines versus generic medicines within a therapeutic group, which is in contrast to some other OECD countries. For example, reimbursement schemes restricted the use of patented statins in several countries such as Sweden, Finland, Norway and Netherlands (Pettersson et al. 2012; Martikainen et al. 2010; Sakshaug et al. 2007; Ohlsson et al. 2011).

1.4.6 Pricing of New Medicines

While most recent PBS pricing policies have been targeting the generic market there are growing concerns about the high prices requested for new medicines by the pharmaceutical industry. An analysis of drivers of the PBS expenditure showed that the changes in prices of existing medicines had reduced PBS expenditure (Department of Health and Ageing and Medicines Australia 2013). However, listings of new medicines increased PBS expenditure. Anticancer and immunomodulating agents, along with medicines that act on nervous system and sensory organs, accounted for 80 % of the PBS growth in 2010–2011 (Department of Health and Ageing and Medicines Australia 2013). PBS expenditure on anticancer drugs rose from $65 million in 1999–2000 to $466 million in 2011–2012, an average increase of 19 % per year (Karikios et al. 2014). In 2013, the listing of three cancer medicines, ipilimumab for advanced melanoma, abiraterone for advanced prostate cancer and oral vinorelbine for advanced breast cancer is estimated to cost the Australian government more than $430 million over 4 years (Australian Government, Department of Health and Ageing 2013a).

In response to the high prices of some new medicines, Australia has implemented managed entry agreements for a number of medicines, with the aim of allowing access to patients for treatment of conditions found to be cost effective, but to limit use outside of these indications. Some agreements are pricing arrangements that involve price or volume rebate, while others are outcome agreements requiring patients to meet health targets for continued subsidy. In February 2013, there were at least 71 medicines with special pricing arrangements in place (Vitry and Roughead 2014). A total of 28 medicines were subject to continuation rules involving documentation of adequate benefit in patients. Provisional funding of new medicines conditional on the later provision of favourable scientific evidence is also currently being trialled in Australia. In 2012, the PBAC recommended the listing of ipilimumab for the treatment of melanoma subject to a risk-sharing arrangement that would involve the '*implementation of a mechanism to verify the anticipated overall survival benefits of ipilimumab in real world clinical practice in Australia... The sponsor would be expected to rebate the cost of difference in performance between observed versus predicted benefits of ipilimumab*' (Pharmaceutical Benefits Advisory Committee 2013b). The special pricing agreements are confidential so the prices paid by Australia cannot be compared with prices paid in other countries (Cheema et al. 2012).

1.4.7 Impact of Pricing Policies on Patient Accessibility

In 2010–2011, patient contributions to the cost of medicines amounted to $1.6 billion for PBS-listed medicines, $1.7 billion for under co-payment prescriptions and $962 million for private prescriptions of non-PBS-listed medicines (Australian Institute of Health and Welfare 2013). Patient contributions as a percentage of the cost of PBS-listed medicines rose slightly from 6.3 to 6.7 % between 2001–2002 and 2011–2012 (Senate Community Affairs References Committee 2014). Between 2000 and 2014, the concessional co-payment for pharmaceuticals increased from $3.30 in 2000 to $6.00 in 2014 (4.4 % average annual change, higher than the 2.8 % increase in the Consumer Price Index) and the general co-payment increased from $20.60 to $36.90 (4.5 % average annual change) (Senate Community Affairs References Committee 2014).

In 2014, the Senate Community Affairs References committee examined the out-of-pocket costs for consumers of Australian healthcare, including medicine costs (Senate Community Affairs References Committee 2014). Submissions and witnesses expressed concern about the impact of further increases in pharmaceutical co-payments on patient access to health care because existing out-of-pocket costs had been shown to affect accessibility of medicines. Australia spends 1.3 % of household consumption on out-of-pocket pharmaceutical costs compared to the OECD average of 1.1 % (Lam 2014). Almost half of out-of-pockets expenses related to health care is spent on prescription medicines, through the co-payments, payment for medicines which are priced under the co-payment thresholds and payment for private (non-subsidised) prescriptions (Lam 2014). Co-payments do appear to have an effect on medicine use. An Australian study found that the 21 % increase in the co-payments in 2005 reduced prescription medicine use for some therapies (Hynd et al. 2008). A 2011–2012 survey undertaken by the National Health Performance Authority showed that the number of adults who reported that they did not fill a medical prescription due to cost ranged from 5 to 15 % (National Health Performance Authority 2013). In 2012–2013, 8.5 % of people given a prescription by their GP delayed or did not fill it due to cost (CoAG Reform Council 2014).

In 2012–2013, 72 % of prescriptions for general patients had a dispensed price less than the general co-payment (Pharmacy Guild of Australia 2014c). For such products, pharmacists are entitled to set prices arbitrarily, though most consumers have little understanding of the potential for price competition in these circumstances. A recent study compared the prices of 31 prescription medicines that were priced under the general co-payment price between banner group pharmacies with open discounting policies and community pharmacies without (Thai et al. 2014). Before April 2012, banner group pharmacies provided discounts to patients of around 40 % per prescription compared to the PBS listed price, whereas other pharmacies provided discounts of around 15 %. Total price savings were on average $9 per prescription at banner group pharmacies and $3.50 at other pharmacies. Percentage discounts did not change greatly after the April 2012 price reductions. Questions have been raised on whether discounting practices may impact adversely on the extent and quality of professional services provided by pharmacists such as counselling. However, no assessment of the effect on practice has been undertaken.

1.5 Ongoing Debates on Pricing Policies

There have been a lot of debates over the last 2 years on future pricing policy options. In 2014, health policies including pharmaceutical policies have been a contentious budget issue for the government. A National Commission of Audit set up in October 2013 to review the performance, functions and roles of the Commonwealth government released its final reports in February and March 2014 (Australian Government, National Commission of Audit 2014) after having received 289 submissions from individuals, organisations and businesses. An inquiry from the Senate Community Affairs References committee that examined the out-of-pocket costs in Australian healthcare released its conclusions in August

2014 (Senate Community Affairs References Committee 2014) after it was proposed in the budget to set-up new co-payments for a number of Medicare services such as visits to general practitioners and increases in co-payments for pharmaceuticals.

There are conflicting opinions on whether or not the growth of the government expenditure on the PBS is sustainable and whether additional pricing policies are required to contain further growth. Since 2004–2005, government PBS expenditure has risen by $2.9 billion to $8.9 billion in 2010–2011 (annual growth rate of around 7 %) (Department of Health and Ageing and Medicines Australia 2013). However, in the year to end of June 2013, Commonwealth expenditure on the PBS decreased by 2.1 % compared to the previous year, while the number of PBS prescriptions increased by 1.2 % (PBS Information Management Section and Pharmaceutical Policy Branch 2013). The deceleration of government PBS expenditure and decreases realised from 2012 to 2013 is principally explained by changes in the pricing of generics over the past decade. Given generic medicine prices have fallen significantly, there is less opportunity to gain cost savings from further generic competition, thus future growth rates may start to increase.

Despite savings achieved, PBS pricing policies are still being criticised by a number of academic teams and the Consumers Health Forum, the peak health consumer organisation in Australia. In March 2013, the Grattan Institute's report, 'Australia's bad drug deal', compared the 2013 prices of 73 drug-dose combinations between Australia and New Zealand (Duckett et al. 2013). It found that the average Australian wholesale price was eight times more expensive than the New Zealand wholesale price. It concluded that if the government benchmarked the prices of generic drugs against prices paid overseas it could save more than $1 billion a year in payments to manufacturers. Australian public hospitals were also able to achieve significantly lower prices than the PBS through tendering and negotiations with suppliers through state health and public sector purchasing agencies. The Grattan Institute estimated that if the PBS were to purchase medicines at the prices available to public hospitals, this would lead to savings between $750 million to $1.2 billion a year (Duckett et al. 2013). New Zealand operates a tendering system for medicines and may only subsidize the lowest price product, which partially explains the then Health Minister criticism of the Grattan institute report stating that "*New-Zealand may get a good price for generic medicines but with much less choice for patients*" (Plibersek 2013).

In September 2013, Consumers Health Forum, the peak health consumer organisation in Australia launched a campaign '*Ticking Away...Medicine Savings Australians Never See*' with an online site showing the mounting cost of Australia's high generic medicines prices (Consumers Health Forum of Australia 2014a). Comparisons between PBS prices and prices in UK and NZ for the top 18 most costly generic medicines are provided and updated quarterly. Consumers Health Forum estimated that more than $1 billion a year could be saved if Australia paid the same prices for medicines as the United Kingdom.

These criticisms highlighted several issues. First, while the first generic of a medicine PBS-listed automatically triggers a 16 % price reduction, the price reduction is small compared to the ones applied to European countries which are closer to 50 % of the price of the original branded medicine (Puig-Junoy 2010; Simoens 2007). In some Canadian provinces the price of six generic medicines decreased by 82 % following patent expiry (Duckett et al. 2013). The Consumers Health Forum argue that even with the latest 2014 pricing measures the prices Australia pays for medicines remain significantly higher than those in the UK, NZ and Canada and recommends reducing the time between price disclosures from 12 to 3 months, which is what occurs in the UK (Consumers Health Forum of Australia 2014a, b).

Second, the de-linking of the prices of medicines in the F1 formulary from the prices of medicines in the F2 formulary may mean discounts on prices that were originally deemed cost-effective are not consistent for medicines across the formularies. For example, in July 2005, atorvastatin (F1 formulary) was granted a price differential of 12.5 % with simvastatin (F2 formulary) on the basis of its superior effect in lowering LDL-cholesterol. By 2012, the price differential was about 30 % above the price differential considered to be cost-effective and this has since increased further (Australian Government and Department of Health 2012). The adverse impact of de-linking of F1 and F2 formularies on overall pharmaceutical expenditures is further compounded when the volume of prescriptions for F1 medicines is greater than for F2 medicines in the same therapeutic class. The case of statins is an interesting illustration of the de-linking artefact. Lipid modifying agents, mainly statins, have been the medicine group with the highest government cost over recent years. After the first EAPD in April 2012, the monthly price of 40 mg simvastatin decreased by more than 50 % to just under $14, this price being the third highest price in comparison to 13 OECD countries (Committee for Economic Development of Australia 2013). However, off-patent simvastatin and pravastatin in F2 constituted only 22 % of statins use in 2011 with the remaining use being patented statins listed in F1. It has been estimated that the PBS expenditure could have been reduced by $1,087 million prior to 2009 if use of off-patent statins had matched that of England (Clarke 2012; Committee for Economic Development of Australia 2013).

De-linking of the prices of fixed dose combination medicines and individual components has also been raised as an issue (Clarke and Avery 2014). Fixed dose combination medicines are listed on the PBS on the basis of cost minimisation. While the initial price of a combination product is generally lower than the total price of the separate components, prices of the fixed dose combinations may not remained linked with the separate components over time. If there are multiple brands of the fixed dose combination product, price disclosure is calculated based on the wholesale costs of the combination products, not the individual components. If there are reductions in the individual components separate to the fixed dose products, then individual components can end up over time price more cheaply than the fixed dose product (Clarke and Avery 2014). There has been growth in expenditure on fixed dose combination products over the last 12 years rising from $150 million in 2000 to more than $600 million in 2012 (Clarke and Avery 2014) representing around 10 % of total government PBS expenditure (Department of

Health and Ageing and Medicines Australia 2013). It was estimated that the overall additional cost to government cost of listing diabetes and cardiovascular combination medicines was around $120 million annually compared with the sum of the costs of individual components (Clarke and Avery 2014).

Industry and pharmacy stakeholders consider that the Australian pricing policies have achieved enough savings so far and consider that further cuts in medicines prices would have adverse consequences for community pharmacies and the pharmaceutical industry.

The Pharmacy Guild of Australia considers that professional services such as the provision of advice on minor ailments and other health issues or the provision of dose administration aids, which used to be cross-subsidised by dispensing remuneration and trading terms, are at risk if further price reductions occur (Pharmacy Guild of Australia 2014c). The Guild claims the price disclosure policy, by lowering pharmacist remuneration levels and removing trading terms, makes the provision of professional services under the existing model of no or low cost to consumers that is becoming unviable (Pharmacy Guild of Australia 2014c). The Guild believes that further acceleration of price disclosure threatens the future viability of pharmacies (Quilty 2014). These claims have been made despite the government payments to pharmacy to enable business restructure in response to the price reforms.

A report to Medicines Australia found that the 2007 PBS reform package and the 2010 PBS reform were likely to deliver $14.5 billion and $3.4 billion savings respectively in the period 2017–18 (Sweeny 2013). Medicines Australia warns that further price cuts may oblige '*restructuring and staff reductions they've had to make to maintain a viable presence here*' as well as cause medicine shortages (Medicines Australia 2014). The Generic Medicines Industry Association claims that further accelerated price disclosure will reduce the time window for suppliers of generic medicines to recoup their investment from entering the market and may ultimately decrease supply of generic medicines to the Australian market (Generic Medicines Industry Association 2014). In the absence of independent economic modelling, it is difficult to ascertain the likelihood of these potential threats to the Australian pharmaceutical industry being realized.

1.6 Conclusion

Australia has a comprehensive universal pharmaceutical funding program that covers both use of medicines in the community sector, as well as use in private hospitals and use by outpatients and patients on discharge from public hospitals in most states and territories. Reference pricing and value based pricing have been the main policies used for the pricing of subsidised medicines for more than two decades. Generic medicine price reforms have included mandatory price reductions and price disclosure cycles with the objective to align PBS prices for generic medicines with pharmacy purchase prices. Overall, these policies have been effective in decreasing medicines prices and the growth rate in pharmaceutical expenditure. However, there are still higher prices of generic medicines in Australia compared to New Zealand and the United Kingdom. De-linking of the prices of the F1 and F2 formularies, and of fixed dose combination medicines and individual components has resulted in variable discounts in prices not consistent with the reference pricing policy. The current community pharmacy remuneration model that links pharmacy remuneration to the prices of medicines may need to be adjusted so that professional pharmacy services remain appropriately rewarded. The high prices requested for new medicines may now represent the most pressing challenge faced by the Australian PBS and will require further development of pricing agreements.

Acknowledgement The first part of this chapter was originally drafted by Ass Prof Hans Lofgren (School of Humanities and Social Sciences, Deakin University, Melbourne) who passed away unexpectedly in July 2014. Hans was a much admired scholar, very attentive to others and still humble. It has been a great privilege to work with him and to help finishing what he had started for this book on pharmaceutical prices. All our thoughts are with Hans, his wife, children and grandchildren.

References

Australian Productivity Commission (2001) International pharmaceutical price differences. http://www.pc.gov.au/projects/study/pbsprices/docs/finalreport. Accessed 19 Sept 2014

Australian Institute of Health and Welfare (2012) Australia's health 2012. AIHW. http://www.aihw.gov.au/publication-detail/?id=10737422172. Accessed 19 Sept 2014

Australian Institute of Health and Welfare (2013) Health expenditure Australia 2011–2012. http://www.aihw.gov.au/WorkArea/DownloadAsset.aspx?id=60129544656. Accessed 13 Sept 2014

Australian Government, Department of Health (2010) Memorandum of understanding between the Commonwealth of Australia and Medicines Australia. http://www.health.gov.au/internet/main/publishing.nsf/Content/further-PBS-reforms-Agreement. Accessed 14 June 2013

Australian Government, Department of Health (2012) Review of statin therapies. http://www.pbs.gov.au/info/industry/listing/elements/pbac-meetings/psd/2012-07/review-of-statin-therapies. Accessed 15 Sept 2014

Australian Government, Department of Health (2014) Fees, patient contributions and safety net thresholds. History of PBS copayments and safety net thresholds. http://www.pbs.gov.au/info/healthpro/explanatory-notes/front/fee. Accessed 24 April 2014

Australian Government, Department of Health (2014a) Aboriginal health services and the Pharmaceutical Benefits Scheme (PBS). http://www.health.gov.au/internet/main/publishing.nsf/Content/health-pbs-indigenous. Accessed 13 Sept 2014

Australian Government, Department of Health (2014b) Browse by brand premium. http://www.pbs.gov.au/browse/brand-premium. Accessed 15 Sept 2014

Australian Government, Department of Health (2014c) Life Saving Drugs Programme (LSDP). http://www.health.gov.au/lsdp. Accessed 13 Sept 2014

Australian Government, Department of Health (2014d) National Medicines Policy. http://www.health.gov.au/nationalmedicinespolicy. Accessed 15 Sept 2014

Australian Government, Department of Health (2014e) Pharmaceutical benefits for palliative care. http://www.pbs.gov.au/browse/palliative-care. Accessed 13 Sept 2014

Australian Government, Department of Health (2014f) Pharmaceutical Benefits Scheme (PBS) growth hormone programme. http://www.pbs.gov.au/info/browse/section-100/growth-hormone-programme. Accessed 19 Sept 2014

Australian Government, Department of Health (2014g) Pharmacy location rules. Applicant's handbook. Version 1.1, March 2014. http://www.health.gov.au/internet/main/publishing.nsf/Content/DDB409EBB18FCE8FCA257BF0001D3C0C/$File/pharmacy-location-rules-handbook-v1.1-march-2014.pdf. Accessed 13 Sept 2014

Australian Government, Department of Health (2014h) Price disclosure (SPD). http://www.pbs.gov.au/info/industry/pricing/price-disclosure-spd. Accessed 14 Sept 2014

Australian Government, Department of Health (2014i) Quality use of medicines. http://www.health.gov.au/internet/main/publishing.nsf/Content/nmp-quality.htm-copy2. Accessed 15 Sept 2014

Australian Government, Department of Health (2014j) Report to parliament on the collection of PBS/RPBS under co-payment prescription data 2012–2013. http://www.health.gov.au/internet/main/publishing.nsf/Content/14DEA08914F167C0CA257BF0001C96FC/$File/report-on-collection-pbs-under-co-payments-2012-13.pdf. Accessed 13 Sept 2013

Australian Government, Department of Health (2014k) Termination of the Pharmaceutical Benefits Pricing Authority (PBPA). http://www.pbs.gov.au/info/news/2014/03/termination-of-pbpa. Accessed 14 Sept 2014

Australian Government, Department of Health and Ageing (2005) Questions and answers on new pricing and listing arrangements for generic medicines on the Pharmaceutical Benefits Scheme (PBS). http://www.health.gov.au/internet/main/publishing.nsf/Content/8464B883F90180E1CA25732B0048D610/$File/qa_newpricing.pdf. Accessed 20 Sept 2011

Australian Government, Department of Health and Ageing (2010) The impact of PBS reform. http://www.pbs.gov.au/info/industry/useful-resources/impact-of-pbs-eform

Australian Government, Department of Health and Ageing (2011) Annual report 2010–2011. http://content.webarchive.nla.gov.au/gov/wayback/20140212092902/http://www.health.gov.au/internet/main/publishing.nsf/Content/FEB608DDB709DAC5CA257BF0001C6C8A/$File/DoHA%20Annual%20Report%202010-11.pdf. Accessed 15 Sept 2014

Australian Government, Department of Health and Ageing (2012a) Annual report 2011–2012. http://webarchive.nla.gov.au/gov/20140212095112/http://www.health.gov.au/internet/main/publishing.nsf/Content/Annual%20Reports-3. Accessed 14 Sept 2014

Australian Government, Department of Health and Ageing (2012b) Price reductions for main, first transitional and second transitional cycles. http://www.pbs.gov.au/info/industry/pricing/eapd/price-reductions. Accessed 24 Aug 2012

Australian Government, Department of Health and Ageing (2013a) Annual report 2012–2013. http://www.health.gov.au/internet/main/publishing.nsf/Content/annual-report2012-13. Accessed 18 Dec 2013

Australian Government, Department of Health and Ageing (2013b) Price reductions for second main cycle. http://www.pbs.gov.au/info/industry/pricing/eapd/price-reductions-for-second-main-cycle. Accessed 15 June 2013

Australian Government, Department of Industry (2014) Regulation and pricing in the pharmaceuticals industry. http://www.industry.gov.au/industry/PharmaceuticalsandHealthTechnologies/Pharmaceuticals/Pages/RegulationandPricingInthePharmaceuticalsIndustry.aspx Accessed 13 Sept 2014

Australian Government, Department of Health (2014a) Drug Utilisation Sub Committee (DUSC). http://www.pbs.gov.au/info/industry/listing/participants/drug-utilisation-subcommittee. Accessed 15 Sept 2014

Australian Government, Department of Health (2014b) Post-market reviews of pharmaceutical benefits scheme subsidised medicines. http://www.pbs.gov.au/info/reviews/subsidised-medicines-reviews. Accessed 15 Sept 2014

Australian Government, National Commission of Audit (2014) Towards responsible government. The report of the National Commission of Audit. http://www.ncoa.gov.au/report/docs/phase_one_report.pdf. Accessed 13 Sept 2014

Australian Government, Department of Health, Therapeutic Goods Administration (2014a) About the TGA. Department of Health. http://www.tga.gov.au/about/index.htm#.U1nhLSTHHY8. Accessed 25 April

Australian Government, Department of Health, Therapeutics Goods Administration (2014b) Australian register of therapeutic goods. http://www.tga.gov.au/industry/artg.htm. Accessed 13 Sept 2014

Australian Government, Department of Human Services, Medicare (2014c) Late stage metastatic cancer. http://www.medicareaustralia.gov.au/provider/patients/late-breast-cancer.jsp#N10009. Accessed 19 Sept 2014

Australian Government, Department of Human Services, Medicare (2014d) Pricing of PBS medicine. http://www.medicareaustralia.gov.au/provider/pbs/pharmacists/pricing.jsp. Accessed 14 Sept 2014

Beecroft G (2007) Generic drug policy in Australia: a community pharmacy perspective. Australia and New Zealand Health Policy 4:7. doi:10.1186/1743-8462-4-7

Bulfone L (2009) High prices for generics in Australia: more competition might help. Australian Health Review 33(2):200–214

Cheema PK, Gavura S, Migus M, Godman B, Yeung L, Trudeau ME (2012) International variability in the reimbursement of cancer drugs by publically funded drug programs. Current Oncology 19(3):e165–e176. doi:10.3747/co.19.946

Chim L, Kelly PJ, Salkeld G, Stockler MR (2010) Are cancer drugs less likely to be recommended for listing by the Pharmaceutical Benefits Advisory Committee in Australia? Pharmacoeconomics 28(6):463–475

Clarke PM (2012) Challenges and opportunities for the Pharmaceutical Benefits Scheme. Med J Aust 196(3):153–154

Clarke PM, Avery AB (2014) Evaluating the costs and benefits of using combination therapies. Med J Aust 200(9):518–520. doi:10.5694/mja14.00199

Clarke PM, Fitzgerald EM (2010) Expiry of patent protection on statins: effects on pharmaceutical expenditure in Australia. Med J Aust 192(11):633–636

CoAG Reform Council (2014) Healthcare in Australia 2012–2013: Five years of performance. Report to the Council of Australian Governments. http://www.coagreformcouncil.gov.au/sites/default/files/files/Healthcare%20in%20Australia%202012-13%20Five%20years%20of%20performance%20REVISED%20WA%20SNAPSHOT.pdf. Accessed 15 Sept 2014

Committee for Economic Development of Australia (2013) Healthcare: Reform or ration. https://www.ceda.com.au/media/302619/healthcarefinal1.pdf. Accessed 19 Sept 2014

Commonwealth of Australia, Pharmacy Guild of Australia (2010) The fifth community pharmacy agreement between the Commonwealth of Australia and the Pharmacy Guild of Australia https://www.health.gov.au/internet/main/publishing.nsf/Content/8D21C5E188499A03CA257BF0001C963A/$File/5CPA%20Agreement%2005%20August%202010.pdf. Accessed 13 Sept 2014

Consumers Health Forum of Australia (2014a) Medicines savings—a good start… much more to do. http://ourhealth.org.au/medicines-savings-a-good-start-much-more-do. Accessed 15 Sept 2014

Consumers Health Forum of Australia (2014b) Submission to the National Commission of Audit. http://www.ncoa.gov.au/docs/submission-consumers-health-forum-of-australia.pdf. Accessed 15 Sept 2014

Council of Australian Governments (2012) National Health Care Agreement 2012. http://www.federalfinancialrelations.gov.au/content/npa/healthcare/national-agreement.pdf. Accessed 25 April 2014

Department of Health and Ageing, Medicines Australia (2013) Joint monitoring report on trends in and drivers of Pharmaceuticals Benefits Scheme expenditure. http://www.pbs.gov.au/publication/reports/trends-in-and-drivers-of-pbs-expenditure.docx. Accessed 14 Sept 2014

Duckett SJ, Breadon P, Ginnivan L, Venkataraman P (2013) Australia's bad drug deal: high pharmaceutical prices. Grattan Institute, Melbourne

Fenna A (2012) Centralising dynamics in Australian federalism. Australian Journal of Politics & History 58(4):580–590. doi:10.1111/j.1467-8497.2012.01654.x

Feros P (2011) Price deflation: outbreaks and antidotes. The Australian Journal of Pharmacy 92 (1093):60–63

Generic Medicines Industry Association (2014) The devastating impact of cost cutting on the generic medicines industry. http://www.gmia.com.au/wp-content/uploads/2014/03/GMiA-Fact-Sheet-3-Devastating-Impact-of-Accelerated-Price-Disclosure-Feb14.pdf. Accessed 15 Sept 2014

Godman B, Wettermark B, van Woerkom M, Fraeyman J, Alvarez-Madrazo S, Berg C, Bishop I, Bucsics A, Campbell S, Finlayson A (2014) Multiple policies to enhance prescribing efficiency for established medicines in Europe with a particular focus on demand-side measures: findings and future implications. Frontiers in Pharmacology 5:106

Hynd A, Roughead EE, Preen DB, Glover J, Bulsara M, Semmens J (2008) The impact of co-payment increases on dispensings of government-subsidised medicines in Australia. Pharmacoepidemiol Drug Saf 17(11):1091–1099. doi:10.1002/pds.1670

PBS Information Management Section, Pharmaceutical Policy Branch (2013) Expenditure and prescriptions twelve months to 30 June 2013. Department of Health. http://www.pbs.gov.au/statistics/2012-2013-files/expenditure-and-prescriptions-12-months-to-30-06-2013.pdf. Accessed 24 April 2014

Karikios DJ, Schofield D, Salkeld G, Mann KP, Trotman J, Stockler MR (2014) Rising cost of anticancer drugs in Australia. Intern Med J 44(5):458–463. doi:10.1111/imj.12399

Lam M (2014) Half of out-of-pockets due to scripts. Pharma in focus. http://www.pharmainfocus.com.au/. Accessed 19 Sept 2014

Lofgren H (2009) Generic medicines in Australia: business dynamics and recent policy reform. Southern Med Review 2(2):24–28

Martikainen JE, Saastamoinen LK, Korhonen MJ, Enlund H, Helin-Salmivaara A (2010) Impact of restricted reimbursement on the use of statins in Finland. A register-based study. Med Care 48(9):761–766. doi:10.1097/MLR.0b013e3181e41bcb

Mauskopf J, Chirila C, Masaquel C, Boye KS, Bowman L, Birt J, Grainger D (2013) Relationship between financial impact and coverage of drugs in Australia. Int J Technol Assess Health Care 29(1):92–100. doi:10.1017/s0266462312000724

Medicines Australia (2010) The Australian pharmaceuticals industry. Winds of change http://medicinesaustralia.com.au/files/2011/03/20100603-pub-MedicinesAustralia-winds-of-Change.pdf. Accessed 13 Sept 2014

Medicines Australia (2014) 'Let them eat cake' the wrong PBS recipe. http://medicinesaustralia.com.au/media-events/from-the-chief-executive/. Accessed 19 Sept 2014

National Health Performance Authority (2013) Healthy Communities: Australians' experiences with access to health care in 2011–2012. http://www.nhpa.gov.au/internet/nhpa/publishing.nsf/Content/Our-reports. Accessed 15 Sept 2014

Ohlsson H, Vervloet M, van Dijk L (2011) Practice variation in a longitudinal perspective: a multilevel analysis of the prescription of simvastatin in general practices between 2003 and 2009. Eur J Clin Pharmacol 67(12):1205–1211. doi:10.1007/s00228-011-1082-8

Organisation for Economic Co-operation and Development (OECD) (2013) OECD Factbook 2013: Economic, Environmental and Social Statistics. Life expectancy. http://www.oecd-ilibrary.org/sites/factbook-2013-en/12/01/01/index.html;jsessionid=18hxihifu0815.x-oecd-live-01?itemId=/content/chapter/factbook-2013-95-en&_csp_=2e12af00b8816149004be44b35212040. Accessed 13 Sept 2014

Pettersson B, Hoffmann M, Wandell P, Levin LA (2012) Utilization and costs of lipid modifying therapies following health technology assessment for the new reimbursement scheme in Sweden. Health Policy 104(1):84–91. doi:10.1016/j.healthpol.2011.10.010

Pharmaceutical Benefits Advisory Committee (2009) PBAC Review of bDMARDs for the treatment of severe active rheumatoid arthritis. http://www.health.gov.au/internet/main/publishing.nsf/Content/pbac-psd-bdmards-dec09. Accessed 14 June 2013

Pharmaceutical Benefit Advisory Committee (2013a) PBAC recommendations from the review of pharmaceutical benefits scheme anti-dementia drugs to treat Alzheimer disease. http://www.pbs.gov.au/info/reviews/pbac-minutes-alzheimers. Accessed 14 June 2013

Pharmaceutical Benefits Advisory Committee (2013b) November 2012 PBAC outcomes—Positive recommendations. http://www.health.gov.au/internet/main/publishing.nsf/content/health-pbs-general-listing-committee3.htm. Accessed 14 June 2013

Pharmaceutical Benefits Pricing Authority (2013) Appendix 2: pharmaceutical benefits pricing authority annual report for the year ended 30 June 2013. http://www.health.gov.au/internet/main/publishing.nsf/Content/53FCED10EAD1C98CCA257C0500786C41/$File/Appendix%202%20Pharmaceutical%20Benefits%20Pricing%20Authority%20Annual%20Report.pdf. Accessed 14 Sept 2014

Pharmacy Guild of Australia (2014a) About 5CPA. http://5cpa.com.au/about-5cpa/. Accessed 13 Sept 2014

Pharmacy Guild of Australia (2014b) Pharmacy innovations in e-health. http://www.guild.org.au/docs/default-source/public-documents/issues-and-resources/Fact-Sheets/pharmacy-innovations-in-ehealth.pdf?sfvrsn=0. Accessed 14 Sept 2014

Pharmacy Guild of Australia (2014c) Submission to Senate Standing Committees on Community Affairs Inquiry: out-of-pockets costs in Australian healthcare http://www.aph.gov.au/Parliamentary_Business/Committees/Senate/Community_Affairs/Australian_healthcare/Submissions. Accessed 15 Sept 2014

Plibersek T (2013) Transcript: doorstop on the price of medicines/antimicrobial resistance—Senate Courtyard, Parliament House, Canberra. http://pandora.nla.gov.au/pan/131355/20130702-1129/www.health.gov.au/internet/ministers/publishing.nsf/Content/tr-yr13-tp-tpsp130318b86c.htm?OpenDocument&yr=2013&mth=03. Accessed 19 Sept 2014

Puig-Junoy J (2010) Impact of European pharmaceutical price regulation on generic price competition: a review. Pharmacoeconomics 28(8):649–663. doi:10.2165/11535360-000000000-00000

Quilty D (2014) Pharmaceuticals, pharmacists and profits: the Pharmacy Guild perspective. Australian Prescriber 2014

Sakshaug S, Furu K, Karlstad O, Ronning M, Skurtveit S (2007) Switching statins in Norway after new reimbursement policy—a nationwide prescription study. Br J Clin Pharmacol 64 (4):476–481. doi:10.1111/j.1365-2125.2007.02907.x

Senate Community Affairs References Committee (2014) Out-of-pocket costs in Australian healthcare. http://www.aph.gov.au/Parliamentary_Business/Committees/Senate/Community_Affairs/Australian_healthcare/Report. Accessed 13 Sept 2014

Simoens S (2007) International comparison of generic medicine prices. Curr Med Res Opin 23 (11):2647–2654. doi:10.1185/030079907X233395

Simoens S, De Coster S (2006) Sustaining generic medicines markets in Europe. Katholieke Universiteit Leuven, Leuven

Spinks JM, Richardson JR (2011) Paying the right price for pharmaceuticals: a case study of why the comparator matters. Aust Health Rev 35(3):267–272, doi: AH10930 [pii] 10.1071/AH10930

Sweeny K (2013) The impact of further PBS reforms: report to medicines Australia. Victoria University, Melbourne

Thai LP, Vitry AI, Moss JR (2014) Discounting of medicines in Australian community pharmacies. Aust Health Rev. doi:10.1071/AH14012

The Commonwealth of Australia (2011) Framework for the introduction of parallel TGA and PBAC processes. http://www.pbs.gov.au/info/publication/factsheets/shared/framework-for-introduction-of-parallel-TGA-and-PBAC-processes. Accessed 28 June 2014

The Hon Peter Dutton MP, Minister for Health, Minister for Sport (2013) Media release. Australians to access more affordable medicines sooner. http://www.health.gov.au/internet/ministers/publishing.nsf/Content/4084C89B3E2171EBCA257C140001CA8C/$File/PD007.pdf. Accessed 18 Dec 2013

Vitry A, Roughead E (2014) Managed entry agreements for pharmaceuticals in Australia. Health Policy 117:345–352. doi:10.1016/j.healthpol.2014.05.005

Willis E, Reynolds L, Keleher H (eds) (2012) Understanding the Australian health care system. Elsevier, Sydney

World Health Organization (2014) Global Health Observatory (GHO). http://www.who.int/gho/en/. Accessed 19 Sept 2014

Chapter 2
Drug Pricing in Canada

Joel Lexchin

Abstract Drug pricing in Canada is a divided responsibility between the federal and provincial governments. The price of patented medicines is largely controlled at the federal level through the Patented Medicine Prices Review Board that sets a maximum introductory price for new medicines and then limits the rate of rise of those prices to the rate of inflation. The provinces and territories have a minimal role in pricing of this group of medicines through product listing agreements. Generic drug prices, on-the-other hand, are solely the responsibility of the provinces and territories that set the prices for these products at a certain percentage of the price of the originator product. Separate from these bodies, is a federal health technology assessment process that considers clinical efficacy as well as cost-effectiveness but this process only makes recommendations about funding to the participating provincial, territorial and federal drug plans. Although private insurance pays for over one-third of all drug costs, it has very little role in either setting prices or containing costs. Overall Canada has among the highest drug costs among developed countries but a lack of drug insurance means that up to 35 % of low income people without insurance do not fill their prescriptions.

2.1 Introduction

Health care in Canada is a complicated matter owing to the federal nature of the country and the way that the constitution divides power between the provinces and the federal government. Making the situation even more complex is the wording of the Canada Health Act that sets out which aspects of health care delivery are

J. Lexchin (✉)
Faculty of Health, School of Health Policy and Management, York University, 4700 Keele Street, Toronto, ON, Canada M3J 1P3

Emergency Department, University Health Network, 190 Elizabeth Street, Toronto, ON, Canada M5G 2C4

Faculty of Medicine, Department of Family and Community Medicine, University of Toronto, 263 McCaul Street, Third Floor, Toronto, ON, Canada M5T 1W7
e-mail: jlexchin@yorku.ca

Z.-U.-D. Babar (ed.), *Pharmaceutical Prices in the 21st Century*,
DOI 10.1007/978-3-319-12169-7_2

eligible for federal funding and which are solely reliant on provincial funding (Government of Canada 2012). Then there is the way that Canada has chosen to regulate the prices of patented and generic drugs and finally the role of health technology assessment and the role of the private insurance companies. This chapter explores all of these points and looks at how successful Canada has been at controlling drug costs and ends by examining whether or not drugs are affordable for all segments of the Canadian population.

2.2 Overview of the Canadian Health Care System

There actually is no Canadian national health care system. Under the Canadian constitution, written in 1867, "the provinces were responsible for establishing, maintaining and managing hospitals, asylums, charities and charitable institutions, and the federal government was given jurisdiction over marine hospitals and quarantine" (Canada's Health Care System 2014). As a result, as health care became more important provinces individually developed their own mechanisms for funding and delivering health care. The beginning of publicly funded hospital care came in Saskatchewan in 1947 followed by federal legislation that provided for federal funding for half the cost of hospital care provided that the provinces agreed to offer universal coverage through a publicly administered system. Saskatchewan expanded its system to include universal public coverage for physician services in 1962 with the federal government once again following suit in 1966 with legislation to pay for 50 % of the cost to any province (Canada's Health Care System 2014; Government of Canada 1966).

These two pieces of federal legislation were consolidated in 1984 in the Canada Health Act (CHA). The CHA lays out five conditions for the provision of federal funding to the provinces: portability (insurance continues when people move from province to province), accessibility (people cannot be charged extra for any service that is covered), universality (all Canadian citizens and permanent residents are automatically covered), comprehensiveness (all necessary medical services are covered), and public administration (the health care system is administered on a public not-for profit basis) (Canada's Health Care System 2014). Although the CHA says nothing about the way that health care should be delivered almost all hospitals in Canada are run by private not-for profit corporations that are not investor owned and almost all of their funding comes from the provincial government (Sutherland et al. 2013). Doctors are not state employees but also receive nearly all of their income from the publicly run system (Blomqvist and Busby 2013).

While virtually all doctor and hospital services are covered without any form of patient copayment, it is important to note that aside from drugs administered while patients are in hospital, the CHA is silent about payment for prescriptions drugs. Canada is unique as being the only developed country with a national health care system that does not also cover drug costs. Therefore, as described below, each province has developed its own system for public payment, with the resultant provincial variation in what drugs are covered, what groups of the population are eligible for public insurance and what level of copayment, deductibles and user fees are levied. Further complicating the situation is that prices for patented drugs, i.e., brand-name drugs, are controlled differently from prices for generic drugs.

2.3 Pharmacy Services

As of 2011, there were a total of 8,869 pharmacies in Canada and of these 5,476 were part of a chain, with the remainder split almost equally between independently owned stores and pharmacy services located in food and other mass merchandising stores (IMS Brogan 2012). There are no publicly owned or private not-for profit pharmacies in Canada.

There were just over 30,600 pharmacists in 2012 with three-quarters working in community pharmacies and the remainder employed in hospitals and other health care facilities. "Most pharmacists reported their position as staff pharmacist, with approximately 30 % reporting themselves as pharmacy owners/managers" (Canadian Institute for Health Information 2013b). Pharmacy services are considered part of the delivery of health care and as such pharmacists and pharmacies are under the control of provincial governments.

2.4 Pharmaceutical Industry Ownership

The pharmaceutical industry in Canada is dominated by the subsidiaries of multinational companies. Out of the top ten companies in 2012, seven were multinational subsidiaries and three were generic companies of which two (Apotex and Pharmascience) were Canadian owned (see Table 2.1).

The brand-name industry is represented by Canada's Research-Based Pharmaceutical Companies with 56 members. Although there is a scattering of small Canadian owned start up companies the vast majority are foreign owned (Canada's Research-Based Pharmaceutical Companies 2014). As of 2006, there were 15 generic suppliers in Canada with 13 having manufacturing plants in the country; seven of the top ten companies were foreign based (Canadian Generic Drug Sector Study 2007). The Canadian Generic Pharmaceutical Association (CGPA) represents a subset of the generic industry and has nine members with a mix of Canadian and foreign owned companies (Canadian Generic Pharmaceutical Association 2014). Sandoz, one of the CGPA companies is actually owned by Novartis, a Swiss based brand-name company. There are no publicly owned generic or brand-name pharmaceutical companies.

Table 2.1 Industry ownership and sales, 2012

Rank	Company	Total sales (C $ billions)	Market share (%)	Brand-name or generic	Ownership (Canadian or foreign)
1	Johnson & Johnson	1.89	8.6	Brand	Foreign
2	Pfizer	1.60	7.2	Brand	Foreign
3	Apotex	1.27	5.7	Generic	Canadian
4	AstraZeneca	1.22	5.5	Brand	Foreign
5	Merck	1.11	5.0	Brand	Foreign
6	Teva	1.03	4.7	Generic	Foreign
7	Novartis	0.99	4.5	Brand	Foreign
8	Abbott	0.95	4.3	Brand	Foreign
9	GlaxoSmithKline	0.95	4.3	Brand	Foreign
10	Pharmascience	0.77	3.5	Generic	Canadian

Source: Industry Canada (2013)

Nearly all of the active ingredients that go into both brand and generic drugs are imported into Canada and manufacturing consists largely of combining the active ingredient with the excipients into the various dosage forms.

2.5 Canadian Drug Regulation

Health Canada is the federal department with the responsibility for approving new drugs for marketing, through two of its branches. The Therapeutic Products Directorate approves and monitors prescription and non-prescription drugs derived from chemical manufacturing whereas the Biologics and Genetic Therapies Directorate is responsible for biological and radiopharmaceutical drugs including blood and blood products, viral and bacterial vaccines, genetic therapeutic products, tissues, organs and xenografts. While dealing with different types of products, both Directorates function in an almost identical manner in terms of analyzing the laboratory, preclinical and clinical data that the drug companies submit when they fill a New Drug Submission. The basis for approving a new drug is efficacy, safety and manufacturing quality. Health Canada has no involvement in pricing issues (Lexchin 2008).

2.6 Patented Drug Pricing

2.6.1 *Compulsory Licensing*

Up until the early 1990s Canada allowed the import of active ingredients through a compulsory license in order to encourage competition and lower the price for brand-name drugs. During the 1960s, a series of three reports all pointed out that drug prices in Canada were among the highest in the world and all three reports identified patent protection as one of the major reasons for this situation (Restrictive Trade Practices Commission 1963; Royal Commission on Health Services 1964; Canada House of Commons 1967). The decision of the Liberal government of the day was to allow companies to receive a compulsory license to import a drug into Canada. Based on figures in the Report of the Commission of Inquiry into the Pharmaceutical Industry (the Eastman Report), in 1983 the multinationals had lost only 3.1 % of the Canadian market to generic competition but compulsory licensing was responsible for a reduction of $211 million in a total drug bill of $1.6 billion (Commission of Inquiry on the Pharmaceutical Industry 1985).

The compulsory licensing system significantly increased the availability of generic drugs and could lead to a price reduction on individual drugs of as much as 80 % depending on the number of generic competitors and the availability of low priced generics allowed for the development and expansion of provincial public drug plans (Lexchin 1993a). However, a combination of pressure from the United States (US) and free trade agreements—the Free Trade Agreement (Canada and the US), the North American Free Trade Agreement (Canada, Mexico and the US) and the Trade Related Aspects of Intellectual Property Rights Agreement, one of the agreements administered by the World Trade Organization, lead to first the weakening of compulsory licensing in 1987 and its ultimate abandonment in 1993 (Lexchin 1993b, 1997).

2.6.2 *Patented Medicine Prices Review Board*

Once the government made the decision to end the use of compulsory licensing it was faced with the question of how to ensure that drug prices were set at an affordable level. Having used the patent system for almost a quarter of a century, the government chose to continue to use the patent system to regulate prices for patented drugs and created the Patented Medicine Prices Review Board (PMPRB) in 1988. The PMPRB is a federal agency that operates at arms length from the Ministry of Health. The authority of the PMPRB extends over the $12.8 billion in sales of patented drugs or 59.3 % of total drug sales in Canada (Patented Medicine Prices Review Board 2013). "Under the Patent Act, patentees are required to file price and sales information about their patented drug products at introduction and twice a year thereafter for each strength of each dosage form of each patented drug product sold in Canada" until the patent expires (Patented Medicine Prices Review 2014b).

Once this information is received, the product is assessed by PMPRB's Human Drug Advisory Panel (HDAP) to determine if it is a line extension, i.e., a new presentation of an existing product, or a new active substance (NAS), i.e., a molecule never marketed before in any form in Canada. If the product is a line extension it is priced in line with the already existing presentation of the medicine. If it is a NAS then the HDAP rates its therapeutic value and based on that rating the PMPRB applies a series of criteria in its guidelines including the price of existing products in the same therapeutic class and the median price in seven comparator countries (France, Germany, Italy, Sweden, Switzerland, United Kingdom and United States) to determine the maximum average potential price (MAPP) for the drug (Patented Medicine Prices Review 2014b). The MAPP is the maximum allowable introductory price for the drug. If the price that the company proposes is at or below the MAPP then no further action is taken but if the price exceeds the MAPP then the PMPRB first enters into negotiations with the company for a Voluntary Compliance Undertaking to reduce the price. If those negotiations are unsuccessful then the PMPRB can use its quasi-judicial powers to hold a public hearing. If the hearing finds that the price is excessive, the PMPRB may issue an order to reduce the price. PMPRB decisions are subject to judicial review in the Federal Court of Canada.

Finally, the PMPRB limits the rate of rise of prices of individual products to the rate of rise in the Consumer Price Index (CPI) over any 3 year period. Just examining the increase in prices for individual products, the PMPRB has been successful in controlling drug prices in Canada, with general price inflation, as measured by the CPI, exceeding the average increase in patented drug prices almost every year since 1988 (see Table 2.2).

At the same time, Canadian prices are higher than those in four out of the seven comparator countries (Patented Medicine Prices Review Board 2013). At over $700 per person per year (US$ purchasing power parity), Canada spends more per capita on pharmaceuticals than any other country in the world except the United States (US) (OECD 2013). Similarly when measured against comparator countries in the Organisation for Economic Co-operation and Development (OECD), Canada's growth in drug spending per capita (in real terms) between 2000 and 2009 was 4.3 % per year compared to the OECD average of 3.5 %. Although this rate fell to −0.3 % per year from 2009 to 2011, the OECD average fell to −0.9 % (OECD 2013). The high per capita expenditure, despite the control over introductory prices for patented drugs and the limitation on the rate of rise of their price, reflects the fact that the price of individual drugs is only one factor influencing expenditures. Far more important are "increased volume of use and changes in the mix of treatments being used…accounting for average annual growth of 6.2 % and 2.0 %, respectively. Both volume and mix effects were due in part to changes in treatment guidelines, increased disease prevalence and the uptake of new drugs" (Canadian Institute for Health Information 2012).

Table 2.2 Annual rate of change of patented drug prices and consumer price index, 1988–2012

Year	Average annual change patented drug prices	Average change consumer price index
1988	4.2	3.9
1989	1.9	5.1
1990	2.8	4.8
1991	3.3	5.6
1992	2.2	1.4
1993	0.1	1.9
1994	−0.7	0.1
1995	−1.9	2.2
1996	−2.2	1.5
1997	0.04	1.7
1998	−0.1	1.0
1999	0.2	1.8
2000	0.4	2.7
2001	−0.03	2.5
2002	−0.1	2.2
2003	0.1	2.8
2004	0.7	1.8
2005	0.5	2.2
2006	−0.2	2.0
2007	0.0	2.2
2008	−0.1	2.3
2009	0.2	0.3
2010	−0.5	1.8
2011	−0.1	2.9
2012	0.6	1.5

Source: Patented Medicine Prices Review Board (2013) and Statistics Canada (2014)

There are also inherent deficiencies in the PMPRB process that help to contribute to the high per capita expenditure level in Canada. When generic equivalents are marketed in Canada, the brand-name companies do not reduce their prices in an attempt to compete on price (Lexchin 2004). Since the PMPRB allows companies to set prices for new patented medicines up to the highest amount charged for other medicines in the same therapeutic market (Patented Medicine Prices Review 2014a) by not lowering brand-name prices, companies thereby enable new entrants into the same therapeutic market to charge higher prices. Lexchin has shown how this feature of the PMPRB guidelines concretely affects introductory prices. The mean introductory price of 33 new medications was 95.9 % of the price of existing brand-name products and 91.5 % of the price of the most expensive brand-name product in their class (Lexchin 2006).

Gagnon and Hébert criticize the comparator countries that the PMPRB uses noting that the list includes the four countries with the most expensive prices worldwide: Germany, Sweden, Switzerland and US. Since the Canadian price is

Table 2.3 Average foreign-to-Canadian price ratio at market exchange rates for patented drugs, 2005

	Country	Ratio
PMPRB comparator countries	France	0.85
	Germany	0.96
	Italy	0.75
	Switzerland	1.09
	United Kingdom	0.90
	United States	1.69
Non-comparator countries	Australia	0.78
	Finland	0.88
	Netherlands	0.85
	New Zealand	0.79
	Spain	0.73

Source: Patented Medicine Prices Review Board (2006)

the median of the seven comparator countries, they conclude that the PMPRB guidelines ensure that the price of patented medicines in Canada are normally the fourth most expensive price worldwide (Gagnon and Hébert 2010). Using other comparator countries could significantly affect the Canadian price. In 2006, the PMPRB conducted bilateral comparisons of the price of patented drugs in Canada and 11 other OECD countries including 6 of the 7 comparator countries that the PMPRB uses. (Sweden was excluded.) The mean of the average prices for the 6 comparator countries compared to the Canadian price was 1.04 whereas had all 11 countries been used the mean would have been 0.91 (Patented Medicine Prices Review 2006) (see Table 2.3).

2.7 Health Technology Assessment

In 2003, the Common Drug Review (CDR), operating as part of the Canadian Agency for Drugs and Technology in Health (CADTH), was established. The CDR provides advice to all of the provincial drug plans, except the one operated by the province of Quebec, the three territorial and six federal drug plans about the clinical efficacy and cost-effectiveness of a drug against other drug therapies so that public funds are optimally used. The CDR is funded by federal, provincial (except Quebec) and territorial governments and is governed by a 13-member jurisdictional Board of Directors appointed by the Federal/Provincial/Territorial Deputy Ministers of Health (Standing Committee on Health of the House of Commons 2007).

CDR reviews submissions from manufacturers for new drugs, new combination products, and drugs with new indications and in addition, the Formulary Working Group (composed of representatives from the federal, provincial, and territorial publicly funded drug plans and other related health organizations) or one or more of the participating drug plans "may request through a submission: (1) a review of the listing status of a particular drug that is already listed on one or more formularies,

(2) a class review, or (3) a drug-related review other than that described in (1) and (2), and which may include a request for the review of a new drug or an old drug that is not currently listed on any participating Drug Plan formulary" (Common Drug Review 2013).

When CDR receives a submission it contracts a team that prepares a clinical review, including a systematic review of all relevant published and unpublished randomized controlled trials and in addition, examines and critiques the manufacturer's pharmacoeconomic evaluation. The review team then prepares a report for the Canadian Expert Drug Advisory Committee (CEDAC), a body appointed by the Board of Directors for CADTH (see http://www.cadth.ca/index.php/en/cdr/committees/cedac). CEDAC uses the review to assess the clinical and economic value of the product and then makes a recommendation to the participating drug plans about listing taking into consideration the medication's effectiveness, safety and cost-effectiveness compared to existing therapies (Tierney and Manns 2008). There are four different types of recommendations that the CDR can make: unrestricted listing, list in a manner similar to other drugs in the class, list with criteria and do not list. CDR recommendations are not binding on any of the participating drug plans, which are free to make their own funding decisions (Morgan et al. 2006).

Between May 2004 when the CDR made its first recommendation and May 2009, it considered 53 submissions and made a recommendation for listing in some form for 24 of these. Participating drug plans listed between 7 and 25 of these drugs and several drugs were listed on one or more formularies despite being given a "do not list" recommendation. (Quebec listed 12 of the 29 drugs given a "do not list" recommendation.) "The percent agreement between recommendations and decisions ranged from 60.4 to 96.2 %, irrespective of how agreement was defined" (Gamble et al. 2011).

A process similar to the one used by CDR is in place for providing advice to provincial and territorial plans about oncology drugs, the pan-Canadian Oncology Drug Review and as of April 1, 2014 responsibility for its administration was transferred to CADTH (Pan-Canadian Oncology Drug Review 2014).

2.8 Provincial Drug Formularies

Since coverage for medicines is not included under the CHA, each province and territory has developed its own public drug plan. Drug companies apply to get their drugs (patented, non-patented brand-name and generic) onto provincial formularies but there are differences in the number of new patented drugs that achieve listing. Out of 198 new patented drugs approved between May 1999 and May 2009, 152 (76.8 %) were listed on one or more formularies but the number listed on individual formularies varied from a low of 65 (32.8 %) to a high of 132 (66.7 %) (Gamble et al. 2011). When generic drugs are included, the variation in listing in 2006 ranged from 55 % of 796 drugs to 73 %. Rates of bilateral formulary agreement went from a low of 49 % to a high of 65 % depending on the provinces being compared. However, when national expenditure weights are applied to the drugs listed on the individual formularies then drugs listed on any of the nine provincial formularies (Prince Edward Island, the smallest of the ten provinces was excluded) accounted for an expenditure weighted share of 77 % of the market, suggesting that provincial drug coverage is more consistent than it would seem on the surface (Morgan et al. 2009).

2.8.1 Product Listing Agreements

Although the PMPRB sets a national price for patented drugs the provincial governments have started to play a role in how much they will pay for some of these drugs that they list on their formularies. Companies apply to have their drugs listed on provincial formularies and as part of that process produce pharmacoeconomic studies to show the value for money for their medicines. If the price of the product is felt to exceed its therapeutic value, i.e., it is not cost effective, then increasingly Canadian provinces are entering into product listing agreements (PLAs) with companies. These PLAs lead to lower, but confidential prices that may be achieved through "rebates that may or may not be tied to drug expenditures, utilization patterns or health outcomes" (Morgan et al. 2013b). According to a recent study into PLAs, they are being used by at least seven out of ten Canadian provinces although to varying degrees. Out of 12 drugs with a negative recommendation from the CDR, ten were funded with a PLA in at least one province (Morgan et al. 2013b). While PLAs reduce the price for drugs to the provinces, people who have to pay out-of-pocket or who are covered by private insurance do not benefit from these reduced prices.

2.8.2 Reference-Based Pricing

British Columbia is the only province to use reference-based pricing (RBP) to set and control drug prices in certain drug classes. The system was set up in 1995 and now covers five therapeutic classes of drugs. The assumption underlying RBP is that in certain drug classes the medications are essentially equally safe and effective and can be interchanged although they are not bioequivalent as generic are. A reference price is established for the class and RBP covers the cost of drugs priced at or below the reference price; if a physician prescribes a more expensive medication, the patient pays the difference. Overall, a Cochrane review found that RBP can reduce third party drug expenditures by inducing a shift in drug use towards less expensive drugs (Aaserud et al. 2006). The introduction of RBP for angiotensin converting enzyme inhibitors (drugs used to treat hypertension, congestive heart failure and coronary artery disease) lead to a saving of 6 % of all cardiovascular drug expenditures by the British Columbia drug plan (Schneeweiss et al. 2002). However, there have not been any recent evaluations of the effects of RBP to see if there are ongoing savings from the policy.

2.9 Generic Drug Pricing

Generic drugs account for just over 63 % of prescriptions filled in Canada but represent slightly less than 25 % of the expenditures on medications (Canadian Generic Pharmaceutical Association 2013). Previous reports have documented the high price of Canadian generics compared to those in other countries. In 2007, Canadian prices were higher than those in 11 other OECD countries (Patented Medicine Prices Review Board 2010) (see Table 2.4).

One reason for the higher Canadian prices is the level of generic competition in the market. Countries such as the US that have much larger populations tend to attract more generic companies into the market leading to lower prices. However, there still is substantial competition in Canada; work done by the PMPRB indicates that Canada ranks in the middle of 6 countries studied in terms of the average number of generic suppliers for each non-patented product (Canadian Generic Drug Sector Study 2007). The main reason for the higher Canadian prices is that competition among the generic companies takes place at the level of pharmacies and particularly pharmacy chains. Because of the dominance of pharmacy chains and franchises in the Canadian market they have been able to demand high rebates from generic manufacturers in return for stocking their products. Average rebates have been estimated to be 40 % and may be as high as 80 % for individual generic products (Competition Bureau Canada 2007).

The main mechanisms used by public drug plans to set the price that they will pay for generic products are capping the formulary price at a percentage of the brand name price and specifying a maximum reimbursable cost for a drug or group

Table 2.4 Average foreign-to-Canadian price ratios at market exchange rates, by bilateral comparator, 2007

Country	Ratio
Australia	0.95
France	0.63
Germany	0.57
Italy	0.71
Netherlands	0.77
New Zealand	0.19
Spain	0.56
Sweden	0.45
Switzerland	0.74
United Kingdom	0.63
United States	0.47

Source: Patented Medicine Prices Review Board (2010)

of interchangeable drugs. With a maximum reimbursable cost approach the plans obtain the cost of the generic from the manufacturer and use that cost to determine an appropriate formulary price (Bell et al. 2010).

In recent years provincial plans have significantly decreased what they will pay for generic drugs. Ontario has gone from 50 to 25 % of the originator price (with 20 % for the top ten drugs) and other provinces are at 25 and 35 %, although some are still paying 65 % of the originator price and when British Columbia reduced prices to 35 %, it granted over 600 exemptions for specific products (Law and Kratzer 2013). Despite these reductions Canadian generic prices still remain excessive. If Ontario paid prices available for generics in either New Zealand or the US Department of Veterans Affairs for the top 82 generics it covered, then it would have reduced it expenditures on these products from $190 to $61 million (Law 2013).

Most recently there is an interprovincial program to reduce generic prices, the Generic Pricing Initiative. Initially the program targeted six widely used drugs and set a price cap at 18 % of the originator price. When fully implemented this program could save up to $100 million annually Canada-wide (Council of the Federation 2013). As of April 1, 2014 four additional drugs were added (Ontario Public Drug Programs 2014).

2.10 Role of Private Insurance Companies

Twenty-three million Canadians (68 % of the population) have some form of private insurance coverage for medications (Canadian Life and Health Insurance Association 2012) and over one-third (35.4 %) of total prescription drug expenditures in Canada is covered by private insurance (Canadian Institute for Health Information 2013a), but these plans have little role in controlling drug prices or overall expenditures. In fact, over the period 2003–2012 private expenditures rose faster than public expenditures in 8 of the 10 years (Canadian Institute for Health Information 2013a). One of the key reasons that private insurers pay little attention to costs is because "the majority of private drug benefit plans are administered for companies by outside firms—mainly insurance companies—that are often paid a percentage of plan costs" leaving them no incentive to rein in prices (Silversides 2009).

Law and colleagues point out the weaknesses in how private insurers approach the issue of costs (Law et al. 2014). Private insurers are much more likely to list new drugs on their formularies compared to public plans. An analysis of new drugs approved by Health Canada between 2004 and 2011 found that 81 % of new drugs were insured by at least one private plan compared to 47 % by at least one public plan (CHPI 2013). Listing newer and typically more expensive drugs is only advantageous if these drugs offer significant therapeutic advantages over existing products but out of 336 NAS approved by Health Canada between January 1, 2000 and March 31, 2012 only 31 met that criterion (Lexchin 2014).

Private plans often pay prices that are in excess of the manufacturer's list price. Although some provinces try to ensure that generic prices are equivalent in the public and private sector, a Competition Bureau report found that prices in private plans are 10 % higher than those in public plans for non-patented brand name drugs and 7 % higher for generic drugs (Competition Bureau Canada 2007). This difference in prices extends to patented brand-name products. In a "claims review of a large employer, drug prices submitted by pharmacies for certain brand drugs ranged from 9.2 to 37.2 % more than the. . .list price; and certain generic drugs were priced between 45 and 102.9 % more than the. . .list price. In other words, some pharmacies charged 102.9 % more for the same drug, in the same quantity, to the same drug plan" (Stevenson 2011) and the plan paid that price.

While all public drug plans require mandatory generic substitution only 67 % of employees belonged to private plans that had this requirement and only 19 % of employees were part of a private plan that used a multitiered formulary, i.e., a formulary that places drugs into different tiers with the first tier requiring the lowest copayment and typically including mostly generic drugs (Kratzer et al. 2013). According to Law and colleagues "[t]he very limited use of managed formularies—a list of the drugs covered by the Plan—in the past by private drug plans. . .has made it difficult, if not impossible, for insurers to negotiate. . .preferred discounts or rebates in exchange for preferential listing status. Industry estimates also suggest that the limited use of formularies resulted in private plans paying $3.9 billion more for drugs in 2012 where equally effective therapeutic alternatives were available" (Law et al. 2014).

2.11 Impact of Pricing on Accessibility

Provincial plans pay 38.5 % ($10,677.1 million) of total prescription drug costs in Canada, federal and social security funds pay an additional 6.0 % ($1,652.5 million), leaving private insurance to cover 35.4 % ($9,825.4 million) and out-of-pocket payment at 20.1 % ($5,578.5 million) (Canadian Institute for Health Information 2013a). While provincial drug plans are the largest payers they only cover about 25 % of the population (Demers et al. 2008). Estimates are that 13 % of the Canadian population is either uninsured or underinsured for prescription drug costs and people with no drug coverage and paying out of pocket are usually those with minimum wage jobs (Applied Management in Association with Fraser Group Tristat Resources 2000).

The individual prescription drug programs in each province vary considerably in their design in terms of who is eligible for coverage, what drugs are covered and how much people have to pay in the form of deductibles, copayments and user fees. Provincial plans are based on age (usually covering people 65 and older), income level (coverage on a sliding scale below a certain individual or family income) and employment (if employers offer health benefits to their workers then they must offer drug insurance and employees are obligated to purchase the insurance).

In addition, all provinces cover social assistance recipients although sometimes these people are required to pay a co-payment (Daw and Morgan 2012; Morgan et al. 2013a).

Simulations were constructed to show the variation in costs to people in different provinces. One example was for a 65 year old woman whose family income was below the national average and who was taking medications for diabetes, hypertension and insomnia. Her annual out-of-pocket costs ranged from $8 to $504 depending on what province she lived in. A 40 year old social assistance recipient taking drugs for hypertension and high cholesterol would get his drugs for free in some provinces but would pay up to $200 in another. Overall, seniors, depending on their income, paid 35 % or less of their drug costs in two provinces but up to 100 % in others (Demers et al. 2008). These figures are based on the drug plans as of December 2006 and while plans have changed since then it is likely that this level of variation still exists. In recent years, "[u]niversal income-based catastrophic coverage appears to be emerging as an implicit national standard for provincial pharmacare. However, due to the variation and high level of patient cost-sharing required under these programs, convergence on this model does not equate to substantial progress towards expanding coverage or reducing interprovincial disparities" (Daw and Morgan 2012).

Cost related non-adherence to prescription medications across Canada is about 5.1 % (Kennedy and Morgan 2006) but this figure hides significant within-country differences. In Quebec where drug insurance is mandatory (either through employment or the provincial government) cost related non-adherence was 4.4 %. In Ontario where there was coverage for those 65 and over and social assistance recipients it was 8.8 % and in provinces with income-based coverage it was 12.1 % (Kennedy and Morgan 2009). Not surprisingly, cost-related non-adherence is significantly related to income and having insurance coverage. For those with a high income (annual household income >$80,000) and insurance it was 3.6 % while for those with a low income (annual household income <$20,000) and no insurance it was 35.6 % or ten times greater (Law et al. 2012).

2.12 Conclusion

Although superficially it would seem that Canada has been successful at controlling the price of patented medicines, a deeper examination and per capita expenditures shows that the mechanism that is used is deeply flawed and leads to Canadian prices being among the highest of all of the OECD countries. Similarly, despite recent moves by some of the provinces, generic prices remain much higher than those in places such as New Zealand or those from the US Veterans Affairs. Private insurance companies, despite playing a major role in paying for drugs have no incentive for trying to help contain costs because they often paid a percentage of how much the plan spends. The complicated federal nature of the country also means that while there is a health technology assessment process, participation is voluntary on the part of federal, provincial and territorial drug plans, and although all of them aside from Quebec have chosen to opt in, they are free to ignore the advice that comes out of the process. The lack of a federal role in ensuring coverage for drug costs means that each province and territory has its own unique plan with a divergence from province to province in terms of who is covered, what drugs are listed on formularies and how much people need to pay out of pocket in the form of copayments, user fees or deductibles. The ultimate result is that many lower income people who lack insurance forego filling the prescriptions that they receive.

References

Aaserud M, Austvoll-Dahlgren A, Kösters J, Oxman A, Ramsay C, Sturm H (2006) Pharmaceutical policies: effects of reference pricing, other pricing, and purchasing policies. Cochrane Database Syst Rev (2): CD005979. doi:10.1002/14651858.CD005979

Applied Management in Association with Fraser Group Tristat Resources (2000) Canadian's access to insurance for prescription medicines, vol 2, The uninsured and the under-insured. Health Canada, Ottawa

Bell C, Griller D, Lawson J, Lovren D (2010) Generic drug pricing and access in Canada: what are the implications? Health Council of Canada, Toronto

Blomqvist Å, Busby C (2013) Paying hospital-based doctors: fee for whose service? Commentary No. 392. C.D. Howe Institute, Toronto

Canada House of Commons (1967) Second (final) report of the special committee of the House of Commons on drug costs and prices. Canada House of Commons, Ottawa

Canada's Research-Based Pharmaceutical Companies (2014) Member profiles. Rx&D. http://www.canadapharma.org/en/about-rxd/membership/rxd-members. Accessed 8 May 2014

Canada's Health Care System (2014) Health Canada. http://www.hc-sc.gc.ca/hcs-sss/pubs/system-regime/2011-hcs-sss/index-eng.php. Accessed 7 May 2014

Canadian Generic Pharmaceutical Association (2013) The value of generic prescription medicines: are you taking full advantage. CGPA. http://www.canadiangenerics.ca/en/advocacy/docs/ValueofGenericPrescriptionMedicine2013.pdf. Accessed 8 May 2014

Canadian Generic Pharmaceutical Association (2014) About CGPA. CPGA. http://www.canadiangenerics.ca/en/about/members.asp. Accessed 8 May 2014

Canadian Institute for Health Information (2012) Drivers of prescription drug spending in Canada. CIHI, Ottawa

Canadian Institute for Health Information (2013a) Drug expenditure in Canada, 1985 to 2012. CIHI, Ottawa

Canadian Institute for Health Information (2013b) Pharmacist workforce, 2012—provincial/territorial highlights. CIHI, Ottawa

CHPI (2013) How good is your drug insurance? Comparing federal, provincial and private-sector plans, 2004–2011. Annual report—2013 edition. Toronto

Commission of Inquiry on the Pharmaceutical Industry (1985) Report. Ottawa

Common Drug Review (2013) Procedure for Common Drug Review. Canadian Agency for Drugs and Technology in Health, Ottawa

Competition Bureau Canada (2007) Canadian generic drug sector study. Gatineau

Council of the Federation (2013) Provinces and territories seek significant cost savings for Canadians on generic drugs. http://www.councilofthefederation.ca/phocadownload/newsroom-2013/nr-cof-generic_drugs_final-jan_18.pdf. Accessed 8 May 2014

Daw J, Morgan S (2012) Stitching the gaps in the Canadian public drug coverage patchwork? A review of provincial pharmacare policy changes from 2000 to 2010. Health Policy 104:19–26

Demers V, Melo M, Jackevicius C, Cox J, Kalavrouziotis D, Rinfret S, Humphries K, Johansen H, Tu J, Pilote L (2008) Comparison of provincial prescription drug plans and the impact on patients' annual drug expenditures. CMAJ 178:405–409

Gagnon M-A, Hébert G (2010) The economic case for universal pharmacare: costs and benefits of publicly funded drug coverage for all Canadians. Canadian Centre for Policy Alternatives, Ottawa

Gamble J-M, Weir D, Johnson J, Eurich D (2011) Analysis of drug coverage before and after the implementation of Canada's Common Drug Review. CMAJ 183:E1259–E1266

Government of Canada (1966) Medical Care Act. R.S.C. 1970, c. M-8. Queen's Printer, Ottawa

Government of Canada (2012) Canada Health Act. R.S.C. 1985, c. C-6. Queen's Printer, Ottawa

Canadian Life and Health Insurance Association (2012) Backgrounder—Canadian life and health insurance industry drug pooling agreement. CLHIA. http://www.clhia.ca/domino/html/clhia/CLHIA_LP4W_LND_Webstation.nsf/resources/Drug_Protection/$file/backgrounder.pdf. Accessed 8 May 2014

IMS Brogan (2012) Retail pharmacies by outlet type, Canada, 2005–2011

Industry Canada (2013) Pharmaceutical industry profile. Industry Canada. http://www.ic.gc.ca/eic/site/lsg-pdsv.nsf/eng/h_hn01703.html. Accessed 9 May 2014

Kennedy J, Morgan S (2006) A cross-national study of prescription nonadherence due to cost: data from the joint Canada–United States survey of health. Clin Ther 28:1217–1224

Kennedy J, Morgan S (2009) Cost-related prescription nonadherence in the United States and Canada: a system-level comparison using the 2007 international health policy survey in seven countries. Clin Ther 31:213–219

Kratzer J, McGrail K, Strumpf E, Law M (2013) Cost-control mechanisms in Canadian private drug plans. Healthcare Policy 9(1):35–43

Law M (2013) Money left on the table: generic drug prices in Canada. Healthcare Policy 8 (3):17–25

Law M, Kratzer J (2013) The road to competitive generic drug prices in Canada. CMAJ 185:1141–1144

Law M, Cheng L, Dhalla I, Heard D, Morgan S (2012) The effect of cost on adherence to prescription medications in Canada. CMAJ 184:297–302

Law M, Kratzer J, Dhalla I (2014) The increasing inefficiency of private health insurance in Canada. CMAJ 186:E470–E474. doi:10.1503/cmaj.130913

Lexchin J (1993a) The effect of generic competition on the price of prescription drugs in the province of Ontario. CMAJ 148:35–38

Lexchin J (1993b) Pharmaceuticals, patents and politics: Canada and Bill C-22. Int J Health Serv 149:1401–1407

Lexchin J (1997) After compulsory licensing: coming issues in Canadian pharmaceutical policy and politics. Health Policy 40:69–80

Lexchin J (2004) The effect of generic competition on the price of brand-name drugs. Health Policy 68:47–54

Lexchin J (2006) Do manufacturers of brand-name drugs engage in price competition? An analysis of introductory prices. CMAJ 174:1120–1121

Lexchin J (2008) New directions in Canadian drug regulation: whose interests are being served? In: O'Donovan O, Glavanis-Grantham K (eds) Power, politics and pharmaceuticals. Cork University Press, Cork, pp 153–170

Lexchin J (2014) Postmarket safety in Canada: are significant therapeutic advances and biologics less safe than other drugs? A cohort study. BMJ Open 4:e004289

Morgan SG, McMahon M, Mitton C, Roughead E, Kirk R, Kanavos P, Menon D (2006) Centralized drug review processes in Australia, Canada, New Zealand, and the United Kingdom. Health Aff 25(2):337–347

Morgan S, Hanley G, Raymond C, Blais R (2009) Breadth, depth and agreement among provincial formularies in Canada. Healthcare Policy 4(4):e162–e184

Morgan S, Daw J, Law M (2013a) Rethinking pharmacare in Canada. C.D. Howe Institute, Toronto

Morgan S, Friesen M, Thomson P, Daw J (2013b) Use of product listing agreements by Canadian provincial drug benefit plans. Healthcare Policy 8(4):45–57

OECD (2013) Health at a glance 2013: OECD indicators. OECD Publishing

Ontario Public Drug Programs (2014) Executive Officer Notice: Pan-Canadian competitive value price initiative for generic drugs. Ministry of Health and Long-Term Care. http://www.health.gov.on.ca/en/pro/programs/drugs/opdp_eo/notices/exec_office_20140310.pdf. Accessed 8 May 2014

Pan-Canadian Oncology Drug Review (2014) About the Pan-Canadian Oncology Drug Review. pCODR. http://www.pcodr.ca/wcpc/portal/Home/AboutpCODR?_afrLoop=324795520801000&lang=en&_afrWindowMode=0&_adf.ctrl-state=n4wxkb1b8_458. Accessed 8 May 2014

Patented Medicine Prices Review Board (2006) Non-patented prescription drug prices reporting: Canadian and foreign price trends. PMPRB, Ottawa

Patented Medicine Prices Review Board (2010) Generic drugs in Canada: price trends and international price comparisons, 2007. PMPRB, Ottawa

Patented Medicine Prices Review Board (2013) Annual report 2012. PMPRB, Ottawa

Patented Medicine Prices Review Board (2014a) Compendium of policies, guidelines and procedures—reissued June 2013. PMPRB. http://www.pmprb-cepmb.gc.ca/english/View.asp?x=1733. Accessed 8 May 2014

Patented Medicine Prices Review Board (2014b) Regulating prices. PMRPB. http://www.pmprb-cepmb.gc.ca/english/View.asp?x=1440. Accessed 8 May 2014

Restrictive Trade Practices Commission (1963) Report concerning the manufacture, distribution and sale of drugs. Queen's Printer, Ottawa

Royal Commission on Health Services (1964) Report. Queen's Printer, Ottawa

Schneeweiss S, Soumerai S, Maclure M (2002) Reference drug pricing. CMAJ 167:126–127

Silversides A (2009) Ontario's law curbing the cost of generic drugs sparks changes. CMAJ 181: E43–E45

Standing Committee on Health of the House of Commons (2007) Prescription drugs part 1—common drug review: an F/P/T process. Standing Committee on Health of the House of Commons, Ottawa

Statistics Canada (2014) Consumer price index, historical summary. Statistics Canada. http://www.statcan.gc.ca/tables-tableaux/sum-som/l01/cst01/econ46a-eng.htm. Accessed 8 May 2014

Stevenson H (2011) An end to blank cheques: getting more value out of employer drug plans. Reformulary Group, Toronto

Sutherland J, Crump R, Repin N, Hellsten E (2013) Paying for hospital services: a hard look at the options. Commentary No. 378. Toronto

Tierney M, Manns B (2008) Optimizing the use of prescription drugs in Canada through the Common Drug Review. CMAJ 178:432–435

Chapter 3
Pharmaceutical Pricing Policies in China

Yu Fang

Abstract This chapter describes China's drug pricing system, which affects the overall health system, pharmaceutical industry, and drug price setting and regulation. China's thousands of domestic drug companies account for approximately 70 % of the market. However, the Chinese pharmaceutical industry is characterized as having a low market concentration, weak international trading competitiveness, and a lack of domestically developed patented pharmaceuticals. Between 1998 and 2013, the government intervened to directly set prices on 32 occasions. Each time, the average price reduction across therapeutic categories was approximately 20 %. These cuts have had a significant impact on the Chinese pharmaceutical industry. The number of drugs subject to price controls in China rose to 2,700 in 2013; these drugs only account for 20 % of all medicines, but represent 60 % of the total value of all drugs sold. Although the government has substantially improved drug price management, further steps are required to make the pricing system more scientific, rational, and transparent.

3.1 Chinese Healthcare System

As the largest developing country in the world, China's medical and healthcare system is of vital importance to its population of over 1.3 billion. However, it is also a major issue in people's continuing well-being. Although the medical care system and the health of Chinese citizens have improved since the launch of economic reform in the late 1970s, access to basic healthcare by most Chinese has not kept pace with the country's economic growth (Yip and Hsiao 2009). Dramatic changes have occurred in both the social and economic structures associated with health-sector reform. These include a decreased reliance on state funding (Hsiao 2007), the decentralization of public health services, increased autonomy of health facilities, and increased freedom of movement of health workers. Disparities between urban

Y. Fang (✉)
Department of Pharmacy Administration, School of Pharmacy, Health Science Center, Xi'an Jiaotong University, Xi'an, China
e-mail: yufang@mail.xjtu.edu.cn

Z.-U.-D. Babar (ed.), *Pharmaceutical Prices in the 21st Century*,
DOI 10.1007/978-3-319-12169-7_3

and rural areas and between different regions have increased and healthcare expenditure has grown (Chen 2009).

In 2009, China's national healthcare expenditure amounted to US$ 240 billion, or approximately 5 % of gross domestic product (GDP). More than 40 % of this expenditure was on medicines, which is one of the highest proportions in the world. The disproportionately high pharmaceutical expenditure sets China apart from most comparators. For example, pharmaceutical expenditure accounts for approximately 17 % of total health expenditures in Organization for Economic Cooperation and Development (OECD) countries (OECD Library 2010). The high cost of medical products continues to be considered the major obstacle in accessing healthcare in China (Sun et al. 2008; Zhang 2010).

The reform of China's medical and healthcare system continues to best ensure the implementation of basic medical and healthcare systems (both urban and rural), and to guarantee that every resident has access to safe, effective, convenient, and affordable basic medical and health services. In doing so, China has enjoyed a number of recent achievements. In 2009, the Chinese government announced a systematic plan to achieve universal access to healthcare by 2020. This reform is anchored in five interdependent areas: (1) expanding coverage to insure more than 90 % of the population; (2) establishing a national essential medicines system to meet the primary medical needs of all Chinese; (3) improving the primary care delivery system to provide basic healthcare and to manage referrals to specialist care and hospitals; (4) making public health services available and equal for all; and (5) piloting public hospital reforms (Communist Party of China Central Committee, State Council 2009).

Since the beginning of the new healthcare reform in 2009, the average health of Chinese people has improved. Judging from important indicators that measure national health, the health of Chinese people is now among the top in developing countries. In 2010, the average life expectancy was 74.8 years (72.4 years for males and 77.4 years for females), maternal mortality rates fell from 51.3 per 100,000 in 2002 to 24.5 per 100,000 in 2012, and infant mortality rates and the mortality rate of children under five have continued their downward trend. The former fell from 29.2 per 1,000 in 2002 to 10.3 per 1,000 in 2012, and the latter, from 34.9 per 1,000 to 13.2 per 1,000, exceeding UN Millennium Development Goals in this regard (Ministry of Health 2014).

China's reform process has also seen the implementation of medical and healthcare systems covering both urban and rural residents. The first was a public health service system, covering disease prevention and control, health education, maternity and child care, mental health, health emergency response, blood collection and supply, health supervision, family planning, and other specialized public health services. The system is based on community-level healthcare networks that provide public health services. The second is a medical care system. In rural areas, this system refers to a three-level medical service network that comprises the county hospital, township hospitals, and village clinics. The county hospital is the main provider, and township hospitals and village clinics provide a base service. In cities and towns, the medical care system represents a new urban medical health service system that features the division of responsibilities as well as cooperation among various types of hospitals at all levels and community healthcare centers. The third is a medical security system. This system comprises basic medical security, supported by many forms of supplementary medical insurance and commercial health insurance. The basic medical security system covers basic medical insurance for employed urban residents and basic medical insurance for non-working urban residents. The system also includes new types of rural cooperative medical care (covering rural populations) and urban–rural medical aid (which covers people suffering from economic difficulties). Finally, the fourth system is a pharmaceutical supply system that covers the production, circulation, price control, procurement, dispatch, and use of pharmaceuticals. Recent work under the supply service has focused on establishing a national system for essential drugs (State Council 2013).

China's health financing structure is being constantly improved. Health expenditure comes from a number of sources including the government's general tax revenue, social medical insurance, commercial health insurance, and residents' out-of-pocket spending. In 2011, the total health expenditure in China reached US$ 376.94 billion, US$ 279.77 per capita. The total expenditure accounted for 5.1 % of the country's GDP. In comparable prices, China's health expenditure grew by an average annual rate of 11.32 % from 1978 to 2011. Individual out-of-pocket spending declined from 57.7 % in 2002 to 34.8 % in 2011, showing that health financing is effective in areas of risk protection and re-distribution.

Furthermore, health resources are being sustainably developed. By the end of 2011, there were 954,000 medical and healthcare institutions around the country, an increase of 148,000 since 2003. Licensed doctors (assistants) reached 2,466,000, or 1.8 per 1,000 people, as compared with 1.5 per 1,000 people in 2002. Registered nurses totaled 2,244,000, or 1.7 per 1,000 people, as compared with 1 per 1,000 people in 2002. The number of hospital beds reached 5,160,000, or 3.8 per 1,000 people, as compared with 2.5 per 1,000 people in 2002.

Marked improvements have also been seen in the utilization of medical and health services. In 2011, medical institutions throughout the country have 6.27 billion outpatients visits, and admitted 150 million inpatients, as compared with 2.15 billion and 59.91 million in 2002, respectively. In 2011, Chinese citizens visited medical institutions for treatment an average of 4.6 times and 11.3 of every 100 were hospitalized. Furthermore, the utilization rate of hospital beds reached 88.5 % and the average hospital stay was 10.3 days. These figures show that it has become increasingly convenient to see a doctor and medical services are more accessible. In 2011, 83.3 % of all households (80.8 % in rural areas) could reach a medical institution within a 15-min journey, as compared with 80.7 % in 2002. Medical service quality management and control systems have been significantly improved (State Council 2012).

3.2 China's Pharmaceutical Industry

China established a strong pharmaceutical industry, and has become one of the largest pharmaceutical producers in the world. The Chinese pharmaceutical industry has been growing at an average annual rate of 16.72 % over the last few decades. As of June 2012, 4,706 pharmaceutical manufacturers were licensed in China, including more than 1,500 manufacturers of traditional Chinese medicine. However, the industry is still small-scale with a scattered geographical layout, duplicated production processes, and outdated manufacturing technology and management structures. Most are small companies that manufacture non-branded generics as well as traditional Chinese medicine. The largest group of producers is located in southeast China, and the rest are relatively dispersed across the territory. The sector is dominated by basic technology and simple production methods. Many of the larger producers are government-owned enterprises, characterized by overproduction, outmoded methods, and constant operating losses. The very large number of government-owned producers raises the potentially thorny question of conflict of interest, as manufacturers and regulators report to the same government authorities.

The Chinese pharmaceutical industry also has a low market concentration and weak international trading competitiveness, coupled with a lack of domestically developed patented pharmaceuticals. The thousands of domestic producers account for approximately 70 % of the market (in terms of value). In 2011, the ten largest domestic companies only accounted for 14.3 % of the market (Guo 2013). This is in contrast to most OECD countries where the ten largest companies typically dominate the market. Despite the relative backwardness of the industry, the balance of the domestic market and the size of the export market have been steadily shifting in favor of domestic producers. There is relatively little R&D and innovation, a weakness that the government is attempting to change by encouraging joint ventures with multinational companies.

Multinational drug manufacturers view China as an opportune and important market, based largely on its sheer size. Faced with restrictive drug policies and sophisticated cost-containment strategies in their own markets, virtually every major international manufacturer has a presence in China, usually through joint ventures. These enterprises employ sophisticated teams of marketing professionals, sales representatives, and lobbyists. The Chinese association of research-based multinational manufacturers reports that half of their members' revenues come from innovative drugs. The other half comes from the sale of well-known off-patent generic drugs that have large followings among patients and health professionals.

During the last decade, experts consistently predicted that China would be the second largest prescription drug market in the world by 2015. Instead, China's growth experienced a 20 % decline in 2013. Several factors are thought to have been responsible for this, including a greater emphasis on promoting Chinese R&D as well as recent crackdowns on corruption. Although China's R&D spending is only one-third that of the United States, it is increasing by 25 % each year. Thus, US and Western European pharmaceutical companies are facing greater competition from Chinese pharmaceuticals. Another factor impacting on companies working in China are recent allegations of bribes by foreign pharmaceutical companies to Chinese doctors. As Chinese authorities continue to investigate a number of foreign pharmaceutical companies, many are opting out of the Chinese market.

However, there are strong indicators that growth in China will continue despite the slowdown. Healthcare reforms along with continued government investment are designed to ultimately provide basic healthcare for more than 90 % of the Chinese population. Moreover, the number of Chinese citizens earning US$ 5,000 or more a year is expected to reach 339 million by 2016 (The Language of Science 2014).

3.3 Drug Price Setting and Regulation

3.3.1 Drug Price Regulatory Authorities

The National Development and Reform Commission (NDRC), previously the powerful former state planning commission, is in charge of the pricing of all medical drugs and devices included in the drug formularies associated with publicly funded insurance programs. Products not covered in the drug formularies can be determined freely by market forces. Although drugs included in the state drug formulary list account for 20 % of the approximately 10,000 available products, they represent 60–70 % of the value of all market sales.

Drug price regulation is jointly administrated by NDRC agencies at both national and provincial levels. Currently, approximately 1,900 drugs are as category A drugs, and their pricing is determined by the NDRC at a national level. Approximately 800 or 15 % of drugs are classified as category B, and their price ceilings are left to the discretion of provincial governments. In 2005, pricing regulatory responsibility for over-the-counter drugs was delegated from the NDRC to provincial pricing bureaus, and they can now set prices according to local health-care priorities and requirements (Liu et al. 2009).

3.3.2 Evolving Drug Price Control in China

Strategies to control pharmaceutical costs have evolved through several phases since the founding of the Peoples' Republic of China. During the era of the planned economy prior to 1978, all pharmaceutical prices were set by the government. When the early stages of China's economic transition began in the 1980s, prices were largely left to the market. However, in response to perceived problems of market-based pricing—including price increases, poor quality control, corruption, and kickbacks—the government recentralized much of pharmaceutical pricing in 1997. A series of policy measures were enacted between 1996 and 2007, including a new pharmaceutical law, various decrees on how pricing would be adjusted, and several approaches to setting and adjusting prices (Yu et al. 2010).

There are two primary drug pricing regulations: (1) uniform price ceilings applicable to generics to meet good manufacturing practice (GMP) standards; and (2) "independent pricing policy" for specified pharmaceutical products, largely patented medicines, off-patent originators, domestic primary generics, and subsequent generics of obviously superior quality. In 2001, the NDRC issued regulations, permitting drugs that demonstrate a better treatment rate at a lower cost than generics or similar drugs to apply for independent pricing under a special pricing system. This system allows companies to request special higher pricing if they can show significant safety and efficacy benefits compared with similar drugs. In recent years, the independent pricing policy has played a positive role in motivating manufacturers to improve drug quality and undergo incremental innovation.

The government intervened and set prices on 32 occasions between 1998 and 2013. Each time, the average price reduction across therapeutic categories equaled 20 %. These cuts have had a significant impact on the Chinese pharmaceutical industry. From 2003 to 2006, the average profit percentage in the pharmaceutical industry decreased from 9.7 to 6.3 % (Wang 2007). Furthermore, the number of drugs subject to price controls rose from roughly 1,500 to 2,700 during this decade (1,900 products were regulated by central government and 800 by local governments). By 2013, these drugs only represented about 20 % of all medicines but 60 % of the value of all drugs sold.

Drug prices remain uncontrolled because of several flaws in China's healthcare system. First, the drug distribution system is congested with middlemen who operate between the drug makers and hospitals, and they inflate the cost of the drugs several times over. Second, revenues for hospitals in China are heavily dependent on drug sales because of inadequate government funding. On average, government subsidies cover only 10 % of hospital expenses. Because the government allows hospitals to mark up their drug prices by 15 %, they tend to buy more expensive drugs. This could potentially change when the healthcare reform is implemented (Meng et al. 2005).

Although the mandated price cuts have significantly affected the industry, its impact on actual pricing has been limited. When the price of a drug is reduced, hospitals and retailers switch to alternative brands. As a result, sales typically decline or products are even withdrawn from the market. When the profit margin of a drug is substantially eroded, many manufacturers will stop producing that product. Furthermore, uniform pricing cuts have occurred because of the lack of comprehensive reform in the rational use of medicine, insurance coverage policy, and the China Food and Drug Administration (CFDA) approval policy for "new" drugs. Many manufacturers may opt to change the packaging, form, or specification of the drug, registering it as a new one to avoid the former's price restrictions, whereas "old" drugs have been removed from the market because of low profit margins.

In April 2007, around 100 Chinese pharmaceutical companies filed a complaint with the State Council concerning the price cut policy, stating that domestic hospitals (which are financed through profits from drug sales) are the root cause of high drug costs in China (Beijing Business Today 2007). The NDRC set 2011 as the deadline to resolve this problem. It is expected that price ceiling regulations will be introduced for all prescription drugs at different stages in the supply chain, including ex-factory, wholesale, and retail, in an attempt to keep healthcare costs down and to prevent irregularities and price manipulation through distribution channels. A pilot model is currently under way in Guangdong Province. There is also news that the NDRC is considering implementing a "fixed-price increase" policy. Under this policy, hospitals will earn a fixed and independent service fee for each prescription they dispense thus "equalizing" the incentives for prescribing more expensive medicines (Economic Observation 2008).

There have been recent discussions regarding healthcare reforms involving preferential pricing policies for innovative drug products; however, it remains unclear how this will fit in with other pricing measures the government will adopt. As drug pricing regulations will continue to have a major impact on the industry, corporate strategies must take these into account (Pirce Waterhouse Cooper 2009).

3.3.3 Drug Pricing Setting Principles

The Drug Administration Law of the People's Republic of China, and Regulations for Implementation of the Drug Administration Law of the People's Republic of China state that a drug price is determined as follows.

Article 48: For drug pricing, the State exercises a system under which the prices are fixed or guided by the government or regulated by the market. For drugs listed in the directory of drugs for national basic medical insurance and drugs not listed in the directory but monopolistically manufactured and distributed, their prices shall be fixed or guided by the government; the prices of other drugs shall be regulated by the market.

Article 55: For drugs the prices of which are fixed or guided by the government, the competent pricing department of the government shall, on the pricing principle stipulated in the Pricing Law of the People's Republic of China and on the basis of average social cost, supply and demand in the market, and public affordability, rationally fix and adjust the prices, in order to ensure that price is commensurate with quality, eliminate excessively high price, and protect the legitimate interests of users. The government shall organize experts in pharmaceutical, medical, economic and other fields to conduct assessment, and if necessary, it shall solicit comments from drug manufacturers, drug distributors, medical institutions, citizens, and other relevant units and persons.

Article 56: For drugs the prices of which are adjustable with the market according to law, drug manufacturers, drug distributors and medical institutions shall fix the prices on the principles of fairness, rationality, good faith and commensuration of price with quality, in order to provide the users with drugs of reasonable prices.

In practice, the factory price set by manufacturers is usually much higher than the actual production cost because the government pricing authority does not have the capacity to check these costs. Different prices for the same drug exist in different areas because of local competition, procurement transparency, and local protection. For medicines with market pricing, the retail price is set based on production costs and market supply and demand. Wholesalers, retail pharmacies, and hospitals can set the actual selling price but cannot exceed the retail price set by the manufacturer (Wang 2007).

3.3.4 Drug Price Setting Methodologies

In 2006, the NDRC announced a series of measures to consolidate prices for pharmaceuticals as well as for medical services.

1. Further reductions in drug prices. All drug prices were adjusted in a comprehensive manner and the prices of some expensive items were reduced. Prices were raised for some inexpensive drugs with a high clinical demand that manufacturers had not been willing to produce because of low profitability. Rules to regulate differential price setting were established to prohibit manufacturers from changing dosages, strengths, and packaging to avoid price controls. All hospitals above the county level are required to limit their markup to no more than 15 % (except traditional Chinese medicines, which can be gradually increased up to 25 %).
2. Implementation of the ratified ex-manufacturer price. To ensure the scientific characteristics of government price setting and to control excessive profits from drug distribution, certain drugs were selected with high distribution price differentials. The prices of these drugs were reduced to reduce retail prices.
3. Drug price adjusted by the market. To improve transparency, the government suggested that manufacturers add retail price labels on drug packaging. These prices would reflect approved prices (including any increases of the adjusted price), limitations on the price differential, and restrictions on excess profits. Any market-adjusted pricing for prescription drugs must be incorporated into the government pricing system.
4. Rational adjustments to prices for medical services. Adjustments were made to increase the price of medical services (to reflect the true value of the required technical skill and labor) while the fee schedule for high-tech examination procedures was reduced.
5. Standardization of hospital norms for treatment and medication and the revision and improvement of clinical guidelines. Physicians were directed to write prescriptions using generic names (active ingredients by molecule name) and this

was gradually extended to generic drugs. The aim was to de-link the relationship between hospital revenue and personal income, and to promote competition for medical and pharmacy services (NDRC 2006).

In April 2007, the NDRC announced that pharmaceutical costs would be monitored more closely. Further improvements in pricing methods were announced, and the number of price-controlled drugs was expanded to include virtually all prescription drugs. These new guidelines were more responsive to manufacturers' arguments that drug pricing should reflect the costs of manufacturing inputs, distribution and marketing expenses, and reasonable profit margins. Manufacturers are now permitted to set prices for new drugs (as well as for some existing drugs) based on their assessment of costs. However, once set, these prices are now closely monitored by central government. Foreign pharmaceutical manufacturers are also allowed to set prices, taking into account actual costs related to sales, rebates, commissions, and promotions.

The NDRC has adopted a wider range of pricing methodologies, including the following.

1. Differential pricing. A drug's differential price is based on the price ratio value of forms ($K = 1.9 \log_2 X$), strengths ($K = 1.7 \log_2 X$), and packages ($K = 1.95 \log_2 X$), where X = ratio (i.e., defined test drug strengths/the standard drug strengths). For the same medicine, this will be influenced by factors such as average production costs, production techniques, and the efficiency and effectiveness of clinical application, convenience, and treatment cost.
2. Combined pricing. A combined pricing policy uses both the fixed-margin (15 %) added-pricing method and the fixed-value added-pricing method. Low-price drugs use the 15 % margin for added-pricing. When a drug price reaches a threshold, a high-price drug will only have a fixed margin, usually less than a 15 % markup. In principle, this should work to hold the price down. To illustrate the application of combined pricing in setting differential prices in the distribution process, suppose that the drug price is RMB 1,000 and the markup rate is 15 % (i.e., RMB 150) as set by the government. The final drug price would then be RMB 1,000 + RMB 150 = RMB 1,150. To limit the retail price (i.e., because the price of the drug is greater than RMB 1,000), the distribution markup would be restricted to the fixed margin of RMB 75. Thus, in this case, the final retail price would be reduced to RMB 1,075.
3. Reducing the profit margin on distribution. An estimated 30 % of drug costs are attributed to the manufacturing process (ex-factory price), 55 % to the cost of commercial distribution (commissions and rebates), and 15 % to retail markup at the point of sale (the hospital). In principle, if drugs were provided directly from the manufacturer to the hospital, the distributors' share could be reduced and significant savings could be passed on (The World Bank 2010a).

3.4 Generic Policy

In China, there are no requirements for generic substitution or favorable terms for registering generics, and there is no policy to promote the prescription of international nonproprietary name (INN) generics. However, in the prescription management strategies issued by the Chinese Ministry of Health (MOH) (MOH 2007), the government suggested that doctors should prescribe using INNs. Meanwhile, the Chinese government implemented its Essential Medicine Policy in 2009 to promote the usage of low-cost generics. In August 2009, the MOH issued a National Essential Medicine List (NEML), which included 307 generic drugs: 205 Western medicines and 102 traditional Chinese medicines (MOH 2009). In 2012, a new NEML (2012 edition) (The Ministry of Health 2012) was released. The new list consists of three parts: chemical medicines and biological products (317), Chinese proprietary medicines (203), and prepared slices of Chinese crude drugs The number of chemical medicines and biological products in the list is approaching that registered in the WHO current model list of essential medicines. The list places an equal emphasis on both traditional Chinese medicine and Western medicine. To meet the demand of patients, the MOH has stated that all primary healthcare institutions in urban and rural areas must acquire and use essential medicines. The ministry has also set specific utilization rates of essential medicines for other healthcare institutions: in secondary and tertiary hospitals, at least 40 % and 30 %, respectively, of all medicines used should be NEML drugs, and the inpatient and outpatient sales of essential medicines should be no less than 30 % and 20 % of their total drug sales, respectively (Shaanxi Provincial Government 2010). Patients are also allowed to purchase prescribed drugs in retail pharmacies. Individual provinces can apply the NEML to its local reimbursable medicines list and the reimbursement percentage of essential medicines must be 5–10 % higher than that of non-essential medicines.

The central government has instructed provincial governments to engage in public online bidding for medicines to achieve the lowest possible purchasing prices for medicines used to treat the most frequent and prevalent medical conditions. For example, Shaanxi Province has established a coordinating center (the Shaanxi Provincial Center for Medicine Procurement) in charge of the "unified bidding, unified distribution, and unified pricing" of essential medicines. In February 2010, the center announced the bidding results of 367 drug suppliers for 1,034 products (Xian Bureau of Health 2011). Compared with NDRC reference prices, the average Shaanxi bidding prices were lower by 46.1 % (The Shaanxi Provincial Government 2012). Under highly centralized bidding, wholesale drug distributors' distribution costs are set at 5 % of drug prices. Because drug sales revenues were replaced by a zero-markup policy, the shift inevitably led to a serious drop in income for hospitals (Guan et al. 2011). To maintain the normal operation of grass-roots healthcare institutions, multiple measures have been taken to meet the revenue: direct subsidies by central, provincial, and municipal level governments, higher user fees, and higher insurance payments for medical services.

Generic drugs play a central role in China's essential medicines policy, but their utilization and availability need to be improved, as do production and perception. There are a number of ways these can be achieved.

1. Subsidize production. Several subsidized policies could be used to support the production of generic medicines, such as compensation to the pharmaceutical companies that manufacture essential medicines, low-interest loans to manufacturers, support for R&D, and lower VAT or tax exemptions.
2. International nonproprietary names (INNs). The use of INNs should be expanded and pricing standardized for equivalent ingredients.
3. Select a designated list of approved generic manufacturers. To ensure the quality of essential medicines, designated manufacturers should be carefully screened and selected at provincial and municipal levels. Designated manufacturers would facilitate economies of scale in production, helping to further reduce production costs. The selection of designated manufacturers has been held up, largely through resistance from the pharmaceutical sector. However, necessary criteria have been agreed to as part of the selection process of manufacturers to participate in the newly mandated programs for bulk purchasing. This step needs to be followed through.
4. Ensure quality. In every aspect of manufacturing and distribution, the principle must be enshrined: quality first, then price. There can no leeway in conformity with strict good manufacturing practice standards—a message that must be widely disseminated among those who prescribe and use these medicines.
5. Simplify the package. The MOH and CFDA should encourage pharmaceutical manufacturers to simplify drug packaging.

3.5 The Impact of Pricing on Public Health

In both 2010 and 2012, two cross-sectional surveys (Yang and Fang 2010; Fang 2012) on medicine availability and prices in Shaanxi Province were conducted using a standard methodology developed by WHO and Health Action International (WHO/HAI) (WHO, Health Action International 2008). A total of 44 medicines were surveyed in both years: 27 selected from WHO/HAI core global and regional lists (representing medicines for common acute and chronic conditions), and 17 locally selected supplementary medicines chosen for their local importance and disease burden (The Shaanxi Department of Health 2012; Department of Health 2013). Sectors surveyed included public hospitals and private retail pharmacies. As required by the WHO/HAI survey method, data were collected on the availability and price of both the originator brand (OB) and the lowest-priced generic (LPG) equivalent.

Availability was reported as the percentage of facilities where each product was found on the day of data collection. Medicine prices were expressed as median unit prices (MUPs) in RMB (yuan unit price refers to the price per individual tablet, capsule, milliliter [e.g., for injections and liquids]), gram [for creams] or dose [for inhalers]) (WHO, Health Action International 2008).

The results showed that the average availability of surveyed medicines was low in both public and private sectors. Furthermore, the availability of essential medicines decreased from 2010 to 2012, particularly in primary hospitals. The MUPs of OBs and their generic equivalents decreased significantly from 2010 to 2012 in primary hospitals in comparison with secondary and tertiary hospitals. In the private sector, the median percentage decrease in price between 2010 and 2012 for 38 LPGs was 4.7 % compared with a larger median decrease of 7.9 % for 16 OBs. Inflation-adjusted medicine prices were also lower and more affordable in comparison with local wages. However, there were concerning decreases in 2012 (from the already low 2010 levels) in the availability of medicines in both the public and private sectors. A long-term, stable, and consistent information system is required to monitor the further impacts of the implementation of the Chinese essential medicine policy.

3.6 Future Direction for Drug Price Setting

3.6.1 Improving Methods for Pricing Drugs

In formulating the Healthy China 2020 master plan (January 2008), the government substantially improved drug price management, making the pricing system more scientific, rational, and transparent. Efforts along these lines should be continued.

1. The pharmacoeconomic valuation method should be used to select and price essential medicines. (The less-sophisticated selection/pricing method used presently is based on the traditionally narrow criteria of clinical necessity, safety and efficacy, price, and the balance between Western and traditional Chinese medicine.)
2. Drug price policies must be specified by category of drugs, for example, innovative drugs, breakthrough drugs, orphan drugs, and low-price generic drugs.
3. Other objectives of price-setting policies should be strengthened, for example, the need to fully protect and encourage innovation, facilitate healthy market competition, and continuing support for traditional Chinese medicines.
4. The so-called individual drug price-setting system should be abolished. The time lag between the pricing of originator drugs (i.e., those for which patents have expired) and generic medicines should be shortened.
5. Gradually reduce the scope of government price setting, from approximately 2,400 items (representing a 20 % market share and 60–70 % of its value) to all prescription drugs. It is not realistic to audit production costs for every medicine, even using a standard panel drug as a benchmark.

6. The drug reimbursement list can and should vary according to the basic insurance packages offered by existing insurance schemes (i.e., urban employee basic medical insurance, urban resident basic medical insurance, and the new rural cooperative medical system). Realistically, these will not be merged nor their pricing fully standardized within the near term.
7. The general principle of pricing methods is that they should be consistently working to close the gap between branded and generic medicines (The World Bank 2010b).

3.6.2 Implementing Zero Markup

The zero-markup rate policy for drugs does not work independently, and should be combined with government budgetary management and the separation of revenue and expenditure accounts. Another important issue is related to the incentives of professionals. Where the economic linkage between prescribing and health center revenue is blocked, the performance evaluation of health workers can serve as an important tool to establish alternative compensations (The World Bank 2010b).

A zero-markup policy is likely to reduce medical insurance expenditure and can help to cut unnecessary utilization. However, a close eye must be kept on the sustainability of the policy, primarily because a mechanism has not yet been designed to compensate hospitals for their lost revenues.

The extent to which the zero markup succeeds realistically depends on offsetting subsidies. Government financial support is uncertain, and its allocation may be geographically uneven. The amount of subsidy that a hospital or community health center (CHC) receives would depend on the number and volume of zero-markup drugs described by each CHC.

The zero-markup policy faces considerable political challenges under China's health reform. Most CHCs oppose zero markup because of fears that pharmaceutical revenues will be lost. In addition, many patients fail to perceive any substantial benefits. The zero-markup policy needs to be combined with government budgetary management and the separation of revenue and expenditure accounts. Unless the separation of CHC revenue and expenditure accounts is implemented and local governments fully support implementation, the policy is unlikely to be sustainable.

3.6.3 More Effective Use of Bulk (Pooled) Purchasing

A relatively small number of top drugs account for a disproportionately large share of hospital pharmaceutical sales. If bulk-purchasing systems were effectively implemented for these drugs, substantial savings would accrue.

To establish the production and supply system of essential medicines, the government could conduct bulk purchasing using market competition. When organizing designated production, a supervision system will help to avoid market monopolies and government corruption.

The distribution system of essential medicines could entail both government-exclusive selling rights and market circulation. The distribution system of essential medicines should be gradually shifted toward government purchasing, unified distribution, and no markup for hospital-sold essential medicines. All bidding and pooled purchasing fees should be borne by the government.

3.6.4 Continued Learning from International Experience

There is much to be learned from international experience in the area of cost containment. Virtually every government has employed either direct or indirect interventions to control pharmaceutical prices. China can benefit from these experiences, especially with regard to setting maximum prices, price negotiation, reference prices, profit controls, volume-based price policy and application of pharmacoeconomics evaluation. On issues relating to the prices of imported drugs, China should select several Asian or OECD countries at a similar economic level and undertake rigorous comparative price analyses.

3.7 Conclusion

The Chinese government changed its drug pricing policy from controlling the entire cascade of prices for all pharmaceuticals to controlling retail prices for selected products only. Although the mandated price cuts since 1998 have significantly affected the industry, its impact on actual pricing has been limited. To tackle the root cause of unaffordable health care—rapid cost inflation caused by an irrational and wasteful health care delivery system, the Chinese government announced in 2009 a systematic plan to achieve universal access to healthcare by 2020. Of the five main priorities of this plan, the establishment of a national essential medicines system to meet basic needs for treatment and prevention and ensuring drug safety, quality, and supply were particularly emphasized. The solution is to establish a comprehensive and balanced national medicine policy which reconciles the interests of different players in the pharmaceutical sector and guides the whole process: drug production, distribution, consumption and pricing. Although there is only limited evidence available, the implementation of the national essential medicines system in China have been characterized by relative reductions in medicine prices but lower availability of drugs on the National Essential Medicine List in the public and private sectors, especially in primary hospitals. It is critical for government to regulate industry with patient's-need-oriented production, not profit-oriented, and increase financial support to hospitals to break the present incentive system and increase salaries for doctors to prevent rebates. Also, improving transparency and providing adequate price and quality information to empower patients are crucial. In the long run, the government should improve drug price management by continuously learning from international experiences.

References

Beijing Business Today (2007) Analysis of pharmaceutical companies' activity—a document criticizing the drug cuts policy handed to the State Council for the second time

Chen Z (2009) Launch of the health-care reform plan in China. Lancet 373:1322–1324

Communist Party of China Central Committee. State Council (2009) Opinions of the Communist Party of China Central Committee and the State Council on Deepening the Health Care System Reform. Government of the People's Republic of China, Beijing

Economic Observation (2008) NDRC plans a new medical reform on the "markup limited" policy

Fang Y (2012) Medicine prices, availability and affordability survey in Shaanxi Province, Western China. http://www.haiweb.org/medicineprices/surveys/201203CNX/sdocs/2012_Shaanxi_survey_report_FINAL.pdf. Accessed 20 Mar 2014

Guan X, Liang H, Xue Y, Shi L (2011) An analysis of China's national essential medicines policy. J Public Health Policy 3:305–319

Guo C (2013). Pharmaceutical industry and distribution in China. http://chinahealthreform.org/index.php/report/10-researchreport/1659-2013-07-22-03-07-25.html. Accessed 14 Mar 2014

Hsiao WC (2007) The political economy of Chinese health system reform. Health Econ Policy Law 2:241–249

Liu GG, Fukuda T, Lee CE, Chen V, Zheng Q, Kamae I (2009) Evidence-based decision-making on medical technologies in China, Japan, and Singapore. Value Health 12(Suppl 3):S12–S17

Meng Q, Cheng G, Silver L, Sun X, Rehnberg C, Tomson G (2005) The impact of China's retail drug price control policy on hospital expenditures: a case study in two Shandong hospitals. Health Policy Plan 20:185–196

Ministry of Health (2014) Yearbook of Chinese health statistics 2013. http://www.moh.gov.cn/ewebeditor/uploadfile/2014/04/20140430131845405.pdf. Accessed 12 Apr 2014

NDRC (2006) Further consolidation of the market for pharmaceuticals and medical services

OECD Library. Health at a glance: Europe 2010 (2010) http://www.oecd-ilibrary.org/social-issues-migration-health/health-at-a-glance-europe-2010_health_glance-2010-en. Accessed 15 Apr 2014

Pirce Waterhouse Cooper (2009) Investing in China's pharmaceutical industry. 2nd ed. http://www.pwc.com/en_GX/gx/pharma-life-sciences/assets/en-pharma_03-26-small.pdf. Accessed 24 May 2014

Sun Q, Santoro MA, Meng Q, Liu C, Eggleston K (2008) Pharmaceutical policy in China. Health Aff 27:1042–1050

The Department of Health (2013) China's health statistics yearbook 2012. China Statistics Press, Beijing

The Language of Science. China's Pharma Industry Outlook (2014) http://www.languageconnections.com/wp2/chinas-pharma-industry-outlook. Accessed 27 May 2014

The Ministry of Health (2009) National essential medicines list (primary care section) 2009 edition. http://www.moh.gov.cn/publicfiles/business/htmlfiles/mohywzc/s3580/200908/42506.html. Accessed 5 May 2014

The Ministry of Health (2012) National essential medicines list (primary care section) 2012 edition. http://www.moh.gov.cn/publicfiles/business/htmlfiles/mohywzc/s3580/200908/42506.html. Accessed 5 May 2014

The Shaanxi Department of Health (2012) The notice of the regulation on the distribution and use of essential medicines in primary healthcare institutions. http://www.sxhealth.gov.cn/xxxx.asp?no1=12612. Accessed 17 May 2014

The Shaanxi Provincial Government (2010) The implementation of essential medicine policy in Shaanxi Province. http://www.shaanxi.gov.cn/0/1/6/17/953/958/79488.htm. Accessed 25 Apr 2014

The Shaanxi Provincial Government (2012) White Paper: Medical and Health Services in Shaanxi Province. http://www.sndrc.gov.cn/view.jsp?ID=17733. Accessed 28 Apr 2014

The State Council. (2012) Medical and health services in China. http://news.xinhuanet.com/politics/2012-12/27/c_124156559.htm. Accessed 12 Apr 2014

The State Council (2013) Opinion on strengthening and improving the essential drugs system and the new system of grass-roots operation. http://www.moh.gov.cn/tigs/s8340/201309/d0497b2cded74fef81608720410688bd.shtml. Accessed 15 July 2014.

The World Bank (2010) Financing, pricing, and utilization of pharmaceuticals in China: the road to reform

The World Bank (2010) A generic drug policy as cornerstone to essential medicines in China

Wang Z (2007) China's pharmaceutical price policies and practices. Dissertation

WHO, Health Action International (2008) Measuring medicine prices, availability, affordability and price components. 2008 edition. http://www.haiweb.org/medicineprices/manual/documents.html. Accessed 20 Mar 2014

Xian Bureau of Health (2011) Fundamental knowledge of essential medicines. http://www.xawsj.gov.cn/ptl/trs_ci_id_302192.html. Accessed 12 May 2014

Yang S, Fang Y (2010) Medicine prices, availability and affordability survey in Shaanxi Province, Western China. http://www.haiweb.org/medicineprices/surveys/201009CNX/sdocs/survey_report_shaanxi_Final.pdf. Accessed 20 Mar 2014

Yip W, Hsiao WC (2009) China's health care reform: a tentative assessment. China Econ Rev 20:613–619

Yu X, Li C, Shi Y, Yu M (2010) Pharmaceutical supply chain in China: current issues and implications for health system reform. Health Policy 97:8–15

Zhang H (2010) China's irrational medical pricing scheme. Lancet 375:726

Chapter 4
Pharmaceutical Pricing in Egypt

Heba Wanis

Abstract This chapter discusses medicine pricing in Egypt. Historically, medicines were subject to compulsory pricing, later formulated into a legislation that was based on cost-plus and mark up regulation. In 2009, external reference pricing was introduced and later combined with mark-up regulation in a more recent legislation in 2012. Despite the clear legislations, their implementation continues to be a challenge to the government which makes medicine pricing a nontransparent and confused element of pharmaceutical regulation. In a country with high private out-of-pocket expenditure on medicines, affordability remains a major determinant of access to medicines. The local pharmaceutical industry, which is the main provider of inexpensive generic medicines, suffers the confusion of pricing policies, and often risk operating at a loss. The chapter addresses medicine pricing from several angles in an attempt to provide a comprehensive, yet critical, reading of the Egyptian scene.

Abbreviations

API	Active Pharmaceutical Ingredient
CAJ	Court of Administrative Justice
CAPA	Central Administration for Pharmaceutical Affairs
CAPMAS	Central Agency for Population Mobilisation and Statistics
EDA	Egyptian Drug Authority
EGP	Egyptian Pound
EIPR	Egyptian Initiative for Personal Rights
ERP	External Reference Pricing
GDP	Gross Domestic Product
HAI	Health Action International
HIO	Health Insurance Organisation
IP	Intellectual Property
ISPOR	International Society for Pharmacoeconomics and Outcomes Research
MNCs	Multinational Corporations

H. Wanis (✉)
Right to Health Programme, Egyptian Initiative for Personal Rights, Cairo, Egypt
e-mail: heba@eipr.org

Z.-U.-D. Babar (ed.), *Pharmaceutical Prices in the 21st Century*,
DOI 10.1007/978-3-319-12169-7_4

MOHP	Ministry of Health and Population
TDL	Tender Drug List
THE	Total Health Expenditure
TRIPS	Trade-related Aspects of Intellectual Property Rights
USD	United States Dollar
WHO	World Health Organisation

4.1 The Health System in Egypt

4.1.1 Introduction

The Arab Republic of Egypt is a lower-middle income country with a population size of over 86 million (CAPMAS 2014). The gross domestic product (GDP) of Egypt is USD 262 billion and there is 26 % of the population living under the national poverty line of USD 1.56 per day (CAPMAS 2013).

The health system in Egypt is fragmented with multiple service providers (ISPOR 2012). The Ministry of Health and Population (MOHP) lies at the centre as the main service provider. Services are subsidised through public funding, and are delivered through different establishments managed and overseen by the MOHP, such as public hospitals, teaching (university) hospitals and hospitals belonging to the Health Insurance Organisation (HIO), which is the public health insurance system. The coverage of HIO, however, is limited to about 55 % of the population and covers only employees of the formal sector (ISPOR 2012). Services in government facilities, including medicines, are provided either for free or against a small fee. Those who do not have insurance coverage can benefit from the Programme for Treatment at the Expense of the State, which was initiated by the government with an independent budget (ISPOR 2012).

4.1.2 Expenditure on Health and Pharmaceuticals

Total Health Expenditure (THE) constitutes about 6 % of Egypt's GDP, of which the government covers nearly 44 % (WHO and HAI 2008). The low budget of the MOHP remains a major challenge facing better and more comprehensive health coverage. According to National Health Accounts in 2009, the MOHP was allocated only 4.3 % of public budget, most of which gets spent on salaries (MOH and WHO 2011). This low budget is reflected in the MOHP inability to cater for the healthcare needs of all Egyptians, and certainly in the quality of its facilities and service provision. Patients, accordingly, resort to private healthcare providers preferring to pay out-of-pocket for a service with guaranteed quality. That said, out-of-pocket expenditure on heath constitutes a large proportion of total expenditure in Egypt, constituting 71.8 % (MOH and WHO 2011).

In 2009, expenditure on pharmaceuticals constituted 34.2 % of THE. Private out-of-pocket expenditure on pharmaceuticals was nearly 77 % of total expenditure on pharmaceuticals (MOH and WHO 2011). There have been recent calls to raise the budget of the MOHP. The new Egyptian Constitution states in Article 18 that health should be allocated at least 3 % of gross national product (GNP) (Egypt 2014).

4.2 Pharmaceutical Sector

4.2.1 Pharmaceutical Industry

Egypt has the largest pharmaceutical industry base in the Arab and MENA region (Al-Ali 2002). Its sizeable infrastructure and historical expertise has developed since the late 1930s. Pharmaceutical manufacturing in Egypt is primarily based on packaging of imported active pharmaceutical ingredients (APIs) and repackaging of finished dosage forms, with some local production of APIs (MOH and WHO 2011).

Annual size of pharmaceutical production in Egypt reached EGP 15 billion in 2009, which was equivalent to USD 2.7 billion at the time (Bank of Alexandria 2010). At present, the local industry covers around 82 % of the needs of the market, providing affordable medicines to the Egyptians. The remaining 18 % are imported pharmaceuticals (Mehanna 2014).

There is currently 119 licensed pharmaceutical manufacturers in Egypt (MOH and WHO 2011). These companies belong to three categories: (1) public sector companies; (2) local private sector companies; and (3) multinational corporations (MNCs). Public sector pharmaceutical companies operate under the umbrella of the Holding Company for Pharmaceuticals, Chemicals and Medical Appliances (HoldiPharma). The HoldiPharma umbrella covers 12 affiliate companies, and 11 partnerships, as joint ventures, with shares of different sizes (HoldiPharma 2009).

4.2.2 Pharmaceutical Market

Although Egypt's pharmaceutical expenditure per capita is one of the lowest in the MENA region, it is still the largest market of pharmaceuticals among African and Arab countries (AmCham 2012). In 2010, pharmaceutical sales reached USD 3 billion (AmCham 2012). Expenditure on pharmaceuticals is expected to reach USD 4.24 billion by the end of 2014, and enjoys an annual growth rate estimated at 11.4 % (Bank of Alexandria 2010).

In terms of market share, MNCs have nearly 30 % of local sales through their domestic manufacturing facilities and 35 % through licensing agreements with local companies, whereas the remaining 35 % belong to generic production of local companies (Bank of Alexandria 2010).

Looking at the pharmaceutical trade balance, Egypt is a net importer of pharmaceuticals, with a trade deficit of USD 966 million in 2010. The majority of imported pharmaceuticals are finished products, making 73 %, followed by antibiotics which account for 9.3 %, and blood products and vaccines which account for 8.6 % (AmCham 2012). As for exports, Egypt exports mostly to developing countries with Africa alone receiving 22.4 % of exports. The HoldiPharma companies alone export to more than 50 countries (AmCham 2012).

The Egyptian pharmaceutical market is expected to continue to grow. Reasons for this include the increasing prevalence of non-communicable diseases, which require long term and relatively expensive treatment, and the widespread use of generic medicines, which improve access and increase consumption (AmCham 2012).

4.3 Drug Regulation

Egypt has a well established drug regulatory system which was necessitated by the fast growing pharmaceutical industry in the mid-twentieth century. The official drug regulatory body in Egypt is the Egyptian Drug Authority (EDA), operating under the umbrella of the MOHP (Fig. 4.1). There is an existing National Medicines Policy, which was updated in 2005; however, there is no clear implementation plan for it (MOH and WHO 2011).

The EDA comprises three principal, independent yet complementary, organisations:

1. Central Administration of Pharmaceutical Affairs (CAPA), which comes at the forefront of drug regulation being mandated with critical responsibilities such as registration and pricing of medicines, and inspection of pharmacies and manufacturing facilities. The CAPA hosts four departments for Registration; Licensing and Pharmacists' services; Inspection and Control; and Importation and Exportation.
2. National Organisation for Drug Control & Research (NODCAR), which is the national quality control authority. NODCAR is responsible for quality control of pharmaceutical products, raw materials, medical devices, cosmetics, insecticides, medicinal plants and products from natural origin. The Organisation hosts several laboratories which carry out the necessary testing for all pharmaceutical products under registration, which seek to be marketed in Egypt, whether locally manufactured or imported (EDA 2009a).
3. National Organisation For research & Control of Biologicals (NORCB), which is responsible for marketing authorisation and licensing activities related to

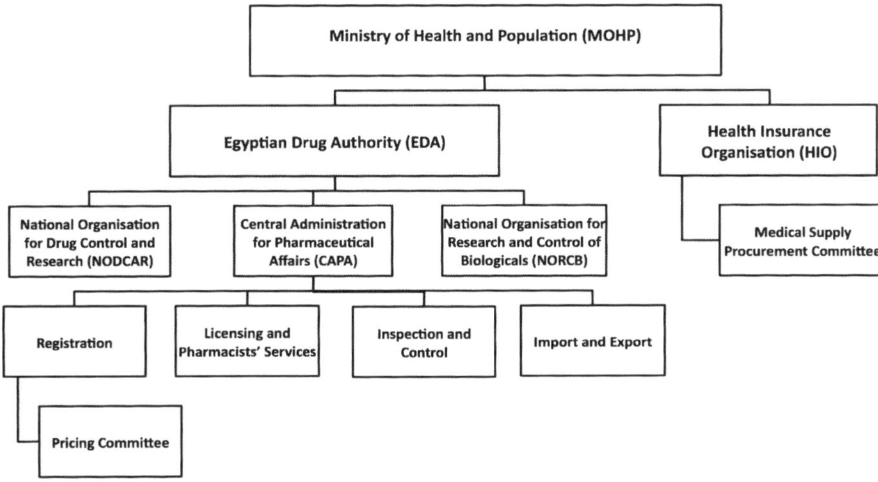

Fig. 4.1 Regulation and procurement of medicines in Egypt. *Source*: ISPOR 2012

biological products; laboratory assessment; post marketing activities including surveillance of adverse events following immunisation; GMP inspection related to manufacturing of biological products; granting authorisation and approval of clinical trials of vaccines and biologicals (EDA 2009b).

4.4 Medicine Pricing in Egypt

4.4.1 Context

Egypt has long enjoyed some of the lowest retail drug prices compared to other countries in the region (Bahgat and Wright 2010). Medicine pricing has been regulated by a strong legislative framework since the 1950s (Egypt 1950). Historically, a strict compulsory pricing policy has been in place, with mark up regulation and profit control, with the aim of making medicines affordable to the lowest socioeconomic segments of the population.

The pricing of medicines is mandated to the Registration Department of the CAPA. Pricing is governed by special legislation in the form of a Ministerial Decree issued by the Minister of Health specifically for this purpose, which is Ministerial Decree 499/2012 on Pricing of Human Pharmaceutical Preparations (EDA 2009a).

The process of medicine pricing in Egypt entails a wide space of negotiations between the government, represented by an appointed Pricing Committee, and pharmaceutical companies. This continues to happen despite the detailed legislative texts governing the pricing process. This will be further explained in the next sections.

4.4.2 *Pricing Legislation*

Before discussing the current pricing system in Egypt, it is important to examine how the pricing policy has developed and how this has been translated into different legislations. It is also worth noting here that the pricing process discussed below concerns retail prices, which patients have to pay when privately purchasing medicines.

4.4.2.1 Development of Pricing Legislation

Since the 1960s, medicine pricing was subject to special procedures to guarantee affordability. Pricing was mandated to the Egyptian General Foundation of Pharmaceuticals and Chemical Products, which took the full responsibility for the pharmaceutical system at the time. A special Pricing Committee was established by the Minister of Health to set prices or mark up for locally produced and imported pharmaceutical products. It is not clear, however, if anything different from compulsory pricing was applied then (Egypt 1962a, b).

Later, cost-plus and mark up regulation were put in place by two ministerial decrees in 1990 and 1991. This pricing system was based on economic cost. It specified profit margins for producers, distributors and pharmacists, and presented a detailed breakdown of the pricing process under direct costs, indirect costs, profit margin of the manufacturer, discount of expedited payment and distribution expenses, public retail price and revisions of product prices (Egypt 1991 and MOH 1991). For this pricing system to function, pharmaceutical manufacturers were required to submit proof of production costs and purchase invoices to be used for price calculations.

In recent years, pricing policies have significantly changed with the introduction of external reference pricing (ERP) in 2009, and later in combination with mark-up regulation in 2012.

In 2009, decree 373/2009 distinguished between branded and generic medicines. Branded, or innovator, medicines refer to those primarily produced by MNCs; and they are either imported or produced locally under licence, whereas generic medicines refer to locally produced off-patent medicines. Branded medicines were priced at 10 % less than the least price where they are marketed. The decree provided a guiding list of 36 countries to use as reference countries. The same list is used in the current pricing system (see list in Table 4.1). Generic medicines were priced at a mark down percentage of the price of the branded medicine, 30, 40 or 60 %, depending on the level of the quality certification of their manufacturing plant (MOH 2009).

This pricing decree has been replaced by a more recent one, decree 499/2012, which is currently in force, and will be discussed in the next section.

Table 4.1 Summary of the pricing system currently in force in Egypt (Decree 499/2012)

1. For the purposes of this decree, human pharmaceutical preparations are categorised as follows:
(a) Innovator: a product composed of an innovative active pharmaceutical ingredient
(b) Imported generic: a generic/similar to an innovator and is imported as a finished product
(c) Local generic; a generic/similar to an innovator that is manufactured in Egypt
(d) Bulk products: a product which is manufactured abroad and gets packaged in local manufacturing plants
2. The proprietor of the product submits to the Central Administration for Pharmaceutical Affairs (CAPA) a list of the product prices in the countries where it is circulated, indicating the retail prices in individual countries, including all discounts. The CAPA contacts the designated government offices of the countries in the guiding list (annexed to the decree) in order to verify the prices submitted by the applicant. The Pricing Committee has the right to refer to the price of the product in countries other than the ones in the provided list
3. Innovator products are priced according to the following:
(a) Its lowest retail price in countries where it circulates
(b) In case it circulates in less than five countries, it is priced at whichever lower price based on either:
– A comparative study between the product and its alternatives; or
– The lowest retail price in the five countries where it circulates
4. Local and imported generic products, from reference and non-reference countries, are priced for the public at the following mark down percentages from the innovator product selling price:
(a) 35 %: applies for the first five generic products to be priced
(b) 40 %: for any other generic products which follow
This applies to generic products whose innovator products had been priced prior to the issuing of this decree, with the condition that the new price does not exceed that of the last generic product that got priced. Pharmaceutical compositions with eleven or less generic versions are exempted from this point
5. Imported high-technology generic products are priced for the public at the following mark down percentages from the innovator product selling price:
(a) 30 % for generic products imported from a reference country, so that the price does not exceed the selling price in its country of origin or any country where it circulates
(b) 35 % for generic products imported from non-reference countries, so that the price does not exceed the selling price in its country of origin or any country where it circulates
6. Profit margins for pharmacists and distributors are set as follows:
(a) Products in the Essential Medicines List:
– Distributor's profit margin: 7.86 % of ex-factory price
– Pharmacist's profit margin: 25 % of ex-factory price
(b) Subsidized products (imported or locally produced):
– Distributor's profit margin: 4 % of ex-factory price
– Pharmacist's profit margin: 10 % of ex-factory price
(c) Imported products (special imports or individual purchases):
In case the public selling price is less than EGP 500 per box, profit margins are set as follows:
– Distributor's profit margin:
8.8 % of importer's selling price
6.4 % of public selling price
– Pharmacist's profit margin:

(continued)

Table 4.1 (continued)

22.9 % of distributor's selling price
18 % of public selling price
In case the public selling price exceeds EGP 500 per box, profit margins are set as follows:
– Distributor's profit margin:
6.4 % of importer's selling price
4.8 % of public selling price
With a maximum profit of EGP 150 for the distributor, deducting the difference from public selling price for the benefit of the patient
– Pharmacist's profit margin:
18.5 % of distributor's selling price
15 % of public selling price
With a maximum profit of EGP 450 for the pharmacist, deducting the difference from public selling price for the benefit of the patient
(d) Local and bulk products (raw material):
– Distributor's profit margin:
8.8 % of ex-factory price
– Pharmacist's profit margin:
30 % of distributor's selling price
25 % of public selling price
In case of cash payment, a further 4.5 % of ex-factory price is added as an expedited payment charge
7. The pharmacist's mark-up is to be raised by 1 % annually on all products which were priced according to the previous pricing system until the new mark-up percentages are reached for imported and locally produced products. The distributor's mark-up is to be raised on all products priced according to the previous pricing system 1 year after this decree is enforced
8. For high-technology products, the CAPA has the right to request comparative economic studies. The CAPA also has the right to change the price in case a lower price is found in any country, compared to the price which was originally considered, before registration of the product is final
9. Prices are valid for a period of 5 years. Companies are responsible for the renewal of prices of their products 3 months before the expiry of the 5-year period. The older price remains in effect until a new one is issued by the Pricing Committee
10. In case of changes to the concentration or packet size of an already registered (and priced) product, percentage of price changes follow a guiding table annexed to the decree. Tablets and capsules are priced in units of strips, with the exception of antibiotics
11. The CAPA is mandated with the lowering of prices of imported innovator products which were previously priced, in case they are marketed in any other country at a price lower than that the one in Egypt. In this case, lowering of the prices of generic versions of such products will apply
12. Price revisions can take place in the following cases:
(a) Currency exchange fluctuations of average 15 % up or down within 1 year
(b) If a company requests price revisions of its products, not exceeding 5 % of its products per year
13. Ministerial Decree no. 373/2009 on the Pricing of Human Pharmaceutical Preparations is terminated, whereas Ministerial Decrees 314/1991 on Pricing of Nutritional Supplements, and 842/2012 on the Composition of the Medicines and Nutritional Supplements Pricing Committee remain in force

(continued)

Table 4.1 (continued)

Annexes		
Annex 1		
List of countries: Algeria, Austria, Argentina, Bahrain, Belgium, Canada, Cyprus, Denmark, Finland, France, Germany, Greece, Hungary, India, Iran, Ireland, Italy, Japan, Jordan, Kingdom of Saudi Arabia, Kuwait, Lebanon, Morocco, Netherlands, Norway, Oman, Philippines, Poland, Portugal, Spain, Sudan, Sweden, Switzerland, Turkey, United Arab Emirates and United Kingdom		
Annex 2		
1. Pricing a new concentration to an already priced pharmaceutical product:		
Dosage Form	Ratio of concentrations	Percentage of price change (up or down)
Tablets, capsules and sachets	2:1	18
	3:1	24
	4:1	30
Syrups and oral solutions	2:1	15
	3:1	20
	4:1	30
Ampoules and vials	2:1	20
	3:1	25
	4:1	30
2. Pricing a new pack or pack size of an already priced pharmaceutical product:		
Dosage Form	Ratio of pack sizes	Percentage of price change (up or down)
Tablets, capsules and sachets	2:1	12
	3:1	14
	4:1	15
	5:1	20
Syrups and oral solutions	2:1	13
	3:1	15
	4:1	18
	5:1	20
Ampoules and vials	2:1	15
	3:1	20
	4:1	20
	5:1	20
Ointments, creams, and topical preparations	2:1	12
	3:1	24
	4:1	27
	5:1	30
Rectal and vaginal suppositories	2:1	13
	3:1	16
	4:1	20
	5:1	24

Source: Ministerial Decree 499/2012 on Pricing of Human Pharmaceutical Preparations (MOHP 2012a). Unofficial translation by the author.

4.4.2.2 How Medicines Are Priced

The current pricing system, in force since July 2012, combines ERP with mark up regulation, detailing profit margins for pharmacists and distributors. Table 4.1 provides a summary of the text of pricing decree 499/2012.

The decree categorises finished pharmaceutical products as "innovator", "imported generic", "local generic" products, and distinguishes them from raw material to which the decree refers as "bulk" products (MOHP 2012a). The market price of a branded medicine is determined according to the least selling price where the product is marketed. A list of 36 countries is provided as annex to the decree for guiding purposes, and it is the same as that of the preceding decree. In case the product is marketed in less than five countries, pricing should be done either following a comparative study between the product in question and its therapeutic alternatives, or as per the least of the prices in those five countries. The applicant would submit to CAPA a list of market prices of the product in countries where it is registered, including all discounts, if any (Article 2, MOHP 2012a). The Pricing Committee can refer to any country where the product is marketed, and the CAPA can always communicate with official bodies in these countries to verify the prices submitted (CAPA 2014).

As for generic products, whether imported and locally produced, they are subject to a mark down percentages from the branded product price: 35 % for the first five generic products who apply for pricing, and 40 % for the remaining generic products in the "box". Imported "high technology" generic products are subject to a 30 and 35 % mark down of their branded version in reference and non-reference countries respectively (Article 5, MOHP 2012a).

Profit margins for pharmacists and distributors for different pharmaceutical products categories are specified as follows: (1) medicines in the Essential Medicines List; (2) Subsidized products, both imported and locally produced; (3) Imported products, including "special import" and individual orders; (4) Locally produced products and "bulk".

According to decree 499/2012, pricing revisions are done every 5 years; however, there are cases when revisions are necessitated: (1) currency exchange fluctuations of average 15 % up or down in 1 year; (2) when a company requests price revisions of its products, not exceeding 5 % of its products per year.

4.4.3 Who Prices Medicines in Egypt?

Pricing of medicines is mandated to an independent nominated committee, the Drug Pricing Committee. The Director of CAPA is the de facto head of the Committee, by position.

The Pricing Committee was established in 1976 (Ministerial Decree 404/1976), and since then its membership has been determined by ministerial decrees. There is no specific term for its membership, given that it remains at the discretion of the Minister. The latest decree on the composition of the Committee was in 2011, Ministerial Decree 842/2011, which replaced decree 298/2006 which was 5 years earlier (MOHP 2011). Additional members could be appointed to join the Committee, also with a decree; this is the case with five newly appointed members who joined the existing Committee following a decree in 2012 (MOHP 2012b).

The Committee currently comprises a heavy representation of academia: the dean of a pharmacy school, professors of pharmaceutics, pharmacology, surgery, accounting, management. Besides, there is a representative of ministries of Finance, Trade and Industry and Social Solidarity, and the Pharmacists' Syndicate (MOHP 2011 and MOHP 2012b).

The Pricing Committee lacks certain important areas of expertise which could be of use in carrying out its mandate. Missing expertise includes pharmacoeconomics and health technology assessment, which were identified as new and useful domains but not yet applied to the work of CAPA or the Pricing Committee (CAPA 2014).

4.4.3.1 How the Pricing Committee Works

It is the responsibility of the Committee to set prices of all pharmaceutical products and nutritional supplements circulating in Egypt. The National Drug Policy instructs the Pricing Committee on the regulation and control of medicine prices based on the following factors: (1) cost of manufacturing/importation plus a fixed mark up; (2) control of profit margins, fixing mark ups for importers/manufacturers, distributors and pharmacies; (3) price comparisons with other countries or other products in the same therapeutic group; and (4) direct price negotiations with producers of patented pharmaceutical products and other single source medicines without therapeutic alternatives (Bahgat and Wright 2010 after MOH 2004–2005).

Despite the rather clear medicine pricing legislations in Egypt, there has always been a wide space for negotiations between the government, represented by the Pricing Committee, and pharmaceutical manufacturers. And the Committee has been known to apply a conservative pricing policy.

In cases when following the pricing legislation in force would cause a medicine to be priced at a relatively high price, the Committee would arbitrarily set a lower price and start a process of price negotiations with the producing company. The net result is that the Committee enforces pricing legislations only partially in order to serve the purpose of maintaining a low ceiling of medicine prices on the market (Adly 2014).

Pricing of medicines used to come towards the end of their registration process. However, this policy has been changed, because it was common that registered medicines never get marketed in case the price set by the Committee is found to be too low by the producing company. Now the pricing process runs in parallel to the registration process. And agreeing on a price has become a determinant of whether the product will end up on the market one day.

Decisions of the Pricing Committee are considered final, although they still need to be cleared by the Minister of Health. Ministers, however, do not usually approve decisions with price raises, according to a senior pricing official (CAPA 2014). Committee decisions cannot be appealed, and companies usually have to accept them, otherwise their product registration file would be indefinitely suspended, in which case they risk losing their product market authorisation altogether (CAPA 2014).

4.4.4 Public Procurement of Medicines

The Egyptian government has always been able to procure medicines for use within the public sector at relatively low prices compared to private sector prices and international reference prices (WHO and HAI 2007). It is worth noting here that there is little information available on pricing of medicines for public procurement. Procurement of medicines and health technology products in the public sector follows a Tender Drug List (TDL) system. Only products included in the TDL are purchased, hence reimbursed, for use within the government facilities, namely the MOHP and HIO outlets (ISPOR 2012). That said, not all pharmaceutical products registered by the CAPA can be purchased for government use. However, for a product to compete in a MOHP tender, it has to be registered with the CAPA. Purchasing is done through calls for tenders, or reverse auctions, where price is a major determinant of which product gets selected.

The development and update of the TDL is mandated to a technical committee called the Procurement Committee, which operates under the CAPA. The Procurement Committee decides which pharmaceutical and health technology products get listed in the TDL. Decisions are based on the needs of public hospitals and primary care units on the one hand, and the bids submitted by pharmaceutical companies on the other hand (ISPOR 2012).

Companies and wholesalers submit bids with price offers for APIs identified as needed by the MOHP. The Procurement Committee examines the technical aspects of product applications, such as pharmacokinetics, safety and efficacy. The financial aspects of bids are referred to a different committee within the MOHP, which ensures that the submitted price of each API does not exceed an estimated price set by the procurement section within the CAPA. This is done in a rather arbitrary manner, because there is no mechanism which regulates these estimated prices from the government side (ISPOR 2012). Pharmaceutical products with acceptable technical offers and the lowest prices get selected by the Procurement Committee, and join the TDL for 2 years.

Public sector procurement was found to be an effective mechanism, not only for obtaining low prices for purchases, but also for transferring these low prices to the benefits of the patients, given the low fees charged at public health facilities (WHO and HAI 2007). There is a significant difference between private sector prices, that is, pharmacy retail prices, compared to prices for government procurement, with the former being considerably higher. Pharmacy prices for the lowest priced generics were found to be 68 % higher compared to procurement prices in the public sector (WHO and HAI 2007). However, this "efficient" government procurement system applies mostly to generic medicines, leaving branded medicines out of its scope (WHO and HAI 2008). There is the exception of imported medicines, which get procured only for use within the MOHP and HIO facilities (ISPOR 2012).

4.5 Impact of Pricing on Access to Medicines

This section examines the current medicine pricing system from different perspectives, and attempts to explore its the impact on public health in terms of access to medicines. The recent, and rather frequent, changes to the pricing system in Egypt have revealed the interlinks between the different players in the pharmaceutical scene. Securing access to affordable medicines in Egypt necessitates taking into consideration the interests of all parties involved when designing a pricing policy, namely patients and local generic industry. Affordability comes at the forefront as a major determinant of access, given that patients are more likely to pay for their treatment out-of-pocket. In the meantime, the conservative implementation of pricing legislation was heavily criticised by the Egyptian pharmaceutical industry.

4.5.1 Affordability

There is little research done on medicine affordability in Egypt and its effect on access to medicines. In addition to this, there is no evidence that the current medicine pricing system is based on affordability studies.

Affordability varies significantly between public and private sectors in Egypt. Purchasing generic products in the public sector for a one month's treatment of a chronic condition would cost an unskilled government worker less than half a day's wage, whereas in the private sector it would cost the same worker up to 12.6 days' wage (WHO and HAI 2007). These calculations date back to 2007 before pricing decrees 373/2009 and 499/2012 were issued. It is not clear how affordability of medicines has changed with the current pricing system, which was strongly speculated to raise prices on the market.

The indicator which the CAPA often uses to measure affordability is medicine price "categories". Registered medicines are grouped as categories based on price ranges in which they fall. The more the number of medicines which fall in the lower price segments, the higher the evidence of affordability. The segmentation of registered medicines showed that 35 % of them are priced at less than EGP 5.00 (less than USD 0.70), and that 75 % of all medicines on the market are priced at less than EGP 20.00 (less than USD 2.80). Price segments go as far as EGP >1,000, equivalent to USD >140, which constitute 0.5 % of registered medicines (Bayoumi 2008).

While the categorisation of medicine prices could give a rough idea about the level of medicine prices, it has got substantive limitations in providing reliable evidence for affordability. It does not reveal the distribution of therapeutic categories across price segments. Certain therapeutic categories might be completely absent from the lower price ranges forcing patients to pay what is beyond their affordability because no generic alternatives exist in a lower price segment. Also, the unit price used by the CAPA, does not take into consideration the cost of long term treatment in case of chronic diseases. This particularly applies to the most expensive products, falling in the last category which does not have a price ceiling.

The introduction of decree 373/2009 was perceived as a threat to the right to health of Egyptians by subjecting medicine prices to global market forces. It was subject to strong reactions by analysts, academics and civil society groups. Some argued that the MOHP placed medicine pricing in the hands of regulatory authorities of other countries which do not share Egypt's economic situation or ceilings of affordability (Abu Bakr and Abdel Raziq 2009). Besides, the MOHP had not consulted patient groups before this decree was issued, whereas they had consulted pharmaceutical companies (EIPR 2009).

Seen as a threat to access to medicines, decree 373/2009 was challenged before court by the civil society in Egypt. A case was filed before the Administrative Court by the Egyptian Initiative for Personal Rights (EIPR), an independent civil society think-tank. The EIPR claimed that applying this new pricing mechanism based on ERP would gradually deprive Egyptians of affordable medicines, hence threatening their right to health. The Court ruled with the suspension of decree 373/2009. Following this, the MOHP appealed, and the Egyptian Association for Pharmaceutical Producers petitioned to support its appeal (EIPR 2010). The decree came back to force, until it was replaced by decree 499/2012 three years later (EIPR 2013).

4.5.2 *Local Generic Industry*

The medicine pricing system was changed in 2009 and 2012 in order to resolve the complexities of the cost-plus system, longstanding at the time. The new system was aimed at providing "very clear, easy and transparent way of pricing medicines" (Abu Bakr and Abdel Raziq 2009). Under the old cost-plus system, the government claimed that pharmaceutical companies submitted fake purchase invoices for their raw materials in order to claim as high as possible cost of production. Besides, validating the actual costs of production was a challenging task which consumed too much time and effort by the Pricing Committee. On the other hand, pharmaceutical companies always accused the Pricing Committee of being non-transparent (Abu Bakr and Abdel Raziq 2009).

Local pharmaceutical manufacturers criticised decree 499/2012, particularly its mark up regulation element. The Chamber of Pharmaceutical Industries filed a case against the Minister of Health challenging the decree. The case claimed that the pricing decree specified profit margin for the pharmacies and distributors, raising market prices of medicines, hence “maximising the profits of pharmacists and distributors at the cost of the profits pharmaceutical manufacturers and importers”. According to the case, this is a breach of pricing of medicines based on economic cost which realises the “balance of rights” between pharmaceutical companies and patients, and negatively affects investment in the pharmaceutical sector and the competitiveness of Egyptian medicines in Arab and African countries (CAJ 2013). There were claims against regulating prices of medicines produced by companies compliant to the investment law; however, court considered medicine pricing to be an exception to the rule, for socioeconomic considerations particularly “social solidarity and consumer protection” (CAJ 2013). The Court refused the request to annul the decree and it continues to be in force.

4.5.3 The Technical Challenge of the Pricing Process

Academia and civil society in Egypt raised concerns regarding the implementation of the current pricing decree 499/2012. These included the lack of administrative capacity for its implementation, particularly concerning accessing accurate information on market prices from other countries for referencing (EIPR 2013). One more challenge is that discounts made to governments often remain confidential, making it difficult to obtain real prices for referencing (Jack 2013).

A senior official at the Pricing Department of the CAPA has emphasised the difficulty of complying with decree 499/2012 since the time it was issued, despite the presence of a technical support team that conducts the necessary research for the Pricing Committee (CAPA 2014). The result is the inconsistent or selective implementation of the pricing decree, which pharmaceutical companies have been criticising demanding that a clear system be put in place (CAPA 2014).

4.5.4 Availability: Registered, But Not Marketed, Medicines

It is common in Egypt that pharmaceutical products get registered with the CAPA, hence obtain a market authorisation, however, do not make it to the market. At the time that preceded the introduction of the pricing system which is now in force, nearly 22 % of all registered medicines could not make it to the market. This was attributed to the complexity of the cost-plus system at the time, and to the fact that pricing was done at the end of the registration process (Abu Bakr and Abdel Raziq 2009). The CAPA now does registration and pricing in parallel to avoid these marketing gaps (CAPA 2014). However, the problem persists with the current pricing decree.

Registration of pharmaceuticals in Egypt follows what is called a "box" system, whereby there is a maximum number of 12 products per pharmaceutical composition allowed on the market: 1 branded/innovator product, and 11 generic products. The 12 products thus constitute a "box" in that sense.

According to the pricing decree 499/2012, the first five generic products get priced at a 35 % mark down of the price of that of the innovator's, and the ones which follow at 40 % mark down of the same price. Within a given "box", the Pricing Committee tends to strictly observe descending prices depending on registration date. The later the registration date the lower the price given to the generic product. It is common to have long waiting lists of other products for registration in case a product falls out of the "box". This happens in case a pharmaceutical company registers a product and does not market it for a period of 1 year (Adly 2014).

The system is implemented in a manner which limits generic competition. And at the same time, it does not guarantee that all registered products will be available on the market because of the pricing policy applied. In case a product is registered, but gets priced at too low a price which does not satisfy the producer, there is no guarantee that it will be marketed. The system in this case falls short of ensuring the availability of an adequate number of generic products per pharmaceutical composition.

4.5.5 Availability of Medicines: Shortages

The pharmaceutical market has been suffering frequent shortages, always hitting medicines in the lowest price categories. Out of 13,000 registered products, only 8,000 are actually available on the market (Mehanna 2014).

Rising costs of imported raw material, overheads and salary increases, investment in meeting manufacturing specifications, inflation and exchange rate of the Egyptian Pound against foreign currency, were among the identified causes by companies, which might cause certain production lines to operate at a loss (Adly 2014). The public pharmaceutical Business Sector currently produces over 600 pharmaceutical products at a loss. This cannot last for too long, and gradually, cheaper medicines will disappear from the market altogether leaving behind expensive ones (Adly 2014). There are estimates that 31 % of all locally produced medicines are manufactured at a loss, and only big manufacturers can absorb such high loss and continue to operate (Mehanna 2014). Often, companies which risk operating at a loss, due to restrictive pricing decisions, seek to protect their registration files by producing one or two batches of the medicine per year, which explains the frequent shortage of certain products (Adly 2014).

Ultimately, the rigid, non transparent and conservative pricing system of the government was blamed by local companies, and even perceived as a threat to the industry (Hussein 2014). On the other hand, the MOHP is always reluctant about slight price increases for fear of public reactions, and shortages continue to be common in the Egyptian market.

4.5.6 Other Options to Ensure Access to Medicines

The fact there is no adequate health insurance coverage, or a clearly enforced pricing policy in place has lead to the emergence of other mechanisms on which the Egyptian government has been relying to ensure affordability and access to medicines. Unsustainable as they may seem, such mechanisms undoubtedly, bring in some balance to the confused scene.

Subsidisation of certain pharmaceutical categories is one protective measure against overpriced medicines. These include medicines for renal failure, hepatitis and high blood pressure, in addition to insulin and infant milk. The total value of subsidy reaches EGP 120 million in 2007, for instance. The government has commissioned a distribution company, owned by HoldiPharma, to distribute the medicines at subsidised prices to pharmacies (Bahgat and Wright 2010).

Another mechanism is treatment at the expense of the government. Patients who are outside the coverage of the national HIO, resort to this option when they cannot afford costly treatment such as in cases of cancer and transplants.

Following the enforcement of the Agreement on Trade-related Aspects of Intellectual Property Rights (TRIPS Agreement), the Egyptian Law 82/2002 on the Protection of Intellectual Property Rights ordered the establishment of a fund for subsidising medicines, called a Medicine Prices Stabilisation Fund, in anticipation of rising medicine prices (Article 18, Egypt 2002). The Fund aims at maintaining stability of prices of medicines, not intended for export, ensuring access and affordability in the case of unexpected price increases. However, this Fund has not been operationalised since the law came to force (Bahgat and Wright 2010).

A signatory to the TRIPS Agreement, Egypt can possibly use measures such as compulsory licensing or government use, to secure access to affordable medicines. Despite the stipulation of these measures in the Egyptian national intellectual property (IP) law, decision makers seem to prefer to stay away from them.

Recently, the Egyptian government negotiated with Gilead Sciences Inc. to register, price and procure sofosbuvir, an oral direct acting antiviral for the treatment of viral hepatitis C. Generic manufacturers in Egypt expressed interest in locally producing sofosbuvir; however, MOHP officials were concerned about the violation of the IP rights of Gilead, despite the absence of a patent for sofosbuvir in Egypt (Al-Hadidi 2014 and CAPA 2014). With a prevalence rate of 14.7 %, viral hepatitis C creates a significant social and economic burden in both the public and private sectors. Unfortunately, measures in the TRIPS Agreement to ensure less expensive HCV treatment were overlooked by the government (Wanis 2014).

4.6 Conclusion

The Egyptian government has invested in developing the medicine pricing over the recent years, shifting it from a system which was based on cost-plus and mark-up regulation to one which is based on ERP in combination with mark-up regulation. Despite this, pricing legislation remains to be seen as disconnected from the reality of the pharmaceutical scene in Egypt, and there remains a wide gap between legislation and its implementation.

Pricing legislation in Egypt needs to be based on national pricing surveys and affordability studies to ensure that medicine remains affordable to the whole population. Based on this, the government should be able to decide on the best possible combination of pricing mechanisms which suit the Egyptian setting. This should ensure that medicines in the Egyptian market remain affordable to the whole population, namely to the lower economic segments who do not have adequate insurance coverage, or who lack it altogether.

The protection and development of the local generic industry should be within sight of the Egyptian government as a long term vision when designing pricing policies. Pricing mechanisms should be regularly revised to accommodate for rise in production costs. This should help protect the local industry and encourage it to continue to supply the domestic market with medicines of affordable prices, and avoid shortages which is a recurrent problem in the Egyptian pharmaceutical market.

References

Abu Bakr K, Abdel Raziq S (2009) Al-Gabali: Al-fasad Huwwa Sabab Ilgha' Nizam Al-Tas'ir Al-qadim Wa Sa-ataraja' An Al-qarar Al-jadid Idha Thabata Fashaluh (Al-Gabali: corruption is the reason why the old pricing system has been terminated, and I will reconsider it if it failed). Al-Shorouk, 4 November 2009

Adly H (2014) CEO and Chairman, Egyptian company for blood transfusion services. Interview on 17 April 2014

Al-Ali N (2002) The Egyptian pharmaceutical industry after TRIPS—a practitioner's view. Fordham Int Law J 26:274

Al-Hadidi D (2014) Minister of Health meets representatives of a pharmaceutical company which produces a new HCV treatment to negotiate the possibility of making it available in Egypt. Al-Youm Al-Sabea Newspaper, 5 February 2014

AmCham (American Chamber of Commerce in Egypt) (2012) Healthcare and pharmaceuticals in Egypt. Business Studies and Analysis Centre, Cairo

Bahgat H, Wright R (2010) Access to medicines in Egypt: a human rights approach to IP, trade and health. In: Rizk N, Shaver L (eds) Access to knowledge in Egypt: new research on intellectual property, innovation and development. Bloomsbury Academic, New York, pp 56–91

Bank of Alexandria (2010) Sectoral survey: pharmaceutical industry in Egypt. November 2010. http://www.alexbank.com/Uploads/documents/research/pharmaceutical%20industry%20in%20Egypt.pdf. Accessed 19 April 2014

Bayoumi A (2008) Pharmaceutical pricing policy in Egypt (PowerPoint presentation). http://212.100.220.58/NR/rdonlyres/A20FBE06-0695-421A-A4D6-9CB9D50A9E76/0/PharmaceuticalPricingPolicyinEgypt.pdf. Accessed 13 April 2014

CAJ (Court of Administrative Justice) (2013) Decision of Court of Administrative Justice, First Circuit, case no. 53307/66, Chamber of Pharmaceutical Industries and Association of Egyptian Pharmaceutical Manufacturers vs. Minister of Health and Director of the Central Administration for Pharmaceutical Affairs, issued 26 February 2013

CAPA (Central Administration for Pharmaceutical Affairs) (2014) Senior official at the Pricing Department, Central Administration for Pharmaceutical Affairs. Name withheld upon request. Interview, 17 April 2014

CAPMAS (Central Agency for Population Mobilisation and Statistics) (2013) Poverty indicators according to data of income, expenditure and consumption 2012–2013. http://www.capmas.gov.eg/pepo/a.pdf. Accessed 26 April 2014

CAPMAS (Central Agency for Population Mobilisation and Statistics) (2014) Population size of Egypt. http://www.capmas.gov.eg/?lang=2. Accessed 14 April 2014

EDA (Egyptian Drug Authority) (2009) Egyptian Drug Authority. http://www.eda.mohp.gov.eg/. Accessed 5 May 2014

EDA (Egyptian Drug Authority) (2009) National Organisation for Research and Control of Biologicals. http://www.eda.mohp.gov.eg/About/NORCBI.doc. Accessed 5 May 2014

Egypt, Arab Republic of (1950) Law No. 163/1950 on compulsory pricing and profit regulation. Official Gazette, extraordinary issue (60), 14 September 1950

Egypt, Arab Republic of (1962) Explanatory Note of Law 113/1962 on re-organising import, manufacture and trade of medicines, and medical chemicals and necessities. Official Gazette (168), 25 July 1962

Egypt, Arab Republic of (1962) Presidential Decision with Law 113/1962 on re-organising import, manufacture and trade of medicines, and medical chemicals and necessities. Official Gazette (168), 25 July 1962

Egypt, Arab Republic of (1991) Minister of Health Decision 314/1991 on rules and principles of pricing of locally produced medicines and pharmaceutical preparations and profit regulation thereof. Official Gazette (272), 1 December 1991

Egypt, Arab Republic of (2002) Law 82/2002 on the Protection of Intellectual Property Rights. Official Gazette (22), 2 June 2002

Egypt, Arab Republic of (2014) The constitution of the Arab Republic of Egypt. http://www.sis.gov.eg/Newvr/consttt%202014.pdf

EIPR (Egyptian Initiative for Personal Rights) (2009) Facts about the new drug-pricing decree: the decree threatens citizens' right to health. http://eipr.org/en/report/2009/12/15/671. Accessed 15 Jan 2013

EIPR (Egyptian Initiative for Personal Rights) (2010) Pharmaceutical companies intervene in support of the government in the drug pricing case: price reductions for 40 drugs are not a result of the new pricing system; the minister's decree is in the interest of business. http://eipr.org/node/911. Accessed 10 June 2010

EIPR (Egyptian Initiative for Personal Rights) (2013) Pricing Decree 499/2012: where is it from the right to medicine? http://eipr.org/sites/default/files/reports/pdf/right_to_medicine.pdf

HoldiPharma (The Holding Company for Pharmaceuticals, Chemicals and Medical Appliances) (2009) Company history. http://www.holdipharma.com.eg/ar/home/pages/companyhistory.aspx?. Accessed 7 May 2014

Hussein H (2014) Ghorfat Sena'at Addawa'a: Nantather Al-Hokouma Al Qadema Lehal Azmat Tas'eer Al Adweya (Pharmaceutical Manufacturers' Chamber: waiting for the next government to solve the drug pricing crisis). 10 January 2014. http://www.shorouknews.com/news/view.aspx?cdate=10012014&id=01185fd5-9f12-49ce-859b-456a6df553be. Accessed 13 April 2014

ISPOR (The International Society for Pharmacoeconomics and Outcomes Research) (2012) ISPOR Global Health Care Systems Road Map: Egypt. May 2012. http://www.ispor.org/htaroadmaps/egyptph.asp

Jack A (2013) Comparing drug prices across borders a difficult task. Financial Times 11 August 2013

Mehanna M (2014) Former President of the Chamber of Pharmaceutical Industries, Mustaqbal Sena'at Ad-dawa' fi Misr (The future of the pharmaceutical industry in Egypt) Hawla Al-Ahdath TV Programme, Al-Tahrir TV Channel. https://www.youtube.com/watch?v=MuOgIU-XJO4. Accessed 5 Feb 2014

MOH (Ministry of Health) (1991) Decree 150/1990. Official Gazette (4), 5 January 1991

MOH (Ministry of Health) (2004–2005) National Drug Policy

MOH (Ministry of Health) (2009) Ministerial Decree 373/2009 on pricing of human pharmaceutical preparations. Official Gazette (220), 24 September 2009

MOH and WHO (Ministry of Health and the World Health Organisation) (2011) Egypt Pharmaceutical Country Profile. http://www.who.int/medicines/areas/coordination/Egypt_PSCPNarrativeQuestionnaire_27112011.pdf. Accessed 30 July 2013

MOHP (Ministry of Health and Population) (2011) Ministerial Decree 842/2011 on the re-appointment of the medicines and nutritional supplements Pricing Committee. Official Gazette (284), 17 December 2011

MOHP (Ministry of Health and Population) (2012) Decree 499/2012 on pricing of human pharmaceutical preparations. Official Gazette (153), 3 July 2012

MOHP (Ministry of Health and Population) (2012) Decree 712/2012 on appointing extra members to the medicines and nutritional supplements Pricing Committee. Official Gazette (227), 3 October 2012

Wanis H (2014) No sofosbuvir patent in Egypt, but Gilead deal still expensive. South-North Development Monitor (SUNS), Issue 7782, 10 April 2014. http://www.twnside.org.sg/title2/health.info/2014/hi140402.htm

WHO and HAI (World Health Organisation and Health Action International) (2007) Medicine prices in Egypt. Unpublished report submitted at the WHO/HAI Post-medicine Survey Workshop, Cairo, January 2007

WHO and HAI (World Health Organisation and Health Action International) (2008) Medicine prices, availability, affordability and price components: a synthesis report of medicine price surveys undertaken in selected countries of the WHO Eastern Mediterranean Region. Annex 2

Chapter 5
Pharmaceutical Pricing in Ethiopia

Eskinder Eshetu Ali, Anwarul-Hassan Gilani, and Teferi Gedif

Abstract The Ethiopian health care system is under constant reforms that evidently continued to increase the health service coverage and improve the quality of life of the population. As a result of such expansions, the size of the pharmaceutical market is expected to double in less than a decade. However, low level of access to essential medicines is still a problem. The main reasons for the problem of access being: (1) erratic supply of pharmaceuticals especially in public health facilities and (2) unaffordable prices of essential medicines for the poor. Although the government is in the process of instituting social health insurance, households' out of pocket expenditure on medicines constitutes a major share of their health care spending. The pharmaceutical pricing situation is characterized by absence of clear medicines pricing policy, high retail markups, and high variation in prices of medicines. Pharmaceutical prices are not controlled by the government and there is no system for pharmacoeconomic evaluation. Hence appropriate pricing policies complemented by a proper system of pharmacoeconomic evaluation should be introduced.

5.1 Introduction

The Federal Democratic Republic of Ethiopia is an East African country with a total surface area of 1.1 million square kilometers. In 2013 the population size of the country was projected to be about 86.6 million with close to 83 % engaged in agriculture. Administratively, the country is divided into nine autonomous National Regional States and two City Administrations which are further divided into 611 districts called '*woredas*'. The *woredas* are divided into 15,000 *kebeles*—the

E.E. Ali (✉) • T. Gedif
Department of Pharmaceutics and Social Pharmacy, School of Pharmacy, College of Health Sciences, Addis Ababa University, Addis Ababa, Ethiopia
e-mail: eskeshet@gmail.com; tgedif@gmail.com

A.-H. Gilani
Department of Pharmacy, College of Health Sciences, Mekele University, Mekele, Ethiopia
e-mail: anwarhgilani@yahoo.com

Z.-U.-D. Babar (ed.), *Pharmaceutical Prices in the 21st Century*,
DOI 10.1007/978-3-319-12169-7_5

lowest administrative units in the government structure (CSA 2013). With the current double digit economic growth, the country is expected to transform itself from agriculture based to an industrially led economy in a short period of time (MoFED 2010a).

In this chapter, a general description is given on the situation of pharmaceutical pricing in Ethiopia. The chapter starts by a brief account of the setup of the health care system followed by the health care financing system in the country. Available evidence on availability, affordability and pricing of pharmaceuticals will then follow. The chapter also discusses the status of health outcomes research in Ethiopia.

5.2 The Ethiopian Health Care System

The Ethiopian health care system is undergoing tremendous changes. Since the 1997/98 Ethiopian Fiscal Year[1] (EFY), the government has been implementing the Health Sector Development Program (HSDP) in four phases. Execution of the final phase is expected to end in 2014/15. Thus far the government has been successful in decentralizing the health care system (FMOH 2005a, 2010a). As a result, the Federal Ministry of Health (FMOH) and Regional Health Bureaus (RHBs) now focus more on policy making and provision of technical support to *woreda* health offices which are engaged in the management and coordination of primary health care services (FMOH 2012a). In an effort to make health care more accessible to the society, the referral system of public health facilities has changed to a three tier structure from its previous four tier pyramid. The health care system in Ethiopia is also augmented by different levels of clinics and hospitals operated by private for profit and nongovernmental organizations (NGOs) (FMOH 2010a, b).

The three tier referral system is characterized by a first level of Primary Health Care Unit (PHCU) which has different structures in urban and rural areas. In rural parts of the country, the PHCU is comprised of a primary hospital serving 60,000–100,000 people; and up to four health centers serving 15,000–25,000 people each. Under a rural health center, there are five satellite health posts each serving 3,000–5,000 people. A health center, with a capacity of serving 40,000 people makes the PHCU in urban areas. The second referral level for both the rural and urban population is a general hospital with population coverage of 1–1.5 million; and the third is a specialized hospital that covers 3.5–5 million people (FMOH 2010a, b).

Health promotion, preventive and curative services are provided at all levels of the referral system. However, more emphasis is given to preventive services in the

[1] The Ethiopian Fiscal Year starts in July of each year. The country uses its own calendar which is late by 7–8 years from the rest of the world and the New Year begins in September. Thus the Fiscal year touches 2 Gregorian calendar years.

areas of maternal and child health, infectious diseases, and other locally important conditions as we move down the referral system. There is also a major difference between the referral levels in terms of the relative emphasis on services; the number and expertise of professionals; sophistication of diagnostic capacity; availability of different types of medical equipment, medical supplies and medicines; availability and level of surgical services, and availability and capacity of inpatient services (FMOH 2010a, b).

A unique feature of the primary health care system in Ethiopia is the Health Extension Program (HEP). It is a community outreach program based in health posts in rural parts of the country and health centers in urban areas. The HEP upholds the principles of primary health care and its main objective is to improve access to essential health services to households by adopting local technologies and the skill and wisdom of the community. Each health post has two female Health Extension Workers (HEWs) who are expected to spend at least 75 % of their time in community outreach activities. The HEWs visit households for health education and other health promotion activities. Another interesting aspect of the HEP is the recent activity of organizing the community into a five member health development 'army'. The main objective of having the 'army' is to promote safe health practices like hygiene and environmental sanitation by households and bring behavioral changes to increase health care utilization especially that of maternal and child health (Admassie et al. 2009; Admasu 2013; Elias and Accorsi 2013).

In the past 17 years since the commencement of HSDP, the government of Ethiopia has made significant progress in increasing the number of health care facilities. The numbers of health posts, health centers and all levels of hospitals have respectively reached to 16,048; 3,245 and 127 by the year 2012/2013. The baseline number of health facilities in the 1996/97 EFY was 76 health posts, 412 health centers and 82 hospitals (FMOH 2010a, 2013). The huge amount of investment on health posts and health centers shows the government's focus on improving accessibility of primary health care to the Ethiopian population (World Bank 2005).

Another important achievement of the Ethiopian government is its success in achieving Millennium Development Goal 4. In September 2013 it was announced that the country was successful in reducing its under-five mortality to 68/1,000 live births from 204/1,000 live births in 1990 (UNICEF 2013). The maternal mortality rate has also declined to 676/100,000 in 2011 from about 871/100,000 live births in 2001/02. The coverage for antenatal care (at least one visit) and deliveries attended by skilled health personnel reached 42.6 % and 28.6 % respectively. In 2011, the national contraceptive prevalence rate for currently married women was found to be 29 % and the government targets to increase it to 66 % by 2015. Despite these improvements, some of the indicators show that the country needs to work hard to make the health services better even by Sub Saharan African standards (FMOH 2010a; CSA and ICF International 2012).

Looking at the demographic situation of the country, young people constitute one third of the total population. This implies the need for reproductive health services. The major reproductive health problems faced by the young population in the country are gender inequality, early marriage, female genital mutilation, unwanted pregnancy, unsafe abortion, and Sexually Transmitted Diseases (STDs) including Human Immunodeficiency Virus (HIV)/Acquired Immunodeficiency Syndrome (AIDS) (FMOH 2010a).

Communicable diseases are still a big concern in Ethiopia. The adult HIV prevalence in 2009/10 was estimated to be 2.4 %. With an estimated 1.1 million people living with HIV, its prevalence in Ethiopia is high. Malaria and tuberculosis (TB) are also regarded among the major causes of mortality and morbidity in the country (MoFED 2010b). With the increasing economic development and urbanization, the prevalence of chronic non-communicable diseases is also on the rise, creating a double burden on the already constrained health care resources (Misganaw et al. 2012; Muluneh et al. 2012; Weldearegawi et al. 2013).

5.3 Health Care Financing in Ethiopia

Financing of the health system in Ethiopia is hugely dependent on international donations which cover nearly half of the national health expenditure. Households' out of pocket spending which covers up to 34 % of the overall health expenditure in the country is the second largest contributor. Generally, HIV/AIDS, malaria, reproductive health, child health and TB are priority areas of the national health expenditure accounting for about 19 %, 15 %, 14 %, 11 % and 4 % respectively of the overall expenditure in the year 2011 (Wamai 2009; Barnett and Tefera 2010; FMOH 2010c, 2014). According to a 2007 report, the government expenditure on medicines is very low (only 10 % of the close to 2.5 billion Ethiopian Birr spent on drugs at the time). At that time 47 % of the country's total drug expenditures were out of pocket with the remaining covered by donors and NGOs (FMOH/WHO 2007).

The government of Ethiopia is currently implementing health care financing reform. The components of this reform can be categorized into two. The first one comprises of strategies that help to generate additional revenue and make health facilities more efficient. Revenue retention, establishment of private wings in public hospitals, outsourcing of non clinical services and user fee setting and revision can be included in this category. The second category contains strategies that are meant to protect the public from the financial hardships of ill health. This includes the institution of health insurance, fee waiver and exemption systems. Currently, the implementation of the reforms is at different stages in the different regional states of the country (FMOH 2005b, 2013; Zelelew 2012; Ali 2014).

Services such as diagnosis, follow-up and supply of medicines for Tuberculosis (TB); prenatal, family planning, delivery and postnatal services in PHCUs; immunization of mothers and children; HIV Voluntary Counseling and Testing (VCT), treatment of HIV; leprosy management; epidemic follow-up and control; fistula management; immunization and treatment of health professionals to reduce risk related to occupational hazards are currently provided free of charge in public health facilities for all Ethiopians (Amhara National Regional State Council 2005; FMOH 2005b; Zelelew 2012).

Currently, two types of public health insurance systems are being instituted in the country. These are Social Health Insurance (SHI) scheme for the formal sector employees and pensioners and Community Based Health Insurance (CBHI) for citizens in the informal and agriculture sectors (FMOH 2008; Ali 2014). Finances for these schemes are to be pulled from contributions by members, employers and the government (House of Peoples Representatives of Ethiopia 2010a; Council of Ministers 2012; Ali 2014).

CBHIs are established at the *woreda* and *kebele* level while the SHI will be established at national level and will have regional subsidiaries. CBHI is currently in the pilot phase of implementation since 2011 and 143,852 households with a total of 608,675 beneficiaries were enrolled in the scheme by July 2013 (Ministry of Labor and Social Affairs 2012; FMOH 2013). The implementation of the SHI scheme is expected to start in the near future, although the relevant legal and administrative measures are being put in place since August 2010 (House of Peoples Representatives of Ethiopia 2010a; Council of Ministers 2012). Despite variations from place to place and restrictions in the types of specific services, these insurance schemes are generally expected to cover inpatient, outpatient, delivery, surgical services; diagnostic services and generic drugs included in the reimbursement list of the insurance agency (Council of Ministers 2012).

5.4 Pharmaceutical Pricing and the Pharmaceutical Sector in Ethiopia

5.4.1 Pharmaceutical Sector in Ethiopia

The pharmaceutical sector is guided by the National Drug Policy which was endorsed in November 1993 by the then transitional government of Ethiopia (Transitional Government of Ethiopia 1993). Although it might need some revision due to the changes in the global arena of pharmaceuticals, the policy gives a comprehensive direction to the way the pharmaceutical sector should be governed. The Food, Medicines, Healthcare Administration and Control Authority (FMHACA) is the main regulator of pharmaceuticals used for human consumption. It is a subsidiary of the Federal Ministry of Health (FMOH) and delegates some aspects of pharmaceuticals' regulation to the regional and *woreda* health offices (House of Peoples Representatives of Ethiopia 2010b; FMOH 2012b).

The government owned Pharmaceuticals Fund and Supply Agency (PFSA) is the largest purchaser and supplier of pharmaceuticals and medical equipment for government owned health facilities in the country (Sutton and Kellow 2010). Public health facilities are generally obliged to buy pharmaceuticals only from PFSA. However, PFSA permits health facilities to buy from private suppliers if the product is out of stock at its stores (House of Peoples Representatives of Ethiopia 2007). With the exception of out of stock products at PFSA stores, the private importers and wholesalers in the country generally supply pharmaceuticals for private health facilities and drug retail outlets. Overall there are 92 wholesalers and 114 importers supplying pharmaceuticals in the country (FMHACA 2013a).

The size of the pharmaceutical market in Ethiopia has been increasing over the past decade and continues to grow at a speed significantly higher than the global average. In 2006, the total national expenditure on drugs was 2.4 billion Ethiopian Birr (about 274.32 million USD-the exchange rate at the time was 1 Birr to 0.1143 USD). This figure has increased to around 7 billion Ethiopian Birr (about 377.3 million USD-the exchange rate at the time was 1 Birr to 0.0539 USD) in 2013 and is expected to be more than double the 2013 value in 2018 (FMOH/WHO 2007; Naidoo 2012; FMOH 2013).

With 80 % of the country's demand for medicines covered by imports, Ethiopia's local pharmaceutical production capacity is very low (Sutton and Kellow 2010). Currently, production of pharmaceuticals and medical supplies is undertaken by private manufacturers. Until recently there were 13 pharmaceutical manufacturers in the country (UNCTAD 2011; FMOH 2012c). Around 90 % of the raw materials used in local pharmaceutical production are imported accounting for at least 40 % of production costs. This affects the price competitiveness of local producers with imported finished dosage forms (UNCTAD 2011; Vaughan and Gebremichael 2011).

The structure of the pharmaceutical retail system is unique in Ethiopia. It is a tiered system of pharmaceutical retail outlets which somehow corresponds to the three tier referral system in the country. Accordingly there are three levels of retail outlets and these are 'pharmacies', 'drug stores' and 'rural drug vendors' (FMHACA 2013b). Unlike the primary health care facilities, the majority of pharmaceutical retail outlets in Ethiopia are owned by the private sector. All of the rural drug vendors, 85 % of 'pharmacies', and 81 % of 'drug stores' are under private ownership (World Bank 2005). Although chain pharmacies are emerging, many of the medicines retail outlets are independently owned by pharmacists or non-pharmacist business people who are required to hire a licensed pharmacist and/or pharmacy technician (FMHACA 2013b). A 2011 report indicated that there were, 400 'pharmacies', 1,888 'drug stores' and 1,884 'rural drug vendors' in the country (FMOH 2012c).

The types of medicines they are allowed to handle, the required experience and training level of professionals, geographical location and requirements of physical infrastructure determine the level of a drug retail outlet. For example a 'pharmacy' is to be managed under the responsibility of a licensed pharmacist. The pharmacist should have at least a Bachelor level education and a minimum experience of 3 years to be licensed to run a pharmacy. Other pharmacists, druggists and other support staff can be employed under the licensed pharmacist. A 'pharmacy' stocks the highest number of registered medicines in the country (FMHACA 2012a, 2013b). A 'drug store' on the other hand is managed under the responsibility of a licensed pharmacist with a minimum of 1 year experience or a druggist (undergraduate diploma level training in pharmacy) with a minimum of 3 years of experience. The types of medicines that a ‘drug store’ can stock are lesser than a ‘pharmacy’ (FMHACA 2012b, 2013b). A ‘rural drug vendor’ is the lowest level of pharmaceutical retail outlet and is managed under the responsibility of a licensed druggist with a minimum of 1 year experience or licensed pharmacy technician (a certificate level training in pharmacy) with at least 3 years of experience. The stock of this level of retail outlet is restricted to basic essential medicines (FMHACA 2011, 2013b).

The public health facilities in the country starting from health centers to the different levels of hospitals have pharmacy sections which are headed by pharmacists. The pharmaceutical services in these facilities are organized into three case teams as inpatient, outpatient and emergency pharmacy case teams. Each of these case teams is to be led by registered pharmacists. The health posts only handle very small number of essential pharmaceuticals and the HEWs are responsible for them. Private hospitals are also required to have a pharmacy unit which gives service to inpatients, outpatients and emergency room (FMHACA 2010a; FMOH 2010d).

5.4.2 Pharmaceutical Pricing in Ethiopia

According to a World Bank (2005) report, pharmaceutical products comprise a huge portion (up to 60 %) of household health expenditures in Ethiopia. This is partly because of ineffective financial protection mechanisms and erratic supply systems. Unavailability of essential medicines in public facilities forces even those with fee waiver privileges to buy from expensive private sources (Engida and Haile-Mariam 2002; Woldie et al. 2005; Carasso et al. 2009; Barnett and Tefera 2010). Although it is not well studied in Ethiopia, the economic, psychosocial and medical consequences are enormous when poor people are forced to pay for medicines and other aspects of health care by their own (Liu et al. 2003; Lexchin and Grootendorst 2004; Wang et al. 2006; Wagner et al. 2011).

It can generally be said that the pharmaceutical pricing system in Ethiopia is based on the principles of free market and there is no direct control of prices by the government (FMOH/WHO 2005). However, government is involved in provision of some medicines free of charge to ensure access to treatments for priority public health concerns. Medicines used in the treatment of TB (6 Active Pharmaceutical Ingredients in 11 different dosages and dosage forms), HIV (11 Active Pharmaceutical Ingredients in 34 different dosages and dosage forms), opportunistic infections related to HIV (22 Active Pharmaceutical Ingredients in 45 different dosages and dosage forms), leprosy (4 Active Pharmaceutical Ingredients in 5 different dosages and dosage forms), epidemics (based on the need), health professionals’ occupational hazards (based on the need) and those used for maternal and child health (25 Active Pharmaceutical Ingredients in 31 different dosages and dosage forms) are provided freely to those who need them (Amhara National Regional State Council 2005; FMOH 2005b; Zelelew 2012). Moreover, the government supply agency gives priority for local manufacturers during the tendering process of pharmaceuticals. The agency supports local manufacturers by different strategies. Among these strategies are: (1) providing 25 % local preference margin in international tenders (2) disbursing an advance payment of 30 % of the tender value if local manufacturers win international bid; and (3) signing tripartite agreement with the development bank of Ethiopia that allows the winning local manufacturer to borrow 70 % of the bid value in advance (Assefa et al. 2013; FMOH 2013).

A 2004 World Health Organization/Health Action International (WHO/HAI) pricing survey reported that Ethiopia had relatively cheaper generic patient prices, procurement prices and innovator brand product prices compared to other African countries. It should however be noted that the median prices of lowest price generic equivalents in public health facilities and private pharmacies were 35 and 125 % above the international reference prices although public procurement prices for most sold and lowest price generic products were lower than the international reference prices by 29 % and 39 %, respectively (FMOH/WHO 2005). A more recent study in the capital Addis Ababa and Benishangul Gumuz (a regional state found in the western periphery of the country) also found that the lowest priced generic drug was 2.7 and 3.7 times higher than the international reference price in retail outlets of the capital and the peripheral city respectively (Nuru 2009).

Although the 2004 study showed relatively lesser prices of medicines compared to the rest of Africa, affordability was an issue especially in case of innovator brand products. For example, the lowest paid government worker had to work for 4.1 days, and 10.3 days in order to purchase innovator brand of a course of Amoxicillin and a 1 month supply of Glibenclamide from private pharmacies respectively. In both cases the lowest paid government worker would have to pay 0.9 days worth of wage to buy the lowest priced generic equivalents from the same source (FMOH/WHO 2005). This should be seen in conjunction with the fact that in some parts of the country, at least one in six patients is forced to purchase drugs in the private sector, where drugs can be twice as expensive as their public sector counterparts (Carasso et al. 2009; Gutema and Shikur 2011). According to Nuru (2009) people who are unable to pay for their medicines may forego their treatment or potentially resort to the informal sector where quality and safety of medicines cannot be guaranteed.

According to the 2004 national survey, the major contributors to the final price patients have to pay were retail mark-ups (between 93.7 % and 271.5 % mark-ups on public procurement prices of most sold and lowest price generics respectively) and wholesale markups (between 20 and 40 % of the landed costs of imported products and 5 and 10 % of the ex-factory prices of locally manufactured products) (FMOH/WHO 2005). The 2009 survey done in Addis Ababa and Benishangul Gumuz revealed that retail pharmacy markups were 25–55 % for innovator brand products and 25–247 % for generics (Nuru 2009). At this point it is important to note that, there is no clear pharmaceutical pricing policy in Ethiopia (FMOH/WHO 2005; Gutema and Shikur 2011).

Another important factor to consider here is the fact that the country imports close to 80 % of its medicines (World Bank 2005; MoFED 2010a). This has huge implications on the price of medicines in the face of fast devaluing national currency. Assuming that the international price of the medicines does not change, this roughly means that the retail price of most of the medicines would continue to increase at a rate the birr is devaluing (PCI 2010).

5.4.3 The Situation of Generic Medicines and Pharmacoeconomics in Ethiopia

Unlike the situation of pharmaceutical pricing, the national drug policy of Ethiopia specifically favors generic medicines. The policy allows generic substitution by pharmacists (Transitional Government of Ethiopia 1993). National Essential Lists of Medicines have been prepared in generic names and health facilities are expected to develop facility specific formularies. The procurement of pharmaceuticals by the national supply agency and that of health facilities is done based on the national essential medicines list or facility specific formularies (FMHACA 2010b, c).

Although the regulatory authority asserts that due emphasis is given to the quality safety, efficacy and relative costs of medicines when preparing the national essential medicines list, there is no proper cost effectiveness evaluation (FMHACA 2010b, c). Moreover, there is no specific unit in the health system or a separate organization that is entrusted with doing health technology assessment in the country. It can generally be said that the concepts of health economics, pharmacoeconomics and health outcomes research are not well integrated into the Ethiopian health care system. Thus the country relies on prices data and expert opinion on costs to select pharmaceuticals. However, there are unique cases where international organizations like WHO conduct program specific economic evaluations. In addition the higher learning institutions of the country seldom conduct such evaluations as part of their academic exercise not necessarily linked to government decision making (Zergaw et al. 2002; Tekola et al. 2006; Griffiths et al. 2009).

Nevertheless, it is expected that this trend will change with the establishment of public health insurance systems in the country. Since the financial viability of the insurance system will mainly depend on provision of cost effective health care services, it will soon be imperative to integrate the principles of health economics in the day to day workings of the system. As health insurance is still under establishment, it is also a great opportunity for Ethiopia to learn from experiences of other countries and institute a strong health technology assessment body.

5.5 Conclusion

With the expansion of health care facilities and the ever increasing population size, the Ethiopian pharmaceutical market is expected to expand at a fast rate. In this regard pharmaceutical prices are crucial aspects of policy making because prices are important predictors of the size of the pharmaceutical market and accessibility of essential medicines. Apart from the supply of limited number of essential medicines for the treatment of priority public health concerns free of charge, the Ethiopian government does not directly control pharmaceutical prices. Moreover, there is no clear pharmaceutical pricing policy. Although limited, the already available data shows high retail and wholesale markups and variability of drug prices between private and public health facilities. Affordability of pharmaceuticals is also a concern in the country. Although generic medicines are promoted, there is no strong system for the pharmacoeconomic evaluation of medicines and pharmaceutical services. Thus, pharmaceutical pricing policy appropriate for the existing economic and health care system in the country and strong pharmacoeconomic evaluation institutions are recommended.

References

Admassie A, Abebaw D, Woldemichael A (2009) Impact evaluation of the Ethiopian health services extension programme. J Dev Eff 1(4):430–449

Admasu K (2013) The implementation of the health development army: challenges, perspectives and lessons learned with a focus on Tigray's experience. Fed Democr Republic Ethiopia Ministry Health Q Health Bull 5(1):3–7

Ali E (2014) Health care financing in Ethiopia: implications on access to essential medicines. Value Health Reg Issues 4c:37–40. http://www.valuehealthregionalissues.com/webfiles/images/journals/vhri/VHRI_164.pdf. Accessed 30 Aug 2014

Amhara National Regional State Council (2005) The Amhara national regional state health service provision and administration proclamation. Zikre Hig of the Council of the Amhara National Regional State, Bahir Dar

Assefa H, Bienen D, Ciuriak D (2013) Ethiopia's investment prospects: a sectoral overview. Afr Rev Econ Finan 4(2):203–246

Barnett I, Tefera B (2010) Poor households' experiences and perception of user fees for healthcare: a mixed-method study from Ethiopia. Young Lives, London

Carasso B, Lagarde M, Tesfaye A et al (2009) Availability of essential medicines in Ethiopia: an efficiency-equity trade-off? Trop Med Int Health 14:1394–1400

Council of Ministers (2012) Social health insurance council of ministers regulation no. 271/2012. Federal Negarit Gazeta of the Federal Democratic Republic of Ethiopia, Addis Ababa

CSA (2013) Annual statistical abstract. http://www.csa.gov.et/newcsaweb/images/documents/pdf_files/nationalstatisticsabstract/2012/2012%20POPULATION.pdf. Accessed 29 Apr 2014

CSA, ICF International (2012) Ethiopia demographic and health survey, 2011. Central Statistical Agency of Ethiopia, Addis Ababa

Elias N, Accorsi S (2013) Countdown to 2015: the performance of the health sector in the second year of HSDP IV (EFY 2004). Fed Democr Republic Ethiopia Ministry Health Q Health Bull 5 (1):8–20

Engida E, Haile-Mariam D (2002) Assessment of the free health care provision system in Bahir Dar area, northern Ethiopia. Ethiop J Health Dev 16(2):173–182

FMHACA (2010a) Minimum standards for health posts, health centers, primary hospitals, general hospitals and specialized hospitals. Food, Medicines and Healthcare Administration and Control Authority, Addis Ababa

FMHACA (2010b) List of medicines for Ethiopia, 6th edn. Food Medicines Healthcare Administration and Control Authority, Addis Ababa

FMHACA (2010c) List of essential medicines for Ethiopia, 4th edn. Food Medicines Healthcare Administration and Control Authority, Addis Ababa

FMHACA (2011) List of medicines for rural drug vendor, 4th edn. Food Medicines Healthcare Administration and Control Authority, Addis Ababa

FMHACA (2012a) List of medicines for community pharmacy, 4th edn. Food Medicines Healthcare Administration and Control Authority, Addis Ababa

FMHACA (2012b) List of medicines for drug shop, 4th edn. Food Medicines Healthcare Administration and Control Authority, Addis Ababa

FMHACA (2013a) List of importers and/or wholesalers in Ethiopia. http://www.fmhaca.gov.et/otherdocuments.html. Accessed 30 Apr 2014

FMHACA (2013b) Model directive for licensing or drug retail outlets. http://www.fmhaca.gov.et/documents/Medicine%20Retail%20outlet%20model%20%202013.pdf. Accessed 30 Apr 2014

FMOH (2005a) Health sector development plan III. Planning and Programming Department, Federal Ministry of Health, Addis Ababa

FMOH (2005b) Implementation manual for health care financing reforms. Federal Ministry of Health, Addis Ababa

FMOH (2008) Health insurance strategy. Planning and Programming Department, Federal Ministry of Health, Addis Ababa

FMOH (2010a) Health sector development program IV. Federal Democratic Republic of Ethiopia Ministry of Health, Addis Ababa

FMOH (2010b) Guideline for implementation of a patient referral system. Medical Services Directorate of the Federal Ministry of Health, Addis Ababa

FMOH (2010c) Ethiopia's fourth national health accounts. Federal Democratic Republic of Ethiopia Ministry of Health, Addis Ababa

FMOH (2010d) Ethiopian hospital reform implementation guidelines. Federal Democratic Republic of Ethiopia Ministry of Health, Addis Ababa

FMOH (2012a) Health services providers. http://www.moh.gov.et/hsp. Accessed 15 Apr 2014

FMOH (2012b) Food, medicine and health care administration and control authority. http://www.moh.gov.et/web/pages/fmhcaca. Accessed 3 June 2014

FMOH (2012c) Health and health related indicators. Federal Democratic Republic of Ethiopia Ministry of Health, Policy Planning Directorate, Addis Ababa

FMOH (2013) Health sector development programme IV: annual performance report. http://www.moh.gov.et/documents/26765/1612928/Annual+Performance+Report+EFY2005/edac28ed-1365-4d9a-b734-ac4fc352d e5e?version=1.0. Accessed 15 Apr 2014

FMOH (2014) Ethiopia's fifth national health accounts. Federal Democratic Republic of Ethiopia Ministry of Health, Addis Ababa

FMOH/WHO (2005) Survey on prices of medicines in Ethiopia. Federal Ministry of Health/World Health Organization, Addis Ababa

FMOH/WHO (2007) Drug financing in Ethiopia. Federal Ministry of Health/World Health Organization, Addis Ababa

Griffiths U, Korczak V, Ayalew D et al (2009) Incremental system costs of introducing combined DTwP–hepatitis B–Hib vaccine into national immunization services in Ethiopia. Vaccine 27:1426–1432

Gutema G, Shikur M (2011) The private public divide on the economics of essential medicines in Mekelle, Northern Ethiopia: a critical analysis on the national drug policy outcomes. IJAPR 2:630–638

House of Peoples Representatives of Ethiopia (2007) Drug fund and pharmaceuticals supply agency establishment proclamation. Federal Negarit Gazeta of the Federal Democratic Republic of Ethiopia, Addis Ababa

House of Peoples Representatives of Ethiopia (2010a) Social health insurance proclamation. Federal Negarit Gazeta of the Federal Democratic Republic of Ethiopia, Addis Ababa

House of Peoples Representatives of Ethiopia (2010b) Food, medicine and health care administration and control proclamation. Federal Negarit Gazeta of the Federal Democratic Republic of Ethiopia, Addis Ababa

Lexchin J, Grootendorst P (2004) The effects of prescription drug user fees on drug and health services use and health status: a review of the evidence. Int J Health Serv 34(1):101–122

Liu Y, Rao K, Hsiao W (2003) Medical expenditure and rural impoverishment in China. J Health Popul Nutr 21(3):216–222

Ministry of Labor and Social Affairs (2012) National social protection policy of Ethiopia. Federal Democratic Republic of Ethiopia, Ministry of Labor and Social Affairs, Addis Ababa

Misganaw A, Haile-Mariam D, Araya T (2012) The double mortality burden among adults in Addis Ababa, Ethiopia, 2006–2009. Prev Chronic Dis 9:E84

MoFED (2010a) Growth and transformation plan. Ministry of Finance and Economic Development of the Federal Democratic Republic of Ethiopia. http://www.mofed.gov.et/English/Resources/Documents/GTP%20English2.pdf. Accessed 29 Apr 2014

MoFED (2010b) Ethiopia: 2010 MDGs report trends and prospects for meeting MDGs by 2015. http://www.phe-ethiopia.org/pdf/MDGs_Report.pdf. Accessed 30 Apr 2014

Muluneh A, Haileamlak A, Tessema F et al (2012) Population based survey of chronic non-communicable diseases at Gilgel Gibe field research center, Southwest Ethiopia. Ethiop J Health Sci 22(Special Issue):7–18

Naidoo S (2012) High growth rates expected for the Ethiopian pharmaceutical market, but it's not all smooth sailing—unpacking the challenges. http://www.frost.com/prod/servlet/market-insightprint.pag?docid=267359592. Accessed 31 July 2014

Nuru M (2009) Cost as a barrier to access: availability, affordability and identifying component cost of essential medicines. Thesis, Addis Ababa University, School of Graduate Studies, Addis Ababa

PCI (2010) Ethiopia: business and economic updates. Precise Consult International LLC, Addis Ababa

Sutton J, Kellow N (2010) An enterprise map of Ethiopia. International Growth Centre in Association with the London Publishing Partnership, London

Tekola F, Haile-Mariam D, Davey G (2006) Economic costs of endemic non-filarial elephantiasis in Wolaita Zone, Ethiopia. Trop Med Int Health 11(7):1136–1144

Transitional Government of Ethiopia (1993) National drug policy of the transitional government of Ethiopia. http://www.fmhaca.gov.et/documents/drugPOLICY.pdf. Accessed 30 Apr 2014

UNCTAD (2011) Local production of pharmaceuticals and related technology transfer in developing countries: a series of case studies by the UNCTAD secretariat. United Nations, New York

UNICEF (2013) Ethiopia meets MDG 4 by cutting under 5 mortality by two-thirds since 1990. http://www.unicef.org/ethiopia/events_13459.html. Accessed 30 July 2014

Vaughan S, Gebremichael M (2011) Rethinking business and politics in Ethiopia: the role of EFFORT, the endowment fund for the rehabilitation of Tigray. Overseas Development Institute on behalf of the Africa Power and Politics Programme (APPP), London

Wagner A, Graves A, Reiss S et al (2011) Access to care and medicines, burden of health care expenditures, and risk protection: results from the world health survey. Health Policy 100:151–158

Wamai R (2009) Reviewing Ethiopia's health system development. JMAJ 52(4):279–286

Wang H, Zhang L, Hsiao W (2006) Ill health and its potential influence on household consumptions in rural China. Health Policy 78:167–177

Weldearegawi B, Ashebir Y, Gebeye E et al (2013) Emerging chronic non-communicable diseases in rural communities of Northern Ethiopia: evidence using population-based verbal autopsy method in Kilite Awlaelo surveillance site. Health Policy Plan 28(8):891–898

Woldie M, Jirra C, Tegegn A (2005) An assessment of the free health care provision system in Jimma town, southwest Ethiopia. Ethiop J Health Dev 19(3):188–194

World Bank (2005) Ethiopia—a country status report on health and poverty: main report. The World Bank Group, African Region Human Development and Ministry of Health, Ethiopia

Zelelew H (2012) Health care financing reform in Ethiopia: improving quality and equity. http://www.healthsystems2020.org/content/resource/detail/85865/. Accessed 26 Mar 2014

Zergaw A, Haile-Mariam D, Ali A (2002) Cost-effectiveness analysis of health care interventions in Meskanena Mareko Wereda, Ethiopia. Ethiop J Health Dev 16(3):267–276

Chapter 6
Drug Prices in Finland

Katja M. Hakkarainen, Akseli Kivioja, and Leena K. Saastamoinen

Abstract In Finland, primary and secondary healthcare services are provided to all residents by municipalities, small local governing areas. The municipal health services cover drug treatments administered during primary and secondary healthcare visits. As healthcare units procure such drugs directly from pharmaceutical companies through competitive bidding, purchase prices vary. In 2013, drugs procured by healthcare units represented 18 % of the total pharmaceutical expenditure in Finland. The municipal health services are complemented with National Health Insurance, a universal public insurance for all residents. National Health Insurance reimburses curative drugs dispensed at community pharmacies, at basic (35 %) or special (65 or 100 %) levels depending on the illness and drug necessity. Drugs are included in the insurance based on manufacturers' applications for reimbursement status and a reasonable wholesale price, from the Pharmaceuticals Pricing Board under the Ministry of Social Affairs and Health. Products with new active ingredients require a health economic evaluation as part of the application. With or without reimbursements, drug prices are the same in all community pharmacies, consisting of a wholesale price, standardised pharmacy-margins, a value added tax, and a fixed dispensing fee. In 2013, prescription-only drugs purchased from community pharmacies represented 71 % and non-prescription drugs 12 % of the total pharmaceutical expenditure in Finland. In 2013, 63 % of the total costs of drugs dispensed at community pharmacies were reimbursed to patients. Under generic substitution, pharmacies substitute prescribed drugs with cheaper substitutable drugs. In the reference price system, the cheapest substitutable drug also determines the maximum reimbursement for patients.

K.M. Hakkarainen (✉)
Nordic Health Economics, Gothenburg, Sweden

Nordic School of Public Health NHV, Gothenburg, Sweden
e-mail: katja.hakkarainen@nordichealtheconomics.se; info@nordichealtheconomics.se

A. Kivioja
Farenta 3 Oy, Vantaa, Finland

L.K. Saastamoinen
The Social Insurance Institution, Helsinki, Finland

Z.-U.-D. Babar (ed.), *Pharmaceutical Prices in the 21st Century*,
DOI 10.1007/978-3-319-12169-7_6

6.1 The Health System in Finland

Finland is a country of 5.4 million people, located in the northeast of Europe. It has been a Member State of the European Union since 1995. Finland is highly industrialised and considered a high-income country by the World Bank (World Bank 2014). The average life expectancy in Finland has improved throughout the twentieth century, and especially during the last three decades, reaching 77.5 years for men and 83.4 years for women in 2012 (Statistics Finland 2013). Significant public health challenges include cardiovascular diseases, diabetes, obesity, chronic lung diseases, cancers, musculoskeletal diseases and mental health disorders (Vuorenkoski et al. 2008; Ministry of Social Affairs and Health 2013a).

In Finland, universal healthcare is provided to all residents, regardless of for example age, income, nationality, or place of residency in Finland. The constitution of Finland (Ministry of Justice 1999) is the foundation of the country's health services, according to which: "*Everyone shall be guaranteed by an act the right to basic subsistence in the event of unemployment, illness, and disability and during old age as well as at the birth of a child or the loss of a provider. The public authorities shall guarantee for everyone, as provided in more detail by an act, adequate social, health and medical services and promote the health of the population.*" Health services aim at promoting and maintaining the health, well-being, work capacity, functional capacity and social security of the population (Ministry of Social Affairs and Health 2013b). Health services also aim at reducing health inequalities. The current social and health policy focuses on improving social sustainability, through enhancing the strong foundation for welfare, access to welfare for all, and healthy and safe living environments (Ministry of Social Affairs and Health 2011a).

Public healthcare in Finland is funded by municipal financing of primary and secondary healthcare services and complemented with the obligatory National Health Insurance covering for example drugs dispensed at community pharmacies (Vuorenkoski et al. 2008; National Institute of Health and Welfare 2014a, b). In 2012, this public sector funding constituted 75 % of the total expenditure on health (National Institute of Health and Welfare 2014a, b).

More than 300 self-governing municipalities—local governments with a median number of 5,900 inhabitants (Association of Finnish Local and Regional Authorities 2013)—are by law responsible for providing necessary primary and secondary health services to their residents (Vuorenkoski et al. 2008; National Institute of Health and Welfare 2014a, b). Thus, the provision of healthcare services is decentralised to the municipalities which have a significant degree of autonomy in organising services. For primary healthcare, municipalities must have a health centre providing physician, nursing, and other primary care services locally. Municipalities may also run health centres collaboratively with other municipalities. To provide secondary care services, municipalities have formed 21 hospital districts, which are financed and managed by their member municipalities.

Municipal financing of public healthcare is mainly funded by municipal income tax (Vuorenkoski et al. 2008; National Institute of Health and Welfare 2014a), the level of which the democratically elected local council of each municipality decides. Municipalities also receive state subsidies from the Government for the provision of healthcare services under municipal financing (Vuorenkoski et al. 2008; National Institute of Health and Welfare 2014a).

The second public financing mechanism, the National Health Insurance, is a universal insurance for all residents reimbursing the costs of health services excluded from municipal financing, such as the costs of prescribed outpatient drugs, transportation, sickness allowances, private healthcare services, and occupational healthcare (Vuorenkoski et al. 2008; Ministry of Social Affairs and Health 2010a). The National Health Insurance is run by and paid through the Social Insurance Institution (Kela) (Ministry of Social Affairs and Health 2010a). Funding for the National Health Insurance is gained from the insured residents (37 % in 2011), employers (35 %), the Government (27 %), and the European Union and investments (1 %) (Social Insurance Institution 2012). The contribution gained from insured residents is collected through income taxation (Vuorenkoski et al. 2008). In addition to public services, National Health Insurance reimburses about a third of private health services (National Institute of Health and Welfare 2014a). Few Finnish residents have private health insurance.

Employers are by law obligated to provide free of charge preventive occupational healthcare services for their employees (Ministry of Social Affairs and Health 2009). Of the costs associated with providing these services, the National Health Insurance reimburses employers for approximately 40 %. Some employers also voluntarily provide curative outpatient services for their employees. Occupational healthcare accounts for approximately 18 % of all outpatient physician visits among adults (National Institute of Health and Welfare 2014c).

In addition to public funding, patients pay co-payments for both municipal healthcare services and for services covered by National Health Insurance, with set annual limits for patients (Vuorenkoski et al. 2008; National Institute of Health and Welfare 2014a). In 2012, patients themselves covered 19 % of the total expenditure on health (National Institute of Health and Welfare 2014a). Within municipal financing, patient co-payments represented 8 % of the total expenditure on primary care services, and 4 % of expenditure on secondary care services (National Institute of Health and Welfare 2014a). However, if the income of an individual or a household is considered inadequate for the patient co-payments, municipal social assistance may also contribute towards the co-payments.

The total expenditure on health as a percentage of the gross domestic product (GDP) in Finland was 9.1 % in 2012 (National Institute of Health and Welfare 2014a). In the latest comparison among the countries of the Organisation for Economic Co-operation and Development (OECD) in 2011, Finland's healthcare expenditure was average, with respect to both per capita expenditure and expenditure related to the GDP (Organisation for Economic Co-operation and Development 2013).

According to several indicators of quality of care, such as surgical complications and unplanned hospital re-admissions, the Finnish healthcare system provides good quality services compared to the average among the OECD countries (Organisation for Economic Co-operation and Development 2013). The Finnish health system has, however, been criticised for long waiting times (Vuorenkoski et al. 2008; Organisation for Economic Co-operation and Development 2013). Further, Finland's dual public financing of health services has been criticised for inefficient service production and challenges in cost-shifting, particularly in pharmaceutical care where dispensed drugs and drugs administered during healthcare visits have different public funders (Vuorenkoski et al. 2008). An ongoing reform suggests changing the basis of municipal financing and arranging primary and secondary care services by decreasing the number of governing areas to five by 2017 (Ministry of Social Affairs and Health 2014a). The reform aims at uniting primary and secondary care services as well as other social and health services.

6.2 The Pharmaceutical System in Finland

In 2013, the total pharmaceutical expenditure in Finland was €2 824 million, consisting of pharmaceuticals and other medical non-durables purchased from community pharmacies and drugs sold to health centres and hospitals (Personal communication, Tinna Voipio, Finnish Medicines Agency, 30 July 2014). Of the total pharmaceutical expenditure, prescription-only drugs purchased from community pharmacies represented 71 % (retail prices), non-prescription drugs purchased from community pharmacies 12 % (retail prices), and drugs procured by health centres and hospitals 18 % (wholesale prices) (Personal communication, Tinna Voipio, Finnish Medicines Agency, 30 July 2014). In 2012, the total pharmaceutical expenditure represented 16 % of Finland's total healthcare costs (Fig. 6.1) (National Institute of Health and Welfare 2014a).

In Finland drugs dispensed at community pharmacies are reimbursed by National Health Insurance, while drug treatments administered in health centres and hospitals are covered by municipal financing. Non-prescription drugs purchased from community pharmacies are paid by patients themselves. In 2012, drug reimbursements through National Health Insurance represented 67 % of the total costs of drugs dispensed at community pharmacies (Finnish Medicines Agency and Social Insurance Institution 2013). In July 2014, 5,006 drug packages (unique strength, formulation and package size) had a reimbursement status, excluding drugs supplied under a special permit by the Finnish Medicines Agency, clinical nutritional products and basic topical ointments (Pharmaceuticals Pricing Board 2014). The list of reimbursed products is available at the Pharmaceuticals Pricing Board (PPB) website (Pharmaceuticals Pricing Board 2014).

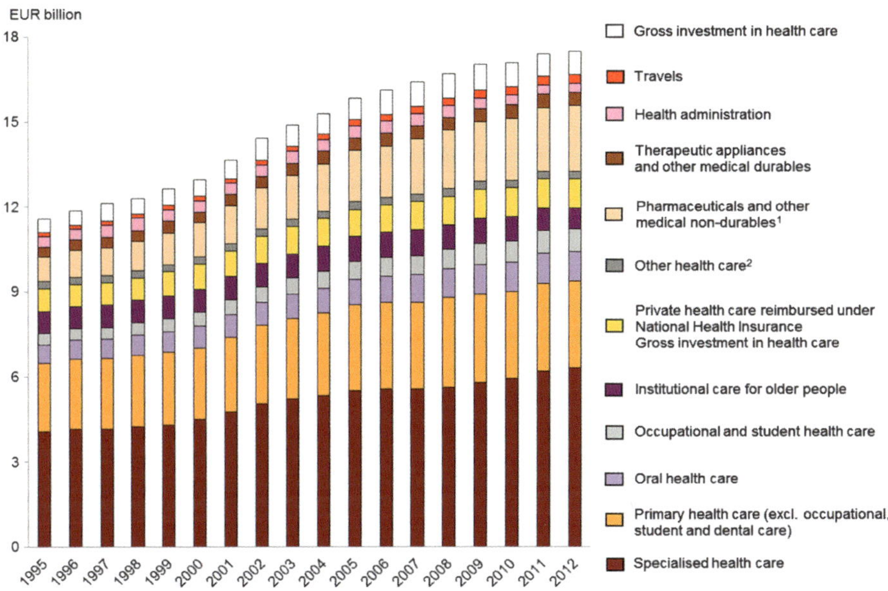

Fig. 6.1 Healthcare costs in Finland in 1995–2012, in 2012 prices (National Institute of Health and Welfare 2014a, permission for reproduction from the Social Insurance Institution). [1]Includes drugs purchased from community pharmacies and drugs procured by health centres and hospitals. [2]Includes institutional care for people with intellectual disabilities, provided by municipalities or purchased by municipalities from private providers, and healthcare provided by Defence Forces and the prison service administration (excluding dental care)

6.2.1 Drugs Purchased from Community Pharmacies

Drugs for outpatient care are sold exclusively in community pharmacies. The only exceptions are nicotine replacement products, which may also be sold in grocery stores, kiosks and petrol stations. Only pharmacists (Master's degree in pharmacy) or assistant pharmacists (Bachelor's degree in pharmacy) can dispense drugs or provide medication counselling. In 2013, there were 617 community pharmacies and their 199 subsidiaries (Association of Finnish Pharmacies 2014a). Each of these 816 community pharmacy units serve on average 6,617 inhabitants. The pharmacies are spread across the country, with at least one pharmacy in almost every municipality. The number and locations of pharmacies are regulated by the Finnish Medicines Agency, with the aim of securing the provision of drugs and pharmaceutical services equally across the country.

A community pharmacy license is required for private ownership of a pharmacy (Association of Finnish Pharmacies 2014a; Ministry of Social Affairs and Health 2010b). Through an application procedure, the Finnish Medicines Agency grants the license to the applicant considered best qualified. Only pharmacists (Master's degree in pharmacy) registered in Finland may be granted a pharmacy license. Once a pharmacist gains a pharmacy licence to a specific pharmacy, the pharmacist

Table 6.1 Construction of drug prices in community pharmacies

Wholesale price, €	Retail price in pharmacy, exclusive of tax (10 %)
Prescription drugs	
0–9.25	1.45 × wholesale price
9.26–46.25	1.35 × wholesale price + €0.92
46.26–100.91	1.25 × wholesale price + €5.54
100.92–420.47	1.15 × wholesale price + €15.63
Over 420.47	1.1 × wholesale price + €36.65
Dispensing fee €2.17 per product, exclusive of tax (10 %)	
Non-prescription drugs	
0–9.25	1.5 × wholesale price + €0.50
9.26–46.25	1.4 × wholesale price + €1.43
46.26–100.91	1.3 × wholesale price + €6.05
100.92–420.47	1.2 × wholesale price + €16.15
Over 420.47	1.125 × wholesale price + €47.68
Dispensing fee €2.17 per product, if prescribed and dispensed, exclusive of tax (10 %)	

becomes the new owner of the pharmacy and must buy at least the stock from the previous owner. One pharmacist may own only one pharmacy, but the pharmacy may have up to three smaller subsidiary pharmacies. The pharmacy license is terminated when the pharmacy owner reaches the age of 68 years.

In addition to the privately owned pharmacies, the University of Helsinki and the University of Eastern Finland providing pharmacy education have the authority to operate community pharmacies (Ministry of Social Affairs and Health 2010b). The Helsinki University Pharmacy also runs 16 subsidiary pharmacies, in addition to the main pharmacy (University Pharmacy 2013).

Community pharmacies purchase drugs from wholesale companies, with regulated wholesale prices for reimbursed drugs, and the drugs are sold to consumers with regulated pharmacy margins, as described in the following paragraphs below (Table 6.1). When reimbursed drugs are dispensed, community pharmacies issue the reimbursements and provide the reimbursements to patients at the time of dispensing. Afterwards, pharmacies apply for reimbursements from Kela, the public institution administrating the reimbursements of dispensed drugs.

6.2.2 Drugs Administered in Health Centres and Hospitals

Pharmaceutical services in public hospitals and health centres are organised and provided by hospital pharmacies and the medicine dispensaries owned by the municipalities (Aaltonen et al. 2012). Hospital pharmacies procure drugs from pharmaceutical companies, maintain storage, compound, and deliver drugs and drug information. Drugs cannot, however, be sold to patients in hospitals and health centres.

All hospitals must have an essential drugs list in order to ensure rational drug use (Finnish Medicines Agency 2012). The lists of essential drugs standardise and guide procurement. Expert panels with medical specialists and pharmacists in institutions compile the essential lists according to clinical practice guidelines and other scientific evidence.

6.3 Authorities Governing Regulation, Sale, Pricing and Use of Medicines in Finland

Several regulatory authorities, subordinated to the Ministry of Social Affairs and Health, are responsible for regulating and controlling the manufacturing, sale, quality, safety, and pricing of drugs and prescribing and dispensing. The most central of these authorities are the Finnish Medicines Agency and the Pharmaceuticals Pricing Board (PPB).

The Finnish Medicines Agency is responsible for the general planning and direction of pharmaceutical policy, and controlling of pharmaceuticals, pharmaceutical industry and community pharmacies. Marketing authorisations for medicinal products are granted by the Finnish Medicines Agency. The Agency also grants licences for community pharmacies and conducts inspections of community pharmacies and pharmaceutical companies.

The PPB is the authority overseeing drug pricing in community pharmacies and drug reimbursements through National Health Insurance. For dispensed drugs at community pharmacies, the PPB determines which drugs gain reimbursement status and confirms the reimbursable wholesale price of said drugs. The PPB has seven members from the Ministry of Social Affairs and Health, Kela, the Finnish Medicines Agency, the National Institute for Health and Welfare and the Ministry of Finance (Ministry of Social Affairs and Health 2010b). The PPB must have pharmaceutical, legal, medicinal and economic expertise. In addition, the PPB has a PPB expert group, including persons with expertise in medicine, pharmacology, health economics and health insurance. The expert group may be consulted in decision making.

Two other authorities under the Ministry of Social Affairs and Health also contribute to governing drug utilisation as a whole: the National Supervisory Authority for Welfare and Health, and the National Institute for Health and Welfare. The National Supervisory Authority for Welfare and Health controls and supervises healthcare practice, for example, grants practice licences for health professionals and evaluates medical errors. Enhancing the implementation of pharmaceutical policies into the health system as a whole is overseen by the National Institute for Health and Welfare.

Kela, the Social Insurance Institution of Finland, administers the National Health Insurance, including reimbursements of dispensed drugs. Apart from the drug reimbursement scheme, other schemes administered by Kela include family benefits, student benefits, unemployment security, housing benefits, assistance for immigrants, and basic pensions. Kela operates under the supervision of the Parliament. Although Kela is an administrative institution rather than a regulatory authority, Kela establishes practical rules and procedures for patients and community pharmacies in order to administer reimbursements of dispensed drugs.

Apart from the determined tasks of the above mentioned authorities, the Ministry of Social Affairs and Health proposes laws regulating prices and reimbursement of drugs, including the Medicines Act (Ministry of Social Affairs and Health 2010b) and the Health Insurance Act (Ministry of Social Affairs and Health 2010a).

6.4 How Drug Prices Are Determined

6.4.1 *Drugs Purchased from Community Pharmacies*

In outpatient care, the retail prices of drugs sold at community pharmacies consist of a wholesale price, regulated pharmacy-margins, a value added tax (10 %), and a standard dispensing fee (Ministry of Social Affairs and Health 2013c). Drug prices are the same in every pharmacy. For drugs that are not reimbursed, manufacturers may freely determine wholesale prices. If a manufacturer, however, wants to include a drug into the reimbursement scheme, the manufacturer must apply for a reasonable wholesale price for the drug, from the PPB (Finnish Medicines Agency and Social Insurance Institution 2013; Pharmaceuticals Pricing Board 2013a; Ministry of Social Affairs and Health 2010b). Based on the application, the reasonable wholesale price is then confirmed or rejected by the PPB, as described in the following paragraphs of this chapter. The pharmacy-margins, the value added tax, and the dispensing fee are regulated by the Government Decree on the Price List of Drugs (Table 6.1) (Ministry of Social Affairs and Health 2013c). The pharmacy-margins differ for prescription and non-prescription drugs, with slightly higher pharmacy-margins for non-prescription drugs.

The retail prices and the reimbursements of drugs currently on market in Finland are available through the website of Kela (Social Insurance Institution 2014).

6.4.2 *Drugs Administered in Health Centres and Hospitals*

According to legislation, drugs used in health centres and hospitals are procured through competitive bidding directly from pharmaceutical companies (Pharma Industry Finland 2014). Thus, purchase prices from pharmaceutical companies to health centres and hospitals vary. Most hospital pharmacies collaborate in larger areas for the procurement of their drugs. In these cases, one larger unit, such as a hospital pharmacy of a large university hospital, organises the bidding and comparing of tenders given by pharmaceutical companies. Cooperative bidding decreases drug costs and the workload of individual hospitals. As drugs administered during healthcare visits are included in the health centre or hospital budgets, such drugs are free of charge to patients. Patients still pay a small co-payment for the healthcare visit as a whole.

6.5 Reimbursement of Drugs in Community Pharmacies

Drugs dispensed at community pharmacies may be reimbursed at three reimbursement levels: basic reimbursement of 35 %, special reimbursement of 65 %, or special reimbursement of 100 % (Ministry of Social Affairs and Health 2010a). Drugs can be dispensed for a maximum of three months' treatment duration at one time.

Whether drugs can be reimbursed at the basic or special reimbursement levels is decided by the Pharmaceuticals Pricing Board (PPB) (see Sect. 6.6). Drugs for other uses than *treating* diseases cannot be reimbursed (Ministry of Social Affairs and Health 2010a). For example, contraceptives are not reimbursed when prescribed solely for birth-control, but when prescribed for *treating* for example severe acne or hirsutism they can be reimbursable. Furthermore, drugs used for temporary conditions or conditions with mild symptoms are not reimbursed, such as small packages of sedatives for temporary use. Traditional herbal or homeopathic products are not eligible for reimbursement.

6.5.1 Basic Reimbursement (35 %)

Most drugs are reimbursed at the basic level: 35 % of the retail price of the drug (Ministry of Social Affairs and Health 2010a). Drugs under basic reimbursement are mainly prescription drugs, such as antibiotics and drugs for allergy. Some non-prescription drugs are also reimbursed, provided that the drug is prescribed, such as some laxatives (e.g. lactulose solution) and topical corticosteroids (e.g. hydrocortisone cream). Drugs reimbursed at the basic level are generally reimbursed for all indications, with few exceptions of restricted reimbursements.

6.5.2 Special Reimbursement (65 or 100 %)

A Government Decree specifies diseases for which drugs can be reimbursed at the special reimbursement levels (Table 6.2) (Ministry of Social Affairs and Health 2010a, 2013d). The lower special reimbursement level—65 % of the retail price—is for drugs for *treating severe and chronic* diseases, such as chronic asthma (Table 6.2). Drugs with the higher special reimbursement are for *severe and chronic*

Table 6.2 Diseases that entitle patients to special reimbursements, 65 or 100 % of drug[a] costs

Lower special reimbursement (65 % of retail price) of dispensed drugs[a]	Higher special reimbursement (100 % of retail price[b]) of dispensed drugs[a]
Chronic asthma ja other chronic obstructive lung diseases	Adrenal cortical hypofunction
Chronic arrhythmias cardiac dysrhythmias	Aplastic anaemia
Chronic heart failure	Breast cancer
Chronic hypertension	Chronic bleeding disorders
Chronic ischaemic heart disease and related dyslipidaemia	Chronic metabolic disturbances of vitamin D
Disseminated connective tissue diseases, rheumatoid arthritis and comparable conditions	Congenital metabolic disturbances
Gout	Diabetes insipidus
Inherited severe dyslipidaemias	Diabetes mellitus
Severe, long-term narcolepsy	Epilepsy and comparable spasms
Ulcerative colitis ja Crohn's disease	General erythroderma
	Glaucoma
	Gynaecological cancers
	Hypogammaglobulinaemia
	Hypoparathyroidism
	Anterior pituitary hypofunction
	Hypothyroidism
	Idiopathic thrombocytopenia or granulocytopenia
	Behavioural disorders associated with mental retardation
	Leukaemias and other malignant diseases of the blood and bone marrow as well as malignant diseases of the lymphatic system
	Multiple sclerosis
	Myasthenia gravis
	Other malignant tumours not mentioned elsewhere
	Parkinson's disease and comparable ataxia
	Pemphigus
	Pernicious anaemia and other vitamin B12 malabsorption
	Post-transplant conditions in organ or tissue transplants
	Prostate cancer
	Sarcoidosis
	Severe anaemia related to kidney failure
	Severe, chronic pancreatic insufficiency
	Severe hypogonadism

(continued)

Table 6.2 (continued)

Lower special reimbursement (65 % of retail price) of dispensed drugs[a]	Higher special reimbursement (100 % of retail price[b]) of dispensed drugs[a]
	Severe psychosis and other severe mental disorders
	Trigeminal or glossopharyngeal neuralgia
	Uraemia requiring dialysis

[a]Only drugs with a special reimbursement status, granted by the Pharmaceuticals Pricing Board (PPB), are reimbursed at the special level
[b]€3 co-payment per purchased drug

diseases and considered *essential for the patient*. Diseases with the higher special reimbursement include cancers, diabetes, multiple sclerosis, glaucoma, and epilepsy (Table 6.2). For drugs with the higher special reimbursement, 100 % of the retail price is reimbursed, but patients pay a €3 co-payment for each drug purchased at one time.

Marketing authorisation holders must apply for the special reimbursement status for their products from the Pharmaceuticals Pricing Board (PPB), as described in Sect. 6.6. Thus, drugs indicated for treating the specified indications (Table 6.2) are not automatically reimbursed at the special levels. A patient is entitled for special reimbursement, if the dispensed drug has a special reimbursement status and the patient has a disease that entitles the patient to special reimbursement (Table 6.2), proved by a physician's statement.

6.5.3 Restricted Reimbursements

A limited number of drugs, less than 100, are reimbursed only to patients with specific indications or to otherwise specified patient groups (Ministry of Social Affairs and Health 2010a). This is called *restricted basic* or *restricted special* reimbursement. For example, interferon beta, glatiramer acetate and teriflunomide are reimbursed only for treatment resistant multiple sclerosis. Other examples are fertility drugs, which are automatically reimbursed at the basic level only for women under 43 years of age. An example of a drug with restricted special reimbursement is the growth hormone somatropin, which is reimbursed at the special level only for growth retardation in children with renal insufficiency.

6.5.4 Annual Limit for Patients' Out-of-Pocket Drug Expenses

In the beginning of each calendar year, patients receive the drug reimbursements at basic (35 %) or special (65 or 100 %) levels and the rest is being paid out-of-pocket by patients. However, patients only have to pay co-payments for reimbursed drugs until they reach a maximum amount in a given calendar year (€610 in 2014). After reaching this annual limit for patients' out-of-pocket drug expenses, Kela covers the full costs of all reimbursed drugs for such patients, though a small €1.50 patient co-payment applies to each dispensed drug.

6.6 Application for Reasonable Wholesale Price and Reimbursement Status for Drugs Dispensed at Community Pharmacies

A dispensed drug can be reimbursed in a community pharmacy through the National Health Insurance if the drug has both a reasonable wholesale price and reimbursement status confirmed by the Pharmaceuticals Pricing Board (PPB), subordinated to the Ministry of Social Affairs and Health (Finnish Medicines Agency and Social Insurance Institution 2013; Pharmaceuticals Pricing Board 2013a; Ministry of Social Affairs and Health 2010b). Pharmaceutical companies submit an application to the PPB for the reasonable wholesale price and reimbursement status, after a marketing authorisation for the product has been granted. However, no confirmation of a reasonable wholesale price is required for marketing medicinal products without reimbursement. In that case, wholesale prices are freely determined by pharmaceutical companies.

The application for a reasonable wholesale price and reimbursement status shall include clarifications on the therapeutic value and the benefits of the drug compared with other medicinal products or treatments used for treating the same disease (Ministry of Social Affairs and Health 2010b; Pharmaceuticals Pricing Board 2013a). Furthermore, a statement of the average daily dose and cost, an estimate of the sales of the product, and a statement of cost-effectiveness must be included. Other required documents in the application include a market forecast, information regarding patent protection, and a clarification of wholesale prices and reimbursement in other states of the European Economic Area.

6.6.1 Health Economic Evaluation

Since 1998, a health economic evaluation has been required when pharmaceutical companies apply for reimbursement status and reasonable wholesale price for a new active medicinal substance (Pharmaceuticals Pricing Board 2013b). A health economic evaluation may also be included in applications, should the applicant or the PPB deem it necessary. A health economic evaluation is, for example, often required for products with new indications, even if the active substance is not new. The guidelines for the health economic evaluation are available at the PPB website (Pharmaceuticals Pricing Board 2013b).

6.6.2 *Reasonable Wholesale Price*

In the application, the applicant suggests and justifies a reasonable wholesale price, which the PPB either accepts or rejects. According to the Health Insurance Act (Ministry of Social Affairs and Health 2010a), the PPB compares the applied wholesale price to the prices of other medicinal products available in Finland for the same indication and to the prices of the same product in other countries of the European Economic Area. The PPB also compares the treatment costs with the overall benefits gained by the patient, healthcare system and in turn society as a whole. The benefits and costs of other treatment options available in Finland are also reviewed. In addition, the PPB considers available funds for reimbursements through the National Health Insurance, when deciding about the reasonable wholesale price.

6.6.3 *Basic (35 %) or Special (65 or 100 %) Reimbursement Status*

The applicant applies for a basic (35 %) or one of the special (65 or 100 %) reimbursement statuses for the product, which the PPB either accepts or rejects (Pharmaceuticals Pricing Board 2013a). The applicant must also clarify whether the reimbursement is to be restricted to certain indications or patient groups. The PPB can grant drug reimbursements only based on indications that are approved by the marketing authorisation authorities.

According to the Health Insurance Act, the PPB can approve a reimbursement status only for medicinal products that are indicated for *treating* diseases (Ministry of Social Affairs and Health 2010a), as described under Sect. 6.5 on reimbursement of dispensed drugs. Further, the PPB cannot grant reimbursement for products with minimal therapeutic value, products for temporary conditions or conditions with mild symptoms, or traditional herbal and homeopathic products.

The PPB can approve a special reimbursement status only for products for a *severe and chronic* indication listed in the Government Decree on special reimbursed indications (Table 6.2.) (Ministry of Social Affairs and Health 2010a, 2013d). Further, the special reimbursement can generally be approved only after the medicinal product has had the basic reimbursement for at least two years (Ministry of Social Affairs and Health 2010a). According to the Health Insurance Act, the PPB shall in their decision making on the special reimbursement consider the nature of the disease, the necessity and cost-effectiveness of the product, and proof of the product's therapeutic value in practice and through research. The PPB also considers available funds for the special reimbursement.

The PPB may restrict the basic or special reimbursement of a medicinal product to more specifically defined indications or patient groups, if the product has proven significant therapeutic value for such patients, but not enough for other patients. Restricted reimbursement is also used for particularly expensive medicinal product and when extensive use of the product would cause unreasonable costs.

6.6.4 Determining the Reasonable Wholesale Price and Reimbursement Status

After the PPB has received the application, the PPB secretariat starts the evaluation process by acquiring an opinion from Kela. An appointed, permanent PPB expert group may also provide their expert opinion. The applicant is informed of the various evaluations before the PPB announces its decision. The applicant may provide additional material during the evaluation process and adjust the suggested wholesale price before the PPB's decision is presented. Thereafter, the PPB decides on the approval or rejection of the applied wholesale price and on the inclusion of the product in the reimbursement scheme.

The PPB shall present its decision on the reasonable wholesale price and reimbursement status within 180 days after receiving a complete application. If approved, the reimbursement and reasonable wholesale price are valid for a maximum of five years. After that, a renewal application must be submitted to the PPB in order to maintain the reimbursement status.

6.7 Generic Substitution for Drugs Dispensed at Community Pharmacies

Generic substitution was introduced in Finland in 2003 (Ministry of Social Affairs and Health 2003a). Under generic substitution, community pharmacies are obligated to offer patients less expensive substitutable alternatives for dispensed drugs. Drugs may become substitutable, if they "*contain the same quantity of the same active agent and are biologically equivalent*" (Finnish Medicines Agency 2014). The Finnish Medicines Agency maintains quarterly lists of substitutable products. Until 2009, patients could decline the substitution and gain the normal reimbursement (35, 65 or 100 %) also for the most expensive substitutable drugs. According to a doctoral thesis (Heikkilä 2013), most physicians and patients perceived the voluntary generic substitution positively and considered it to save drug expenses.

In the currently valid reference price system introduced in 2009, patients' reimbursements are calculated from a specified reference price (Ministry of Social Affairs and Health 2010b). The reference price is determined according to the price of the cheapest substitutable drug. If the price of the lowest priced substitutable drug is less than €40, then the reference price becomes this lowest price plus €1.50. If the lowest price among substitutable drugs exceeds €40, the reference price is this price plus €2.00. Community pharmacies must offer patients substitutable drugs that have the same or lower price than the reference price, i.e. products within the reference price. When a product within the reference price is dispensed, the patient's reimbursement is calculated from the retail price of the product (Fig. 6.2). However, if the price of a product exceeds the reference price and the patient declines substitution, the reimbursement is calculated from the reference price (Fig. 6.2). Thus, the patient has to pay co-payment based on the reference price and the difference between the reference price and the retail price of the more expensive product. This difference does not count towards the patient's annual limit for out-of-pocket expenses for dispensed drugs. If the physician forbids generic substitution in the prescription due to medical reasons, Kela pays the reimbursement based on the retail price, even if the price exceeded the reference price.

Pharmaceutical companies inform Kela of the prices of substitutable drugs on a quarterly basis. In turn, Kela publishes the informed prices and forwards them to the PPB and to community pharmacies. The PPB then determines the reference prices for each quarter of the year.

6.8 The Impact of Pricing on Public Health

The Finnish reimbursement system facilitates medicines affordability for all (Ministry of Social Affairs and Health 2010a). Also, the annual limit for out-of-pocket expenses aims at preventing unreasonable drug costs for the individuals. Nevertheless, patient co-payments finance a large part of the pharmaceutical costs, which is considered an important limitation of the reimbursement system (Aaltonen et al. 2012). In 2012, the share of the public financing of drugs purchased from community pharmacies in Finland was 56 %, lower than on average in EU-15-countries (64 %) (OECD, Organisation for Economic Co-operation and Development 2014). Also, the annual limit for patients' out-of-pocket expenses of dispensed drugs, €610 in 2014, is relatively high (Aaltonen et al. 2012). On average, 11 % of the population has experienced at least one occasion during a year when lack of money prevented them from purchasing their drugs (Aaltonen et al. 2014). The share of patients with economical barriers to purchasing drugs is even larger among those who receive social benefits, such as sickness allowances (32 %) or lower unemployment benefit (37 %). These percentages are rather high, when compared to other Western European countries (Kemp et al. 2010; Schoen et al. 2010).

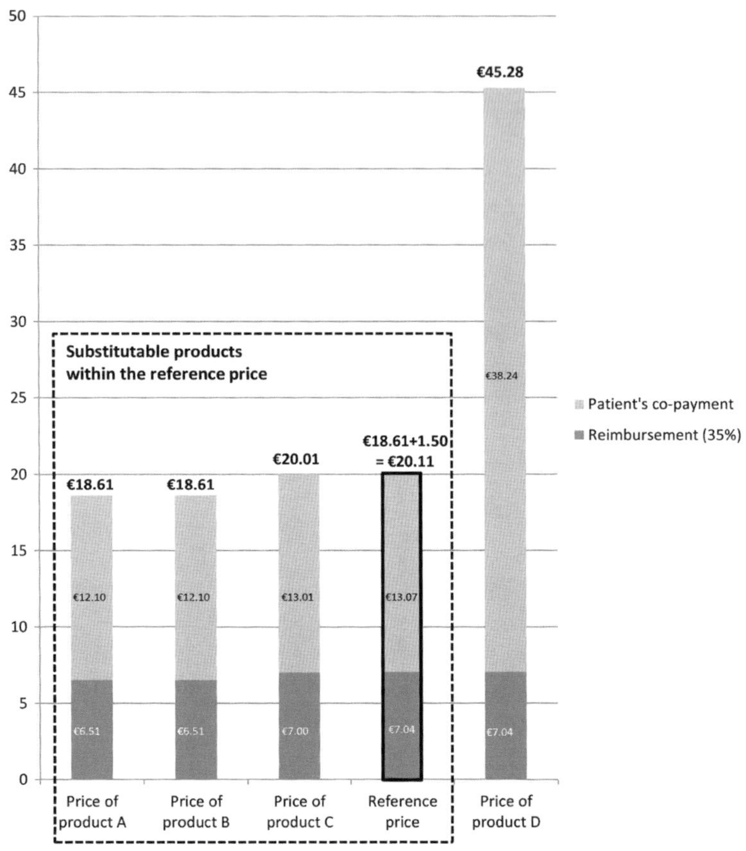

Fig. 6.2 Example of the reference price system. A patient is prescribed simvastatin 20 mg 100 tablets, with the product D in the prescription. The patient is entitled for the 35 % basic reimbursement. Products A–D are substitutable. The reference price is the retail price of the cheapest product (A or B) €18.61 plus €1.50, totalling €20.11. As the product D (€45.28) is not within the reference price, reimbursement cannot be given for the full price of product D. If the patient accepts substitution to a product within the reference price, A, B or C, the 35 % reimbursement is calculated from the retail price of the dispensed product. If the patient declines the substitution and is dispensed the product D, the patient gets a €7.04 reimbursement, calculated as 35 % of the reference price. Thus, the patient has to pay in total €38.24 out-of-pocket, consisting of the co-payment according to the reference price (€13.07) plus the difference between the retail price of the product D and the reference price (€45.28 – 20.11 = €25.17)

However, municipalities may pay social support towards the patient co-payments of dispensed drugs for residents with the lowest income.

One of the goals of the Finnish drug reimbursement system is to enhance rational prescribing (Aaltonen et al. 2012). The special reimbursement system, where the higher reimbursement is subjected to more severe diseases, channels the reimbursements to more cost-effective medicinal treatments and to patients who have higher morbidity. Restrictions in reimbursements also channel reimbursements to patients who most likely benefit from specific drugs. In 2012, these patients with special or restricted reimbursements, who had a physician's statement on the specific indications, received 82 % of all drug reimbursement payments (Finnish Medicines Agency and Social Insurance Institution 2013). Although this system supports rational prescribing, the system requires a great deal of administrative work.

In recent decades, pharmaceutical expenditure in Finland increased more quickly than health expenditure in general (Organisation for Economic Co-operation and Development 2010). Driving forces behind the increase have included the aging population and the introduction of new, expensive drugs (Organisation for Economic Co-operation and Development 2010; Ess et al. 2003). Thus, limiting public pharmaceutical expenditure and sharing the limited financial resources as efficiently and rationally as possible have been central goals of the Finnish pharmaceutical policy during recent decades (Ministry of Social Affairs and Health 2003b, 2011b). Consequently, several cost containment methods have been introduced. Patients' share of the costs of dispensed drugs was increased in 1992–1994 by decreasing the reimbursement percentage and increasing the patient co-payments. In 2013, the patients' share was revisited again, as the reimbursement percentage was further decreased. Followed by the cost containment methods, the share of pharmaceutical costs of the health expenditure has decreased since 2004, being currently among the lowest in the EU (Association of Finnish Pharmacies 2014b). More changes to patients' reimbursement of prescribed drugs are expected in 2015, when a new reform will be introduced (Ministry of Social Affairs and Health 2014b). For example, from 2015 onwards patients must pay an annual threshold payment of €40 before any reimbursements for a dispensed drugs could be claimed. However, it is expected that after reaching the threshold, the basic reimbursement level for prescribed drugs would increase from 35 to 45 %.

6.9 Conclusion

In the Finnish health system, like in many European countries, pricing and financing differ for drugs sold in community pharmacies and for drugs administrated in health centres and hospitals. For drugs sold in community pharmacies, wholesale prices of reimbursed, dispensed drugs are determined by the same health authority that determines the reimbursement status of drugs, while pharmaceutical companies may freely decide the wholesale prices of non-reimbursed drugs. Retail prices, based on the wholesale prices, are by law fixed for all drugs sold in community pharmacies. Reimbursed drugs are financed through the public, obligatory National Health Insurance. On the contrary, drugs administered in health centres and hospitals are covered by local public funding through 320 municipalities. As healthcare units buy such drugs from pharmaceutical companies through competitive bidding, purchase prices from pharmaceutical companies to healthcare units vary. Beyond general co-payments, healthcare units cannot charge patients for these drugs. This dual financing of drug treatments, by the National Health Insurance and by the numerous local municipalities, has been criticised and is considered as inefficient. An ongoing reform aims at uniting health services by decreasing the number of local governing entities. To decrease pharmaceutical expenditure, several reforms since the early nineties have decreased patients' reimbursements and have resulted in price cuts in wholesale prices. More changes to patients' reimbursement of prescribed drugs are expected in 2015, when a new reform will be introduced. The implementation of these reforms will remain a challenge in the coming years.

Acknowledgement The authors would like to acknowledge Dr. Jaana E. Martikainen and Dr. Zaheer-Ud-Din Babar for their constructive comments on the content and Ms. Myriah Lesko for the English proof reading of this chapter.

References

Aaltonen K, Saastamoinen LK, Koskinen H, Martikainen JE (2012) Is dual financing a problem in pharmaceutical services? (In Finnish: Onko monikanavaisuus lääkehuollon ongelma?). In: Mikkola H, Blomgren J, Hiilamo H (eds) National or local? Words about social and healthcare (In Finnish: Kansallista vai paikallista? Puheenvuoroja sosiaali- ja terveydenhuollosta). Research Department of the Social Insurance Institution, Helsinki, pp 204–215

Aaltonen K, Miettinen J, Airio I, Martikainen JE, Saastamoinen LK, Bell S, Hartikainen S, Norris P (2014) Cost-related barriers to use of health services and prescription medicines in Finland: a cross-sectional survey. Eur J Publ Health (in press)

Association of Finnish Local and Regional Authorities (2013) The number of cities and municipalities (In Finnish: Kaupunkien ja kuntien lukumäärä) [Homepage of Association of Finnish Local and Regional Authorities]. http://www.kunnat.net/fi/tietopankit/tilastot/aluejaot/kuntien-lukumaara/Sivut/default.aspx. Accessed 3 Aug 2014

Association of Finnish Pharmacies (2014a) Annual review 2013, Association of Finnish Pharmacies, Helsinki. http://www.apteekkariliitto.fi/media/pdf/afp_annual_review_2013_web.pdf. Accessed 3 Aug 2014

Association of Finnish Pharmacies (2014b) Drug prices decrease, food prices increase (In Finnish: Lääkkeet halpenevat, ruoka kallistuu), Association of Finnish Pharmacies, Helsinki. http://www.apteekkariliitto.fi/fi/media/tiedotteet/laakkeet-halpenevat-ruoka-kallistuu.html. Accessed 3 Aug 2014

Ess SM, Schneeweiss S, Szucs TD (2003) European healthcare policies for controlling drug expenditure. Pharmacoeconomics 21(2):89–103

Finnish Medicines Agency (2012) Regulation 6/2012 (In Finnish: Määräys 6/2012)

Finnish Medicines Agency (2014) Criteria used in compiling the list [Homepage of Finnish Medicines Agency]. http://www.fimea.fi/medicines/substitutable_medicinal_products/criteria_used_in_compiling_the_list. Accessed 3 Aug 2014

Finnish Medicines Agency & Social Insurance Institution (2013) Finnish statistics on medicines 2012, Finnish Medicines Agency; Social Insurance Institution, Helsinki. http://www.fimea.fi/download/24954_SLT_2012_net.pdf. Accessed 3 Aug 2014

Heikkilä R (2013) Generic substitution from the perspective of consumers and physicians in Finland. Publications of the University of Eastern Finland, Kuopio

Kemp A, Roughead E, Preen D, Glover J, Semmens J (2010) Determinants of self-reported medicine underuse due to cost: a comparison of seven countries. J Health Serv Res Policy 15(2):106–114

Ministry of Justice (1999) The Constitution of Finland 731/1999. http://www.finlex.fi/en/laki/kaannokset/1999/en19990731.pdf. Accessed 3 Aug 2014

Ministry of Social Affairs and Health (2003a) Medicines Act 395/1987

Ministry of Social Affairs and Health (2003b) Pharmaceutical Policy 2010, Ministry of Social Affairs and Health, Helsinki. http://www.stm.fi/c/document_library/get_file?folderId=28707&name=DLFE-3623.pdf&title=Laakepolitiikka_2010__tiivistelma_fi.pdf. Accessed 3 Aug 2014

Ministry of Social Affairs and Health (2009) Occupational Health Care Act 1383/2001. http://www.finlex.fi/en/laki/kaannokset/2001/en20011383.pdf. Accessed 3 Aug 2014

Ministry of Social Affairs and Health (2010a) Health Insurance Act 1224/2004. http://www.stm.fi/c/document_library/get_file?folderId=1175755&name=DLFE-17023.pdf. Accessed 3 Aug 2014

Ministry of Social Affairs and Health (2010b) Medicines Act 395/1987. http://www.fimea.fi/download/18580_Laakelaki_englanniksi_paivitetty_5_2011.pdf. Accessed 3 Aug 2014

Ministry of Social Affairs and Health (2011a) Socially sustainable Finland 2020—strategy for social and health policy (In Finnish: Sosiaalisesti kestävä Suomi 2020—Sosiaali- ja terveyspolitiikan strategia). Ministry of Social Affairs and Health, Helsinki

Ministry of Social Affairs and Health (2011b) Medicines Policy 2020, Ministry of Social Affairs and Health, Helsinki. http://www.stm.fi/c/document_library/get_file?folderId=2765155&name=DLFE-14405.pdf. Accessed 3 Aug 2014

Ministry of Social Affairs and Health (2013a) Health care in Finland, Ministry of Social Affairs and Health, Tampere. http://www.stm.fi/c/document_library/get_file?folderId=6511570&name=DLFE-26813.pdf. Accessed 3 Aug 2014

Ministry of Social Affairs and Health (2013b) Health services [Homepage of Ministry of Social Affairs and Health]. http://www.stm.fi/en/social_and_health_services/health_services. Accessed 3 Aug 2014

Ministry of Social Affairs and Health (2013c) Government Decree 713/2013 (In Finnish: Valtioneuvoston asetus 713/2013)

Ministry of Social Affairs and Health (2013d) Government Decree 25/2013 (In Finnish: Valtioneuvoston asetus 25/2013)

Ministry of Social Affairs and Health (2014a) Social welfare and health care reform [Homepage of Ministry of Social Affairs and Health]. http://www.stm.fi/en/ministry/strategies/service_structures. Accessed 3 Aug 2014

Ministry of Social Affairs and Health (2014b) The Government's bill to the Parliament on amendments to the Health Insurance Act, Draft, 5 March 2014 (In Finnish: Hallituksen esitys eduskunnalle laiksi sairausvakuutuslain muuttamisesta, Luonnos 5.3.2014)

National Institute of Health and Welfare (2014a) Health expenditure and financing 2012, National Institute of Health and Welfare, Helsinki. http://urn.fi/URN:NBN:fi-fe2014032823255. Accessed 3 Aug 2014

National Institute of Health and Welfare (2014b) Statistical Yearbook on Social Welfare and Health Care 2013, National Institute of Health and Welfare, Tampere. http://urn.fi/URN:ISBN:978-952-302-046-7. Accessed 3 Aug 2014

National Institute of Health and Welfare (2014c) Private services (In Finnish: Yksityiset palvelut) [Homepage of National Institute of Health and Welfare]. http://www.thl.fi/fi_FI/web/kaventaja-fi/eriarvoisuus/palvelujarjestelma/terveyspalvelut/yksityiset-palvelut. Accessed 3 Aug 2014

Organisation for Economic Co-operation and Development (2010) Health at a glance: Europe 2010, OECD Publishing, Paris. http://dx.doi.org/10.1787/health_glance-2010-en. Accessed 3 Aug 2014

Organisation for Economic Co-operation and Development (2013) Health at glance 2013: OECD Indicators, OECD Publishing, Paris. http://dx.doi.org/10.1787/health_glance-2013-en. Accessed 3 Aug 2014

Organisation for Economic Co-operation and Development (2014) Health policies and data, OECD Publishing, Paris. http://www.oecd.org/els/health-systems/. Accessed 3 Aug 2014

Pharma Industry Finland (2014) Hospital medicines [Homepage of Pharma Industry Finland]. http://www.pif.fi/en/medical-care/hospital-medicines. Accessed 3 Aug 2014

Pharmaceuticals Pricing Board (2013a) Application instructions—reimbursement status and wholesale price for a medicinal product subjected to marketing authorization, Pharmaceuticals Pricing Board, Helsinki. http://www.stm.fi/c/document_library/get_file?folderId=71804&name=DLFE-26220.pdf. Accessed 3 Aug 2014

Pharmaceuticals Pricing Board (2013b) Application instructions—health economic evaluation, Pharmaceuticals Pricing Board, Helsinki. http://www.stm.fi/c/document_library/get_file?folderId=71837&name=DLFE-26705.pdf. Accessed 3 Aug 2014

Pharmaceuticals Pricing Board (2014) Pharmaceuticals Pricing Board Notices 2014—July 1st (July 3rd 2014), Pharmaceuticals Pricing Board, Helsinki. http://www.stm.fi/en/ministry/boards/pharmaboard/notices/2014. Accessed 3 Aug 2014

Schoen C, Osborn R, Squires D, Doty MM, Pierson R, Applebaum S (2010) How health insurance design affects access to care and costs, by income, in eleven countries. Health Aff 29 (12):2323–2334

Social Insurance Institution (2012) Funding [Homepage of Social Insurance Institution]. http://www.kela.fi/web/en/funding. Accessed 3 Aug 2014

Social Insurance Institution (2014) Medicinal products database [Homepage of Social Insurance Institution]. https://easiointi.kela.fi/laakekys_app/LaakekysApplication?kieli=en. Accessed 3 Aug 2014

Statistics Finland (2013) Life expectancy (In Finnish: Elinajanodote) [Homepage of Statistics Finland]. http://www.tilastokeskus.fi/org/historia/elinajanodote.html. Accessed 3 Aug 2014

University Pharmacy (2013) University Pharmacy [Homepage of University Pharmacy]. http://www.yliopistonapteekki.fi/fi/apteekkipalvelut/pages/english.aspx. Accessed 3 Aug 2014

Vuorenkoski L, Mladovsky P, Mossialos E (2008) Finland: health system review. Health Syst Transit 10(4):1–168

World Bank (2014) Finland [Homepage of World Bank]. http://data.worldbank.org/country/finland. Accessed 3 Aug 2014

Chapter 7
Pharmaceutical Prices in India

Sudip Chaudhuri

Abstract The contribution of India in making patented drugs more affordable has been recognised widely. Though the prices of patented drugs are lower in India, the retail markets suffer from several imperfections. As a result, despite the existence of large number of manufacturers, substantial price differences exist between different brands of the same drug. In India medicines are purchased mainly by the people themselves rather than by the government or through health insurance. Because of limited public health and insurance facilities, access to medicines has been low in India. India has drug price control in some form or the other since 1963. But India adopted a selective approach—while some drugs are under control, competing drugs have been kept out of control. This provided the opportunity to manufacturers to stop or reduce the manufacture and sale of drugs under control and promote the competing ones out of control. After 2005, India has re-introduced product patent protection. MNCs have started selling new patented drugs at exorbitant prices but these are yet to be included under price control. India has been able to restrict product patents by exempting grant of patents under certain conditions. But potentially the more effective instrument of compulsory licensing has remained unutilized in India.

Price depends on market structure. In pharmaceuticals, product patents play a very important role. Pharmaceuticals companies—mostly multinational corporations (MNCs) from developed countries such as Pfizer and GlaxoSmithKline—who obtain product patents can prevent others from manufacturing and marketing these medicines and hence as a monopolist can charge a very high price. When patents expire (or when patents are not obtained), other companies can enter the market and the resultant competition leads to lower prices.[1]

Professor of Economics, Indian Institute of Management Calcutta. This is an outcome of the research project, "State, globalization and industrial development in India: the political economy of regulation and deregulation", coordinated by the Norwegian Institute of International Affairs.

[1] See any standard economics textbook (for example, Paul A Samuelson and W A Nordhaus, *Economics*, McGraw Hill) for the theoretical link between price and market structure.

S. Chaudhuri (✉)
Indian Institute of Management Calcutta, Kolkata, India
e-mail: sudip@iimcal.ac.in

Z.-U.-D. Babar (ed.), *Pharmaceutical Prices in the 21st Century*,
DOI 10.1007/978-3-319-12169-7_7

Before 1972, India effectively, had a product patent regime in drugs. In 1972, when the Patents and Designs Act, 1911 was replaced by the Patents Act, 1970, drug product patent protection was abolished. From 1 January 2005, product patents have again been introduced in India, to comply with the requirements under the Agreement on Trade Related Aspects of Intellectual Property Rights (TRIPS) of the World Trade Organization. Before the 1970s, while the MNCs themselves were not very keen on manufacturing in India, they used their patent rights to prevent Indian companies from manufacturing. As a result, on the one hand the industry remained underdeveloped and on the other hand the monopolies led to high prices. An American Senate Committee (Kefauver Committee) in fact found in the 1960s that India was among the highest priced nations in the world in pharmaceuticals.[2] The abolition of product patents eliminated the monopoly power of the MNCs. Supported by the government, the pharmaceutical industry in India developed primarily through the efforts of Indian generic companies such as Cipla, Ranbaxy, Dr Reddys Laboratories. India emerged as a major player in the global pharmaceutical industry with prices of patented drugs being one of the lowest in the world.[3] Perhaps the best known international example is the fall in the prices of antiretroviral drugs (ARVs) used for the treatment of HIV/AIDS. Before supplies from India started, the price of one of the most important ARV combination (stavudine + lamivudine + nevirapine), in the patent protected countries exceeded US $10,000 per person per year. Due to the competition provided by Indian generic companies such as Cipla, Hetero, Aurobindo, prices reduced to below US $100 within a few years making it possible to treat a much larger number of people with ARVs.[4]

In the domestic market in India, in the absence of patents, how did prices behave? Drug price control has been in operation in India in some form or the other since 1963. India has issued several Drug (Prices Control) Order (DPCO)—in 1970, 1979, 1987, 1995. Another DPCO has been issued in 2013 after India re-introduced product patent protection in pharmaceuticals. But as we will see below this does not cover the pries of patented medicines. To what extent have prices gone up in the patent protected monopoly markets in India? Under the TRIPS agreement, countries enjoy some flexibilities including providing compulsory licences to non-patentees under certain conditions. To what extent has India used such flexibilities to ensure to regulate prices? Price control is not forbidden under any of the WTO agreements. What steps have India taken to control the prices of patented medicines?

This paper tries to analyse these issues. In Sect. 7.1, we will discuss the structure of pharmaceutical markets and how prices are determined. We will also discuss how medicine purchase is financed and the implications for access to medicines. In Sect. 7.2, we will analyse the impact of price control measures for generic medicines adopted in India, particularly under the latest DPCO (2013). Section 7.3 will focus on the patent protected monopoly markets after 2005.

---

[2] Cited by Kidron (1965), p. 251.

[3] See Chaudhuri (2005), Chapter 2 for an account of the rise and growth of the Indian pharmaceutical industry.

[4] MSF, *Untangling the Web of Antiretroviral Price Reductions* (various editions).

7.1 Structure of Generic Markets, Prices and Financing

If patent protected markets are compared with monopoly, generic markets are often compared with competition. Under perfect competition, profit maximizing firms do not have the market power to charge a price higher than the marginal cost—competition among the firms bids down the price to the level of the marginal cost. But the model of perfect competition is based on the following crucial assumptions, particularly presence of large number of sellers, individually too small to have any significant impact on the supplies, product homogeneity and perfect information.[5]

To understand the price structure in the Indian pharmaceutical industry, it is important to make a distinction between the market for bulk drugs and formulations. Bulk drugs are the active pharmaceutical ingredients (APIs) present in a drug and formulations are finished dosage forms such as tablets, capsules, ointments, injections etc.

The bulk drugs market closely resembles a perfectly competitive market. There are a large number of firms. Both the buyers and the sellers are firms. Unlike in the case of the formulations market as discussed later, those who buy bulk drugs are aware not only of the prices charged by the different firms but also of their quality reputation. The buyers can avoid the poor quality producers and shop around in the market to buy from the cheapest reliable supplier. Such competition among the firms has resulted in very low bulk drugs prices. For a wide range of drugs, the market prices in fact, were found to be lower than the prices which were fixed by the government under DPCO (Chaudhuri 2005).

The formulations market can be broadly classified into the following three markets: (i) the retail market where the consumer pays the full price; (ii) the retail market where the consumer is reimbursed partially or fully by the health insurer, private or public, and (iii) the institutional market where drugs are purchased by institutional buyers such as public health authorities, hospitals. These markets differ with respect to demand conditions—the extent to which the demand is sensitive to the price. In the first market, as we will discuss below, the demand is quite insensitive to the price level—the consumers operating individually do not exercise any bargaining power vis-à-vis the firms with significant market power. But in the other two cases, the demand is sensitive to the price level-the insurer or the institutional buyer can exercise significant market power to influence the price.

7.1.1 Retail Formulations Market Where Consumer Pays the Full Price

A large number of companies sell products in these markets in India in different dosage forms and strengths under different brand names. As can be seen from Table 7.1, 369 brands are available for Ofloxacin, an anti-infective medicine;

[5] See Footnote 1 above.

Table 7.1 Number of brands in retail formulations market in India

Molecule	Therapeutic group	No. of brands
Ofloxacin	Anti-infective	369
Azithromycin	Anti-infective	306
Paracetamol	Pain/analgesics	295
Cefixime	Anti-infective	277
Omeprazole	Gastro intestinal	245
Diclofenac	Pain/analgesics	226
Cetirizine	Respiratory	221
Amoxycillin	Anti-infective	210
Albendazole	Anti-parasitic	198
Ondansetron	Gastro intestinal	164
Atrovastatin	Cardiac	149
Clotrimazole	Derma	120
Metformin	Anti-diabetic	100
Nandrolone	Hormones	86
Amlodipine	Cardiac	84
Folic acid	Blood related	71
Atenolol	Cardiac	60
Pregabalin	Neuo/CNS	54
Chloroquine	Anti-malarial	53
Carbamazepine	Neuo/CNS	39
Enoxaparin	Cardiac	38
Mathotrexate	Anti-cancer	25
Docetaxel	Anti-cancer	25
Gemcitabine	Anti-cancer	21

Source and *Notes*: Calculated from *Sales audit data* of AIOCD Pharmasofttech AWACS Pvt. (hence forth referred to as AIOCD-AWACS). All the products of the molecule sold in 2010 in different dosage forms and strengths and by different companies have been included here

245 brands for Omeprazole (gastro-intestinal), 198 brands for Albendazole (anti-parasitic), 84 brands for Amlodipine (cardiac), 54 brands for Pregablin (neuro/CNS) and so on. Even for the newer anti-cancer drugs which are relatively higher priced, 25 brands are available for Mathotrexate and 21 brands for Gemcitabine.

Multiple sellers have been possible in India because of the absence of product patent protection. Because of competition, prices of drugs have been much lower in India compared to those in the countries practicing product patent production. But the existence of a large number of formulation sellers has not resulted in competitive prices in the sense that substantial price differential exists between different brands of the same product as Table 7.2 shows. In Table 7.2 we have considered only the important brands, each accounting for 1 % or more of the market. Despite the availability of 50 brands in Diclofenac injection (25 mg/mL), the prices varied between Rs 3.88 (maximum) and Rs 0.16 (minimum) making the former costlier by

Table 7.2 Price differential in selected formulation products in India

Product	No. of important brands	Maximum price to retailer (Rs)	Minimum price to retailer (Rs)	Extent to which maximum price higher compared to minimum price (%)	Ceiling price, DPCO 2013 (Rs)	Extent to which ceiling price lower compared to maximum price (%)
Diclofenac injection 25 mg/mL	50	3.88	0.16	2,325.0	1.32	66.0
Ofloxacin tablets 200 mg	35	26.69	1.14	2,241.2	4.2	84.2
Diclofenac tablets 50 mg	21	3.55	0.19	1,768.4	1.7	52.7
Alprazolam tablets 0.5 mg	27	3.39	0.19	1,684.2	1.7	49.0
Povidone iodine ointment 5 %	17	3.35	0.25	1,240.0	1.4	57.9
Omeprazole capsules 20 mg	26	7.6	0.57	1,233.3	2.6	65.8
Ondansetron tablets 4 mg	23	7.5	0.6	1,150.0	4.1	45.2
Albendazole tablets 400 mg	32	14.02	1.15	1,119.1	7.9	43.9
Amlodipine tablets 2.5 mg	34	3.34	0.31	977.4	1.8	47.6
Atenolol tablets 50 mg	21	3.2	0.31	932.3	1.8	44.1
Tramadol injection 50 mg/mL	27	17.49	1.75	899.4	10.1	42.1
Azithromycin tablets 500 mg	7	39.38	4.16	846.6	17.1	56.5
Atorvastatin tablets 10 mg	45	7.97	1.09	631.2	5.1	36.0
Cefixime tablets 100 mg	48	18	2.7	566.7	6.6	63.2
Metformin tablets 500 mg	44	2.31	0.38	507.9	1.4	41.6
Amoxicillin capsules 500 mg	18	8.88	1.55	472.9	5.3	40.9
Ondansetron injection 2 mg/mL	31	11.81	2.1	462.4	6.4	46.1

(continued)

Table 7.2 (continued)

Product	No. of important brands	Maximum price to retailer (Rs)	Minimum price to retailer (Rs)	Extent to which maximum price higher compared to minimum price (%)	Ceiling price, DPCO 2013 (Rs)	Extent to which ceiling price lower compared to maximum price (%)
Azithromycin suspension 100 mg/5 mL	35	2.73	0.51	435.3	1.3	50.9
Amoxicillin trihydrate + clavulanic acid potassium salt tablets 625 mg	47	41.42	8.37	394.9	19.4	53.3
Metoprolol tablets 25 mg	30	5.31	1.09	387.2	2.9	45.2
Sodium valproate tablets 500 mg	29	7.85	3.04	158.2	6.2	21.1
Enoxaparin injection 40 mg	17	655.27	260.78	151.3	378.8	42.2
Fluoxetine hydrochloride capsules 20	11	4	2.15	86.0	3.0	25.3
Cetrizine tablets 10 mg	35	3.07	1.81	69.6	1.6	49.2

Source: "Working Sheet Related to Price Notified" on different dates in 2013, available under "Archives" in the website of the National Pharmaceutical Pricing Authority (NPPA) (http://www.nppaindia.nic.in)

Notes: In col (2) only brands accounting for 1 % or more of the market sales have been considered. Retailers margin and local taxes need to be added to the prices in cols (3), (4) and (6) to get the retail market price

2,325 % compared to the latter. Other examples include Omeprazole capsules, 20 mg (1,233 % costlier among 26 brands); Cefixime tablets 100 mg (568 % costlier among 48 brands); Ondansetron injection, 2 mg/mL (462 % costlier among 31 brands); Enoxaparin injection, 40 mg (151 % costlier among 17 brands) and Cetrizine tablets, 10 mg (70 % costlier among 35 brands) (Table 7.2).

In a perfectly competitive market, the firms are price takers—no one is large enough or significant enough to influence the price. But the retail formulation market in India does not satisfy some of the critical conditions of a perfectly competitive market. The price behaviour in the retail formulations markets reflects the imperfections in the market—buyers do not have knowledge about the prices and quality of all other products available in the market. In India the quality of drugs manufactured, sold, and distributed are regulated under the provisions of the Drugs and Cosmetics Act, 1940 and Rules, 1945, as amended from time to time. There are elaborate legal and administrative provisions for regulating the quality of medicines manufactured and sold in India. But implementation is still weak though substantial improvements have been made particularly after GMP (Schedule M) has been made mandatory. As a result, medicines available in the market manufactured by different firms are not perceived to be equally safe and effective. The retail formulations market in India is essentially a branded generics market. The larger and more reputed firms differentiate their products through branding and promote their products to doctors, not in generic names but in brand names. Doctors and consumers are often not aware of the lower priced less promoted products. Even when they are aware, doctors and public confidence appears to be more with the branded products of reputed firms. This enables some firms to charge a price higher than that of others and still maintain higher market shares.[6]

7.1.2 *Bargaining Power of Insurers and Organized Buyers*

In the retail market where the consumer is reimbursed partially or fully by the health insurer, or in the institutional market where drugs are purchased by organized buyers such as public health authorities, the insurer or the organized buyer can exercise some market power which can influence the price as we will see below.

One common method is to have a 'formulary' of approved drugs. The stipulation can be that only the expenditure on the drugs included in the formulary will be reimbursed. The insurer may exclude costly branded products from the formulary. Unlike in the case of retail sales where the consumers may be sceptical about the quality of cheaper products, the insurer may carry out its own analysis and checks and include only those drugs, which satisfy the quality criterion. But as we will see below, the penetration of insurance in India has been extremely low.

Similarly, institutional buyers of drugs—for example, public health authorities, hospitals, NGOs, or large companies—can shop around for their requirements and get better prices. Institutional buyers can float tenders for buying drugs and can benefit from the competition among the sellers. In countries such as India, a common complaint against such institutional purchases is that the quality of the drug is compromised with. It is said that many of these companies are able to supply

[6] For selected formulations, D G Shah ("Myths about pharmaceutical industry", Indian Pharmaceutical Alliance, May 2012) has shown that brand leaders are not the costliest. But the same data also shows that brand leaders are not the cheapest. The point is that there are products in the market which are cheaper but sold less.

drugs at such a low price because they do not take adequate care and do not spend the required amounts for producing quality products in certified plants. The experience in Tamil Nadu, for example shows that it is possible to achieve substantial saving through pooled purchase without compromising with quality. The state government medicine procurement agency, Tamil Nadu Medical Services Corporation (TNMSC) restricts bids to manufacturers who have the capacity and the capability to supply quality products (Lalitha 2008). But despite that the prices of the drugs procured by TNMSC have been significantly below the retail prices, particularly compared to those of leading brands (Selvaraj et al. 2012, Table 1). For example whereas the average retail price of the three highest priced brands for ciprofloxacin, 50 mg, 10 tablets was Rs 88.60, TNMSC was able to purchase it at Rs 9.82. Similarly prices were respectively Rs 59.30 and Rs 0.75 for Glimepride, 1 mg, 10 tablets; Rs 12.70 and Rs 1.85 for Ranitidine, 150 mg, 10 tablets etc. In India, however as we will now discuss the institutional drug market is quite limited.

7.1.3 Drug Financing and Accessibility in India

For drugs to be accessible what is important is not only the level of drug prices but also whether finances are available to pay for the cost of drugs. If prices are lower, then costs go down but it still may be beyond the paying capacity of those who need them. In such cases it is important to ensure proper finances to pay for the cost of the drugs. Purchase of drugs is financed by the consumers themselves, by the government, or through private or social/national insurance. Public health facilities providing free or partially free medicines care and/or subsidized insurance cannot only influence prices, as explained above, it can shift the financial burden from the poor who are unable to afford the cost themselves and, thus, improve accessibility.

In India medicines are purchased mainly by the people themselves rather than by the government or through insurance. In 2004 only 8.99 % of medicine prescriptions were supplied free for hospitalized patients and 5.34 % for out-patients. The proportion of prescriptions where medicines were provided partially free was also quite low at 16.38 % and 3.38 % respectively in the same year. As a result, 71.79 % of the prescriptions in hospitalized cases and 65.27 % of that for out-patients had to be purchased by the people themselves (Table 7.3). The same table also shows that the situation has worsened over time. The proportion of supply of free medicines was much higher earlier in 1995–1996 and particularly in 1986–1987. Similarly out of pocket purchase of medicines was lower for hospitalized patients earlier. In some states, particularly in Tamil Nadu the situation is much better. Since 1995 about 260 essential medicines are supplied free to all patients visiting public health facilities (constituting about 40 % of the total number of patients). TNMSC not only procures medicines in bulk at very competitive prices. It also ensures proper

Table 7.3 Trends in access to medicines in India, 1986–1987 to 2004

Period	Free medicines (%)	Partly free (%)	On payment (%)	Not received (%)	Total (%)
In-patient					
1986–1987	31.20	15.00	40.95	12.85	100
1995–1996	12.29	13.15	67.75	6.80	100
2004	8.99	16.38	71.79	2.84	100
Out-patient					
1986–1987	17.98	4.36	65.55	12.11	100
1995–1996	7.21	2.71	79.32	10.76	100
2004	5.34	3.38	65.27	26.01	100

Source: *National Sample Survey Rounds*, 60, 52 and 42, cited in Planning Commission Expert Group (2011), p. 118

distribution to avoid shortages in the different centres. But for the low procurement prices it would have been difficult to provide access given the financial constraints which governments face.[7]

Not only is the scope of health insurance extremely limited in India. Both private insurance as well as social insurance (for example the Central government sponsored Rashtriya Bhima Suraksha Yojana, Rajiv Aarogyasri in Andhra Pradesh, Vajpayee Aarogyasri in Karnataka and the Kalaignar scheme in Tamil Nadu) are restricted to hospitalization cases (Planning Commission Expert Group 2011, p. 121). There is practically no insurance coverage for out-patients. The fact that these patients themselves are required to bear the cost of medicines with no insurance coverage has led to situations where they are unable to buy the medicines. By 2004 for more than a fourth of out-patient prescriptions, they did not get medicines because they could not afford to buy these medicines (Table 7.3).

7.2 Drug Price Control in India

7.2.1 History of Drug Price Control in India

Drug price control began in India in 1963 when the drug prices were frozen under the Defence of India Rules following the war with China.[8] Since then under the Essential Commodities Act, 1955, the government has issued the following Orders:

[7] See the *Report of the Working Group on Drugs & Food Regulations for Formulation of 12th Five Year Plan*, p. 26 (Ministry of Health & Family Welfare (2011).

[8] See Chaudhuri (2005), chapter 8 for the detailed history.

1. Drugs Prices (Display & Control) Order, 1966;
2. Drugs (Prices Control) Order, 1970;
3. Drugs (Prices Control) Order, 1979;
4. Drugs (Prices Control) Order, 1987;
5. Drugs (Prices Control) Order, 1995; and
6. Drugs (Prices Control) Order, 2013.

The entire period since 1963 can be classified into the following periods:

1. 1963–1979; the period of elaborate price freeze and selective price fixation, covered by the Orders of 1966 and 1970;
2. 1979–1987: the period of elaborate price fixation, covered by the Order of 1979;
3. 1987–2013: the period of liberalization of price control starting with the Order of 1987 and intensified with the Order of 1995
4. Since 2013: transition from cost based pricing to market based pricing.

The Drugs Prices (Display & Control) Order, 1966 provided for selective increases in drug prices on prior approval of the government. But the government was not empowered to reduce the prices of any drugs. By an amendment in 1968, firms were allowed the freedom to fix, with prior government approval the prices of new drugs. But no guidelines were issued and hence manufacturers were practically free to fix the prices of new products as if there were no price control. Under the Drug Prices Control Order (DPCO), 1970 the government acquired for the first time the right to fix the maximum selling prices of bulk drugs. Government fixed the prices of 18 bulk drugs and froze the prices of other bulk drugs—prices could not be increased without the approval of the government. For formulations, a formula was announced for fixing the prices based on material cost, conversion cost and packaging charges.

Unlike under DPCO, 1970, which practically covered the entire drug industry, since DPCO, 1979 a selective approach has been adopted. The basic structure of the DPCOs remained practically unchanged between 1979 and 2013. The DPCOs differ from each other basically with respect to the number of scheduled drugs (i.e., those listed in the DPCO for the purpose of price control), the degree of mark-up over cost permitted for formulation pricing and the rate of return allowed for bulk-drug pricing. The degree of mark-ups and the rate of return permitted have been enhanced and the span of control has been diluted over the years. Under DPCO, 1995 which preceded the current DPCO, 2013, the prices of 74 bulk drugs—such as sulphamethoxazole, vitamin C, insulin, insulin, ibuprofen, captopril, norfloxacin, cloxacilin—and the formulations based on these bulk drugs were controlled. Bulk drug prices were fixed on the basis of actual costs. The manufacturing units were provided any one of the following post-tax returns: (i) 14 % on net worth; (ii) 22 % of capital employed; and (iii) internal rate of return of 12 % based on long term marginal costing for new plants. In case of the production from basic stage, an additional 4 % return is provided to the return on net worth or capital employed. The prices of formulations were fixed not on the basis of unit-wise costs but by using the following formula:

Retail price = (material cost + conversion cost + cost of the packing material + packing charges) × (1 + MAPE/100) + excise duty, where MAPE is the maximum allowable post-manufacturing expenses, which includes trade margin and margin for the manufacturer.

The impact of DPCOs on drug prices has been a very controversial topic in India. A number of studies have analysed the behavior of formulation prices. The conclusions vary a great deal because of the differences in the methodologies employed and also because of the different time points considered. The broad conclusion that can be reached is that DPCO, 1995 succeeded in keeping the prices of controlled drugs more under check than it has for the decontrolled drugs.[9]

7.2.2 Drug (Prices Control) Order, 2013

DPCO, 1995 radically changed the criteria for selecting the drugs under price control. Rather than considering the essentiality of the drug, it adopted the economic criteria based on turnover of drugs, number of producers and market share. The criteria used were such that the number of bulk drugs under price control went down from 142 under DPCO, 1987 (and 347 under DPCO, 1979) to 74 under DPCO, 1995. The *Pharmaceutical Policy, 2002* attempted to further liberalize the span of control over pricing. The turnover limit was enhanced from Rs 40 million to Rs 250 million. The other criteria including that on market share was also liberalized.[10] This would have reduced the number of drugs under control to less than 35 (Selvaraj et al. 2012). The 2002 policy was challenged in the court of law and ultimately the Supreme Court directed the government not to implement this policy. The Court asked the government to "formulate appropriate criteria for ensuring essential and life saving drugs not to fall out of price control". Thereafter after deliberations at different levels, the government announced the *National Pharmaceuticals Pricing Policy, 2012*. This made three important changes to the drug price control regime in the country:

1. Drugs under price control are to be decided not by the economic criteria but on the essentiality of the drugs. The *National List of Essential Medicines, 2011* (NLEM) is to be used for the purpose.
2. Only the prices of formulations will be regulated not the prices of bulk drugs
3. The prices of formulations will be regulated through "market based pricing" rather than through "cost based pricing".[11]

---

[9] For a more detailed history and the impact of different DPCOs, see Chaudhuri (2005), chapter 8.

[10] The text of the 2002 Policy is available in the website of the National Pharmaceutical Pricing Authority (http://www.nppaindia.nic.in/index1.html).

[11] The text of the 2012 Policy is available in the website of the National Pharmaceutical Pricing Authority (http://www.nppaindia.nic.in/index1.html).

The government introduced DPCO, 2013 to implement the 2012 policy. In line with the latter, the important provisions of DPCO, 2013 are as follows:

1. Government will fix the ceiling prices of the 348 drugs (only formulations) listed in the NLEM.
2. The ceiling prices will be fixed on the basis of the market based data provided by the IMS Health, a private sector market research company. The ceiling prices will be the simple average of the prices of the all the brands with market share of 1 % or above. Market share will be calculated on the basis of moving annual turnover.
3. The ceiling prices fixed will be allowed an annual change depending on the changes in the Wholesale Price Index.[12]

If we compare the ceiling prices with the prices of the costliest brands, as government has done to find out the impact of DPCO, 2013,[13] we do find that prices have decreased substantially in many cases—84.2 % for Ofloxacin tablets 200 mg, 65.8 % for Omeprazole Capsules 20 mg, 56.5 % for Azithromycin Tablets 500 mg, 47.6 % for Amlodipine Tablets 2.5 mg, 36 % for Atorvastatin tablets 10 mg and 21.1 % for Sodium Valproate tablets 500 mg (Table 7.2, col (6)). But in view of the multiple brands with different prices available in the market, the gain of consumers depends on how much they have purchased at what price. If we compare not with the maximum prices but with the aggregate sales of the products before and after price control, we find that the gain is much less. Thus for Atorvastatin, 10 mg tablets, whereas the price decrease is 36 % the decrease in market sales (if all those who charged a higher price now charge the ceiling price), is only 15 %. This actually measures the collective gain of the consumers (and the loss of the producers). Similarly the consumer gain is 15 % for Azithromycin tablets, 500 mg (compared to 47.6 % price decrease); 15.1 % for Amoxicillin Trihydrate + Clavulanic Acid Potassium Salt tablets, 625 mg (compared to 53.3 % price decrease) and 22 % for Omeprazole capsules 20 mg (compared to 56.5 % price decrease) (Backliwal 2013).[14]

But if we consider the impact on the formulations market as a whole, the impact of DPCO, 2013 is very low—the erosion in the market value will be only 2.2 %. For different therapeutic groups, the erosion varies between 0.5 % in respiratory drugs and 5.6 % in vaccines (Table 7.4). The major reason why the impact is marginal is that the market value of the formulations under price control constitutes only 18 %

[12] See the text of DPCO, 2013 (available at http://www.nppaindia.nic.in/index1.html) for other features including the details of alternative steps, where there are less than five manufacturers having 1 % or more market share and in case of no reduction in the average price.

[13] While notifying the ceiling prices fixed, the government also provided the worksheets used for calculating the ceiling prices. In these worksheets government has also calculated the extent of decrease of the ceiling price. To do so government considered the ceiling price compared to the maximum price among the important brands.

[14] The author is the Managing Director, IMS Health—South Asia and the calculations are based on IMS Health, *Total Sales Audit March 2013*.

Table 7.4 Impact of DPCO, 2013

	MAT value pre-DPCO, 2013 (Rs crores)	MAT value post-DPCO, 2013 (Rs crores)	Value erosion (Rs Crores) (col (2)—col (3))	Value erosion (%) (col (4) as % of col (2))
Total market	72,762	71,166	1,597	2.2
Anti-infectives	11,892	11,420	472	4.0
Cardiac	8,505	8,246	259	3.0
Gastro intestinal	7,613	7,476	137	1.8
Neuro/CNS	4,322	4,206	117	2.7
Dermatology	4,012	3,907	106	2.6
Gynaecology	4,073	3,985	89	2.2
Pain/analgesics	5,936	5,855	81	1.4
Vaccines	1,387	1,309	78	5.6
Hormones	1,285	1,214	71	5.5
Anti diabetic	5,000	4,942	59	1.2
Respiratory	5,711	5,680	31	0.5
Blood related	771	743	28	3.7

Source and Note: Backliwal (2013). MAT figures based on IMS Health, *Total Sales Audit March 2013*

of the total market—the remaining 82 % of the market is out of price control. Keeping such a huge proportion of the market outside price control is one of the most important lacunas of DPCO, 2013.

Questions have also been raised about the market based approach used in fixing prices under DPCO, 2013. As we have discussed above, the Indian retail formulations market suffers from several imperfections. Medicines are sold under brand names and the prices depend on the marketing power of the companies promoting the brands rather than on costs of production. Not surprisingly therefore as Srinivasan and Phadke (2013, Table 1) shows, the ceiling prices fixed under the market based approach would be much higher than what would have been the case if DPCO, 1995 cost norms were followed. Considering the prices at which TNMSC procures drugs as the ex-factory cost price, the same authors also report that some manufacturers will be earning huge profit margins. They argue that what is required is cost based pricing providing the manufacturers reasonable returns. On the other hand the industry has always been critical of cost based pricing. The basic issue is that costs vary a great deal between firms depending on the type of plants, the expenditure on R&D etc.[15] The larger firms in the domestic markets are also major exporters to regulated markets abroad. To satisfy the regulatory requirements of

[15] Note submitted to Bhattacharjea and Sindhwani (2013), by D G Shah of the Indian Pharmaceutical Alliance, p. 50.

these markets they are required to set up plants at a much higher costs. They are also required to incur marketing and other expenses to enter and grow in foreign countries. Industry argues that the way price control has been practiced in India and the uncertainty associated with what is to be controlled and how have not been conducive for investments for growth of the industry. In the absence of a vibrant generic industry it will be more difficult to use TRIPS flexibilities such as compulsory licensing and control the high prices of patented medicines (see below).

The objective of price control is not merely to control the price but to ensure that people can access the medicines at these prices. A basic problem in India has been that even when price control measures have succeeded in reducing prices or keeping these under check, access to essential medicines has not improved necessarily. A basic tendency which has been observed among manufacturers is to stop or reduce the manufacture and sales of controlled drugs and promote drugs outside price control (Chaudhuri 2005, Srinivasan et al. 2013). This has been possible because of the selective approach adopted under DPCO, 2013 (as well as in the previous ones). Under DPCO, 2013, only the prices of dosage forms, strengths and ingredients specifically listed in NLEM are to be controlled. This excludes a large number of formulations which compete against those listed in NLEM. Consider anti-diabetic drugs for example. Only Insulin injections, 40 IU/ML, Glibenclamide tablets, 2.5 and 5 mg and Metformin tablets, 500 mg are listed. NLEM does not include other anti-diabetic drugs sold in the market, for example Gliclazide and Glimepiride, It does not include other strengths of the same medicine, for example Metformin tablets, 1,000, 850 or 250 mg. Neither does it include Metformin sold in combinations with other drugs, for example Gliclazide and Glimepiride. In view of this, manufacturers can respond to lower prices of Metformin, 500 mg tablets, for example under price control by promoting and selling not only other drugs not under price control but the same medicine in other strengths and combinations. Combinations drugs are a major problem in India. Much of these are irrational not justified therapeutically but are promoted for commercial reasons including for bypassing DPCOs. Medicines in retail markets in India are sold much more in combinations with other drugs rather than as single ingredient drugs. For Glibenclamide, for example, only one-third of the total sales are as Glibenclamide alone—the remaining two-thirds are in combination with other drugs (Selvaraj and Farooqui 2012).

In most countries where price control has been effective, control on prices is associated with some other mechanisms to ensure availability and accessibility. The provisions of DPCOs in India have undergone several changes. But none of the changes in the past has tackled the basic problem. Government has not been able to discipline the firms. Nor has the government changed the incentive structure to discourage violations.

DPCO, 2013 incorporates some positive features in this regard. Under paragraph 15, the pricing of new drugs containing new strengths, combinations need to be approved by the government. And it has also been declared that government will approve these depending on the recommendations of experts on rational basis. This however does not include the pricing of non-scheduled formulations already being marketed. For the existing formulations, under paragraph 19 of DPCO, 2013, "... the Government may, in case of extra-ordinary circumstances, if it considers necessary so to do in public interest, fix the ceiling price or retail price of any Drug ...." Observing that prices of drugs other than those specified in NLEM, have gone up by more than 25 % of the simple average, NPPA has fixed the ceiling prices of 108 other formulation covering 50 anti-diabetic and cardiac medicines in July 2014. This includes not only the drugs not included in NLEM such as Gliclazide, Glimepiride, Sitagliptin, Lisinopril but also other strengths of drugs specified in NLEM, for example Metformin 1,000, 250, 850 mg, Amlodipine, 10 mg, Atorvastatin 20, 40 and 80 mg etc.[16] If government monitors also the prices of drugs of other therapeutic groups and combination drugs, and takes corrective action, then firms will find it more difficult to take advantage of loopholes and bypass price control.

A better designed price control regime surely can make drugs more affordable. But in India where out of pocket expenditure is very high as mentioned above, if poor people are unable to afford even the lower prices, access to medicines does not improve. What is required is not only lower prices. What is equally important is that proper financing arrangements need to be made for example by improving public health facilities and providing subsidized insurance. The pharmaceutical policy of 2012 does acknowledge this problem and has highlighted the importance of supplementing price control with other steps. But such steps are conspicuous by its absence—no specific action has been initiated before or after DPCO, 2013.

7.3 Regulation of Prices of Patented Drugs

In a product patent regime, as we have in India since 2005, the prices of new patented drugs will depend on:

- What prices the MNCs holding the patents would charge
- What steps can be taken to regulate such prices through price control or price negotiation or
- What steps are taken to provide competition from generic producers by using the flexibilities provided under TRIPS

MNCs have started marketing in India monopoly drugs at exorbitant prices. A 50 mL injection of Roche's anti-cancer drug Herceptin (generic name: trastumuzab), for example costs Rs 135,200. Among the other high priced drugs are Merck's Erbitux (cetuximab) (Rs 87,920), Bristol-Myers-Squibb's Ixempra (ixabepilone) (Rs 66,430), Pfizer's Macugen (pegaptanib) (Rs 45,350), Sanofi-

[16] "NPPA has fixed the prices of Antidiabetic & Cardiovascular in respect of 108 non-scheduled formulation packs under Paragraph 19 of DPCO, 2013 in related Notification/order dated 10.7.2014" (in http://nppaindia.nic.in/whatsnew.htm).

Aventis' Fasturtec (rasburicase) (Rs 45,000) Roche's Avastin (bevicizumab) (Rs 37,180). There are six products costing between Rs 10,000 and Rs 45,000 (for example Wyeth's Enbrel (etanercept): Rs 15,761), eight products between Rs 10,000 and Rs 1,000 (GSK's Tykerb (lapatinib): Rs 4,468), another six products between Rs 100 and Rs 1,000 (for example Bayer's Xarelto (rivaroxaban): Rs 480) and only eight products with prices below Rs 100 (for example MSD's Januvia (sitagliptin): Rs 43) (Chaudhuri 2012, Table 7). It may also be noted that in therapeutic categories such as cardiac and anti-diabetic, where different molecules are available in the market, the prices of the monopoly molecules are relatively low, for example, sitagliptin. But for life threatening diseases such as cancer, for essential drugs without effective substitutes, prices are exorbitant as in the cases trastuzumab, cetuximab, ixabepilone etc.

Price control is not forbidden under TRIPS or any other agreement of the WTO. The Pharmaceutical Policy of 2012 and DPCO of 2013 do not cover patented drugs. Government has expressed the intention to control these through a separate mechanism. Committees have been appointed to look into the issues of price regulation of patented drugs and reports are available but no concrete action has yet been taken.[17]

Where India has made some progress is in using some of the flexibilities provided under TRIPS. Two important flexibilities which TRIPS permit to mitigate the negative effects of product patent protection on market competition and prices are:

1. Exemptions from grant of patents in certain cases and
2. Compulsory licences to non-patentees under certain conditions.[18]

Under Article 27(1) of TRIPS, patents will have to be provided for inventions, which are 'new, involve an inventive step and are capable of industrial application'. The agreement, however, does not define these terms. This provides some flexibility. Developing countries can interpret these terms so as to restrict the number of patents. Developed countries, for example, the USA, follow very liberal patent standards. Patents are granted not only for NCEs and NBEs involved in the new drugs. Secondary patents can also be taken for new formulations, new combinations and new uses of existing NCEs/NBEs. CIPR (2002, p. 49) had pointed out that there is no compulsion under TRIPS for the developing countries to follow the liberal patent standards of developed countries. The aim should be to ensure that patents are granted for true technical contributions and not for blocking innovation and legitimate competition by generic producers.

India has used this flexibility by amending Section 3 of the Patents Act. Under Section 3(d), "the mere discovery of a new form of a known substance which does

[17] "Report of the Committee on Price Negotiations for Patented Drugs", February 2013 available at the website of the Department of Pharmaceuticals, www.pharmaceuticals.gov.in.

[18] Other flexibilities relate to: some exceptions to patent rights, data protection, using competition laws, parallel importation etc. (see Chaudhuri (2005), chapter 3; Musungu and Oh (2006)).

not result in the enhancement of the known efficacy of that substance or the mere discovery of any new property or new use for a known substance . . ." will not be treated as an invention and is not patentable in India. It has been further clarified that: "salts, esters, ethers, polymorphs, metabolites, pure form, particle size, isomers, mixtures of isomers, complexes, combinations and other derivatives of known substance shall be considered to be the same substance, unless they differ significantly in properties with regard to efficacy". Thus India does not grant patents for new uses. Nor will patents be granted for new formulations/combinations/chemical derivatives of NCEs "unless they differ significantly in properties with regard to efficacy."

The most famous Section 3(d) case in India is the denial of product patent to Novartis for its anti-cancer drug, imatinib mesylate (brand name Glivec of Novartis) (Chaudhuri 2013). Patents have been rejected under this section for a number of other drugs too including Rosiglitazone, Atorvastatin, Erlotinib polymorph (Park 2010, Table 3). This has permitted competition and hence lower prices. In imatinib mesylate for example there are 14 generic companies marketing it—Cipla, Natco, Intas, Sun etc. And 400 mg tablets are available at prices varying between Rs 170 and Rs 432 (AIOCD-AWACS database referred in Table 7.1).

While section 3(d) has played quite an useful role in India in recent years, the policy option which is much more potent and sustainable in the longer run in compulsory licensing. Compulsory licensing is a permission given by the government to a non-patentee to manufacture a drug without (or even against) patentee's consent. As is widely recognised, compulsory licensing is one of the ways in which TRIPS attempts to strike a balance between promoting access to existing drugs and promoting R&D into new drugs. If generic companies are given licenses to produce a patented drug on payment of royalty, then competition among manufacturers would drive down prices, but the royalty paid to the innovators would continue to provide funds and the incentive for R&D. Under Section 84 of India's Patent Act as amended in line with TRIPS, a compulsory licence can be obtained on the ground that the product is not available at a "reasonably affordable price". There is no doubt that the prices charged by MNCs for some of the drugs are beyond the reach of even more affluent sections of the society. But till now only one compulsory licence has been granted to one generic company, Natco for Sorafenib (Bayer's brand name: Nexavar). Compulsory licence application for another drug, Dasatinib (Bristol-Myers Squibb's brand name Sprycel) has been rejected by the Patent Office (Nair et al. 2014). It has been widely reported that the US government on behalf of the MNCs has been putting pressure on India not to grant compulsory licences and to dilute the patentability standards being followed by India. In the *Special 301 Report for the year 2014* of USA, India has been classified as a "Priority watch list country" to intensify pressure on India.[19]

---

[19] "US Opposition to Section (d) of the Indian Patent Act", Statement by Minister of State (Independent Charge), Ministry of Commerce & Industry, in Rajya Sabha, 30 July, 2014 (http://pib.nic.in/newsite/PrintRelease.aspx?relid=107612).

One important difference between price control measures and compulsory licensing may be noted. The former, if properly implemented, makes drugs more affordable but does not provide any room for generic companies. The latter not only makes the prices more affordable through competition. It also ensures some space to generic companies, which is vital for their long term sustenance.

References

Backliwal A (2013) DPCO 2013 will equally affect domestic as well multinational pharma companies. Express Pharma, Financial Express, 19 June. http://pharma.financialexpress.com/sections/management/2289-dpco-2013-will-equally-affect-domestic-as-well-multinational-pharma-companies

Bhattacharjea A, Sindhwani F (2013) Competition issues in the Indian Pharmaceuticals Sector. A report submitted to Consumer Unity & Trust Society, Jaipur

Chaudhuri S (2005) The WTO and India's pharmaceuticals industry: patent protection TRIPS and developing countries. Oxford University, New Delhi

Chaudhuri S (2012) Multinationals and monopolies: pharmaceutical industry in India after TRIPS. Economic and Political Weekly, March 24

Chaudhuri S (2013) The larger implications of the Novartis-Glivec judgment. Economic and Political Weekly, April 27

CIPR (2002) Integrating intellectual property rights and development policy. Commission on intellectual property rights. DFID, London

Kidron M (1965) Foreign investments in India. Oxford University, London

Lalitha N (2008) Tamil Nadu Government intervention and the prices of medicines. Economic and Political Weekly, January 5, pp 66–71

Musungu S, Oh C (2006) The use of flexibilities in TRIPS by developing countries: can they promote access to medicines? South Centre, Geneva

Nair GG, Fernandes A, Nair K (2014) Landmark pharma patent jurisprudence in India. J Intellect Prop Rig 19:79–88

Park C (2010) The implementation of India's patent law: a review of patents granted by the Indian patent office. In: Chaudhuri S, Park C, Gopakumar KM (eds) Five years into the product patent regime: India's response. United Nations Development Programme, New York. http://content.undp.org/go/cms-service/download/publication/?version¼live&id¼3089934

Planning Commission Expert Group (2011) High level expert group report on Universal Health Coverage for India. Planning Commission, New Delhi (Chairman: K Srinath Reddy)

Selvaraj S, Farooqui HH (2012) Draft Drug Price Policy 2011. Legitimising unaffordable medicine prices? Economic and Political Weekly, November 17

Selvaraj S et al (2012) Pharmaceutical pricing policy: a critique. Economic and Political Weekly, January 28

Srinivasan S, Phadke A (2013) Pharma Policy 2012 and its discontents. Economic and Political Weekly, January 5

Srinivasan S, Srikrishna T, Phadke A (2013) Drug price control order 2013. As good as a leaky bucket. Economic and Political Weekly, June 29

Chapter 8
Pharmaceutical Pricing Policies in Italy

Claudio Jommi and Paola Minghetti

Abstract This chapter provides an overview of drug price and reimbursement regulations in Italy within the general context of Italian pharmaceutical policy.

Reimbursement and ex-factory prices are negotiated by the National Drug Agency and the relevant company, whereas the distribution margins and VAT (Value Added Tax) are set by law. The pharmaceutical companies are free to set prices for non-reimbursable (prescription-only and non-prescription) drugs.

Disease burden, comparative risk-benefit profiles and drug budget impacts are the key parameters considered in the negotiation process of ex-factory prices. Many drug price approvals are accompanied by managed market entry contracts, including financially based contracts (e.g., price-volume agreements) and outcome-based contracts (especially for cancer drugs). Generic reference pricing has been applied since 2001, while therapeutic reference pricing, temporarily introduced by regions, has not been allowed since October 2007. Regions, local health authorities and hospital trusts play important roles in managing market access to drugs: despite they cannot change list prices chosen at the national level, they implemented aggressive procurement policies to reduce actual prices and policies aimed at promoting prescribing behavior that favors cheaper drugs.

Pricing policy has doubtlessly improved in the last 20 years (i.e., after the 1993–1994 scandals that revealed that companies, policy makers and top public officials constructed an illegal system to set prices), with a profound cultural change, an increasing role played by evidence-based medicine and, more generally, by technical competence. However, there are some critical factors that should be addressed in the future political agenda. A clearer pathway to defining innovation, increased transparency of assessment and appraisal processes, a more rational distribution of competencies between central and regional authorities, and a softer approach to drug budgets, with an explicit recognition of the impact of drugs in the use (and

C. Jommi (✉)
Department of Pharmaceutical Sciences, Università del Piemonte Orientale and Pharmaceutical Observatory, Cergas, Università Bocconi, Milan, Italy
e-mail: claudio.jommi@pharm.unipmn.it

P. Minghetti
Department of Pharmaceutical Sciences, Università degli Studi di Milano, Milan, Italy
e-mail: paola.minghetti@unimi.it

Z.-U.-D. Babar (ed.), *Pharmaceutical Prices in the 21st Century*,
DOI 10.1007/978-3-319-12169-7_8

cost) of other health care services (and vice versa), may further improve the Italian drug pricing policy.

8.1 Introduction

The Italian health care system has adopted, since 1978, a "Beveridge" or "National Health Service" model (Servizio Sanitario Nazionale—SSN), where the State is the most important financer, via general tax levies, and provider of health care services. Regions have played an important role since the very beginning of the SSN constitution, but their role was strengthened first by one reform in 1992/1993 and second by a more radical reform of Constitutional Law in 2001. Decentralization and financial accountability of regions have been a matter of conflict between the central and the regional governments and have also affected the pharmaceutical market: although prices and reimbursements are decided at the national level, many regions have introduced barriers to market access (including regional formularies, aggressive procurement policies, and prescription targets for GPs (General Practitioners)).

The pharmaceutical market for reimbursable drugs is strongly regulated, and cost-containment has been the main driver of pharmaceutical policies. Pricing and reimbursement are simultaneously negotiated by the National Drug Agency (Agenzia Italiana del Farmaco—AIFA) and the company holding the Marketing Authorization (MA). Managed market entry agreements (MMEA) usually accompany market access for new and expensive drugs. Many actions have been put in place to govern prescribing behavior, including guidelines, therapeutic protocols and prescription targets. Drug distribution is highly regulated and regulation cover pharmacies' locations, properties and chains, remuneration of pharmacists and wholesalers, and substitution rights.

This chapter provides an analysis of price and reimbursement (P&R) regulations in Italy within the general context of the Italian pharmaceutical market and policies. The first and second sections illustrate the Italian health care and pharmaceutical systems, respectively. In the third paragraph the main regulatory authority (AIFA) is described. The following section provides a general overview of pharmaceutical policies and drugs P&R. Section 8.6 illustrates P&R negotiation. Section 8.7 focuses on MMEA, which play an important role in P&R negotiation. In the two following sections, reasons for possible differences between list and actual prices paid by hospitals and how prices change over time are discussed. Empirical evidence of the impact of pharmaceutical pricing policies is illustrated in Sect. 8.10, and a special paragraph (Sect. 8.11) is devoted to generics. The final paragraph discusses the pros and cons of the Italian regulatory context and future prospects for pharmaceutical policy in Italy.

8.2 The Italian Health Care System

In 2013, Italy's population was 59,685,227 inhabitants with a mean age of 44 years. Twenty-one percent the population is over 64 years, 64.7 % are between 15 and 64 years and the population's annual growth rate is 0.6 %. Italy is divided into 20 regions,[1] 8 of which account for approximately 80 % of the overall population (www.istat.it, accessed July 26, 2014).

The Italian health care system was modeled as a National Health Service (SSN), primarily funded by national and regional taxes, in 1978 (Law 883/78).

The SSN is intended to provide for public and preventive care, including promotion of health education of all citizens, education and training of health professionals, food and drink hygiene, work safety, and actions against pollution, and primary and secondary care through an efficient and uniform health system covering the entire population.

Providers of health services are both public (most hospitals and some outpatient and community services) and private (some hospitals, many outpatient and community services, community pharmacies and GPs). Relationships between private providers who work on behalf of the SSN and for the SSN itself are regulated by national contracts.

Since the early 1990s (DL.vo 502/1992 and DL.vo 517/1993), the SSN has been experiencing a devolution of power that has transferred legislative, administrative and, to a certain extent, fiscal power to the 21 regions (Fattore 1999; Jommi et al. 2001; Anessi Pessina et al. 2004; France and Taroni 2005). The central government has retained regulation over the determination of "essential levels of care," i.e., the benefits package that each region is expected to cover, general contracts for SSN employees, contracts with community pharmacies and GPs, and P&R of pharmaceuticals. In addition, the central government, after a complex negotiation between the Minister of Health, the Minister of Finance and the regional governments, chooses the total budget for the SSN and its allocation among regions. All other aspects are regulated by the regions: they have almost full control over the provision of services, funding mechanisms and regulation, and are responsible for guaranteeing the "essential levels of care" within the resources determined at the national level. Decentralization was accelerated with an amendment to Constitutional Law in 2001 (Law 3/2001, as integrated by Law 131/2003). Regions may select the overall structures of their (regional) health care systems (e.g., introducing a purchaser/provider split, managing accreditation of providers and most of the cost-containment methods), provided that they offer the benefit package determined by the central government. Regions are also fully responsible for health care budgets allocated by the central government. If the budget is exceeded, regions may use cost-sharing, taxes, and cost-containment to cover the

[1] The Autonomous Region of Trentino Alto Adige is divided into two Provinces (Trento and Bolzano) that autonomously govern their health care systems. Hence, from the health care system viewpoint, there are 21 "regions."

Table 8.1 Health expenditure indicators in Italy

	Per capita health expenditure (Euro, 2012)	Per capita public health expenditure (Euro, 2012)	Health expenditure to GDP (2012)	Public health expenditure to GDP (2012)
Italy	3,040	2,376	9.2 %	7.2 %
Average EU-15	4,220	3,287	10.0 %	7.6 %
Average Europe	3,262	2,473	8.8 %	6.6 %
	Health expenditure (CAGR 1995–2012)	Public health expenditure (CAGR 1995–2012)	Public health expenditure to total health expenditure (2012)	Out-of-pocket expenditure to total private health expenditure (2012)
Italy	4.3 %	4.7 %	78.2 %	92.7 %
Average EU-15	5.5 %	5.5 %	76.5 %	68.9 %
Average Europe	6.3 %	6.2 %	74.4 %	74.2 %

Legend: *CAGR* compound annual growth rate, *GDP* gross domestic products
Source: Our elaboration on the WHO Global Health Expenditure Database (http://apps.who.int/nha/en/, accessed 2 May, 2014)

deficit (Tediosi et al. 2009). Regional budget accountability has been softened in recent years due to huge differences across regional deficits, with most Northern and Central Regions remaining within their budgets and the Southern ones well over theirs. If a region has a substantial deficit, it may require partial coverage of the deficit by the central government, provided that it creates and follows a turnaround plan approved by the central government.

The SSN's economic indicators are quite good: the per capita public health expenditure, public health expenditure to GDP ratio and health expenditure growth rate are all lower than in most other EU countries (Table 8.1). Despite cost-containment actions, public coverage of health care costs is still quite high. The salient feature of SSN's is that most of the private expenditure is paid out-of-pocket, i.e., no third-party payers are involved (for-profit and not-for-profit health insurance companies).

Primary care is provided by independent SSN-contracted GPs. Patients are free to choose their GPs, who act as gatekeepers, and there is a maximum of 1,500 patients per GP. GP payment is based 75 % on capitation and 25 % on incentive schemes. Primary care is undergoing important changes aimed at improving networking and GP groups.

In-patient services are provided by public and private hospitals. The latter may be fully or partially contracted by the SSN and are generally for-profit. Public and private hospitals accounted for 80.7 % and 19.3 % of SSN beds, respectively, in 2010 (Guerrazzi and Ricci 2013). In the past, the SSN has relied on a fully vertical integrated model for health care services: most services (including hospitals) were managed by Local Health Authorities (LHAs). Since the 1992/1993 reform, regions are free to split public hospitals from LHAs, thus making them independent. The former has become a provider of services and the latter, commissioners ("quasi-market" model). Outpatient services are provided by hospitals and public and accredited private ambulatories. Preventive care is mostly managed by LHAs. A fee-for-service system has been introduced for both independent hospitals and accredited private providers for inpatient (classified according to the Diagnosis Related Group—DRG—system) and outpatient services.

Cost sharing is applied to all outpatient services, excluding GP visits and including access to emergency rooms, should this access be non-urgent. Inpatient services are free at the point of delivery. Cost sharing on all reimbursed drugs is decided by regions and takes the form of a co-payment (fixed charge per prescription), whereas co-insurance on generic drugs due to the reference pricing system is set centrally (see Sect. 8.5).

8.3 The Pharmaceutical System

In 2013, Italy was the third largest pharmaceutical market in Europe, after Germany and France, and the sixth worldwide (Farmindustria 2014).

Pharmaceutical expenditures reached 25.3 billion Euros in 2013 (423 Euros per capita). The retail market and drugs procured by hospitals accounted for 67 % and 33 % of the total market, respectively. The SSN covers 53 % of the retail market expenditure, whereas drugs procured by hospitals are fully covered by the SSN: as a whole, public coverage of drug expenditure is 68 % (Table 8.2).

Private expenditure on reimbursable drugs (cost-sharing + reimbursable drugs privately purchased by patients), prescription-only non-reimbursable drugs, and non-prescription drugs accounts for 32 %, 37 % and 31 % of the private drug expenditure, respectively. Non-prescription drugs may be sold to pharmacies (92 % of the relevant market), para-pharmacies (4.9 %) and mass retailers (2.5 %).

Drugs procured by hospitals are either used in inpatient setting (64 % of the relevant market) or are distributed to patients who use them outside of the inpatient setting (home care, first therapeutic cycle at the patient's discharge from the hospital, drugs administered in outpatient settings—e.g., epoetin for patients with chronic renal failure, etc.) (36 %).

From 2001 to 2013, public drug expenditures increased less than health expenditures (Fig. 8.1). Drugs account for 15.2 % of the total SSN expenditure in 2013 (18.3 % in 2002). The annual growth rates of the pharmaceutical SSN expenditures and total SSN expenditures were 1.9 % and 3.2 %, respectively.

The growth in drug expenditure has been driven by hospital procurement, while retail drug expenditure fell by 20 % from 2001 to 2013 (Fig. 8.2). This trend is primarily due to the fact that most new and expensive products are launched into the hospital market. In addition, the share of retail drugs procured and distributed by hospitals has been growing.

Off-patent drugs represent 64.2 % and 41.5 % of the SSN retail market in volume and value, respectively (Table 8.3). Generics accounted in 2013 for 14.9 % of the total SSN retail market, i.e., 36 % of the off-patent market.

Table 8.2 Pharmaceutical expenditure in Italy (2013)

Drug expenditure	Million Euros	% on the relevant market
Total drug expenditure	25,212	
– Retail market	16,847	67 % on Total drug expenditure
– Procured by hospitals	8,425	33 % on Total drug expenditure
SSN drug expenditure	17,288	68 % on Total drug expenditure
– SSN retail drug expenditure	8,863	51 % on SSN drug expenditure
– SSN hospital drug expenditure	8,425	49 % on SSN drug expenditure
(a) Inpatient	5,422	64 % on SSN hospital drug expenditure
(b) Other settings	3,003	36 % on SSN hospital drug expenditure
Private drug expenditure (only retail)	7,984	32 % on Total drug expenditure
– Reimbursable drugs	2,578	32 % on Private drug expenditure
(a) Cost-sharing on SSN prescriptions	1,436	56 % on Private drug expenditure on reimbursable drugs
Regional cost-sharing	558	39 % on Cost-sharing on SSN prescriptions
Reference pricing	878	61 % on Cost-sharing on SSN prescriptions
(b) Private prescriptions for reimbursable	1,142	44 % on Private drug expenditure on reimbursable drugs
– Non-reimbursable drugs	5,406	68 % on Private drug expenditure
(a) Prescription-only drugs	2,966	55 % on Private non-reimbursable drug expenditure
(b) Non-prescription drugs	2,440	45 % on Private non-reimbursable drug expenditure
Community pharmacies	2,257	93 % on Private non-reimbursable non-prescription drug expenditure
Para-pharmacies	120	5 % on Private non-reimbursable non-prescription drug expenditure
Mass retailers	62	3 % on Private non-reimbursable non-prescription drug expenditure

Source: Our elaboration of AIFA (2014) and Assosalute (2014)

There are 311 pharmaceutical companies based in Italy that are represented by the relevant association ("Farmindustria"). In 2013, the industry employed 72,300 people; 9.6 % were employed in R&D, compared to an average of 21.7 % in the other main EU countries. Production of drugs and vaccines has grown by 16 % in the last 5 years, but most of this production has been absorbed by exports, which account for 71 % of the production value (50 % in 2008).

Drug distribution is managed by 110 wholesalers (despite a huge reduction in recent years, the wholesale drug market is still very fragmented)[2] and 18,039 community pharmacies (of which 91 % are privately owned and 9 % are owned

[2] www.adfsalute.it. Accessed 25 July 2014.

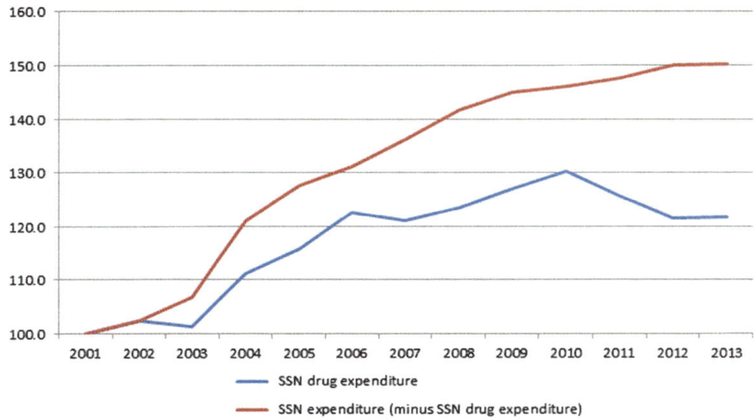

Fig. 8.1 SSN pharmaceutical expenditure versus SSN total expenditure (2001 = 100). *Source*: Our elaboration of AIFA (2014), Armeni and Ferré (2013) and MEF (2014)

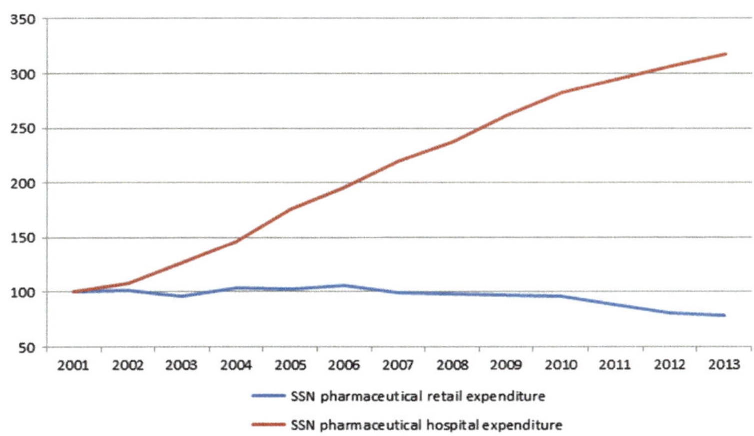

Fig. 8.2 SSN pharmaceutical retail expenditure versus SSN pharmaceutical hospital expenditure (2001 = 100). *Source*: Our elaboration of AIFA (2014) and MEF, various years

by municipalities[3]). Since 2006 (Law Decree 223/2006), para-pharmacies (3,156 in 2014) and gross retailers (340 areas in gross retailers) (Assosalute 2014) are authorized to distribute non-prescription drugs, provided that sales are supervised by a pharmacist and that a separate area for drug sales is created. The market share of non-prescription drugs sold outside of pharmacies is still very limited. The number of pharmacies is determined by law, according to demographic and geographic criteria (one pharmacy per 3,300 inhabitants and a minimum distance of 200 m between two retailers). Private pharmacies should be owned by pharmacists

[3] www.federfarma.it. Accessed 25 July 2014.

Table 8.3 SSN pharmaceutical retail expenditure: patent-protected versus off-patent drugs (%)

	2007	2008	2009	2010	2011	2012	2013
Total retail	100.0	100.0	100.0	100.0	100.0	100.0	100.0
– In patent	80.4	72.9	72.2	69.6	67.8	62.3	58.5
– Off patent	19.6	27.1	27.8	30.4	32.2	37.7	41.5
Branded	14.8	20.7	20.7	22.0	22.7	24.3	26.6
Generics	4.7	6.4	7.1	8.4	9.5	13.4	14.9
Total off patent	100.0	100.0	100.0	100.0	100.0	100.0	100.0
– Branded	75.5	76.4	74.5	72.4	70.5	64.5	64.1
– Generics	24.0	23.6	25.5	27.6	29.5	35.5	35.9

Source: Our elaboration of AIFA (2014)

(Marchetti and Minghetti 1992) and small pharmacy chains have been allowed since 2006 (with a maximum of four pharmacies per chain in the same province). Other, larger chains have been created as a result of the ability of large wholesalers (including Boots and Admenta) to manage public pharmacies. Private and public pharmacies are represented by Federfarma and Assofarm, respectively. Internet sales have recently been authorized, but are limited to non-prescription drugs, and the seller must be a pharmacy. Doctors are not allowed to distribute drugs.

8.4 Drugs Regulatory Authorities

Market access is regulated by the Italian Medicines Agency (AIFA),[4] but regions also play an important role in governing the pharmaceutical market.

AIFA was created in July 2004 (Law 326/2003). Unlike most other countries where drug agencies are only focused on regulatory issues (market authorization, inspections, and pharmaco-surveillance), AIFA covers the whole spectrum of market access tools, including manufacturing authorization, P&R for all (reimbursable) drugs, MMEA and guidelines (named “AIFA Notes”) that only allow reimbursements to some of the patients covered by the license.

AIFA is an autonomous agency from organizational, financial and administrative perspectives, and is under the direction and surveillance of the Minister of Health and the Minister of Finance. It cooperates with regions, which are represented in AIFA’s governing bodies and technical units.

AIFA is governed by a General Director appointed by the Minister of Health and a Management Board, composed of the President, who is appointed by the Minister of Health (in agreement with the State-Regions Conference), and four members, of whom two are appointed by the Minister of Health and two are appointed by the State-Regions Conference. AIFA is split into five units: Pre-Marketing

[4] www.agenziafarmaco.gov.

Authorization, Marketing Authorization, Post-Marketing Surveillance, Pharmaceutical Strategy and Policy, Inspections and Certification, and Administrative Affairs.

P&R is managed by the P&R Office of the Pharmaceutical Strategy and Policy Unit. The P&R Office is supported by two technical consulting committees: the Technical Scientific Committee (CTS) that provides a consultative opinion on drug administrative classifications and reimbursement (it is composed of 11 members appointed by the Minister of Health, the Minister of Finance and the State-Regions Conference); the Committee for P&R (CPR) that supports AIFA in the management of the P&R dossier (it includes ten members appointed by the Minister of Health, the Minister of Finance and the State-Regions Conference). Besides the two technical consulting committees, AIFA relies on (1) four technical units ("Segretariati di Supporto e Coordinamento"). One of these units is focused on P&R: it supports the activities of CTS and CPR and provides for full integration of the two committees and the P&R Office; (2) six consultant committees composed of clinicians who represent major therapeutic areas.

Many pharmaceutical policies are managed on a regional level, including binding regional formularies, guidelines on drug procurement by hospitals, direct distribution of drugs by hospitals, clinical governance, prescription targets for GPs, and regulations of information and advice provided by the pharmaceutical companies' representatives (Jommi et al. 2013). Most of these policies are managed by the General Director of the Regional Departments of Health, supported by the relevant Pharmaceutical Unit.

8.5 Pharmaceutical Policies and Drug Pricing Set-Up

A flow chart of the market access for pharmaceuticals is provided in Fig. 8.3.

From a reimbursement perspective, pharmaceuticals are divided into three categories: Class A (Table 8.4):, which includes pharmaceuticals for severe and chronic diseases reimbursed by the SSN in all settings; Class H, which includes drugs reimbursed only if used in hospital setting; most of them (78 %) may only be used in hospitals for health reasons; Class C, which includes both prescription-only and non-prescription drugs not covered by the SSN, with exception of specific patients (e.g., patients affected by rare diseases).

Class A and H represent the list of reimbursable drugs (positive list—Prontuario Farmaceutico Nazionale). Regions may decide to reimburse drugs classified as Class C if they demonstrate having enough regional funds and if they have already covered drugs in Classes A and H.

Prescription drugs are divided into three main categories: drugs that can be used only in hospital settings; prescription-only drugs that can also be used outside of hospitals: for most of them, the prescription is managed by the GP and is "repeatable" i.e., the same prescription may be used for 6 months with a maximum of ten requests per drug (few prescriptions are not repeatable, or are not allowed to be prescribed by GPs because of a complex diagnosis, the risk of abuse or important

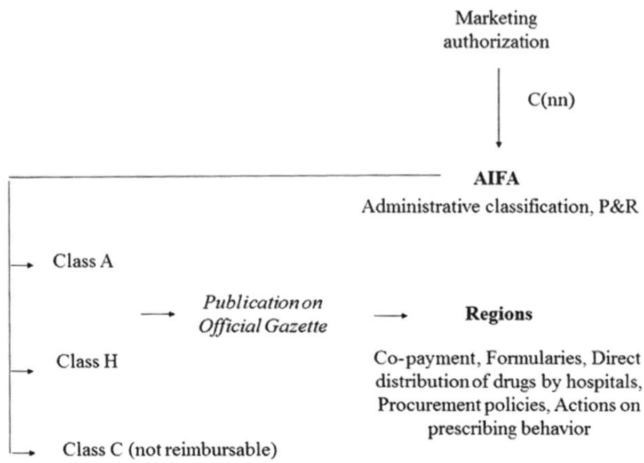

Fig. 8.3 Market access for pharmaceuticals in Italy

Table 8.4 Number of drugs according to reimbursement and prescription statuses

Class A	8,177	53.9 %
Class H	1,397	9.2 %
Class C	5,606	36.9 %
Drugs that may only be used in hospital settings	1,949	12.8 %
Normal prescription (GP, repeatable)	10,253	67.5 %
Special prescriptions	1,227	8.1 %
Non-prescription non-advertisable	867	5.7 %
Non-prescription advertisable	884	5.8 %
Total drugs	15,180	100.0 %

Source: Our elaboration of AIFA (2014)

side effects; special prescriptions are provided for narcotic drugs); non-prescription drugs that may be advertised (OTC) or not advertised to the general public.

Pharmaceutical policy has been strongly influenced by the presence of a national spending cap on drugs (set as a percentage of public health funds) that was enforced by law in 2001 and has been changed many times (Fattore and Jommi 2008). At present, pharmaceuticals are subject to a budget on Class A drugs not used in hospital setting (11.35 % of public health funds) ("retail drugs budget") and a budget on all Class H and Class A drugs used in hospital settings (3.5 % of public health funds) ("hospital drugs budget"). Should the retail drugs budget be overrun, the pharmaceutical industry and distributors must pay back the difference. In a case where spending on hospital drugs is over the budget, regions and the pharmaceutical industry are in charge of covering the deficit (50 % each). Since 2007 (Law 222/2007), each pharmaceutical company has been given a budget, based on the national drug budget for the current year and market shares in the previous year; if the actual SSN drug spending is over the budget, each company will contribute to the payback in proportion to its actual revenue (compared to its budget). Innovative and orphan drugs are exempt from the payback requirement; if they exceed the budget, their payback is distributed among other brand-name products.

In brief, P&R in Italy are characterized by the following features.

Reimbursement and ex-factory prices are simultaneously negotiated by AIFA and the relevant company; because this negotiation takes 1 year on average (347 days according to Efpia-IMS data) (Efpia 2011), beginning in 2013 market access was accelerated by allowing drugs to be marketed once they were approved (they are included in a "limbo" Class $C_{(nn)}$ that stands for "Drugs whose price and reimbursement has not yet been negotiated") and waiting for price and reimbursement negotiations; the relevant expenditure is covered by patients unless the region and industry have negotiated a temporary reimbursement arrangement. If AIFA and the industry do not reach an agreement the drug is classified as Class C.

The main criteria used in the negotiation are the disease burden, the place in therapy and availability of alternative treatments, the risk-benefit profile, the therapeutic added value, and the impact on the drug budget. For most new drugs, MMEA are agreed on; for some drugs, more than one contract is negotiated.

Cost-sharing for drugs was abolished at the national level in 2001, but regions are free to introduce cost-sharing to cover possible health care spending deficits. In 16 out of the 21 regions, cost-sharing has been introduced in the form of co-payments (fixed charges per prescription). Regional cost-sharing accounts for 5 % of gross SSN retail drug spending in 2013 (AIFA 2014). Finally, generic reference prices were introduced at the national level in 2001 (Decree 347/2001). Products sharing the same generic molecule and package (same active ingredients, pharmaceutical form, route of administration, dose and quantity of molecules per dose) are reimbursed at the lowest available price (Ghislandi et al. 2005). Patients are required to pay the possible difference between the price of the prescription and the reference value. Since 2005, if a product is priced higher than the reference level, pharmacists are obliged to inform patients of the existence of cheaper substitutes, unless the prescriber indicates "non-substitutable" on the prescription form. If patients accept substitution, pharmacists are obliged to dispense the cheapest product, which will be fully reimbursed. Cost-sharing for drugs subject to reference pricing accounts for 7.8 % of gross SSN retail spending in 2013 (AIFA 2014). Exemptions to cost-sharing are decided by regions and are usually applied to people suffering from chronic diseases and rare diseases, elderly people, disabled people, and people with low family incomes.

Distribution margins for reimbursable drugs are regulated by law. At present (Law 122/2010), wholesalers and pharmacists receive a 3 % and a 30.35 % margin, respectively, on the final price before the VAT (10 %). The distribution margin for generics is 8 % higher (and margins for the industry are 8 % lower) than for other drugs. If the drug is covered by the SSN, pharmacists are subject to a progressive discount ranging from 3.75 % (when the drug's final price is under 25.82 Euros) to 19 % (if the price is over 154.94): hence, actual margins for pharmacists range from 26.6 to 11.35 %. Further discounts have been temporarily imposed to address cost-containment, whereas pharmacies with low turnover and that are located in rural areas benefit from reduced discounts. A reform of pharmacist and wholesaler remunerations stating that remuneration for reimbursed drugs should generally rely on a fee per drug dispensed was announced in 2010 (Law 122/2010). Implementation of the reform has been postponed many times and it is now expected to be introduced in 2015.

The industry is free to set prices for non-reimbursable drugs, but industry is allowed to increase prices in each odd-numbered year. Distribution margins for non-reimbursable drugs are free. Whereas the final price of non-reimbursable prescription drugs is the same all over the country, prices for OTC and other non-prescription drugs may differ across pharmacies and other points of delivery (para-pharmacies and gross retailers).

8.6 How Prices Are Set and Which Entities Are Involved in Price Negotiations

Ex-factory prices for all reimbursable drugs are negotiated by AIFA and the company holding the marketing authorization. The company is invited to submit a file to the P&R Office of AIFA with the following data (Delibera CIPE 3/2001): general information on the drug, i.e., mechanism of action, posology and route of administration, length of treatment/number of cycles, approved indication; disease burden/seriousness; place in therapy and availability of therapeutic alternatives; relative (comparative) risk-benefit profile; summary of the clinical evidence; pharmaco-surveillance data from other countries where the product has been launched before Italy; prices in other EU countries; impact on drug budget, i.e., number of expected patients, total market for the target population, expected market share of the new drug; suggested measures to reduce the impact on the budget (e.g., discounts); industrial parameters (investments in research and development and production in Italy; drugs exports); cost-efficacy data, considered useful for orphan and highly innovative drugs.

Disease relevance (drugs for minor diseases are usually not reimbursed), comparators (and their prices), therapeutic added value, and the impact on drug budget are the most important parameters considered in the negotiation. Cost-efficacy is usually disregarded, and industrial parameters seem to not be taken into account.

Disease relevance, place in therapy and added value are also used to categorize a drug as “innovative.” An innovative drug has two main advantages: its revenue is excluded from payback if the relevant (retail or hospital) budget is overrun and it may be prescribed even if it is not listed in regional formularies. The assessment of innovativeness (Motola et al. 2005), formally adopted in 2007 (AIFA 2007), has been criticized for being too broad, not transparently managed and more oriented toward assessing a drug indicated for diseases without alternatives (e.g., rare diseases) as innovative than a drug providing important added value to existing alternatives. Despite these criticisms, new criteria to assess innovativeness have not been implemented yet despite multiple announcements about them.

Files provided by companies are first scrutinized by the CTS, who suggests an administrative classification and reimbursement status. Next, the dossier is analyzed by the P&R Office of AIFA, with the support of the P&R "Segretariato" and, if necessary, the support of the relevant consultant committee and the P&R Committee. In principle, the negotiation process can be entirely managed online, but P&R Committee hearings to discuss the most controversial parts of the dossier are common. If an agreement is reached, it is formally approved by the CTS and the AIFA Management Board and published on the Gazzetta Ufficiale (Official Gazette, Official Journal of the Italian Republic). If an agreement is not reached, the drug is classified as Class C and is not reimbursed by the SSN.

In principle, the whole process should take 90 days, not including a "clock stop" chosen by AIFA to obtain further information. According to Efpia/IMS Health data, the P&R negotiation takes a longer time (347 days on average). This market access delay is certainly caused by the length of the negotiation process, but it can also be due to a delay in the dossier submission. Market access delays for oncology drugs are even longer (422 days on average), but 40 % of this delay is caused by submission postponement (Russo et al. 2010).

8.7 Managed Market Entry Agreements

Managed Market Entry Agreement (MMEA) have been extensively used because of the necessity of making drugs available (and covered by payers) with insufficient evidence for new drugs, uncertainty at market launch and the need to limit the budget impact of new drugs. The taxonomy of these agreements has been illustrated in recent reviews (Morel et al. 2013; Carlson et al. 2010). MMEA may be (1) financial-based or outcome-based when the price or reimbursement status, or both, depends on the financial and clinical impact, respectively, and (2) -population-based or patient-based when the drug's performance is measured on the population as an aggregate or on each individual patient, respectively (Fig. 8.4).

In Italy, most new drugs are approved with an MMEA. They are both financial-based (price-volume agreements or total spending cap/capping on the annual cost per patient treated, discounts on first cycles) and outcome-based contracts (only in the form of performance-linked reimbursement). Outcome-based contracts have been applied to oncological drugs—e.g., everolimus has been approved with a performance-linked reimbursement contract that requires a payback to hospitals from Novartis should patients not respond after 3/6 months of treatment for advanced renal carcinoma/HER2 negative advanced breast cancer and pNET, respectively—and could rely on drugs registries as an information tool for patients follow-up. To date, 25 drugs have been subject to such contracts. Registries have

Fig. 8.4 Taxonomy of managed market entry agreements

	POPULATION LEVEL	PATIENT LEVEL
FINANCIAL-BASED	Discounts Price/volume agreements	Capping Discounts on first cycles
OUTCOME-BASED	Coverage with evidence development	Performance-linked reimbursement

been implemented for a broader number of drugs (46) to govern the prescription of expensive drugs.[5]

Many times, multiple MMEA are negotiated: e.g., vemurafenib, approved for the treatment of advanced and inoperable melanoma in BRAF-mutated patients, has been approved with a performance-linked reimbursement contract and a spending cap of 36 million Euros for 2 years. Roche has also agreed to provide the relevant biomarker free at the point of delivery.[6]

8.8 Official Prices Are Not the Actual Transaction Prices

Ex-factory list prices negotiated by AIFA and the relevant pharmaceutical companies (plus distribution margins and VAT) represent the official price covered by the SSN for drugs used at the retail level.

Actual prices paid by hospitals may differ from the official prices for two reasons.

First, hidden discounts may be negotiated with AIFA as part of the MMEA strategy. These discounts are unknown to the general public, but regions and hospitals are informed of them because the discounted price represents the maximum price of drug procurement.

Second, hospitals may require and companies provide further discounts. Procurement policies have become very aggressive in recent years for cost-containments reasons: most hospitals are joining networks (even at the regional level) to increase their bargaining power. Many times tenders refer to the molecule (thus including originators, co-marketers and generics, if the patent has expired) or even the therapeutic class (including molecules with the same indication/mechanism of action—e.g., statins). There are no official data on the average discounts

[5] http://www.agenziafarmaco.gov.it/it/content/registri-farmaci-sottoposti-monitoraggio. Accessed 25 July 2014.

[6] http://www.gazzettaufficiale.biz/atti/2013/20130129/13A04712.htm. Accessed 25 July 2014.

and actual prices paid by the SSN. A recent analysis, focused on off-patent biotechnological drugs and biosimilars in eight regions where drug procurement is centralized, found that the average discount on the bid price (which can be lower than the price negotiated with AIFA) was 61.4 % for epoetin, 59.9 % for filgrastim and 17.4 % for somatropin (Curto et al. 2014).

8.9 Medicine Prices Change Over Time

Medicine price changes over time are influenced by four factors.

The price/reimbursement contract between AIFA and the pharmaceutical companies lasts 2 years, unless it is defined differently (e.g., if a 1 year price-volume agreement is negotiated). Price (and reimbursement) conditions are renewed for another 2 years, unless AIFA or manufacturers provide new evidence 3 months before the deadline of the contract. This has never produced, to the best of our knowledge, an increase in prices, but has possibly resulted in price-cuts.

Second, should there be an extension to the indication of the drug that noticeably increases the number of patients (and volume sold), AIFA asks the company for a price cut.

Third, in the last 10 years, patent protections for many molecules have expired, and are no longer protected by the Italian Supplementary Patent Certificate (Certificato Protettivo Complementare, CPC). This certificate was introduced in 1991 and guaranteed a patent protection extension over the European Supplementary Patent Certificate (18 years compared to 5 years). The latter has cancelled any previous national legislation over patent protection (including the Italian CPC), but has not had any retroactive impact on drugs with patent protections that were already extended (Garattini and Ghislandi 2006). Actually, after 18 years (i.e., in 2010), the impact of the Italian CPC has diminished. Many molecules whose patent expired many years ago elsewhere are now off-patent in Italy as well. Generication together with reference pricing has contributed to a huge decrease in prices.

Finally, pharmaceutical price cuts have been extensively used as cost-containment measures (Ghislandi et al. 2005). While administrative price cuts prevailed in the second half of the 1990s, subsequent years have seen the implementation of more complex actions. The most important one, named cut-off and approved in 2003, provided for a maximum price per DDD (Defined Daily Dosage) per therapeutic class (IV or sub-VI ATC) and delisted all products with a price per DDD over a maximum level: most companies were forced to lower prices to avoid delisting and losing reimbursability.

As a result, in the last 12 years, price variations for retail drugs covered by the SSN have always been negative (Fig. 8.5) and unit prices are lower in Italy than in most other EU countries both for retail drugs (Department of Health 2012) and hospital list prices (Jommi and Costa 2013).

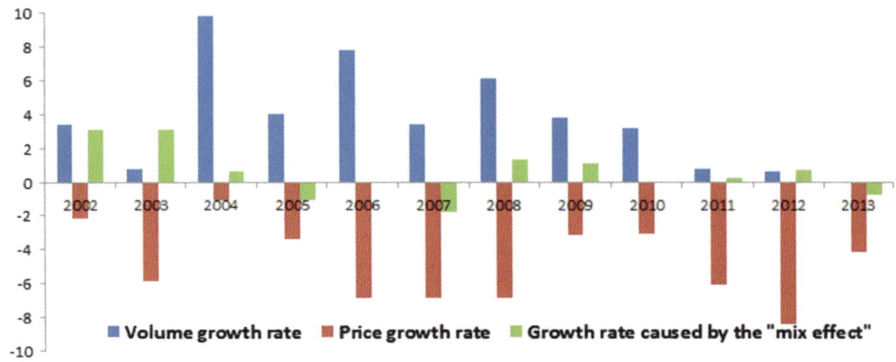

Fig. 8.5 The impact of volume, price and mix effects on the growth rate of gross expenditure. *Source*: Our elaboration of AIFA, various years (2006–2013). *Legend*: Volume effect is measured in DDDs, Mix effects stands for an increase in the use of more expensive drugs at the expense of cheaper ones for the same indication

8.10 The Impact of Pricing on Public Health

There are no available data on the effects of pricing policies on public health. However, some data have been published on equity issues, access to drugs and economic impacts of policies.

As far as equity is concerned, it must be firstly noted that public coverage of retail pharmaceutical spending has fallen from 67.6 % in 2001 to 50.3 % in 2013. This is mostly caused by an increase in cost-sharing. There is also a huge difference across regions in public coverage of pharmaceutical expenditure, ranging from 48.2 % in northern regions (min 45.2 %) to 53.9 % in the southern ones (max 58.5 %); these differences are mostly motivated by important differences in private expenditure for reimbursable drugs and in the use of non-reimbursable drugs for minor diseases. Finally, access to new and expensive drugs has been affected by important delays to their inclusion in regional formularies (Jommi et al. 2013).

Empirical evidence regarding the impact of pharmaceutical policies and access issues in Italy is rather limited. A study on regional cost-sharing conducted from 2001 to 2003 found that an increase in the co-payment by one Euro reduced the per capita number of prescriptions by 4 % and the per capita public pharmaceutical expenditure by 3.4 %, thus revealing demand-price elasticity (Fiorio and Siciliani 2010). Another study explored how and to what extent cost-sharing influences patients' decisions on medication use: a large proportion of Italian patients (66.5 %) showed cost sensitivity (Atella et al. 2005). A more recent study (Ghislandi et al. 2013) found that generic reference pricing has reduced average prices by 13 % more than off-patent drugs not affected by reference pricing (i.e., that were genericated before the generic reference price was introduced). Moreover, each entry of a new generic was associated with a price drop of approximately 2.8 %: i.e., the more generics there are, the higher the effect of reference pricing on price competition. The final study of note investigated factors influencing market access and penetration for oncology drugs: regional formularies, high prices and a substantial impact on the drug budget are correlated with slower market access, whereas the stipulations of an MMEA improve market access (Russo et al. 2010).

8.11 The Case of Generic Medicines

The term "generics" was introduced for the first time in 1996 (Law 425/1996). A generic is defined as a product with "the same qualitative and quantitative composition in active substances and the same pharmaceutical form as the reference medicinal product, and whose bioequivalence with the reference medicinal product has been demonstrated by appropriate bioavailability studies." The same law stated that the price of the generic product should be set at least 20 % lower than the price of the original.

In general, the procedure for generic pricing does not differ from other drugs. However, according to a recent Decree (April, 4, 2013), companies holding market authorizations for generic and biosimilar drugs are not obliged to negotiate prices if generic/biosimilar prices are set 30–50 % and 45–70 % lower than the original drug in Classes H and A, respectively. Larger markets require higher discounts to avoid negotiation.

As mentioned before, generic reference prices were introduced in 2001. In the same year, the Minister of Health launched an informational campaign to inform patients of generics through a publication sent by mail to each family. AIFA carried out a second pro-generic media campaign aimed at patients in 2007.

Generic substitution by pharmacists was introduced in 2005. Substitution is mandatory for pharmacists unless the prescriber states "non-substitutable" on the prescription form (aut-idem clause) and the patient refuses substitution. In addition, distribution margins for generics have been set 8 % higher than other drugs since 2009 (Law 79/2009).

Mandatory generic prescriptions (i.e., prescription of the molecule, possibly followed by the brand name) were introduced in 2012 (Law 135/2012) and partially amended by Law 221/2012 for case of first prescriptions for chronic diseases, and new prescriptions for non-chronic diseases. Law 221/2012 has also states that physicians should inform patients about the availability of cheaper drugs if they want to prescribe a product priced above the reference price.

Additionally, regions have implemented actions to favor the prescription of off-patent molecules. Prescription targets for off-patent drugs within the same therapeutic class (e.g., statins, β-blockers, sartans, selective serotonin reuptake inhibitors), with the associated sanctions (if targets are not reached) or incentives (if targets are reached), have been implemented mainly in the southern regions, where medical doctors are more used to prescribing new drugs covered by patent protections and avoiding generics. Regions were also temporarily allowed to introduce therapeutic reference pricing, i.e., reference prices by therapeutic class, with patients required to cover the difference between the actual prescribed drug price and its reference value. Eight regions introduced a therapeutic reference price for proton pump inhibitors. Therapeutic reference prices were abolished in October 2007.

Despite the fact that the retail market is now mostly off-patent (off-patent drugs represent 64.2 % and 41.5 % of the total SSN retail market in volume and value, respectively) and many actions have been put in place that favor generics, the market share for generics has grown but is still limited (14.9 % of the total SSN retail market, i.e., 36 % of the off-patent market—Table 8.3). The modest performance of generics can be attributed to a long tradition of brand name prescriptions, and the circumstance that, owing to reference pricing, public expenditure is unaffected by the decision to prescribe a generic or its originator.

8.12 Conclusion

After the scandals in 1993 and 1994 showed that companies, policy makers and top public officers constructed an illegal system to set prices, Italian pharmaceutical policy has been revised to reflect a new approach more oriented toward evidence-based medicine and cost containment. Despite unquestionable achievements in terms of health policy goals (structural inclusion of evidence-based medicine in the decision-making process) and cost containment, there are some critical issues that remain unaddressed.

First, dynamic efficiency (i.e., allocating sufficient resources to make the industry continuously invest in innovation) and the introduction of appropriate incentives to encourage competitive research and development have been neglected. There is a huge discussion around the role of price regulation in promoting dynamic allocative efficiency and territory attractiveness, and the authors agree with the principle that pricing of new drugs should not incorporate industrial objectives. However, it is clear that the unstable regulatory environment and cost-containment imperatives have reduced Italy's attractiveness for R&D (Jommi and Paruzzolo 2007; Gehring et al. 2013).

Second, short-term cost-containment policies have dominated in recent years. This approach has been accompanied by silo budgeting, determined by the existence of drug budgets. A silo budget pushes payers to disregard the impact of drugs on other health care services, e.g., whether a drug may reduce admissions to hospitals, with important savings for the SSN. Such an approach is manageable if this impact is not significant, but may be seriously challenged when new and innovative drugs for a large target population produce important savings in other health care services; this circumstance may develop surrounding new drugs for Hepatitis C.

Third, problems arising from the distribution of power between the central state and the regions remain unresolved. Despite regulations put in place to reduce conflicts and to better clarify what the competencies of AIFA and the regions are, the latter are still accountable for their health care budgets and will systematically challenge decisions made by AIFA if these decisions undermine their financial equilibrium. A clearer definition of competencies at the national, regional and local levels would reduce fragmentation of assessments that may undermine horizontal equity. In addition, it would avoid duplication of assessments based on the same information, thus reducing administrative costs. However, this may not be enough because regional authorities are accountable for managing their health care budgets. In multi-tier regulations, collaboration among different levels and a higher level of transparency are needed. Any decision made at the central level may be legitimately challenged at the regional level if regions do not know the rationale behind these decisions. Unlike other HTA Organizations (e.g., NICE—National Institute for Health and Care Excellence; SMC—Scottish Medicine Consortium; HAS—Haute Autorité de Santé, French National Authority for Health; GBA—Gemeinsamer Bundesausschuss, Federal Joint Committee; IQWIG—Institut für Qualität und Wirtschaftlichkeit im Gesundheitswesen, Institute for Quality and Efficiency in Healthcare), AIFA does not publish any appraisal document to illustrate the rationale for (and evidence behind) the decisions that are made. Once an appraisal report has been published and discussed, the exclusion of new drugs from formularies or delayed approvals at the regional and local levels will be more difficult to justify (Jommi et al. 2013).

References

AIFA (2007) Gruppo di lavoro sull'innovatività dei farmaci. Criteri per l'attribuzione del grado di innovazione terapeutica dei nuovi farmaci ed elementi per la integrazione del dossier per l'ammissione alla rimborsabilità (documento approvato dalla CTS il 10 luglio 2007). http://www.agenziafarmaco.gov.it/allegati/documento_integrale.pdf. AIFA. Accessed 25 July 2014

AIFA (2014) Ossmed. L'uso dei Farmaci in Italia. Rapporto Nazionale Anno 2013–2006. Roma, 2014 and various years. http://www.agenziafarmaco.gov.it/it/content/osservatorio-sull%E2%80%99impiego-dei-medicinali-osmed. Accessed 25 July 2014

Anessi Pessina E, Jommi C, Cantù E (2004) Phasing out market mechanisms in the Italian NHS. Public Money Manag 24(5):309–316

Armeni P, Ferré F (2013) La spesa sanitaria: composizione ed evoluzione. In: CERGAS (ed) Rapporto OASI 2013. Osservatorio sulle Aziende e sul Sistema sanitario Italiano. Egea, Milano, pp 183–221. http://www.cergas.unibocconi.it/. Accessed 25 July 2014

Assosalute (2014) Numeri e Indici dell'Automedicazione, Milano. http://assosalute.federchimica.it/homepage-anifa/pubblicazioni/numeri-e-indici.aspx. Accessed 25 July 2014

Atella V, Schafheutle E, Noyce P, Hassell K (2005) Affordability of medicines and patients' cost-reducing behaviour: empirical evidence based on SUR estimates from Italy and the UK. Appl Health Econ Health Policy 4(1):23–35

Carlson JJ, Sullivan SD, Garrison LP et al (2010) Linking payment to health outcomes: a taxonomy and examination of performance-based reimbursement schemes between healthcare payers and manufacturers. Health Policy 96(3):179–190

Curto S, Ghislandi S, van de Vooren K et al (2014) Regional tenders on biosimilars in Italy: an empirical analysis of awarded prices. Health Policy 116(2–3):182–187

Department of Health (2012) The pharmaceutical price regulation scheme, eleventh report to the parliament. HSMO, Londra. https://www.gov.uk/government/publications/pharmaceutical-price-regulation-scheme-11th-report-to-parliament. Accessed 25 July 2014

Efpia (2011) Patients' W.A.I.T. indicator. Report. http://www.efpia.eu/documents/33/64/Market-Access-Delays. Accessed 25 July 2014

Farmindustria (2014) Indicatori Farmaceutici, Roma. https://www.farmindustria.it/. Accessed 25 July 2014

Fattore G (1999) Cost-containment and reforms in the Italian National Health Service. In: Mossialos E, Le Grand J (eds) Health care and cost containment in the European Union. Ashgate, Aldershot, pp 513–546

Fattore G, Jommi C (2008) The last decade of Italian pharmaceutical policy: instability or consolidation? Pharmacoeconomics 26:5–15

MEF Ministero dell'Economia e delle Finanze (2014) Documento di Economia e Finanza. http://www.mef.gov.it/doc-finanza-pubblica/def/2014/documenti/DEF_Sezione_II_-_Analisi_e_tendenze_della_finanza_pubblica_.pdf. Accessed 25 July 2014

Fiorio CV, Siciliani L (2010) Co-payments and the demand for pharmaceuticals: evidence from Italy. Special issue on health econometrics. Econ Model 27:835–841

France G, Taroni F (2005) The evolution of health-policy making in Italy. J Health Polit Policy Law 30(1–2):169–187

Garattini L, Ghislandi S (2006) Off-patent drugs in Italy: a short-sighted view? Eur J Health Econ 7(1):79–83

Gehring M, Taylor RS, Mellody M et al (2013) Factors influencing clinical trial site selection in Europe: the Survey of Attitudes towards Trial sites in Europe (the SAT-EU Study). BMJ Open 3(11):e002957

Ghislandi S, Krulichova I, Garattini L (2005) Pharmaceutical policy in Italy: towards a structural change? Health Policy 72(1):53–73

Ghislandi S, Armeni P, Jommi C (2013) The impact of generic reference pricing in Italy, a decade on. Eur J Health Econ 14(6):959–969

Guerrazzi C, Ricci A (2013) La struttura e le attività del SSN. In: CERGAS (ed) Rapporto OASI 2013. Osservatorio sulle Aziende e sul Sistema sanitario Italiano. Egea, Milano, p 111–181. http://www.cergas.unibocconi.it/. Accessed 25 July 2014

Jommi C, Costa F (2013) I prezzi a ricavo industria dei farmaci rimborsabili: l'Italia a confronto con i principali paesi Ue. Politiche Sanitarie 14(2):55–66

Jommi C, Paruzzolo S (2007) Public administration and R&D localisation by pharmaceutical and biotech companies: a theoretical framework and the Italian case study. Health Policy 81(1):117–130

Jommi C, Cantù E, Anessi Pessina E (2001) New funding arrangements in the Italian National Health Service. Int J Health Plann Manage 6(4):347–368

Jommi C, Costa E, Michelon A et al (2013) Multi-tier drugs assessment in a decentralised health care system. The Italian case-study. Health Policy 112:241–247

Marchetti M, Minghetti P (1992) Italy. In: Spivey RN, Wertheimer AI, Rucker TD (eds) International pharmaceutical services. The drug industry and pharmacy practice in twenty-three major counties of the world. PPP, New York, pp 281–302

Morel T, Arickx F, Befrits G et al (2013) Reconciling uncertainty of costs and outcomes with the need for access to orphan medicinal products: a comparative study of managed entry agreements across seven European countries. Orphanet J Rare Dis 8:198

Motola D, De Ponti F, Rossi P et al (2005) Therapeutic innovation in the European Union: analysis of the drugs approved by the EMEA between 1995 and 2003. Br J Clin Pharmacol 59 (4):475–478

Russo P, Mennini FS, Siviero PD, Rasi G (2010) Time to market and patient access to new oncology products in Italy: a multistep pathway from European context to regional health care providers. Ann Oncol 21(10):2081–7

Tediosi F, Gabriele S, Longo F (2009) Governing decentralization in health care under tough budget constraint: what can we learn from the Italian experience? Health Policy 90:303–312

Chapter 9
Pharmaceutical Pricing Policies in South Korea

Iyn-Hyang Lee and Karen Bloor

Abstract South Korean healthcare system has experienced an unprecedented growth and transformation in the span 15 years. The landmarks were the unification of insurance funds, and the separation of prescribing and dispensing of drugs (SPD). Several pricing policies have been introduced, revised and abolished to attempt to address unexpected increases in pharmaceutical expenditure which followed the separation of prescribing and dispensing of medicines. This chapter outlines the health care and pharmaceutical systems in South Korea, details pricing policies in the latest decade and reviews the effectiveness of these policies. While having a long-lasting history in pharmaceutical price control, South Korea has often introduced policies with a weak scientific basis and then abolished them without proper assessment and evaluation. Some evidence suggests that price controls have reduced pharmaceutical costs in the short-term, but evidence on the long-term impacts are largely absent. Given the cause of current cost inflation, i.e., increased use of pharmaceuticals and an ageing population, society needs a policy consensus to control prices and encourage rational prescribing.

9.1 Introduction

The Republic of Korea (hereafter South Korea or Korea) was viewed as one of the 'tiger economies' as a result of rapid export-led growth in the latter half of the twentieth century. Social health insurance was introduced in 1977 and covered the whole population by 1989 (NHIC and HIRA 2007). But South Korea's health care system faces challenges similar to those in many other developed countries. In particular, chronic conditions are increasing significantly as the population ages. This is contributing to expenditure inflation in health care, particularly in the cost of

I.-H. Lee (✉)
College of Pharmacy, Yeungnam University, Gyeongsangbuk-do, South Korea
e-mail: leeiynhyang@ynu.ac.kr

K. Bloor
Department of Health Sciences, University of York, York, UK
e-mail: karen.bloor@york.ac.uk

Z.-U.-D. Babar (ed.), *Pharmaceutical Prices in the 21st Century*,
DOI 10.1007/978-3-319-12169-7_9

pharmaceuticals. Policy makers in Korea, like in other countries, have implemented numerous reforms to address cost inflation and perceived inefficiency, with varying success. Reforms in the area of pharmaceutical expenditure include the unification of insurance funds, and the separation of prescribing and dispensing of drugs (SPD), a substantial policy change that was implemented in 2000 (Kwon and Reich 2005; Hwang 2006). Different pricing policies have been introduced, revised and abolished in attempts to address unexpected increases in pharmaceutical expenditure following the SPD. In this chapter, the healthcare and pharmaceutical systems in South Korea are outlined, pricing policies in the latest decade are described and the effectiveness of these policies is reviewed.

9.2 The Korean Health Care System

Most of the Korean population is covered by a mandatory National Health Insurance (NHI) scheme (Fig. 9.1), complemented by a Medical Aid (MedAid) system which provides comprehensive coverage to low income households. In 2012, the whole population was covered either by the NHI (97 %) or by MedAid (3 %) (NHIS and HIRA 2012). The NHI fund is made up of beneficiaries' contributions (85 %), and other sources, mostly public tax (15 % in 2012) (NHIS and HIRA 2012). Patients generally enjoy substantial freedom of choice among health care providers if they were willing to pay a premium fee. Currently, most Korean healthcare providers are engaged in private practice and are paid on a fee-for-service basis. A diagnosis-related group (DRG) payment system has been expanded since July 2012 (HIRA 2013). There are no publicly funded community pharmacies and few public hospitals. Only 8.5 % of hospitals and 20.6 % of acute beds were publicly managed in 2005 (MOHW 2006) and the situation has since changed little (Yonhapnews 2011).

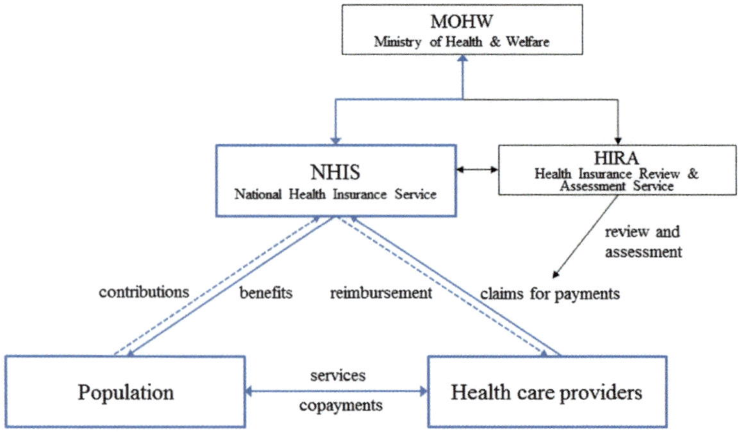

Fig. 9.1 Flows of funds and services in the Korean health care system

Key statistics summarizing the Korean healthcare system are presented in Table 9.1. Life expectancy was 81.1 in 2011 (OECD 2013b), and the share of the population over 65 years of age increased from 7.2 % in 2000 to 11.8 % in 2012. Although the ageing population is still smaller than in other developed societies, it has increased substantially—at least twice as fast as in Japan or Germany (Lee 2010). This brings about similar challenges to those seen in other developed countries' health care systems, including health expenditure inflation. Total health expenditure increased from 5.1 to 7.2 % of GDP between 2001 and 2011. However, it is still below the international average of 9.5 % (of GDP) in OECD countries (OECD 2013a). High private expenditure has been the subject of strong criticism in South Korea (Choi et al. 2005; Lee 2005; OECD 2007). Patients are required to pay nearly half of their health care expenses out-of-pocket at the point of care, including legal copayments and non-subsidized services (Kim and Jung 2005; Kim and Lee 2006).

Table 9.1 Key statistics summarizing the Korean healthcare system

Indicator	2000	2005	2010	2012	Source
Total population, million	47,008	48,138	49,410	50,004	OECD Factbook
Population aged over 65 years, %	7.2	9.1	11.0	11.8	OECD Factbook
Life expectancy at birth, total	76.0	78.5	80.6	81.1 (2011)	OECD Factbook
Life expectancy at birth, female	79.6	81.9	84.1	84.5 (2011)	OECD Factbook
Life expectancy at birth, male	72.3	75.1	77.2	77.7 (2011)	OECD Factbook
GDP per capita in US$ PPP	16,439	22,783	28,613	30,800	OECD Factbook
Total health expenditure, % GDP	5.1 (2001)	5.7	7.1	7.2 (2011)	KOSIS
Public health expenditure, % of total	54.9 (2001)	52.6	57.7	56.9 (2011)	KOSIS
Private health expenditure, % of total	45.1 (2001)	47.4	42.3	43.1 (2011)	KOSIS
Pharmaceutical expenditure, % of total	25.1 (2003)	22.4	20.5	20.2 (2011)	OECD Health Statistics
Pharmaceutical expenditure per capita, US$ PPP	137	287	427	445 (2011)	OECD Health Statistics
Number of acute care beds per 1,000 population	4.2 (2003)	4.6	5.5	5.9 (2011)	OECD Health Statistics
Practising doctors per 1,000 population	1.3	1.6	2.0	2.1	OECD Health Statistics
Practising pharmacists per 1,000 population	–	0.6	0.7	0.7	OECD Health Statistics
Number of visits to GPs per capita per year	–	11.8	12.9	13.2 (2011)	OECD Health Statistics

PPP purchasing power parity, *GDP* gross domestic product, *KOSIS* Korean Statistical Information Service

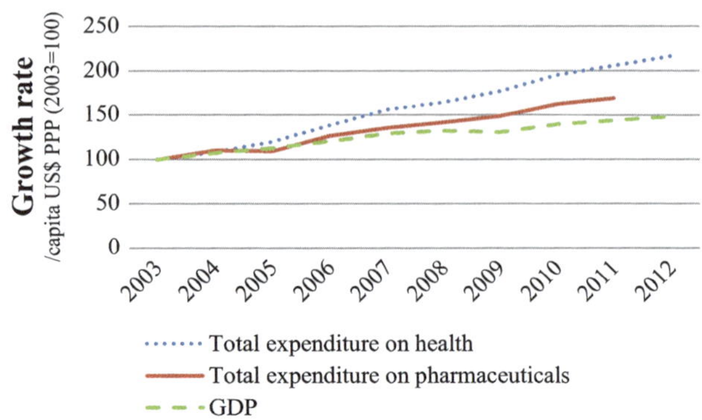

Fig. 9.2 Trends in pharmaceutical expenditure per capita (purchasing power parity) in comparison with total healthcare expenditure and the Korean economy, 2003–2012. *Data source*: OECD.Stat (2014)

Pharmaceutical expenditure has increased faster than general economic growth since 2005 (Fig. 9.2). In 2011 pharmaceutical expenditure per capita was US$445 PPP,[1] a lower absolute value than most industrialized countries but the growth rate between 2005 and 2011 was 55 %, the second highest in the OECD and 2–3 times higher than France (18 %), Germany (25 %), the Netherlands (20 %), and the US (22 %) (OECD 2013c).

9.3 Pharmaceuticals in South Korea

Since the late 1990s, South Korea has experienced an unprecedented transformation in the organization and regulation of the pharmaceuticals market. There have been several recent significant changes in pharmaceutical policy, the most important of which was the separation of prescribing and dispensing of drugs (SPD) from July 2000 onwards.

9.3.1 The Korean Pharmaceutical Market

South Korea is a small part of the world market for pharmaceuticals, accounting for about 1.8 % of global sales in 2011. The Korean pharmaceutical market was around 18.9 trillion KRW (US$17 billion[2] in 2014) in 2011 (KHIDI 2013). The Korean pharmaceutical industry is characterized by small businesses. The share of national GDP made up by the pharmaceutical industry has been around 1.5 % since 2005 (KHIDI 2004, 2007, 2013). In 2011, 638 manufacturers produced pharmaceuticals, among whom the top 15 producers represented 40.8 % of annual sales (KHIDI 2013).

[1] Values adjusted by purchasing power parity (PPP) to eliminate price level differences in inter-country comparisons, equalising currencies by using a basket of goods and services.

[2] US$1 = 1,100 KRW in 2014.

Overall R&D investments of the top 20 producers were around 10 % in 2011, less than the average 16 % of the international top 20 patent holders (KHIDI 2013). Korean companies conventionally make more efforts to sell generics and, as a result, the volume share of generics in the pharmaceutical market is relatively high, over 40 % (Lee et al. 2014).

9.3.2 Distribution Structure of Pharmaceuticals

The distribution structure of pharmaceuticals in Korea is complicated and until recently far from transparent. There were 1,889 wholesalers in the Korean pharmaceutical market in 2011 (HIRA 2012). This has increased steadily since a de-regulation measure in the beginning of 2000 (DailyPharm 2000). Community pharmacies are managed privately. Only registered pharmacists are eligible to establish a community pharmacy. Community pharmacies can contract with both manufacturers and wholesalers to acquire pharmaceutical stocks. Sizable not-for-profit hospitals usually purchase pharmaceuticals through an annual open bidding system. They generally provide a pre-defined formulary, encompassing a set of potential manufacturers for each chemical ingredient (from one, in cases of patented products, to five or more for off-patented products). The final product chosen under contract is delegated to wholesalers. Little is known about the selection process by wholesalers, which remains the scope of private business.

9.3.3 Pharmaceutical Regulatory Authorities

Table 9.2 shows the key government bodies involved in regulating pharmaceuticals in Korea. The ***Ministry of Health and Welfare (MOHW)*** authorises national pharmaceutical policies, working with arms' length bodies and advisory committees. The ***Ministry of Food and Drug Safety (MFDS)*** is an organization similar to the U.S. Food and Drugs Administration (FDA) and is responsible for the safety and pharmacological effectiveness of drugs. Accelerated licensing is possible under the supervision of the *Korean Orphan Drug Centre (KODC)* in cases of urgent patient need. The *Korea Institute of Drug Safety & Risk Management (KIDS)* is an independent body, established in 2012 to monitor pharmacovigilance activity (KIDS 2013).

The ***National Health Insurance Service (NHIS)*** is a single payer in the Korean healthcare system, responsible for administration of the NHI and MedAid in terms of eligibility, billing and management of health insurance funds. The ***Health Insurance Review & Assessment Service (HIRA)*** is an independent agency for reviewing medical claims. Health care providers are reimbursed directly by the NHIS, based on prescriptions obtained from the patients after evaluation by HIRA (as illustrated in Fig. 9.1). Before the existence of HIRA there was no way for the

Table 9.2 Government bodies regulating pharmaceutical use and reimbursement in South Korea

Name	Role	Notes
Ministry of Health & Welfare (MOHW)	Establishing national pharmaceutical policies	Since 1948
Central Pharmaceutical Affairs Council (CPAC)	Core decision advisory committee on pharmaceuticals	Since 1963
Ministry of Food and Drug Safety (MFDS)	Safety control	Independent from the ministry since 1998; formerly Korea Food & Drug Administration (KFDA), raised to the status of a ministry in 2013
National Health Insurance Service (NHIS)	Administering the national health insurance system	Established in 1998 to merge fragmented sources of funds; full integration was completed in July 2003; formerly National Health Insurance Cooperation (NHIC)
Committee on the health insurance policy (CHIP)	Core decision advisory committee over the NHI reimbursement rules	Since 2002
Health Insurance Review & Assessment Service (HIRA)	Reviewing and assessing insurance claims	Restructured from the National Federation of Medical Insurance in 2000
National Evidence-based Healthcare Collaborating Agency (NECA)	Synthesizing and disseminating evidence on cost-effectiveness	Since 2009

NHIS to intervene in pricing, and critics described it as a 'cashier' rather than an active purchaser (DailyPharm 2004b). Following the introduction of a positive list in 2006, HIRA became involved in pricing of patented drugs, through a process described in Sect. 9.4. Another important role of HIRA is to make decisions about the list of reimbursed pharmaceuticals, including establishing reimbursement standards for marketed drugs and assessing the cost-effectiveness of candidate drugs to determine whether or not they are worthy of public subsidy.

The ***National Evidence-based Healthcare Collaborating Agency (NECA)*** is an agency for Health Technology Assessment (HTA) and Comparative Effectiveness Research. This is similar to the National Institute for Health and Care Excellence (NICE) in the UK.

9.3.4 Separation of Prescribing and Dispensing of Drugs

Mandatory separation of prescribing and dispensing was introduced in South Korea differently. No on-site pharmacies are allowed at primary care clinics. In hospitals, in-house pharmacies are responsible for inpatient services. Outpatient dispensing services are allowed for only a small number of specified cases such as emergency episodes, patients with severe disability or with specific groups of disease which are exempt from the SPD regulation (*Korean Pharmaceutical Affairs Law, provision 23*). Additionally, there are regional exceptions due to lack of institutions in some remote districts.

The SPD has created a 'cultural revolution' in every aspect of the Korean pharmaceutical market. Technically, it verified the function of health professionals as prescribers or dispensers, but in reality this has been much more than just separation. Firstly, a number of policy changes were needed to support the SPD. This included price regulation (the Maximum Allowable Price at Actual Transaction Price system, MAP-ATP) and regulation to standardize produces (the Bio-equivalence Validation Program, BVP) (Chung and Kim 2005). Separation of prescribing and dispensing of drugs resulted in increase in pharmaceutical expenditures. To contain pharmaceutical expenditures, two projects were started namely the Better Prescribing Project (BPP) and the Pharmaceutical Expenditure Rationalization Plan (PERP).

The BPP, a national prescribing monitoring and feedback program, has generated informative data around prescribing practices nationwide since 2001, which has been published since 2002. Variables include the rate of antibiotics prescribed for the common cold, the rate of injections prescribed, the number of items per prescription and costs per prescription, and the rate of pre-defined drugs prescribed by diagnosis.

The PERP was enacted on 29 December 2006 with the goal of minimizing unnecessary drug expenses by modifying prescribing behavior and by promoting transparency in the market. It was a comprehensive package of pharmaceutical regulations consisting of four sub-domains: *price control*, *volume control*, *quality control* and *the restructure of the pharmaceutical market*. Before the PERP, regulations tended to be inconsistent and sometimes conflicting, so the PERP was an attempt to rationalize and harmonize policy in this area.

9.4 Drug Pricing

In the Korean market, pharmaceutical manufacturers are free to set prices of those drugs, which are not reimbursed. Since 1999, retail pharmacists have also set their own prices for the medicines which are not reimbursed (*Korean Pharmaceutical Affairs Law*; *provision 78*). Prices of reimbursed drugs have been regulated since the beginning of the National Health Insurance (NHI) system. Following the separation of prescribing and dispensing, prescription-only-medicines (POMs) that are mostly reimbursed by the government are no longer allowed to be sold without authorized prescriptions. The market prices for POMs that have a 70–80 % market share are governed by the Maximum Allowable Price (MAP) system (KHIDI 2013).

9.4.1 *How Are the Maximum Allowable Prices Determined?*

The MAP, which has been in force since the beginning of the NHI, is a form of price cap that sets an upper limit of remuneration for each pharmaceutical product. It is decided at the ministerial level through a process involving several government bodies. Generally, different rules apply to on- and off-patent original drugs, and generics. During the last decade, there were two substantial changes in pricing policy: the PERP in 2006 and the Single Price System in 2012.

Before the PERP, when prices for new chemical entities (NCEs) were determined, a cross-national price comparison was employed. The average wholesale prices in seven industrialized countries[3] were considered as the international comparator (hereafter, A7 average price system). This was thought to be potentially inflationary as it compared drug prices with countries with much stronger economies than South Korea (Bae and Kim 2001; Chung 2002; Lee 2006). Moreover, the prices of generics after patent expiry might also have been higher because of the Korean Linkage Price System (LPS).[4] Under the LPS, the price for generics (from the first to the fifth products to enter the market) was set at a maximum 80 % of the price of the off-patent original products. The price for the sixth and later generic comers would not exceed 90 % of the price of the cheapest existing generic products with identical substances, form and strength. Mounting opinion in favor of reducing pharmaceutical prices to an affordable level for Korean patients (Kim 2002; Lee 2006; DailyPharm 2004a; People's Solidarity for Participatory Democracy 1998; Korean Pharmacists for Democratic Society 2006) resulted in PERP, which included a positive listing system with the formal requirement of economic evaluation and a price-volume agreement.

9.4.1.1 Positive List System for Insured Pharmaceuticals

From December 2006, the PERP employed a positive listing system for insured pharmaceuticals, and price-volume agreements for new chemical entities (NCEs). Under the positive list system, the authorities were able to refuse to list a candidate drug that is considered less cost-effective than existing alternatives (*HIRA Guidelines for economic evaluations of pharmaceuticals*). However, owing to the scarcity of economic studies (Choi 2008), a cross-national price comparison seems likely to play some role in pricing for some time to come. Where economic evidence is lacking, Taiwan and Singapore, with similar economic environments to Korea, were added to the group of reference countries for price setting (*Pharmaceutical Price Agreement Guideline, National Health Insurance Corporation Official Instruction 2006-122; provision 11*).

[3] France, Germany, Italy, Japan, Switzerland, the UK and the US.

[4] The first to fifth generic drug is set at less than 80 % of cost for its off-patent alternative. The sixth and later product is set at the 90 % price of the least expensive alternative (*MOHW Official Instructions 2005–14; provision 8*).

9.4.1.2 Price-Volume Agreements for New Chemical Entities

Figure 9.3 illustrates the process of pricing pharmaceutical products. When pharmaceutical manufacturers apply for listing, HIRA assesses whether a candidate product is more cost-effective than the most frequently used comparator, including drugs or other medical procedures. If HIRA recommend reimbursement, other details for reimbursement have to be determined within 150 days. In cases where listing is refused, each applicant can appeal for re-evaluation. If the candidate drug is a generic, the maximum allowable reimbursement price will be calculated according to a statutory pricing guideline (see the next section for details). If a candidate product is newly developed, with no comparators for pricing, the MOHW refers this to the NHIS to begin a negotiation with applicants to determine an appropriate price. The NHIS price is calculated partly based on the manufacturers' predictions of likely consumption and impact on health expenditure. Pricing can be set without agreements if the candidate drug is viewed as essential for the public, merely with adjustments by the Benefit Coordination Committee (BCC). If manufacturers do not apply for listing even if the products are considered essential, the authorities set prices through the same pathway as if there is a disagreement.

The initial price is reassessed in the second year according to sales volume from pharmaceutical claims data during the first year, a so-called price-volume agreement (*MOHW Official Instruction 2006-165*, *Pharmaceutical Price Agreement Guideline*; *provision 12*). If consumption of a product is 30 % higher than predicted, then the price of the product is lowered in proportion to the increase in volume. From the second year, products with consumption 60 % or greater than the

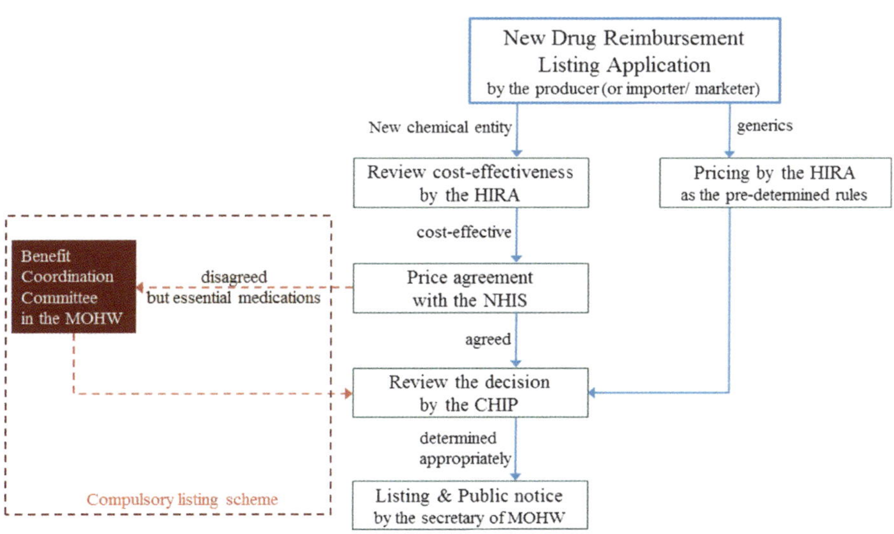

Fig. 9.3 Decision-making process of reimbursement pricing on pharmaceuticals. *CHIP* Committee on the health insurance policy, *HIRA* Health Insurance Review & Assessment Service, *MOHW* Ministry of Health and Welfare, *NHIS* National Health Insurance Service

preceding year are also the target of re-pricing. The rate of re-pricing is limited to a maximum of 10 %. Between 2007 and 2009, consumption of contracted products was between 68 and 487 % more than the expected volume and the impact of re-pricing within a 10 % bound was questioned, with calls for integrating an expenditure target into the price-volume agreement (Kim and Choi 2011).

9.4.1.3 Adjusting the Statutory Pricing Guideline for Off-Patent Products and Generics to a Single Price System

The PERP also adjusted the statutory pricing guideline for off-patent original products and generics. The price for original products would be reduced by 20 % as soon as any generic formulation entered the market after losing patent protection. As shown in Fig. 9.4, the pricing system for ***generics*** was set according to the Principle of the LPS (*MOHW Official Instruction 2001-59*). In reality, the PERP system reduced the price of the off-patent original drugs by 20 %.[5] But the LPS was criticized because even then it allowed high prices for generics (Lee 2013a). A generic product could be registered on the benefit list only if it provided a 20–30 % price cut over its brand counterpart.

In April 2014, the Korean government revised the pricing guideline further by introducing a 'Single Price System (SPS)' (Fig. 9.5). Prices for off-patent originals were again reduced to 70 % on the price when the patent was valid and other generics were priced at 85 % of the off-patent counterparts (equivalent to 59.5 % of the patent price) regardless of their market entry ranking. One year after patent expiry, all pharmaceuticals including off-patent originals and generics are priced at 53.55 % of the price of the original patent products.

9.4.2 *How Are the Maximum Allowable Prices Managed?*

Once the MAP is determined for each pharmaceutical product, it is revised regularly via a price survey to reflect market dynamics. Three major revisions of this process have taken place: Investigating price system; Reporting price system; and Actual Transaction Price (ATP) system (Table 9.3).

During the operation of the investigating or reporting price systems, the differences between the reimbursement price and the actual transaction price were a

[5] For instance, 'GenericA', a generic product of the 'OriginalA' (price 100) was priced at the maximum of 80 (i.e. 0.8 × 100) in the previous system. Now, it is priced at maximum 64 (i.e. 0.8 × 0.8 × 100) because the price of 'OriginalA' is reduced to 80 in the new system.

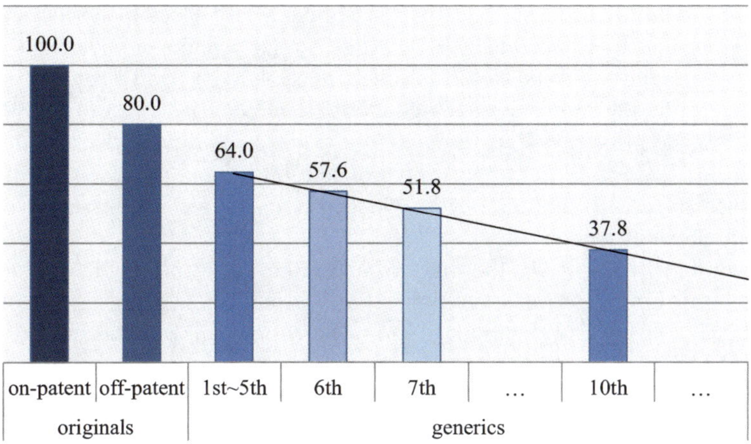

Fig. 9.4 Pricing schedule for pharmaceuticals before April 2014 ('Linkage Price System')

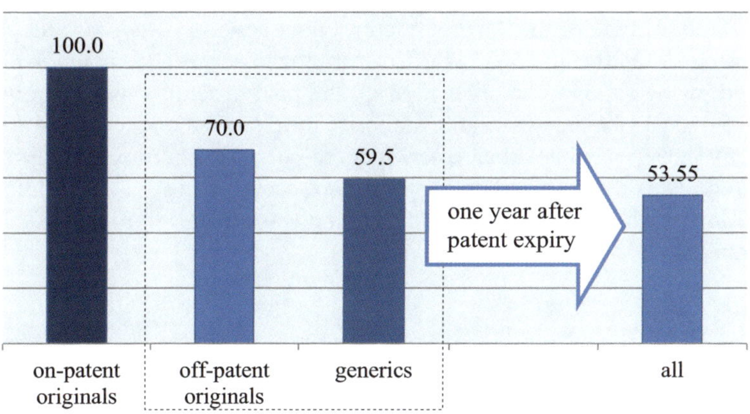

Fig. 9.5 Pricing schedule for pharmaceuticals after the 'Single Price System' in April 2014

Table 9.3 Systems revising the Maximum Allowable Price of pharmaceuticals

System	Active period	The price revision process
Investigating price system	July 1977 to December 1981	Revising prices at ex-factory prices (investigated by the MOHW) plus distribution mark-up 12 % of ingredient costs
Reporting price system	January 1982 to November 1999	Revising prices at ex-factory prices (reported by pharmaceutical manufacturers) plus distribution mark-up 12.3 % (downward to 3.43 % for pre-defined expensive drugs and 5.15 % for other drugs in 1985)
Actual Transaction Price system	November 1999 onwards	Revising prices according to the transaction price between retailers and manufacturers

MOHW Ministry of Health and Welfare, *NHIS* National Health Insurance Service source of income for providers (People's Solidarity for Participatory Democracy 1998, 1999). This was sizeable, over 40 % of the total revenue of physicians' clinics (Ministry of Health & Welfare, 2000 cited by Kwon 2003). To remove such an unmerited profit, the authorities adopted the ATP in 1999 (just prior to the SPD) and thereafter made price revisions three or four times every year. Prices on the MAP list are considered to be the upper-limits of reimbursement and each institution is reimbursed differently for the same product according to its transaction price as long as it does not go over the price cap.

At the start of the ATP, the authorities undertook a thorough assessment of pharmaceutical market prices, and imposed a mandatory cut in drug prices by an average of 30 % (DailyPharm 1999b). Thereafter, all pharmaceutical manufacturers, wholesalers, and retailers (including pharmacies and medical institutions) are required to report their transaction prices quarterly. The NHIS regularly inspects a random sample of prices. When the investigation yields any form of illegal transaction (such as an unusual discount, or a hidden contract), then as a result, reimbursement prices are reduced based on relevant rules and regulations. With the exception of 1 year (September 2002 to August 2003), the MAP has been decided at the weighted average of the ATP of each product across institutions and pharmacies. During 2002/2003 the MAP was frozen at the lowest ATP, a policy which was abolished owing to vigorous opposition by the pharmaceutical industry. Between October 2010 and January 2012, the authority introduced a market-based ATP that financially incentivized healthcare providers to purchase pharmaceuticals at lower prices. While this was expected to contain pharmaceutical costs by facilitating price competition, it was not formally evaluated, and was stopped in February 2012 and finally abolished in February 2014.

9.5 The Impact of Pricing Policies

9.5.1 Do Pricing Policies Reduce Pharmaceutical Prices and/or Pharmaceutical Expenditure?

It is argued that policies have reduced pharmaceutical prices in the Korean insurance market: Jeong et al. (2005) estimated that the ATP reduced pharmaceutical prices by 2.3 % between 2001 and 2003. This was greater than during the reporting price system, which reduced prices by 0.8 % between 1996 and 1997. The authors reported, however, that public expenditure on pharmaceuticals for inpatients increased by 1.4 % due to compensating utilization, resulting in a 3.4–4.5 % increase in overall public pharmaceutical expenditure. The impact of the policy on outpatients was not analyzed. It is unclear whether the growth in utilization was attributed to changes in population morbidity or to marketing activity by the industry. The MOHW officially reported that the MAP-ATP of pharmaceuticals decreased annually by around 5 % from 2000 to 2006 through continuous re-pricing, which achieved savings over 6 years of around 357 billion KRW (US$325 million at 2014 rates) (MOHW 2006). The magnitude of price reduction appeared to decrease, from 7.4 % in 2001 to 0.9 % in 2010 (Lee 2013b). Lee et al. (2012) performed an interrupted time-series analysis exploring the impact of price cut in the PERP and found few changes in overall pharmaceutical utilization and costs following the policy change.

Robust evidence on the long-term effects of the pricing policies is currently lacking. Table 9.4 indicates that the price has affected little the growth of pharmaceutical expenditure during the last decade in South Korea. Price changes varied from −3 to 0.45 % but total drug expenditure increased by 10–16 % between 2003 and 2009. This suggests first, that pricing policies have yielded some control of drug prices; second, that there is seemingly little room for a further price reduction and third, that controlling price alone is not sufficient to control expenditures and perhaps further action is required. With this regard, Korean experts have continuously advised the introduction of new strategies such as risk-sharing schemes, reference pricing and several kinds of budget control measures (Park 2010; Kim and Choi 2011; Kwon and Yang 2011; Lee et al. 2013). Other measures to contain pharmaceutical prices include competition employing profit controls, encouraging generic use, or incentives for R&D activity of the industry (Kim and Lee 2008).

9.5.2 Do Pricing Policies Affect the Pharmaceutical Market?

The MAP removes any incentives for providers to purchase pharmaceuticals at lower prices (Chung 2002; Yang 2002), as the ATP converges upon the MAP from the very beginning of the new measure. In 2005, the ATP was 99.97 % of the MAP in clinics, 99.92 % in pharmacies, 98.31 % in general hospitals, and 98.6 % in tertiary hospitals (Lee 2006). Price competition in the market became virtually non-existent, resulting in the introduction of the market-based ATP in 2010. The market-based ATP reduced transaction prices in hospitals to 88.7–91.7 % and in clinics to 95.3 %, but made little change in pharmacies (99.8 % of the MAP). Since approximately 70 % of pharmaceuticals were distributed at community pharmacies in 2010, the overall discount rate of ATP was smaller, 2.9 % of the MAP (Lee 2013b). The market-based ATP failed to decrease pharmaceutical expenditures as much as expected and officially allowed service providers to obtain double gains in the provision of pharmaceuticals, i.e. incentivized mark-ups as well as service fees (Newsmp 2012; Lee 2013b). In addition, it created transactions costs in terms of monitoring and regulation (Lee 2013b).

Table 9.4 Factors affecting the pharmaceutical expenditure growth in South Korea

Year		2003[a]	2004[a]	2005[a]	2006[b]	2007[b]	2008[b]	2009[b]
Overall growth rate (%)		10.8	14.1	15.2	16.17	12.67	10.37	11.23
Maintenance products	Price	−1.7	0.3	0.5	0.45	−1.9	−3.04	−0.96
	Utilization	−1.6	8.7	4.1	15.01	15.12	13.38	12.0
	Product-mix	11.0	2.0	4.5	−0.8	−0.43	−0.56	−0.93
New products		3.51	2.90	5.90	1.95	1.09	1.44	1.5
Orphan drugs		N/A	N/A	N/A	−0.42	−1.21	−0.84	−0.38

Data sources: [a]2003–2005 Choi (2007), [b]2006–2009 Jang et al. (2010)

9.5.3 Do Pricing Policies Affect Public Health?

Lee et al. (2012) reported that the price cut in the PERP was associated with a rise in the number of patients taking antihyperlipidemics. However, it is unclear whether the price cut would increase the affordability of medicines due to the short time period between the PERP and later policy changes.

Another study reported that repeated price controls between 2008 and 2010 affected the existing increasing trend of patients taking lipid-lowering drugs little, nor did it affect pharmaceutical expenditure (Kwon et al. 2013). One recent study exploring the relationship between the price-cut and utilization of statins indicated that the selection of medicines was linked to physicians' preferences. The reduction in drug prices did not lead to significant changes in expenditures (Lee and Lee 2013).

The main concern of the new price agreement scheme was a delay in patients' access to new products. In 2005, before the PERP, the average time taken from application to a final reimbursement decision was 132 days (DailyPharm 2006). The first year experience after PERP reveals that this could take much longer. There was no agreement made until 10 months after the new procedure began, while the pertinent committee in HIRA recommended public subsidy for 8 candidates among 20 applicants (DailyPharm 2007). Ha et al. (2011) showed that the drug listing took 223 days during 2007–2008 on average. New chemical entities took around 70 days longer in listing than incrementally modified products did.

9.6 Generic Medicines

The volume share of generics in the pharmaceutical market was relatively high even before recent reforms (over 40 %). This figure is comparable with Sweden or the UK, who greatly encourage the use of generics (Simoens and De Coster 2006; Andersson et al. 2007). However, it should be noted that the share of value may be as high as of volume, indicating the low possibility of saving by using generics. This implies that generic policies, which are advocated as useful measures to reduce expenditures, might not be as effective in South Korea if this situation persists (Park et al. 2011).

Table 9.5 demonstrates price differences of generics among selected countries compared to South Korea in 2010 (Kim et al. 2010). Pharmaceutical prices were 22–45 % higher in South Korea than in other countries, as high as Taiwan and the US, indicating that Koreans consume relatively expensive generic products. A body of empirical evidence from national claims analyses verifies the tendency of costly product consumption in the Korean market (Yoon 2008; Park et al. 2011, 2013; Lee et al. 2014). Such market environments were anticipated when the SPD was introduced. One survey reported that doctors expressed concerns for their reputations if SPD let patients take prescriptions away to be dispensed in their catchment

Table 9.5 Average generic prices for pharmaceuticals in selected countries (IMS Health data analysis for 80 ingredients of most frequently used in the South Korean market)

	By purchasing power parity	
Country	Average prices	Volume-weighted average price
South Korea	1	1
Spain	0.601	0.550
Taiwan	1.062	0.955
Germany	0.624	0.562
Italy	0.664	0.643
UK	0.689	0.644
Australia	0.720	0.672
Japan	0.819	0.784
France	0.754	0.696
US	1.497	0.937

Data source: Kim et al. (2010)
Volume-weighted average price = an average price weighted by the amount of utilization

pharmacies, as their prescriptions would be publicly disclosed (DailyPharm 1999a). Academic evidence suggested that the rising expenditure was associated with changing prescribing patterns in favor of more expensive products (Jang et al. 2001; Cho et al. 2001, 2003; Lee and Malone 2003; Kim 2005). Three local studies suggested that the LPS might damage price competition, maintaining relatively high generic prices in Korea (Huh et al. 2006; Jung et al. 2008; Shin and Choi 2008).

9.7 Summary and the Future

Currently, Korean society faces problems common to many other countries, with ageing populations and an increased burden of chronic conditions. This environment is associated with increased use of pharmaceuticals. South Korea has a long tradition in pharmaceutical price control. Unfortunately, rigorous evidence concerning the impact of pricing policies is rarely available to draw clear conclusions for evidence-based policy-making. While there is some evidence suggesting that price controls reduced drug costs over the short term, longer term evaluations are scant. Overall, it seems that price control is a necessary but not sufficient condition for control of total pharmaceutical expenditure.

Price control has been one of two major pharmaceutical policies in South Korea, coupled with patient cost-sharing. Korean authorities have, of course, made considerable efforts during the last decade but have failed to improve the situation so far. They appear to iterate pricing policies—modifying, implementing and eliminating them without appropriate evaluation. For South Korea, it is critical to reach a policy consensus over principles and priorities about regulating pharmaceuticals.

References

Andersson K, Bergstrom G, Petzold MG, Carlsten A (2007) Impact of a generic substitution reform on patients' and society's expenditure for pharmaceuticals. Health Policy 81(2–3): 376–384

Bae E-Y, Kim J-H (2001) Pharmaceutical price regulation in Korea. Korea Institute for Health and Social Affairs, Seoul

Cho J-G, Lee E-K, Kim J-Y, Jang S-M, Bae E-Y, Park H-K, Lee S-J, Kim J-K, Lee Y-H (2001) Evaluation and policy implication of the separation of prescribing and dispensing drugs. Korea Institute for Health and Social Affairs, Seoul

Cho J-G, Choi S-H, Lee S-Y, Yoon K-J (2003) Achievements and policy implication of the separation of prescribing and dispensing drugs. Korea Institute for Health and Social Affairs, Seoul

Choi YJ (2007) Analysis of factors attributing to pharmaceutical expenditure. Health Insurance Review & Assessment Service, Seoul

Choi S-E (2008) Current state and challenges of pharmacoeconomic evaluation in Korea. J Prev Med Public Health 41(2):74–79

Choi S-J, Kim J-H, Lee S-Y (2005) Intensify public share in the National Health Insurance: definition, plan and practice. Health Insur Forum 4(4):2–13

Chung WJ (2002) The political economy of health policy decision-making: Korea's drug pricing policy reform. Korean Assoc Policy Stud 11(4):99–133

Chung WJ, Kim HJ (2005) Interest groups' influence over drug pricing policy reform in South Korea. Yonsei Med J 46(3):321–330

DailyPharm (1999a) Doctors prefer original drugs in case of the introduction of the separation policy. DailyPharm, 8 June 1999

DailyPharm (1999b) Putting the actual acquisition price system into effect in October; 30% price cut. DailyPharm, 1 Sept 1999

DailyPharm (2000) Abolishment of a fund requirement in drug wholesalers. DailyPharm, 12 March 2000

DailyPharm (2004a) Public health organisations, call for abolishing "A7 average pricing". DailyPharm, 11 Feb 2004

DailyPharm (2004b) Urgent needs to provide the information of healthcare utilization. DailyPharm, 12 April 2004

DailyPharm (2006) NCEs, spending 132 days for benefit listing. DailyPharm, 11 Feb 2006

DailyPharm (2007) Four NCEs out of ten registered on the positive list. DailyPharm, 12 Oct 2007

Ha D, Choi Y, Kim DU, Chung KH, Lee EK (2011) A comparative analysis of the impact of a positive list system on new chemical entity drugs and incrementally modified drugs in South Korea. Clin Ther 33(7):926–932

HIRA (2012) Statistics for drug products distribution 2011. Health Insurance Review & Assessment Service, Korea Pharmaceutical Information Service, Seoul

HIRA (2013) About the drug-related group payment. Health Insurance Review & Assessment Service. http://www.hira.or.kr/dummy.do?pgmid=HIRAA030066010000. Accessed 10 May 2014

Huh S-I, Jung J-C, Lee H-Y (2006) A strategy for rationalising pharmaceutical expenditure. National Health Insurance Corporation, Seoul

Hwang G-J (2006) National health insurance: from segmentation to greater equality. In: Pathways to state welfare in Korea: interests, ideas and institutions. Ashgate Publishing, Aldershot, pp 80–111

Jang S-M, Lee E-K, Kim Y, Han E-A, Bae E-Y, Kim J-Y, Lee Y-H, Shin C-W, Song Y-M, Kang Y-H, Hwang K-H (2001) Pharmaceutical utilisation before and after the separation of prescribing and dispensing of drugs; focusing on changes in prescribing behaviour. Korea Institute for Health and Social Affairs, Seoul

Jang S, Park CM, Bae G, Lee HJ, Kim HS (2010) Analysis of factors affecting the change of pharmaceutical expenditure. Health Insurance Review & Assessment Service, Seoul

Jeong H-S, Lee EK, Kim EJ, Ryu G-C, Song YM, Kim SJ (2005) Impact of the purchasing price reimbursement system for insurance drugs upon the health insurer's financial situation. Korean J Health Policy Adm 15(3):40–59

Jung S-W, Lee T-J, Cho B-H (2008) Market competition structure after original drug patent expiry. Korean J Health Econ Policy 14(2):1–25

KHIDI (2004) Health industry year book 2003. Korea Health Industry Development Institute, Seoul

KHIDI (2007) Health industry year book 2006. Korea Health Industry Development Institute, Seoul

KHIDI (2013) Health industry year book 2013. Korea Health Industry Development Institute, Osong

KIDS (2013) About KIDS. Korea Institute of Drug Safety & Risk Management. https://www.drugsafe.or.kr/iwt/ds/en/introduction/EgovGreeting.do. Accessed 10 May 2014

Kim J-H (2002) History of Korean pharmaceutical pricing and challenges. Monthly Consumers. http://www.consumer.or.kr/magazine/mz_view.html?num=41

Kim S-O (2005) Realities in expensive drug prescribing and its determinants. Health Insur Forum 4(4):57–83

Kim S-O, Choi S-E (2011) Improving price-volume arrangement system by linking expenditure target with pharmaceutical price negotiation. Korean J Health Econ Policy 17(3):1–21

Kim J-H, Jung J-C (2005) Survey of out-of-pocket in the National Health Insurance system. Health Insur Forum 4(1):74–88

Kim J-H, Lee H-Y (2006) Survey of out-of-pocket in the National Health Insurance system 2005. Health Insur Forum 5(4):42–58

Kim W, Lee K (2008) Drug price policy under national health insurance: a win-win strategy. Korean Soc Secur Stud 24(4):65–88

Kim S-J, Kwon S-M, Jung Y, Heo J-H (2010) International comparison of generic medicine prices. Korean J Health Econ Policy 16(3):41–62

Korean Pharmacists for Democratic Society (2006) Introduce a proper positive list system to remove drug price premium. Korean Pharmacists for Democratic Society, Korea

Korean Statistical Information Services (2014) Health expenditure. National Statistical Office. http://kosis.kr/statisticsList/statisticsList_03List.jsp?vwcd=MT_RTITLE&parmTabId=M_03_01#SubCont. Accessed 30 June 2014

Kwon S (2003) Pharmaceutical reform and physician strikes in Korea: separation of drug prescribing and dispensing. Soc Sci Med 57(3):529–538

Kwon S, Reich MR (2005) The changing process and politics of health policy in Korea. J Health Polit Policy Law 30(6):1003–1026

Kwon H-Y, Yang B-M (2011) Fixed budget for pharmaceuticals. Korean J Health Econ Policy 17(1):25–45

Kwon H-Y, Hong J-M, Godman B, Yang B-M (2013) Price cuts and drug spending in South Korea: the case of antihyperlipidemic agents. Health Policy 112(3):217–226. doi:10.1016/j.healthpol.2013.08.011

Lee S-Y (2005) Reforms of the health care delivery system in transition. Health Insur Forum 4(2):16–34

Lee E-K (2006) Reimbursement pricing and some policy implications. Health Insur Forum 5(2):2–14

Lee I-H (2010) Evaluating pharmaceutical policy in South Korea. University of York, York

Lee I-H (2013a) Evidence-based pharmaceutical policy-making; a challenging task? Vivid voices from Korean experts. Korean J Clin Pharm 23(3):185–195

Lee JH (2013b) The review of market-based Actual Transaction Price system. SungKyunKwan University, Suwon

Lee H-J, Lee T-J (2013) Impact of price control on drug expenditure and factors associated with the drug switch among statins: analysis of HIRA-NPS data. Health Policy Manage 23(2):112–123

Lee EK, Malone DC (2003) Comparison of peptic-ulcer drug use and expenditures before and after the implementation of a government policy to separate prescribing and dispensing practices in South Korea. Clin Ther 25(2):578–592

Lee I-H, Bloor K, Hewitt C, Maynard A (2012) The effects of new pricing and copayment schemes for pharmaceuticals in South Korea. Health Policy 104(1):40–49. doi:10.1016/j.healthpol.2011.09.003

Lee JY, Park JH, Shin HH, Ko SK (2013) Reference pricing; case study and implication. Korean Assoc Policy Stud 29(4):201–219

Lee I-H, Park S, Lee EK (2014) Generic utilization in the Korean National Health Insurance market; cost, volume and influencing factors. Yakhak Hoeji 58(2):99–106

MOHW (2006) [MOHW report to the National Assembly 2006]. Ministry of Health & Welfare, Gwacheon

Newsmp (2012) M.P. NamYoon insists the abolishment of market-based Actual Transaction Price system. Newsmp, 8 Oct 2012

NHIC, HIRA (2007) Statistical booklet on 30 year-history of Korean National Health Insurance. National Health Insurance Corporation, Health Insurance Review & Assessment Service, Seoul

NHIS, HIRA (2012) National Health Insurance statistical yearbook. National Health Insurance Service, Health Insurance Review & Assessment Service, Seoul

OECD (2007) How does Korea compare OECD Health Data 2007. Organisation for Economic Co-operation and Development, Paris

OECD (2013a) Health expenditure OECD Factbook 2013: economic, environmental and social statistics. OECD Publishing, Paris

OECD (2013b) Life expectancy at birth, total population. Health: key tables from OECD, no. 11. doi:10.1787/lifexpy-total-table-2013-2-en

OECD (2013c) Pharmaceutical expenditure. Health: key tables from OECD. doi:10.1787/pharmexpcap-table-2013-2-en; 10.1787/pharmexp-table-2013-2-en

OECD.Stat (2014) Organisation for Economic Cooperation and Development. http://www.oecd-ilibrary.org/statistics. Accessed 12 June 2014

Park S (2010) Risk-sharing agreement on the pricing and reimbursement of new drugs. Korean J Health Econ Policy 16(2):125–153

Park S, Jang Y-S, Chae S-M, Park E-J, Kim N-S, Lee EK, Lee I-H (2011) An indepth study of the utilization and costs of pharmaceuticals in South Korea, 2010. Ministry of Health & Welfare, Korea Institute for Health and Social Affairs, Seoul

Park S, Jang Y-S, Park E-J, Chae S-M, Lee Y-S, Ko S-K, Lee EK, Lee I-H (2012) An indepth study of the utilization and costs of pharmaceuticals in South Korea, 2012. Ministry of Health & Welfare, Korea Institute for Health and Social Affairs, Seoul

People's Solidarity for Participatory Democracy (1998) Overestimated drug prices causes more than a trillion won financial loss in the National Health Insurance. Committee on Social Welfare, People's Solidarity for Participatory Democracy, Seoul

People's Solidarity for Participatory Democracy (1999) MOHW should disclosure real transaction prices for pharmaceuticals. Committee on Social Welfare, People's Solidarity for Participatory Democracy, Seoul

Shin J-Y, Choi S-E (2008) The volume and the price of generic drug consumption in Korean prescription drug market. Korean J Health Econ Policy 14(1):103–125

Simoens S, De Coster S (2006) Sustaining generic medicines markets in Europe. Research Centre for Pharmaceutical Care and Pharmaco-economics, Katholieke Universiteit, Leuven

Yang C-Y (2002) A critical analysis of drug pricing and reimburse schemes in Korean medical insurance system. Kukje Kyungje Yongu 8(3):249–265

Yonhapnews (2011) Number of public beds, staying the same for 10 years. Yonhapnews, 18 Oct 2011

Yoon H-S (2008) National Insurance reimbursement pricing scheme: challenges and a strategy for improvement. Korea Development Institute, Seoul

Chapter 10
Pharmaceutical Pricing in Malaysia

Mohamed Azmi Hassali, Ching Siang Tan, Zhi Yen Wong, Fahad Saleem, and Alian A. Alrasheedy

Abstract Malaysia's healthcare system consists of two sectors namely public and private sector. Ministry of Health (MOH) is the main agency providing healthcare services in public sector.

Malaysia pharmaceutical market is dominated by prescription drugs that account for approximately 60 % of the pharmaceutical market share by value. There is no price control mechanism for pharmaceuticals in Malaysia. In fact, drug prices are not regulated in Malaysia and it is left to market forces to foster competition. However, in public sector, few price control strategies are employed by MOH to ensure fair, reasonable, affordable and stable prices of drugs. Despite various strategies formulated, there are challenges that need to be addressed. In public sector, the main challenges include escalating cost of pharmaceuticals as a result of privatization of Government Medical Store, lack of implementation of pro-generics policies and overlapping role of Malaysian Health Technology Assessment (MaHTAS) and Pharmacoeconomic Unit at Pharmaceutical Service Division (PSD) in cost-effectiveness evaluation of drugs. Similarly, in private sector, majority of the private health care providers would not follow the recommended retail price in selling medicines. In conclusion, there are several challenges that need be addressed in order to have a good pharmaceutical pricing strategy in Malaysia.

M.A. Hassali (✉) • C.S. Tan • F. Saleem • A.A. Alrasheedy
Discipline of Social and Administrative Pharmacy, School of Pharmaceutical Sciences, Universiti Sains Malaysia, 11800 Minden, Penang, Malaysia
e-mail: azmihassali@usm.my; azmihassali@gmail.com; chingsiang9@hotmail.com; fahaduob@gmail.com; alian-a@hotmail.com

Z.Y. Wong
Pharmacy Department, Hospital Teluk Intan, Jalan Changkat Jong, 36000 Teluk Intan, Perak, Malaysia
e-mail: wongzy88@gmail.com

Z.-U.-D. Babar (ed.), *Pharmaceutical Prices in the 21st Century*,
DOI 10.1007/978-3-319-12169-7_10

10.1 Introduction

The healthcare delivery system in Malaysia has undergone huge improvements since the country's independence in 1957 and currently a fairly comprehensive range of health services is provided by both public and private sectors. The healthcare services are provided via a dual system (public and private), the public healthcare sector is the main provider and the Ministry of Health (MOH) is the main regulatory and policy-making body (Hassali et al. 2014). Malaysia's public health system is financed mainly through taxation and some general revenue, while the private sector is financed through private health insurance, consumers' out-of pocket spending, nonprofit institution and private institution. This chapter provides an insight regarding drug pricing and pharmaceutical system situation in the country.

10.2 Healthcare System in Malaysia

Malaysia's healthcare system consists of two sectors, namely public and private sector. In the public sector, the Ministry of Health (MOH) is the main provider of healthcare services in the country (Performance Management Delivery Unit 2012). Other ministries providing healthcare services include Ministry of Higher Education, Ministry of Defence, Department of Aboriginal (Orang Asli) Affairs, Department of Social Welfare, Ministry of Home Affairs and Ministry of Housing (Jaafar et al. 2013). Currently, there are 147 public hospitals and 209 private hospitals in Malaysia (Ministry of Health Malaysia 2013). For health clinics, there are 1,025 clinics in public sector and 6,675 clinics in private sector (Ministry of Health Malaysia 2013).

10.2.1 Healthcare Financing in Malaysia

Healthcare delivered by public hospitals and clinics are heavily financed by taxes and other public revenues (Jaafar et al. 2013; Performance Management Delivery Unit 2012). Therefore, patient pay only little amount of money for treatment. In fact, Malaysia citizens have to pay only MYR 1 for each visit to outpatient department and MYR 5 (1 USD = 3.2415 MYR, Consumer Price Index = 106.5) for visiting specialists' clinic (Ministry of Health Malaysia 2014; Central Bank of Malaysia 2013; Department of Statistic Malaysia 2013). In contrast, private sectors are funded mainly by private health insurance, consumers' out-of pocket payment and nonprofit institution (Chua et al. 2010; Jaafar et al. 2013).

There are two types of health insurances available namely private and employee-based (also known as social security funds). There are two main social security funds namely the Social Security Organization (SOCSO) and the Employee Provident Funds (EPF) that provide some health coverage for employees in the private sector (Jaafar et al. 2013).

Under the Employees Provident Fund Act 1991 (Act 452), the EPF is formed to provide retirement benefits for its members (Employees Provident Fund 2013). Private and non-pensionable public sector employees are the EPF members (Employees Provident Fund 2013). The members are required to pay certain amount of money monthly to EPF while employer contributes another portion (Employees Provident Fund 2013). The money can only be withdrawn when the members reach certain age for retirement. However, members are allowed to withdraw certain amount of money from EPF for healthcare purposes.

Government servants who took pension can enjoy free medical care in public hospitals and clinics after they retire. SOSCO provides protection for employees who meet with an accident or suffers from an occupational disease (Social Security Association). These employees are entitled to free treatment at SOCSO panel clinics or government clinics/hospital (Social Security Association). For treatments received from a clinic which is not a SOCSO panel, the employer or employee can apply for reimbursement (Social Security Association). However, the reimbursement is subject to rates determined by SOCSO (Social Security Association).

Private health insurance is voluntary and is mainly used to cover private hospital costs (i.e. 70 % of health insurance expenditure is on hospital care) (Jaafar et al. 2013). Examples of main insurance companies are ING Insurance, National Insurance Association of Malaysia, Life Insurance Association of Malaysia and Private Insurance Association of Malaysia (Jaafar et al. 2013). Private health insurance applies risk rating concept in which they select healthy members (Jaafar et al. 2013). In other words, private health insurance selects policy members who do not have pre-existing illnesses. Policy members are required to pay predetermined monthly premium (Jaafar et al. 2013).

To date, there is no national health insurance system or universal coverage scheme in Malaysia. However, there is a future plan for a universal coverage scheme. In 2009, Malaysian government proposed a universal coverage scheme called '1 care for 1 Malaysia'. However, misinterpretation occurs among media and civil society groups due to provisional nature of the proposal (Bridel 2012). Currently, Ministry of Health is finalising the proposals to enable informed discussion regarding the issue (Bridel 2012). According to the proposal, financing will be derived from combination of mandatory Social Health Insurance (SHI) and government contribution (Bridel 2012). SHI is calculated based on sliding scale as a percentage of income from employee, employer and government (Bridel 2012). Governmental contribution is derived from general taxation. Monthly salary deduction for SHI premiums are estimated to be 9.5 % of household income (Bridel 2012). Summary of Malaysian healthcare system is shown in Table 10.1.

Table 10.1 Schematic overview of the Malaysian healthcare system

<table>
<tr><th>Healthcare</th><th colspan="7">Public healthcare</th><th>Private healthcare</th></tr>
<tr><td rowspan="2">Funding source</td><td colspan="7">(a) Taxes and public revenues</td><td>(a) Private health insurance</td></tr>
<tr><td colspan="7">(b) Minimal co-payment from public</td><td>(b) Social security fund (i.e. SOSCO and EPF)</td></tr>
<tr><td rowspan="7">Providers</td><td rowspan="5">Ministry of Health (MOH)</td><td colspan="6" rowspan="2">Non MOH Hospitals</td><td>(c) Out-of pocket spending</td></tr>
<tr><td>(d) Nonprofit institution and private institution</td></tr>
<tr><td rowspan="3">Ministry of Higher Education</td><td rowspan="3">Ministry of Housing and Local Government</td><td rowspan="3">Ministry of Defence</td><td rowspan="3">Department of Aboriginal Affairs</td><td rowspan="3">Department of Social Welfare</td><td rowspan="3">Ministry of Home Affairs</td><td>(a) Private hospitals</td></tr>
<tr><td>(b) General practitioner clinics</td></tr>
<tr><td>(c) Community pharmacies</td></tr>
<tr><td rowspan="2">District hospitals, state general hospitals, national referral centres, and special institutions</td><td rowspan="2">Teaching hospitals</td><td rowspan="2">Provides environmental health services and limited health services</td><td rowspan="2">Military hospitals and medical centres</td><td rowspan="2">Provide health services to the indigenous community</td><td rowspan="2">Nursing homes for the elderly</td><td rowspan="2">Drug rehabilitation centres</td><td>(d) Dentist</td></tr>
<tr><td>(e) Diagnostic labs</td></tr>
<tr><td>Target group</td><td colspan="3">General population</td><td colspan="4">Specific population</td><td>Population who can afford</td></tr>
</table>

10.2.2 Drug Regulatory Authority in Malaysia

The main drug regulatory authority in Malaysia is the Drug Control Authority (DCA). According to the Regulation 7(1)(a) of the Control of Drugs and Cosmetics (Amendment) Regulations 2006, all products should be registered with the DCA prior to being manufactured, sold, supplied, imported or possessed or administered unless the product is exempted under the specific provisions of the Regulations (National Pharmaceutical Control Bureau 2012b). DCA is executive body of Ministry of Health established under the Control of Drugs and Cosmetics Regulations 1984 with the main aim to ensure the safety, quality and efficacy of pharmaceuticals, health and personal care products that are marketed in Malaysia (National Pharmaceutical Control Bureau 2012a).

There are three stages in registration of pharmaceutical product (Azmi and Alavi 2001). The first stage involves the evaluation of product to ensure that the active ingredient or formulation is already registered with the DCA (Azmi and Alavi 2001). The second stage involves testing the quality of the finished product and it is performed by National Pharmaceutical Control Bureau (NPCB) to ensure the quality of the pharmaceutical product (Azmi and Alavi 2001). The NPCB as DCA secretariat is the agency that develops and implements the regulations concerning the quality, safety and efficacy of medicines (Ministry of Health Malaysia 2007). The third stage involves the evaluation of the application for registration by checking the quality, efficacy and safety of the product, based on the documents and data submitted (Azmi and Alavi 2001). In most of the cases, drug registration process is lengthy and it usually takes between 18 and 36 months after the application is submitted (Azmi and Alavi 2001; Abdul 1999).

10.2.3 Malaysian Medicine Market

Prescription medicines accounted for approximately 60 % of the pharmaceutical market share and it was valued at MYR 4.39bn (US$ 1.4bn, 1 USD = 3.2415 MYR, Consumer Price Index = 106.5) in 2012 (Business Monitor International 2013; Department of Statistic Malaysia 2013; Central Bank of Malaysia 2013). The prescription drugs market is based on strong domestic generic drug sector and imported of patented and generic drugs (Malaysia External Trade Development Corporation 2013). Patented drugs with a strong foothold in the Malaysia market have the largest market share (i.e. about 60 % of prescription sales by value) (Table 10.2) (Business Monitor International 2013).

Table 10.2 Generic and patented drug sales indicators 2009–2011

Year	2009		2010		2011	
Generic vs. Patented	Generic	Patented	Generic	Patented	Generic	Patented
Drug sales (US$ bn)	0.33	0.56	0.44	0.68	0.54	0.77
Drug sales (US$ bn) % change y-o-y	7.1	−4.5	36.1	21.0	23.0	13.7
% of prescription sales	36.81	63.19	39.59	60.41	41.48	58.52
% of total sales	26.80	46.00	28.50	43.48	30.00	42.33

Source: Business Monitor International. Malaysia Pharmaceuticals and Healthcare Report Q3 2013 (Business Monitor International 2013)

10.2.4 Pharmaceutical Industry in Malaysia

The pharmaceutical industry in Malaysia can be divided into three major sectors, namely manufacturing, importation and distribution (Hassali et al. 2009). Multinational companies (MNC) monopolize the importation and distribution sectors whereas the manufacturing sector consists of domestic generic manufacturers and foreign-owned companies with manufacturing site in Malaysia (Hassali et al. 2009; Business Monitor International 2013; Malaysian Industrial Development Authority 2011). Most of the local companies are small and medium-sized companies and involved in the manufacturing of generic drugs, traditional and herbal products (Malaysian Industrial Development Authority 2011). Some of these companies are contract manufacturer for MNCs (Malaysian Industrial Development Authority 2011). Currently, there are over 40 local generic manufacturers in Malaysia (Hassali et al. 2009). The generic drugs are produced mainly to cater domestic consumption (i.e. 33 % of domestic market in value term) (Malaysian-German Chamber of Commerce and Industry 2011; Malaysian Industrial Development Authority 2011).

10.3 Drug Pricing Set-Up and Price Control Mechanisms in Malaysia

10.3.1 Public Sector Pricing

Ministry of Health (MOH), as the largest healthcare service provider, controls and procures medicines at lower prices compared to private healthcare sector. The price control mechanism adopted by the MOH is discussed below.

(a) Public procurement pricing
The MOH Drug Formulary consists of all pharmaceuticals approved by Ministry of Health Drug List Review Panel and it serves as a guide to hospitals to select medicines for their own local formulary (Ministry of Health Malaysia 2012).

It was formulated and implemented in 1983, which consists of 1,224 formulations for use by all health institution in Malaysia (Malaysian Medical Resource 2012). The aim of MOH Drug Formulary is to control the drug usage in MOH by reducing wastage, encourage optimum use of medicines and to enhance rational drug usage (Director General of Health Malaysia 1997). Figure 10.1 illustrates the flow of Drug Formulary reviewed by panels which consists of Director General (DG) of Health as chairman, Deputy DG of medical services, Director of Pharmaceutical Services, eight consultants in public service and three pharmacists in public services (Ngadiman 2013). Listing in the MOH Drug Formulary enables medicines to be made available in the MOH's healthcare facilities. Pharmaceutical companies are required to provide evidence of medical benefit and of low prices in order to gain listing in MOH Drug Formulary. To control and maintain the medicine price after listing into the MOH Drug Formulary, there is an agreement to pharmaceutical companies that there will be no price increment exceeding the quoted price for 1 year (Ministry of Health Malaysia 2008a). The later price increment also must be justified. This price monitoring mechanism has enhanced the medicine price at affordable level in MOH.

(b) Procurement Principles

MOH developed an effective procurement and distribution system (Ministry of Health Malaysia 2008b). The current system of MOH public sector includes three processes namely the national tendering, supply by Concession Company (Approved Product Purchase List) and local purchase at institutional

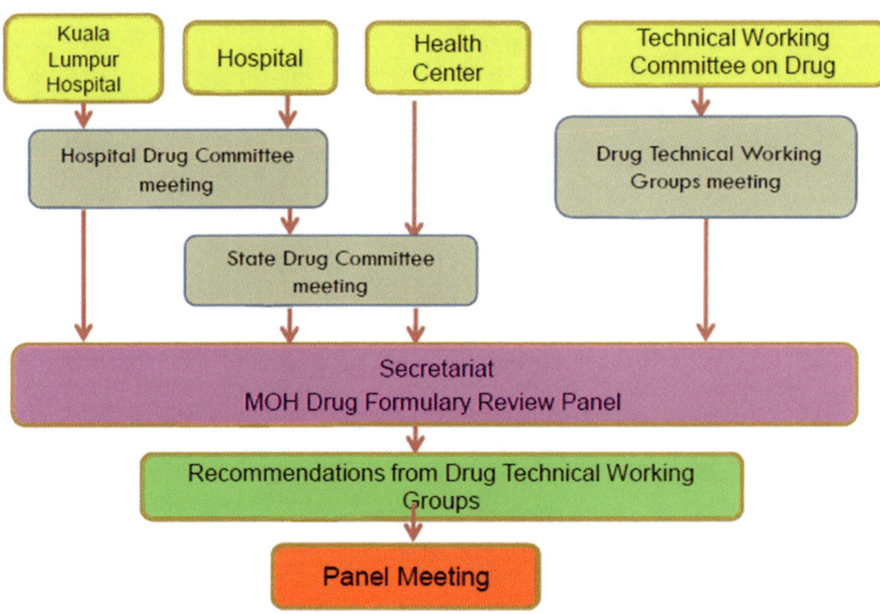

Fig. 10.1 Flow of MOH Drug Formulary review panel. *Adopted*: Ngadiman (2013)

level (Ministry of Health Malaysia 2008b). Those medicine and non-medicine listed in Approved Product Purchase List (APPL) is supplied by Concession Company whereas local purchase at institutional level can be divided into direct purchase and quotation (Table 10.3). Through open tender and price negotiation, a privatized central supplier (i.e. Concession Company) has an agreement with government to provide approximately 73 % of the annual value of drugs to all public healthcare institutions. Within this context, the

Table 10.3 Types of procurement in Malaysia Ministry of Health

No.	Types of procurement	Description	Price evaluation and negotiation process
1.	Supply by Concession Company	• Medicine and non-medicine listed in Approved Product Purchase List (APPL)	• *For multisource products:* Internal (i.e. other public institutions) and external referencing (i.e. International Referencing Pricing, IRP) will be used
		• Price is revised every 3 years	
2.	National tender	• Tender is processed centrally by MOH and prices are Prices valid for 2 years for most items	• *For Single source products*:
		• Open tender	External referencing will be used
		• All contractors intending to participate in local tenders must be registered with the Government	Country of selection will be based on economic status, population size and other factors
		• International tenders will be invited for supplies and services if there are no locally produced supplies or services available	• *For single/sole supplier*: Prices are negotiated further
3.	Local purchase	• Procurement is done at individual Institution/Hospital and Health Centres	• Price for newly listed medicines in MOH Drug Formulary will be approved by the MOH Drug Formulary Panel and controlled for at least 1 year from the date of listing
		• Prices valid at point of purchase or 1 year	
		• There are two types of local purchase namely direct purchase and quotation	
	(a) Direct Purchase	• Refer to procurement if items with value less than MYR 50,000	
		• The requirement of registration is exempted	• The price approved is subjected to fulfilling the criteria of cost-effectiveness and affordability of the MOH in achieving cost-containment
	(b) Quotation	• Refers to procurement of items (i.e. medicine and non-medicine products) that value between MYR 50,000 and MYR 500,000	
		• All suppliers wishing to take part in quotations must be registered with the Government	
		• Minimum of five quotation	

Source: Ministry of Finance Malaysia (2013), Bahri (2013)

particular supplier has a contract to provide MOH nearly 600 items include drugs and medical supplies for a period of 15 years (i.e. until year 2019) (Director General of Health Malaysia 1997). All public institutions (i.e. public hospitals, district hospitals and health clinic) have to purchase all medicine and non-medicine product with the selected company as in 'Request Order Form of the Concession Company'. Monetary penalty will be given to public institution that purchases products from other companies. In fact, the supplier usually supplies drugs with lower prices and usually the prices are revised every 3 years (Asia Pacific Observatory on Health Systems and Policies 2013).

(c) Pharmacoeconomic Evaluation
Moreover, Formulary and Pharmacoeconomic Unit, PSD conducts drug evaluation for formulary listing applications by using pharmacoeconomic principles. In addition, this unit continuously monitors outcome in terms of cost and clinical efficacy for both the new and existing drugs (Hussain 2008; Ministry of Health Malaysia 2012b). The PSD had published pharmacoeconomics guidelines to assist healthcare professionals to make informed decision (Pharmaceutical Services Division Ministry of Health Malaysia 2012b).

(d) Health Technology Assessment
In addition, in order to ensure safe and cost-effective technology is being used in the Ministry of Health institutions in Malaysia, the Malaysian Health Technology Assessment (MaHTAS) was established by Ministry of Health in August 1995 (International Network of Agencies for Health Technology Assessment (INAHTA) 2014). The duties of MaHTAS include (Sivalal 2009): to identify priority issues for HTA, to review the HTA program, approve health technology assessments and to formulate policies related to technology, and to review the dissemination and implementation activities of HTA. The scope of HTA is expanded to include both new and existing technologies including pharmaceuticals, devices and procedures through which healthcare is provided (Sivalal 2009). To date, 43 in-depth assessments have been carried out and 140 rapid assessment reports were produced (Sivalal 2009).

(e) Pro-generics policies
Generic medicines have been widely used especially in public hospital setting and the market share of generic medicine is growing over the years (Business Monitor International 2013). The Generic Medicines Policy in Malaysia National Medicine Policy was launched initially in year 2007 to encourage generic manufacturing, generic prescribing, generic dispensing, generic substitution and generic use in Malaysia (Ministry of Health Malaysia 2007). After few years of implementation, revision was made and revised version of National Medicine Policy was published (Ministry of Health Malaysia 2012a). Recently, in order to transform the country to be a developed-nation by the year 2020, a national blue print of Economic Transformation Program (ETP) was formulated and local generic pharmaceutical industry has been given priority for boosting the country economic transformation (Performance Management Delivery Unit 2013b, c).

10.3.2 Private Sector Pricing

In Malaysia, currently there is no price control mechanism for pharmaceuticals at private retail pharmacies. In fact, drug prices are not regulated in Malaysia and its left to market forces (Bahri 2013; Babar et al 2007). Due to the absence of drug price regulation in Malaysia, pharmaceutical companies, wholesaler and healthcare professional can set their own retail selling price (Hassali et al. 2012; Kolassa 1997; Mahmood and Bukhari 2002).

Historically, high drugs prices have been reported in Malaysia. Within 3 years (1990–1992), a proportionate increase of 7–28 % in medicine prices was reported in Malaysia whereas prices in United Kingdom remained constant during the same time period (Azmi and Alavi 2001). A study conducted by using WHO/HAI drug pricing methodology showed that the innovator brand medicines were 16 times higher than the International Reference Prices (IRP). In addition, the commonly sold generic medicines were 6.89 times higher than IRP (Babar et al. 2007). In line to what is reported earlier, mean retail medicine prices in Penang, Malaysia were 30.3–148.2 % higher than the mean retail drug prices in Australia (Hassali et al. 2012).

In private sector, the dynamic pricing of medicine is partly attributed by the different bonus schemes of products offered by pharmaceutical companies to the community pharmacies. Pharmaceutical companies often offer cheaper price or extra quantities of pharmaceutical products if purchased in a bigger volume. Thus, chain pharmacies and big alliance independent pharmacies have higher purchase volume and better financial support, so they are able to get bonus deals with cheaper pharmaceutical products and able to sell at lower prices (Hassali et al. 2010; Malaysian Pharmaceutical Society 2012). Normally there were two methods of bonus scheme offered by pharmaceutical companies (Malaysian Pharmaceutical Society 2012). First, product bonus incentives, for every 12 boxes of X medicine purchased, 1 box of the same X medicine will be given as free bonus; for every 24 boxes of X medicine purchased, 3 boxes will be given as free bonus and so on. The second method is price discount incentive and there are different pricing for the quantities ordered. For example, for the purchase of less than 10 boxes of X medicine cost certain price; if procured more than 10 boxes of X medicine, then the price would decrease (Gan 2013; Malaysian Pharmaceutical Society and Malaysian community Pharmacy Guild 2013). As a result of individualized strategies and the non existence of drug price regulation, this has resulted in price disparities within the pharmaceutical market where the chain and big independent pharmacies tend to sell medicine in lower price compare to independent pharmacies (Hassali et al. 2010; Kamat and Nichter 1998).

Due to the existence of different bonus schemes to clinics and community pharmacies by pharmaceutical companies, some unethical doctors tended to make quick profit by selling medicine to pharmacy through runner network (Hassali et al. 2013). Runner in pharmaceutical market represents a person without a valid wholesale license and supplies pharmaceuticals or OTC products to community pharmacies. Normally runners get their cheaper stocks either from doctors, through illegal sources (stolen products), parallel import, counterfeit products or products from those community pharmacists who purchased with bonus (Hassali et al. 2013). Community pharmacists tend to purchase medicine from runner network because it is cheaper with no restriction on quantities as compare to wholesaler which are more expensive (Malaysian Pharmaceutical Society 2012). This finding is consistent with what is reported by Babar and colleagues that runners without valid wholesale license tend to buy in bulk and re-sell to retail pharmacy (Babar et al. 2005). This is unfair to those pharmacists who purchased medicine from the valid wholesaler.

As a result of high prices in Malaysia, the Medicine Price Unit (MPU) was set up by Pharmaceutical Service Division (PSD), Ministry of Health in year 2005. The objective of this unit was to oversee and monitor medicine prices in Malaysia. MPU has undertaken few initiatives based on the Malaysian National Medicines Policy (MNMP), to ensure equitable and timely access to good quality essential medicines at affordable price. MNMP was approved by Malaysian Government in year 2006 (Pharmaceutical Services Division Ministry of Health Malaysia 2012a). In order to enhance the implementation of MNMP in terms of medicine cost containment, affordability and accessibility, MPU has to set up a national database on medicine price information. The purpose of national database for medicine price is to provide useful information about the accurate pricing scenario.

Therefore, in year 2005, a baseline medicines price survey was conducted to get an overview of medicine prices price trend in Malaysia based on 238 brands for 30 commonly used medicines over 33 public premises and 35 private premises (Ministry of Health Malaysia 2005). The findings from the preliminary report has shown that medicines of original brands were 47 % cheaper in the public sector compared to the private sector, generic medicine were 60 % cheaper in public sector as compare to private sector as well, wholesale medicine prices in the public sector were 1.3 times higher than International Reference Price (IRP) and gross retail price in the private sector were 4 times higher than IRP. Subsequently a medicine price survey was conducted in year 2006 to cover 100 types of medicines consisting 711 brands. The main findings from this report revealed that the overall medicine prices in the public sector and private sector in East Malaysia were 1 % and 9 % more expensive respectively than Peninsular Malaysia. In addition, the report also had shown that the median price ratio at public sector was found 1.02 times higher than the IRP (Ministry of Health Malaysia 2008a). Since 2006, medicines prices and mark-ups monitoring has been done by Malaysia PSD (Bahri 2013). Besides, in order to curb the escalating medicine prices, medicines in Malaysia are exempted from tariffs and duties (Bahri 2013).

In the year 2010, the Malaysian government offered Competition Act 2010 and the act was effective on business practice since 1st January 2012. It is implemented under the Malaysia Competition Commission (MyCC) to enhance consumer welfare, business practice and business development (Malaysia Competition Commission 2010). The Competition Act 2010 prohibited price discrimination. Hence, some community pharmacies strongly opposed the different bonus scheme for community pharmacies and different pricing for pharmacists and doctors by the pharmaceutical companies (Hassali et al. 2013; Oorjitham 2011). Taking these observations into consideration, community pharmacists demanded the enforcement of Competition Act 2010. They believe that the enforcement of this act would reduce price disparity.

In addition, Pharmaceutical Services Division, Ministry of Health, Malaysia proposed guidelines on "Good Pharmaceutical Trade Practice (GPTP) with the aim to encourage non-discriminatory trade practices across different trade channels in the private healthcare sector (i.e. general practitioners' clinics, community pharmacies and private hospitals) (Malaysian Association of Pharmaceutical Suppliers (MAPS) 2014). In the proposed GPTP, all trade channels in private sectors must enjoy similar pricing and bonus schemes for pharmaceuticals purchased. However, some industry stakeholders are against the proposed GPTP and urge to maintain the same 'free market forces' (Malaysian Association of Pharmaceutical Suppliers (MAPS) 2014).

10.4 The Impact of Pricing on Public Health (Access and Affordability of Medicines for Public)

World Health Organization (WHO) has ranked Malaysia at 49 out of 191 WHO member states for good performance of overall health system (Tandon et al. 2000). Nonetheless, Malaysia is now confronting a challenge of increasing healthcare expenditures over the years. Ministry of Health pharmaceutical expenditure has increased almost 70 % from RM 891 million in 2005 to RM 1.5 billion in 2009 (Asia Pacific Observatory on Health Systems and Policies 2013). Malaysia's healthcare expenditure is expected to be doubled in the next 6 years, reaching up to RM 68.4 billion in 2018 with an annual growth rate of 6.5 % over the 6-year period (Bahrom 2013). The increase in the spending of Ministry of Health is corresponding to the increment in the high usage of medicine, drug cost and to conduct more public health programs (Asia Pacific Observatory on Health Systems and Policies 2013). Government treasury allocates funds to Ministry of Health based on past spending and Consumer Price Index for the necessary increment (Asia Pacific Observatory on Health Systems and Policies 2013). Table 10.4 shown the Ministry of Health was the leading source of public sector health expenditure in 2009 which accounted 82 % of public expenditure (World Health Organization 2011).

Table 10.4 Public health expenditure by source of financing in year 2009[a]

Source	RM million	Percentage (%)
Ministry of Health	14,322	82.4
Ministry of Higher Education	1,766	10.2
Local authorities	129	0.7
Social Security Organization	93	0.5
Ministry of Defence	57	0.3
Employee Provident Funds	40	0.2
General State Government	27	0.2
Other state agencies (including statutory bodies)	10	0.1
Total	17,371	100

[a]*Adopted*: World Health Organization (2011)

10.5 Role of Generic Medicines in Malaysia

In Malaysia, the National Pharmaceutical Control Bureau (NPCB) defined generic medicine as a product that is essentially similar to a currently registered product in Malaysia (National Pharmaceutical Control Bureau 2012b).

Over the years, generic market share continue to grow. For example, the generic medicines sales increased from 0.33 US$ bn in year 2009 to reach 0.54 US$ bn in year 2011 representing 64 % increment over a period of 3 years time (Business Monitor International 2013). Factors that stimulate the growth of Malaysia generic drug market include (1) increasing government spending in purchasing of generics, (2) changing Malaysian population (3) support from the Malaysian government and policies, (4) improved quality of generic products, (5) cost-containment needs and (6) implementation of the ASEAN Free Trade Area (AFTA) agreement, with products from signatory countries to be exempt from import barriers and tariffs (Hassali et al. 2009; Business Monitor International 2013).

Greater use of generic medicine is encouraged as it is one of the effective mechanisms to curb the escalating healthcare cost especially pharmaceutical expenditure (King and Kanavos 2002; Kanavos 2007; Karim et al. 1996; Haas et al. 2005). In Malaysia, generic medicines are 30–90 % cheaper than brand innovator products (Shafie and Hassali 2008). Two policies were formulated by the Malaysian government to improve the usage of generic medicines, including the Malaysian generic medicines policy, the economic transformation program (ETP). In 2006, Malaysia adopted a national medicines policy (NMP), which encourages generic manufacturing, generic prescribing, generic dispensing, generic substitution and generic medicine use in Malaysia (Ministry of Health Malaysia 2007). Moreover, one new strategy was introduced in 2012 to give priority to locally manufactured medicines in terms of pharmaceutical procurement (Ministry of Health Malaysia 2012a). In the current generic medicines policy, which is part of the NMP 2012, healthy price competition in medicines are encouraged via the following strategies (Ministry of Health Malaysia 2012a):

(a) Prescribing by using generic name or International Non-proprietary Name (INN) shall be practiced at all levels
(b) Promoting the use of generic names or INN in procurement of medicines
(c) Priority shall be given to locally manufactured medicines in terms of pharmaceutical procurement
(d) Using the generic names or INN with or without the trade names in labelling for dispensed medicines should be encouraged
(e) Establishment or formation of formulary of interchangeable medicines
(f) For all interchangeable medicines, generic substitution shall be allowed and encouraged
(g) Appropriate incentives or allowances should be introduced to encourage the use and manufacturing of generic medicines in Malaysia.

In 2010, the ETP was formulated as part of Malaysia's National Transformation Program, targeting a Gross National Income per capita of USD $15,000 (Performance Management Delivery Unit 2013a). The ETP's targets will be achieved through the implementation of 12 National Key Economic Areas (NKEA) which include the healthcare sector (Performance Management Delivery Unit 2013a). The government aims to further grow this sector by increasing local generic manufacturing for exports under a listing of entry point projects (EPP) (Performance Management Delivery Unit 2013c). A few of the strategies under EPP were to (Performance Management Delivery Unit 2013b, c):

(a) Promote Malaysia as a member in The Organisation of the Islamic Cooperation and the Pharmaceutical Inspection Convention and Pharmaceutical Inspection Cooperation Scheme (PIC/S) to widen the export opportunities
(b) Upgrade the domestic manufacturing plants
(c) Have good relationships between multinational corporations and domestic manufacturers
(d) Ministry of Health (MOH) off-take procurement agreement with new local manufactured pharmaceuticals. Under this scheme, the MOH will become the main buyer of the manufacturer's future production for 3 years with the condition that the product must be manufactured in Malaysia. The agreement could be extended for another 2 years if the manufacturer demonstrates that the product can be registered and marketed in other countries
(e) Develop comprehensive national pharmaceutical data

Despite the government's continuous effort in improving the utilization of generic medicines, healthcare stakeholders have expressed concerns. Summary of issues from different healthcare stakeholders are shown in Table 10.5.

Table 10.5 Overview of issues from different healthcare stakeholders

Stake holders	Issues
Government or policy maker	• Implementation and support of the use of generic medicines in the country
Generic manufacturers	• Expressed ambiguous perceptions about the effectiveness of Malaysian government policies and regulations in promoting generic medicine
	• Expressed an unclear view of regulatory exception provision (i.e. Bolar provision) in which development of generic medicines was allowed before the branded originator product's patent expired
	• Dissatisfied with level of generic medicine prescribing
	• Patent clustering by branded innovator companies
	• Earlier entry of imported generic medicines
Medical practitioners	• Low level of knowledge of the basis of bioequivalence testing
	• Misconceptions about safety, quality and efficacy of generic medicines
Pharmacists	• Expressed doubts about the quality, safety and efficacy of locally manufactured generic medicines
	• Lack of confidence in Malaysia's generic approval system
	• Mixed results were obtained for generic substitution rate
	• Misconceptions about safety, quality, efficacy and bioequivalence of generic medicines
	• Supporting implementation of generic substitution policy
Consumers	• Lack of knowledge about generic medicine
	• Expressed concerns about safety, efficacy and quality of generic medicines

Adopted from Wong et al. (2014)

10.6 Conclusion

The present review has highlighted that issues related to pharmaceutical pricing. The issues related to price disparity and pharmaceutical product bonusing scheme between practitioners need to be addressed in a transparent manner. Besides that a viable price control mechanism and policy need to be established through good stewardship by all stakeholders involved in healthcare delivery.

References

Abdul LS (1999) Regulations and policies on pharmaceuticals in Malaysia: its impact on healthcare. Kaohsiung J Med Sci 15:S75–S78

Asia Pacific Observatory on Health Systems and Policies (2013) Malaysia health system review [Online]. http://www.wpro.who.int/asia_pacific_observatory/hits/series/Malaysia_Health_Systems_Review2013.pdf. Accessed 20 Nov 2013

Azmi IM, Alavi R (2001) TRIPS, patents, technology transfer, foreign direct investment and the pharmaceutical industry in Malaysia. J World Intellect Prop 4:946–976
Babar ZUD, Izham MIM, Singh H, Bukhari NI (2005) A survey on medicine prices availability, affordability and price components in Malaysia using the WHO/HAI methodology [Online]. Malaysia. http://apps.who.int/medicinedocs/documents/s18599en/s18599en.pdf. Accessed 5 Dec 2012
Babar ZUD, Ibrahim MIM, Singh H, Bukahri NI, Creese A (2007) Evaluating drug prices, availability, affordability, and price components: implications for access to drugs in Malaysia. PLoS Med 4:e82
Bahri S (2013) Use of health economics data in listing and pricing of pharmaceuticals: Ministry of Health perspective. Monash Health Economic Forum 2013. Monash University Malaysia, Bandar Sunway.
Bahrom S (2013) Robust growth seen for healthcare industry [Online]. https://www.freemalaysiatoday.com/category/business/2013/02/06/robust-growth-seen-for-healthcare-industry/. Accessed 11 June 2013
Bridel A (2012) Explaining 1 care: its proposals, rationale and feasibility. http://www.cpps.org.my/upload/CPPS%201Care%20Policy%20Paper.pdf. Accessed 17 Aug 2012
Business Monitor International (2013) Malaysia pharmaceuticals and healthcare report Q3 2013. Business Monitor International Ltd., London
Central Bank of Malaysia (2013) Exchange rate [Online]. http://www.bnm.gov.my/index.php?ch=statistic&pg=stats_exchangerates. Accessed 23 Oct 2013
Chua GN, Hassali MA, Shafie AA, Awaisu A (2010) A survey exploring knowledge and perceptions of general practitioners towards the use of generic medicines in the northern state of Malaysia. Health Policy 95:229–235
Department of Statistic Malaysia (2013) Consumer Price Index Malaysia August 2013 [Online]. http://www.statistics.gov.my/portal/index.php?option=com_content&view=article&id=2105%3Aconsumer-price-index-malaysia-august-2013-updated-18092013&catid=71%3Aconsumer-price-index-malaysia-&Itemid=153&lang=en. Accessed 23 Oct 2013
Director General of Health Malaysia (1997) Essential Drugs Concept- An International Perspective [Online]. http://www.prn.usm.my/old_website/isdb/speech.html. Accessed 26 Nov 2013
Employees Provident Fund (2013) About EPF [Online]. http://www.kwsp.gov.my/portal/en/about-epf/overview-of-the-epf. Accessed 27 Jan 2014
Gan BZ (2013) Say no to inducement to medical prescribers [Online]. https://www.facebook.com/groups/147352308715470/permalink/428227587294606/. Accessed 25 Nov 2013
Haas JS, Phillips KA, Gerstenberger EP, Seger AC (2005) Potential savings from substituting generic drugs for brand-name drugs: medical expenditure panel survey, 1997–2000. Ann Intern Med 142:891–897
Hassali MA, Yuen KH, Ibrahim MIM, Wong JW, Ng BH, San Ho DS (2009) Malaysian pharmaceutical industry: opportunities and challenges. J Generic Med 6:246–252
Hassali MA, Shafie AA, Al-Haddad M, Balamurugan T, Awaisu A, Siow Y (2010) A qualitative study exploring the impact of the pharmaceutical price war among community pharmacies in the state of Penang, Malaysia. J Clin Diagn Res 4:3161–3169
Hassali MA, Shafie AA, Babar ZUD, Khan TM (2012) A study comparing the retail drug prices between Northern Malaysia and Australia. J Pharm Health Serv Res 3:103–107
Hassali MA, Tan CS, Saleem F, Aljadhey H (2013) A qualitative exploration of perceptions toward pharmaceutical price war among community pharmacists in the state of Penang, Malaysia. J Med Mark Device Diagn Pharm Mark 13:44–53
Hassali MA, Alrasheedy AA, Ab Razak BA, Al-Tamimi SK, Saleem F, Haq NU, Aljadhey H (2014) Assessment of general public satisfaction with public healthcare services in Kedah, Malaysia. Australas Med J 7:35
Hussain SH (2008) Drug control and formulary management in Malaysia. Value Health 11: S158–S159

International Network of Agencies for Health Technology Assessment (INAHTA) (2014) MaHTAS—Health Technology Assessment Section, Ministry of Health Malaysia [Online]. http://www.inahta.org/Members/MaHTAs/. Accessed 22 April 2014

Jaafar S, Noh KM, Muttalib KA, Othman NH, Healy J, Maskon K, Abdullah AR, Zainuddin J, Bakar AA, Rahman SSA, Ismail F, Yuen CY, Baba N, Said ZM (2013) Malaysia health system review. Health Syst Transit [Online] 3(1):103. http://www.wpro.who.int/asia_pacific_observatory/hits/series/Malaysia_Health_Systems_Review2013.pdf

Kamat VR, Nichter M (1998) Pharmacies, self-medication and pharmaceutical marketing in Bombay, India. Soc Sci Med 47:779–794

Kanavos P (2007) Do generics offer significant savings to the UK National Health Service? Curr Med Res Opin 23:105–116

Karim SA, Pillai G, Ziqubu-Page T, Cassimjee M, Morar M (1996) Potential savings from generic prescribing and generic substitution in South Africa. Health Policy Plan 11:198–202

King DR, Kanavos P (2002) Encouraging the use of generic medicines: implications for transition economies. Croat Med J 43:462–469

Kolassa E (1997) Prices politic, and problems—a pricing philosophy. J Pharm Mark Pract 1:21–27

Mahmood M, Bukhari N (2002) Pharmaceutical management and marketing. Tariq Academy, Faisalabad, pp 115–144

Malaysia Competition Commission (2010) Competition Act 2010 [Online]. http://www.mycc.gov.my/files/announcement/06c727d2-d538-43ba-99fe-40df475d0a8d.pdf. Accessed 20 Dec 2012

Malaysia External Trade Development Corporation (2013) Pharmaceutical: overview of the industry [Online]. http://www.matrade.gov.my/en/foriegn-buyers-section/69-industry-write-up--products/520-pharmaceutical. Accessed 18 Aug 2013

Malaysian Association of Pharmaceutical Suppliers (MAPS) (2014) Message from the President, June 2014 [Online]. http://www.i-maps.my/1.asp. Accessed 4 Aug 2014

Malaysian Pharmaceutical Society, Malaysian Community Pharmacy Guild (2013) Community pharmacy pricing issues and strategies required. http://www.mcpg.org.my/index.php?root=MjIy&detail=OTA=. Accessed 19 Nov 2013

Malaysian Industrial Development Authority (2011) Guide on pharmaceutical industry in Malaysia. http://www.mida.gov.my/env3/uploads/Publications_pdf/Guide_on_Pharmaceutical/Guide%20Book%20Oct%202011.pdf. Accessed 3 Feb 2013

Malaysian Medical Resource (2012) National Pharmaceutical Formulary 2012 [Online]. http://medicine.com.my/wp/2012/09/national-pharmaceutical-formulary-2012/. Accessed 26 Nov 2013

Malaysian Pharmaceutical Society (2012) An "honest-voice" against unethical promotion [Online]. MPS Announcements, Articles and News Alerts. http://www.mps.org.my/newsmaster.cfm?&menuid=37&action=view&retrieveid=3603. Accessed 15 Dec 2012

Malaysian-German Chamber of Commerce and Industry (2011) "Market Watch 2012" The healthcare sector in Malaysia. http://www.malaysia.ahk.de/fileadmin/ahk_malaysia/Market_reports/The_Healthcare_Sector_in_Malaysia.pdf. Accessed 24 April 2014

Ministry of Finance Malaysia (2013) Malaysia government procurement regime. http://www.treasury.gov.my/pdf/lain-lain/msia_regime.pdf. Accessed 23 Oct 2013

Ministry of Health Malaysia (2005) Malaysian statistics on medicine 2005 [Online]. http://www.crc.gov.my/wp-content/uploads/documents/report/msmreport_2007.pdf. Accessed 19 July 2014

Ministry of Health Malaysia (2007) Malaysian National Medicines Policy. http://www.pharmacy.gov.my/aeimages//File/MNMP_DUNAS.pdf. Accessed 24 April 2014

Ministry of Health Malaysia (2008a) Malaysia's health [Online]. http://www.moh.gov.my/images/gallery/publications/mh/Malaysia%20Health%202008-2.pdf. Accessed 20 July 2014

Ministry of Health Malaysia (2008b) Malaysia's health 2008. http://www.moh.gov.my/images/gallery/publications/mh/Malaysia%20Health%202008-2.pdf. Accessed 6 Nov 2012

Ministry of Health Malaysia (2012a) Malaysian National Medicines Policy. http://www.pharmacy.gov.my/v2/sites/default/files/document-upload/buku-dunas.pdf. Accessed 12 Sept 2014

Ministry of Health Malaysia (2012a) Malaysian National Medicines Policy. http://www.pharmacy.gov.my/v2/sites/default/files/document-upload/buku-dunas.pdf. Accessed 24 April 2014

Ministry of Health Malaysia (2012b) Pharmacoeconomic guideline for Malaysia [Online]. http://www.pharmacy.gov.my/v2/sites/default/files/document-upload/pharmacoeconomic-guideline-malaysia.pdf. Accessed 28 Nov 2013

Ministry of Health Malaysia (2013) Health facts 2013. http://www.moh.gov.my/images/gallery/publications/HEALTH%20FACTS%202013.pdf. Accessed 18 Aug 2013

Ministry of Health Malaysia (2014) Outpatient charges [Online]. http://www.moh.gov.my/english.php/pages/view/151. Accessed 14 Jan 2014

National Pharmaceutical Control Bureau (2012a) About the Drug Control Authority [Online]. http://portal.bpfk.gov.my/index.cfm?&menuid=148&parentid=9. Accessed 13 Dec 2012

National Pharmaceutical Control Bureau (2012b) Drug registration guidance document. http://portal.bpfk.gov.my/aeimages//File/RGDOC_updated_Oct_2012_edited_121112.pdf. Accessed 13 Dec 2012

Ngadiman SA (2013) Financing ARV experience from Malaysia [Online]. https://www.google.com/webhp?source=search_app#q=malaysia+FLOW+OF+MOH+DRUG+FORMULARY+REVIEW+PANEL. Accessed 26 Nov 2013

Oorjitham S (2011) Competition countdown: level playing field [Online]. New Straits Times. http://www.nst.com.my/opinion/columnist/competition-countdown-level-playing-field-1.4678. Accessed 15 Dec 2012

Performance Management Delivery Unit (2012) Healthcare [Online]. http://etp.pemandu.gov.my/upload/Inside%20Investor%20-%20Healthcare.pdf. Accessed 5 March 2014

Performance Management Delivery Unit (2013a) About economic transformation program (ETP) [Online]. http://etp.pemandu.gov.my/About_ETP-@-Overview_of_ETP.aspx. Accessed 21 Nov 2013

Performance Management Delivery Unit (2013b) Healthcare NKEA fact sheet. http://etp.pemandu.gov.my/upload/NKEA_Factsheet_Healthcare.pdf. Accessed 23 Nov 2013

Performance Management Delivery Unit (2013c) National Key Economic Area (NKEA): health care [Online]. http://etp.pemandu.gov.my/upload/LINK_Healthcare_Event.pdf. Accessed 23 Nov 2013

Pharmaceutical Services Division Ministry of Health Malaysia (2012a) Malaysian National Medicines Policy [Online]. http://www.pharmacy.gov.my/v2/en/documents/malaysian-national-medicines-policy-dunas.html. Accessed 21 July 2014

Pharmaceutical Services Division Ministry of Health Malaysia (2012b) Pharmacoeconomic guideline for Malaysia, p 33. http://www.pharmacy.gov.my/v2/sites/default/files/document-upload/pharmacoeconomic-guideline-malaysia.pdf

Shafie AA, Hassali MA (2008) Price comparison between innovator and generic medicines sold by community pharmacies in the state of Penang, Malaysia. J Generic Med 6:35–42

Sivalal S (2009) Health technology assessment in Malaysia. Int J Technol Assess Health Care 25: 224–230

Social Security Association. Medical benefit [Online]. http://www.perkeso.gov.my/en/medical-benefit.html. Accessed 27 Jan 2014

Tandon A, Murray CJ, Lauer JA, Evans DB (2000) Measuring overall health system performance for 191 countries [Online]. http://www.who.int/healthinfo/paper30.pdf. Accessed 11 June 2013

Wong ZY, Hassali MA, Alrasheedy AA, Saleem F, Yahaya AH, Aljadhey H (2014) Malaysian generic pharmaceutical industries: perspective from healthcare stakeholders. J Pharm Health Serv Res. doi:10.1111/jphs.12072

World Health Organization (2011) System of Health Accounts (SHA 2011) [Online]. http://www.who.int/nha/sha_revision/en/. Accessed 20 Nov 2013

Chapter 11
Pharmaceutical Pricing in New Zealand

Rajan Ragupathy, Kate Kilpatrick, and Zaheer-Ud-Din Babar

Abstract All New Zealand residents are covered by a national public health system, and approximately 80 % of all health expenditure is publically financed. A well-regulated system of privately owned pharmacies supplies outpatient pharmaceuticals, while inpatient pharmaceuticals are provided in secondary care facilities. New Zealand does not use pharmaceutical price controls, leaving prices to be determined by negotiation. However, the public health system has a very effective monopsony purchaser, the Pharmaceutical Management Agency of New Zealand (PHARMAC). PHARMAC negotiates the prices of inpatient, outpatient and cancer pharmaceuticals, vaccines and medical devices, and manages a capped national budget for outpatient and cancer pharmaceuticals. PHARMAC also sets (separate) national positive formularies of publically funded outpatient and inpatient pharmaceuticals, and administers access schemes for pharmaceuticals that are not on these formularies. PHARMAC uses a variety of mechanisms to obtain favourable prices, including competitive tendering, sole supply contracts, reference pricing, bundling deals, risk sharing agreements and promoting use of generics. Health technology assessment is used extensively in decision making and price negotiations. As a result, New Zealanders have universal and nationally consistent pharmaceutical coverage, with lower patient pharmaceutical co-payments than many comparable countries.

R. Ragupathy (✉) • K. Kilpatrick
Pharmacy Services, Waikato Hospital, Pembroke Street, Hamilton, New Zealand
e-mail: rajan.ragupathy@gmail.com; katelmkilpatrick@gmail.com

Z.-U.-D. Babar
School of Pharmacy, The University of Auckland, Private Mail Bag 92019, Auckland, New Zealand
e-mail: z.babar@auckland.ac.nz

Z.-U.-D. Babar (ed.), *Pharmaceutical Prices in the 21st Century*,
DOI 10.1007/978-3-319-12169-7_11

11.1 Introduction

This chapter discusses pharmaceutical pricing in New Zealand. The chapter focuses on the universal public health system and the public health system's monopsony pharmaceutical purchaser, the Pharmaceutical Management Agency of New Zealand (PHARMAC).

The structure of the New Zealand health system is briefly described, including financing and service provision. This is followed by an overview of the pharmacy system, including controls on ownership, contractual relationship with the public health system and pharmacy charges to consumers. The remit of Medsafe, the national drug regulatory authority, is also briefly described. The majority of the chapter describes PHARMAC's role within the public health system, its impact on the prices of publically funded medicines, and effects on public health. PHARMAC differs from many other pharmaceutical pricing agencies by integrating formulary setting, budget management, price negotiation and health technology assessment within the same agency. The chapter likewise considers these aspects of New Zealand's pharmaceutical pricing together. The pricing of pharmaceuticals that are not publically funded (and hence outside PHARMAC's remit) is also briefly discussed.

11.2 The New Zealand Health System

All New Zealand residents are covered by a national public health system. New Zealand's per capita health expenditure in 2011 was $3,182 United States Dollar Purchasing Power Parity (USD PPP). This was slightly below the OECD average of $3,322 USD PPP. New Zealand's per capita pharmaceutical expenditure was $284 USD PPP, the fifth lowest in the OECD, and well below the OECD average of $483 USD PPP (The Organisation for Economic Co-operation and Development 2013).

Approximately 80 % of all New Zealand's health expenditure is publically funded (The Commonwealth Fund 2010; The Organisation for Economic Co-operation and Development 2013). The public funding sources are central Government tax revenue (85 %), levies on employers including compulsory accident insurance contributions (7 %), and local Government (8 %) (The Commonwealth Fund 2010). The remaining 20 % of health expenditure largely consists of out-of-pocket patient contributions (co-payments). Private health insurance only accounts for 5 % of all health expenditure (The Organisation for Economic Co-operation and Development 2013).

The central Government tax revenue allocated to health is known as 'Vote Health'. Approximately 19 % of Vote Health is spent on national health programmes, including screening, maternity care and child health services (The New Zealand Ministry of Health 2013a). Over 75 % of Vote Health is allocated to regional organisations known as District Health Boards (DHBs), which are responsible for public health services for the people of their respective regions (The Commonwealth Fund 2010; The New Zealand Ministry of Health 2013a).

Each DHB has a funding arm (responsible for planning, funding and purchasing health services) and a provider arm (responsible for administering and staffing public health facilities) (The Commonwealth Fund 2010). The provider arms of DHBs provide roughly half of New Zealand's health services by value (The Commonwealth Fund 2010). This mainly consists of secondary and tertiary care, and includes pharmaceuticals for inpatient treatment within public hospitals (The Commonwealth Fund 2010).

DHBs also contract health services from private providers. These are mainly primary care providers such as general practitioners, but can also include elective surgical and other secondary care services (The Commonwealth Fund 2010). Most general practices belong to networks called Primary Health Organisations (PHOs), which are funded by DHBs to provide care for their enrolled populations (The Commonwealth Fund 2010). Patients who are enrolled in a PHO pay lower general practice and outpatient prescription co-payments, and 95 % of New Zealanders are enrolled in a PHO (The Commonwealth Fund 2010; The New Zealand Ministry of Health 2014a).

DHBs are responsible for funding outpatient pharmaceuticals, cancer treatments and vaccines for their eligible populations. PHARMAC is responsible for managing this spending on behalf of the DHBs, and ensuring that it remains within a set national budget each year (The Commonwealth Fund 2010; The Pharmaceutical Management Agency of New Zealand (PHARMAC) 2012a). PHARMAC's role is described in more detail in Sect. 11.5 of this chapter. It should be noted that DHB funding for prescription dispensing and other pharmacist services (which is described in Sect. 11.3) is distinct from the funding of pharmaceuticals.

The public health system also covers outpatient, inpatient, maternity and pre-natal care, national screening and immunisation programmes, and other public health services in addition to pharmaceuticals (The New Zealand Ministry of Health 2011b). These are largely publically funded (as described above), although patient co-payments are required for some services (The Commonwealth Fund 2010).

The public health system also covers some dental services, including preventive services for children, emergency care for both children and adults, and basic dental care for low-income adults in some areas (The New Zealand Ministry of Health 2011c). Treatment for injuries resulting from accidents is usually provided by the public health system, but is funded by the Accident Compensation Corporation (ACC), a publically funded no-fault accident compensation scheme that covers all New Zealanders (The New Zealand Ministry of Health 2011a). ACC also funds the treatment costs of injuries resulting from medical treatment, gradual work processes and violent crimes (The Accident Compensation Corporation 2013).

11.3 The New Zealand Pharmacy System

New Zealand pharmacies are an integral part of the New Zealand public health system. There are over 900 pharmacies in New Zealand, which dispense over 50 million prescriptions per year, as well as providing primary health care and facilitating the provision of medicines to thousands of New Zealanders (Pharmaceutical Society of New Zealand 2014). For this reason, the New Zealand pharmacy system is tightly controlled by robust laws and regulations to protect health and disability consumers.

The Medicines Act 1981 sets out strict laws regulating the ownership and operation of pharmacies in New Zealand. Each pharmacy must hold a license, which authorises the establishment of the pharmacy and the provision of pharmacy practice in that pharmacy (Medicines Act 1981). Licenses are issued and controlled by the Licensing Authority at the Ministry of Health (The New Zealand Ministry of Health 2010). Pharmacies that hold a valid license are able to operate a pharmacy if a New Zealand registered pharmacist is present to supervise the pharmacy.

Pharmacies may be owned by individuals, as a partnership or by a company (Medicines Act 1981). Most pharmacies in New Zealand are owned by companies. However, the majority share capital of the company must be held by a New Zealand registered pharmacist or a group of pharmacists. Companies are prohibited from operating or holding majority interest in more than five pharmacies at any one time. Similarly to companies, individuals either alone or in partnership may only operate a pharmacy if the majority interest is held by a pharmacist and held in no more than five pharmacies. There are also restrictions on authorised prescribers holding interests in a pharmacy. No authorised prescriber shall hold an interest in a pharmacy unless permission is given by the licensing authority (Medicines Act 1981). This prevents the delivery of health care being influenced by financial or commercial interests.

Pharmacies have contractual relationships with DHBs to provide specific services to certain patients, such as long term condition services, warfarin monitoring and methadone dispensing (New service model for community pharmacy 2012; New Zealand District Health Boards 2007). Pharmacies receive payments for providing these services in addition to funding for community pharmaceuticals (The Pharmaceutical Management Agency of New Zealand (PHARMAC) 2012b).

In July 2012 the Pharmacy Service model shifted from paying pharmacies based on each dispensing transaction to providing a patient-centered service (New service model for community pharmacy 2012). Pharmacies now receive a core service fee per patient, per pharmacy, per day and then a handling fee for each medicine dispensed (Central Region's Technology Advisory Services 2014). This is paid from the DHB budget via the Ministry of Health's centralised payment service (Pharmaceutical Management Agency of New Zealand (PHARMAC) 2014). This model has been developed to combat growth in pharmacy dispensing costs, which was considered unsustainable by the New Zealand Government (New service model for community pharmacy 2012).

Pharmaceutical products which are listed on the Pharmaceutical Schedule (a nationwide positive formulary of publically funded pharmaceuticals, administered by PHARMAC) will be reimbursed by DHBs. The medicine price listed in the Pharmaceutical Schedule indicates the amount of subsidy paid to community pharmacies for each medicine (before mark-ups and tax) (Wilson et al. 2014). This payment is made from the combined pharmaceutical budget (The Pharmaceutical Management Agency of New Zealand (PHARMAC) 2014b, c). Patients also make a co-payment for funded medicines, which is usually $5 New Zealand Dollars (NZD) per item. This co-payment is paid directly to the community pharmacy and is then subtracted from the pharmacy's invoice to the DHB (i.e. patients pay $5 NZD per item towards their medicines). If the manufacturer's medicine price exceeds the subsidy price, patients will then have to pay a manufacturers fee on top of the usual co-payment fee to receive the medicine (Wilson et al. 2014). This is considered a partially subsidised medicine, and the cost to the patient will vary between pharmacies based on the size of the mark-up the dispensing pharmacy charges (this will be discussed further in Sect. 11.6).

PHARMAC's aim is to publically fund a high volume of medicines across a wide range of therapeutic classes from the available pharmaceutical budget (The Pharmaceutical Management Agency of New Zealand (PHARMAC) 2014b, c). The strategies PHARMAC uses to achieve these goals are discussed in detail in Sect. 11.5 of this chapter.

11.4 Drug Regulatory Authority (Medsafe)

The New Zealand Medicines and Medical Devices Safety Authority (Medsafe) is the authority responsible for regulating all medicines in New Zealand (The New Zealand Medicines and Medical Devices Safety Authority (Medsafe) 2013). Medsafe is responsible for ensuring the safety, efficacy and quality of medicines through pre-marketing evaluation and post-marketing monitoring (The New Zealand Medicines and Medical Devices Safety Authority (Medsafe) 2013).

Medsafe is widely perceived to be an efficient and impartial regulator by key informants familiar with the New Zealand pharmaceutical system. Medsafe is perceived to have a cordial and professional relationship with the pharmaceutical industry that allowed the two to work together effectively, without compromising Medsafe's objectivity (Ragupathy 2013). This opinion was shared by a wide range of informants that included health professionals, pharmaceutical industry representatives, public servants, and elected representatives (Ragupathy 2013). Medsafe is currently harmonising its regulatory activities with the Australian Therapeutic Goods Administration (TGA). The eventual goal is the creation of a joint regulatory agency, the Australia New Zealand Therapeutic Products Agency (ANZTPA), which will regulate medicines in both countries (The Australia New Zealand Therapeutic Products Agency 2014).

Medsafe and PHARMAC each carry out their own evaluations of a given pharmaceutical, and make decisions independently of each other. This means that medicines approved by Medsafe will not necessarily be publically funded. Conversely, PHARMAC can on rare occasions fund medicines that have not been approved by Medsafe, or fund medicines for uses other than those approved by Medsafe (Best Practice Advocacy Centre New Zealand 2013).

11.5 Managing Pharmaceutical Spending in the Public Health System (PHARMAC)

11.5.1 PHARMAC's Role in the Public Health System

PHARMAC is responsible for negotiating the prices of pharmaceuticals used in the public health system, but its role goes much further. PHARMAC's statutory objective is "to secure for eligible people in need of pharmaceuticals, the best health outcomes that are reasonably achievable from pharmaceutical treatment and *from within the amount of funding provided*" (emphasis added) (The New Zealand Parliament 2000).

PHARMAC administers the Pharmaceutical Schedule, a nationwide positive formulary that lists which outpatient and cancer treatments are publically funded, along with special access schemes for some pharmaceuticals that are not on the Pharmaceutical Schedule. PHARMAC also decides the listing (or de-listing) of pharmaceuticals on the Pharmaceutical Schedule, along with variations on the conditions of listing. Neither the Government nor the Judiciary can order or block the listing of any pharmaceutical (Ragupathy 2013; Ragupathy et al. 2012a; Aaltonen et al. 2010; Raftery 2008; Cumming et al. 2010; Morgan et al. 2006).

PHARMAC also manages national pharmaceutical budgets for outpatient pharmaceuticals, and cancer treatments. PHARMAC conducts its own health technology assessments (see Sect. 11.5.3). Budgetary constraints and health technology assessments are incorporated into listing (or de-delisting) decisions and price negotiations (Ragupathy 2013; Ragupathy et al. 2012a; Aaltonen et al. 2010; Raftery 2008; Cumming et al. 2010; Morgan et al. 2006).

Another function of PHARMAC is to manage the funding of pharmaceuticals for patients in exceptional circumstances (i.e. situations not adequately provided for by the Pharmaceutical Schedule) (Pharmaceutical Management Agency (PHARMAC) 2013; Pharmaceutical Management Agency (PHARMAC) 2014a). This is a requirement of PHARMAC set out in the New Zealand Public Health and Disability Act 2000, and funding is from the combined pharmaceutical budget or individual DHB budgets (Pharmaceutical Management Agency (PHARMAC) 2013). The Named Patient Pharmaceutical Assessment (NPPA) is the framework PHARMAC uses to assess applications for subsidising pharmaceuticals in exceptional circumstances. NPPA is not used to provide access to *every* medicine not listed on the Pharmaceutical Schedule, but instead where the patient has unusual clinical circumstances, or if PHARMAC is considering or is likely to consider to fund the pharmaceutical in the future (Pharmaceutical Management Agency (PHARMAC) 2013).

PHARMAC's role is also expanding in ways that are likely to increase its ability to negotiate favourable prices. PHARMAC has been involved in managing inpatient pharmaceutical expenditure within DHBs since the launch of the National Hospital Pharmaceutical Strategy in 2002. The National Hospital Pharmaceutical Strategy included negotiating nationally consistent supply contracts (which reduced inpatient pharmaceutical prices by up to 90 %), along with providing health technology assessments to guide DHBs in their inpatient pharmaceutical formulary listing decisions, and promoting the quality use of medicines. However, each DHB retained final control over its own inpatient pharmaceutical formulary decisions, and managed its own budget for inpatient pharmaceuticals (Tordoff 2007). This led to concerns about variability in access based on where a patient lived, sometimes called 'post-code prescribing' (Ragupathy 2013; Ragupathy et al. 2012b).

In July 2013, all DHBs began using the Hospital Medicines List (HML), a nationally consistent inpatient prescribing formulary managed by PHARMAC. The HML replaced all DHB pharmaceutical formularies, and lists the pharmaceuticals that may be prescribed for inpatients, and the conditions under which these may be prescribed. If a pharmaceutical is not on the HML, it cannot be prescribed except through a Named Patient Pharmaceutical Assessment (NPPA) application, though there is some flexibility for urgent situations (Pharmaceutical Management Agency of New Zealand 2014a).

DHBs currently still manage individual budgets for inpatient pharmaceuticals, but PHARMAC will eventually undertake this role, just as it does for outpatient pharmaceuticals. Where a pharmaceutical is funded for both inpatient and outpatient use, PHARMAC aims to align the conditions under which it may be used in both instances (Pharmaceutical Management Agency (PHARMAC)). It has been argued that aligning the management of inpatient and outpatient pharmaceuticals under one agency makes New Zealand unique in the world (Dew and Davis 2014).

PHARMAC's scope is also moving beyond traditional pharmaceuticals. Since July 2012, PHARMAC has also been responsible for the purchase and management of vaccines, including those on the national childhood immunisation schedule. PHARMAC negotiates vaccine prices with manufacturers and makes listing decisions, as well as deciding changes to eligibility (The New Zealand Ministry of Health 2013b). PHARMAC has also begun taking over the purchasing and management of medical devices from individual DHBs, and is expected to be managing most medical devices by mid-2015 (Pharmaceutical Management Agency (PHARMAC) 2014b).

The concentration of so many powers and health technologies under one agency arguably place PHARMAC in very select company among pharmaceutical pricing agencies, if not actually making PHARMAC *sui generis*. PHARMAC even has the authority to fund pharmaceuticals or treatment protocols that have not been approved by New Zealand's drug regulatory agency (Best Practice Advocacy

Centre New Zealand 2013). Certainly none of the pharmaceutical pricing bodies in Australia, Canada, Finland, the United Kingdom, nor the United States combine nationwide jurisdiction with such broad powers (Ragupathy 2013; Ragupathy et al. 2012a; Aaltonen et al. 2010; Morgan et al. 2006). This gives PHARMAC much stronger levers for controlling pharmaceutical expenditure than many other agencies (Ragupathy et al. 2012a; Aaltonen et al. 2010; Raftery 2008; Cumming et al. 2010).

11.5.2 PHARMAC's Price Negotiation Strategy

In order to fund a large number of medicines, PHARMAC, use a number of techniques to operate within the fixed medicines budget. A central strategy for PHARMAC is promoting competition among pharmaceutical companies in order to keep prices low. Other commercial purchasing strategies include price negotiations, tendering for generic or sole supply contracts, and reference pricing for medicines with similar therapeutic effects (The Pharmaceutical Management Agency of New Zealand (PHARMAC) 2014b, c; Woodfield 2001).

PHARMAC also use price rebates for subsidised medicines and cross-product agreements (bundling) to keep prices low (The Pharmaceutical Management Agency of New Zealand (PHARMAC) 2014b, c; Morgan et al. 2007; Woodfield 2001). Pharmaceutical companies and PHARMAC may negotiate a price for a medicine, and DHBs will purchase the medicines at the stated price. However, after an agreed period of time the DHB will receive a rebate back from the pharmaceutical company, with the deal remaining confidential (The Pharmaceutical Management Agency of New Zealand (PHARMAC) 2014b, c; Management Sciences for Health 2012). A rebate may also be received for expenditure caps; when sales of a subsidised product exceed an agreed limit, the manufacturer will cover all or some of the costs to supply the medicine above the set expenditure cap (Morgan et al. 2007).

In the case of cross-product (bundling) agreements, PHARMAC may only agree to subsidise a new medicine in return for price reduction on one or more medicines already listed on the Pharmaceutical Schedule, produced by the same manufacturer (The Pharmaceutical Management Agency of New Zealand (PHARMAC) 2014b, c; Morgan et al. 2007). The listed price in the Pharmaceutical Schedule for the new medicine will be the manufacturer's international price, not including the overall discount obtained by PHARMAC for subsidising a bundle of medicines (The Pharmaceutical Management Agency of New Zealand (PHARMAC) 2014b, c; Morgan et al. 2007; Woodfield 2001).

Rebates, expenditure caps and cross-product agreements are all techniques which result in the Pharmaceutical Schedule listing a medicine price which is higher than the true price paid by DHBs (Wilson et al. 2014; The Pharmaceutical Management Agency of New Zealand (PHARMAC) 2014b, c). PHARMAC will agree with the manufacturer on the listed price and continue to protect details about the true price paid for the pharmaceutical. This method avoids other buyers (including those in other countries) from knowing what discount PHARMAC negotiated, and thereby requesting equivalent pricing discounts from pharmaceutical companies. These procurement techniques produce a lack of transparency, as the official medicine prices in the Pharmaceutical Schedule are often higher than the actual transactional price. However, these techniques are essential for PHARMAC to contain pharmaceutical expenditure in New Zealand and encourage access to a wide range of subsidised medicines.

11.5.3 PHARMAC's Health Technology Assessment

PHARMAC takes nine decision criteria into account when deciding whether a pharmaceutical will be publically funded, and at what price (The Pharmaceutical Management Agency of New Zealand (PHARMAC) 2006). These are:

1. The health needs of all eligible people within New Zealand
2. The particular health needs of Māori and Pacific People
3. The availability and suitability of existing medicines, therapeutic medical devices and related products and related things
4. The clinical benefits and risks of pharmaceuticals
5. The cost effectiveness of meeting health needs by funding pharmaceuticals rather than using other publicly funded health and disability support services
6. The budgetary impact (in terms of the pharmaceutical budget and the Government's overall health budget) of any changes to the Pharmaceutical Schedule
7. The direct cost to health service users
8. The Government's priorities for health funding, as set out in any objectives notified by the Crown to PHARMAC, or in PHARMAC's Funding Agreement, or elsewhere
9. Such other criteria as PHARMAC thinks fit. PHARMAC will carry out appropriate consultation when it intends to take any such "other criteria" into account (The Pharmaceutical Management Agency of New Zealand (PHARMAC) 2006)

It is worth noting that PHARMAC is carrying out consultation on these decision criteria at the time of writing (The Pharmaceutical Management Agency of New Zealand (PHARMAC) 2014a). Individual criteria may therefore be subject to change. However, PHARMAC's statutory obligation to remain within its capped budget means that health technology assessment (broadly speaking, criteria 3–6) is likely to remain a key part of PHARMAC's strategy.

PHARMAC takes clinical advice from its Pharmacology and Therapeutics Advisory Committee (PTAC). PTAC consists of senior medical practitioners who are highly experienced in their respective fields, and has specialist subcommittees with particular experience in a given field, such as oncology. PTAC members are expected to critically appraise each pharmaceutical's harms and benefits, and the strength of the evidence for these. (Well-designed randomised controlled trials and meta-analyses are the preferred sources of evidence, and the internal validity of the trials as well as their applicability to New Zealand clinical practice are considered). PTAC may recommend that the pharmaceutical be funded with a high, medium or low priority or that it be declined (Grocott et al. 2013). PTAC uses the same nine decision criteria in making its recommendation, but this recommendation is not the final PHARMAC decision (Grocott et al. 2013; Morgan et al. 2006).

PHARMAC also conducts economic evaluation of the pharmaceutical, along with price negotiations. PHARMAC's preferred method of economic evaluation is cost-utility analysis (CUA). This method of economic analysis produces a common outcome measure across all pharmaceutical treatments, namely the cost per Quality Adjusted Life Year (QALY) gained. PHARMAC takes a health system perspective in its economic analyses, which means that all public health system costs (not just pharmaceutical costs) are included in its analyses, along with potential savings (Grocott et al. 2013). Non health system costs (such as foregone tax revenue or increased social welfare spending from a patient's inability to work) are not included (Grocott et al. 2013).

As PHARMAC operates with a capped budget, and cost utility is only one of the decision criteria, PHARMAC does not use a 'cost utility threshold' (a cost per QALY level below which a pharmaceutical is likely to be funded). Between 1999 and 2007, the cost utility of new PHARMAC funding decisions varied from *savings* of NZ $40,000 per QALY to spending of over NZ $200,000 per QALY (Metcalf et al. 2012). Furthermore, New Zealand funded five of the ten pharmaceuticals that the United Kingdom's National Institute for Health and Care Excellence (NICE) had found to have the highest cost per QALY between 1996 and 2005 (Raftery 2008). Having a high cost per QALY doesn't therefore in itself preclude a pharmaceutical from being funded. However, there is widespread agreement among key informants that pharmaceuticals are assessed much more stringently for economic benefit than other New Zealand health investments, including non-pharmaceutical health technologies (Ragupathy et al. 2012b; Babar and Francis 2014).

11.6 Drug Pricing in New Zealand

11.6.1 Pharmaceutical Price Control

Unlike other OECD countries, in New Zealand there is no government price regulation for pharmaceuticals which are not listed on the Pharmaceutical Schedule (Organisation for Economic Co-operation and Development 2010; Kilpatrick et al. 2014). This means that manufacturers are able to set pharmaceutical prices at market entry without any restrictions such as profit controls, volume limitations or international reference pricing (United States Department of Commerce: International Trade Administration 2004).

If a medicine is publically funded, PHARMAC negotiates the price with the manufacturer, and the taxpayer subsidises all or part of the price for the patient. If a medicine is non-funded (i.e. not listed on the Pharmaceutical Schedule), the consumer must pay the full price out-of-pocket to receive the medicine.

The MIMS (Monthly Index of Medical Specialties) New Ethicals—a widely used prescribing reference—lists manufacturer prices for commonly prescribed medicines available in New Zealand (MIMS New Ethicals 2014). A wholesale mark-up is added to the manufacturer's price, which determines the pharmacy purchase price. The pharmacy is then able to add a mark-up to the medicine price which can be at any level (Burden of Disease Epidemiology and Equity and Cost-Effectiveness Programme (BODE)). A recommended mark-up in New Zealand is a multiplier of 1.86, but this is intended as a guide only. In reality community pharmacies may have mark-ups lower or higher than this (MIMS New Ethicals 2014). The total cost to the patient for non-funded medicines includes all three pricing components with no government control, and therefore varies for different medicines purchased at individual community pharmacies within New Zealand.

Recent evidence suggests the lack of government control on New Zealand medicine prices may lead to higher prices for non-funded medicines. In a 2013 study exploring medicine price differences between New Zealand and Europe, New Zealand consistently had high medicine prices compared to sixteen European countries for medicines not listed on the Pharmaceutical Schedule (i.e. medicines not funded in New Zealand) (Kilpatrick et al. 2014). The differences in medicine prices seen in the study are likely attributable to varying Government price controls and reimbursement policies between the countries investigated. The true impact of these findings is not fully known and further research is needed to determine the effect high non-funded medicine prices have on New Zealanders' access to medicine.

In 2012–2013 about 30 % of the New Zealand population had private health insurance (Health Funds Association of New Zealand 2013). Private health insurance can cover the cost of some pharmaceuticals and prescription charges for consumers with comprehensive care policies (Health Funds Association of New Zealand 2013). Private insurers are also able to negotiate medicine prices with pharmaceutical companies, which is especially significant for highly specialised, high cost pharmaceuticals not funded in New Zealand (Lakdawalla and Yin 2013; McCormack et al. 2009). The true cover provided by insurance companies is kept confidential and therefore it is not fully known to what extent non-funded medicines will be paid for by insurance companies. New Zealanders may also be unwilling to obtain private insurance for pharmaceuticals (2012c). Despite this, comprehensive care policies *may* allow some patients with private insurance access to funding for a wider range of pharmaceuticals.

Access to and affordability of medicines that are not publically funded may be a productive area for future research. Such research could include determining the effect high non-funded medicine prices have on New Zealand patients, the effectiveness of private insurance as means of accessing non-funded medicines, and the benefits and pitfalls of policy options such as pharmaceutical price controls for non-funded medicines.

However, as the vast majority of pharmaceutical spending in New Zealand is public spending (The Organisation for Economic Co-operation and Development 2013), the remainder of this chapter will focus on publically funded pharmaceuticals.

11.6.2 PHARMAC's Impact on the Price of Publically Funded Medicines

Medicine prices in New Zealand have significantly fallen since the introduction of PHARMAC in 1993 (The Pharmaceutical Management Agency of New Zealand (PHARMAC) 2014b, c). Figure 11.1 shows the impact PHARMAC has had on drug expenditure over time. The shaded area between the two lines represents the total savings since 2002. Cumulative savings attributed to PHARMAC from 2000 to 2010 was $4.37 billion (NZD) (The Pharmaceutical Management Agency of New Zealand (PHARMAC) 2013). These results are directly related to the purchasing techniques PHARMAC uses, which have been discussed above.

An example of the dramatic price reductions achieved by PHARMAC can be assessed using fluoxetine, a selective serotonin reuptake inhibitor. In 1993 fluoxetine 20 mg capsules cost $1.93 NZD/capsule, but referencing pricing with paroxetine brought the price down to $1.58 (The Pharmaceutical Management Agency of New Zealand PHARMAC and Evans 2008). There was a significant price reduction

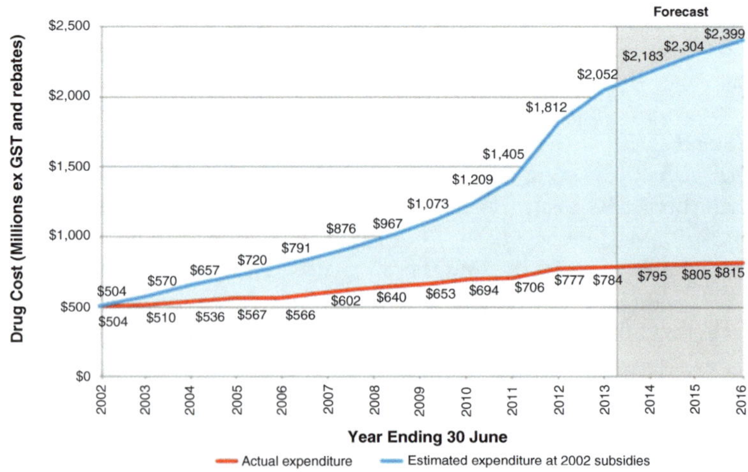

Fig. 11.1 Impact of PHARMAC on drug expenditure over time; actual and predicted expenditure from 2002 to 2016. Drug cost is expressed in millions of New Zealand Dollars excluding GST and rebates (Pharmaceutical Management Agency (PHARMAC) 2013)

on paroxetine which took the price of fluoxetine to $1.12 due to reference pricing. Following this, the introduction of generics in 2000 produced a price of $0.45. Subsequent price reductions, reference pricing and sole supply led to a price of $0.05 in 2004 which is a cumulative reduction of 97 %. In 2012 the price had reduced further to $0.032/capsule (The Pharmaceutical Management Agency of New Zealand (PHARMAC) and Evans 2008). This example shows some of the key techniques used by PHARMAC to achieve significant price reductions over time. Despite this, the lack of transparency for medicine prices published in the Pharmaceutical Schedule makes it impossible to determine the exact medicine price changes over time in New Zealand.

Many OECD countries have policies in place to support the use of generic medicines (Derek et al. 2002). When a patent expires, generic medicines will emerge with lower medicine prices than the originator. New Zealand also has policies in place to support the uptake of generic medicines, and to create competition between different generic manufacturers through tendering (The Pharmaceutical Management Agency of New Zealand (PHARMAC) 2014b, c). In 2013 almost half of all medicines purchased (by volume) were through multi product tendering, which represents 20 % of the combined pharmaceutical budget (The Pharmaceutical Management Agency of New Zealand (PHARMAC)). The large number of medicines available in generic brands produces a significant price saving, which can be reinvested to subsidise other new medicines on the Pharmaceutical Schedule.

11.7 The Impact of Pricing on Public Health (Access and Affordability of Medicines)

The impact of PHARMAC's cost-containment strategies on the health of New Zealanders has been a source of considerable controversy (Ragupathy 2013). At the broadest level, the debate focuses on the impact funding or not funding particular medicines has on New Zealanders' health outcomes, both in absolute terms and relative to comparable countries (Castalia Strategic Advisors 2005; Business and Economic Research Limited (BERL) 2005; Easton 2005). However, linking differences in access to medicines to health outcomes is difficult, due to multiple confounding factors such as differences in demographics, environmental and lifestyle factors, access to screening, and waiting times for treatment (Ragupathy 2013).

There has also (until recently) been a dearth of systematic, peer-reviewed comparisons of New Zealanders' overall access to publically funded medicines relative to comparable countries (Ragupathy 2013). Past controversies have therefore focused on smaller parts of the access picture. These included particular PHARMAC techniques such as sole supply tendering or funding switches for HMG CoA Reductase Inhibitors (statins) (Begg et al. 2003; MacKay 2005), funding for sub-types of medicines such high cost and highly specialised medicines (McCormack et al. 2009), or the funding of medicines for particular indications, such trastuzumab for early stage HER2 positive breast cancer (Isaacs et al. 2007). These controversies had to be considered in light of the fact PHARMAC had considerably expanded the number of publically funded medicines while restraining the growth in pharmaceutical expenditure (Cumming et al. 2010).

In recent years, published studies have compared New Zealand's access to publically funded medicines with publically funded health systems in Finland, Australia, the United Kingdom and the United States (Ragupathy et al. 2012a; Aaltonen et al. 2010; Wonder and Milne 2011). Taken together, these studies do much to clarify the impact of PHARMAC's strategies on public access to medicines.

PHARMAC funded fewer medicines than Finland's public health system in 2007, 471 unique entities compared to 495 (Aaltonen et al. 2010). PHARMAC also funded fewer entities (503) than the Australian Pharmaceutical Benefit's Scheme (567), the United Kingdom's National Health Service (1016) and the United States Department of Veterans Affairs National Formulary (505) in 2007 (Ragupathy et al. 2012a). The above study also compared access to innovative entities that provided important health gains. PHARMAC subsidised 19 of the 65 innovative entities in 2007, compared with 30 by the Pharmaceutical Benefits Scheme (and a further four by the Life Saving Drugs Program, which operates alongside the Pharmaceutical Benefits Scheme in Australia), 58 by the National Health Service, and 20 by the Department of Veterans Affairs National Formulary (Ragupathy et al. 2012a).

A separate comparison of Australia and New Zealand found that PHARMAC only subsidised 59 (43 %) of the 136 new prescription medicines subsidised by the Pharmaceutical Benefits Scheme between 2000 and 2009 (conversely, only four medicines were subsidised by PHARMAC but not the Pharmaceutical Benefits Scheme). The 59 medicines were on average subsidised later by PHARMAC than by the Pharmaceutical Benefits Scheme (mean difference 32.7 months, $p < 0.0001$) (Wonder and Milne 2011).

Though it has been shown that PHARMAC subsidises fewer medicines than its comparators, however its impact on public health and health outcomes is not fully known (Babar and Vitry 2014). Also, while evaluating the impact of PHARMAC on New Zealanders' health, many other factors should be taken into account. These include universality and equity of coverage, the restrictions placed on how subsidised medicines may be prescribed, and patient cost sharing (Ragupathy 2013; Raftery 2008). It is worth noting that unlike the situation in the United States, where publicly funded systems such as Department of Veterans Affairs National Formulary or Medicare only cover selected subsets of the population, PHARMAC covers all New Zealand residents. Similarly, unlike the United Kingdom, where variable decisions by local funding bodies can lead to 'post-code prescribing', PHARMAC's coverage is nationally consistent (Ragupathy 2013).

Over 86 % of the entities subsidised by PHARMAC in 2007 were fully subsidised, which meant most patients only paid a fixed \$3 NZD co-payment for up to 3 months' supply (this co-payment has since been increased to $5 NZD) (Aaltonen et al. 2010). Furthermore, 69 % of entities were fully subsidised without any restrictions on how they could be prescribed. PHARMAC's strategy appears to be providing fully subsidised options across almost all therapeutic areas, including options for symptom relief such as analgesics and antacids (Aaltonen et al. 2010). The co-payments and yearly maximum payments for PHARMAC subsidised medicines are lower than other comparable systems (Ragupathy et al. 2012a; Aaltonen et al. 2010). Co-payments in New Zealand for funded medicines are currently $5 NZD per item, up to a maximum of 20 co-payments per family per year. Once this threshold is met (i.e. once a patient or family spend $100 NZD per year on medicines), patients no longer need to pay the co-payment to receive their medicines (The New Zealand Ministry of Health 2014b). Less than 3 % of New Zealanders spent more than $1,000 USD on out of pocket payments for prescription medicines, compared with 5 % in Australia and 13.2 % in the United States (Morgan and Kennedy 2010). The 10 % of New Zealanders who reported not filling prescriptions or skipping doses in a year because of cost was lower than in Australia (13.4 %) and the United States (23.1 %).

The impact of PHARMAC's strategies on New Zealanders' public health could therefore be seen as a trade-off. A degree of therapeutic choice (including access to new and innovative medicines, and medicines for rare conditions) is traded for equity of access to the medicines that are subsidised, and maximising the affordability of medicines to both patient and taxpayer. Whether the right balance has been struck between these competing priorities is likely to remain a source of debate.

11.8 Country Summary: New Zealand

New Zealand does not rely on legal controls of manufacturers' selling prices, profits or mark-ups to ensure affordable pharmaceutical prices. Rather, the price is determined by the relative negotiating power of the seller and the buyer. Individuals who privately purchase non-funded pharmaceuticals may therefore pay higher prices than in many other countries.

However, the New Zealand pharmaceutical market is dominated by its public health system, and therefore by PHARMAC. PHARMAC's monopsony on publically funded pharmaceuticals and its statutory independence in decision-making give it a very strong bargaining position. PHARMAC leverages these advantages effectively in order to maximise its capped budget, and uses a variety of techniques such as competitive tendering, reference pricing, generic substitution and bundling agreements. Health technology assessment also plays a key role in funding decisions. This has allowed PHARMAC to drastically restrain the growth of New Zealand's pharmaceutical expenditure while expanding access to medicines.

Given PHARMAC's central role in determining New Zealanders' access to pharmaceuticals, controversies about its decisions and processes are inevitable. Despite this, PHARMAC has benefited from a broad political consensus, and this stability has allowed it to focus on negotiating favourable prices. Its role has expanded considerably, and now encompasses outpatient and inpatient pharmaceuticals, cancer treatments, vaccines, and medical devices. PHARMAC is therefore likely to be a feature of the New Zealand health system for many years to come.

Glossary

ACC Accident Compensation Corporation
ANZTPA Australia New Zealand Therapeutic Products Agency
DHB District Health Board
HML Hospital Medicines List
Medsafe New Zealand Medicines and Medical Devices Safety Authority
NICE National Institute for Health and Care Excellence (United Kingdom)
NPPA Named Patient Pharmaceutical Assessment
OECD Organisation for Economic Co-operation and Development
PHARMAC Pharmaceutical Management Agency of New Zealand
PHO Primary Health Organisation
PTAC Pharmacology and Therapeutics Advisory Committee
QALY Quality Adjusted Life Year
TGA Therapeutic Goods Administration (Australia)

References

Aaltonen K, Ragupathy R, Tordoff J, Reith D, Norris P (2010) The impact of pharmaceutical cost containment policies on the range of medicines available and subsidized in Finland and New Zealand. Value Health 13(1):148–156

Babar Z-U-D, Francis S (2014) Identifying priority medicines policy issues for New Zealand. BMJ Open 4(5):e004415

Babar Z-U-D, Vitry A (2014) Differences in Australian and New Zealand medicines funding policies. Australian Prescriber 2014, Online First 8th July. http://www.australianprescriber.com/online-first/54/differences-in-australian-and-new-zealand-medicines-funding-policies

Begg E, Sidwell A, Gardiner S, Nicholls G, Scott R (2003) The sorry saga of statins in New Zealand—pharmacopolitics versus patient care. N Z Med J 116(1170):U360

Best Practice Advocacy Centre New Zealand (2013) Upfront: unapproved medicines and unapproved uses of medicines: keeping prescribers and patients safe. Best Pract J 51

Burden of Disease Epidemiology, Equity and Cost-Effectiveness Programme (BODE) (2011) Costing of pharmaceuticals in New Zealand for health economic studies: backgrounder and protocol for costing. Public Health Monograph Series, No. 20, Technical report no. 6. ISSN: 1178–7139. Department of Public Health, University of Otago, Wellington

Business and Economic Research Limited (BERL) (2005) Independent review of the Castalia report on New Zealand pharmaceutical policies. http://www.pharmac.govt.nz/2006/05/04/040506b.pdf. 2014

Castalia Strategic Advisors (2005) New Zealand pharmaceutical policies: time to take a fresh look. http://www.castalia-advisors.com/files/14634.pdf. 2014

Central Region's Technology Advisory Services Pharmacy Today (2014) New service model for community pharmacy. http://webcache.googleusercontent.com/search?q=cache:tAHjiOt2P7sJ:www.pharmacytoday.co.nz/media/349234/pharmacy_services_agreement_q_a.doc+&cd=1&hl=en&ct=clnk&gl=n. 2014

Cumming J, Mays N, Daubé J (2010) Analysis: how New Zealand has contained expenditure on drugs. BMJ 340:c2441

Derek R, King R, Kanavos P (2002) Encouraging the use of generic medicines: implications for transition economies. Croat Med J 43(4):462–469

Dew K, Davis A (2014) Limits to neoliberal reforms in the health sector: the case of pharmaceutical management in New Zealand. Int J Health Serv 44(1):137–153

Easton B (2005) New Zealand's pharmaceutical policies: a fresh look. http://www.pharmac.govt.nz/2006/05/04/040506a.pdf. 2014

Grocott R, Metcalf S, Alexander P, Werner R (2013) Assessing the value for money of pharmaceuticals in New Zealand—PHARMAC's approach to cost-utility analysis. N Z Med J 126 (1378)

Health Funds Association of New Zealand (2013) Annual review: 2013. http://www.healthfunds.org.nz/pdf/2013-annual-review.pdf. 2014

Isaacs R, Frampton C, Kuper-Hummel M (2007) PHARMAC's funding of 9 weeks Herceptin: many assumptions in a high-risk decision. N Z Med J 120 (1259)

Kilpatrick K, Vogler S, Babar Z (2014) Proceedings of the Waikato Clinical School Biannual Research Seminar, March 2014. Analysis of prices of medicines in Europe and in New Zealand. N Z Med J 127 (1393)

Lakdawalla D, Yin W (2013) Insurers' negotiating leverage and the external effects of Medicare part D. National Bureau of Economic Research, Boston

MacKay P (2005) Is PHARMAC's sole-supply tendering policy harming the health of New Zealanders? N Z Med J 118(1214):U1433

Management Sciences for Health (2012) Pharmaceutical pricing policy. Management Sciences for Health, Medford

McCormack P, Quigley J, Hansen P (2009) Review of access to high cost, highly specialised medicines in New Zealand. Report to Minister of Health, Hon Tony Ryall. Wellington

Medicines Act (1981) Effect of licences. 118, vol. 1e. Wellington

Metcalf S, Rodgers A, Werner R, Schousboe C (2012) PHARMAC has no cost-effectiveness threshold. N Z Med J 125 (1350)

Morgan S, Kennedy J (2010) Prescription drug accessibility and affordability in the United States and abroad. Commonw Fund 89:1–12

Morgan S, McMahon M, Mitton C, Roughead E, Kirk R, Kanavos P, Menon D (2006) Centralized drug review processes in Australia, Canada, New Zealand and the United Kingdom. Health Aff (Millwood) 25(2):337–347

Morgan S, Hanley G, McMahon M, Barer M (2007) Influencing drug prices through formulary-based policies: lessons from New Zealand. Health Policy 3(1):121–140

MIMS New Ethicals (2014) January–June 2014 edn. UBM Medica NZ, Auckland

New service model for community pharmacy (2012). Best Prac J (45)

New Zealand District Health Boards (2007) DHB shared services: pharmacy services agreement for the provision of pharmacy services. http://www.dhbsharedservices.health.nz/site/sig/npsf/toolkit/service-agreements.aspx. 2014

Organisation for Economic Co-operation and Development (2010) Value for money in health spending: drawing all the benefits from pharmaceutical spending

Pharmaceutical Management Agency (2013) Pharmaceutical Management Agency annual report 2012/13. Wellington

Pharmaceutical Management Agency (PHARMAC) (2013) Named patient pharmaceutical assessment (exceptional circumstances) policy. http://www.pharmac.health.nz/assets/nppa-policy-2013-07.pdf

Pharmaceutical Management Agency (PHARMAC) (2014a) Named Patient Pharmaceutical Assessment (NPPA) Questions and Answers for clinicians. http://www.pharmac.health.nz/assets/nppa-clinician-info-sheet.pdf

Pharmaceutical Management Agency (PHARMAC) (2014b) PHARMAC and hospital medical devices. http://www.pharmac.health.nz/medicines/hospital-devices

Pharmaceutical Management Agency of New Zealand (PHARMAC) (2014c) http://www.pharmac.health.nz

Pharmaceutical Society of New Zealand (2014) What is pharmacy? http://www.psnz.org.nz/public/home/careers/intro.aspx

Raftery J (2008) Paying for costly pharmaceuticals: regulation of new drugs in Australia, England and New Zealand. Med J Aust 188(1):26–28

Ragupathy Y (2013) New Zealanders' access to licensed and subsidised medicines compared with a nationwide single payer system in each of Australia, the United Kingdom and the United States. Doctor of Philosophy, University of Otago, Dunedin

Ragupathy R, Aaltonen K, Tordoff J, Norris P, Reith D (2012a) A 3-dimensional view of access to licensed and subsidized medicines under single payer systems in the United States, United Kingdom, Australia and New Zealand. Pharmacoeconomics 30(11):1051–1065

Ragupathy R, Tordoff J, Norris P, Reith D (2012b) Key informants perceptions of how PHARMAC operates in New Zealand. Int J Technol Assess Health Care 28(4):367–373

Ragupathy R, Udin-Babar Z, Chandra H, Daiya M, Girn M, Mirza W, Yousif A (2012c) Proceedings of the Waikato Clinical School biannual research seminar, March 2012. Son of Doctor Strangelove: how we learned to stop worrying and love PHARMAC (New Zealand consumers' perceptions of private insurance for pharmaceuticals). N Z Med J 125(1352)

The Accident Compensation Corporation (2013) ACC frequently asked questions. http://www.acc.co.nz/about-acc/media-centre/frequently-asked-questions/index.htm. Accessed June 2014

The Australia New Zealand Therapeutic Products Agency (2014) Transition to the Australia New Zealand Therapeutic Products Agency. http://www.anztpa.org/index.htm. 2014

The Commonwealth Fund (2010) International profiles of health care systems

The New Zealand Medicines and Medical Devices Safety Authority (Medsafe) (2013) About Medsafe. http://www.medsafe.govt.nz/other/about.asp#pre. 2014

The New Zealand Ministry of Health (2010) Pharmacy licensing. http://www.health.govt.nz/our-work/regulation-health-and-disability-system/medicines-control/pharmacy-licensing. 2014

The New Zealand Ministry of Health (2011a) Accident cover. https://www.health.govt.nz/new-zealand-health-system/publicly-funded-health-and-disability-services/accident-cover. 2014

The New Zealand Ministry of Health (2011b) Publically funded health services. https://www.health.govt.nz/new-zealand-health-system/publicly-funded-health-and-disability-services. 2014

The New Zealand Ministry of Health (2011c) Visiting a dentist. https://www.health.govt.nz/new-zealand-health-system/publicly-funded-health-and-disability-services/visiting-dentist. 2014

The New Zealand Ministry of Health (2013a) Funding. http://www.health.govt.nz/new-zealand-health-system/overview-health-system/funding. 2014

The New Zealand Ministry of Health (2013b) Vaccine purchasing. http://www.health.govt.nz/our-work/preventative-health-wellness/immunisation/immunisation-programme-decisions/vaccine-purchasing. 2014

The New Zealand Ministry of Health (2014a) Enrolment in a primary health organisation. http://www.health.govt.nz/our-work/primary-health-care/about-primary-health-organisations/enrolment-primary-health-organisation. 2014

The New Zealand Ministry of Health (2014b) Prescription charges. http://www.health.govt.nz/your-health/conditions-and-treatments/treatments-and-surgery/medications/prescription-charges. 2014

The New Zealand Parliament (2000) New Zealand public health and disability act, Wellington

The Organisation for Economic Co-operation and Development (2013) Health at a glance 2013-OECD indicators

The Pharmaceutical Management Agency of New Zealand (PHARMAC) (2006) Operating policies and procedures of the Pharmaceutical Management Agency ("PHARMAC"). 3rd ed., Wellington

The Pharmaceutical Management Agency of New Zealand (PHARMAC) (2012a) Introduction to PHARMAC. http://www.pharmac.health.nz/assets/infosheet-01-intro-2013.pdf. 2014

The Pharmaceutical Management Agency of New Zealand (PHARMAC) (2012b) Our place in the system. http://www.pharmac.health.nz/assets/infosheet-01-intro-2013.pdf. 2014

The Pharmaceutical Management Agency of New Zealand (PHARMAC) (2013) PHARMAC's history. http://www.pharmac.health.nz/assets/infosheet-02-history-2013.pdf. 2014

The Pharmaceutical Management Agency of New Zealand (PHARMAC) (2014a) Pharmac's decision criteria—proposal for change. Wellington

The Pharmaceutical Management Agency of New Zealand (PHARMAC) (2014b) Purchasing medicines. http://www.pharmac.health.nz/assets/infosheet-05-purchasing-medicines-2013.pdf

The Pharmaceutical Management Agency of New Zealand (PHARMAC) (2014c) Setting and managing the combined pharmaceutical budget. http://www.pharmac.health.nz/assets/infosheet-08-community-pharm-budget-2013.pdf

The Pharmaceutical Management Agency of New Zealand (PHARMAC), Evans J (2008) Freeing up funds: fluoxetine 20 mg capsules. http://www.pharmac.govt.nz/2008/07/03/Pharmaceutical%20Funding%20presentation.pdf. 2014

Tordoff J (2007) Evaluating the impact of a national hospital pharmaceutical strategy in New Zealand. University of Otago, Dunedin

United States Department of Commerce: International Trade Administration (2004) Pharmaceutical price controls in OECD countries. Implications for U.S. consumers, pricing, research and development, and innovation. Washington

Wilson K, Bloor R, Jennings D (eds) (2014) New Zealand Pharmaceutical Schedule. Pharmaceutical Management Agency, Wellington

Wonder M, Milne R (2011) Access to new medicines in New Zealand compared to Australia. N Z Med J 124(1346)

Woodfield A (2001) Augmenting reference pricing of pharmaceuticals in New Zealand with strategic cross-product agreements. Pharmacoeconomics 19(4):365–377

Chapter 12
Pharmaceutical Pricing Policies in Norway and Sweden

Helle Håkonsen and Karolina Andersson Sundell

Abstract This chapter provides an overview of the organization of pricing, reimbursement of medicines, and the organization of the pharmaceutical systems in the two Scandinavian countries Norway and Sweden. The two countries have many similarities; however, they have also chosen different roads in several aspects. Both countries have a comprehensive tax-based public health insurance covering health services for all inhabitants. This includes medicines provided to cure, alleviate or prevent diseases that have been judged to be in the interest of the public. Pricing of prescribed medicines is strictly regulated in the two countries. More than 70 % of the total pharmaceutical expenditures are paid by a public third-party payer. Both countries experienced dramatic increase in pharmaceutical expenditures in the early 1990s. This set off a series of reforms concerning the pricing and reimbursement of medicines. The fundamental principle for pricing of prescription medicines is maximum pricing at the retail level. Norway applies international reference pricing while Sweden's pricing system is based on health economic evaluations. Pricing is tied to the process of marketing in Norway and to reimbursement in Sweden. Both countries have applied mandatory generic substitution for more than 10 years.

12.1 Introduction

The Scandinavian countries Norway and Sweden have always been closely linked to each other and there has been an extensive migration between the countries. Sweden has approximately twice the population of Norway but in terms of other key characteristics, they are fairly similar (Table 12.1).

H. Håkonsen (✉)
School of Pharmacy, University of Oslo, Oslo, Norway

Institute of Medicine, University of Gothenburg, Gothenburg, Sweden
e-mail: helle.hakonsen@farmasi.uio.no

K. Andersson Sundell
Institute of Medicine, University of Gothenburg, Gothenburg, Sweden
e-mail: karolina.a.sundell@gu.se

Z.-U.-D. Babar (ed.), *Pharmaceutical Prices in the 21st Century*,
DOI 10.1007/978-3-319-12169-7_12

Table 12.1 Overview of key characteristics

	Norway	Sweden
Population	5.0 million	9.6 million
Life expectancy at birth	81.6 (2013)	81.9 (2013)
Elderly rate (above 65 years old)	15.2 % (2011)	18.6 % (2011)
GDP per capita	61,897 USD (2011)	41,761 USD (2011)

Both countries have taken part in the European internal market since 1995; Sweden as a member of the European Union (EU) and Norway through their agreement with the European Economic Area (EEA). However, none of the countries are members of European Monetary Union and hence have their own currency (Norwegian Krone/Swedish Krona). Membership in the EU/EEA has had certain implications for health policy in regards of market authorizations for pharmaceuticals and other regulations regarding competition in the pharmaceutical market. Large reforms in the pharmacy sector in the mid-1990s onwards arose to some extent as a result of these changes (Norris 1998).

Reforms were also introduced as a consequence of a dramatic increase in pharmaceutical expenditures that raised attention in the early 1990s (Hågå and Sverre 2002; Ljungkvist et al. 1997). These reforms included the composition of the reimbursement schemes, introduction of the firm pricing models and stimulation of price competition by reference-based pricing and generic substitution (Gerdtham et al. 1998; Andersson et al. 2006, 2007; Håkonsen et al. 2009a). In Sweden, the reforms also concerned transferring the financial responsibility for reimbursed medicines from the Swedish government to the county councils on regional level (Bergström and Karlberg 2007). On the clinical side, all county councils were obliged to have Drugs and Therapeutics Committees since 1998 (Godman et al. 2009) with the purpose to facilitate and increase rational use of medicines.

This chapter aims to present an overview of the Scandinavian regulations of pharmaceutical pricing. It also discusses how these regulations have developed as results of the changes experienced in the pharmacy systems over the last decades. The first part of the chapter provides a brief introduction to key characteristics of the Scandinavian health care systems including the pharmaceutical benefit schemes. Thereafter, the drug regulatory authorities involved in the two countries and the pharmacy systems are outlined. It also describes how and why extensive deregulation of these systems came about in 2001 (Norway) and 2009 (Sweden). The pharmaceutical pricing policies are discussed in terms of drug pricing set-up for medicines used in outpatient and inpatient care, how the prices are set and in what way the authorities enable price revisions. The last part of the chapter presents the case of generic medicines policies and a brief discussion of how these have been successful for public cost containment.

12.2 Scandinavian Health Systems

12.2.1 Organisation of Health Care

The Scandinavian health care systems have developed gradually in the context of welfare policy where a key characteristic is the predominance of tax-financed public provision (Magnussen et al. 2009). The aim is to improve the general health of the population and reduce mortality and morbidity as well as social inequalities in health. An important aspect of the Scandinavian policy model is to provide access to basic welfare services independently of income and employment status. Membership in the Norwegian National Insurance Scheme ("Folketrygden") or the Swedish National Health Insurance is mandatory for all citizens and indirectly paid through taxation. Health care services, including primary care and hospitals, are financed primarily by block grants from the government[1] (Anell et al. 2012; Bjorvatn 2012; Hågå and Sverre 2002).

In Norway, health care is organized on two levels beneath the central State. The 428 municipalities take care of provision and funding of primary health care, while four regional health authorities (RHAs) are responsible for financing, planning and providing specialized care under the supervisory responsibility of the ministry. In 2014 there were 20 hospitals and 32 hospital pharmacies under the four RHAs, which are non-profit public organizations.

In Sweden the 21 county councils located on regional level are responsible for the provision of health care including medicines to their inhabitants (Anell et al. 2012). The county councils also have a certain proportion of the taxes that they can decide on independently. They are funded both by their own direct taxes and indirect through taxes by money from the government. The county councils collaborate with each other within the Swedish Associations of Local Authorities and Regions (SALAR) which is the counterpart discussing funding with the government.

Primary care is organised around general practitioner (GP) practices or primary health care facilities. All inhabitants are entitled to a regular GP (in Norway) or a primary health care facility which usually involves more than one GP (in Sweden). In Norway GP practices are private but on contract with the municipalities whereas in Sweden primary health care facilities are operated by the county council or by private actors on contracts with the county council (Beckman and Anell 2013; Grasdal and Monstad 2011).

[1] In July 1997 the funding system of Norwegian hospitals was changed to a combination of block grants and activity-based financed reimbursements based on Diagnosis Related Group (DRG) prices, mainly aiming at providing incentives for the hospitals to increase the treatment activity (Bjorvatn 2012).

Table 12.2 Overview of health care and pharmaceutical expenditures in the two countries

	Norway	Sweden
Health expenditures (% of GDP)	9.3 % (2011)	9.5 % (2011)
Pharmaceutical expenditure as a percentage of health expenditures	10.3 % (2011)	14.9 % (2011)
Pharmaceutical expenditure in USD purchasing power parity/per capita	585.3 (2011)	583.7 (2011)
Patient co-payment structure	Joint co-payment for health care and medicines	Separate co-payment for health care and medicines
Medicine co-payment	Fixed proportion of the price (38 % up to the annual ceiling)[a]	Regressive proportion of the price depending on total co-payment paid during the period
Maximum annual co-payment	NOK 2105[b,c]	SEK2200[c]

[a]Low income pensioners and children under 16 are exempted
[b]Includes co-payments for physician consultations, laboratory tests, radiography, etc.
[c]NOK 1 = € 0.12; SEK 1 = € 0.11 (exchange rates of July 3, 2014)

12.2.2 Pharmaceutical Benefit Scheme

The Scandinavian countries have by tradition a large public sector and hence a high degree of public third-party payment for pharmaceuticals. The purpose of the pharmaceutical benefit scheme (PBS) is to ensure equal access to effective drugs in the society. At the same time the PBS encourages clinically rational and cost-effective use of medicines to ensure investments in the health care services.

Table 12.2 shows an overview of health care and pharmaceutical expenditures in Norway and Sweden. The proportion of pharmaceutical expenditures appears low because of the large total expenditures on health. The total pharmaceutical expenditures can be subdivided into prescribed medicines and over-the-counter (OTC) medicines used in outpatient care, and medicines provided in hospitals. Prescribed medicines account for almost 70 % of the total pharmaceutical expenditures and OTC medicines for around 10 %. Medicines funded by hospitals stand for roughly 20 % (LMI 2014; Socialstyrelsen 2014).

The first versions of the PBS established in the mid-50s were intended to cover expensive essential medicines. With time a progressively increasing number of drugs for the treatment of chronic conditions and certain infectious diseases was included. The dimension of the PBS has continued to increase steadily. Among prescribed medicines, between 80 and 90 % of the costs are attributable to medicines included in the PBS (LMI 2014; Socialstyrelsen 2014). Of these, patient co-payments constitute about 20 % or even less while the remaining part is paid by the public third party payer. Thus in total reimbursed prescribed medicines paid by the third party payer account for 50 % of the pharmaceutical expenditures (LMI 2014; Socialstyrelsen 2014).

All inhabitants with a valid personal identification number are entitled to purchase medicines within the PBS. Moreover, EU/EES citizens are included when the need for medicines arise while they are in Norway or Sweden. Co-payments are based on the price of the product (Table 12.2). For refugees and asylum seekers, a special program is applied where the patients pay a fixed fee per filled prescription. The PBS covers medicines primarily for chronic or long-term illnesses (at least 3 months per year) used in outpatient care (Act on Pharmaceutical Benefits 2002; Regulation on reimbursement 2007). Medicines given during hospital stays are incorporated within the health care provided by the RHAs (Norway) or the county councils (Sweden) (Hågå and Sverre 2002; Lundkvist 2002). The medicines need to be prescribed by an authorized prescriber, and must be intended to prevent, diagnose, alleviate, or cure an illness or a symptom of illness. Both countries have positive lists of the products covered by the PBS. There are special tracks for certain infectious diseases for which medicines are provided for free to the patients (e.g. tuberculosis, syphilis or HIV/AIDS) as well as for vaccines included in the national vaccine program. In Norway, short-term therapy and OTC medicines are generally not included in the PBS. OTC medicines used for long-term treatment and certain short-term treatments such as antibiotics are included in the Swedish PBS.

Since 1997, the Swedish county councils have also been responsible for the costs of medicines within the PBS (Jansson and Anell 2006). Many county councils have even decentralized the budget responsibility for medicines within the PBS to health care facilities (Bergström and Karlberg 2007; Jansson and Anell 2006; Sandheimer and Karlberg 2013).

Reimbursement is product specific in both countries.[2] Health economic evaluations are required in the application of inclusion in the PBS. The cost-effectiveness evaluations should apply a societal perspective and include all effects and costs irrespective of who the payer is. Thus it includes indirect costs for production loss such as sickness absence or reduced productivity. An agreed price is a prerequisite for reimbursement. Thus if a price cannot be agreed on reimbursement may not be granted or it can be taken off the product (Act on Pharmaceutical Benefits 2002).

The reimbursement decision is guided by three principles:

- The cost-effectiveness principle—the cost of using a medicine should be reasonable from a medical, humanitarian, and societal economical perspective
- The needs and solidarity principle—those with the largest medical needs shall be granted more of the health care resources than other patient groups.
- The human value principle—the heath care shall show respect to the equal value for all humans

[2] A generic equivalent to an already marketed product on the Norwegian market is given the same reimbursement status as the original product.

Both countries have two main types of reimbursement. The Norwegian reimbursement scheme consists of general and individual reimbursement. General reimbursement accounts for more than 90 % of the reimbursed drug sales. This type of reimbursement is applicable when the product is on the list of reimbursable drugs and shall be used for a diagnosis approved for reimbursement. In some cases additional conditions must be met, e.g. that more cost-effective (preferred) drugs are tried first (Sundar et al. 2006). Individual reimbursement may be appropriate if the patient should be treated with a drug that is not listed on the reimbursement list for the disease in question. To be granted this kind of reimbursement, the prescriber has to apply on behalf of the patient and give a medical justification. There is also an application scheme for expensive drugs on regular prescriptions (the "contribution scheme") (Hågå and Sverre 2002).

In Sweden, the reimbursement status can be either general (most common) or limited. Within the general reimbursement, use for all approved indications of the product is covered. If a product has limited reimbursement, it is only reimbursed when used for a specific indication or in a specific patient group. Reasons for limited reimbursement can be that the product is cost-effective only for a limited patient group or indication. The prescriber is responsible for determining whether the patient is eligible for reimbursement of a product with limited reimbursement but does not have to submit an individual application. In both countries, cost for health care service and medicines are tracked using the individual's unique personal identification number and the Total Population Register with place of residence of all inhabitants (Furu et al. 2010).

12.3 Drug Regulatory Authorities

The Ministries of Health[3] are responsible for determining policy and legislation, national budgeting and planning of the health care systems. The ministries have a number of subordinate agencies taking care of, among other things, execution of drug regulation (including pricing) and provision of health care services (including medicines) within the PBS.

Pharmaceutical products are strictly regulated in the Scandinavian countries. Most tasks related to medicines are handled by the national medicines agencies, i.e. the Norwegian Medicines Agency (NoMA) and the Swedish Medical Products Agency (MPA). The agencies are responsible for drug approval, market authorization, classification, pharmacovigilance and the generic substitution systems. In addition, they are in charge of the permissions to run pharmacies and the quality assurance of the activities in the pharmacies. In Norway, the NoMA is also responsible for pharmaceutical price setting and the reimbursement scheme while

[3] In Norway: The Ministry of Health and Care Services; in Sweden: The Ministry of Health and Social Affairs.

in Sweden, the Dental and Pharmaceutical Benefits Agency is responsible for setting prices and deciding on products to be included in the PBS since 2002.

12.4 The Pharmacy Systems

Historically, the pharmacy markets in Scandinavia, like in the other Nordic countries, have been extensively regulated. From 1953 to 2001, when a new pharmacy act went into effect (Act on Pharmacy 2000), Norway had a system where the number of pharmacies, as well as their location, were strictly controlled by the government (Rudholm 2008). The state-owned Norwegian Medicinal Depot (NMD) was the only approved wholesaler in the market. The new legislation broke the pharmacists' monopoly of pharmacy ownership and was followed by considerable changes in the distribution chain for pharmaceuticals by allowing horizontal integration (i.e. pharmacy chains) and vertical integration between pharmacies and wholesalers (Håkonsen et al. 2009a; Rudholm 2008). This was a consequence of the EEA agreement, which also in several other ways prohibited certain special regulations considered to limit the competition in the market. This included the establishment of pharmacies and the number of drugs allowed to be sold (the "need clause") (Norris 1998). However, it was also a goal to introduce more competitive actors in the market. From the mid-90s onwards the number of pharmacies has more than doubled (Fig. 12.1) and the amount of market authorizations has increased more than fourfold (LMI 2005, 2014).

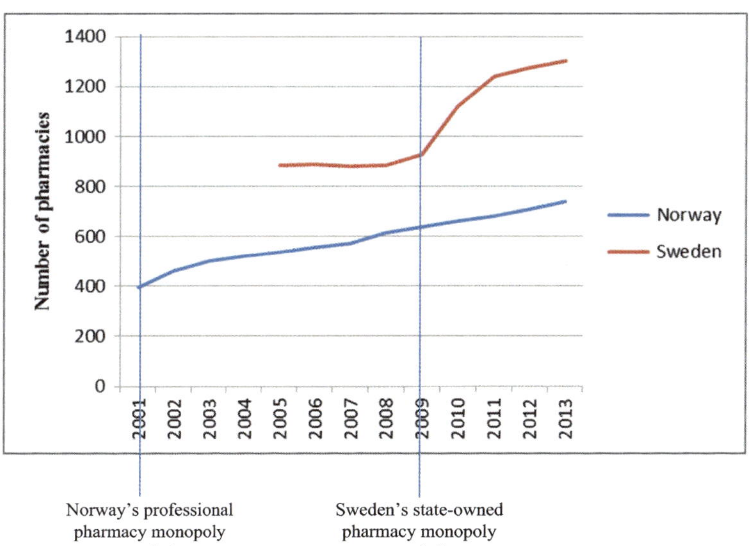

Fig. 12.1 The development of number of pharmacies after the professional ownership monopolies were ended. Sources: The Norwegian Pharmacy Association, Swedish Pharmacy Association

As late as 2009, similar actions were taken in Sweden which had a state-owned monopoly of pharmacies, known as "Apoteket AB" (National Corporation of Swedish Pharmacies), for 40 years. The process of changing the ownership of pharmacies was initiated in 2006 following a government shift from a labour to a conservative/liberal government. Signals that the pharmacy monopoly did not comply with the EU legislation contributed to this change. The number of pharmacies increased from around 900 pharmacies before the reform to around 1,300 pharmacies less than four years after the reform (Fig. 12.1).

Today the pharmacy markets in both countries are dominated by large national or international pharmacy corporations. In Norway, all community pharmacies are privately owned and most of them by one of three large international corporations (Alliance Boots, Celesio and Phoenix). Sweden has seven large corporations in the market, most of them national. One of them (Apoteket AB) is still owned by the government. Pharmaceutical industry and prescribers are denied ownership of pharmacies in both countries (Act on Pharmacy 2000; Act on Sales of Medicinal Products 2009).

The changes that occurred in Scandinavia were a result of much political debate with regards to changing the drug distribution and pharmacy ownership, which took place in the Nordic countries in the 1990s and the 2000s. The deregulation was set off in Iceland in 1996 when a new drug distribution legislation went into effect and liberalized the ownership of community pharmacies (Almarsdóttir et al. 2000). The changes that took place in Norway, Sweden and Iceland can be contrasted to Denmark where no radical changes happened despite political pressure and an economic reform aiming at eliminating all forms of monopolies (Anell 2005; Larsen et al. 2006).

The reforms also ended the pharmacies' retail monopoly on medicines. In 2003 (Norway) and 2009 (Sweden) a selection of OTC medicines was allowed to be sold in places such as supermarkets, gas stations etc. Sold outside the pharmacy, OTCs can only be sold to individuals older than 18 years of age and restrictions apply regarding package size.

In addition to the community pharmacies, there are hospital pharmacies. These are stately-owned in Norway and either run by the large pharmacy corporations or by the county councils in Sweden.

12.5 Pharmaceutical Pricing Set-Up

Both Scandinavian countries have a tradition for balancing clinical and economic interests in their pharmaceutical pricing policies. In Norway regulations on the quality, safety, efficacy and costs of drugs date back to 1928 (Andersson 1992). Pharmaceutical prices are first of all a concern for the PBS since both health care and medicines are mainly publicly financed and private costs are relatively small. However, Norway and Sweden have introduced pharmaceutical price control in different ways due to different traditions for domestic pharmaceutical production.

Both countries started this by introducing reference-based pricing in 1993, followed by more firm and comprehensive pricing models for new medicines in 1995 (Norway) and 1998 (Sweden). In the following decade, international reference pricing in Norway and value-based pricing in Sweden were implemented. Other policies were generic substitution and parallel-import of drugs from less expensive markets such as Greece, Italy and Portugal. Just as for reimbursement, pricing is product specific in both countries.[4]

12.5.1 Medicines Used in Outpatient Care

Norway previously had an explicit goal to achieve a common price level for pharmaceuticals all over the country and at the same time keep the prices at moderate levels by controlling the margins in all parts of the distribution chain (Brekke and Straume 2003). This has later been modified into a goal of achieving as low prices as possible (HOD 2005).

From 2002 onwards drug pricing in Sweden has been part of the reimbursement status process. Pricing has shifted from primarily being in the hands of the manufacturers to be the authorities' responsibility. Two different pricing principles are applied depending on whether the product is subject to generic substitution or not (described in Sects. 12.6.2 and 12.8.2). Health economic evaluations of cost-effectiveness are part of the pricing process for new medicines. These prices should be set in relation to the health economic and therapeutic value of the product. For medicines where the patent has expired, competition striving for low and sustainable prices is the goal.

OTC medicines are subject to free pricing in both countries.

12.5.2 Medicines Provided in Hospital Care

The hospital sector differs from the outpatient market in terms of procurement procedures. In both countries, medicines prescribed for inpatient use are purchased through direct negotiations with manufacturers (Ess et al. 2003; Tordoff et al. 2008). The cost of medicines is included in hospital budgets. The pharmaceutical expenditures account for a limited amount of the hospitals' operating costs. However, the hospitals' share of the total pharmaceutical expenditures is on the rise, totalling 20–25 % of the pharmaceutical market (LMI 2014; Socialstyrelsen 2014). In addition, the medicine use patterns in hospitals are considered important to the manufacturers since they are often reflected in the patients' medicine use after

[4] A generic equivalent to an already marketed product on the Norwegian market is given the same maximum price as the original product.

discharge and thereby indirectly affect the resources spent in primary care. Thus, there is an increasing concern about the importance of cost containment and scale economies in hospitals, and joint procurement and tendering processes have been initiated (Amgros; LIS; Milovanovic et al. 2004; Tordoff et al. 2005).

Tendering in hospitals is legally based on the Act on Public Procurement which was implemented as a result of the EU/EEA agreement in 1995. Most hospitals are owned by the government and organized in hospital trusts financed by the state. Each hospital trust has a drug committee which makes annual recommendations for drug use within restricted hospital budgets and represents the hospital in a nationwide drug procurement cooperation. This cooperation is assigned to perform all contracting, procurement, distribution and logistical operations of pharmaceuticals on behalf of the hospitals and hereby enable the hospital organizations to improve efficiency and reduce costs (LIS).

12.6 How Prices Are Set

12.6.1 Norway: International Reference Pricing for Prescription Drugs

In Norway different strategies for price control have been implemented over the last decades, aiming to reduce prices either directly or indirectly (Håkonsen et al. 2009a). In 1995, it was decided that all prescription drugs must obtain an approved maximum price before marketing. This included patent-protected as well as generic products. The maximum price is set at the pharmacy purchasing price (PPP) level. The pharmacy retail price (PRP) is set by adding the maximum pharmacy mark-ups and value-added tax (VAT) which also are regulated by the Ministry of Health and Care Services (Hågå and Sverre 2002). The pharmaceutical companies, wholesalers and pharmacies are allowed to sell their products to any price at or below the approved maximum price.

Since 2000 international reference pricing has been applied for determination of maximum prices. A price reference is conducted based on prices in nine other EU/EEA countries (Austria, Belgium, Denmark, Finland, Germany, Ireland, The Netherlands, Sweden and The United Kingdom). The applicant is responsible for submitting price data on all marketed packages of the product in the reference countries. The price is set as the average of the three lowest prices. If the product is marketed in less than three countries, existing prices are used (Hågå and Sverre 2002; Håkonsen et al. 2009a). Since package sizes in different countries are not always directly comparable, price comparisons are made on the basis of units, e.g. price per tablet/dose. Local currency prices must be converted into Norwegian Krone (NOK) using the mean exchange rate of the last six whole months, as presented by the Bank of Norway.

In special cases, the calculated maximum price can be considered too low and the price is decided to be scaled up. If certain conditions are met, a price is set based on the documentation of the production costs and any other special conditions related to the basis of the calculation.

Since prices are set at the PPP level, wholesalers are free to negotiate mark-ups with the manufacturers. Mark-ups for generics and parallel imported products are significantly higher than for branded medicines. A "discount sharing model" gives the pharmacies incentives for offering products at lower prices by allowing the pharmacies to keep up to 50 % of the difference between the given maximum price and the actual price. The other part belongs to the customer or the third-party payer. For generic products an additional pricing model is applied when generic competition is established (described in Sect. 12.8.1).

International reference pricing was introduced as a response to the pharmaceutical companies' request for more predictability and transparency in pricing decisions. The consistent use of international reference pricing has led to substantial price reductions on many drugs. It has been considered a stable and predictable strategy by the authorities as well as the industry. In addition, the administrative costs are considered small in comparison to other pricing schemes (Håkonsen et al. 2009a).

12.6.2 Sweden: Cost-Effectiveness Evaluations in Pricing of New Medicines

Different methods for pharmaceutical price control have been applied in Sweden over time. Reference-based pricing was introduced 1993 for medicines where the patent had expired. In 2002 this was reinforced by the introduction of mandatory generic substitution. At the same time health economic evaluations were introduced as a part of the pricing process for new medicines. This has been further developed and now cost-effectiveness data is required to determine price and reimbursement status of the products (Ljungkvist et al. 1997; Andersson 2006; Andersson et al. 2006; Godman et al. 2009). Pricing decisions states a maximum PPP for medicines within the PBS. In addition fixed margins are regulated by the authorities thereby in practice setting the PRP.

Prices of new medicines should be set in relation to the health economic and therapeutic value of the product and assessment of cost-effectiveness is an important part of the pricing process. The pharmaceutical companies are required to submit evidence of cost-effectiveness according to predefined standards upon submitting an application for the product to be included in the PBS (Persson et al. 2012; Drummond et al. 2011). Furthermore, the agency has the task to conduct reviews of the reimbursement status of existing products by therapeutic groups (Wettermark et al. 2010). In these reviews the value and the cost of the products in a therapeutic group are considered.

Table 12.3 Pharmacy margins in the Scandinavian countries

Norway		
	All prescription medicines	
Pharmacy purchase price, PPP (NOK)	Pharmacy sales price (NOK)	
≤200	PPP*1.07 + 25.00[a]	
>200	PPP*1.03	
Sweden		
	Medicines with no generic competition	Medicines with generic competition
Pharmacy purchase price, PPP (SEK)	Pharmacy sales price (SEK)	Pharmacy sales price (SEK)[b]
≤75	PPP*1.20 + 31.25	PPP*1.20 + 31.25 + 13.00
>75–300	PPP*1.03 + 44.00	PPP*1.03 + 44.00 + 13.00
>300–6,000	PPP*1.02 + 47.00	PPP*1.02 + 47.00 + 13.00
>6,000	PPP + 167.00	PPP + 167.00 + 13.00

NOK1 = € 0.12; SEK1 = € 0.11 (exchange rates of July 3, 2014)
[a]Additional fee per package of NOK 10 for narcotic and psychotropic substances
[b]For products where the price was set before October 1, 2013 the add-on for generic medicines is SEK 10.00 instead of SEK 13.00

Sweden applies a different pricing principle for medicines subject to generic substitution as described in Sect. 12.8.2.

12.6.3 Pharmacy Margins

The pharmacy margins are based on the price level of the product and consist of a proportional part based on the PPP plus a flat rate add-on per package. The margins decrease as the price of the product increases, as illustrated in Table 12.3. It can therefore be more profitable for the pharmacies to sell more of rather inexpensive drugs compared to a smaller volume of expensive ones.

Norwegian pharmacy mark-ups are fixed for all prescription medicines regardless of the product's reimbursement status. A VAT of 25 % is added to all prices before sale. A similar but more detailed system is operated in Sweden where there are separate plans of mark-ups for medicines with and without generic competition. Sweden has no VAT on prescription medicines. Mark-ups on OTC medicines are not regulated in any of the countries.

12.7 Price Revisions

In Norway NoMA can initiate price revisions if drug prices are altered in one or more of the reference countries or if a significant change in currency rates occurs. The pharmaceutical companies can apply for price revision for the same reasons. In

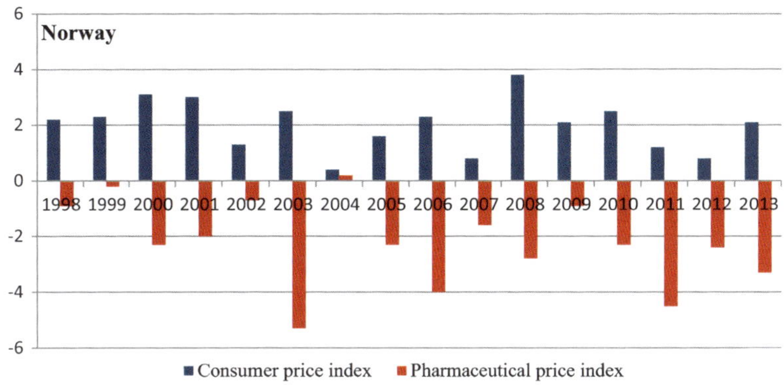

Fig. 12.2 Changes in pharmaceutical prices and the general rate of inflation in Norway 1998–2013. Source: The Norwegian Association of Pharmaceutical Manufacturers

both cases, price revisions should not occur more than once a year. The exception is the prices of recently launched products which within a two-year period can obtain new price data every sixth month from the company in question. This is supposed to ensure that any recent launches in the reference countries are taken into account. If a product is withdrawn from the market in one of the reference countries, this could also form the basis for changing the price.

After the introduction of international reference pricing, systematic price revisions of already marketed drugs were initiated to ensure that drugs with a large turnover were also affected by the new pricing principle (Hågå and Sverre 2002). During the first year, prices of 60 products topping the sales statistics were revised, followed by further 132 drugs the year after. The revisions have led to significant price reductions on many products although price increases have also occurred. This process has since continued on an annual basis. As can been seen from Fig. 12.2, the changes in the Norwegian pharmaceutical price index have been considerable since 2000.

In Sweden the manufacturer can apply for price changes at any time. Price changes might also be initiated by the Dental and Pharmaceutical Benefits Agency within a pharmaceutical review of reimbursed medicines. Several large therapeutic groups have so far been reviewed and this has resulted in products being delisted or prices decreased (Wettermark et al. 2010). For medicines subject to generic substitution the maximum prices within substitutable groups can be revised 6 months after the introduction of generic competition. Maximum prices for substitutable medicines are published on monthly basis. Changes in medicine prices have been moderate in comparison to Norway during the last 15 years (Fig. 12.3).

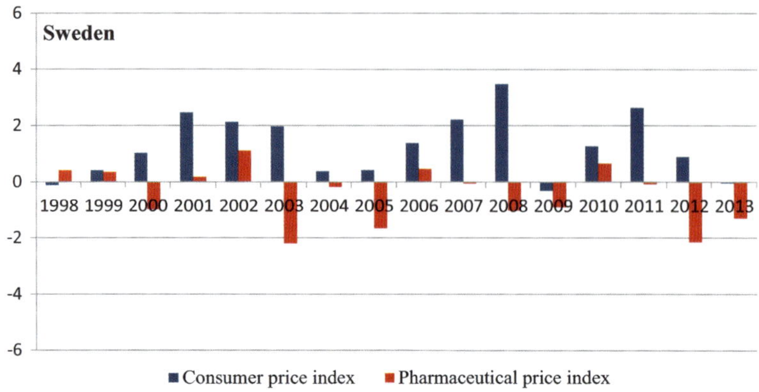

Fig. 12.3 Changes in pharmaceutical prices and the general rate of inflation in Sweden 1998–2013. Source: Statistics Sweden

12.8 The Case of Generic Medicines

Mandatory generic substitution was introduced in Norway and Sweden in 2001 and 2002, respectively, for medicines where the patent has expired and where substitutable products are available on the market. The systems applied for generic substitution are similar in both countries but there are differences in the pricing of generic medicines. The aim of introducing generic substitution was to stimulate price competition in the off-patent market and reduce the growth in public expenditures. It obliged the pharmacies to keep less expensive generics in stock and offer them to the patients unless the price difference is insignificant. The lists of substitutable products contain both generic and parallel imported products and are decided on and continuously updated by the NoMA (Norway) and the MPA (Sweden). Certain drug groups are excluded from the lists. This includes medicines with a narrow therapeutic window or any drug with warfarin or other active ingredients where erroneous use may be life threatening.

Three restrictions to generic substitution are applied. First the generic drugs must be approved as bio equivalent by the NoMA or the MPA. Secondly, the patient has the freedom to refuse substitution if she/he pays the corresponding price difference, and thirdly, the physicians have the right to exclude individual patients due to special medical reasons. Additionally, in Sweden the pharmacists can restrict substitution due to certain reasons such as split tablets.

If substitution is restricted by either the prescriber (or the pharmacist), the cost of the dispensed product is fully included in the patient co-payment. However, if the patient refuses substitution he/she has to pay the price difference between the cheapest available product and the dispensed product out-of-pocket. This price difference is not included in the patient's total co-payment.

Norwegian physicians are encouraged to prescribe by active ingredient (perform generic prescribing). However, in Sweden generic prescribing is not allowed.

12.8.1 Pricing of Generics in Norway

To increase the effect of generic substitution, an incentive-based pricing model was introduced in 2003 (the "index price model"). This included the generic products with the highest turnover in the reimbursement system. An index price for each substance was set equal to the average of the three lowest reported wholesale purchase prices of that substance from the previous 3-month period plus a fixed wholesale and retail margin. The index price was reimbursed regardless of the actual retail price. If the patient refused to switch to a cheaper product, he/she had to pay for the price difference in addition to the co-payment. This was intended to give economic incentives for patients who agreed to substitute and for pharmacies which offered cheaper products. The aim of adjusting prices below the index price was to obtain a reduction in prices in the following months. The model led to moderate savings for the PBS due to some distributional effects. However, the savings were less than expected mainly since the model was not adjusted to the vertical integration between pharmacies and wholesalers. The model was replaced by a direct price control model called the "stepped price model" in 2005 (Håkonsen et al. 2009a).

Within the stepped price model the maximum reimbursement price for both branded and generic prescription drugs is reduced in a stepwise matter once the patent has expired (Table 12.4). The size of the price cuts depends on annual sales prior to generic competition and the time since this was established. The pricing is based on PRP; implying that mark-ups are not regulated.

The sale of generic drugs has increased considerably since 2001 and has by 2013 reached 45 % of the market shares (in defined daily doses). In the generic interchangeable market the market shares of generics have stabilized around 70 % by volume and nearly 50 % by price (LMI 2014). Generic substitution is acknowledged as an important measure of cost containment in the society although close attention is paid to potential side effects of the system such as erroneous medicine use and medication errors in hospitals (Håkonsen et al. 2009b, 2010; Håkonsen and Toverud 2011).

Table 12.4 Overview of the stepped price model

Sales PRP (12 months before generic competition)	First price reduction step (at the time of establishment of generic competition)	Second price reduction step (6 months after generic competition)	Third price reduction step (18 months or more after generic competition)	
<NOK 100 Mio.	35 %	59 %	>NOK 15 Mio.	69 %
>NOK 100 Mio.	35 %	81 %	>NOK 30 Mio.	86 %
			>NOK 100 Mio.	90 %

Source: The Norwegian Medicines Agency

12.8.2 Pricing of Generics in Sweden

Initially in 2002, medicines eligible for generic substitution were also subject to reference-based pricing. Thus the product with the lowest price would get large market shares (Andersson et al. 2005). This set off a series of price changes contributing to decreased reference-prices for many products. During the same period of time the patent for several blockbuster medicines expired. Together this resulted in the previously increasing pharmaceutical expenditures levelling off for both the patients and the public third party payers (Andersson et al. 2007).

The current pricing policy for generics is more static and applies a maximum price. Today, a maximum price for a group of substitutable medicines is set by the Dental and Pharmaceutical Benefits Agency for substitutable products where (1) the price of the generic products is below 70 % of the original price of the original brand product, and (2) generics have been sold on the market for at least 4 months. If these prerequisites are met, the maximum price is set to 35 % of the original price of the original brand product. This price is applicable for all substitutable products of the (original brand) including parallel exported medicines.

The sales of non-branded drugs as a share of total sales have risen considerably the last decade. This has resulted in significant price reductions (Andersson et al. 2007). By 2012, generics accounted for 49 % of the medicines sold by volume and 15 % by price in the Swedish market.

12.9 Conclusion

Over the last three decades Norwegian and Swedish authorities have implemented several pharmaceutical pricing policies in order to increase predictability and transparency in pricing decisions. Since medicines are mainly publicly financed, prices are a concern for the public benefit schemes and hospitals. More than 70 % of the total pharmaceutical expenditures are paid by a public third-part payer. For prescribed medicines included in the benefit schemes, the patients pay less than 20 % of the cost.

The fundamental principles for pricing of prescription medicines are maximum pricing at the retail level. Norway applies international reference pricing. In Sweden health economic evaluations are mandatory in pricing decisions in order to document the values being paid for by the public. The pricing systems also include regulation of the pharmacies' margins. Thus the impact by pharmacies on pricing of prescribed medicines is insignificant. Pricing and market authorization is handled by one governmental authority in Norway whereas in Sweden these tasks are handled by separate authorities.

References

Act on Pharmaceutical Benefits (2002: 160) Ministry of Health and Social Affairs, 2002 [in Swedish]

Act on Pharmacy (2000-06-02-39) Ministry of Health and Care Services, 2000 [in Norwegian]

Act on Sales of Medicinal Products (2009:366) Ministry of Health and Social Affairs, 2009 [in Swedish]

Almarsdóttir AB, Morgall JM, Grímsson A (2000) Cost containment of pharmaceutical use in Iceland: the impact of liberalization and user charges. J Health Serv Res Policy 5(2):109–113

Amgros. About Amgros. http://www.amgros.dk/en. Accessed 14 July 2014

Andersson F (1992) Norway's pivotal role in regulatory health economics and pharmaceutical cost containment—what can other countries learn? Health Policy 21(1):17–34

Andersson K (2006) Swedish pharmaceutical benefit reforms: analyses of implementation, pharmaceutical sales patterns and expenditures. Göteborg University, Göteborg

Andersson K, Sonesson C, Petzold M, Carlsten A, Lönnroth K (2005) What are the obstacles to generic substitution? An assessment of the behaviour of prescribers, patients and pharmacies during the first year of generic substitution in Sweden. Pharmacoepidemiol Drug Saf 14 (5):341–348

Andersson K, Petzold MG, Sonesson C, Lönnroth K, Carlsten A (2006) Do policy changes in the pharmaceutical reimbursement schedule affect drug expenditures? Interrupted time series analysis of cost, volume and cost per volume trends in Sweden 1986-2002. Health Policy 79 (2–3):231–243

Andersson K, Bergström G, Petzold MG, Carlsten A (2007) Impact of a generic substitution reform on patients' and society's expenditure for pharmaceuticals. Health Policy 81:376–384

Anell A (2005) Deregulating the pharmacy market: the case of Iceland and Norway. Health Policy 75(1):9–17

Anell A, Glenngård AH, Merkur S (2012) Sweden—health system review. Health Syst Transit 14 (5):1–159

Beckman A, Anell A (2013) Changes in health care utilisation following a reform involving choice and privatisation in Swedish primary care: a five-year follow-up of GP-visits. BMC Health Serv Res 13:452

Bergström G, Karlberg I (2007) Decentralized responsibility for costs of outpatient prescription pharmaceuticals in Sweden. Assessment of models for decentralized financing of subsidies from a management perspective. Health Policy 81(2–3):358–367

Bjorvatn A (2012) Making incentives work: hospital organisation and performance. Scand J Public Health 40(5):449–456

Brekke KR, Straume OR (2003) Pris- og avanseregulering i legemiddelmarkedet: en prinsipiell diskusjon og en vurdering av den norske modellen. Notat 20/2003. Rokkansenteret, Bergen [in Norwegian]

Drummond M, Jönsson B, Rutten F, Stargardt T (2011) Reimbursement of pharmaceuticals: reference pricing versus health technology assessment. Eur J Health Econ 12(3):263–271

Ess S, Schneeweiss S, Szucs T (2003) European healthcare policies for controlling drug expenditure. Pharmacoeconomics 21(2):89–103

Furu K, Wettermark B, Andersen M, Martikainen JE, Almarsdottir AB, Sørensen HT (2010) The Nordic countries as a cohort for pharmacoepidemiological research. Basic Clin Pharmacol Toxicol 106(2):86–94

Gerdtham UG, Johannesson M, Gunnarsson B, Marcusson M, Henriksson F (1998) The effect of changes in treatment patterns on drug expenditure. Pharmacoeconomics 13(1 Pt 2):127–134

Godman B, Wettermark B, Hoffmann M, Andersson K, Haycox A, Gustafsson LL (2009) Multifaceted national and regional drug reforms and initiatives in ambulatory care in Sweden: global relevance. Expert Rev Pharmacoecon Outcomes Res 9(1):65–83

Grasdal AL, Monstad K (2011) Inequity in the use of physician services in Norway before and after introducing patient lists in primary care. Int J Equity Health 15(10):25

Hågå A, Sverre JM (2002) Pricing and reimbursement of pharmaceuticals in Norway. Eur J Health Econ 3(3):215–220

Håkonsen H, Toverud EL (2011) Special challenges for drug adherence following generic substitution for Pakistani immigrants living in Norway. Eur J Clin Pharmacol 67(2):193–201

Håkonsen H, Horn AM, Toverud EL (2009a) Price control as a strategy for pharmaceutical cost containment—what has been achieved in Norway in the period 1994-2004? Health Policy 90 (2–3):277–285

Håkonsen H, Eilertsen M, Borge H, Toverud EL (2009b) Generic substitution: additional challenge for adherence in hypertensive patients? Curr Med Res Opin 25(10):2515–2521

Håkonsen H, Hopen HS, Abelsen L, Ek B, Toverud EL (2010) Generic substitution: a potential risk factor for medication errors in hospitals. Adv Ther 27(2):118–126

HOD (Ministry of Health and Care Services) (2005) White paper no. 18 (2004-2005). Rett kurs mot riktig legemiddelbruk. Legemiddelpolitikken, Oslo [in Norwegian]

Jansson S, Anell A (2006) The impact of decentralised drug-budgets in Sweden—a survey of physicians' attitudes towards costs and cost-effectiveness. Health Policy 76(3):299–311

Larsen JB, Vrangbaek K, Traulsen JM (2006) Advocacy coalitions and pharmacy policy in Denmark—solid cores with fuzzy edges. Soc Sci Med 63(1):212–224

LIS (Drug Procurement Cooperation). About LIS. http://www.lisnorway.no/sider/tekst.asp?id=english. Accessed 14 July 2014

Ljungkvist MO, Andersson D, Gunnarsson B (1997) Cost and utilisation of pharmaceuticals in Sweden. Health Policy 41(Suppl):S55–S69

LMI (The Norwegian Association of Pharmaceutical Manufacturers) (2005) Facts and figures 2005. http://www.lmi.no/dm_documents/tall_og_fakta_2005_v5_05gsfb2279v5.pdf. Accessed 1 July 2014

LMI (The Norwegian Association of Pharmaceutical Manufacturers) (2014) Facts and figures. http://legemiddelstatistikk.com/2014/index.html. Accessed 1 July 2014

Lundkvist J (2002) Pricing and reimbursement of drugs in Sweden. Eur J Health Econ 3:66–70

Magnussen J, Vrangbäk K, Saltman RB (2009) Nordic health care systems. Recent reforms and current policy challenges. Open University Press, McGraw Hill, Glasgow. http://www.euro.who.int/__data/assets/pdf_file/0011/98417/E93429.pdf. Accessed 15 July 2014

Milovanovic DR, Pavlovic R, Folic M, Jankovic SM (2004) Public drug procurement: the lessons from a drug tender in a teaching hospital of a transition country. Eur J Clin Pharmacol 60 (3):149–153

NoMA (The Norwegian Medicines Agency). Guidelines for pricing. http://www.legemiddelverket.no/Blaa_resept_og_pris/pris-paa-legemidler/maksimalpris/Documents/Retningslinjer%20for%20prisfastsettelse.pdf. Accessed 3 July 2014 [in Norwegian]

Norris P (1998) The impact of European harmonisation on Norwegian drug policy. Health Policy 43(1):65–81

Persson U, Svensson J, Pettersson B (2012) A new reimbursement system for innovative pharmaceuticals combining value-based and free market pricing. Appl Health Econ Health Policy 10 (4):217–225

Regulation on reimbursement of essential medicines etc. (Blåreseptforskriften) (FOR-2007-06-28-814) Ministry of Health and Care Services, 2007 [in Norwegian]

Rudholm N (2008) Entry of new pharmacies in the deregulated Norwegian pharmaceuticals market—consequences for costs and availability. Health Policy 87(2):258–263

Sandheimer C, Karlberg I (2013) Ten years experience with models for financing of outpatient prescriptions. Health Policy Technol 2(4):188–195

Socialstyrelsen (2014) Läkemedelsförsäljningen i Sverige - analys och prognos http://www.socialstyrelsen.se/Lists/Artikelkatalog/Attachments/19428/2014-4-16.pdf. Accessed 3 July 14 [in Swedish]

Sundar T, Thuestad AB, Thomassen PT, Røshol H, Hjelme K, Andestad U, Bryn E (2006) Reimbursement prescription system in poor state? Tidsskr Nor Laegeforen 126(13):1759–1761 [in Norwegian]

Tordoff JM, Norris PT, Reith DM (2005) Managing prices for hospital pharmaceuticals: a successful strategy for New Zealand? Value Health 8(3):201–208

Tordoff JM, Norris PT, Reith DM (2008) "Price management" and its impact on hospital pharmaceutical expenditure and the availability of medicines in New Zealand hospitals. Value Health 11(7):1214–1226

Wettermark B, Godman B, Neovius M, Hedberg N, Mellgren TO, Kahan T (2010) Initial effects of a reimbursement restriction to improve the cost-effectiveness of antihypertensive treatment. Health Policy 94(3):221–229

Chapter 13
Pharmaceutical Pricing Policies in Qatar

Mohamed Izham Mohamed Ibrahim

Abstract Qatar is the world's highest per capita income non-OECD country. The country has established the National Health Strategy 2011–2016 (NHS), which is aligned with the Qatar National Vision 2030 that will advance Qatar's Healthcare Vision of creating a world-class, patient-centered healthcare system. There has been a huge increase in public spending on healthcare, and it is the highest per capita health expenditure in the region. The National Health Insurance Scheme is a strong platform to ensure a healthy population with access to affordable healthcare. Public sector drug procurement is carried out through closed international tenders, GCC bulk procurement and direct purchasing. The Qatari pharmaceutical market reached a value of QR 1.43 billion (USD 392.6 million) in 2010. The spending on medicines and pharmaceuticals in 2009 and 2010 out of the total public sector spending was USD 138 million (9 %) and USD 143 million (8 %), respectively. Medicines dispensed at the Hamad Medical Corporation health institutions are priced differently for Qataris and non-Qataris. The development of the pharmaceutical market is shaped by the decision of the Supreme Council of Health (SCH) to abolish government controls over the pricing of medicines and to allow more importing agents and suppliers in the country. Qatar has adopted an open market system. The retail prices of medicines remain among the highest in the region. There is no policy on the bioequivalence of generic medicines, but the government is promoting the use of generic medicines. There is extensive use of branded medicines in Qatar's healthcare facilities. A high share of imported and branded medicines, which are trusted and preferred by prescribers and consumers, has increased the Qatari government's healthcare spending. SCH's attempt to remove price controls had affected the affordability of medicines as the prices of some drugs have increased and are inconsistent across facilities. The government has had to implement price controls, although it abstained from explicitly fixing prices.

M.I. Mohamed Ibrahim (✉)
College of Pharmacy, Qatar University, P.O. Box 2713, Doha, Qatar
e-mail: mohamedizham@qu.edu.qa

Z.-U.-D. Babar (ed.), *Pharmaceutical Prices in the 21st Century*,
DOI 10.1007/978-3-319-12169-7_13

13.1 Country Profile

The State of Qatar is located on the western coast of the Persian Gulf on a 160-km-long peninsula. Together with total islands, the country occupies a total area of 11,493 km^2. The estimated population in 2012 was 2.05 million (approximately 1.2 million were males above 15 years of age, and slightly more than 300,000 were females above 15 years of age), and approximately 70 % of the total population were expatriates. In 2012, life expectancy at birth was 78.2 years. Between 1990 and 2012, the annual population growth rate was 6.6 % and estimated to be 1.7 % for the period 2012–2030 (Table 13.1) (UNICEF n.d.). More information is included in Table 13.1.

Qatar is the world's highest per capita income non-OECD country, and in the past several years, it has experienced persistent high real gross domestic product (GDP) growth. In addition, the country has the lowest unemployment rate due to the oil and gas industry. In 2012, GDP per capital (PPP) is estimated at USD103,900 vs. USD93,300 (est) in 2010 (Index Mundi 2013; World Bank 2014). The average annual GDP per capita growth rate for 1990–2012 was 0.9 % (UNICEF n.d.).

Table 13.1 Country general indicators

Indicator	Data (2010 statistics)	Data (2012 statistics)
Total population	1,759,000	2,051,000
Life expectancy at birth m/f (years)	78/79	79/80
Probability of dying under five (per 1,000 live births)	8	7
Probability of dying between 15 and 60 years m/f (per 1,000 population)	69/48	73/51
Total national expenditure on health as % of GDP (excluding health expenditure of the private sector)	2.1	1.9 (2011)
Per capita total expenditure on health at average exchange rate (USD)	1,489	1,805
Government expenditure on health as % of overall government expenditure	6.9	5.3 (adjusted based on the rate for the last 3 years)
Out of pocket health expenditure (% of private expenditure on health)	71.0	52.2
Density of pharmaceutical personnel (per 10,000) population	12.59 (2006 statistics)	na
Number of beds in government hospitals	1,667	na
Number of beds in private hospitals	366	na
Total hospital beds in the country (per 1,000 people)	1.2	1.2
Gross domestic product (purchasing power parity, USD)	158.5 billion	191 billion
Gross domestic product per capita (current USD)	72,773	93,825

Source: World Health Organization (n.d.a, n.d.b), General Secretariat for Development Planning of Qatar (2014), World Bank (2014), Hamad Medical Corporation (2012)

Based on the revenues from oil and gas, Qatar has built a sophisticated healthcare and social infrastructure. The investment in social and healthcare development has contributed significantly to the health and wellbeing of Qatar's people. The proportion of health expenditure excluding the private sector was 3.1 % of GDP (Bener and Al Mazroei 2010). According to UNICEF (n.d.), the Qatar Ministry of Development Planning and Statistics (MDP&S) forecasted that real GDP in 2013 will grow by 5.3 % due to the revision in expected output of oil and gas. Consumer price inflation will rise, but stay moderate; consumer prices rose by 3.5 % in May 2013 compared with the same month in 2012. The country's Advisory Council approved a draft law for the formation of a Health and Education Fund with working capital of QR 360 billion, which will be funded directly through government revenues each year. The main purpose of this funding is to provide sustainable financial resources and support for developing the country's health and education sectors. High expenditures are also expected for the construction of new healthcare centers and education facilities (GSDP 2012). According to the Human Development Index 2013, the Qatar value index reached 0.851, ranking Qatar 31st of the 187 countries worldwide (vs. 37th/187 in 2011) (UNDP 2014).

From another positive perspective, in the Middle Eastern and North African (MENA) region, Qatar ranked first in the Global Peace Index (GPI) for six consecutive years (2009–2014). Qatar leads other Arab countries and ranks 22nd globally among 162 countries covered by the GPI (Ministry of Interior of Qatar 2014).

13.2 Healthcare System

13.2.1 National Healthcare System

Qatar desires to manage and develop an integrated healthcare system according to world-class standards in order to improve the health of Qatar's population. The plans are to improve the health and extend the lifespan of all of its people and to meet the requirements of present and future generations. Overall healthcare services are intended to be accessible and affordable to the entire population. The healthcare system is available to all, regardless of residency or nationality (Hamad Medical Corporation n.d.).

13.2.2 Healthcare Authority

The Qatar Supreme Council of Health (SCH), established in 2005, is an agency responsible and committed to providing quality and effective healthcare services. The SCH does not provide clinical services. It oversees the services delivered by public institutions such as Hamad Medical Corporation, Primary Health Care

Corporation and the private sector (Ministry of Foreign Affairs of Qatar 2014) to ensure that standards are met and performance targets achieved. It also oversees public health programs related to the control of infectious diseases, and coordinates with other agencies on environmental and public safety promotion. It develops and regulates policies in areas such as licensure and credentialing, information technology, health insurance and continuing medical education (Ministry of Foreign Affairs of Qatar 2014).

The SCH is headed by a Chief Executive Officer and Board of Directors, and several directorates as the following areas: Human Resources; Administrative and Financial Affairs; Communication and Media; Contracts and Procurement; E-Health and Information Technology; Facilities & General Services Department; Finance, Health Financing and Insurance; Health Planning & Assessment; Healthcare Quality Management; Legal Affairs; Medical Commission; Medical Relation and Treatment Abroad; National Health Committee for Disaster Management; Pharmacy and Drug Control; Public Health; and Qatar Council of Health Practitioners.

13.2.3 General Health Indicators

In general, life expectancy of the Qatar population has increased, although many people live with debilitating non-communicable diseases (NCDs), such as diabetes, cancer and heart disease (Tables 13.1 and 13.2). Qatar has committed to combat the widespread prevalence of NCDs and the morbidity associated with these diseases (National Health Strategy 2011–2016; Qatar National Vision 2030). Table 13.2 also demonstrates that the health services and personnel have improved over the years.

There are 10 public, private and semi-public hospitals, 23 health centers, and 317 private, individual and multiple clinics. Hospital beds per 1,000 people have augmented from 1.2 beds in 2009 to 1.3 beds in 2011. The total doctors' number has increased from 3.11 doctors per 1,000 people in 2006 to 4.03 generalist doctors in 2010 (GSDP 2012).

The country established the National Health Strategy 2011–2016 (NHS), a comprehensive program of reforms aligned with the Qatar National Vision 2030 that will advance Qatar's Healthcare Vision of creating a world-class, patient-centered healthcare system. There are seven strategy goals under this initiative (National Health Strategy 2011–2016; Qatar National Vision 2030).

The NHS provides a framework and guiding work plan, under seven goals, with 35 specific projects and associated implementation plans to achieve the goals of Qatar National Vision (2030). It is a strategy for reform with far-reaching and fundamental changes across Qatar's overall healthcare system.

Table 13.2 Health service performance and diseases in Qatar during the period 1998–2012[a]

Variables	Year 1998	2003	2008	2010	2012
Leading causes of deaths (%):					
Cardiovascular	na	36.2	20.3	14.5	na
Traffic accidents; poisoning	15.6	17.8	22.4	na	na
Cancer	10.1	9.2	9.0	na	na
Endocrine, nutritional and metabolic	na	3.1	12.0	5.2	na
Diseases congenital malformation	6.2	5.8	3.1	na	na
Other causes	28.8	35.0	45.9	na	na
Incidence rates of selected infectious diseases/10,000:					
Measles	2.14	0.33	0.70	na	na
Rubella	na	0.68	0.48	0.85	na
Meningococcal infection	0.15	0.79	0.85	na	na
Typhoid paratyphoid	0.29	0.97	0.81	na	na
Malaria	na	4.88	1.28	1.49	na
Viral hepatitis	1.80	21.17	12.32	na	na
Pulmonary tuberculosis	na	2.56	2.18	2.11	na
Chicken pox	29.01	31.31	39.07	na	na
Mumps	na	1.99	1.33	2.04	na
Shigellosis	0.0	0.76	0.33	na	na
Hospital services:					
Primary health care centers (No.)	32	30	30	30	30
Population/center	16,979	24,138	48,282	na	na
Hospitals (No.)	na	3	10	12	14
Beds (No.)	1,253	1,468	2,023	2,218	2,613
Beds per 1,000 population (No.)	na	2.31	2.03	1.40	1.43
Rate of bed occupancy	na	78.0	75.5	81.3	na
Average days of stay	6.8	6.9	4.7	10.8	7.4
Discharge daily average	na	124	140	167	na
Population/operation	34.01	36.96	51.53	na	na
Population/daycare surgery	61.27	48.6	94.61	na	na
Percentage of hospital deliveries	98.24	98.44	98.34	na	na
Consultation length in minutes per patient	5.8 ± 2.4	6.6 ± 2.1	6.9 ± 2.5	na	
Personnel:					
Physicians (No.)	968	1,624	3,259	na	na
Physician/bed	0.8	1.1	1.6	na	na
Nurse/bed	1.9	2.8	4.2	na	na
Population/physician	561	446	444	na	na
Population/dentist	3,528	2,577	1,786	na	na
Population/pharmacist	na	1,386	991	1,099	na
Population/nurse	226	179	172	na	na

Note: *na* = not available
Source: [a]Annual Health Report. Vital Health Statistics, Bener and Al Mazroei (2010), Hamad Medical Corporation (2012)

13.2.4 Medical Service Facilities Provider

HMC was established in 1982 and is one of the region's most well-known specialized medical institutions. HMC manages three general hospitals (Al Khor Hospital (149 beds), Al Wakra Hospital (350 beds) and the Cuban Hospital (75 beds)) and five specialist hospitals (Hamad General Hospital (616 beds), Rumailah Hospital (362 beds), Women's Hospital (334 beds), the National Center for Cancer Care and Research and Heart Hospital (120 beds)), which look after patients with the most prevalent conditions, including heart conditions, cancer, rehabilitation, and provide specialist treatment for women and children. It was awarded the Joints Commission International (JCI) certification for quality health facilities. In addition, under the Qatar Foundation, the country has now a developed an ultramodern, all-digital academic medical center, i.e., Sidra Medical and Research Center, which focuses on patient care for women and children in Qatar.

In addition to Hamad Medical Corporation as a non-profit healthcare provider, there are also a number of private medical service facilities providing healthcare to the public, e.g., Al Ahli Hospital, Al-Emadi Hospital, American Hospital, and Doha Clinic Hospital. Private practices and clinics offer a full range of medical services, from specialist consultations to dentistry to home nursing care, rehabilitation, hospital procedures and surgeries.

The primary healthcare services in Qatar are an essential part of the country's plan for socioeconomic development and first level contact of individuals, families and the community with the national health system. The primary healthcare services provided through the health centers are distributed across the country with a referral system to hospitals and to promote the health of the population (Hamad Medical Corporation 2012).

Qatar's Preventive Health Department is responsible for carrying out a comprehensive vaccination program for newborns, infants and children; immunization and food and quarantine watch control; fighting infectious diseases; providing health education in the field of mother and child care; and protecting environmental health and safety. Other than contagious diseases, a section for incommunicable diseases was set up comprising three units: a tobacco control unit, a chronic diseases and accidents control unit and a statistics and nutrition unit (Hamad Medical Corporation 2014).

13.2.5 Health Expenditure

Qatar's healthcare sector has grown steadily since the opening of the country's first hospital almost 50 years ago. According to recent World Health Statistics reports by the World Health Organization, there has been a massive increase in public spending on healthcare in Qatar in the last years, and the country is currently at the top of the per capita health expenditure list among the Gulf Cooperation Council countries (World Health Organization n.d.a).

The total expenditure on health is 2.5 % of GDP, with public spending (2007–2011) allocated to health at 1.6 % of GDP (UNICEF n.d.). In terms of healthcare expenditures, healthcare spending per capita in Qatar is the highest in the Middle East at USD 935 quoting figures from the World Health Organization (WHO-EMRO n.d.b). There has been an enormous increase in public healthcare spending since 1991.

According to the Qatar Health Accounts (QHA) 2011 study, Qatari households spend far more than non-Qatari households on health, although the difference in health expenditure is gradually decreasing (Qatar Health Accounts 2011). Qatari household health expenditure increased by approximately 25 % between 2006 and 2010, while it increased by 58 % for non-Qatari households (both at the individual and household levels) Qatar Health Accounts 2009 & 2010. This is due to the increasing population and demand. In addition, the use of private sector services has also caused a rise in expenditure due to the lack of coverage under the national health insurance scheme. It is reported that 10 % of Qataris and 9 % of non-Qataris do not have a regular healthcare provider due to the high cost.

In addition, the QHA (2011) noted that the HMC spent a billion Qatari riyals on health care in 1991. The total expenditure of the Ministry of Public Health and Hamad Medical Corporation reached QR 1.3 billion in 2002–2003 with an increase of 99.6 % compared to 1990–1991. In 2004, the HMC and NHA together spent QR 1.67 billion (USD458 million) on health care, while the figure was QR 1.3 billion in 2003. Between 2000 and 2004, spending by HMC and NHA has grown as high as 71 %. The budget allocated for public health for the 2006–2007 financial year was QR 3.8 billion, out of which QR 239 million was set aside for public works in the health sector. Expenditure on the health sector in the 2003–2004 financial year amounted to QR 1.5 billion, an increase over the QR 655.5 m in 1990–1991. These amounts do not include health-related public work projects. While the budget allocated to public health for the fiscal year 2006–2007 was QR 3.8 billion, QR 239 m out of this went toward public work in the health sector.

13.2.6 National Health Insurance and Coverage

A comprehensive overview of the Qatar national health insurance scheme was provided by Jones and Shlah (Clyde & Co 2013). The National Health Insurance Company (NHIC) is a fully owned government entity. The NHIC manages and operates the social health insurance scheme in Qatar. The scheme provides mandatory health insurance coverage through a network of public and private providers. The organization has also appointed a third-party administrator and subcontractors to manage the scheme.

All nationals and expatriates are able to obtain free health care. However, rising costs and increased pressure on the budget led the Qatar government in 1999 to require nationals and expatriates to purchase health cards. The costs to purchase cards are low and do not come close to meeting the actual cost of health provision, but signal an erosion of the all-embracing free welfare system. This change in the government's approach to the public provision of healthcare is reflected in the establishment of Qatar's first private hospital, built at an estimated cost of USD27.5 m.

The National Health Insurance Scheme is an embodiment of Qatar's National Vision 2030 and the National Health Strategy 2011–2016 to ensure a healthy population with access to affordable health care. This scheme provides universal health care to members offering a choice of providers from both the public and private sectors. The scheme is expected to be fully launched by 2015; it will cover all individuals living in Qatar, including nationals, non-nationals and even visitors. The Health Insurance Scheme was enacted through issuance of Law No. 7 of 2013 concerning the Social Health Insurance Scheme (the Health Insurance Law). The Health Insurance Law was published in the official gazette—Issue No. 10 dated 16 June 2013 (National Health Insurance Council 2014). According to the new law there will be "Basic and Additional Health Services"; basic health services include preventative, therapeutic and rehabilitative services and medical tests, as per Table 13.3. Accredited health insurance companies will be entitled to offer insurance coverage for additional health services, they will not cover the basic health services.

A national health insurance scheme, accessible to all citizens, residents and visitors, is in the process of being implemented in five phases (the Health Insurance Scheme). The Health Insurance Scheme is to be rolled out in five phases up to 2015 (Table 13.4). The SCH has indicated that expatriates (non-national residents) will be enrolled in the Health Insurance Scheme upon renewal of their residence permits; their employer or sponsor needs to pay a premium. The government is responsible for paying health insurance premiums for Qatari nationals. Visitors are responsible for paying their own health insurance premiums for the duration of their stay in the country. Beneficiaries of the Health Insurance Scheme will be able to obtain services from both public and private healthcare providers. Phase 1 of the Health Insurance Scheme was launched in July 2013. This phase covers Qatari females of age 12 and above, for maternity, gynecology and related healthcare (Supreme Council of Health n.d.a).

13.3 Pharmacy System

13.3.1 Pharmacy Authority

The Pharmacy and Drug Control Department (PDCA) manages, implements and regulates pharmaceutical policy, law and practice in the country. The subunits within PDCA are the drug registration section, drug release section, inspection

Table 13.3 Basic and additional health coverage for Qataris vs. non-Qataris

Qatari nationals	Residents (non-national)	Visitors
• General medicine services	• General medicine services	Accident and emergency services
• Preventive healthcare services	• Preventive health care services	
• Accident and emergency services	• Accident and emergency services	
• Inpatient and outpatient services	• Inpatient and outpatient services	
• Laboratory, radiology and medical examination services	• Laboratory, radiology and medical examination services	
• Maternity and delivery services	• Maternity and delivery services	
• Pharmacy services	• Pharmacy services	
• Basic dental and vision services	• Basic dental and ophthalmological services	
• Treatment of neurological disorders and diseases	• Treatment of neurological disorders and diseases	
• Home health care and private nursing	• Home health care and private nursing	
• Speech disorders, occupational diseases, Palliative care	• Speech disorders, occupational diseases, Palliative care	
• Organ transplantation		
• Death agony care		
• Durable medical devices		
• Infertility treatment and family planning		

and narcotic section, and quality control laboratory. The Pharmacy and Drug Control Department is accountable for recommending drug policy to the higher authority, registration of drug agents and importers, registration of drug companies and their products, and registration of herbal products, dietary supplements and medicated cosmetics. It controls narcotics and psychotropic drugs via import, storage and dispensing control and the quality of registered drugs, herbal products and dietary supplement via laboratory analysis. The PDCA is also engaged in inspection of private (community) pharmacies, drugstores, herbal stores, and drug manufacturing companies to make sure that they are operating according to the pharmacy law and related regulations, scheduling the community pharmacies working hours in collaboration with other concerned authorities in the country (Supreme Council of Health n.d.c).

13.3.2 Pharmacy Practice in Qatar

The pharmacy practice in Qatar has rapidly advanced in recent years due to a number of national initiatives that have included accreditation programs of healthcare services, i.e., under JCI, opening the college of pharmacy, the first and

Table 13.4 Five phases of the health insurance scheme

Phase	Date of implementation	Groups covered	Services covered	Providers in the network
1	July 2013	Qatari women aged 12+ years	Gynecology, obstetrics, maternity and related women's health conditions	• HMC Women's Hospital • Al Emadi Hospital • Doha Clinic Hospital • Al Ahli Hospital • Al Wakra Hospital • The Cuban Hospital • Al Khor Hospital
2	Q1 2014	All Qatari nationals	All services	Select HMC and private providers
3	Q3 2014	All Qatari nationals	All services	Select HMC and private providers
4	Q1 2015	All Qatari nationals, white-collar expatriates and visitors	All services	Select HMC and private providers
5	TBD 2015	All Qatari nationals, white-collar and blue-collar expatriates and visitors	All services	Select HMC and expanded private providers + three designated purpose-built single male laborers' hospitals

only pharmacy college in the country, and a trend to employ those holding advanced degrees in pharmacy practice, e.g., the PharmD. From a policy point of view, Qatar's National Health Strategy of 2011–2016, which states its vision of developing a comprehensive world-class healthcare system, includes disease management, health insurance and integration between both the government and private sectors. To improve efficiency and access and to decease dependence on hospitals for filling prescriptions, the strategy also promotes a community pharmacy network supported by appropriate policy and processes (National Health Services 2011–2016).

13.3.3 Pharmacy Workforce

The majority of pharmacy practitioners in Qatar are foreigners with degrees from Egypt, India, Sudan or Jordan (Kheir et al. 2008). The primary focus areas for these pharmacists are in private community pharmacies, public hospitals, primary healthcare settings and private clinics mentioned in the sections above (Tables 13.5 and 13.6). According to the PDCA list (2011), there are approximately

Table 13.5 Pharmacist workforce in hospitals in Qatar (2012 data)

Hospital	No. of pharmacists
l-Amal Hospital	23
Al-Wakra Hospital	36
Hamad General Hospital	122
Heart Hospital	22
North Area Hospital	36
Rumailah Hospital	24
Women's Hospital	45
HMC corporate	4

Table 13.6 Pharmacists working in Primary Health Centers in Qatar (2012 data)

Pharmacy workforce	Number (%)
Pharmacist	160 (75.8)
Assistant pharmacist (diploma)	33 (15.6)
Technologist (science)	18 (8.6)
Total	211 (100)

160 registered community pharmacies in the country and 44 pharmacies within a private hospital or private medical clinic.

The rate of pharmacists for every 1,000 people of the total population has shown a slight increase from 1.14 in 2006 to 1.17 in 2010 (Statistics Authority 2011; HMC 2012).

13.3.4 Pharmacy Practice Regulations

There is no independent professional pharmacy association that controls the pharmaceutical practice and represents or promotes the profession of pharmacy in Qatar (Wilbur 2010). These roles fall under the prerogative of the SCH, and a Pharmacy Law provides the legal framework that governs the practice. The pharmacy laws are as follows: prescription medicine, pharmacists' registration and practice in Qatar, and pharmacy ownership.

13.4 Qatar Pharmaceutical Profile

13.4.1 Pharmaceutical Supply

Drug procurement, storage, and supply follow organized and well-established protocols. The rules and regulations governing these inventory-related activities are generally similar to those in other neighboring Middle Eastern countries; and several Gulf countries (members of the GCC) purchase their annual quota of medicines through a joint procurement process. This process imposes the political commitment of their member states. The country ensures a cost-effective procurement process through the adoption of a centralized tendering system. In a study conducted in Qatar, practicing pharmacists felt that the regulatory procedures for the procurement, storage, marketing, and pricing of medications are acceptable and they appeared to be satisfied with the processes associated with dispensing medications in retail settings, public clinics, and public hospital outpatient pharmacies (Kheir and Fahey 2011; El Hajj et al. 2011).

Most medicines are imported. Public sector drug procurement is carried out through closed international tenders, GCC bulk procurement and direct purchasing. If the amount is less than QR 500,000, procurement is through direct purchase; if more than QR 500,000, it is through tender. Medicines are also purchased through the GCC committee to get better prices with all Gulf countries. Emergency supplies are provided directly from local pharmaceutical distributors to government hospitals. There is a special non-restricted procedure of procuring medicines for the Qataris. SCH through Pharmacy and Drug Control Department (PDCD) ensures medicines in the country are of good quality, safe and effective. Not all medicines registered in PDCD are available in HMC and vice versa. According to PDCA, there are approximately 4,470 registered pharmaceutical products (Table 13.7) in Qatar (final list updated on April 24, 2014) that are supplied and distributed by 18 registered companies; Ebn Sina Medical Company is the largest suppliers (SCH n.d.b). It is the leading distributor of pharmaceuticals that has a market share of 50 % and operates its own network of pharmacies. It represents most multinational drug manufacturers and supplies both the public and private sectors (Business Monitor International 2013).

In addition, Sidra Medical and Research Center's Procurement and Contracts (P&C) Department manages the sourcing of its goods and services, including pharmaceutical supplies.

Medicines dispensed at the HMC health institutions are charged accordingly. For nationals (and exempted individuals such as GCC, if the mother is Qatari), medicines are free of charge and are now covered by the new insurance system. For non-nationals who are residents they only have to pay 10–20 % of the HMC prices.

Medicines in the public sector, i.e., hospitals, are selected through the pharmacy & therapeutic committee. If a medicine is requested to be included in the formulary, there is a form that should be completed. It will then be discussed and approved in the hospital P&T committee. Next it will be forwarded to the corporate committee for approval before it can be purchased. At the country level, there is a medicine list, but HMC hospitals have their own hospital-based formulary.

13.4.2 Pharmaceutical Market

Qatar imported USD 280.2 million worth of pharmaceutical products in 2010, translating into an annual average of 16.3 % from 2008. Although pharmaceutical

Table 13.7 Profile of registered drugs in Qatar

No.	Profile	Number of items
1	Branded: Generic	50:50 (approx.)
2	Dosage form	
	Tablet	1,638
	Capsule	474
	Ointment	285
	Syrup	183
	Cream	149
	Suspension	78
	Gel	65
	Suppositories	57
	Inhaler	21
	Others (e.g., injectable items, infusion, solution)	1,520
4	Country of manufacturer	
	European + North America + Australia	2,235
	Within the Middle East	1,170
	Other countries (e.g., India, China, Japan, Brazil, Mexico)	1,065

Source: SCH (n.d.d)

exports have multiplied ten times between 2008 and 2011, the export figure is negligible in comparison to imports (Alpen Capital 2013).

In 2009, Qatar Pharma began production and is presumably the only local pharmaceutical manufacturing company that operates on a reasonable scale. However, domestic drug production is gradually gaining momentum in the country.

The Qatari government favors increasing local production. SCH stipulates all doctors to prescribe medicines only by their generic names in order to promote expansion of generic drugs in the market, hence leaving the final choice of generic or branded drugs to the patients. However, it remains to be seen whether generic drugs are able to penetrate the country with the rich and brand conscious consumer base.

The report expects that the Qatari pharmaceutical industry will benefit from the forthcoming implementation of the national health insurance program, which envisions covering all residents and visitors in the country under the scheme.

Furthermore, potential signing of a free trade agreement between the GCC and India, thus paving the way for cheaper imports of generics, can alter the structure of the pharmaceutical industry in the country.

The GCC pharmaceutical industry is expected to experience sustainable growth in the medium to long term. Increased domestic production, foreign investment, and consumption of generics are likely to support the market's evolution (Alpen Capital 2013).

The growing number of lifestyle-related chronic diseases has increased demand for high-value prescription medication in Qatar. People are also becoming increasingly aware of personal health care, which has boosted sales of OTC products such as cold and flu medication, analgesics, digestives, and topical creams.

However, regulations on advertising and retail sales through licensed pharmacies have only partially stunted the growth of the OTC segment. Under Qatari laws, some OTC drugs are categorized as prescription medicines, while some drugs generally available under prescription only are dispensed OTC (NHSQ 2014).

The Qatari pharmaceutical market reached a value of 1.43 billion riyals (USD392.6 million) in 2010, valued at USD379 million in 2012 and is forecasted to grow an average of 12.6 % a year to 2015, when it will be worth 2.58 billion riyals (Business Monitor International 2011, 2013).

Qatar will continue to rely on imported medicines, and it is projected that the emirate will become a billion-dollar pharmaceutical market in 2019, reaching a value of QR 3.99 billion (USD1.10 billion) by 2020. Business Monitor International (2011, 2013) forecast strong growth for pharmaceutical sales in Qatar, projecting annual increases averaging 10.1 % to 2014, when it expects the market to be worth QR 1.37 billion compared to QR 848 million in 2009 (Alpen Capital 2013).

Under the present system, registered importers are responsible for medicines' quality and they are required to produce documentation showing that the drugs conform to international standards and are approved for sale in neighboring countries such as United Arab Emirates (UAE), Saudi Arabia and Kuwait. Opening up the market to more companies will create an enormous challenge in terms of monitoring for quality. Qatar has very limited pharmaceutical manufacturing. According to SCH, Qatar has 17 suppliers and seven pharmaceutical importers (Business Monitor International 2013). At the moment, the country has QatarPharma, a pharmaceutical company that is focusing more on intravenous solutions and is projected to have four more new drug manufacturers to produce tablets, syrups and injectable. Other pharmaceutical companies under establishment are Qatar Al-Hayat, Q-Med; Al-Mutamayyiz Factory for pharmaceutical products, Doha Factory for pharmaceutical products, and factory for medical solutions and intravenous nutrients (all five have been granted for initial approval) (The Peninsula 2012). This move is aimed to reduce dependence on imported medicines.

13.4.3 Medicine Expenditure

Qatar's public sector expenditure in 2009 was USD1,596 million and USD1,757 million in 2010. Out of this total public sector expenditure of both years, the spending on medicines and pharmaceuticals was USD138 million (9 %) and USD143 million (8 %), respectively. This shows a 3.6 % increase (Business Monitor International 2013).

13.5 Medicine Pricing

The issue of medicine pricing is under the jurisdiction of SCH. The Pharmacy and Drug Control Department at the Supreme Council of Health (SCH) is the sole authority to fix prices for medicines. Qatar has implemented a free market system. To bring down prices of medicines and to ensure a continuous supply, all registered and licensed importers as well as dealers in drug importations have been allowed to fix retail prices of the medicines as against the initial price control being done by the council.

13.5.1 History

Drug prices are determined by the Pharmacy and Medical Control Department, Qatar Ministry of Health under the Law No. (7) of 1990. The medicine pricing considerations are based on the following aspects:

1. Original value for medicines
2. Value of insurance for the medicines
3. Wages of freight to the port in Qatar
4. Value of custom fee
5. Expenses of unloading, excluding the demurrage

The pricing process included 10 % profit margin to importers and nearly 30 % margin to retailers. The retailers received stocks from wholesalers with the prices printed on each pack of medicines. Retail outlets were bound to keep the printed prices. The foreign currency exchange rate was fixed.

Under the initial registration law of 1986, by Pharmacy and Medical Control Department, SCH, products have to be registered with the Pharmacy and Drug Control Department at the SCH. Licensed dealers that were controlled by 18 licensed agents were allowed to import medicines only from the country of origin. Qatar's pharmaceutical market relies heavily on imports; imported products are, by default, more expensive. The old law and procedures have caused few problems. The Qatari market faced a shortage of certain drugs; and high drug prices, which were said to be among the highest in the region. Suggested solutions were to liberalize imports and open market to the competition in order to allow more businessmen to enter the industry, which could result in increased availability of all types of medicines and this would in turn decrease drug prices.

13.5.2 New Changes in Law

The development of Qatar's pharmaceutical market is shaped by the decision made by the SCH to abolish government controls over the pricing of medicines and to allow more importing agents in the country. Prior to this new initiative, there was a small number of importing agents that had caused high pharmaceutical prices (Business Monitor International 2011). It is an open market system. In April 2011, the Law No. (7) of 1990 by the Pharmacy and Medical Control Department was reviewed and repealed. Government control over retail prices of all medicines sold in Qatar was withdrawn, which permits importers to establish their own prices. Free pricing has provided a way for medicine supply chain companies to increase their margins and counter foreign-exchange fluctuations.

As part of Qatar's public health strategy for 2011–2016, and based on complaints by consumers about high prices and non-availability of some drugs, a new law was enacted. In addition, many consumers and pharmacists complain about the government's move to issue price controls on medicines without more licensed drug importing companies to stop the existing monopoly in the market. The market is seeing an unprecedented increase in medicine prices even though it is anticipated that the elimination of a medicine price ceiling would help decrease drug prices. Retailers criticize that they have been at the receiving end, when the SCH put a price cap to curb a unilateral rise in medicine prices imposed by some wholesalers. The retailer's profit margin has been reduced to 10 %, which was previously nearly 27 % (Business Monitor International 2011).

The regulations previously made the retailers' stock only the most expensive drugs in order to maximize their profit margins. The new system provides an opportunity for lower-priced branded drugs and generics to move into Qatar's pharmaceutical market. Nevertheless, the market's value at consumer prices will result from both upward (including healthcare modernization and high per capita GDP) and downward pressures. The main downward pressure is the fact that open market competition on drug prices, and the availability of cheaper alternative drugs, should drive down artificially inflated prices, although this is unlikely to happen rapidly. SCH has stated that drug manufacturers will still need to obtain import licenses by meeting stringent regulatory conditions. The retailers and distributors are unlikely to reduce prices or go for cheaper drugs if they think it will affect their businesses' profitability. There is also likely to be a degree of consumer loyalty to branded drugs, particularly among those with high incomes and private general practitioners. According to the Business Monitor International (2011), it is expected that the country's pharmaceutical market will post a compound annual growth rate (CAGR) of 16.07 % in the 2009–2014 period, to reach QR 2.61 billion (USD716 m) in value, boosted by a strong economy.

Drug prices in Qatar have rapidly increased by approximately 30 % following the introduction of new free-pricing legislation that was intended to reduce the cost of medicines (IHS 2011). The law ended government control over retail prices of all medicines sold in Qatar and allows importers to establish their own prices.

Previously, the official prices, which were set by the PDCD of the SCH, were widely considered to be too high.

However, according to anecdotal reports from the Peninsula (2011), Gulf Times (2011) and Taylor (2010, 2011), consumers were surprised to find that wholesalers had increased product prices by as much as 30 % within days of the ending of government controls. Consumers interviewed have complained that medicine prices from retail pharmacies such as asthma medicine has increased from QR 42 to QR 60 (QR 1 = USD0.274), anticholesterol agent increased from QR 240 to QR 373, and medicine for diabetes has increased by more than QR 100. The same brand of Loratadine syrup (100 mL) an antihistamine for allergy, ranged between QR 22 and QR 25 at three different outlets. Similarly, 60 mL of paracetamol syrup for children from the same maker cost anywhere from QR 7 to QR 12. A bottle of an OTC drug containing 96 tablets to cure indigestion and heartburn was also being sold at different prices—from QR 9 to QR 11—in three of the medicine stores visited. While some local pharmacies were selling a strip of ten paracetamol tablets of the same brand for QR 4 and QR 5, others were providing the same for as high as QR 11. A similar brand of one strip of ten 200-mg tablets of Ibuprofen, which is used to reduce fever, pain or inflammation caused by conditions such as headache, toothache, back pain, arthritis, menstrual cramps or minor injury, was being sold over the counter at prices ranging from QR 4.50 to QR 7. In yet another example of the pricing discrepancy, an anti-decongestant for children (75 mL) was found selling for QR 7 and QR 19 at two drug stores. Sun-screen costs QR 104 when another cream that produced similar results was available at a supermarket for only QR 10. A mystery shopper study conducted by Qatar University College of Pharmacy on a simple acute upper respiratory infection conducted by two simulated clients illustrated that the cost of medications dispensed to them ranged from QR 7 to QR 88.75 (Mohamed Ibrahim et al. 2014). Inquiries by Gulf Times at a number of local pharmacies confirmed that some OTC drugs from the same manufacturer were being sold at various prices in different shops. Furthermore, Gulf News reported the difference in medicine prices (Table 13.8) before and after the introduction of the new law (Gulf Times 2013).

In the past, retailers were required to charge the prices set by the PDCD, which were printed on the packs received from wholesalers, but since the change in the law retailers have been free to set their own price levels based on the price lists supplied by wholesalers (The Peninsula 2011). However, retailers are unclear whether they are free to fix their own prices and they are following the lists of wholesale and retail prices issued by wholesalers and showing these lists to consumers.

The PDCD cannot intervene over the price increases because it no longer has any control over drug pricing issues. However, the cabinet has also approved legislation suggested by the SCH that seeks to boost competition in the market by ending the monopoly held by the 18 suppliers/distributors currently licensed to bring medicines into the country. It is believed that these market liberalization measures will again reduce drug prices (Alpen Capital 2013).

Table 13.8 Selected products with price increase in Qatar

	Previous price (QR)	Post April 2011 price (QR)	% change
Lipitor (atorvastatin; 10 mg)	163.75	219.00	33.7
Norvasc (amlodipine; 5 mg)	85.50	92.00	7.6
Januvia (sitagliptin; 100 mg)	323.75	400.00	24.0
Augmentin (amoxicillin and clavulanate)	140.00	154.00	10.0

Source: Gulf News

On the other end, several pharmacists said that they would be forced to sell cosmetics, instead of medicines, to overcome the losses caused by a major cut in their profit margin imposed by the SCH. Initially, the PDCD was the sole authority to fix the prices of medicines in Qatar by issuing a rate list to wholesalers, who sell the stocks to retailers with prices printed on each pack of drugs. The retail outlets were then bound to keep the printed prices and not allowed to inflate prices on their own. Even the wholesalers could not increase prices without the PDCD's authorization. During the price fixing era, most retailers used to claim that they were selling medicines with very low income margin and that their profits were not commensurate with the overhead costs and shop rents.

It has been indicated that medicines prices in Qatar are high due to the monopoly maintained by current distributors. There was lack of competitive market to ensure increased supply of medicines and pharmaceutical products which failed to help beat down drug prices. Retail prices of medicines in Qatar remain among the highest in the region despite the abolition of the drug pricing law by the PDCD in April 2011 (Gulf Times 2011). The move had aimed to bring down the retail prices of OTC medicines in local pharmacies across the country. The officials also mentioned that plans to establish four new pharmaceutical companies in the country would help reduce drug prices (Gulf Times 2014).

13.6 Generic Medicines Policy

Qatar's pharmaceutical market is not able to support its own needs and is likely to remain highly dependent on imports, providing significant opportunities for multinational branded drug makers to penetrate its market. Government tends to purchase branded products; however, the share of the generic drug market is increasing (Business Monitor International 2013). There is no policy on generic medicines bioequivalent, but the government is promoting the use of generic medicines. HMC is using brands mainly because of prescribers' preference, patient trust and unavailability of a bioequivalence center in Qatar. There are no criteria to select generics such as FDA orange book (USA FDA 2014).

Observations show that there is extensive use of branded medicines in Qatar's healthcare facilities. Anecdotal evidence has also indicated that due to the preference and cultural aspects to use branded medications among both clinicians and patients, the usage of generic drugs is low. This contributed to additional healthcare costs that could have been avoided. Under the National Health Strategy 2011–2016 (Project 5.4), the government has focus on generic medicines use awareness in the country. SCH has proposed several behavioral and utilization studies to assess issues regarding generic medicines among public and healthcare providers, i.e., levels of utilization, perception, knowledge, and practice.

It is estimated that the value of Qatar's drug expenditure at consumer prices in 2009 was QAR 848 million (USD233 million), having posted double-digit growth in relation to the previous year (Business Monitor International 2010). Prescription drugs continued to dominate the market, accounting for close to 90 % of sales by value. By 2014, drug expenditures are forecasted to increase by a compound annual growth rate of 11.16 %, in both US dollar and local currency terms, as the latter is linked to the former to reach QAR 1.44 billion (USD400 million).

In Arab States, the World Bank report warns of the impact of poverty and the huge disparity in wealth in the Middle East. Rich and wealthy Arabs are needed to undertake a related approach at the very least through investing their wealth in productive projects, e.g., pharmaceutical companies for generic medicines in Arab countries or in countries and regions of the marginalized and poor. That way, Arabs can bridge the gap between people lacking basic needs, e.g., essential medicines and life requirements rather than relying on imports of branded medicines from abroad forever, which is the case in all Arab countries, especially the six GCC states.

The multinational pharmaceutical companies have been successful in the Qatari market due to people's high brand consciousness for both prescription and OTC (over-the-counter) medicines. There is low interest among multinational manufacturers to set up manufacturing plants in the country due to the small market size. Instead, the country prefers to import medicines from the MENA and Asian countries.

13.7 Conclusions

A high share of imported and branded medicines, caused by prescriber and consumer trust and preference, has inflated healthcare spending of the Qatari government, the main buyer of medicines, and consumers. A small market size and high income per capita has affected government's strategy to curb high medicine prices in the country. SCH's attempt to remove price controls had affected the affordability of medicines as the prices of some drugs have increased. The government had to enforce price controls, although it abstained from explicitly fixing the prices.

References

Alpen Capital, GCC Pharmaceutical Industry (2013) Dubai

Bener A, Al Mazroei A (2010) Health services management in Qatar. Croat Med J 51:85–88

Business Monitor International. Qatar pharmaceuticals and healthcare report Q2, London

Business Monitor International. Qatar pharmaceuticals and healthcare report 2011, London

Business Monitor International. Qatar pharmaceuticals & healthcare report, Business Monitor International Q3 2013, London

El Hajj MS, Kheir N, Zaidan M et al (2011) Pharmacist characteristics, medication use perceptions, and professional satisfaction: a first national survey in the state of Qatar. J Healthcare Leadership 3:9–28. https://www.dovepress.com/pharmacist-characteristics-medication-use-perceptions-and-professional-peer-reviewed-article-JHL-recommendation1

General Secretariat for Development Planning of Qatar (GSDP). Qatar population status, 2012. Minister of development planning and statistics, Qatar. http://www.gsdp.gov.qa/portal/page/portal/ppc/PPC_home/ppc_news/ppc_files_upload/populations_status_2012_en.pdf. Accessed 26 Mar 2014

General Secretariat for Development Planning of Qatar (GSDP). Qatar Economic Outlook 2013–2014. Minister of development planning and statistics, Qatar

General Secretariat for Development Planning of Qatar. Qatar National Vision 2030, Doha

Gulf Times (2011) New law aims to cut drug prices. http://www.gulf-times.com/qatar/178/details/27071/new-law-aims-to-cut-drug-prices. Accessed: 3 Apr 2014

Gulf Times (2013) Pharmacies sell same medicine at different prices. http://www.gulf-times.com/qatar/178/details/340439. Accessed 3 Apr 2014

Gulf Times (2014) Medicine prices set to drop in Qatar. http://www.gulf-times.com/qatar/178/details/383096/medicine-prices-set-to-drop-in-qatar. Accessed 3 Apr 2014

Hamad Medical Corporation. HMC annual report 2012. Doha

Hamad Medical Corporation. http://www.hmc.org.qa/en/. Accessed 25 Apr 2014

Hamad Medical Corporation. National health strategy. http://www.hmc.org.qa/en/hcp/healthcare_in_qatar/national_health_strategy/national_health_strategy.aspx. Accessed 15 Apr 2014

IHS (2011) http://www.ihs.com/products/global-insight/industry-economic-report.aspx?id=1065929679. Accessed 12 June 2014

Index Mundi. Qatar Economy Profile (2013) http://www.indexmundi.com/qatar/economy_profile.html. Accessed 3 June 2014

Jones W, Shlah R. Qatar national health insurance scheme update. http://www.clydeco.com/insight/updates/qatar-national-health-insurance-scheme-update. Accessed 10 May 2014

Kheir N, Fahey M (2011) Pharmacy practice in Qatar: challenges and opportunities. Southern Med Rev 4(2):92–96

Kheir N, Zaidan M, Younes H, El Hajj M, Wilbur K, Jewesson P (2008) Pharmacy education and practice in 13 middle eastern countries. Am J Pharm Educ 72:1–13

Ministry of Foreign Affairs, Qatar. Health services. http://www.mofa.gov.qa/en/Qatar/Pages/Health.aspx. Accessed: 5 Apr 2014

Ministry of Interior, Qatar. http://www.moi.gov.qa/site/english/index.html. Accessed 30 Apr 2014

Mohamed Ibrahim MI et al (2014) How do community pharmacists in Qatar respond to patients presenting with symptoms of acute respiratory tract infections? J Pharmacy Practice Res 44:62–63

National Health Strategy (2011–2016) Supreme Council of Health, Qatar. http://www.nhsq.info/strategy-goals-and-projects/national-health-policy/healthcare-products-regulation/news-details?item=81&backArt=286. Accessed 19 Mar 2014

National Health Insurance Council. http://www.nhic.qa/. Accessed 3 May 2014

National Health Strategy Qatar. http://www.nhsq.info/strategy-goals-and-projects/national-health-policy/healthcare-products-regulation/news-details?item=81&backArt=286. Accessed 12 June 2014

Qatar Health Accounts. Qatar national health accounts. Report 2009 & 2010. Supreme Council of Health, Qatar. http://www.nhsq.info/app/media/1148

Qatar Health Accounts. Qatar national health accounts. Report—2011. Supreme Council of Health, Qatar

Qatar Statistics Authority (QSA). Annual Statistical Abstract, 2011. Minister of Development Planning and Statistics, Qatar. http://www.gsdp.gov.qa

Supreme Council of Health, Qatar (n.d.a) http://www.sch.gov.qa/health-services/services-to-healthcare-professionals/pharmacy-n-drug-control. Accessed 16 Mar 2014

Supreme Council of Health, Qatar (n.d.b) http://www.sch.gov.qa/health-services/services-to-healthcare-professionals/pharmacy-n-drug-control/drug-registration/registered-drug-list. Accessed 18 Mar 2014

Supreme Council of Health, Qatar (n.d.c) http://www.sch.gov.qa/sch/En/content.jsp?menuId=24&CSRT=6635171528762819683. Accessed 28 Mar 2014

Supreme Council of Health (n.d.d) Annual health report, Qatar. Vital health statistics. Doha

Taylor L. Qatar abolishes drug price-fixing. Pharma Times: World News. 12 Oct 2010

Taylor L. Qatar drug prices soar after law change. Pharma Times: World News. 31 May 2011

The Peninsula. Five firms get approval for manufacturing drugs. 15 May 2012

The Peninsula. SCH price cap hurting pharmacies: traders. The Peninsula Thursday, 24 Nov 2011

UNICEF (n.d.) http://www.unicef.org/infobycountry/qatar_statistics.html. Accessed 23 Feb 2014

United Nations Development Programme (2014). Human development index. http://hdr.undp.org/en/content/table-1-human-development-index-and-its-components. Accessed 3 Nov 2014

USA FDA. Orange Book: approved drug products with therapeutic equivalence evaluations. http://www.accessdata.fda.gov/scripts/cder/ob/. Accessed 15 June 2014

Wilbur K (2010) Continuing professional pharmacy development needs assessment of Qatar pharmacists. Int J Pharm Pract 18(4):236–241

World Bank. http://www.data.worldbank.org. Accessed 21 Mar 2014

World Health Organization (n.d.a) Global health observatory. http://apps.who.int/gho/data/?theme=main. Accessed 12 Mar 2014

World Health Organization (n.d.b) http://www.who.int/countries/qat/en/. Accessed 10 Apr 2014

Chapter 14
Pharmaceutical Pricing in South Africa

Andy Gray and Fatima Suleman

Abstract South Africa has implemented a number of important medicine pricing interventions in the post-apartheid era, informed by the 1996 National Drug Policy. Despite considerable resistance, firstly from the transnational pharmaceutical industry but later from a wider range of stakeholders, a number of legal reforms have been successfully implemented. However, many of these interventions have limitations. Generic utilization in the private health sector has increased over time, but can still be improved. Maximum dispensing fees have been introduced, but may need to be complemented by more sophisticated professional remuneration models that more effectively advance the responsible use of medicines. The single exit price mechanism, with annual adjustments, may need reconsideration and refinement. Proposals for external reference pricing are in the final stages of preparation. Greater use of pharmacoeconomic evaluations will help to inform rational selection and reimbursement policies, especially as the country moves towards a National Health Insurance model. The state tender system will also need to be reconsidered, as the separation between public and private healthcare financing and delivery becomes blurred.

14.1 Introduction

This chapter first provides a context for the pharmaceutical pricing interventions that have been introduced in South Africa in the post-apartheid era (since the transition to democratic rule in 1994), by outlining the existing and anticipated features of the health system in the country. The pharmaceutical system, from manufacturing/importing to final dispensing, is described in brief. The nature of the medicines regulatory system, and plans for the immediate future, are then

A. Gray (✉)
Division of Pharmacology, Discipline of Pharmaceutical Sciences, University of KwaZulu-Natal, Durban, South Africa
e-mail: graya1@ukzn.ac.za

F. Suleman
Division of Pharmacy Practice, Discipline of Pharmaceutical Sciences, University of KwaZulu-Natal, Durban, South Africa

Z.-U.-D. Babar (ed.), *Pharmaceutical Prices in the 21st Century*,
DOI 10.1007/978-3-319-12169-7_14

outlined. The post-apartheid health policy environment is then described, with emphasis on the National Drug Policy, which was issued in 1996. Since 1994, South Africa has implemented a number of legislative reforms aimed at improving access to essential medicines, including strong pro-generic policies and an extensive set of pharmaceutical pricing reforms. This process has not been without hurdles, including litigation, and is still considered to be a work in progress.

14.2 The Health System: In Context

The Republic of South Africa is a large (1.2 million km^2) country located at the southern end of the African continent. It has a population of approximately 53 million people, of whom 80 % are black Africans (Statistics South Africa). Approximately 9 % each of the population are White and of mixed race (so-called Coloured), respectively, and some 2.5 % are descendants of migrants from the Indian sub-continent. South Africa is regarded as an upper middle-income country. The total fertility rate is low by African standards, at 2.3. Although there are large under-populated areas, the overall population density is 43.4 /km^2. The single largest population (24 % of the total) resides in the Gauteng Province, which is the economic powerhouse, centred around Johannesburg and Pretoria. Almost 20 % are resident in KwaZulu-Natal Province. Although about two-thirds of the population is urbanized, there are still significant numbers living in poorly-resourced rural areas, particularly those that were designated as "bantustans" (or homelands) during the apartheid era. In the Limpopo Province, almost 90 % of the population is still living in rural areas.

The health system in South Africa still reflects the legacy of the policy of racial segregation and discrimination that was entrenched by the apartheid regime between 1948 and 1994, but also the consequences of earlier colonial policies and practices. Prior to 1994, health services in South Africa were provided in a fragmented manner, as dictated by the apartheid policy of separate development for different races. There were 14 different health departments providing mainly curative services through hospitals (Coovadia et al. 2009). After the democratic transition in 1994, a concerted effort was made to create a unitary healthcare system. However, as South Africa has a quasi-federal Constitution, there are now nine provincial departments of health, with overall policy-making and co-ordination vested in a national Department of Health. However, the division between an over-loaded public sector and a better-resourced private sector has persisted. The public sector is largely funded by the state from the fiscus, and caters to the uninsured. The private sector is funded largely from medical scheme (insurance) premiums and out-of-pocket payments and caters mostly (but not exclusively) to the beneficiaries of such schemes. In 2012, about 44 million of the population were dependent on the public sector, while less than 9 million were insured by 93 separate medical schemes (Council for Medical Schemes 2013). The division is clearly depicted in the per capita expenditure on health per annum, which was ZAR 2,667 in the public sector in 2011, and ZAR 11,048 in the private sector (Day and Gray 2013).

14.2.1 The Pharmaceutical System

South Africa has a large and highly developed pharmaceutical system, including all steps from limited local production of active pharmaceutical ingredients (APIs) and extensive facilities for producing finished pharmaceutical products (FPPs), to highly developed distribution and wholesaling services, and a well-developed community and hospital pharmacy network. Local production is almost entirely dependent on imported APIs, with only a limited range of locally-produced APIs. As of July 2013 the South African Medicines Control Council (MCC) had licensed 259 entities as manufacturers, importers and/or exporters of medicines, secondary packers or testing laboratories (or in at least 1 of these categories) (South African Medicines Control Council 2013). Of these, 77 entities were listed as manufacturers of medicines, meaning that some element of local production was involved. The list included locally registered subsidiaries or offices of both transnational pharmaceutical concerns and international generic pharmaceutical manufacturers. In addition, the MCC listed 194 pharmaceutical wholesalers and 1 pharmaceutical bond store.

All medicines sold in South Africa have to be registered by the MCC, a statutory regulatory authority located within the national Department of Health. The MCC operates in terms of an Act of Parliament (the Medicines and Related Substances Act (Act 101 of 1965), as amended), supplemented by Regulations issued by the Minister of Health, and its own detailed guidelines. The MCC is required to only consider issues of quality, efficacy and safety, and there is no linkage between patent status and regulatory approval. The MCC is in the process of transitioning to a new structure, to be styled as the South African Health Products Regulatory Authority. Under the new system, which will be co-funded from increased user fees, decision-making will vest in the staff of the Authority, rather than in the appointed members of the Council. The legislation to give effect to these changes is before Parliament, but has yet to be finalized (Minister of Health 2014).

In the private sector, medicines supply to the public is through a network of community and private hospital pharmacies, with a number of prescribers also licensed to dispense medicines to their own patients. All community and hospital pharmacies have to be licensed by the Department of Health and registered with the South African Pharmacy Council (SAPC; the responsible statutory body). In April 2014, the SAPC recorded the registration of 3,025 community pharmacies, 259 institutional pharmacies in the private sector (predominantly located in private hospitals), and 640 institutional pharmacies in the public sector (predominantly located in public sector hospitals, but also in larger community health centres) (South African Pharmacy Council 2014). Private hospital pharmacies are generally owned by the hospital group, of which three dominate in the local market. Community pharmacy ownership has been opened to non-pharmacists, and recent years have seen the development of two major pharmacy chains and the establishment of in-house pharmacies within large supermarkets. Each pharmacy is, nonetheless, under the continuous personal supervision of a pharmacist.

The SAPC also recorded the registration of 247 manufacturing pharmacies and 235 wholesale pharmacies. The latter would have included at least some of the pharmaceutical depots operated in the public sector (of which there are ten provincial depots as at April 2014, as well as stores maintained by the military and prison authorities). In the private sector both wholesaler and distributor models co-exist. A wholesaler generally stocks a full range of medicines, and takes ownership of such stock from suppliers. A distributor generally operates on behalf of a limited range of suppliers and holds stock on consignment, without taking ownership.

14.3 National Drug Policy

The immediate post-1994 period was characterized by intense policymaking activity, including the publication of a National Drugs Policy for South Africa (NDP) in 1996 (Department of Health 1996). The NDP addressed health, economic and national development objectives, but the over-riding aim was "to ensure the availability and accessibility of essential drugs to all citizens". When the then Minister of Health initiated the development of the NDP, she instructed the responsible policy committee to "develop a pricing plan for drugs used in South Africa in the public and private sectors". This process was rushed and incomplete (Gray et al. 2002). The policy document therefore outlined some elements, but was not detailed in all respects. It called for the establishment of a Pricing Committee (with an indicative composition), and then committed to "total transparency in the pricing structure of pharmaceutical manufacturers, wholesalers, providers of services, such as dispensers of drugs, as well as private clinics and hospitals". The detailed description was limited to the following statements: "A non-discriminatory pricing system will be introduced and, if necessary, enforced. The wholesale and retail percentage mark-up system will be replaced with a pricing system based on a fixed professional fee."

It is important to note that this policy was intended to apply only to the private sector, as medicines procurement in the public sector continued to be based on a national competitive tender process, limited to locally registered products. In the public sector, medicines are not charged for individually. At primary care level, all services are free, and in hospitals a means-tested and capped daily fee is levied.

Nonetheless, the NDP did also address other cost-drivers in relation to pharmaceuticals. The policy therefore called for the maintenance of a database to monitor costs compared with other developing and developed countries, for the regulation of price increases; for the provision, in certain circumstances, of public sector stock to the private sector; for the promotion of generic substitution; for measures to improve rational medicines use; and for increased control of pharmaceutical marketing practices (Gray 2009).

As will be seen, the implementation of these policies, once translated into legislative reforms, has been highly contested. South Africa has embarked on the even more challenging process of introducing a system of integrated universal coverage with a national health insurance scheme. Such changes will require that the current divisions between the public and private health sectors are considerably blurred and eventually removed, and that a single medicines pricing system applies across the health system.

14.4 Medicines-Related Legislative Reform Since 1994

14.4.1 The 1997 Amendment Act: Delayed by Litigation

The first attempted to provide a legislative platform for the policy changes signaled in the 1996 NDP came with the Medicines and Related Substances Control Amendment Act (Act 90 of 1997) (Republic of South Africa 1997). This enabling piece of legislation provided for the creation of a ministerially-appointed Pricing Committee. It also introduced three related interventions directed at the pricing of medicines in the private sector. First, it established that all medicines should be sold in the private sector (that is, to any purchaser other than the state), at a disclosed single exit price, unrelated to the volume purchased. In order to make this meaningful, it introduced a ban on the provision of samples or of any bonus stock of any description, and outlawed all incentive schemes. Lastly, it provided for a regulated, annual maximum adjustment in the single exit price of all medicines. Act 90 of 1997 also introduced mandatory offer of generic substitution (in all sectors), with a negative list of non-substitutable medicines to be stipulated by the MCC. More controversially, the Act appeared, at first reading, to allow the Minister of Health to issue compulsory licences for medicines, without regard to the Patents Act. The pricing interventions were scheduled to come into effect 1 year after promulgation of the Act, which would also allow for the determination, through Regulations to be issued by the Minister of Health, of maximum dispensing fees for pharmacists and licensed dispensing practitioners.

Acts of Parliament do not come into effect as soon as they are passed, but require an implementation date to be set by the President, in the form of a promulgation notice. Before the 1997 Amendment Act could be brought into effect, this step was interdicted by the Pharmaceutical Manufacturers' Association and 39 of its member companies, representing the majority of the transnational pharmaceutical industry active in South Africa at that time (Pharmaceutical Manufacturers' Association of South Africa 2001). Due to a protracted process of exchange of documents, the case was only set down for oral argument in January 2001. At that point, the newly-established AIDS advocacy group, the Treatment Action Campaign, joined as an *amicus curiae* (a friend of the court). This resulted in another delay, but when the court reconvened in April, the complainants withdrew their case. The case was thus never decided upon by a court of law, but was regarded as an important victory for the government, assisted by those who advocated access to affordable essential medicines. The new Minister of Health brought another set of amendments to the Medicines Act to Parliament in 2002, and the legislative changes first delineated in the NDP were brought into effect from May 2003 (Republic of South Africa 2002). The pricing interventions could therefore only come into effect a year later, in 2004.

14.4.2 The Challenges of Implementation: More Litigation

Although the key provision in Act 90 of 1997 which precipitated the court action was that related to intellectual property, the Act also introduced other important provisions aimed at improving access to medicines ('tHoen 2002). The first of these was the provision for mandatory offer of generic substitution. All dispensers of a prescription in South Africa are obliged to offer a generic substitute if one exists. The dispenser (whether a pharmacist or a licensed dispensing prescriber) cannot substitute a more expensive option for a cheaper one, and must respect the wishes of the patient. In addition, the prescriber may indicate that substitution may not be done, by indicating "do not substitute" in his/her own handwriting. The MCC also provides a list of non-substitutable medicines. Over time, this list has been amended, and it now lists only biosimilars as non-substitutable. The 2002 Amendment Act introduced a requirement for the dispenser to take reasonable steps to inform the prescriber if substitution has occurred, but only after making the substitution and recording this fact in the prescription record. The entire generic substitution scheme therefore came into effect in May 2003, when the two Amendment Acts were promulgated by the President.

The direct pricing intervention, however, was scheduled to come into effect a year later, in 2004. The necessary subordinate legislation (Regulations issued by the Minister of Health) were published for comment in mid-January 2004, allowing barely enough time for the required 3-month comment period before the final versions were issued on 30 April 2004. The scheme was intended to come into effect on 2 May 2004. The Act itself had provided for the appointment of a Pricing Committee (with a designated composition). On their recommendations, the Minister was enabled to make regulations "on the introduction of a transparent pricing system for all medicines and Scheduled substances sold in the Republic". Firstly, the Minister was required to publish "an appropriate dispensing fee" to be charged by a pharmacist or by a licensed dispensing prescriber, and "on an appropriate fee to be charged by wholesalers or distributors". The "transparent pricing system" was to be based on "a single exit price", defined as "the only price at which manufacturers shall sell medicines and Scheduled substances to any person other than the State".

Instead of the fixed professional fee envisaged in the policy, a capped fee (26 % to a maximum of ZAR26 per item) was initially prescribed, together with a price freeze (locking factory gate prices at the weighted average of 2003 prices offered to the private sector). Importantly, the pharmaceutical industry had succeeded in altering a draft regulation which sought to impose an immediate 50 % cut in the factory gate price to one which ensured a cost-neutral price freeze, with the promise of annual review. In order to prevent perverse incentives being offered which would undermine the single exit price, unrelated to volume, the Act also provided that "[n] o person shall supply any medicine according to a bonus system, rebate system or any other incentive scheme". The prospect of a reference pricing system, or at least a one-off benchmarking exercise, was also signaled, but not described in detail.

The challenge to the regulatory scheme came from pharmacists in the community and private hospital arenas instead. Two linked cases were heard by a full bench in the Cape High Court, and rejected by the majority (New Clicks South Africa (Pty) Ltd 2005). The Supreme Court of Appeal overthrew the Cape High Court decision and the entire set of Regulations was declared "invalid and of no force and effect" (Pharmaceutical Society of South Africa 2005). The Minister of Health in turn appealed to the Constitutional Court. The case was joined, as *amici curiae*, by the Treatment Action Campaign and Innovative Medicines South Africa (a pharmaceutical industry grouping, representing a number of transnational manufacturers and resulting from a split of the Pharmaceutical Manufacturers' Association). The majority held that the dispensing fee was not "appropriate" (Minister of Health 2005). Critically, the Chief Justice wrote that, while some evidence had been provided that the proposed dispensing fee would result in damage to the viability of pharmacies (and in particular, rural pharmacies and courier pharmacies), the onus was on the Minister (as advised by the Pricing Committee) to show that their scheme would not have this effect. After a protracted process, final dispensing fees were eventually determined, and have been subsequently adjusted to take some account of changes in the costs of providing such services. The fees are based on a fixed amount and a percentage component, varied by four bands of single exit prices. The tier structure and variables for income and expenses for calculation of the dispensing fees are based on an agreement between pharmacists' stakeholders and government.

An international benchmarking system, in which the prices of innovator products will be compared with those in a basket of countries (Australia, Canada, New Zealand, Spain, together with South Africa), has been proposed but not yet implemented. A final draft version of the regulations, which dealt with concerns previously raised by the industry, was published for comment in May 2014 (Minister of Health 2014). There is no indication as yet regarding the acceptability of the methodology to either pharmaceutical manufacturers or funders. A phased approach has been proposed. In phase 1, it is proposed that the interim benchmark price will be the average of prices in the five country basket, if this is lower than the South African ex-manufacturer price. However, in this period, which will last for 2 years, if the South African ex-manufacturer single exit price is lower than the average of prices in the basket, that price will be retained. In phase 2, the final benchmark price will be lowest price in the basket. Provision has been made for exemption from the benchmark in certain circumstances. Importantly, the draft methodology has allowed for the use of weighted prices for those manufacturers who trade in both the public and private sectors. However, all newly introduced medicines, first marketed after the final regulations are published, will have to comply with the final benchmark immediately, and will not benefit from the phased approach.

Benchmarking has already been used in the public sector, but in a very different form. Medicines for the public sector are procured by means of competitive tender processes. The 2010–2012 antiretroviral tender introduced a benchmarking step, in which indicative global best prices were provided before tenders were invited. This process has now been repeated for other tenders issued by the National Department of Health, including for new vaccines.

Another element which has been described in detail in subordinate legislation is the requirement for the submission of pharmacoeconomic analyses to justify the initial launch prices of new medicines (National Department of Health 2013). To date, the submission of such data remains voluntary, and no medicines have yet been deemed to have unacceptable prices. The prices of newly launched patent protected medicines, generally brought to the market by transnational innovator firms, therefore remain unregulated. Such medicines may not be included easily in the public sector Essential Medicines List, and may be refused reimbursement or attract considerable co-payments in the private sector.

14.5 Effects of the Pharmaceutical Pricing Interventions

The initial single exit price, applied from 2004, was a cost-neutral compromise from the initial government intention to force a 50 % reduction in prices. Although the method for determining the quantum of the maximal annual adjustment of the single exit price policy implied the application of a predetermined formula (based, for example, on consumer price inflation and the exchange rate between the local currency and major global currency), and this was the basis for negotiation between the manufacturers and government, the regulations allowed the Minister of Health to take other aspects into consideration. Thus the annual adjustments (as shown in Table 14.1 below) were not always as desired by the manufacturers. Adjustments could only be published after the court challenges to the dispensing fees were settled, and so only commenced from 2007. Calls were issued each year for inputs from industry. At times, the adjustments were capped at the level of the prevailing consumer price inflation rate, but they have varied widely, from a zero adjustment in 2011 to a high of 13.2 % in 2009. From a base of ZAR 100 in 2004, the single exit price would now be at a level of ZAR 155.76 in 2014. However, that mechanism of control will have had no effect on the launch prices of newly registered and marketed medicines. It is for this reason that the proposed international benchmarking exercise is being watched with such interest. However, it should also be noted that every manufacturer does not take advantage of the full single exit price adjustment for every product in its portfolio. For reasons of competition, price increases may be less than the maximum allowed in some cases.

Table 14.1 Single exit price adjustments since 2007 (after the court challenge)

Year	Single exit price adjustment (maximal change in single exit prices, to be applied during the year following the determination)
2007	5.2 %
2008	6.5 %
2009	13.2 %
2010	7.4 %
2011	0 %
2012	2.14 %
2013	5.8 %
2014	5.82 %

The volatility in exchange rates been of considerable concern, especially since the significant changes experienced by many emerging market currencies after 2013. As a result, the SEP Adjustment methodology is once again under review in 2014. Currently, wholesalers and distributors are paid a logistics fee by manufacturers, from the factory-gate single exit price. Although a single fee is disclosed on the price list made available on a national Department of Health web site (http://www.mpr.gov.za/), not all logistics service providers are able to negotiate the same fee. There have been efforts to separate the ex-manufacturer price and logistics fee components within the single exit price calculation, but there has been no consensus on how this can be done. There is also uncertainty as to whether this is allowed under the current legislation framework. The possibility has been floated on separate adjustments for originator medicines, fully imported generic medicines and locally produced generic products.

As with many countries, it is difficult to show whether local prices are higher or lower than in other comparable countries, with similar sized economies. An attempt was made to apply the WHO/HAI pricing methodology in a survey conducted in the Gauteng province in 2004 (before the final application of the pricing regulations, but 6 months after the application of the first single exit price) (Xiphu and Mpanza 2004). This survey showed that, in the private community pharmacy sector and for a basket of 42 selected medicines, the median price ratio (in relation to the 2003 Management Sciences for Health international reference price) was 24.91 for innovator brands, 6.82 for the most sold generic, and 6.52 for the lowest priced generic. The corresponding ratios were very similar when the survey was based on private hospital prices, as would be expected (26.35; 6.82; 6.45). However when applied to medicines procured by the public sector, on tender, the results were very different. The median price ratio was 1.64 for innovator brands, 1.85 for the most sold generic, and 1.62 for the lowest priced generic.

No comparable study has been conducted since 2004. At least in relation to innovator brands that are still under patent, the proposed international benchmarking exercise will provide significant data. The 2004 survey also drew attention to the contribution of South Africa's 14 % value-added tax, which has remained constant since that time. Although there have been calls for exemption of all medicines, or at least essential medicines, this has been resisted by the Treasury, partly on the basis that it would only benefit the insured elite. This argument ignores the possibility of out-of-pocket purchases of medicines by the uninsured, including medicines obtained from community pharmacies and dispensing medical practitioners.

As was outlined above, the quantum of the dispensing fee has been highly contested. Even though a final dispensing fee for pharmacists was established in 2006, the adjustment of this fee structure over time has remained controversial. Requests for commercial information from community pharmacists have not resulted in the submission of sufficient data to allow for recalibration of the fee structure, and adjustments have been more closely tied to general inflation measures. The evolution of the fee structure for pharmacists, in South African Rand, is shown in Table 14.2. Although this is a maximum fee which cannot be exceeded, a number of medical schemes have negotiated lower dispensing fees with preferred providers, including the community pharmacy chains. The ability of pharmacists in independent practice to extract the maximum fee is therefore constrained. In addition to the dispensing fee, the South African Pharmacy Council has published a list of non-distributive services for which pharmacists in community and hospital practice may levy a professional fee. While theoretically available, such fees have not embraced by funders and are therefore rarely levied.

Table 14.2 Evolution of the maximum dispensing fee for pharmacists 2004–2013

Year	Single exit price breakpoints	Maximum dispensing fee (as a fixed amount or a percentage of the single exit price, or a combination of these)
2004	Less than R100	26 %
	R100 or more	R26.00
2006	Less than R75	R4.00 + 33 %
	R75 and more, but less than R250	R25.00 + 6 %
	R250 and more, but less than R1000	R33.00 + 3 %
	R1000 and more	R50.00 + 1.5 %
2010	Less than R75	R6.00 + 46 %
	R75 and more, but less than R200	R15.75 + 33 %
	R200 and more, but less than R700	R51.00 + 15 %
	R700 and more	R121.00 + 5 %
2013	Less than R80	R6.40 + 46 %
	R80 and more, but less than R216	R16.00 + 33 %
	R216 and more, but less than R756	R55.00 + 15 %
	R756 and more	R131.00 + 5 %

The private hospital sector in South Africa has chosen not to levy the dispensing fee at all, selling medicines at the single exit price only. This has required the entire pharmaceutical service in such hospitals to be funded from the bed and operating theatre fees. Data from the Council for Medical Schemes have shown that expenditure in the private hospital sector has outstripped that on medical specialists and any other category of provider since 2000. The entire private healthcare sector is the subject of an inquiry by the Competition Commission of South Africa, which will commence in 2014.

The maximum dispensing fee system also applied to prescribers who were licensed to dispense, but on a different scale altogether. This system has also been contested, but less successfully than in the case of community pharmacy. Nonetheless, the policy stance in favour of restricting dispensing by prescribers, which was first signaled in the 1996 National Drug Policy and legislated for in the 1997 Amendment Act, has been seriously eroded by court challenges. The provisions which required an applicant for a dispensing licence to demonstrate that there was need for the service were struck down by the Constitutional Court in 2005 (The Affordable Medicines Trust 2005). Over time, the total number of licensed dispensing practitioners has returned to the levels that existed before the policy was introduced. However, the role of the medicine pricing regulations in this arena has been limited, as such practitioners provide an all-inclusive service for a flat fee, including the provision of basic medicines.

An area of more importance has been that of generic penetration, in response to the legal requirements for mandatory offer of generic substitution by all dispensers. While the public sector has always been more dependent on generic medicines, as the use of a competitive bid system relies on the existence of competitors and the Essential Medicines List has been skewed towards older products, less likely to be on patent, the private sector has seen significant brand loyalty and a tendency towards the use of branded medicines. In the 1980s, even before the generic policy was developed, the Pharmaceutical Society of South Africa introduced a maximum medical aid price (MMAP) mechanism, as a form of internal reference pricing (Boyce and Bartlett 1990). This scheme was adopted by a number of medical schemes, as well as by some of the provinces, which were then using private sector pharmacies to serve selected ambulatory patients.

Evidence of the extent to which the private sector has embraced generic medicines is not easily obtained. In 2012, South Africa's insured population was served by 93 separate medical schemes (Council for Medical Schemes 2013). Although some schemes are self-administered, other use the services of an administrator and many use managed care organisations. Five administrators are responsible for 83.8 % of the market (excluding the self-administered schemes). One of the managed care organisations has, in contrast to its competitors, chosen to place significant data on medicines utilisation in the public domain. The Mediscor Medicines Review has been published annually since 2002. In 2012, Mediscor provided pharmaceutical benefit management (PBM) services to 32 medical schemes, and a total of 1.6 million beneficiaries (Mediscor 2013). The changes in generic market penetration reported by Mediscor since 2004, as measured by the volume of prescriptions for generic brands, innovator brands with valid patents, and

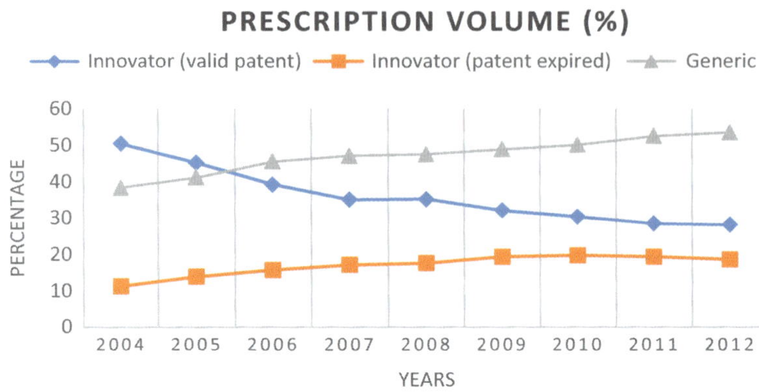

Fig. 14.1 Generic penetration (as reported in the Mediscor Medicines Reviews 2004–2012)

innovator brands with expired patents, are shown in Fig. 14.1. The increase in generic penetration after the policy change was implemented can be seen. The situation for the entire country, including the public sector, would likely show generic penetration beyond the level reported by this single PBM. However, there is still room for improvement.

The Mediscor reports have also provided evidence of the growing effect of newly launched, expensive (and often biological) medicines on the private sector market. In 2011, of the top ten new chemical entities reimbursed by Mediscor-administered schemes, three were antiretrovirals, and two were biologicals (an epoetin and cetuximab). Whereas existing medicines cost on average ZAR132 per item in 2011, new chemical entities (including those launched in the 5 years preceding the report) cost on average ZAR482 per item. Oncology products, while presenting 9.5 % of total medicines expenditure, cost on average ZAR1855 per item in the same year.

14.6 Ongoing Debates and Prospects

If measured against the intentions of the 1996 National Drug Policy, it is clear that the implementation of the 1997 Amendment Act and the development of the necessary subordinate legislation has delivered in some regards, but not in all.

The pro-generic policy has resulted in an increase in generic utilization in the private sector, but not to the degree which has been achieved in major developed country markets, notably in the United States. One of the key problems that remains is the lack of access to an equivalent of the FDA's Orange Book, which clearly indicates the basis for generic registration, the identity of reference products, and hence the basis for interchangeability. The non-substitutable list has been rationalized, but the restriction of options in relation to biosimilar medicines may prove to be premature and require further reconsideration. Managed care interventions in the private sector have assisted in driving greater use of generics, but are hampered by the outdated treatment algorithms that are imposed for certain chronic conditions (Nicolosi and Gray 2009).

In terms of private sector pricing, the single exit price mechanism and the publication of annual adjustments has provided the state with a powerful tool, but one that is lacking in relation to the prices of new medicines at launch. In that regard, much is expected from the international benchmarking exercise, but also from the application of pharmacoeconomic analyses. The latter provision, while in place, is not yet binding on manufacturers and requires not only considerable resources in order to prepare such submissions, but also considerable capacity to critically assess the submissions and make defensible determinations on that basis. In this regard, the capacity of the Pricing Committee and its secretariat will need significant attention. There will also have to be far more transparent documentation of the basis for decisions taken by these structures, which inform the actions taken by the Minister.

Transparency was a key principle outlined in the policy. While the fees levied by dispensers are now transparent to patients and funders, the logistics fee remains opaque and problematic. The processes of determining adjustments in the single exit price and in the dispensing fee also need attention, and more transparent documentation. The 1996 National Drug Policy expressed a preference for a professional fee that was not linked to the value of the medicine. That has not proven easy to implement. In time, more attention will also need to be paid to the development of more sophisticated remuneration models that promote the responsible use of medicines.

There is ongoing concern about the persistence of perverse incentives in the medicines market. While some elements of the South African system, such as the ban on sampling, have been effectively implemented, there are still concerns about the proliferation of additional fees paid to pharmacies by manufacturers that may constitute inappropriate bonusing or incentive schemes.

As South Africa continues with its planned introduction of National Health Insurance, the stark separation between the public and private sector systems will need to be addressed. One way in which this may occur is a greater reliance on a single medicines selection process, backed by more explicit health technology assessment processes. In this regard, the early experiences with the pharmacoeconomic evaluations will be instructive. Increasingly, private sector stakeholders are being included in the Expert Review Committees that serve the National Essential Medicines List Committee. A single national essential medicines list, applicable both to the public sector and to medical schemes, may well be possible. In time, hard choices will need to be made about the future of the state tender system for medicines. A reimbursement list, informed by pharmacoeconomic data, may well be a future option for a unified health system.

Returning to the issues that precipitated the court actions that delayed implementation of the 1997 Amendment Act, South Africa has also finally embarked on a review of its intellectual property policies and laws (Minister of Trade and Industry 2013). The intent is to introduce reforms that will enable the country to make full use of the flexibilities provided for in the Agreement on Trade-related Aspects of Intellectual Property (TRIPS), as well as to introduce an effective patent examination system. It is worth reflecting on the fact that South Africa has not yet issued a compulsory or government use licence for a medicine. The success of the antiretroviral treatment programme has been based on the ability to access affordable generic medicines, but these have become available as a result of voluntary licensing (sometimes under duress from activists) and non-enforcement of patents, not from explicit government action.

14.7 Conclusion

South Africa developed a comprehensive National Drug Policy in 1996, which included a number of policy choices relevant to medicines pricing. While the implementation of those policies has not been without challenge, including repeated litigation in South African courts, a number of interventions have been successfully applied. South Africa has managed to ban the use of medicine samples, has limited the scale of price increases over the years, has managed to promote increased use of generic medicines, and has proposed mechanisms for external reference pricing and for increasing use of health technology assessment in medicines selection and pricing. In the public sector, the use of indicative reference prices has contributed to the ability of the state tender system to obtain competitive prices for medicines. However, as the country moves towards universal healthcare coverage, it will need to find ways of merging the strongest elements of all of these policies, in order to ensure sustainable access to quality, affordable, essential medicines.

References

Boyce D, Bartlett G (1990) The maximum medical aid price programme. A review of the concept and of its ability to reduce expenditure on medicines. S Afr Med J 78(3):147–151

Coovadia H, Jewkes R, Barron P, Sanders D, McIntyre D (2009) The health and health system of South Africa: historical roots of current public health challenges. Lancet 374:817–834

Council for Medical Schemes (2013) Annual report 2012/2013. Pretoria

Day C, Gray A (2013) Health and related indicators. In: Padarath A, English R (eds) South African health review 2012/2013. Health Systems Trust, Durban

Department of Health (1996) National Drug Policy for South Africa. Pretoria

Gray AL (2009) Medicine pricing interventions—the South African experience. South Med Rev 2 (2):1–5

Gray A, Matsebula T, Blaauw D, Schneider H, Gilson L (2002) Policy change in a context of transition: drug policy in South Africa 1989–1999. Centre for Health Policy, University of the Witwatersrand, Johannesburg

Mediscor (2013) Mediscor Medicines Review 2012. Johannesburg

Minister of Health. Medicines and Related Substances Act (101/2014): regulations relating to a transparent pricing system for medicines and scheduled substances: (Benchmark Methodology). Government Notice R.354, Government Gazette No. 37625, 12 May 2014

Minister of Health. Medicines and Related Substances Amendment Bill (Bill 6 of 2014)

Minister of Health and Another v New Clicks South Africa (Pty) Ltd and Others CCT59/04 2005 (2) SA 311 (CC)

Minister of Trade and Industry. Draft National Policy on Intellectual Property, 2013. General Notice No. 918, Government Gazette No. 36816, 4 September 2013

National Department of Health. Publication of the guidelines for pharmacoeconomic submissions. Government Notice No. R.68, Government Gazette No. 36118, 1 February 2013

New Clicks South Africa (Pty) Ltd v Tshabalala-Msimang and Another; Pharmaceutical Society of South Africa and Others v Minister of Health and Another 2005 (3) SA 231 (C)

Nicolosi E, Gray A (2009) Potential cost savings from generic medicines—protecting the prescribed minimum benefits. SA Fam Pract 51(1):59–63

Pharmaceutical Manufacturers' Association of South Africa and others v President of the Republic of South Africa and others. Transvaal Provincial Division (2001) (case no: 4183/98)

Pharmaceutical Society of South Africa v Minister of Health and Another; New Clicks South Africa (Pty) Ltd and Others v Minister of Health and Another 2005 (3) SA 238; 2005 (6) BCLR 576 (SCA)

Republic of South Africa. Medicines and Related Substances Amendment Act (Act 40 of 2002)

Republic of South Africa. Medicines and Related Substances Control Amendment Act (Act 90 of 1997)

South African Medicines Control Council (2013) Licenses issued in terms of section 22C of the Medicines and related Substances Act, 1965. Manufacturers, importers, exporters, wholesalers, distributors. Pretoria

South African Pharmacy Council statistics page (2014). http://www.pharmcouncil.co.za/B_Statistics.asp. Accessed 30 Apr 2014

Statistics South Africa. Census in Brief 2011. https://www.statssa.gov.za/Census2011/Products/Census_2011_Census_in_brief.pdf. Accessed 30 Apr 2014

'tHoen E (2002) TRIPS, pharmaceutical patents, and access to essential medicines: a long way from Seattle to Doha. Chicago J Int Law 3(1):27–46

The Affordable Medicines Trust v the Minister of Health and Others 2005 JOL 13932 (CC)

Xiphu L, Mpanza N (2004) Medicine prices survey in the Gauteng Province in South Africa. National Department of Health

Chapter 15
Politics, Reforms, and Regulation of Pharma Prices and Expenditures in Turkey over the 2000s

Ipek Eren Vural

Abstract This chapter provides a political economy perspective on reforms of pharma price and expenditure control in Turkey over the 2000s. This is carried out through (a) embedding the description of the properties of pharma price control and health care system within their broader socio-political context, and (b) exposing the social struggles underpinning these polices.

Over the 2000s, changes in pharma price and expenditure control policies in Turkey supplemented the neoliberal reforms within the health care system. External reference pricing system (ERP) introduced in 2004 consolidated the power of transnational pharma capital in pricing. While over the period 2004–2008 changes in pharma price and expenditure control policies alongside growing public financing of health care significantly expanded pharma market and sales, since 2009, amidst the spiralling impacts of global financial crisis, increasing stringency of pharma price and control policies appeared to have circumvented favourable accumulation prospects for both local and transnational pharma capital. The latter set of policies indicate how public policies mediate contradictory interests of capital within the processes of accumulation. In due course, however, pharma pricing policies is increasingly enmeshed with fluctuations in exchange rate markets, threatening access to vital drugs used in the treatment of chronic diseases, and raising concerns about both the quality of locally produced drugs and possible anti competitive practices amongst producers of certain groups of pharma products.

I. Eren Vural (✉)
Department of Political Science and Public Administration, Middle East Technical University, Ankara, Turkey
e-mail: ieren@metu.edu.tr

Z.-U.-D. Babar (ed.), *Pharmaceutical Prices in the 21st Century*,
DOI 10.1007/978-3-319-12169-7_15

15.1 Introduction

Over the 2000s, against the background of a short-term capital led economic growth model, Turkish health care system experienced extensive neoliberal reforms. The reforms expanded access to and demand for health care services, endorsed private health care provision while generating a growing public budget for such provision. Changes in pharma price and expenditure control policies supplemented market creation objective of these reforms. External reference pricing system (ERP) introduced in 2004, for regulating maximum market prices of pharmaceuticals, significantly consolidated the power of transnational pharma capital in pricing. Together with other neoliberal reforms in health care, and growing public health expenditures, pharma price and expenditure control policies expanded pharma market and sales, for both original products originating from transnational capital and generic products associated mostly but not exclusively by domestic pharma capital. At first glance, the phenomenal growth in public health care and pharma expenditures during this period may appear contradictory with neoliberalism, and the restrictive fiscal policies generally associated with short-term capital led growth model. In effect, however, such public expenditure sustained inflows of capital into the health care system and supported the creation of private health care markets. Moreover, growing public health care expenditures also garnered public consent for neoliberal reforms both within the health care system and in the wider economy.

Since 2009, amidst the spiralling impacts of the global financial crisis, the Turkish government significantly increased the stringency of its pharma price and expenditure control policies. Successive price cuts, increases in compulsory discounts imposed on both generic and patented drugs within the public reimbursement system, and the freezing of exchange rate adjustments despite rapid fluctuations of the Turkish lira appeared to have circumvented the favourable accumulation prospects for both transnational and local pharma capital. I argue that such policies do not imply a rift or irony within the neoliberal restructuring process but rather signal its consolidation. In due course, however, pharma pricing policies is increasingly enmeshed with fluctuations in exchange rate markets, threatening access to vital drugs used in the treatment of chronic diseases, and raising concerns about both the quality of locally produced drugs, and anti competitive practices within the pharma industry between manufacturers of different groups of products.

The outline of the chapter is as follows. The second section accounts for the continuing significance of pharma price and expenditure controls in both developed and developing economies despite successive waves of liberalisation observed since the 1980s. This is done through locating pharma price and expenditure control policies within their broader context of social reproduction in capitalist economies. The third section describes the content of neoliberal reforms in the Turkish health care provision and financing system over the period 2003–2008. It also presents a current overview of pharma industry, and pharmaceutical distribution chain. The fourth section analyses the changes in pharma pricing and expenditure control policies that supplemented the reforms in health care provision and financing. It evaluates the drivers and nature of policy changes as well as their impacts over the period 2004–2008. The fifth section reviews the increasing stringency of pharma price and expenditure control policies since 2009 under the impacts of the global financial crisis. Final section evaluates the sources and impacts of this more stringent regulation on public pharma expenditures, access to vital drugs, and public health.

15.2 Significance of Pharma Price Controls: An Overview of the Theoretical Approach

Why are pharmaceutical prices and expenditures still controlled through different systems in most economies despite successive waves of liberalisation in trade, investment and financial regimes since the 1980s?

This question requires us to locate pharma price and expenditure policies within their broader context of social reproduction within capitalist economies. As with public policies regulating health care provision and financing (Gough 1975), pharma price and expenditure policies affect social reproduction of labour power, private profitability, accumulation, distribution of income and contribute towards generation of social consensus in capitalist social formations. Such effects of pharma price and expenditure policies highlight the sources of conflicting class interests that lie at the bottom of these policies. As such, formation and implementation of pharma price and expenditure policies are underpinned by intense class struggles involving: (a) inter class struggles between the capital and the dominated classes, (b) intra class struggles amongst the local and transnational fractions of pharmaceutical capital, as well as struggles between the pharmaceutical capital and the wider fractions of capital at both the national and transnational levels. Which dimension of pharma price and control policies (i.e. social reproduction of labour power, generation of social consensus, profitability, accumulation, redistribution) predominate in any one policy context is thus down to the precise conjuncture of class struggles as these are framed by general characteristics of dominant accumulation strategies across different historical periods.[1]

Viewed from this perspective changes in pharmaceutical price control policies in Turkey, were shaped by struggles between the local and transnational fractions of pharmaceutical capital on the one hand and the dominated classes on the other. Social categories, such as the medical doctors and pharmacists, have also been

[1] This argument is an extension of the relational conceptualisation of the state that views it as a material condensation of class relationship of forces, and state policies, such as pharma price and expenditure control policies, as expressions of those relationships (Poulantzas 1978).

influential participants through their peak professional associations. Such struggles and their outcomes were crystallised in government policies towards the sector and in policy implementation by relevant state authorities such as the Ministry of Health, Ministry of Finance, Trade and Industry and so on. Moreover, outcomes of the wider struggles at the national level, between different fractions of Turkish capital and transnational capital on the one hand, and the dominated classes on the other, over important issues such as the growth models, and accumulation regimes not only framed the content of different pharma price control policies but also conditioned, sustained or undermined struggles over alternative policy choices. Examples on how wider social struggles at the national level affect sectoral politics within pharma industry is abundant including, liberalisation of the economy in the 1980s, Turkey's ongoing membership negotiations with the EU (c.f. Eren Vural 2013), and most recently, as discussed in this chapter, the consolidation of a short-term capital led growth pattern since the 2000s.

15.3 Neoliberal Reforms and Pharma Price and Expenditure Control Policies over the 2000s

Over the 2000s, short-term capital led growth model was consolidated in Turkey. This entailed provision of high real interests rates to attract inflows of foreign capital and sustain domestic capital accumulation (Yeldan 2009; Ergunes 2009). To secure investor confidence, the model was supported by government commitment to a restrictive monetary and fiscal policy (Epstein and Yeldan 2006). Politically, this model of development was sustained by a class alliance between the transnational financial capital and the internationalised fractions of the Turkish capital that sought to integrate into global circuits of production (Karakas-Gultekin and Ercan 2008).

Over the 2000s, short term capital led growth model in Turkey intensified the retreat of state from public service provision and a concomitant refocusing of public policies on the generation of new markets and assets for capital investment (c.f. Fine 2008). Within the Turkish health care system, this took the form of extensive neoliberal restructuring of health care provision and financing which was realized under a series of structural reforms initiated in 2003 under the so-called "Health Transformation Program (HTP)".

Throughout the chapter, I analyse the nature and implementation of these reforms in two periods. During the first period of 2003–2008, neoliberal restructuring entailed creation/consolidation of markets for private health care provision while significantly broadening their public financing. The second period starting with 2009 corresponds to consolidation of neoliberal reforms that aims at maintaining their long-term sustainability.

15.3.1 Neoliberal Reforms in Health Care Provision and Financing System

Between 2003 and 2008, reforms focussed on reorganisation of the health care provision and financing systems, including changes in pharmaceutical price and expenditure control policies. Prior to the reforms, both health care provision and financing systems in Turkey were characterised by a high degree of institutional fragmentation. A wide range of public, semi public, non profit institutions and private sector were involved in health care provision, including Ministry of Health, public social security institutions, municipalities, state ministries, economic enterprises, and university hospitals. Health care financing system was equally fragmented with three occupationally segregated public health insurance schemes providing differential access to their beneficiaries.

Reforms unified all public health care provision units under the control of Ministry of Health. Further administrative and financial decentralisation of Ministry of Health affiliated public health units urged them to compete for patients both with each other and with increasing number of private sector health care providers. To sustain the latter, generous investment subsidies provided to the private sector since the 1990s were expanded. Overall the reforms expanded investments by both transnational and local capital in health care provision and financing. The number of private hospitals recorded drastic increase over the period 2002–2011 growing at an compound annual rate of seven per cent (Ministry of Health 2013). Burgeoned by the reforms, private hospital sector attracted transnational finance in the form of private equity fund investments. Over the period 2007–2013 a total of 21 acquisitions and private equity investments were recorded in the private hospital sector, more than ninety per cent of which was realised by transnational financial investors. Meanwhile, within health care financing sector, transnational financial investments were directed towards private insurance sector.

Noeliberal reforms also generated a split between the provision and financing of health care services. Health care financing was centralised under the newly established Social Security Institution (SSI), which unified the previously independent three public social security schemes. SSI, thus, emerged as the single public purchaser of health care services and pharmaceuticals from both public and private health care providers, with extensive market power. The institutional market for health care services was further expanded through the implementation in 2008 of a contribution-based general health insurance system, universal in coverage. As of 2012, the percentage of population covered by SSI increased to 99 % (ISPA & Deloitte 2014:26). Reorganisation of health care provision and financing thus increased the access and demand for health care services, and broadened the public financing of private health service delivery. Over the period 2002–2012, the number of visits to health care providers per patient grew at a compound annual growth rate of ten per cent, from three visits in 2002, to eight visits in 2012 (Ministry of Health 2013).

15.3.2 Health Care Reforms and the Pharma Industry

Neoliberal health care reforms in the 2000s generated new transformational dynamics within the pharma industry in Turkey. The latter had already gone through successive restructuring following the liberalisation of trade and investment regimes in the 1980s, Turkey's revived integration process with the EU since the 1990s, and a stronger intellectual property regime (IPR) since the turn of the new millennium.

Pharma industry in Turkey historically had sophisticated manufacturing capability. In 2013, locally produced drugs accounted for 74 % of the pharma sales volume (Table 15.2). Local pharmaceutical capital, however, have always remained dependent on foreign technology and imports of APIs, either from transnationals or from other external sources. That dependency was strengthened with successive waves of liberalisation in trade and investment regimes during the 1980s, when nascent local production of active pharmaceutical ingredients (APIs) was dislocated and manufacturing specialisation of the industry was readjusted towards formulation drugs (Eren Vural 2013). The same period, especially the aftermath of the completion of Customs Union with the EU in 1996, saw increased penetration of transnational pharma capital into the industry. This had largely focused on imports into Turkey and strengthening collaboration with local pharmaceutical capital, with the consequence of transnationals gaining an increased share in market sales, as well as a rising share of original and licensed products in terms of sales volume and value (Eren 2002). Finally, in 1999, patent protection for pharmaceutical products and processes became binding and a stronger intellectual property regime entered into force. Since then local pharmaceutical capital focussed on generic production, while R&D activities geared towards incremental innovation and exports as well as further strengthening of ties with the transnational pharmaceutical capital emerged as the main survival strategies for the larger and more internationalised local pharmaceutical firms (Eren Vural 2013). Meanwhile, for small-sized local pharma firms that cannot fund such R&D, purchases of product dossiers from foreign sources, alongside importing activities for formulation and resale, have emerged as a more cost-conscious and realistic alternative (c.f. Eren Vural 2013).

There are currently 77 production units in the Turkish pharma industry, 17 of which belong to transnationals, and all manufactures at international standards. There are 300 firms in the industry, employing 30,000 people and marketing around 6000 products (IEIS 2014).

Over the 2000s, pharma industry in Turkey attracted a new wave of transnational entry. A stronger IPR environment and Turkey's EU membership negotiations were important triggers of this new wave of entry. Also important in generating this new wave of entry were the growing public health care expenditures and a favorable pharma price control policy, as will be explained in the following section. Unlike the earlier waves of transnational penetration into the industry, which had focused mainly on imports into Turkey and collaboration with local generics firms, this

Table 15.1 Pharmaceutical imports and exports 1980–2010 in US$ million

	Total			APIs		Formulation	
	Imports	Exports	Ex/imp	Imports	Exports	Imports	Exports
1980	93	4	4	91	2	2	2
1985	149	13	9	137	10	8	3
1990	470	90	19	386	23	18	67
1995	660	61	9	496	24	25	37
1996	979	105	11	717	56	27	49
1997	982	98	10	668	39	32	59
1998	1,180	129	11	769	61	42	68
1999	1,337	128	10	785	67	41	62
2000	1,511	140	9	828	69	683	71
2001	1,534	132	9	836	83	698	49
2002	1,716	180	10	874	94	842	86
2003	2,419	88	4	1,231	21	1,188	66
2004	2,710	331	12	1,379	145	1,330	186
2005	2,845	282	10	1,409	65	1,436	217
2006	3,036	313	10	1,433	66	1,602	247
2007	3,524	358	10	1,660	69	1,863	288
2008	4,360	421	10	2,057	85	2,303	336
2009	4,533	310	7	1,300	11	3,233	299
2010	4,032	356	9	1,028	31	3,004	325

Source: Compiled from Republic of Turkey, Ministry of Health, Health Statistics Yearbooks, 2004, 2008, 2010

second wave of transnational entry was characterized by acquisition of local generics firms by the transnationals. A total of 20 takeovers took place between 1999 and 2013, with both large and small local generics firms targeted (Eren Vural 2013).

Strengthening of IPRs and transnational entry arose at the time of (and possibly caused) increasing import dependence in the local industry, as well as contraction in the market share of locally produced drugs (Eren Vural 2013). During the 2000s, the strong growth in formulation imports generated a new form of dependency. The growth in the value of imported formulation drugs is greater than both the growth in total pharmaceutical imports and in API imports (see Table 15.1). The value of imported formulation drugs increased from US$683 million in 2000 to US$3,004 million in 2010, with an annual compound growth rate of 15 %. This compares with an annual compound growth rate for total pharmaceutical imports and API imports over the same period of 10 % and 2 % respectively (see Table 15.1). The share of formulation drug imports in total pharmaceutical imports increased from 45 % in 2000 to 53 % in 2008, and up to 74 % in 2010. Meanwhile the share of APIs in total imports declined from 55 % in 2000 to 47 % in 2008, and 25 % in 2010.

The growing dominance of imported formulation drugs can also be (Eren Vural 2013) observed in the composition of market sales volume and value, which indicates that imported formulation drugs are replacing locally produced products (The Boston Consulting Group 2011). While in 2005 imported formulation drugs

Table 15.2 Percentage of imported and locally produced pharmaceuticals in the Turkish pharmaceutical market, 2005–2013

	2005	2006	2007	2008	2009	2010	2011	2012	2013
Sales value									
% of imported drugs	42	46	48	50	52	52	49.8	50.3	52.3
% of locally produced	58	54	52	50	48	48	50.2	49.7	47.7
Sales volume									
% of imported drugs	15	17	18	20	22	23	24.6	25	26
% of locally produced drugs	85	83	82	80	78	77	75.4	75	74

Source: Calculated from IMS Dataview, IMS Health, www.imshealth.com

constituted 15 % of sales volume and 42 % of sales value, in 2010 the share of imported formulation drugs in sales volume and value both increased, to 23 % and 52 % respectively (see Table 15.2). Increased import dependency of the local pharmaceutical industry can also be observed in the export to import ratio of the industry, which is approximately 10 % (see Table 15.1).

Formulation drug sector recorded some improvement in its exports. The value of these exports increased from US$71 million in 2000 to US$325 million dollars in 2010, with an annual compound growth rate of 16 % (see Table 15.1). This improvement, however, have so far remained behind the steep rise in imports.

All products (patented and generics) within the Turkish pharma market are branded, which have historically contributed to high levels of promotional expenditures, intensifying concentration levels and oligopolistic market behaviour in the industry (Kirim 1985; Eren 2002). Despite successive waves of market penetration by transnationals over the last decade, as of 2013, the first ten firms controlled forty-one per cent of the total market sales in value, while the market share of first twenty firms reached sixty-two per cent (Author's calculation from IMS Market View Data).

15.3.3 Health Care Reforms and Pharmaceutical Distribution Chain

Pharma distribution chain in Turkey flows from manufacturers/importers down to wholesalers and then to retail pharmacies. Within the wholesaler market, there are two segments. Tenderer wholesalers, which supply hospitals, and pharmacy selling wholesalers (OECD DAF 2014). There are around four hundred wholesalers however, concentration levels, especially within the pharmacy selling segment is very high (Ibid). The market share of two nation-wide operating wholesaler networks is more than 70 %. The third largest share within the wholesaler market, reportedly controlling 18 % of the market, belongs to the Pharmacists Cooperatives, which are owned and managed by the pharmacists (Bilgin 2011). The remaining wholesalers thus operate on a small and local scale with low market shares. Large scale wholesalers, and also pharmaceutical manufacturers/importers supplying them extend their market shares by offering discounts, promotional free products, and favourable payment terms to retail pharmacies. Such favourable terms provide important incentives for pharmacists who have generic substitution rights at the dispensing level to channel sales accordingly.

At the retail distribution level, there are 25,000 pharmacies. Pharmacies are all privately owned and ran by pharmacists and chain pharmacies are not allowed. Drugs cannot be sold outside the pharmacies. Profit margins of both wholesalers and pharmacists are regulated through price control schemes (see next section). Hospitals have their own pharmacies for supplying inpatients. Neoliberal health care reforms, which unified and expanded health care coverage, allowed public reimbursement of all outpatient prescriptions dispensed from private pharmacies. This significantly expanded sales volume at the retail pharmacy end of the distribution chain (Celik and Seiter 2008).

15.4 Reforms in Pharma Price and Expenditure Control Policies

Between 2004–2008, changes in pharma price and expenditure control policies supplemented the neoliberal reforms in health care. Before the reforms, the Ministry of Health regulated maximum market prices of pharmaceuticals through a cost plus control scheme while the three different social security schemes, mentioned earlier, had their own uncoordinated cost containment measures. Following the reforms, two levels of price controls became binding for pharmaceuticals. The first is the controls over maximum market prices of pharmaceuticals regulated through External Reference Pricing System and implemented by the Ministry of Health. The second is a set of supply side expenditure control measures implemented by the SSI, which following the centralisation of health care financing mentioned earlier, emerged as Turkey's monopsonistic public purchaser of health services and pharmaceuticals.

15.4.1 External Reference Pricing System

Pharmaceutical prices have always been regulated through Decisions of Council of Ministers in Turkey. Following this tradition in February 2004, a Council of Ministers Decision introduced a new pharma price control scheme, which was largely compatible with market creation objectives of reforms realized in the health care provision and financing systems.[2]

[2] For an alternative view see Mercan (2012).

The new scheme displaced the previous cost-plus price regulation for pharmaceuticals and introduced External Price Benchmarking (ERP) (c.f. Espin et al. 2011). It regulated maximum market prices (including the product launching prices and price revisions) of pharmaceuticals (Council of Ministers 2004). As in all previous schemes, the Ministry of Health was designated as the main regulatory authority for pharma price controls. Again like previous schemes, the General Directorate of Pharmaceuticals and Pharmacies (GDDP) within the Ministry of Health, and a Pricing Department within this Directorate were reinstated as main implementing bodies. However, more recently in November 2011, a newly founded Pharmaceutical and Medical Devices Agency of Turkey, affiliated to the Ministry of Health, took over functions previously performed by the GDDP, including the pricing of pharmaceuticals.

Within the new ERP system the Ministry of Health for the first time, started to use the prices of pharmaceutical products in a predetermined set of EU countries (the so called reference countries, which were declared as Spain, Portugal, Greece, Italy, for 2004, and which can be subject to change) to derive a reference price, which is then used to set the price of the product in Turkey. The price control scheme adopted a new criterion of original versus generic drugs, to differentiate drugs for pricing purposes (Council of Ministers 2004).[3] The new scheme stated that the reference price of an original drug in Turkey would be set according to 100 % of its cheapest price amongst the predetermined list of five EU countries.[4] The reference price of the original drug determined as such was also to be used to set the prices of its generic equivalents, which could take up to 80 % of the reference price at most (ibid). Retail price of pharmaceuticals were founded by adding wholesaler and pharmacists profitability mark-ups on top of reference price, plus an 8 % value added tax (VAT). While previous price control schemes had adopted fixed margins to regulate profitability in the distribution chain, the new price control scheme introduced regressive margins, providing progressively lower percentage of profit on more expensive products. Depending on the sale to the wholesaler price of drugs, the profitability margins allowed for wholesalers thus ranged between 2 and 9 % while for the pharmacists they ranged between 12 and 25 % (Council of Ministers 2009a). These profitability margins are still valid at the time of writing.

Regulation of maximum market prices through the ERP system covered all patented and generic drugs. This is still valid at the time of writing although

[3] In the Price Communique issued by the Ministry of Health an original product was defined as a product whose efficiency, quality and safety had been proved and was licensed for the first time in the world market. A generic product in turn was defined as a product, which has the same active ingredients, same effectiveness and safety with the original product. The main distinguishing feature of the original products in the wording of 2004 price control scheme is the first time world marketing criterion rather than patent protection. Price Control Communication, Ministry of Health 3 March 2004.

[4] These ceilings were reduced in the aftermath of Council of Ministers (2009b). See Sect. 15.5 and also Table 15.2.

some alternative options are being considered in policy circles. Certain groups of products, however, are excluded from ERP regulation. These include products older than 20 years, and whose prices are equal to or below 6.79 TL, non-prescription drugs, blood products, medicinal foods, radio-pharmaceuticals, enteral formulations, and drugs that are not placed in public reimbursement lists.

As the new scheme indexed drug prices to the cheapest reference price amongst five EU countries, exchange rate fluctuations and the subsequent need for price revisions emerged as a potential source of instability during policy implementation. Still, before the emergence of global financial crisis in late 2007, when the short-term capital led growth model was in its earlier phase, and the capital inflows were abundant, overvaluation of the Turkish lira maintained this instability under control. The new price control scheme adopted Euro as the monetary unit in the calculation of reference prices and authorized a Price Evaluation Commission to decide all increases and reductions in drug prices. The Commission, consisted of representatives from Ministry of Health, Social Security Institution, Ministry of Finance, Development, Prime Ministry Undersecretariat of Treasury. An important function of the Commission was to fix a Euro Term Value that would be used for reference price conversions over a period of 3 months.[5] During this earlier phase of implementation, price revisions were allowed whenever fluctuations in the fixed Euro Term Value exceeded 5 % over a period of 30 days. (For a current overview of ERP system in Turkey see Table 15.3.)

15.4.2 Health Care Reforms and the Public Reimbursement System

Neoliberal health care reforms, which expanded the public financing of health care services also systematized rules applying to public reimbursement of health care services. From 2007 onwards, the SSI started to issue annual Health Implementation Guidelines (HIG) that standardised rules applying to purchases of health services and products from both the public and private health care providers and introduced a series of cost containment measures. Fixed price payments for outpatient and inpatient procedures were introduced for Ministry of Health affiliated hospitals, university hospitals, and private hospitals that contracted with the SSI (Tatar et al. 2011). In relation to pharmaceuticals, reimbursement rules and cost containment measures included: (a) a positive list of drugs to be partially or fully reimbursed by the Institution, (b) mandatory discount rates imposed on producers/importers of both original and generic drugs for inclusion in the positive list, and (c) an internal reference pricing system that defines reimbursement ceilings for generically equivalent clusters of drugs (Turkoglu 2008, c.f. Dickson and Redwood 1998).

[5] This was explicitly allowed in the 2007 Price Decision.

Table 15.3 Current implementation of the external reference pricing system in Turkey

Institution regulating pharma prices	Pharmaceutical and Medical Devices Institution
	Ministry of Health
Regulation method used to set the national price	External Reference Pricing System
Criteria used for deciding the number reference countries	Multiple countries, a minimum of five, maximum of ten EU member and/or candidate countries to be announced each year.[a] Reference countries announced may be changed with two months prior notice
Ad hoc criteria for including non EU countries as reference countries	When drugs to be priced are produced or imported from non EU countries (i.e. India) where there are lower prices, the lowest importer prices in the country of origin applies
Criteria used for selecting specific countries as reference countries	Countries with low and accessible prices as well as countries with similar social properties including population, age distribution of the population, common illnesses
Type of price used for setting the National Target Price	Sale to the wholesaler price in the reference country
Formula to derive the National Target Price from the prices in reference countries	For patented drugs 100 % of the lowest sale to the wholesaler price amongst the reference countries
	For generics and off patent drugs 60 % of the lowest sale to the wholesaler price amongst the reference countries
Monetary unit used in calculating reference prices	Euro
Exchange rate used in calculation of reference prices	Euro Term Value: a fixed value of Euro that is used in calculating reference prices
	Euro Term Value Range: a currency band that is introduced to minimize the impacts of fluctuations in exchange rate on national prices. The lower limit of the band is the Euro Term Value, while its upper limit is 10 % above the Euro Term Value
Authority responsible with price revisions	Price Evaluation Committee consisting of representatives of Ministries of Health, Finance, Development, Treasury, and Social Security Institution, meets regularly every 3 months, decides all changes in drug prices including increases and reductions
Price revisions due to fluctuations in the exchange rate	Price revisions are considered by an extraordinary meeting of the Price Evaluation Committee when arithmetic average of exchange rate fluctuations observed over a period of 90 days exceed 15 % of the Euro Term Value or decline 5 % below the Euro Term Value. No revisions are envisaged when fluctuations remain within the currency band

(continued)

Table 15.3 (continued)

Price revisions due to changes in reference prices in reference countries	The declines reaching to 3 % of the total reference price in the reference countries have to be reported to the Ministry of Health by the firms marketing those products in Turkey. Failure to do so exposes firms concerned to financial compensation and criminal charges
Sources of price information used by the Ministry of Health	Asking applicants for international certificate prices, public official databases, ad hoc requesting of specific price information to authorities in other countries

Source: Most of the criteria used in this table for identifying the characteristics of the external reference pricing system is adapted from Espin, Rovira & de Labry (2011:27) while multiple additional criteria was included by the author herself

Table reflects the most current implementation practice of the external reference pricing system, including the latest changes introduced to the Price Decision on 10th November 2011, and to the Price Communique on 14th of April 2012

[a]Price Decision No. 2007/12325 with changes introduced in 10th of November 2011. Ministry of Health 2012

As a result of these principles, public sector reimbursement prices came to differ significantly from market prices. An interministerial Reimbursement Commission was formed, and is still active at the time of writing, for identifying reimbursement rules, and list of reimbursable drugs, It contains representatives from Ministries of Finance, Development, Health, the Undersecretariat of Treasury at the Prime Minister's Office, and the SSI as well as major stakeholders such as representatives from the pharma industry and officials from selected universities and hospitals. The Commission is aided by a subcommittee of Medical and Economic Evaluation, which provides technical support and makes recommendations for inclusion of new drugs into the positive list (Tatar et al. 2011; Celik and Seiter 2008). More recently, pharma-economic analysis became a prerequisite for companies applying to enter into the positive list alongside general information and clinical data about the drug (Tatar et al. 2011). Assessment of originals and new indications are carried out against the available scientific literature, next to the data provided by the companies, while reviews of applications abroad, comparisons with existing technologies and expert opinions are also used (Kilicaslan 2013). Cost effectiveness analysis remains admittedly low, as budget impact assessment exclude relative direct to indirect costs and defined thresholds (Kilicaslan 2013).

The positive list used by SSI is brand-based (Celik and Seiter 2008). Mandatory discount rates are required from both manufacturers willing to enter into the positive list, as well as private pharmacies willing to contract with SSI to supply its beneficiaries are applied. For the year 2007, for example, the Institution required an 11 % discount from all generic and original drug producers and importers[6] while for newer original products whose active ingredient was younger than 6 years; the

[6] Discounts were to implemented on the retail prices (including the VAT) at the dispensing pharmacies.

discount rate was a more favourable 4 %. Manufacturers may and do offer larger discounts in order to speed up the bureaucratic procedures to enter the positive list (Interviews 1) As will be noted in further sections, increases in these mandatory discount rates since 2009, as part of the global budget negotiated with the industry, generated increasing contestation between the industry and the government.

Discounts required from pharmacies are applied on the price determined after the manufacturers' discount. Progressive discount rates required from pharmacies are negotiated on their behalf with the SSI by the Union of Chambers of Pharmacists. They are based on the value of the pharmacies' previous years sales excluding VAT. The discount rates at the time of writing in 2014 range between 1 and 3 % for pharmacies with medium and highest annual sales while pharmacies with lowest annual sales are exempt from discounts (HIG 2013).

SSI also implements a reference pricing system, using generically equivalent clustering. This type of clustering involves the assignment of reference prices to products containing identical active ingredients/molecules in identical amounts.[7] Currently there are 333 groups (Kilicaslan 2013). In 2007, the Institution set the reimbursement ceiling as the 22 % of the cheapest drug in the same therapeutic equivalent group that consist of products which contain the same active ingredient and used in the treatment of the same indication. As new generic drugs enter the list and the clusters, the cheapest price changes, and the reimbursement amount by the Institution is adjusted. Generic drugs offering prices 5 % cheaper than the cheapest price in a group go through a rapid assessment procedure (Kilicaslan 2013).

As a result of these cost containment measures implemented by the SSI market prices (the official maximum prices issued by The Ministry of Health) and transaction prices (public sector reimbursement prices) differ substantially. Tenders by private and public hospitals from wholesalers or manufacturers also generate important reductions, which further increases the variability of transaction prices.

Ministry of Health and SSI coordinate their pricing activities through allowing official representation for each other in decision making processes carried out within important Commissions such as the Price Evaluation Committee, and the Reimbursement Committee. Representatives of other state ministries responsible for economic policy, such as Ministry of Finance, the Prime Ministry Undersecretariat of Treasury, Ministry of Development, are also involved in the crucial pricing decisions through their membership in both of these Commissions. Pharma firms and their associations are involved in both levels of price control, both informally and formally—through representation for example in Reimbursement Committee.

[7] Clustering of drugs on which reimbursement limits are imposed may be organised according to two principles, the so-called generically equivalent clustering and therapeutically equivalent clustering (Dickson and Redwood 1998). In the former, branded and generic drugs containing identical and bioequivalent active ingredients in identical or similar formulations and pack size are selected to form clusters, while in the latter therapeutically interchangeable or comparable drugs of different chemical structures are selected to form clusters (Dickson and Redwood 1998).

15.4.3 *Sources Underpinning the Shift Towards the ERP System*

The most influential actor that spurred the adoption of the new ERP for regulating pharma prices in 2004 had been the transnational pharma capital. Both direct pressures by transnational capital and influence through their associations such as PhRMA, EFPIA on Turkish government to change the cost-plus pricing system for pharmaceuticals were common during this period. Turkey's ongoing membership negotiations with the EU catalysed the influence of transnational pharmaceutical capital. An important manifestation of the latter during the adoption of the new price control scheme had been the Trade Barriers Regulation (TBR) investigation initiated against Turkey by the European Commission concerning "discriminatory treatment of imported products in terms of pricing, local production requirements, marketing approvals, and distribution policies" (TEB Haberler 2004; EC 2004). The investigation was opened in response to a complaint filed by the European Federation of Pharmaceutical Association (EFPIA), the representative of European transnational pharmaceutical companies. The EFPIA alleged that Turkish pricing scheme of 1984 was implemented by the Turkish authorities in non-uniform, non-transparent and arbitrary manner, in violation of Trade Barriers Regulation (EC 2004). The new price control scheme was introduced 2 months after the initiation of this investigation. Indeed the Health Minister by then Recep Akdag, in one of the progress reports published by his Ministry announced that the New Price Decision issued in February 2004 ruled out the all criticisms of the European Commission investigation opened up against the Turkish government (Akdag 2008:91).

15.4.4 *Evaluation of the Nature of Changes in Pharma Price Control System*

Over the period 2004–2008, the ERP system consolidated the power of transnational capital in pharma pricing. In all previous price control schemes "the place of production" based on territories of the national market, such as the locally produced versus imported products, was taken as the primary criteria to distinguish different drugs in the market, with higher margins allowed for locally produced drugs plus some other protectionist practices against the imported drugs. Displacing the traditional distinction between locally produced versus imported drugs and substituting it with original versus generic drugs, the new price control scheme endorsed a mode of regulation compatible primarily with international rather than national accumulation. The distinction between original and generic drugs, which has long been advocated by the transnational pharmaceutical capital, is developed on the basis of ownership of knowledge exclusivities (i.e. intellectual property rights), and proceeds primarily on the presumption of a global rather a national market for drugs. Given the fact that local pharma capital concentrates on generic production and has meager research and development capabilities (Eren Vural 2013), higher prices attributed to the original drugs is a manifestation of displacement of priorities in the pricing scheme. The new pricing criterion thus naturalized the supremacy of intellectual property rights (IPRs) and complemented the legal changes at the turn of the decade, which provided TRIPs plus protection for IPRs.

Moreover, the ERP generated a policy framework where transnational pharmaceutical capital (vis a vis for example the local pharmaceutical capital) is at a greater advantage to influence pricing decisions through the global strategies available to it. This is because throughout the 1990s, and 2000s, an increasing number of countries started to use ERP systems for setting pharmaceutical prices in their own national markets (Danzon 1997; Jacobzone 2000). Recent studies (Espin et al. 2011; Kanavos et al. 2011) announced that 24 out of 30 OECD countries, and 24 out of 27 member states of the European Union (with the exception of U.K., Sweden, Germany) use it as a mechanism to set pharmaceutical prices. As an OECD (2008) study revealed increased reliance on ERP systems to set pharmaceutical prices evolved in tandem with the development of new strategies by the transnational pharmaceutical capital to maximize profits from global sales. Whereas in the past pharmaceutical transnational capital relied on differential pricing to segment markets, they now prefer to launch their products first in countries where they can set high prices relatively freely, such as for example, U.S., U.K., Germany, and refrain from launching products in relatively lower priced countries (OECD 2008; Kanavos et al. 2011). Higher prices negotiated in markets where there is no or relatively freer price controls then become the reference price for other countries (Docteur 2008). As increasing number of countries benchmark each others' prices, comparisons for setting pharma prices become "circular" (Mossialos et al. 2006) making it easier for transnational pharmaceutical capital to standardize prices across different markets (OECD 2008; Kanavos et al. 2011). As such, spread of ERP systems across countries generate an overall greater potential for transnational pharma capital selling in international markets to influence pricing decisions while the local pharma capital who produce and sell in national markets are devoid of global strategies available to the former. In the Turkish case, similar strategies adopted by the transnational pharma capital to prevent diffusion of low prices to other national markets became more evident since 2011, as will be discussed in more detail in Sect. 15.6 of this chapter.

15.4.5 Evaluation on Implementation Practice of the Pharma Price Control and Expenditure Policies over the 2004–2008

Initiated within the context of short-term capital led growth pattern consolidated in Turkey during the 2000s, the new price control scheme generated important reductions in pharma prices, partly due to the overvaluation of the Turkish Lira.

Another important source of reductions during this period was the reduction in the rate of value added tax on drugs from 18 to 8 %. Although there were limited clashes between the government and transnational companies with regards to the adjustment of exchange rates, the new scheme was praised by all sections of the pharma capital and the successive rounds of price reductions was aired by the media as the achievement of the new scheme.

While the new price control scheme generated a greater scope of influence for transnational pharmaceutical capital, it also provided important opportunities for the domestic pharma capital. This was true especially during the first period of its implementation between 2004 and 2008. Regarding the pricing of generic products for example, the maximum ceiling price of up to 80 % of the original product's cheapest reference price amongst the five EU countries was highly generous compared with international standards (Interview 3, Guclu 2007). Such generous prices for generics had important implications some of which were actualised. First, while reference prices were maximum ceiling prices and some generic products received prices lower than 80 % of the reference price, such high price margins allowed for generic products had a significant effect to limit price competition between the original and generic products (Guclu 2007). Following the introduction of reimbursement policies by the SSI in 2007, one can argue as Guclu 2007 does that low price differentials between the original and generic drugs also prevented the exclusion of original products from the scope of reimbursement lists and thus sustained the sales of original products. Second, such high price margins allowed for generic products could also be seen as an incentive provided by the administration for local manufacturers, who following the entry into force of patent protection in Turkey in 1999, predominantly became engaged in generic production. Third, while being an incentive for the local manufacturers, high price margins allowed for the generic producers through the price control scheme (alongside with other factors such as the on-going health reforms which extended increased the scope of the institutional health market, and increased public health expenditures), also provided important incentive for transnational acquisitions of local generic firms (Eren Vural 2013).

Reforms of health care financing and provision improved important deficiencies in the fragmented nature of the Turkish health care financing system which was elsewhere identified as inflating health care expenditures, including pharmaceutical expenditures (Eren 2002). This being said, cost containment measures especially in the period 2003–2009 were relatively generous and overall sustained the creation of new markets of private health care targeted by the reforms. Overall, health care reforms significantly expanded both the pharmaceutical market and public pharmaceutical expenditure (see Figs. 15.1, 15.2, and 15.3). Total public health expenditure increased from US$6 billion in 2002 to US$25 billion in 2009, with an annual compound growth rate of 19 % (Fig. 15.1). With an average annual growth rate of 8.8 % for health expenditures over the period 1998–2007, Turkey ranked first among all OECD countries in terms of real growth in per capita health expenditure (OECD 2010:105).

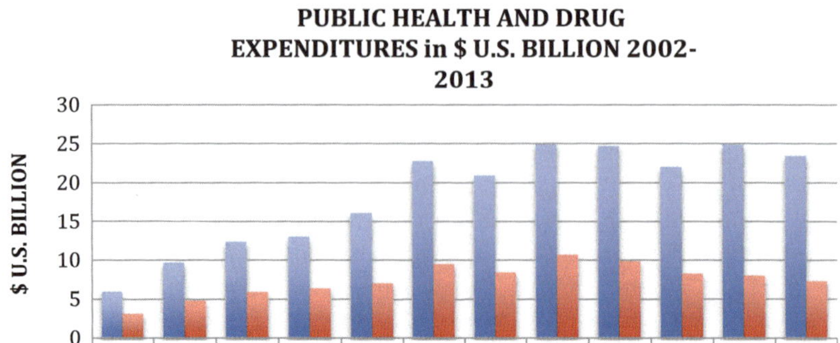

	2002	2003	2004	2005	2006	2007	2008	2009	2010	2011	2012	2013
PUBLIC HEALTH EXPENDITURES	6	10	12	13	16	23	21	25	25	22	25	23
PUBLIC PHARMA EXPENDITURES	3	5	6	6	7	10	8	11	10	8	8	7

Fig. 15.1 Total public health and drug expenditures 2002–2013 in US$ million. *Source*: Turkoglu 2008, Ministry of Finance www.bumko.gov.tr, December 2009, 2010, 2012, 2013 Budget Realisations, Detailed Expenditures, Social Security Institution, May 2011, December 2013 Monthly Bulletin. Absolute Turkish Lira values in these sources are converted into US dollars, using the indicative selling exchange rates values announced by the Turkish Central Bank at the final working day at the end of each year. Total public health and drug expenditures include expenditure by the Social Security Institution, government ministries and Green Card expenditures

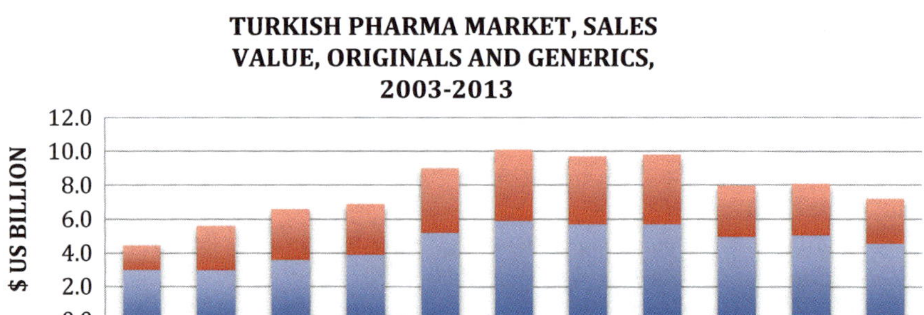

	2003	2004	2005	2006	2007	2008	2009	2010	2011	2012	2013
GENERIC	1.4	2.6	3.0	3.0	3.8	4.2	4.0	4.1	3.0	3.0	2.6
ORIGINAL	3.0	3.0	3.6	3.9	5.2	5.9	5.7	5.7	5.0	5.0	4.6

Fig. 15.2 Turkish prescription market sales 2003–2013 in value US$ billion. The values for 2004–2010 are derived from Business Monitor International, cited in Deloitte (2010) Turkish Healthcare Industry Report. Pharma market sales date for the years 2003, 2011–2013 is calculated from IMS, IEIS value in Turkish liras, which was converted into US$ using the selling exchange rate value announced by the Central Bank of Turkey on the last working day of each respective year. Respective value shares of the generic and original drugs were calculated by sales value percentage shares provided by the IMS, IEIS data

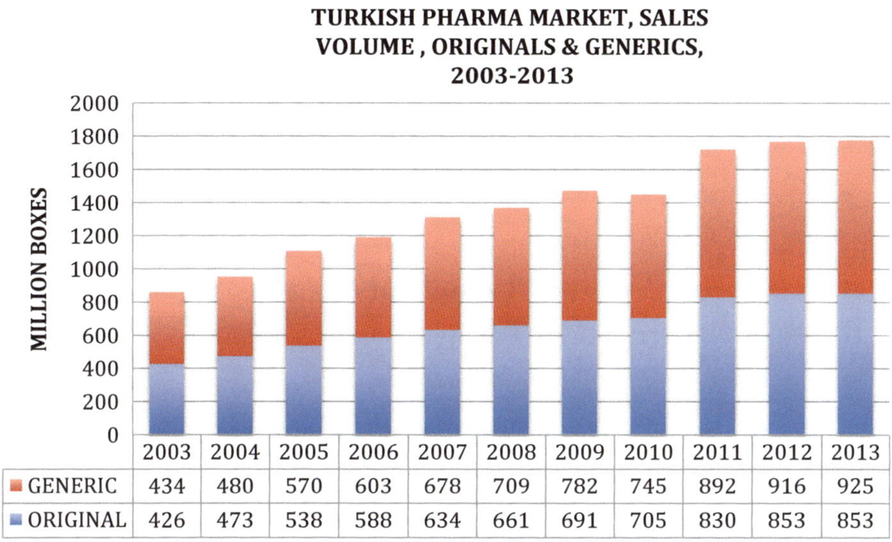

	2003	2004	2005	2006	2007	2008	2009	2010	2011	2012	2013
GENERIC	434	480	570	603	678	709	782	745	892	916	925
ORIGINAL	426	473	538	588	634	661	691	705	830	853	853

Fig. 15.3 Turkish prescription market sales 2003–2013 in volume of million boxes. *Source*: Data for 2003–2009 is taken from IMS, IEIS cited in Deloitte (2010) Turkish Healthcare Industry Report, p. 12. Sales volume data for 2003, 2010, 2011–2013 is taken from IMS data, respective sales volume of generic and original drugs is calculated from the percentage market share data provided by IEIS

Neoliberal health care reforms boosted public pharma expenditure and pharma market sales. They also secured growth for generic formulation sector of the industry. Total public pharmaceutical expenditure increased from US$3 billion in 2002 to US$11 billion in 2009, with an annual compound growth rate of 19 %. In 2009 the share of pharmaceutical expenditures within total public health expenditure stood at 46 % (Fig. 15.1).

Turkish prescription market sales increased in value from US$4.4 billion in 2003, to US$9.7 billion in 2009, with a compound annual growth rate of almost 14 % (Fig. 15.2). Similar growth was seen in sales volumes, which went from 860 million boxes in 2003 to 1.42 billion boxes in 2009 (Fig. 15.3). Given this, Turkey rapidly rose from being the 18th largest pharmaceutical market in the world in 2003 to being the twelfth largest market in 2008 (IMS, cited in Deloitte 2010). Within the EU, Turkey emerged as the sixth largest market (PricewaterhouseCoopers 2010).

Analyses of market sales for original and generic drugs until 2010 also reveal strong growth in value and volume for both groups. For example, generic drug sales increased in value from US$1.4 billion in 2003 to US$4 billion in 2009, with an annual compound growth rate of 19 % (Fig. 15.2). Their share in total sales value increased from 32.2 to 41 %. Over the same period, in terms of sales volume, generic drug sales increased from 434 million boxes to 782 million boxes, with an annual compound growth rate of 10 %, the share in sales volume increasing from 50.5 % in 2003 to 55 in 2009 (Fig. 15.2). As for original drugs, the value of sales of original drugs increased from US$3 billion in 2003 to US$5.7 billion in 2009, with an annual compound growth rate of 11 % (Fig. 15.2). The share of original products in sales value, however, declined from 67.8 % in 2003 to 59 % in 2009. In terms of sales volume, sales of original drugs increased from 426 million boxes to 691 million boxes, with an annual compound growth rate of 8.3 %, while their shares in sales volume declined from 49.5 % in 2003 to 48.5 in 2009 (Fig. 15.3).

15.5 Financial Crisis and Consolidation of Neoliberal Reforms in Pharma Price and Expenditure Policies

The second period of neoliberal restructuring in the Turkish health care system since the end of 2009, witnessed increasing stringency of pharma price and expenditure controls. In this section I review multiple changes introduced to restrain costs, which are still effective at the time of writing, while the next section is devoted to an evaluation of their outcomes.

In December 2009, amidst the spiralling impacts of the global financial crisis, the government forced the pharma industry to accept a global budget to fix its public pharma expenditures over a period of 3 years 2010–2012. Based on 2008 realisation, a seven per cent growth in public pharma expenditures over three years 2010–2012 was offered to the industry. Public pharma expenditures for 2009 were fixed at 16 billion TLs, the pharma expenditures forecasted for 2010 was limited to 14.6 billion TLs, and 15.6 billion TLs for 2011, and finally 16.7 billion TLs for the year 2012 (Kaya 2010).[8] Global budget negotiated between the industry and the government laid the ground for the imposition of price cuts and mandatory discount increases on all drugs both patented and generics first in December 2009 and then successively in 2010 and 2011.

The initial wave of price cuts were introduced in December 2009 through a change in price control scheme. This entailed significant reductions in the maximum prices that can be received by pharmaceuticals (Council of Ministers 2009b). Before the changes, all original drugs were allowed to get the 100 % of their cheapest price amongst the five European reference countries (i.e. the reference price), while the generic drugs whose prices are indexed to their originals, were then allowed up to 80 % of the originals' price. Following the changes, only original drugs, which did not have generic equivalents in the market due to patent protection or data exclusivity, were allowed 100 % of the reference price. Meanwhile, the maximum ceiling prices that can be received by original drugs with generic equivalents in the market was reduced down to 66 % of their reference price. Ceiling prices that can be received by the generics were also reduced to 66 % of

[8] Protocol detailed a series of further reductions in reference price ceilings used in external reference pricing, and increases in mandatory discounts when actual expenditure exceeds the amounts determined in the budget.

the cheapest reference price (Council of Ministers 2009b). The regulation thus equalised the maximum ceiling prices of the originals and generics following a generic entry into the market. While it introduced an approximately 34 % reduction in the prices of the original drugs that came to encounter generic competition, it also involved an approximately 14 % reduction in the maximum ceiling prices of the generic products.

Moreover, against the background of rapid depreciation of Turkish Lira amidst the global financial crisis, an equally powerful price cut was introduced through stiffening the requirements for price revisions generated by exchange rate fluctuations. While the price control scheme previously allowed revisions when the exchange rate fluctuations over a period of 30 days exceeded the fixed Euro Term Value by 5 %, the amendments increased both the extent and duration of necessary fluctuations for upward price revisions. It thus introduced a currency band—known as Term Euro Value Range—which allowed the government to avoid price revisions as long as the fluctuations remain above 10 % of the fixed value of Euro (Euro Term Value) (Council of Ministers 2009b). The new system, which is still in force at the time of writing, thus allows upward price revisions only when arithmetic average of fluctuations observed over a period of 90 days exceeds the fixed Euro Term Value by 15 %.

In addition to these price cuts, the SSI imposed an additional compulsory discount of 12 % on top of the then existing 11 % on sales of original drugs to the Institution. Even more significant, it reduced the reimbursement ceiling used in its reference pricing system. Whereas before it fully reimbursed drugs priced 22 % above the cheapest drug in each generically equivalent cluster, following amendments this reimbursement ceiling was reduced to 15 % above the cheapest drug in each cluster.

Controversies over pharma price and expenditure control increased further throughout 2010 and 2011, with additional reductions and discounts imposed by the Ministry of Health and SSI. In December 2010, an additional 9.5 % discount on all drugs (both patented and generics) was negotiated with the industry (Teksoz 2010) As such, the discount rate for original drugs with no generic equivalents was increased from 23 to 32.5 % on retail prices, for original drugs with generic equivalents and all other generic drugs the discount rate was increased from 11 to 20.5 % (see Table 15.4). A year later, in November 2011, the government introduced even further price reductions and discount increases claiming that over 2 years 2010–2011, the global budget for pharmaceuticals was surpassed for an amount of 1.2 billion TLs (Memurlar Net 2011).[9] Ceilings used in the calculation of reference price by the Ministry of Health were reduced from 66 % of the cheapest price amongst the five EU countries to 60 % (see Table 15.5). Discounts imposed by the SSI were even more radical. The Institution increased the discount rate on

[9] The concerned decisions were taken in the Economic Coordination Council, which includes the members of the Ministry of Labour and Social Security, Ministry of Health, Undersecretariat of Treasury, the Ministry of Finance, Ministry of Economy.

Table 15.4 SSI measures to contain pharma expenditure

Reimbursement by SSI	2004	2009	2010	2011
Compulsory discounts				
Original drugs	6 % for the first year, then 11 %	23 %	32.5 %	41 %
Off patent and generic drugs	11 %	11 %	20.5 %	28 %
Internal reference pricing reimbursement ceiling	22 %	15 %		10 %

Source: SSI 2007, 2009, 2010, 2011

Table 15.5 Changes in the ERP System amidst the financial crisis

ERP System	2004	2009 December	2011
% of reference price allowed			
Original on patent drugs	100	100	100
Original off patent drugs	100	66	60
Generics	80	66	60
Revisions of Euro Term Value[a]	Revision whenever fluctuations in Euro Term Value observed over a period of 30 days exceeded 5 %	Upward revisions whenever fluctuations observed over a period of 90 days exceed 15 % of the Euro Term Value	

Source: 2005 Price Communique, Council of Ministers 2004, 2007, 2009b, 2011.
[a]Euro set as the official monetary unit for price conversions. Euro Term Value corresponded to the value of Euro fixed by the Pricing Commission that was based on the sales values of Euro published by the Central Bank as indicators in the Official Gazette

original drugs without generic equivalents from 32.5 % up to 41 %. For all other original and generic drugs the discount rate was increased from 20.5 to 28 %. Moreover, the SSI further reduced the reimbursement ceiling used in internal reference pricing from 15 % down to 10 % (see Table 15.4).

15.6 Evaluations of the Changes in Pharma Price and Expenditure Controls Since 2009

Increasing stringency of pharma price and expenditure control policies does not indicate a rift in the process of neoliberal restructuring within the health care system (c.f. Mercan 2012). Rather, it reveals the embeddedness of neoliberal health care reforms within the requirements of short-term capital led economic growth model, which became more binding following the impacts of the global financial crisis in

2007. As became evident also in the Turkish case, short-term capital led economic growth model, entails a vicious circle. High real rates of interest attract inflows of foreign capital which leads to appreciation of the local currency, and a subsequent import boom, leading to a deterioration of current account deficits. The latter then results in an erosion of investor confidence, followed by capital outflows, and possibly a crisis (Yeldan 2007). In 2009, reversal of short term capital flows amidst global financial crisis, coupled with high current account deficits forced the Turkish government to restrict its public expenditures and deficits to stabilise the short-term capital led growth model. As noted earlier, the government's preference to continue with this particular growth model, in turn, can be seen as a reflection of the determination of a wider class alliance at the national level, including the internationalised fractions of the Turkish capital and the transnational financial capital to maintain the short term capital led growth model intact amidst the global crisis. In this sense, increasing stringency of price and expenditure controls can be seen as a reflection on pharma policy of wider struggles over a particular economic growth model. It, thus, reveals how public policies mediate contradictory interests of capital within the processes of accumulation (c.f. Bryan 1995).

A brief analysis of public pharma expenditure as well as original and generic sales value and volume distribution of Turkish pharma market reveals that the price cuts and discounts had some success in restricting public pharma expenditures. Unlike the period between 2003 and 2009, compound annual growth rates for public pharma expenditures between 2010 and 2013 turned negative (see Fig. 15.1). Public pharma expenditures declined from US$10 billion dollars in 2010 down to US$7 billion dollars in 2013, and the percentage of annual decline over the same period reached 9 %. Even when changes in public pharma expenditures are calculated in real Turkish Lira values (2003=100), given the fact that TL depreciated significantly vis a vis the US$ over the period concerned, compound annual decline in public pharma expenditure between 2010–2013 is 1.4% .

Over the same period, Turkish pharma market sales value as well as shares of original and generic drugs show similar shrinkage, while sales volume continued to record fair growth. In US$ terms, sales value in Turkish pharmaceutical market over the period 2010–2013 declined from 9.8 billion down to 7.2 billion, recording an annual percentage decline of 10 %. Likewise sales of original drugs declined from 5.7 billion dollars down to 4.6 billion dollars, recording an annual percentage decline of 7 %. Shrinkage in the share of generics is more noticeable declining form 4.1 billion dollars down to 2.6 billion dollars recording an annual percentage decline of 13 %. When same calculations are carried out in real Turkish lira values (2003=100), compound annual decline in pharma market total sales value, and in sales values for originals and generics over the period 2010–2013 are found respectively as 1 %, 0.6 % and 1.4 %.

In terms of sales volume, however, a fair amount of growth continues. Sales volume of pharma products in the Turkish market over the period 2010–2013 increased from 1,450 million boxes to 1,778 million boxes with a compound annual growth rate of 7 %. Sales volume of originals over the same period increased from 705 million boxes to 853 million boxes with a compound annual growth rate of 6 %.

Sales volume of generics over the same period increased from 745 million boxes in 2010 to 925 million boxes in 2013 with a compound annual growth rate of 7 %.

The impacts of price reductions and discounts introduced since 2009 had been variable across different drugs groups, and their manufacturers. Impacts on original drugs under patent protection had been relatively negligible as the high bargaining power of the transnational capital producing them was able to avoid most stringent measures. Following the imposition in 2011 of further discounts of 9.5 % by SSI, the transnational manufacturers of this group of drugs formally demanded that the additional discounts on 450 drugs were lifted. Increasing the strength of this demand, they slowed down the sales of vital drugs used in the treatment of cancer, diabetes, and cardiovascular diseases. Abrupt drug shortages used in the treatment of chronic diseases resulted in growing public discontent that was lively aired by the media. In the event the government had to step down. SSI lifted the additional discounts of 9.5 % on more than half of the drugs, i.e. 267 drugs, demanded by the transnational companies (NTVMSNBC 2011 (Zaman Daily, 6 Jan 2012)).

Despite this many transnationals, continued to withhold their innovative drugs from the Turkish market, which at the time of writing still maintained shortages in vital drugs. In addition to increased discounts and price cuts which reduced profitability, another factor that discourages transnationals to launch innovative drugs in the currently restricted price environment of Turkey is the likely diffusion of these lower prices towards higher priced markets through ERP systems now used by an increasing number of countries. Representatives of transnational companies and also domestic pharma capital in deed offered the Turkish government to maintain confidential rebates so long as these were not published in price lists (Boyacigoglu 2013). Given the insistence of government on official discounts, representatives of transnational companies declare that delays incurred in introduction of new drugs would continue, noting that out of the 165 new active principles that were introduced to the markets in the EU and US since 2005, only 48 (30 %) were introduced in Turkey while 115 new active principles (70 %) remained out of reach in the Turkish market (Tan 2013:14)

In order to overcome shortages in withdrawn or withheld drugs required for treatment of chronic diseases such as cancer, the SSI revived a long existing protocol with the Union of Turkish Chamber of Pharmacists, which allows the latter to import drugs from other countries. While this measure provided some access, the delays incurred in the process as well as the costs of importing the drugs proved formidable.

Meanwhile manufacturers of off patent original and generic drugs also "withdrew their old and cheap drugs from the market because of low profit margins" which expanded access shortages in vital innovative drugs to old and cheap (but) critical drugs (Oner 2013). In November 2013, a total of 730 drugs, which were licensed and included in positive list, were not available in the Turkish market (Alp 2013).

Moreover a report announced by the Turkish Competition Authority in September 2013 warned that recent price cuts introduced by Ministry of Health, which allows a maximum of 60 % of the reference price for both generics and off patent originals, could intensify anti-competitive practices amongst the manufacturers of these group of drugs (i.e. off patent original and generics) (OECD 2014:7). Prevention of generic entry, which might ensue from coordination of activities by manufacturers of generic and off patent originals, the Report stated, could offset the initial regulatory objective of spurring price competition (OECD DAF 2014:7). A basis for such coordination, the report warned, already existed within the scope of co marketing agreements (ibid).

Beyond the price cuts and increases in mandatory discounts, the government's most contested measure had been the freezing of exchange rate adjustments. Given the rapid fluctuations in the value of Turkish lira, the industry claimed losses caused by delays in exchange rate adjustments amount to 20 %. Exchange rate related losses incurred by the industry, recently raised concerns about the quality of locally produced drugs. Such concerns were raised following a warning issued by the CEO and owner of the leading local pharmaceutical company in both market value and sales volume, which stated that labour shedding in the pharma industry, caused by price cuts, and losses, rapidly expanded towards the quality control personnel in pharma firms, and that many pharma firms increasingly relied on cheaper raw materials in order to cut down costs (Sefer 2013). While to date no known official investigation followed this warning, statements by such an authoritative figure in the industry significantly shook the public trust in locally produced drugs.

A final impact of price controls, especially of internal reference pricing implemented by the SSI concerns the rising number of incremental innovations carried out mostly by domestic generic drug producers. Incremental innovation entails modifications of existing chemical entities for the development of new formulations and compositions, which provide benefits to patients such as reducing side effects, and increasing comfort in treatment (OECD 2008:195) Current Turkish IPR regime allows patenting of such innovations. While whether such patents allow higher prices for innovators at product launch, which is regulated by the Ministry of Health through external reference pricing system, is ambiguous, incremental innovators acknowledge that the real target for their incremental innovations is to increase their market share within the SSI sales. Exclusivities granted by the patents for such incrementally modified drugs prevent the substitution of their products with other lower priced generics by the pharmacists at the retail end of the distribution chain. In an environment where prices are continually drawn downwards, exclusivities provided by patents for incrementally modified drugs, emerge as an important opportunity to expand their products sales and market shares within SSI purchases.

15.7 Conclusion

Increasing stringency of pharma price and expenditure controls since 2009 reflect the embeddedness of neoliberal health care restructuring within the short term capital led growth model consolidated in Turkey since the 2000s. Abundant inflows of short term capital before the global economic crisis in 2007 facilitated the growing public health care expenditures, which supported the creation of private health care markets and expanded pharma market and sales. While the phenomenal growth in public health expenditures may appear in contradiction with neoliberalism and restrictive fiscal policies associated with short term capital led model, in effect, it generated inflows of capital into the health care system by sustaining creation of private health care markets and expanding pharma market and sales. More importantly, growth in public pharma and health expenditures also garnered public consent for neoliberal reforms both within the health care system and in the wider economy.

Since 2009, the government increased the stringency of its pharma pricing and control policies, to reduce its public expenditures and stabilise short term capital led growth model. Government's preference to continue with this particular growth model reflects the determination of a wider class alliance at the national level, including the internationalised fractions of the Turkish capital and the transnational capital, to sustain this short term capital led growth in tact amidst its global crisis. While increasing stringency of pharma price and expenditure control policies generate increased contestations between the pharma capital and the state, it does not constitute a rift or irony within the process of neoliberal restructuring (c.f. Mercan 2012). Rather, increasing stringency of pharma price and expenditure control policies reveal how public policies mediate contradictory interests of capital within the processes of accumulation (c.f. Bryan 1995). In due course, however, pharma pricing policies is increasingly enmeshed with fluctuations in exchange rate markets, threatening access to vital drugs used in the treatment of chronic diseases, and raising concerns about the quality of locally produced drugs, as well as intensification of anti competitive practices amongst the manufacturers of generic and off patent original drugs. All with tremendous implications for public health.

Interviews

Interview 1. Local company executives, 25 August 2011, Istanbul.

Interview 2. Local company executive, 7 September 2011, Istanbul.

Interview 3. Local company executives, 16 November 2011, Istanbul.

Interview 4. Local company executive, 1 December 2011, Istanbul.

Interview 5. Pricing Expert, Pricing Cost Analyses Department, General Directorate of Pharmaceuticals and Pharmacies, 31st of October 2011.

References

Akdag R (ed) (2008) Health transformation program: Turkey, progress report. Ministry of Health Publications. www.kalite.saglik.gov.tr/. . ./turkiyeSDP.pdf. Accessed 17 July 2012

Alp A (2013) 735 Ilac Piyasada Bulunmuyor. Hurriyet Daily, 21 Nov 2013. http://www.hurriyet.com.tr/saglik-yasam/25163521.asp. Accessed 6 July 2014

Bilgin A (2011) Ilac Tedarik Zincirinde Depolarin Yeri. Presentation at Mersin University. www.slideserve.com/duff/la-tedar-k-z-nc-r-nde-depolarin-yer. Accessed 10 Nov 2014

Boratav KE, Yeldan A, Kose H (2000) Globalisation distribution and social policy: Turkey 1980–1998. CEPA working paper series I, Working paper no. 20

Boyacigoglu H (2013) Iilacta Turkiyeye Fiat Arttir Baskisi. Radikal Daily, 26 Nov 2013. http://www.radikal.com.tr/Ekonomi/Ilacta Turkiye'ye 'Fiat Arttir' baskisi. Accessed 6 July 2014

Bryan D (1995) The chase across the globe: international accumulation and the contradictions for nation states. Westview Press, Boulder

Celik Y, Seiter A (2008) Turkey: pharmaceutical sector analysis, health nutrition and population. World Bank

Council of Ministers (2004) Decision on pricing of pharmaceuticals, 2004/6781. Official Gazette, 14 Feb 2004

Council of Ministers (2007) Decision on pricing of pharmaceuticals, 2007/12325. Official Gazette, 30 June 2007

Council of Ministers (2009a) Decision changing the pricing of pharmaceuticals, 2009/14577. Official Gazette, 17 Jan 2009

Council of Ministers (2009b) Decision changing the pricing of pharmaceuticals, 2009/15434. Official Gazette, 3 Dec 2009

Council of Ministers (2011) Decision changing the pricing of pharmaceuticals. Official Gazette, 10 Nov 2011

Danzon PM (1997) Pharmaceutical price regulation: national policies versus global interests. AEI, Washington, DC

Deloitte (2010) Turkish healthcare industry report. Republic of Turkey Prime Ministry Investment Support & Promotion Agency. http://www.invest.gov.tr/en-us/infocenter/publications/Documents/HEALTHCARE.INDUSTRY.pdf. Accessed 5 Nov 2011

Dickson M, Redwood H (1998) Pharmaceutical reference prices: how do they work in practice. Pharmaeconomics 14(5):471–479

Docteur E (2008) Pharmaceutical pricing policy in a global market. Workshop on current pharmaceuticals challenges, European Health Forum, Gastein, Austria. http://www.ehfg.org/fileadmin/ehfg/website/Archiv/2008/powerpoints/ws2/08_ws2_Docteur.pdf. Accessed 11 Oct 2014

Epstein G, Yeldan E (2006) Developing policy alternatives to inflation targeting, the new façade of neoliberal conditionality: an introduction. www.bagimsizsosyalbilimciler.org/Yazilar_Uye/EpYeDec06.pdf

Eren I (2002) Transnationalisation of the Turkish pharmaceutical industry. Unpublished Ph.D. thesis, University of Sussex

Eren Vural I (2013) Neoliberalism, intellectual property rights, and the Turkish pharmaceutical industry in the 2000s. In: Lofgren H, Williams O (eds) The new political economy of pharmaceuticals: production, innovation, and TRIPs in the global south. Palgrave Macmillan, Basingstoke, pp 221–245

Ergunes N (2009) Global integration of the Turkish economy in the era of financialisation. Research on money and finance discussion papers: 8 Feb. www.researchonmoneyandfinance.org

Espin J, Rovira J, Olry de Labry A et al. (2011) External reference pricing, Working paper 1. In: WHO HAI project on medicine prices and availability. Review series on pharmaceutical pricing policies and interventions, May 2011. http://www.haiweb.org/medicineprices/05062011/ERP%20final%20May2011.pdf. Accessed 7 July 2014

European Commission (2004) Directorate general for trade, report to the Trade Barriers Regulation Committee, TBR proceedings concerning Turkish practices affecting trade in pharmaceutical products. Non confidential version

Fine B (2008) From financialisation to neoliberalism: engaging neoliberalism. eprints.soas.ac.uk/54413/1/Coimbra.pdf. Accessed 11 Mar 2013

Gough I (1975) State expenditures in advanced capitalism new left review, I/92, July–Aug, pp 53–92

Guclu S (2007) Jenerik Ilac Fiatlari Gercek Maliyet Uzerinden Hesaplanmalidir. http://www.ced.org.tr/v2/ecz-sedat-guclu/jenerik-ilac-fiyatlari-gercek-maliyet-uzerinden-hesaplanmalidir. Accessed 16 July 2012

HIG (2013) Health Implementation Guideline 2013. http://www.sgk.gov.tr/wps/portal/tr/mevzuat/yururlukteki_mevzuat/tebligler. Accessed 18 Mar 2014

IEIS (2014) Turkiye Ilac Endustrisi. http://www.ieis.org.tr/ieis/tr/turkiye_ilac_endustrisi. Accessed 11 Oct 2014

Investment Support and Promotion Agency (ISPA) & Deloitte (2014) Health care industry in Turkey

Jacobzone S (2000) 'Pharmaceutical policies in OECD countries: reconciling social and industrial goals' labour market and social policy, occasional papers no. 40, OECD. Directorate for Education, Employment, Labour and Social Affairs. DEELSA/ELSA/WD (2001)1

Kanavos P, Vandoros S, Irwin R, Nicod E, Casson M (2011) Differences in costs of and access to pharmaceutical products in the EU. European Parliament, Directorate General for Internal Policies, Economic and Scientific Policy, Environment, Public and Food Safety Commission

Karakas-Gultekin D, Ercan F (2008) Turkiye'de uluslararasilasma surecindeki Sermayenin uretken ve para Sermaye Arasindaki zaman yonelimli stratejik tercihi. Iktisat Isletme ve Finans 23(262):35–55

Kaya Y (2010) The affects of global crisis to the pharma market and reimbursement in Turkey. ISPOR presentation delivered in the 13th ISPOR Europe conference. http://www.kfd.org.tr/?q=node/776 Accessed 18 July 2012

Kilicaslan H (2013) Use of pharmacoeconomics in drug reimbursement in Turkey. Conference presentation at the symposium on pharmacoeconomics: basic principles and valuation of health states, 24 May 2013, Istanbul Cerrahpasa Faculty of Medicine, Organised by Turkish Pharmacological Society. www.tfd.org/pharmacoeconoimcs/presentations.htm. Accessed 5 July 2014

Kirim SA (1985) The internationalisation of capital and industrialisation in third world: a case study of the Turkish pharmaceutical industry towards appraising the oligopoly approach to multinational corporations. Unpublished Ph.D. thesis, Norwich, University of East Anglia, School of Development Studies

Memurlar Net (2011) Vatandas Ilac Sikintisi Yasamayacak 13 Aralik 2011. http://www.memurlar.net/haber/212393. Accessed 24 July 2012

Mercan SA (2012) Turkiye'de Saglik Sisteminin Neoliberal Yeniden Yapilandirilma Surecinde Kamu Ilac Politikalari: Devlet Mudahalesinin Degisen Bicimleri. Praksis No. 30–31, pp 167–198

Ministry of Health of Turkey (2012) Communique regarding changes in the communique on pricing of pharmaceuticals, Official Gazette No: 28264, 14 Apr 2012

Ministry of Health of Turkey (2013) 2012 Statistical yearbook. http://sbu.saglik.gov.tr/Ekutuphane/kitaplar/hsy2012/pdf. Accessed 27 Nov 2014

Mossialos E, Brogan D, Walley T (2006) Pharmaceutical pricing in Europe: weighing up the options. Int Soc Secur Rev 59(3):1–24

NTVMSNBC (2011) News line solution for the drug crisis (Ilac Krizine Cozum Formulu), 15 Dec 2011

OECD (2008) Pharmaceutical pricing policies in a global market. OECD health policy studies. http://www.oecd.org/document/36/0.3746.en_2649_33929_41000996_1_1_1_1.00.htm

OECD (2010) Health at a glance: Europe 2010. OECD, Paris. http://dx.doi.org/10.1787/health_glance_2010_en. Accessed 22 Feb 2012

OECD DAF (2014) Competition issues in the distribution of pharmaceuticals: contribution from Turkey, DAF/COMP/GF/WD(2014)51. www.oecd.org/competition/competition-distribution-pharmaceuticals.htm. Accessed 22 July 2014

Oner GZ (2013) Pharmacoeconomics, healthcare policy, and limited resources. Conference presentation at the symposium on pharmacoeconomics: basic principles and valuation of health states, 24 May 2013. Istanbul Cerrahpasa Faculty of Medicine, organised by Turkish Pharmacological Society. www.tfd.org/pharmacoeconoimcs/presentations.htm. Accessed 5 July 2014

Poulantzas N (1978, reproduced 2000) State, power and socialism. Verso, London
PriceWaterhousecoopers (2010) Ilac sektoru birlesme ve satin almalari: 2006–2009 donemi incelemesi. http://www.pwc.com/tr_TR/TR/publications/Assets/Pharmacy09TUR.pdf. Accessed 8 Jan 2012
Sefer L (2013) Nasil Guvenecegiz? Hurriyet Daily, 15 Nov 2013. www.hurriyet.com.tr/ekonomi/25123261.asp. Accessed 6 July 2014
SSI (2007) Health Implementation Guidelines (HIG), Official Gazette No: 26532, 25 May 2007
SSI (2009) Health Implementation Guidelines (HIG), Official Gazette No: 27422, 4 Dec 2009
SSI (2010) Health Implementation Guidelines (HIG), Official Gazette No: 27782, 11 Dec 2010
SSI (2011) Health Implementation Guidelines (HIG), Official Gazette No: 28106, 5 Nov 2011
Tan M (2013) Pharmacoeconomics and pharma. Conference presentation at the symposium on pharmacoeconomics: basic principles and valuation of health states, 24 May 2013. Istanbul Cerrahpasa Faculty of Medicine, Organised by Turkish Pharmacological Society. www.tfd.org/pharmacoeconoimcs/presentations.htm. Accessed 5 July 2014
Tatar M, Mollahaliloglu S, Sahin B, Aydin S, Maresso A, Hernandez-Quevedo C (2011) Turkey health system review. Health systems in transition, vol 13, no 6. European Observatory on Health Systems and Policies
TEB Haberler (2004) Ocak Subat. On price control scheme
Teksoz T (2010) Affects of global crisis to the pharma market in Turkey. Presented in pharmaceutical and medical device pricing and reimbursement in Turkey. http://www.ozanbatigun.com/?page_id=90. Accessed 19 July 2012
Turkoglu S (2008) New regulations and principles of reimbursement in Turkey. Pharmaeconomics and rational drug use. 1st ISPOR International Summer School, 16–20 Nisan, Antalya
Yeldan E (2007) Globalisation as the hegemonic concept of neoliberal ideology. In: Kose A, Senses F (eds) Neoliberal globalisation as new imperialism. Nova Science, New York, pp 41–54
Yeldan E (2009) Kapitalizmin Yeniden Finansallaşmasi ve2007/2008 Krizi: Türkiye Krizin Neresinde? Calisma ve Toplum, 2009/1, pp 11–28

Chapter 16
Pharmaceutical Pricing Policies in the Gulf Countries' Council (GCC) and the United Arab Emirates (UAE)

Ranya Shaban Ibrahim Hasan and Charon Lessing

Abstract Established in 1971, the United Arab Emirates is a federation of seven emirates, lying on the southeast end of the Arabian Peninsula, and home to some nine million people. It is the second largest economy in the Arab world, with a gross domestic product (GDP) of $377 billion in 2012.

The government of the UAE spends more per capita on healthcare than all other Arab states except Qatar, but less than some other developed nations. Data from a 2006 survey showed the UAE government was buying high priced originator brand pharmaceuticals when lower priced generic pharmaceuticals were available, whilst originator and generic medicines in the private sector were high in comparison with international prices and largely unaffordable to low income earners.

Within the framework of a market-driven economy promoted by the Gulf Cooperation Council (GCC) states, the Health Ministers of the GCC including the UAE have introduced a number of legislative and regulatory reforms intended to regulate medicine prices whilst still delivering safe and effective medicines. In 2008, a Strategic Framework was implemented by the UAE Ministry of Health which focused on strengthening regulatory practices and improving technical performance and upgrading health facilities. Alongside this wider health strategy, pharmaceutical policies and reforms were also initiated to improve accessibility to affordable medicines.

This chapter describes the pharmaceutical pricing and accessibility legislative reforms in GCC member states, and the impact therein, focusing especially on pricing policies in the United Arab Emirates.

R.S.I. Hasan (✉)
Health Professions Organization Section, Ministry of Health, Dubai, United Arab Emirates
e-mail: dr.ranyahasan@gmail.com

C. Lessing
Health Systems Section, School of Population Health, University of Auckland, Auckland, New Zealand

Z.-U.-D. Babar (ed.), *Pharmaceutical Prices in the 21st Century*,
DOI 10.1007/978-3-319-12169-7_16

16.1 Introduction

The United Arab Emirates (UAE) is a confederation of seven emirates; Abu Dhabi, Dubai, Sharjah, Ajman, Umm al-Qaiwain, Ra's al-Khaimah and Fujairah, and is governed by the Federal Supreme Council composed of the ruler of each emirate. Each emirate has its own local government, and a constitutional relationship with the Federal Supreme Council (UAE Government). The Gross Domestic Product (GDP) of the UAE in 2012 was US$384 billion, one third of which is derived from oil revenues. A proportion of each emirate's revenue is allocated to the UAE central budget (Medical and Health Care Services). The total population of UAE is just less than ten million, the majority of whom are expatriates (mostly South Asian nationals), with a high net migration. Almost two-thirds of the total population reside in either Abu Dhabi or Dubai in urban areas.

The UAE is a member of the political and economic union, the Cooperation Council for the Arab States of the Gulf (or 'Gulf Cooperation Council'), along with all Arab states of the Arabian Gulf excepting Iraq. Member states of the GCC (United Arab Emirates, the Kingdom of Saudi Arabia, Qatar, Bahrain, Oman, Kuwait) and recently the Yemen are all represented on the Council of Ministers of Health in the GCC. One of the objectives of the Council is to reduce dependence on imported medicines, lower medicine prices and stimulate the domestic manufacturing segment of member states (Medical and Health Care Services).

16.1.1 Overview of the UAE Health Sector

The health care system in the UAE has evolved over the years from the late 1970s (Medical and Health Care Services). Life expectancy at birth is 78 years (2012), the highest amongst Arab countries. The proportion of the population over the age of 65 years is less than 1 %; however, the population is ageing (World Development Indicators). The UAE has a high UNDP Human Development Index ranking, an indicator of human development and extent of inequality, with a literacy rate of 91 % (Human Development Reports). Health expenditure per capita was US$1,343 in 2012, and expenditure on health as a percentage of GDP was 2.8 %, possibly reflecting expenditure confined only to emirate nationals (World Development Indicators). Compared with other countries, the UAE spends more per capita on healthcare than other Arab states except Qatar, but lower than some other developed nations (see Fig. 16.1).

The UAE health system includes government and private sector hospitals, and day care centres and primary health clinics. Most hospitals in the UAE operate a walk-in outpatient department. The provision of and regulation services in Abu Dhabi and Dubai Entities are under met by the Health Authority Abu Dhabi (HAAD), Abu Dhabi Health Services Company (SEHA) and Dubai Health Authority respectively.

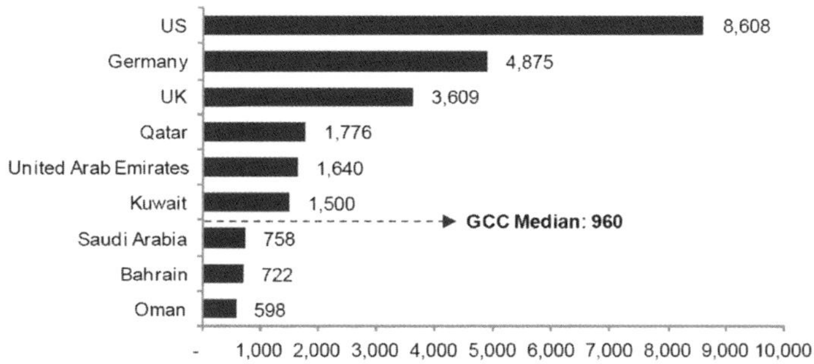

Fig. 16.1 GCC and UAE Healthcare per capita spend (US$, 2011) adapted from (World Development Indicators)

Only local Emirate citizens have access to free healthcare provision, whilst expatriates receive subsidised health care and are encouraged to purchase private healthcare insurance. By law, employers must provide health insurance coverage for employees and their families (Medical and Health Care Services; Koornneef et al. 2012). The major burden of illness in the UAE relates to chronic diseases including cardiovascular disease and diabetes, which also account for a large proportion of reasons for mortality (Koornneef et al. 2012).

In both the Executive Council's Policy Agenda 2007–2008 and the Economic Vision 2030 for Abu Dhabi the vision for healthcare in the UAE has been outlined, and focuses on strengthening regulatory practices and improving technical performance and upgrading health facilities (Koornneef et al. 2012).

16.1.2 Overview of the UAE Pharmaceutical Sector

The pharmaceutical sector in the UAE is highly regulated with prescription medicines requiring a valid prescription for dispensing. Per capita expenditure on medicines was the highest in the UAE in 2012 amongst members of the GCC, with an expenditure of US$80 per capita in the Emirate of Abu Dhabi reported (Abuelkhair et al. 2012). There is, however, a reliance on imported medicines with both doctor familiarity and patient preference weighing heavily on choice, as well as the presence of around 90 multinational pharmaceutical companies in the UAE (Alpen Capital Group). Local manufacture of medicines is undertaken by a limited number of companies accounting for less than one fifth of local pharmaceutical sales. Export of pharmaceutical preparations to Middle Eastern, North African and South East Asian countries by these local companies does, however, take place (Alpen Capital Group).

Government (public sector) pharmacies are primarily found within government hospitals serving both in-patient and outpatient supply. Pharmacies in the private sector dispense prescription medicines as well as supply over the counter medicines and other general items such as baby products and cosmetics. By law, a licensed pharmacist must always be physically present when the pharmacies are open for business. Pharmacists with a university degree and 2 years of experience can be licensed to operate private pharmacies after passing further examinations. In remote areas, assistant pharmacists are able to apply for licenses. In 2011 there were 1,227 community pharmacies in the UAE, reflecting a rapid increase in number over the years with the demand for health care services rising due to an increasing population (Hasan et al. 2011).

Pharmaceuticals are provided free of charge to Emirate nationals via the Thiqa insurance system, one of three insurance schemes in the UAE (Abuelkhair et al. 2012; Rayes et al. 2014). Since 2009, the Abu Dhabi Health Authority has required prescribing in the generic name only; however the dispensing pharmacist is able to choose between the available brands with the prescription still being fully reimbursed (Abuelkhair et al. 2012; Rayes et al. 2014; HAI). In addition the consumption of generic medicines is being promoted, including curtailing advertising, banning direct marketing of medicines and incentivizing the establishment of domestic manufacturing plants (Alpen Capital Group).

The formal medicine registration and pricing processes are detailed in the following sections.

16.2 Registration of Medicines

16.2.1 The Gulf Central Committee for Drug Registration

The Cooperation Council for the Arab States of the Gulf (GCC) has introduced a number of legislative and regulatory reforms to decrease and regulate medicine prices within Gulf States. To improve coordination of pharmaceutical policies within member states, the Central Drug Registration (CDR) committee has been established as a part of the Executive Board of the Council of the Ministers of Health (see Fig. 16.2). The aim of this board is to ensure regular and adequate supply of good quality medicines at affordable prices and promote the rational use of medicines in the whole Gulf area (Alpen Capital Group).

The GCC-Drug Registration Committee consists of two members from each state from whom a Chairman is annually nominated. The Committee has a permanent, full-time secretariat and two non-voting consultant advisors, and is responsible for reviewing and approving the registration of pharmaceutical companies and their products (Bawazir 2010).

In additional to aiming at harmonizing medicine prices within all member states, the Committee is also unifying regulatory processes including Good Manufacturing and Good Laboratory Practices, guidelines for bioequivalence, stability and biosimilar requirements, and regulations regarding registration of sera and antivenum, vaccines, blood products and radiopharmaceuticals. Guidelines for

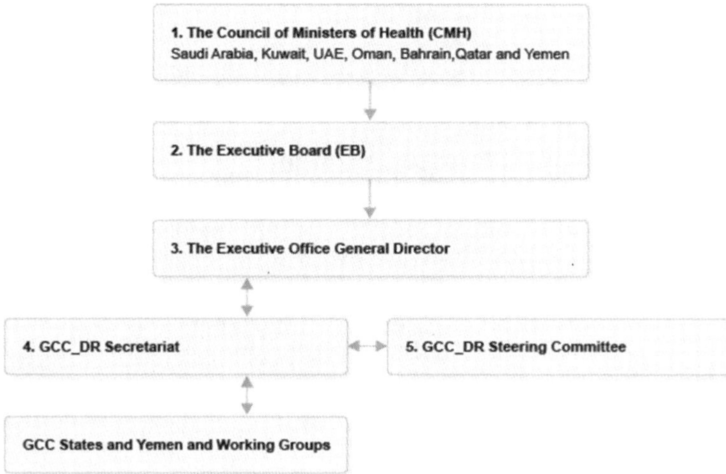

Fig. 16.2 Organizational framework for the GCC-DR operation (UAE Government; The Executive Board of the Health Ministers Council for GCC States)

post-marketing surveillance, pharmacovigilance and clinical trials are also being harmonized (The Executive Board of the Health Ministers Council for GCC States; Pateriya et al. 2011; The International Conference on Harmonization of Technical Requirements for Registration of Pharmaceuticals for Human Use).

Product registration with the GCC process enables the registration of that product within the GCC member states. Once registered centrally, the parent company must submit the certificate of the GCC registration plus two samples of the product and a Price Certificate for national registration and approval.

16.2.2 Pharmaceutical Product Registration in the UAE

The Ministry of Health (MOH) is the pharmaceutical regulatory authority in the UAE. To ensure the quality, efficacy and safety of medicines, both the pharmaceutical manufacturer and the products it produces must be registered in either the GCC or in the UAE by complying with established standards and quality testing. Most medicines must be registered prior to marketing in the UAE. The validity of the registration of the product is 5 years, following which time it must be renewed.

Locally produced medicines from UAE pharmaceutical manufacturers can be distributed directly to retailers and health care facilities or indirectly through wholesalers or distributors. Foreign pharmaceutical companies are not permitted to distribute products directly in the UAE, but must use domestic pharmaceutical importers and distributors. Additionally, all pharmaceutical international companies and local companies must have an agent or scientific office in the UAE to ensure the post marketing surveillance.

16.3 Pharmaceutical Pricing

16.3.1 Pharmaceutical Pricing Policy in the GCC

In 2012 the GCC Executive Ministers' Council decided to implement a unified price (including shipment and insurance) in a common currency for pharmaceutical products exported to GCC countries. Within the GCC a mechanism is being developed to adjust profit margins between the various agents and restrict price rises due to foreign currency fluctuations, a move likely to have a sizeable impact on all the distributors and pharmacies in the industry value chain in the UAE (The Executive Board of the Health Ministers Council for GCC States; Emad Abdul Hameed, Ittihad Newspaper).

A staged approach has been adopted to review prices in the GCC with a single therapeutic class of medicines (e.g. cardiovascular system medicines) being reviewed at a time.

The pricing policy formalized by the Kingdom of Saudi Arabia is used as the reference for the GCC member states, including the UAE. The Pricing Committee in the Saudi Food and Drug Authority has established a database called the Middle East Medicine Prices Database or 'MedPrice' which is a repository of medicine prices within a range of countries.

In addition to using the lowest of CIF prices in 30 countries (see Fig. 16.3: *Saudi FDA Form 30*), the Saudi FDA considers the therapeutic significance of the

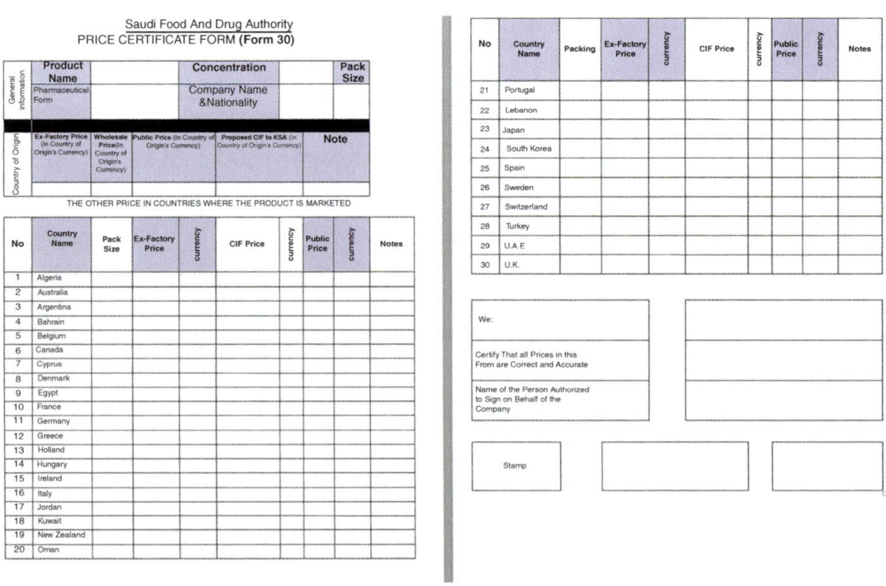
Saudi Food And Drug Authority
PRICE CERTIFICATE FORM **(Form 30)**

General information	Product Name		Concentration		Pack Size
	Pharmaceutical Form		Company Name &Nationality		

Country of Origin	Ex-Factory Price (In Country of Origin's Currency)	Wholesale Price(In Country of Origin's Currency)	Public Price (in Country of Origin's Currency)	Proposed CIF to KSA (In Country of Origin's Currency)	Note

THE OTHER PRICE IN COUNTRIES WHERE THE PRODUCT IS MARKETED

No	Country Name	Pack Size	Ex-Factory Price	currency	CIF Price	currency	Public Price	currency	Notes
1	Algeria								
2	Australia								
3	Argentina								
4	Bahrain								
5	Belgium								
6	Canada								
7	Cyprus								
8	Denmark								
9	Egypt								
10	France								
11	Germany								
12	Greece								
13	Holland								
14	Hungary								
15	Ireland								
16	Italy								
17	Jordan								
18	Kuwait								
19	New Zealand								
20	Oman								

No	Country Name	Packing	Ex-Factory Price	currency	CIF Price	currency	Public Price	currency	Notes
21	Portugal								
22	Lebanon								
23	Japan								
24	South Korea								
25	Spain								
26	Sweden								
27	Switzerland								
28	Turkey								
29	U.A.E								
30	U.K.								

We:	
Certify That all Prices in this From are Correct and Accurate	
Name of the Person Authorized to Sign on Behalf of the Company	

Stamp		

Fig. 16.3 Saudi FDA Form 30 (Drug Authority & Saudi Arabia)

preparation, prices of similar registered medicines and pharmaco-economic evidence.

16.3.2 Pharmaceutical Pricing Policy in the UAE

A survey in 2006 revealed the prices of a sample of 25 medicines in the UAE were higher than international reference prices, leading to activities designed to lower prices especially for chronic conditions (HAI; Cameron et al. 2011). In the same year, the UAE Ministry of Health established a Drug Price Management Division with four dedicated staff, with a principle objective of reducing medicine prices including prices within the private sector.

Prices are set using external benchmarking (international reference pricing) for originator brand products, and with generics priced at a percentage less than the originator brand price. Furthermore, priority is given to generic product applications where there are less than six generic equivalents in the marketplace. Penalties may be applied if pharmaceutical companies withhold registered products from the market.

In line with the GCC staged-approach to pricing reductions, the UAE aims at price reductions of the order of 40 % and has similarly adopted a staged approach. Of more than 7,000 pharmaceutical preparations in the UAE, less than 100 are expected to be unaffected by price changes, whilst 6,632 should decrease in price and the balance (329) may experience an increase.

Current limitations experienced by the Drug Price Management Division include the infancy of pricing policies being adopted and the lack of a formal Technology Assessment process to support decision-making. Instead, the federal Ministry of Health sets medicine prices for the country. The Assistant Undersecretary is supported by representatives from government hospitals such as Tawam and Khalifa Hospital and other parties in setting prices.

16.3.3 UAE Pricing Requirements/Process

The UAE largely follows pricing procedures of the Kingdom of Saudi Arabia (KSA) as the reference strategy for the GCC. Where a product is not registered in the KSA the same procedure is followed for pricing using all available price information, and setting a temporary registration certificate until the product is registered and priced in the KSA.

16.3.3.1 Documentation Required

Except for products originating in GCC members states or locally manufactured products, strict requirements must be met before a certified Price Certificate will be accepted in the UAE. Formal documentation must originate from the country of origin of the finished product, be recent (less than 1 year old) and be specific for the UAE. For each pack-size of the preparation the ex-factory price, approved CIF (cost, insurance and freight) price in other GCC states and that proposed for the UAE, and wholesale (pharmacy purchase price) and retail (price to the patient) prices in the country of origin must be supplied. Documentation must also be attested by the health authority of Chamber of Commerce in the country of origin and also by the embassy of the UAE in the country of origin. Abridged requirements apply to local or GCC products.

16.3.3.2 Price Calculation

The proposed retail (public) price is calculated from the proposed UAE CIF price using the prevailing regulations regarding agent and pharmacy mark-ups and the official exchange rates of foreign currencies. In the case of locally manufactured products the ex-factory price is used instead of the CIF.

$$\begin{aligned} \textit{Proposed Retail (public) price} = {} & (\textit{CIF price in US\$} \times \textit{Exchange rate}) \\ & + (\textit{Agent mark-up}) + (\textit{Pharmacy mark-up}) \end{aligned}$$

The Ministry of Health adopts a single annual exchange rate for its calculations, which in 2014 is 3.67. The permitted wholesalers or agent mark-up is 1.15, whilst additional pharmacy mark-ups of 1.17–1.24 are permitted (amount depends on the base wholesale price). Where there is no wholesale/agent fee, the pharmacy may use mark-up rates of 1.35–1.43 in most instances. Margins for medicines used in chronic conditions and anti-viral preparations are limited to 1.15 (wholesale) and 1.33 (retail).

16.3.3.3 Price Comparison

Reference pricing is used to interpret the calculated price, using the ex-factory price, price in the country of origin, prices in other GCC states, latest prices available in other standard references (such as the United Kingdom), and prices of chemically or pharmacological similar products already registered in the UAE.

Except for in exceptional circumstances for innovator products the final UAE price should not exceed that in other GCC member states, international benchmarked prices and must not exceed the ex-factory price by more than 20 %.

For generic products, in addition, locally produced generic products must be lower than the price of the innovator or market leader product by at least 30 %, and for imported generics must be lower by at least 40 %.

16.3.3.4 The Decision-Making Process

A data sheet showing the product details, the proposed CIF price, the calculations & comparisons thereof, with the available reference prices based on the prevailing regulation is prepared for each pack.

Proposed prices are then screened by an internal committee of the Pricing Unit Supervisor, Registration & Pricing Section Head and Registration & Drug Control Department Director, and the CIF price acceptable for each pack based on the prevailing criteria is noted. If the proposed price is not acceptable, the applicant will be asked to decrease the price to an acceptable level, through letters issued by the Department Director. If not responded positively within 2 weeks, the product will be taken to the Pricing Committee for decision without further notice being given.

In its regular meetings, the Pricing Committee will discuss and approve proposed prices for registration, with formal minutes of the meeting prepared and recorded.

If enough reference prices are not available at the time of first pricing of an essential or life-saving product, the committee may approve the proposed price temporarily, in order to make it available for treatment in the country at the earliest possible time. This price will be reviewed and revised, if necessary, as and when reference prices are available, and the parent company and/or the distributor are obliged to furnish such information to the ministry as soon as it is available.

The committee may reject the proposed price or defer pricing a product, if it deems necessary, and will inform the applicant of this decision. Resubmission of the application is accepted, and an appeals process is available to the pharmaceutical company.

The Pricing Committee also considers price reviews, either regarding the wholesale and retail mark-ups or the product price.

16.4 Ministerial Decree Following Approval

A Ministerial Decree, approving the price recommended by the Pricing Committee will be issued after each pricing meeting. The legislative and associated instruments in the United Arab Emirates are intended to ensure transparency of medicine pricing, through price declarations and publication of price information online and by distributing circulars among the pharmaceutical companies.

Notices signed by the Assistant Undersecretary for the Medical Practice & License Sector, citing the approved wholesale and retail prices of the products, will be issued for official and public distribution. Effective dates for the prices are stated in the document. Conditions, if any, regarding the import and marketing of any product are also specified in this circular.

The final approved CIF price for the product in the UAE will be communicated to the parent company and authorized distributor as a CIF letter from the ministry's Department Director.

The final price published by the ministry is binding and authorized distributors must display the approved public price as a price sticker together with the distributor name on each pack of the product. Any violation, either by increasing or decreasing the approved price, as well as tampering of the price sticker will lead to disciplinary action.

16.5 The Impact of Pricing on Public Health

Data from a 2006 survey showed very high medicine prices were paid by patients in the private sector (HAI). Prices for originator brands were more than 20 times higher than international reference prices in the private sector and more than five times higher (i.e. 400 %) in the public sector. Per capita expenditure on pharmaceuticals has been the highest of other Arab countries in the UAE, and pharmaceutical expenditure accounted for 35 % of total health expenditure in the emirate of Abu Dhabi for example (Abuelkhair et al. 2012).

Although the widely implemented health insurance schemes may have lessened the impact of high prices on the patient, such high medicine's costs are a burden to the national UAE economy. With the implementation of collaborative regulation and pricing policies in the member states of the GCC, it is expected that prices will decrease by around 40 %.

Amongst the vulnerable population especially a fall in prices will increase accessibility of essential medicines, especially those which are required for management of chronic conditions.

16.6 Conclusion

Core to the economic progress of the United Arab Emirates within the health sector is the initiation of pricing policies and membership of the Central Drug Registration of the GCC within the Executive Board of the Council of the Ministers of Health.

With a move towards a market economy, UAE has promoted availability of quality and affordable medicines, whilst allowing pharmaceutical companies' freedom to set prices of their products based on market prices. Policies to promote the uptake of generic medicines and indeed to improve local manufacturing will further enhance the overall pharmacy policies of the UAE.

Amongst the challenges that remain, more research is required to compare prices between the public and private sectors, between the seven emirates, and amongst the GCC and wider international community. An evaluation of pricing policies to establish the best mechanism for controls is also required. Another challenge is the continual revision of legislation and enforcement to cope with an ever-changing marketplace.

Acknowledgements Many thanks and special appreciation to Dr. Amin Hussain Al Amir the Assistant Under Secretary of the Public Health Policies and Licensing Sector in the Ministry of Health—UAE for his wide vision to implement such policy that gets UAE to be number one in the world for the mentioned goals in the chapter. The authors wish to acknowledge the members of the Pricing Committee for their valuable time and effort, and acknowledge Dr. Amal Al Awadhi, Head of Drug Department at the UAE-MOH and Dr. K. M. Abdulsamad, Pricing Section. Special Thanks goes to Dr. Magdi Abdou for his efforts and support.

References

Abuelkhair M, Abdu S, Godman B et al (2012) Imperative to consider multiple initiatives to maximize prescribing efficiency from generic availability: case history from Abu Dhabi. Expert Rev Pharmacoecon Outcomes Res 12(1):115–124

Alpen Capital Group. GCC pharmaceutical industry report. 31 Mar 2013. http://www.alpencapital.com/downloads/GCC%20Pharmaceuticals%20Industry%20Report%202013_31%20March%202013.pdf. Accessed 12 Aug 2014

Bawazir S (2010) Saudi Food and Drug Authority, Saudi Arabia. Presentation at ICDRA 2010. Singapore. http://www.who.int/medicines/areas/quality_safety/regulation_legislation/PL2_2.pdf. Accessed 13 Aug 2014

Cameron A et al (2011) The world medicines situation 2011: medicines prices, availability and affordability. World Health Organization, Geneva

Emad Abdul Hameed. Press Release. Ittihad Newspaper. 14 June 2013

HAI. Medicine prices, availability, affordability and price components: UAE. http://www.haiweb.org/medicineprices/surveys/200612AE/sdocs/EMP-UAE-summary-new%20pricing.pdf. Accessed 12 Aug 2014

Hasan S, Sulieman H, Chapman C et al (2011) Community pharmacy in the United Arab Emirates: characteristics and workforce issues. Int J Pharm Pract 19(6):392–399

Human Development Reports. United Nations Development Programme. http://hdr.undp.org/en. Accessed 12 Aug 2014

Koornneef EJ, Robben PBM, Al Seiari MB et al (2012) Health system reform in the Emirate of Abu Dhabi, United Arab Emirates. Health Policy 108(2–3):115–121

Medical and Health Care Services. UAE Government. http://www.government.ae/en/web/guest/medical_and_health_care. Accessed 12 Aug 2014

Pateriya S, Janodia MD, Deshpande PB et al (2011) Regulatory aspects of pharmaceuticals' exports in Gulf Cooperation Council countries. J Young Pharmacists 3(2):155–162

Rayes IK, Hassali MA, Abduelkarem AR (2014) The role of pharmacists in developing countries: the current scenario in the United Arab Emirates. Saudi Pharm J. ISSN 1319-0164. http://dx.doi.org/10.1016/j.jsps.2014.02.004

Saudi Food and Drug Authority, Saudi Arabia. http://www.sfda.gov.sa/en/drug/Pages/default.aspx. Accessed 13 Aug 2014

The Executive Board of the Health Ministers' Council for GCC States. http://sgh.org.sa/en-us/home.aspx

The International Conference on Harmonization of Technical Requirements for Registration of Pharmaceuticals for Human Use (ICH). http://www.ich.org/

UAE Government. http://www.uaeinteract.com/government. Accessed 12 Aug 2014

World Development Indicators. World Bank. http://data.worldbank.org/products/wdi. Accessed 12 Aug 2014

Chapter 17
The Healthcare System and Pharmaceutical Prices in United States

Albert I. Wertheimer and Ming-Yi Huang

Abstract In the United States, pharmaceuticals are manufactured or distributed by many hundreds of companies, all in private hands. Prices of pharmaceuticals are set by manufacturers and there is no governmental involvement. Pharmaceutical products leaving the manufacturers factory are sent to wholesaler organizations or directly to the warehouses of chain pharmacy corporations, mail service pharmacies or to other large purchasers such as hospitals, clinics, and health maintenance organizations. Hospitals generally purchased their pharmaceutical products at lower prices than are available to community pharmacies. In order to get even lower prices, hospitals have joined together to form buying groups to obtain even lower prices by using their bargaining power. The significant and increasing health care expenditure forces private payers in the U.S. to start to request clinical and economic data from manufacturers to support coverage and reimbursement decisions. Economic evaluation measures efficiency of health programs or health technologies by comparing costs and outcomes across different alternatives. Techniques for economic evaluation include cost-effectiveness analysis, cost-utility analysis, and benefit-cost analysis. While economic evaluation focusing on efficiency, another technique, budget impact model, assesses the affordability of adopting a new program or technique. However, in order not to hinder patient's access to care, it is prohibited by law to use the findings from health technology assessment such as cost-effectiveness analysis in coverage decisions for federal programs.

The health care system of the United States is often referred to as a non-system. It is quite complex and composed of components in the private sector, and systems run by governmental agencies, the military and private not for profit organizations as

A.I. Wertheimer (✉)
Temple University School of Pharmacy, Philadelphia, PA 19140, USA
e-mail: albertw@erols.com

M.-Y. Huang
Temple University School of Pharmacy, Philadelphia, PA 19140, USA

Merck & Co., Inc., West Point, PA, USA

Z.-U.-D. Babar (ed.), *Pharmaceutical Prices in the 21st Century*,
DOI 10.1007/978-3-319-12169-7_17

well as religious groups. Above all, the overall economic system in the United States is free enterprise, capitalism. These various systems in organizations coexist, often with little or no communication among them. That is why the term, non-system has been applied since there is so little coordination and with resulting duplication, waste and overlap.

Pharmaceuticals are manufactured or distributed by many hundreds of companies, all in private hands. The research intensive branded pharmaceutical companies number less than 100 and are responsible for most all of the research and development activities taking place in the pharmaceutical industry in the United States. There are several hundred other pharmaceutical manufacturers who specialize in generic drugs or over-the-counter drugs or in the biotechnology area. In 2012, US spent 71.5 % of total medicine spending on branded drugs and 28.5 % on generics, while 84 % of prescriptions were dispensed for generic drugs (IMS Institute for Healthcare Informatics 2013). In addition there are small numbers of firms that specialize in liquids or ointments or parenteral solutions. All of the entries in the pharmaceutical manufacturing space are privately owned, for-profit enterprises.

Of the 310 million residents of the United States, around 200 million receive health insurance as a benefit from their employers or self-purchased. Another 50 million persons are eligible for coverage under a program called Medicaid which is for medically indigent, low income individuals. In addition, there are about 50 million persons whose healthcare is mostly paid for by a federal government program called Medicare. Medicare is not a poverty program but rather a government mandated insurance program where persons contribute to a fund during their working years, and then receive benefits after retirement, around the age of 65. Among the above insured which are not mutually exclusive, about 40 million persons are covered by more than one health insurance plans. If one were to calculate these preceding numbers, it is clear that there are another 50 million persons who do not have health insurance (U.S. Census Bureau 2013). Many of those persons cannot afford to pay the premiums and some others were young and healthy elect to not buy health insurance and gamble that they will be healthy.

The typical citizen receives health insurance as a portion of their compensation from their employers. The employer offers workers a variety of plans, with differing copayments, benefit levels, deductible amounts, and with various contributions from the employee him or herself. The patient might go to their primary care physician and pay a nominal fee of $10–20. The physician would send the bill to the insurance company or managed care organization for the remaining $80. This scheme works the same with dentists, hospitals, physical therapy, and most other health services.

The Medicaid program is very similar to what was just described above except that the physician bills a state agency that administers the program on behalf of that state and the federal government (http://www.medicaid.gov/Federal-Policy-Guidance/Federal-Policy-Guidance.html). Similarly, the Medicare program is operated by the federal government and invoices are sent to them for services provided to senior citizens who have enrolled in the program (http://www.cms.gov/Medicare/Medicare-General-Information/MedicareGenInfo/index.html). The different services within the military operate their own clinics and hospitals for the servicemen and their families while they are in active duty. Another large organization is the veterans administration which cares for servicemen who served previously. They are entitled to lifetime care from a network of veterans hospitals and clinics scattered through many if not most medium and large sized communities in the United States.

This description would be incomplete if there were no mention of for-profit healthcare institutions. Today we see a large number of investor owned hospitals, nursing homes, dialysis centers, clinical laboratories and imaging facilities. These entities must compete with the not-for-profit religious and local government operations.

In recent years, the indemnity insurance programs so commonly seen during the twentieth century have been replaced by somewhat similar organizations called managed care organizations (MCOs) which have made efforts to streamline the provision of healthcare services and to achieve economies of scale as well as efficiencies in the delivery of personal health services. They become involved in decisions about which hospitals will be used, what surgeons will be utilized and they review outcomes to constantly strive to increase the efficiency and effectiveness of their system. That is necessary because they compete with other managed care organizations in selling programs to employers. In order to compete they are forced to extract discounts from physicians, pharmacies, hospitals and most all other provider groups. Aetna, Cigna, Kaiser Permanente, United Healthcare, WellPoint, and Humana are the largest MCOs and cover more than half of the employer-sponsored health plan members in the United States (Sullivan et al. 2009). MCOs usually contract with pharmacy benefit managers (PBM), which are third party organization that provide prescription drug management service for health plans.

17.1 Pharmacy System of the United States

Pharmaceutical products leaving the manufacturers factory are sent usually to wholesaler organizations (around two-thirds of manufacturers' shipments) but in some cases, shipments are made directly to the warehouses of chain pharmacy corporations (30 %), mail service pharmacies (2 %) and to other large purchasers such as hospitals, clinics, health maintenance organizations, nursing homes or federal facilities (Congressional Budget 2007). There has been great consolidation in the wholesale drug field in recent years, leaving us today with three large and nationwide wholesalers who compete with perhaps 50 other local and regional wholesalers. Many more of this letter group existed previously but they have either gone out of business when the owner retired or they have been purchased by the larger national wholesaler chains.

The wholesalers sell their products to community pharmacies and to hospitals. There are about 60,000 community pharmacies in the US and that number is divided roughly equally by individually owned pharmacies as well as pharmacies operated by chain pharmacy corporations. The largest chain pharmacies are Walgreens which operates more than 8,000 stores (http://news.walgreens.com/article_display.cfm?article_id=1044), *followed by* CVS with more than 7,000 stores (http://pdf.secdatabase.com/2440/0001104659-13-011354.pdf) and Rite-Aid with around 4,500 stores (https://www.riteaid.com/corporate/news). There are a number of regional chains and the remainder of the community pharmacies are sold proprietorships or partnerships operated by one or several pharmacists or others. It should be noted that there are no rules in the United States regarding pharmacy ownership. A qualified pharmacist must be in charge but need not be the owner.

Hospitals, except for the for-profit ones, generally purchased their pharmaceutical products at lower prices than are available to community pharmacies. This is part of a long-standing tradition that since most hospitals are non-profit, or governmental or religious, that they should receive reduced prices. In order to get even lower prices, hospitals have joined together to form buying groups referred to as GPOs (group purchasing organizations) which endeavor to obtain even lower prices by using their bargaining power as very large purchasers. Usually, they obtain prices lower than what an individual 300 bed hospital would be able to obtain.

The drug regulatory authority in the United States is called the food and drug administration. It regulates drugs, devices, diagnostics, vaccines, cosmetics, animal products, tobacco products, foods and nuclear products. The only role for this federal government agency is to assure the safety and efficacy of pharmaceutical products. It was organized in 1906 and legislation that various points as expanded its mission and tightened its regulations and requirements (http://www.fda.gov/regulatoryinformation/legislation/ucm148690.htm). The 50 state governments play overall in pharmaceutical regulation whatsoever. The state governments license and inspect practitioners, and healthcare facilities within that state. It should be pointed out because it is unusual throughout the world, that the federal government has no role in the pricing of pharmaceuticals. This task is handled through the marketplace where prices are set by manufacturers and if a product is not commercially successful, manufacturer as the opportunity of reducing the price or providing discounts or rebates aimed at making the product more attractive to potential buyers.

The FDA is involved in the testing of new drug candidates from preclinical testing in animals and then testing in phase 1 using healthy volunteers to decide safety and proper dosage levels. In phase 2 clinical trials, small numbers of patients with the disease or condition for which the drug is indicated are used to decide efficacy, while safety is continued to be evaluated. Phase 3 is the large-scale multisite clinical trial that should provide sufficient information to the agency to enable it to make a decision as to whether a new pharmaceutical entity should be approved for sale or not. The FDA also requires phase 4 for testing, commonly called post marketing surveillance where the manufacturer must keep records of reported adverse events and other problems and report these according to a specified schedule to the FDA. The FDA must approve the labeling and promotional materials in advance of marketing approvals (http://www.fda.gov/Drugs/ResourcesForYou/Consumers/ucm289601.htm). In addition, the FDA inspects manufacturers to confirm that they meet good manufacturing practices requirements. Distributors are inspected as well as wholesaler facilities.

When the clinical trial phase 3 data have been analyzed and reported, they are sent to the FDA for marketing approval review. This review normally takes at least 1 year and often can be longer. In addition, generic drugs manufacturers apply for an abbreviated new drug application (ANDA) where only bioequivalence requires proof (http://www.fda.gov/newsevents/testimony/ucm115033.htm). It is assumed that the active ingredient is identical to the one in the originator product and therefore only the bio availability is tested. Because of the usual number of ANDA applications pending at the FDA, it typically takes about 3 years for a generic drug to be approved for marketing.

Self-medication drugs called over-the-counter drugs or OTC's are sold without a positions prescription in any retail establishment including mail order, vending machines and in hotel gift shops, grocery stores, etc. Under normal circumstances, OTC drugs are pharmaceutical products that have been widely and safely used as prescription drugs for a number of years (http://www.fda.gov/Drugs/ResourcesForYou/SpecialFeatures/ucm342560.htm). When the manufacturer or the FDA sense that the product can be used safely in an unsupervised fashion by consumers, it is transferred to the OTC category and this is overseen by the Federal Trade Commission which looks for inappropriate or misleading claims or other statements about side effects or benefits.

17.2 Drug Pricing in the United States

In the United States as was mentioned previously, there is no governmental involvement regarding prices of pharmaceuticals and the marketplace becomes the arbiter of competition and success. Pharmaceutical pricing combines science and a bit of art. To some it is a large mystery but in most cases, one looks at the price of competing products and ascertains how successful those other products appear to be. If there is no adequate therapy for a medical problem, then the price of the new product may be rather high. When the early ulcer drugs were compared to the conventional therapy of surgery, we see some of the earliest Pharmacoeconomic studies to guide formulary decision-makers about the inclusion of certain drugs onto the formulary. If a new product joins a crowded market such as with ace inhibitors, it will have a difficult time in replacing the market share of the leading brands unless it has one of two possible attributes; a lower price or superior outcomes. The listed prices for pharmaceuticals are rarely adhered to. Discounts abound from wholesalers and manufacturers and there are frequent special deals available to buyers. In addition, insurers and managed care organizations, because of their size and market prowess are able to obtain further discounts called rebates from manufacturers. Often, to obtain these rebates, managed care organizations must guarantee to a pharmaceutical manufacturer that they will deliver a specified market share percentage for that product. It could be 50 or 70 % or some other number of a therapeutic category. If that target is not achieved, then the ministry organization will expect to pay a higher price.

17.3 Are Official Prices the Actual Transaction Prices?

Wholesale prices are often quoted in catalogs and advertisements as AWP, average wholesale price. AWP is the list price for a drug sold by wholesaler to retailer, which published in commercial publications, such as *Red Book* (Thomson Reuters). However it is well known, that buyers received close to a 20 % discount, on average from that AWP price; therefore; AWP may not be the best price estimate for pharmaceuticals. Obviously, larger purchasers will receive the greatest percentage discount while the small neighborhood independent pharmacy might only receive a 16 or 18 % discount from the AWP price. In order to simplify reimbursements to pharmacies from insurance companies and managed care organizations, these MCOs generally establish the policy where they pay pharmacists the AWP price −15 % to recognize the fact that the pharmacy did not buy the products at the full catalog price. It becomes obvious to all that the pharmacy then receives a fixed dispensing fee from the insurer in addition to keeping the spread between the AWP −15 % payment and the AWP −20 % actual cost to the pharmacy of that product. Of course, these numbers are approximate as each organization has its own individually arrived at policies. Other alternative price estimates include WAC (wholesale acquisition cost) and AMP (average manufacturer price). WAC is another list price, determined by manufacturer for a drug they sold to wholesaler. On the other hand, AMP represents the actual transactions, which is the average price paid by wholesaler to manufacturer and reflects rebates that manufacturer paid back to wholesaler. AMP is reported by manufacturer which is mandated by Congress. Besides wholesaler or direct sales to retail pharmacy, manufacturer may also provide rebates to third-party payers, such as pharmacy benefit manager, health plan, hospital or clinic. These rebates to third-party payer are usually not reflected in the above price estimates (Congressional Budget 2007; Curtiss et al. 2010).

Drug prices in the USA are higher than most other countries in the world. In Canada, branded products are anywhere from 20 to 60 % lower priced than in the United States. That is the same for comparisons of prices between the U.S. and all of Europe, Japan, Australia and New Zealand. In those other countries, government agencies negotiate prices with manufacturers.

17.4 Generics

Prescription drugs in the United States have higher selling prices than in most other countries in the world. The typical cost of a branded pharmaceutical product for a 1-month period of treatment usually exceeds $100. And with generic drugs, this figure is somewhere around $30. Generic drugs become available upon the expiration of the 20 year patent protection period.

17.5 Who or What Is Involved in Setting Prices: Do Prices Change Over Time and How

As mentioned earlier, drug prices in the United States can be decided by manufactures, and they should fall between breakeven price and premium price. The breakeven price is the minimum profitable price level, which can be decided by cost analysis that reflects product discovery, development, manufacture, marketing, and distribution. The premium price is the maximum price that can be rationally charged, which takes into account population size/indication, market crowdedness, product position on the market, and prices of other available treatment options. Since these factors change due to market competition, disease epidemiology, or regulation/policy, drug prices do change over time.

Risk-sharing agreements between drug manufacturer and payer, also known as value-based pricing, is not a new concept but has been used increasingly. The idea is that payer will pay the drug for different prices or cover the drug for different periods of time, based on its future performance. For example, Johnson & Johnson agreed to pay back their UK payer—National Health Service for their anti-cancer drug for multiple myeloma, if patients have no response to their drug after treating for four cycles. Payer uses value-based pricing that attaches their payment to treatment outcomes, as a way to control costs and quality of service. There are barriers that make value-based pricing difficult to implement, such as availability of a good health information system to track outcomes timely, or the difficulty to choose the right outcomes measure in the real-world setting (Neumann et al. 2011; Carlson et al. 2010).

17.6 HTA Process/CER in the United States, How Long Does It Take?

The health expenditure in the U.S. is around 18 % of total Gross Domestic Product (GDP), and is much more higher when comparing to most Western European countries and Canada, which are 9–12 % (http://data.worldbank.org/indicator/SH.XPD.TOTL.ZS). The significant and increasing health care expenditure forces payers to start to ask questions such as: Whether the new or existing treatments worth it? And can we afford it? These questions should be answered by conducting Health Technology Assessment (HTA); however, in the United States, due to the complexity of health care system, or nonsystem, there is neither a single HTA agency nor centralization of HTA process. Therefore, unlike many Western European countries, there is no formal guideline for HTA process in the United States. Academy of Managed Care Pharmacy (AMCP) first published the guidance document in 2001 on evidence required to support formulary listings. The guidance provides framework for Pharmacy and Therapeutics Committees to request appropriate clinical and economic data from manufacturers to support coverage and reimbursement decisions and has been adopted by many largest managed care organizations (MCO) and pharmacy benefit managements (PBM) (http://amcp.org/Tertiary.aspx?id=16065; Spooner et al. 2007). The HTA evidence may affect listing/coverage decision; however, it is not clear how and whether HTA has been used for pricing justification in the U.S.

Economic evaluation is an essential part of HTA, which measure efficiency of health programs or health technologies by comparing costs and outcomes across different alternatives. Techniques that can be used for economic evaluation include cost–effectiveness analysis, cost–utility analysis, and benefit–cost analysis. Cost–effectiveness analysis measures outcomes in disease-specific natural unit (i.e. mmHg reduced for high blood pressure), death prevented, or life-years saved, which allow comparison of treatments for the same disease. Cost–utility analysis measures outcomes in QALY (Quality-adjusted life years), a metric that combines both quantity and quality of life. Since outcomes will be measured in the same standard, regarding diseases or treatments, cost–utility analysis allows evaluation of treatments across different diseases. Benefit–cost analysis measures outcomes in monetary value, which enable the comparison even beyond health care programs (Drummond et al. 2005; Kobelt 2013). While the above analyses measure the efficiency of health programs or health technologies, another technique—budget impact model, which assesses the affordability of adopting a new program or technique, is often used. A new treatment that is efficient or cost-effective compared to the current option, is not always affordable. Budget impact model predicts the financial impact by presenting resource use and costs that comes with new technology uptake (Mauskopf et al. 2007).

For private health plans, each MCO may have different processes and requirements regarding health technology assessment, and these are usually not transparent (Sullivan et al. 2009). The private payers may generate health technology assessment by themselves or review evidence provided by manufacturers, as well as seek advice/service from external HTA organizations, such as Emergency Care Research Institute (ECRI), Hayes Inc., or Blue Cross Blue Shield Association—Technology Evaluation Center (BCBSA TEC) (http://www.npcnow.org/issue/pcori-cer-agencies). WellPoint is the first MCO that published their Health Technology Assessment (HTA) guideline in 2008 and Comparative Effectiveness Research (CER) guideline in 2010 (http://ir.wellpoint.com/phoenix.zhtml?c=130104&p=irol-newsArticle&ID=1429022&highlight=). Both WellPoint's

HTA guideline (http://amcp.org/WorkArea/DownloadAsset.aspx?id=12236) and AMCP formulary submission guideline (http://amcp.org/practice-resources/amcp-format-formulary-submisions.pdf) request cost–effectiveness model and budget impact model to be presented in the dossier as economic evidences for product value.

Several government-sponsored HTA agencies existed to review different government programs. The Office of Technology Assessment (OTA), established in 1972 and closed in 1995, was the first agency to evaluate technologies and programs of a wide range of topics, including health care (Levy and Garrison 2010; http://www.princeton.edu/~ota/ns20/topic_f.html). In 2009, American Recovery and Reinvestment Act (Recovery Act) provided $300 million to Agency for Healthcare Research and Quality (AHRQ) to fund comparative effectiveness research (CER) (http://archive.ahrq.gov/funding/arra/overview/index.html). As the largest federal HTA funder in the U.S., AHRQ partners with external research groups through its Effective Health Care (EHC) Program, including 11 Evidence-Based Practice Centers (EPCs), the Centers for Education and Research on Therapeutics (CERT), and the Developing Evidence to Inform Decisions about Effectiveness (DEcIDE), to generate or review comparative effectiveness evidence which usually takes between 15 and 18 months (Sullivan et al. 2009; http://effectivehealthcare.ahrq.gov/index.cfm/who-is-involved-in-the-effective-health-care-program1/). Then, in 2010, Patient Protection and Affordable Care Act (PPACA) established the Patient Centered Outcomes Research Institute (PCORI), a private, non-profit institution but governed and funded partially by government, to develop and fund CER (http://www.pcori.org/). Statewide, Medicaid Evidence-based Decisions Project (MED), established in 2006 at the Center for Evidence-based Policy of the Oregon Health and Sciences University, has collaborated with 13 state Medicaid agencies to produce evidence to inform decision making (http://www.ohsu.edu/xd/research/centers-institutes/evidence-based-policy-center/med/index.cfm). The other government funded HTA programs include Veteran's Affairs Pharmacy Benefits Management Strategic Healthcare Group (VA PBMSHG) for HTA within VA health system, and Department of Defense Pharmacoeconomic Center (PEC) for military health system (Sullivan et al. 2009; http://www.pbm.va.gov/; http://www.pec.ha.osd.mil/). However, in order not to hinder patient's access to care, it is prohibited to use the findings from health technology assessment to determine "*practice guidelines, coverage recommendations, payment, or policy recommendations*" for federal programs in the U.S. (The Patient Protection and Affordable Care Act (2010); Thorpe 2010).

References

Carlson JJ, Sullivan SD, Garrison LP, Neumann PJ, Veenstra DL (2010) Linking payment to health outcomes: a taxonomy and examination of performance-based reimbursement schemes between healthcare payers and manufacturers. Health Policy 96(3):179–190

U.S. Census Bureau (2013) Income, poverty, and health insurance coverage in the United States 2012

Congressional Budget Office (2007) Prescription drug pricing in the private sector

Curtiss FR, Lettrich P, Fairman KA (2010) What is the price benchmark to replace average wholesale price (AWP)? J Manag Care Pharm 16(7):492–501

Drummond MF, Sculpher MJ, Torrance GW, O'Brien BJ, Stoddart GL (2005) Methods for the economic evaluation of health care programme, 3rd edn. Oxford University Press, Oxford

http://amcp.org/practice-resources/amcp-format-formulary-submisions.pdf. Accessed 15 June 2014

http://amcp.org/Tertiary.aspx?id=16065. Accessed 15 June 2014

http://amcp.org/WorkArea/DownloadAsset.aspx?id=12236. Accessed 15 June 2014

http://archive.ahrq.gov/funding/arra/overview/index.html. Accessed 15 June 2014

http://data.worldbank.org/indicator/SH.XPD.TOTL.ZS. Accessed 15 June 2014

http://effectivehealthcare.ahrq.gov/index.cfm/who-is-involved-in-the-effective-health-care-program1/. Accessed 15 June 2014

http://ir.wellpoint.com/phoenix.zhtml?c=130104&p=irol-newsArticle&ID=1429022&highlight=. Accessed 15 June 2014

http://news.walgreens.com/article_display.cfm?article_id=1044. Accessed 15 June 2014

http://pdf.secdatabase.com/2440/0001104659-13-011354.pdf. Accessed 15 June 2014

http://www.cms.gov/Medicare/Medicare-General-Information/MedicareGenInfo/index.html. Accessed 15 June 2014

http://www.fda.gov/Drugs/ResourcesForYou/Consumers/ucm289601.htm. Accessed 15 June 2014

http://www.fda.gov/Drugs/ResourcesForYou/SpecialFeatures/ucm342560.htm. Accessed 15 June 2014

http://www.fda.gov/newsevents/testimony/ucm115033.htm. Accessed 15 June 2014

http://www.fda.gov/regulatoryinformation/legislation/ucm148690.htm. Accessed 15 June 2014

http://www.medicaid.gov/Federal-Policy-Guidance/Federal-Policy-Guidance.html. Accessed 15 June 2014

http://www.ohsu.edu/xd/research/centers-institutes/evidence-based-policy-center/med/index.cfm. Accessed 15 June 2014

http://www.pbm.va.gov/. Accessed 15 June 2014

http://www.pcori.org/. Accessed 15 June 2014

http://www.pec.ha.osd.mil/. Accessed 15 June 2014

http://www.princeton.edu/~ota/ns20/topic_f.html. Accessed 15 June 2014

https://www.riteaid.com/corporate/news. Accessed 15 June 2014

IMS Institute for Healthcare Informatics (2013) Declining medicine use and costs: for better or worse? A review of the use of medicines in the United States in 2012

Kobelt G (2013) Health economics: an introduction to economic evaluation, 3rd edn. Office of Health Economics, London

Levy AR, Garrison LP Jr (2010) Apples and oranges? Assessing comparative effectiveness and comparative value in the US and other countries. Value Health 13(Suppl 1):S1–S3

Mauskopf JA, Sulluvan SD et al (2007) Principles of good practice for budget impact analysis: report of the ISPOR task force on good research practices—budget impact analysis. Value Health 10:336–347

Neumann PJ, Chambers JD, Simon F, Meckley LM (2011) Risk-sharing arrangements that link payment for drugs to health outcomes are proving hard to implement. Health Aff (Millwood) 30(12):2329–2337

Spooner JJ, Gandhi PK, Connelly SB (2007) AMCP Format dossier requests: manufacturer response and formulary implications for one large health plan. J Manag Care Pharm 13 (1):37–43

Sullivan SD, Watkins J, Sweet B, Ramsey SD (2009) Health technology assessment in health-care decisions in the United States. Value Health 12(Suppl 2):S39–S44

The Patient Protection and Affordable Care Act (2010) Public Law 111–148. 111th United States Congress. Washington, D.C.: United States Government Printing Office. March 23, 2010

Thorpe JH (2010) Comparative effectiveness research and health reform: implications for public health policy and practice. Public Health Rep 125(6):909–912

Chapter 18
Pharmaceutical Pricing Policies in Vietnam

Tuan Anh Nguyen and Elizabeth E. Roughead

Abstract This chapter discusses the pharmaceutical system in Vietnam and the mechanisms for pharmaceutical prices. We include an analysis of the legislative reforms and the impact of the reforms on pharmaceutical prices and accessibility.

Health sector reforms since 1989 have transformed Vietnam's health care system from a publicly funded and provided health care system to public-private mix. With the shift towards a market economy, Vietnam has allowed pharmaceutical companies to set prices of their products based on market forces, subject to stabilization by the State. A number of legislative and regulatory reforms have been introduced to regulate medicine prices in Vietnam, which were intended to ensure transparency of prices along the supply chain, through price declaration and publication of price information. The initiatives, however, have been less successful than expected because they did not address the need for reasonable prices or the need to differentiate between declared, published and selling prices. Further, provisions were not routinely monitored or effectively enforced.

18.1 Introduction

Health sector reforms since 1989 have transformed Vietnam's health care system from a publicly funded and provided health care system to public-private mix. With a shift towards a market economy, Vietnam has allowed pharmaceutical companies to set prices of their products based on market forces, subject to stabilization by the State. A number of legislative and regulatory reforms have been introduced to regulate medicine prices in Vietnam, which were intended to ensure transparency of prices along the supply chain, through price declaration and publication of price information. This chapter provides an analysis of the legislative reforms and the impact of the reforms on pharmaceutical prices and accessibility. It begins with an overview of Vietnam's health care and pharmaceutical systems. A section follows

T.A. Nguyen (✉) • E.E. Roughead
Quality Use of Medicines and Pharmacy Research Centre, School of Pharmacy and Medical Sciences, University of South Australia, Adelaide, SA 5000, Australia
e-mail: Tuan.Nguyen@unisa.edu.au; Libby.Roughead@unisa.edu.au

Z.-U.-D. Babar (ed.), *Pharmaceutical Prices in the 21st Century*,
DOI 10.1007/978-3-319-12169-7_18

on drug regulatory authority, highlighting the function of Vietnam's single drug regulatory authority and its component of drug pricing authority, as well as the timeline for marketing authorization approval for pharmaceuticals. The chapter continues with sections that are devoted to the mechanisms for pharmaceutical prices, including drug pricing set-up, how prices are set and who is involved in price setting, with a focus on the legislative reforms on pharmaceutical pricing. The impact of the reforms on pharmaceutical prices and accessibility is then reviewed, as is an alternative strategy of promoting competition by increasing use of generic medicines in Vietnam. The chapter ends with conclusions and recommendations for future research.

18.2 Vietnam Health Care System

Vietnam's health care system has evolved from health systems established separately in North and South Vietnam. During the war period (1945 to 1975), North Vietnam established an extensive network of primary health care facilities with the aim of achieving universal health care coverage. In urban areas nearly 100 % of the population were covered, as were 75 % of the population in rural areas (Witter 1996). In South Vietnam, a strong private health sector dominated until, upon unification with the North in 1975, private enterprises were banned (Larsson 2003).

Post 1975, Vietnam suffered severe financial pressures, including costly post war reconstruction, an economic blockade by the United States, withdrawal of aid from the former Soviet Union and a rising inflation rate (Chalker 1995; Wolffers 1995; Witter 1996). This had significant impacts on the health care system. The expansion of the network of free public health services that had been set up in North Vietnam to include the South added further economic strain, resulting in poor maintenance of health care facilities and lack of basic equipment and medicines in many health stations and hospitals (Witter 1996). At this time the domestic pharmaceutical industry was only able to meet 30 % of the population's demand for medicines and most essential medicines had to be imported as there was not capacity to manufacture in country (Wolffers 1995).

The economic reform process known as "Doi Moi", initiated in 1986, led to important policy shifts in the health care system in the late 1980s and early 1990s. A number of market-oriented measures were implemented, including the introduction of user fees at public health facilities, legalization of private pharmacy and medical practices, and liberalization of the production and sale of pharmaceuticals (WHO 2007). Free access to health care was gradually replaced by a system of direct payment by patients (Larsson 2003). The provision of free medicines dispensed through the public health system was also discontinued (Larsson 2003). As a result, Vietnam's near universal, publicly funded and provided health services were converted into an unregulated public–private mix (Sepehri et al. 2008).

One result of the country increasing its reliance on market mechanisms was substantial increases in consumer out-of-pocket (OOP) health expenditure (World

Bank 2007). Between 1995 and 2008, OOP expenditure ranged from 55 to 66 % of total health expenditure (WHO 2010). The rising household OOP spending on health was partly because of increasing user fees in public hospitals (MOH of Vietnam, Health Partnership Group 2008). Increases in medicine prices also contributed to the growing magnitude of absolute household OOP expenditure on health.

To address the growth in OOP payments that placed financial barriers to health care access, the government issued a national Health Insurance Decree in 1992, introducing compulsory health insurance for people in salaried employment. Since then, health financing from social health insurance as a percentage of public health expenditure has risen, from 7 % in 1995 to 32 % in 2008 (WHO 2010). In 2008, the Health Insurance Law was passed and came into effect in July 2009. The law stipulated that the government was responsible for fully subsidizing health insurance for children less than 6 years of age, the elderly, and the poor, and for partially subsidizing health insurance for the near-poor and students. The law also provided a roadmap for universal health coverage. By 2011, health care coverage in Vietnam exceeded 64 % of the population (Somanathan et al. 2013). Medicines eligible for public health insurance reimbursement are limited to medicines listed on the schedule issued by the Ministry of Health (MOH). The current schedule comprises 900 western medicines and 57 radioactive substances and marking compounds (MOH of Vietnam 2011). The public health insurance scheme does not cover medicines that are purchased at private retail pharmacies.

18.3 The Pharmaceutical System

The health sector reforms, introduced since 1989, have also impacted on Vietnam's pharmaceutical supply chain, shifting it from a centrally controlled system to a market-oriented system (Larsson 2003). The opening of the country to foreign trade and the liberalization of rules governing pharmaceutical manufacture, sale and distribution led to a 300 % increase in medicine production and a tenfold increase in importation of medicines between 1988 and 1992 (Witter 1996). To improve coordination of pharmaceutical policies the National Drug Policy was promulgated in 1996, with two basic goals; ensuring regular and adequate supply of good quality medicines at affordable prices, and ensuring rational use of medicines (Government of Vietnam 1996b).

To facilitate the implementation of the National Drug Policy, the Drug Administration of Vietnam (DVA) was also established in 1996 with responsibility for state management of pharmaceuticals (Government of Vietnam 1996a). The DVA adopted a roadmap of good practices to ensure the quality of medicines across all aspects of the supply chain. In Vietnam, manufacturers have to comply with the code of Good Manufacturing Practice (GMP), importers with Good Storage Practice (GSP), distributors with GSP and Good Distribution Practice (GDP) and

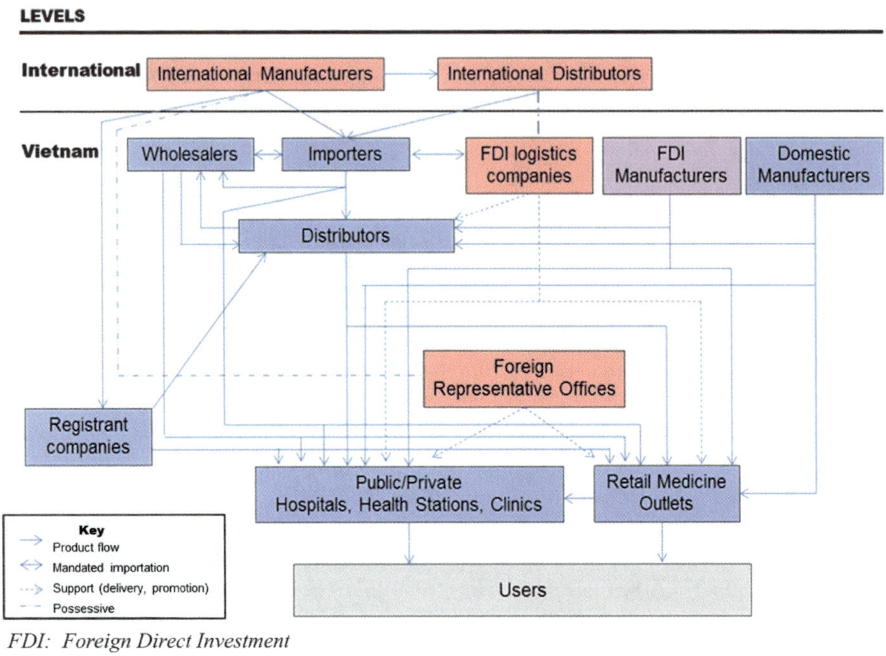

Fig. 18.1 The pharmaceutical supply chain in Vietnam. *Source*: authors' analysis. *FDI* foreign direct investment

retailers with Good Pharmacy Practice (GPP). Figure 18.1 shows a schematic representation of the current pharmaceutical supply chain in Vietnam.

Vietnam's pharmaceutical market is, however, heavily dependent on imports. Imported medicines account for approximately 50 % of the market share, focusing on specialised products. By the end of 2008, there were 10,339 imported medicines covering 909 active substances, averaging 11 brands per active substance (DAV 2009a). The range of imported products is wider than those locally produced, and there is trading duplication of some active substances. For example one substance, cefixime, had 458 imported brands with a valid registration number in Vietnam (MOH of Vietnam 2013).

Domestic medicine production accounts for an increasingly growing market share, rising from 36 % in 2001 to 50 % in 2008 (DAV 2009b). However, the domestic pharmaceutical industry is characterized by limited R&D facilities, insufficient financial capacity and poor management (BMI 2009). Most local pharmaceutical manufacturers comprise small-scale operations with outdated manufacturing technology and duplicated production processes. About 90 % of the raw materials used in domestic production are imported (Cao 2008), thus making domestic medicine prices subject to price fluctuations in international prices, as well as fluctuations in the exchange rates. Nearly 95 % of imported active pharmaceutical ingredients are antibiotics, vitamins, antipyretic, analgesics and anti-spasmodic drugs (MHBS 2010), reflecting a concentration of domestic pharmaceutical production on only some therapeutic classes. By the end of 2008, there were 9,727 locally produced medicines, representing 491 active substances registered for sale in Vietnam, averaging 20 locally produced brands per active substance. Thus, local manufacturers compete for a very limited, and often uneconomic, market share.

Pharmaceutical distribution in Vietnam is a complex activity which involves a number of intermediaries from manufacturers to consumers including:

- 180 domestic pharmaceutical manufacturers (including 22 Foreign Direct Investment (FDI) producers), 90 importers, and 800 domestic wholesalers/distributors (DAV 2009b);
- Three FDI enterprises investing in drug logistics (DAV 2009b);
- 438 foreign pharmaceutical companies (DAV 2009b);
- 39,172 retail medicine outlets, including 9,066 private pharmacies (DAV 2009b);
- 13,460 public health care facilities, including 974 hospitals, 781 regional polyclinics and 10,917 commune health stations (GSO 2009b);
- 74 private hospitals and more than 30,000 private health clinics (MOH of Vietnam, Health Partnership Group 2008).

Locally produced medicines from Vietnam's pharmaceutical manufacturers can be distributed directly to retailers and health care facilities or indirectly through wholesalers or distributors. Vietnamese manufacturers holding a retail license are able to supply medicines directly to end users. Classified as domestic pharmaceutical producers, Foreign Direct Investment producers can directly distribute the products that they manufacture in Vietnam.

Foreign Direct Investment logistic companies and foreign pharmaceutical companies are not permitted to distribute pharmaceutical products directly in Vietnam. Their products have to be sold to domestic pharmaceutical distributors for distribution. Foreign distributors are only permitted to supply their medicines to a local importer. Foreign pharmaceutical manufacturers with a trading license in Vietnam who are not established in Vietnam as an Foreign Direct Investment producer can supply their medicines via their local registrant company or a local importer (MOH of Vietnam 2006) (see Fig. 18.1).

In the retail sector, patients can buy medicines from retail medicine outlets or hospital pharmacies. Accounting for 60–70 % of retail pharmaceutical market share was more than 1,000 public hospital pharmacies and the rest 30–40 % belongs to private pharmacies and other retail medicine outlets (Hải 2008). Pharmacists with a university degree and 5 years of experience can be licensed to operate private pharmacies. In remote areas, assistant pharmacists are able to apply for licenses. By law, licensed pharmacists must always be physically present when the pharmacies are open for business. In practice, licensed pharmacists are not always on duty (Chuc 2002).

The current pharmaceutical distribution network needs reorganisation. The many layers within the distribution network, each contributing a compounding mark-up along the supply chain, serve to inflate the final price of medicines to patients. Unnecessary duplication in manufacturing, importing and trading medicines leads to fierce counterproductive competition for an uneconomic share of an increasingly shrinking market (Nguyen 2011).

18.4 Drug Regulatory Authority

The Drug Administration of Vietnam (DVA) on behalf of the Ministry of Health (MOH) is the pharmaceutical regulatory authority in Vietnam. Most medicines must have product registration, as indicated by a valid registration number prior to marketing in Vietnam. The MOH can allow medicines without a registration number to be marketed on a case-by-case basis, to avoid shortage of medicines. By law, within 6 months from the date of receiving complete and legitimate registration applications, the MOH shall issue medicine marketing authorization for the medicine. To ensure the quality, efficacy and safety of medicines marketed, the pharmaceutical manufacturer must meet the GMP standards and the products must pass laboratory quality testing and clinical trials either in Vietnam or in exporting countries. Where applications fail to meet relevant requirements, the MOH will release written reasons for refusing registration (MOH of Vietnam 2009). By the end of 2011, there were 28,820 medicines registered in Vietnam (MOH of Vietnam 2013).

In 2006, the MOH assigned the DVA to be responsible for assisting the Minister of Health to regulate medicine prices. Accordingly, the Drug Price Management Division was established with four staff. The Drug Price Management Division faces difficulties in the management of prices for medicines, especially because the medicine pricing policies are in the start-up phase and there is currently no requirement for Health Technology Assessment to support medicine pricing.

18.5 Drug Pricing Set-Up

In Vietnam, pharmaceutical pricing policies are classified as public policies, which are developed and implemented to achieve pre-set goals of the government. Therefore, pharmaceutical pricing policies are disseminated in the form of legal documents (Ministry of Health Vietnam and Health Partnership 2011), which can be either legislative or sub-legislative regulatory documents.[1]

[1] Legislative documents comprise the Vietnam Constitution, Laws or Law Sets, and Resolutions of the National Assembly. The sub-legislative regulatory documents include Ordinances, Resolutions of the Standing Committee of the National Assembly (SCONA); Decrees of the government (often issued to elaborate laws/ordinances); and Ministerial Circulars (to guide implementation of Decrees).

Prior to 1989, a strict medicine price control strategy was in place (Simonet 2001). Medicines were sold only via the public sector with one uniform price set by the State Pricing Commission and the MOH (The Council of Ministers 1987; Ministry of Health of Vietnam 1987). Losses in pharmaceutical production and trading due to the one price mechanism were subsidized by the government. In 1987, joint Circular No 28-TT/LB of the State Pricing Commission and the MOH introduced flexibility into medicine pricing by permitting domestically produced medicines to have a different designated price level which was within a price bracket set by the MOH.

In 1989, following the health sector reform, there was a shift to free market pricing for medicines. Joint Circular No 440-TT/LB of the MOH and the State Pricing Commission allowed medicine prices to be set by demand and supply. The change meant government would no longer set prices of medicines and no subsidies would be provided to cover losses in production, trading, importation or exportation. Competition and competitive tendering would be applied with market protection for domestically produced medicines (MOH of Vietnam and State Pricing Commission 1989).

Subsequently, a number of legal instruments and policies were introduced by the Vietnam government, all explicitly referring to free pricing for medicines (i.e. pharmaceutical prices may be freely set by the manufacturers). The legislation and policies could be classified into three groups: (1) the general management of prices of most goods including medicines, (2) the state management of medicine prices, and (3) the state management of medicine prices in public health facilities (see Table 18.1). The next section of this chapter focuses on the key ordinances, decrees and circulars that have been used to influence and control medicine prices in Vietnam.

Table 18.1 Main legislative and sub-legislative documents from January 1989 to December 2013 influencing medicine prices in Vietnam

Groups	Promulgator	Name of regulatory documents	Date of issuance
The general management of prices	NA	Ordinance on Prices No 40/2002/PL-UBTVQH10	26/4/2002
	Gov't	Decree No 170/2003/ND-CP, detailing the implementation of a number of articles of the Ordinance on Prices No 40/2002/PL-UBTVQH10	25/12/2003
	Gov't	Decree No 75/2008/ND-CP, amending and supplementing some articles of Decree No 170/2003/ND-CP on 25 December 2003, detailing the implementation of a number of articles of the Ordinance on Prices	9/6/2008
	NA	Law on Prices No 11/2012/QH13	20/6/2012

(continued)

Table 18.1 (continued)

Groups	Promulgator	Name of regulatory documents	Date of issuance
The state management of medicine prices	MOH and MOF	Circular No 08/2003/TTLT/BYT-BTC guiding the declaration and publication of prices of preventive and curative medicines for human use	25/7/2003
	Gov't	Decree No 120/2004/ND-CP on management of prices of preventive and curative medicines for human use	12/5/2004
	NA	Pharmaceutical Law No 34/2005/QH11	14/6/2005
	Gov't	Decree No 79/2006/ND-CP regulating in detail the implementation of a number of articles of the Pharmaceutical Law	9/8/2006
	MOH, MOF, and MOIT	Joint Circular No 11/2007/TTLT-BYT-BTC-BCT guiding the State management of prices of human-use medicines	31/8/2007
	MOH, MOF, and MOIT	Joint Circular No 50/2011/TTLT-BYT-BTC-BCT guiding the State management of prices of human-use medicines	30/12/2011
The state management of medicine prices in public hospitals	MOH	Decision No 3016/1999/QD-BYT regulating the organisation and operation of hospitals' drug stores	6/10/1999
	MOH and MOIT	Joint Circular No 20/2005/TTLT-BYT-BTC guiding the implementation of bidding for the purchase of medicines in public medical establishments	27/7/2005
	MOH and MOIT	Joint Circular No 10/2007/TTLT-BYT-BTC providing guidance on bidding for the purchase of medicines in public medical establishments	10/8/2007
	MOH	Decision No 24/2008/QĐ-BYT regulating the organisation and operation of hospitals' drug stores	11/07/2008
	MOH	Circular No 15/2011/TT-BYT regulating the organisation and operation of drug retailers inside hospitals	19/04/2011
	MOH and MOIT	Joint Circular No 01/2012/TTLT-BYT-BTC providing guidance on bidding for the purchase of medicines in public medical establishments	19/01/2012

NA National Assembly, *Gov't* Government, *MOH* Ministry of Health, *MOF* Ministry of Finance, *MOIT* Ministry of Industry and Trade

18.6 How Prices Are Set

18.6.1 Free Pricing Principle and State Stabilization of Prices of Essential Goods

In 2002, Ordinance on Prices No 40/2002/PL-UBTVQH10 (Ordinance 40) was issued confirming the free pricing principle for most goods including medicines. It stipulated that "The State respects the right of organisations and individuals involved in production or trade to set prices and compete based on price according to law". The ordinance also stated that the State could implement price stabilization for essential goods by adjusting supply and demand of domestically produced goods, exported and imported goods. Other price stabilisation measures included use of national reserves of goods, controlling inventories, setting maximum or minimum prices, or price brackets, and controlling factors determining price. Goods or services paid in full or partly by the State are subject to State price assessment if they are not purchased via tendering. Price publication at each point of sale along supply chain was also stipulated to increase price transparency, with the ordinance indicating the published price must be the selling price.

The implementation of a number of articles of Ordinance 40 was detailed in subsequent Decrees. Decree No 75/2008/ND-CP (Decree 75) stipulated that the schedule issued by the MOH of medicines used in public health facilities would be subject to State price stabilisation. In addition, prices of all medicines paid by the State or public health insurance would be set by the State. Decree 75 added the requirement of price declaration to the MOH and price publication at each point of sale for medicines subject to State price stabilisation. In 2012, the Law on Prices No 11/2012/QH13, which replaced Ordinance 40, was passed and came into force at the start of 2013. The law reasserted the principle of free pricing and State stabilisation of essential goods. It also stipulated that goods, including medicines under the national reserves scheme, one of the price stabilisation measures regulated in Ordinance 40, would have prices set by the State.

18.6.2 Contextual Development of Medicine Pricing Regulations

In the first quarter of 2003, Vietnam faced a surge in medicine prices. The Drug Price Index (DPI), a component of the consumer price index (CPI) increased by 8.6 %, more than five times the CPI (GSO 2009a). In response, the Vietnam government requested the MOH, in cooperation with the Ministry of Finance, to issue a joint Circular intended to guide the management of prices of essential medicines. The objective was to stabilize medicine prices at a reasonable level (Văn phòng Chính phủ 2003). Subsequently, Circular No 08/2003/TTLT/BYT-BTC (Circular 08) was issued and came into force in August 2003. The regulation broadened the scope of medicines covered beyond essential medicines to include all preventative and curative medicines marketed in Vietnam. Constrained by the free pricing principle, Circular 08 used price declaration and publication as the main mechanism to improve price transparency. Pharmaceutical companies were requested to declare an official wholesale or retail price for their medicines to the MOH. At the point of sale, the companies had to publish their prices for customers' reference. Retail prices were required to be published on the medicine pack and wholesale prices on a board or papers that makes it easy for customers to see. The actual transaction prices must not be higher than the published prices. However, the Circular did not explicitly stipulate that the price to publish is the declared price. Exploiting this regulatory loophole, pharmaceutical companies often published a different price for customers' reference from the price they declared to the MOH.

Despite Circular 08 requirements for price transparency medicine prices kept increasing (GSO 2009a). The circular did not require the declared and published prices to be reasonable or fair prices. Thus, pharmaceutical suppliers declared and published medicine prices as high as the market would bear, resulting in sharp increases in the price of many medicines and another jump on DPI in September and October 2003 (GSO 2009a).

To address this issue government Decree No 120/2004/ND-CP (Decree 120) on the management of prices of preventive and curative medicines for human use was promulgated in June 2004. The Decree included for the first time external reference pricing as the basis for price declaration. Decree 120 also regulated maximum mark-ups for pharmaceutical wholesalers and retailers. Further controls were implemented for medicines directly ordered and purchased by the State without a tender and for medicines purchased by hospitals and other health care institutions that were paid for by the State or by public health insurance. The prices of the former were directly determined by the Minister of Finance and those of the latter were controlled by a tendering process. Subsequent Decrees and Circulars reinforced these approaches included Decree No 79/2006/ND-CP (Decree 79), Joint Circular No 11/2007/TTLT-BYT-BTC-BCT (Circular 11) and Joint Circular No 50/2011/TTLT-BYT-BTC-BCT (Circular 50). Table 18.2 presents a summary of the characteristics of the declaration and publication mechanism used in the pricing regulations of interest.

18.6.3 Ensuring Reasonable or Fair Declared Prices and Published Prices

In this section, we review the effectiveness of the regulation in ensuring reasonable or fair medicine prices and highlight areas where the regulation failed or could have been improved.

Table 18.2 Summary of preconditions of declaration and publication mechanisms used in Vietnam pricing regulations

	The reasonableness of declared prices				Declaration and publication provisions		
	External reference pricing: international comparison standard		Cost plus pricing	Wholesale/ retail mark-ups	Selling prices or published prices not being higher than declared prices	Re-declaration for price increases	Selling prices not being higher than published prices
Circular 08 (2003)	No		No	No	No	No	Yes
Decree 120 (2004)	Highest price	Category base	No	Yes	No	No	Yes
Decree 79 (2006)	Highest price	Category base	No	No	Partly	Yes	Yes
Circular 11 (2007)	Average price	Medicine-to-medicine base	Yes	No	Yes	Yes	Yes
Circular 50 (2011)	Yes but no further information provided		Yes	Yes[a]	Yes	Yes	Yes

[a]Only for medicines sold in retail facilities inside hospitals

18.6.3.1 External Reference Pricing

Decree 120, Decree 79, and Circular 11 all employed external reference pricing as a means of price stabilisation. External reference pricing attempted to ensure that the prices of medicines in Vietnam were reasonable in relation to comparable countries. One of the challenges of implementing external reference pricing came from the fact that no regulations explicitly defined the type of prices for international comparisons (i.e. ex-factory price, wholesale price or retail price, before or after taxes). As price varies along the supply chain (Mossialos and Mrazek 2002), a valid comparison is only achieved when prices are compared at similar levels of the supply chain.

The use of non-specific language also created challenges. Decree 120 and Decree 79 required the price of a medicine sold in Vietnam "*to be not higher than*" prices of medicines of "*the same categories*" sold in comparable countries. This is known as *the highest price* comparison standard, which proved problematic. A strict interpretation of the comparison "*not higher than*" implies that the price in Vietnam could be as high as the highest price among the comparator countries. Using this approach, the Vietnam government could create an opportunity for pharmaceutical suppliers to set *the highest price* from the comparable countries for each medicine, potentially resulting in higher average prices in Vietnam than in the comparator countries. Taking the lowest price in the set or averaging the prices of the medicine among comparator countries is much more commonly used by other countries with experience in external reference pricing system (Nguyen et al. 2014; Espin et al. 2011). In addition, the use of *category* comparisons could also pose dilemmas of definition. Category comparisons mean that comparisons could be applied to different levels of medicine groups such as those that have identical bioactive ingredients, a group of medicines from the same class (i.e. chemically slightly different but related medicines with comparable or identical indications), or a group of medicines used to treat the same condition (Dickson and Redwood 1998; McLaughin 1997; Ioannides-Demos et al. 2002). Other countries only compare the prices of identical medicines in their external reference pricing system (Espin et al. 2011; WHO/HAI 2014).

To overcome these problems, Circular 11 stated *the average price* standard should be used and employed a *medicine-to-medicine* (identical bioactive ingredients) comparison base. The Circular stated that the declared price of a medicine imported into Vietnam was not to be higher than the "*average CIF [Cost, Insurance and Freight] price*" of "*this medicine*" sold in comparator countries. Therefore, the imported medicines were compared to identical products in comparator countries to ensure the price in Vietnam was the average level in comparator countries. One limitation that could arise with this approach is that if the comparator countries include one country with unreasonably high price, the outlier price would affect the mean resulting in a higher average price. Using the *median price* standard would reduce the influence of outliers. An alternative approach is using a larger number of reference countries and taking the average price in the three lowest-priced countries. This approach is employed in Columbia and the Slovak Republic (KEL 2010; OECD 2008).

Decree 120 specified comparator countries as those having similar medical and commercial conditions as Vietnam. It did not, however, nominate the comparator countries, nor specify selection criteria. It was not until Decree 79 that specific criteria were nominated, with statistical indices similar to those of Vietnam. The indices included: (1) per capita gross domestic product (GDP) per year; (2) per capita GDP at purchasing power parity (PPP) per year; and (3) networks of providing services for preventive medicine, medical examination and treatment, functional rehabilitation, and health improvement and medicine supply. Guiding the implementation of the Decree 79, Circular 11 required the government to decide and announce the list of comparators annually. In 2008, the MOH proposed for the first time a list of comparator countries: Thailand, Malaysia, Indonesia, The Philippines and Cambodia. This feature, however, has yet to be implemented due to a number of challenges including lack of resources and difficulty in collecting medicine price information in comparator countries. Another challenge is that, unlike most OECD or European countries that restrict their external reference pricing to on-patent products (WHO/HAI 2014), Vietnam attempted to apply it to all medicines, thus adding further burden on policy implementation and enforcement. Consequently, the external reference pricing system was only included in the legislation and not applied in practice.

18.6.3.2 Cost Plus Pricing

In addition to external reference pricing, Circular 11 and Circular 50 used cost plus pricing techniques to ensure the reasonableness or fairness of declared prices. The circulars stipulated that pricing authorities could use importation or production costs, distribution costs and changes in factors that determine price, including active ingredient costs or exchange rates, to determine if the declared prices were reasonable. No specific formula for calculating the declared price from costs were provided, which made compliance difficult for suppliers.

18.6.3.3 Maximum Distribution Margins

Decree 120 employed maximum distribution margins to ensure the reasonableness of wholesale and retail prices. The decree stipulated that the Ministry of Finance would be responsible for specifying the maximum wholesale and retail mark-up. However, no specification took place because the Ministry of Finance could not issue a subsequent Circular to guide the implementation of Decree 120. As a result, wholesale or retail margins were not effectively regulated.

Maximum retail margins for medicines sold in retail facilities within hospitals were regulated in Circular 50. Circular 50 requested these margins to be compliant with the regulation of Circular No 15/2011/TT-BYT which regulated the organisation and operation of drug retailers inside hospitals. Regressive mark-ups where the percentage mark-up decreases when medicine prices increase were used. A limitation of this approach is that the use of maximum retail margins is only be effective to control retail prices if the wholesale price is also reasonable or fair (Nguyen et al. 2014).

18.6.4 Declared or Published Prices as a Cap for Actual Selling Prices

18.6.4.1 Relationship Between the Declared Price, Published Price and Actual Selling Price

All pricing regulations stipulated that pharmaceutical suppliers must not sell their products at a price higher than the published price. This has enabled the published price to be a ceiling to control the actual selling price. The success of this mechanism has depended on the accuracy or reasonableness of the published price. However, no pricing regulations explicitly stipulated the prices declared to the MOH should be the price to publish for customers' reference. This means that there was no mechanism to ensure a fair or reasonable published price.

To overcome this problem, Circular 11 and Circular 50 directly regulated the relationship between the actual selling prices and the declared prices. The Circulars required medicine producers and importers to declare the final wholesale price of medicines for the entire wholesale chain and wholesalers were not permitted to sell medicines to retailers at prices higher than the declared price. If the declared wholesale price was reasonable, this provision would ensure a fair actual selling wholesale price. To ensure a fair, reasonable retail price retail margin must be regulated. However, the maximum retail margin regulation has not been fully implemented (Decree 120), or regulated (Decree 79 and Circular 11). Circular 50 did regulate retail margins but this provision was for medicines sold in retail outlets inside hospitals only.

18.6.4.2 Re-declaration

Prior to marketing in Vietnam, a medicine must be registered with the MOH with a declared price nominated by the registrant company. The Ministry issues a marketing authorisation, usually valid for 5 years, after which the product must be re-registered. In accepting the declared price, Circular 08 and Decree 120 did not take into account the life-span of the marketing authorisation. The regulations failed to provide for the re-declaration of prices in response to changed economic circumstances, such as adjustments for inflation over the life of the license. Thus, registrants were implicitly encouraged to declare the highest possible price at time of first marketing to accommodate future cost fluctuations.

Overcoming shortcomings of previous pricing regulations, Decree 79, Circular 11 and Circular 50 allowed producers or importers to declare increases in prices with an explanation for the increase prior to their application for re-registration. This provided a legal framework for monitoring increases in medicine prices, as well as ensuring medicine prices remained reasonable throughout the license period. The regulations also permitted suppliers to change their prices after the declaration, thus removing the cost pressure associated with having a fixed price for the entire 5-year approval cycle.

18.6.5 Other Pricing Provisions

Except for Circular 08, all pricing instruments proscribed additional price controls for two targeted medicine groups. The first group included medicines directly ordered and purchased by the State without a tender process. The prices of these medicines were determined directly by the Minister of Finance. The second group comprised medicines purchased by hospitals and other health care institutions that were paid for by the State or health insurance. The prices of these medicines were controlled by a tendering process, first regulated in Joint Circular No 20/2005/TTLT-BYT-BTC in July 2005 and subsequently by Joint Circular No 10/2007/TTLT-BYT-BTC in August 2007 and then Joint Circular No 01/2012/TTLT-BYT-BTC from January 2012. The Circulars stated the successful tender prices were not allowed to be higher than the latest maximum price, which had to be announced every 6 months by the MOH. While proscribed, the MOH has yet to develop a way of determining the maximum price. Thus, currently, tender prices are evaluated against the previous year's prices or previous winning-bid prices (WHO-WPRO 2009). The limitation of this approach is that the previous prices may not have been assessed as reasonable or fair.

While tendering is the main pricing mechanism in public hospitals, tender practices can be problematic in Vietnam. Discriminatory terms and conditions for market entry that favours particular tenderers are sometimes applied in return for gratuities or bribes, all of which confound the free market tender system (Nguyen 2011). The scope of this practice is widespread and can result in significantly inflated tender prices. The successful tender prices are, therefore, often higher than the prevailing market retail price (Pham 2010).

Another confounder is the lack of regulation for the Vietnam Social Insurance (VSI) agency, which is responsible for the reimbursement of medicine costs via public health insurance, Joint Circular No 10/2007/TTLT-BYT-BTC, did not regulate the role of the VSI in the tendering process. As a result, VSI is constrained in its ability to use its purchasing power to negotiate medicine prices. The current tendering regulation Joint Circular No 01/2012/TTLT-BYT-BTC stipulates representatives of VSI participate in the whole tendering process, from planning to approval. However, VSI is yet to establish a decisive role in determining reimbursement prices (Nguyen 2011).

18.7 Who Is Involved in Setting Prices?

Pharmaceutical suppliers and distributors are the primary party involved in setting medicine prices in Vietnam. Subject to the stabilization regulations highlighted in the previous section, pharmaceutical companies set the prices of their products. The pharmaceutical pricing authorities (DAV) do not approve the medicine prices declared by pharmaceutical companies. Instead, they monitor the declared prices as a measure of price stabilization. If they find the declared prices unreasonable, the pharmaceutical pricing authorities will provide pharmaceutical companies with their assessment and request the companies revise the declared prices. Assisting the DVA in assessment are representatives from the Ministry of Finance and Ministry of Industry and Trade.

18.8 Official Prices Are Not the Actual Transaction Prices

Price declaration is the main mechanisms for stabilizing pharmaceutical prices in Vietnam. However, the declared prices may not reflect the selling price. Declared prices are usually maximum prices that can be established within the constraints of the legislation, but companies are free to sell at prices lower than this. The declared prices is sometimes 200 % more than the selling prices (Inspectorate of the MOH of Vietnam 2007).

The shortage of personnel and resources for assessing the reasonableness of declared prices of medicines marketed in Vietnam means that most of the information on medicine prices declared by pharmaceutical companies has not been validated. This was sometime exploited by pharmaceutical companies, also resulting in discrepancies in declared and actual transaction prices as illustrated in the following example (Table 18.3).

The actual transaction CIF price of an imported Celecoxib brand as recorded by the General Department of Vietnam Customs was USD 4.5/box of 100 capsules. However, the declared CIF price was USD 34.4/box, 764 % higher than the actual transaction CIF price (USD 1 = VND 15,700). Without validation from the DAV,

Table 18.3 Price declaration provided to the Drug Administration of Vietnam by a registrant company for a brand of Celecoxib 200 mg

Medicine	Strength	Dosage form	Packing	Declared price in India	Declared CIF price	Declared retail price in Vietnam
Celecoxib	200 mg	Capsule	Box of 10 Strips × 10 capsules	51.0 (USD)	34.4 (USD)	44.6 (USD)

the declared CIF price establishes a declared retail price of USD 44.6/box (approximately 30 % higher than the declared CIF price and still lower than the price in India, which was also declared by the pharmaceutical company and unchecked by the DAV). The officially declared retail price establishes a lower actual selling price of USD 41.4/box to end users in Vietnam, but 920 % higher than the actual transaction imported price (CIF).

18.9 Medicine Prices Change Over Time

Prior to 1989 when strict price controls were in force, medicine prices remained stable over time. The relative stability of medicine prices continued after the market reforms until 2003. Between 2003 and 2004, prices of some medicines soared fourfold (Bộ Tài chính 2004), and the Drug Price Index increased by 13.8 %, almost double the CPI (GSO 2009a). Rising medicine prices have been reported to account for most of the threefold increase in total pharmaceutical expenditure in Vietnam between 2000 and 2005 (World Bank 2007).

In addition to price stabilization, pharmaceutical pricing authorities do use price freezes to slow down price increase of medicines although no legislation stipulated a price freezes provision. The combined effect of all these strategies appears to be having some impact, the DPI after being higher than the CPI for the 5 years (2003 to 2008) has since been kept below the CPI (Fig. 18.2).

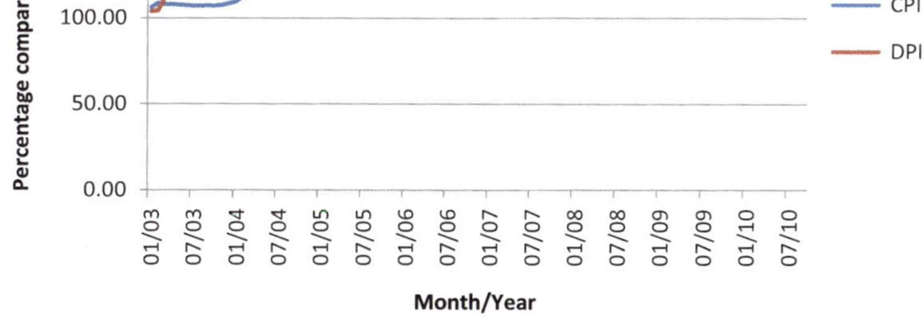

CPI: Consumer Price Index, DPI: Drug Price Index

Fig. 18.2 Drug price index in comparison with consumer price index over time. *Source*: Authors' calculation based on data from the General Statistics Office of Vietnam. *CPI* consumer price index, *DPI* drug price index

18.10 The Impact of Pricing on Public Health

Health care in Vietnam is often less affordable and less accessible for poorer households (Segall et al. 2002; Ladinsky et al. 2000). In order to meet health care costs, many poorer households reduce consumption of essential goods, sell assets and incur debt or fail to use health facilities because of cost barriers (Ensor and Pham 1996). With pharmaceutical expenditure accounting for a large component of total health care costs (Nguyen et al. 2009), the cost of medicines plays a role in impoverishing the poor in Vietnam.

While strategies are now in place to influence medicine pricing in Vietnam, there is evidence that further work needs to be done to make medicines affordable for the population. In assessing the affordability of a standard treatment for pneumonia (using the average retail price of a basket of food sufficient to feed one person per day as the benchmark), Falkenberg et al. (2000) found that the medicines cost people the equivalent price of 2 days of food. Ait-Khaled et al. (2000) also showed the challenges of affordability of inhaled corticosteroids 1 year of treatment for a case of moderate persistent asthma in 1998 was reported to cost a nurse in Vietnam 1.7 months of salary. In Turkey and Algeria however, the same treatment apparently cost a nurse 0.4 months (Ait-Khaled et al. 2000).

A recent study assessing medicine prices, availability and affordability in Vietnam compared the prices of 42 medicines to international reference prices of the same products. The international reference prices were the median of actual procurement prices offered by not-for-profit suppliers or international tender prices to developing countries for multi-sourced products (MSH 2008). Results showed that the procurement prices of the lowest priced generic medicines in the public sector were two times the international reference price and for originator brand medicines they were eight times. Adjusted for purchasing power parity, the prices to patients in the public sector were 11 and 47 times the international reference price for the lowest priced generics and originator brand medicines, respectively. Assessing affordability using the number of days' wages needed by the lowest paid unskilled government worker to purchase a course of treatment for an acute disease or a month's treatment for a chronic disease, the study found that the worker would have had to work 0.7 days to treat an acute respiratory infection with the lowest priced generic amoxicillin (250 mg three times daily in 7 days) but would pay 15.9 days' wages with lowest priced generic ceftriaxone (1 vial 1 g daily in 7 days) in the public sector. Compared to countries in the Western Pacific Region, medicines in Vietnam were much less affordable. The study concluded that medicines were unaffordable for the lowest paid unskilled government worker, and even less so for the population who earned below this benchmark (Nguyen 2011; Nguyen et al. 2009).

18.11 The Case of Generic Medicines

Increased use of generic medicines represents another key strategy used by governments and third party payers to contain medicines costs and improve affordable access to medicines. Vietnam did not have a national generic medicines policy. While the National Drug Policy was adopted in 1996, there were no generic medicines provisions included (Nguyen et al. 2013). In 2009 an Aide Memoire on Strategic Collaboration in Pharmaceuticals was signed by WHO and the Ministry of Health of Vietnam, which included the need for a strategy to develop and promulgate a national generic medicines policy to ensure affordability of safe, high quality medicines (WHO-WPRO 2013). Prior to this, the regulations on prescription-only medicines did require physicians to prescribe using the International Non-proprietary Name (generic name) for "single component" medicines (i.e. one active ingredient medicine) and generic substitution was allowed if pharmacists obtained the acceptance from patients or prescribers (Nguyen 2011).

Barriers to increasing generic medicine use include mistrust in generic medicines in terms of quality, efficacy and safety among physicians, pharmacists and patients. Lack of an assessment of bioequivalence as a regulatory requirement in generic medicines registration and lack of appropriately skilled inspectors and monitoring to ensure the quality of generic medicine products contributes to this mistrust (Nguyen et al. 2013). Lack of knowledge of generic medicines and misconceptions that a cheaper price equates to poorer quality also contributed to low acceptance of generics. In addition, promotional incentives for prescribers from some pharmaceutical companies were reported to influence physician prescribing behaviour, leading to recommendations for more expensive branded products. Vietnam did not have any financial incentives to promote prescribing and dispensing of generic medicines (Nguyen et al. 2013). In addition, the sub-optimal pharmaceutical pricing regimes led to some generic medicines being more expensive than their corresponding originator brands (Nguyen 2011).

18.12 Conclusion

Vietnam has made important economic progress since initiating the Doi Moi reform in 1986 which has had a profound impact on the health care system. With a move towards a market economy, Vietnam promoted free pricing of medicines. Pharmaceutical companies are free to set prices of their products based on market forces, subject to stabilization by the State. Analysis of the vast number of legislative and regulatory reforms demonstrates that, in recent times, substantial improvements have been made in regulations of medicine prices in Vietnam. The legislative and associated instruments in Vietnam were intended to ensure transparency of medicine prices along the supply chain, through the mechanism of price declaration and publication of price information. The initiatives, however, have been less successful than expected because they did not address all the preconditions necessary for the regulations to operate effectively in practice. Additionally, some provisions of the regulations were not monitored or effectively enforced. Consequently, medicine prices remain high in Vietnam and research demonstrates low paid workers would need to forgo more days of wages for courses of treatment for acute or chronic illness than in comparable countries.

While appropriate legislation is pivotal to control medicine prices, it is insufficient as the only means to achieve change. Also critical is the enforcement of legislation and ongoing monitoring. Further research is required to compare between the published prices and the declared prices and to establish the best mechanisms for government controls. The other challenge is the continual revision of legislation and enforcement to cope with changes in the market which can occur quite rapidly. Thus, more work is still needed to ensure reasonable medicines prices in Vietnam that will provide affordable access for the population.

References

Ait-Khaled N, Auregan G, Bencharif N, Mady Camara L, Dagli E, Djankine K, Keita B, Ky C, Mashi S, Ngoran K, Pham DL, Sow O, Yousser M, Zidouni N, Enarson DA (2000) Affordability of inhaled corticosteroids as a potential barrier to treatment of asthma in some developing countries. Int J Tuberc Lung Dis 4(3):268–271

BMI (2009) Vietnam pharmaceuticals and healthcare report Q3 2009. Business Monitor International Ltd., London

Bộ Tài chính (2004) Giá thuốc tăng 100–400 %—Vì sao? Bộ Tài Chính. http://www.mof.gov.vn/Default.aspx?tabid=612&ItemID=14452. Accessed 22 Nov 2006

Cao QM (2008) Pharmaceutical industry development, supply demand balancing solutions to stabilize the Vietnam pharmaceutical market. Papers prepared for pharmaceutical sector conference 2008, Ministry of Health, Hanoi

Chalker J (1995) Vietnam: profit and loss in health care. World Health Forum 16:194–195

Chuc NTK (2002) Towards good pharmacy practice in Hanoi: a multi-intervention study in private sector. Karolineska Institutet, Stockholm

DAV (2009a) Overview of the Vietnam pharmaceutical sector in 2008; operations of foreign pharmaceutical companies in Vietnam and state management orientation in the sector in 2009. Drug Administration of Vietnam, Hanoi

DAV (2009b) Report on Vietnam pharmaceutical sector 2008 and planning for 2009. National pharmaceutical sector conference 2008. Drug Administration of Vietnam, Hanoi

Dickson M, Redwood H (1998) Pharmaceutical reference prices. How do they work in practice? Pharmacoeconomics 14(5):471–479

Ensor T, Pham BS (1996) Access and payment for health care: the poor of northern Vietnam. Int J Health Plann Manage 11:69–83

Espin J, Rovira J, de Labry AO (2011) Review series on pharmaceutical pricing policies and interventions: working paper 1: external reference pricing. WHO/HAI project on medicine prices and availability. WHO/HAI, Geneva

Falkenberg T, Binh NT, Larsson M, Do NT, Tomson G (2000) Pharmaceutical sector in transition-a cross sectional study in Vietnam. Southeast Asian J Trop Med Public Health 31(3):590–597

Government of Vietnam (1996a) Decision No. 547/TTg on 13 August 1996 of the Prime Minister on the establishment of the Drug Administration of Vietnam under the Ministry of Health, Hanoi

Government of Vietnam (1996b) Resolution No. 37-CP of the Government on strategic orientations for public health care and protection in the 1996-2000 period and national drug policy, Hanoi

GSO (2009a) Average consumer price index. Gold and USD price index. General Statistics Office of Vietnam. http://www.gso.gov.vn/default_en.aspx?tabid=472&idmid=3&ItemID=7653. Accessed 16 Jan 2009

GSO (2009b) Number of health establishments by management level. General Statistics Office of Vietnam. http://www.gso.gov.vn/default_en.aspx?tabid=474&idmid=3&ItemID=7747. Accessed 11 May 2009

Hải T (2008) Lũng đoạn giá thuốc tại hơn 1000 nhà thuốc bệnh viện. http://laodong.com.vn/Home/Lung-doan-gia-thuoc-tai-hon-1000-nha-thuoc-benh-vien/20087/97241.laodong. Accessed 22 Dec 2008

Inspectorate of the MOH of Vietnam (2007) The inspection report No 317 of 2 May 2007

Ioannides-Demos L, Ibrahim J, McNeil J (2002) Reference-based pricing schemes: effect on pharmaceutical expenditure, resource utilisation and health outcomes. Pharmacoeconomics 20(9):577–591

KEL (2010) PhRMA's asks regarding special 301, drug pricing and reimbursement. http://keionline.org/node/805. Accessed 19 May 2010

Ladinsky JL, Hoang TN, Volk ND (2000) Changes in the health care system of Vietnam in response to the emerging market economy. J Public Health Policy 21(1):82–98

Larsson M (2003) Antibiotic use and resistance, assessing and improving utilisation and provision of antibiotics and other drugs in Vietnam. Sciences Karolinska Institutet, Stockholm

McLaughin P (1997) Reference-based pricing of prescription drug. Can J Cardiol 13(1):31–32

MHBS (2010) Report on the pharmaceutical sector analysis. MHB Securities, Hanoi

Ministry of Health of Vietnam (1987) Circular No 16/BYT-TT of 7 July 1987 on guiding the implementation of Decision of the Council of Ministers No 104-HDBT of 30 June 1987 on retail prices of curative medicines, Hanoi

Ministry of Health Vietnam, Health Partnership Group (2011) Joint annual health review 2011. Ministry of Health, Hanoi

MOH of Vietnam (2006) Circular 06/2006/TT-BYT of 16 May 2006 guiding the import and export of drugs and cosmetics. Ministry of Health of Vietnam, Hanoi

MOH of Vietnam (2009) Circular No. 22/2009/TT-BYT of 24 November 2009 on guiding medicine registration. Ministry of Health of Vietnam, Hanoi

MOH of Vietnam (2011) Circular No 31/2011/TT-BYT on 11 July 2011 of Ministry of Health issuing and guiding the implementation of the schedule of main medicines used in health facilities, which are reimbursable by Public Health Insurance, 31/2011/TT-BYT, Hanoi

MOH of Vietnam (2013) United Proposal of National Medicines Policy in the period up to 2020 and the vision by 2030. Ministry of Health of Vietnam, Hanoi

MOH of Vietnam, Health Partnership Group (2008) Joint annual health review 2008: health financing in Vietnam. Ministry of Health of Vietnam, Hanoi

MOH of Vietnam, State Pricing Commission (1989) Joint Circular No 440-TT/LB on 14 August 1989 of the Ministry of Health and the State Pricing Commission guiding the implementation of medicine pricing policy

Mossialos E, Mrazek MF (2002) Data needed for developing and monitoring policies. In: Dukes MNG, Haaijer-Ruskamp FM, De Joncheere CP, Rietveld AH (eds) Drugs and money—prices, affordability and cost containment, 7th edn. IOS, Amsterdam, pp 15–27

MSH (2008) International drug price indicator guide. Management Sciences for Health. http://erc.msh.org/mainpage.cfm?file=1.0.htm&module=DMP&language=english. Accessed 6 Jan 2008

Nguyen TA (2011) Medicine prices and pricing policies in Vietnam. School of Public Health and Community Medicine, The University of New South Wales, Sydney

Nguyen AT, Knight R, Mant A, Cao MQ, Auton M (2009) Medicine prices, availability, and affordability in Vietnam. South Med Rev 2(2):2–9

Nguyen TA, Hassali MA, McLachlan A (2013) Generic medicines policies in the Asia Pacific region: ways forward. WHO South-East Asia J Public Health 2(1):72–74

Nguyen TA, Knight R, Roughead EE, Brooks G, Mant A (2014) Policy options for pharmaceutical pricing and purchasing: issues for low- and middle-income countries. Health Policy Plan. doi:10.1093/heapol/czt105

OECD (2008) Pharmaceutical pricing policies in a global market. Centad. http://www.centad.org/seminar/2.%20Price%20regulation/OECD%20Pharma%20pricing%20policies.pdf. Accessed 14 March 2011

Pham LS (2010) Proposal of management of supply, drug reimbursement from health insurance following a centrally planned approach. Social Insurance Magazine. http://www.tapchibaohiemxahoi.org.vn/index.asp?action_menu=ChuyenMuc_Detail&BaiViet_id=1363&MucLuc_ID=649. Accessed 10 Dec 2010

Segall M, Tipping G, Lucas H, Dung TV, Tam NT, Vinh DX, Huong DL (2002) Economic transition should come with a health warning: the case of Vietnam. J Epidemiol Community Health 56:497–505

Sepehri A, Moshiri S, Simpson W, Sarma S (2008) Taking account of context: how important are household characteristics in explaining adult health-seeking behaviour? The case of Vietnam. Health Policy Plan 23:397–407

Simonet D (2001) Une analyse du marché pharmaceutique vietnamien. Cahiers d'études et de recherches francophones/Santé 11(3):155–160

Somanathan A, Dao HL, Tran TV (2013) Integrating the poor into universal health coverage in Vietnam. Universal Health Coverage Studies Series (UNICO)-UNICO Studies Series No. 24. The World Bank, Washington DC

The Council of Ministers (1987) Decision of the Council of Ministers No104/HDBT of 30 June 1987 on retail prices of curative medicines, Hanoi

Văn phòng Chính phủ (2003) Thông báo của Văn phòng Chính phủ số 41/TB-VPCP ngày 28 tháng 3 năm 2003 về ý kiến của Phó Thủ tướng Nguyễn Tấn Dũng tại buổi làm việc về vấn đề tăng giá thuốc, Hà Nội

WHO (2007) Country cooperation strategy: Vietnam 2007-2011. World Health Organization. http://www.wpro.who.int/NR/rdonlyres/D3DCF855-DF91-441B-9EFE-BF286364D02A/0/CCS20072011.pdf. Accessed 5 May 2009

WHO (2010) National health account series. World Health Organization. http://www.who.int/nha/country/vnm.pdf. Accessed 19 Dec 2010

WHO/HAI (2014) Pharmaceutical pricing policies and interventions—policy brief number 1: external reference pricing. Health Action International http://www.haiweb.org/medicineprices/05062011/1_WHOHAI_Policy-Brief_ERP.pdf. Accessed 16 June 2014

WHO-WPRO (2009) Price information exchange for selected medicines in the Western Pacific Region. http://www.piemeds.com/. Accessed 19 November 2010

WHO-WPRO (2013) Essential medicines. WHO in the Western Pacific Region. http://www.wpro.who.int/vietnam/topics/essential_medicines/factsheet/en/index.html. Accessed 7 May 2013

Witter S (1996) 'Doi Moi' and health: the effect of economic reforms on the health system in Vietnam. Int J Health Plann Manage 11:159–172

Wolffers I (1995) The role of pharmaceuticals in the privatization process in Vietnam's health-care system. Soc Sci Med 41(9):1325–1332

World Bank (2007) Vietnam development report 2008: social protection. World Bank. http://www-wds.worldbank.org/external/default/WDSContentServer/WDSP/IB/2008/06/04/000333038_20080604015001/Rendered/PDF/436530WP0REVIS1ction1final01PUBLIC1.pdf. Accessed 21 Feb 2009

Chapter 19
Pharmaceutical Pricing in Europe

Sabine Vogler and Jaana E. Martikainen

Abstract How are medicine prices decided upon in European countries? Which challenges do policy makers face? Which role do reimbursement aspects play in the pricing process? Are there communalities and similarities between European countries? This chapter provides information on pharmaceutical pricing policies in 30 European countries, including all 28 European Union Member States. Key pricing policies at ex-factory price level as well as in the supply chain will be presented. Medicine price data will be provided as an illustrative snapshort.

19.1 Introduction

The right to health, including access to essential medicines, is a human right (Hogerzeil 2004, 2006; Hogerzeil et al. 2006). To ensure access to essential medicines, affordable prices are a major element, together with a rational selection and use of medicines, sustainable financing and reliable health and supply systems (World Health Organization 2004).

This is of relevance for all the countries the world over, no matter whether they are low- and middle-income countries or high-income countries. European countries use the same principles in their pricing policies and funding strategies when they aim to ensure providing their populations with safe, effective and high quality medicines. Many European countries have universal coverage of health care and they have advanced pricing policies. At the same time, they are continuously adjusting their policies in order to achieve the policy aims, particularly in times of economic hardship. This has been true especially during the recent years when

S. Vogler (✉)
Health Economics Department, WHO Collaborating Centre for Pharmaceutical Pricing and Reimbursement Policies, Gesundheit Österreich GmbH/Geschäftsbereich ÖBIG—Austrian Health Institute, Vienna, Austria
e-mail: sabine.vogler@goeg.at

J.E. Martikainen
Research Department, Social Insurance Institution (Kela), Helsinki, Finland

Z.-U.-D. Babar (ed.), *Pharmaceutical Prices in the 21st Century*,
DOI 10.1007/978-3-319-12169-7_19

Europe has been hit by the global financial crisis (Karanikolos et al. 2013; Mladovsky et al. 2012; Stuckler et al. 2011; Vogler et al. 2011b).

European countries show overall similarities in pricing, as well as reimbursement, though there are differences related to the specific policies (Vogler 2012c).

This chapter aims to offer an overview about pricing policies of medicines in the out-patient and in-patient sectors in European countries. The purpose of this chapter is not only to provide background information but also to contribute to an understanding needed when assessing medicine prices in Europe. Data of medicine price comparison will be presented as illustrative examples. This chapter would provide a snapshot of Europe pricing structure by providing a set of data.

19.2 Methodology

19.2.1 Scope of Countries

Europe has approximately 50 countries, the amount differs somewhat depending on the used classification. As of 2014, 28 European countries are members of the European Union (EU), with the latest candidate country, Croatia having acceded to the EU in July 2013.

This European overview will focus on the 28 EU Member States, plus Switzerland and Norway, which are members of the European Free Trade Association (EFTA) and have close links to the EU. Except for Bulgaria, Hungary and Romania, which are upper-middle income economies, all remaining 25 EU Member States as well as Switzerland and Norway are high-income countries according to the classification of the World Bank (The World Bank 2014). Table 19.1 lists these 30 European countries of this chapter, listed in the order of their official abbreviation that we will use.

19.2.2 Data Sources

The information provided here is retrieved from published peer-reviewed articles and from grey literature as well as from unpublished data sources, particularly from information received directly from pricing policy-makers in the countries. A major data source, particularly relevant to ensure recent data, is the Pharmaceutical Pricing and Reimbursement Information (PPRI) network. This is a network of competent authorities for pharmaceutical pricing and reimbursement of 42, mainly European, countries (as of May 2014). A key aim of the PPRI network is to exchange information and experiences on pharmaceutical pricing and reimbursement policies (Vogler et al. 2014a). A major instrument to exchange information among PPRI network members is the so-called PPRI network query that may relate to specific policy questions (e.g. generic pricing policy (PPRI Network Members 2014)) and are regular queries such as the bi-annual ‘PPRI policy monitoring queries’ to assess the policy changes in the European countries (WHO Collaborating Centre for Pharmaceutical Pricing and Reimbursement Policies 2014).

Table 19.1 Thirty European countries surveyed in this chapter

Country	Abbrev.	Geographic position	Country	Abbrev.	Geographic position
Austria	AT	Central	Ireland	IE	Western
Belgium	BE	Western	Italy	IT	Mediterranean
Bulgaria	BG	Western	Lithuania	LT	Nordic/Central—Baltic
Switzerland	CH	Western	Luxemburg	LU	Western
Cyprus	CY	Mediterranean	Latvia	LV	Nordic/Central—Baltic
Czech Republic	CZ	Central	Malta	MT	Mediterranean
Germany	DE	Western	The Netherlands	NL	Western
Denmark	DK	Nordic	Norway	NO	Nordic
Estonia	EE	Nordic/Central—Baltic	Poland	PL	Central
Greece	EL	Mediterranean	Portugal	PT	Mediterranean
Spain	ES	Mediterranean	Romania	RO	Central
Finland	FI	Nordic	Sweden	SE	Nordic
France	FR	Western	Slovenia	SI	Central—Balkans
Croatia	HR	Central—Balkans	Slovakia	SK	Central
Hungary	HU	Central	United Kingdom	UK	Western

Knowledge about pricing in hospitals in European countries was gained in PPRI's sister project Pharmaceutical Health Information System (PHIS) (Hoebert and Mantel-Teuwisse 2011).

The information provided refers to the latest available date, as of the year 2014, where possible.

Medicine price data shown in this chapter were provided by the Pharma Price Information (PPI) service of Gesundheit Österreich GmbH (Austrian Health Institute) (Gesundheit Österreich GmbH).

This paper uses the terminology as defined in the glossary on pharmaceutical terms developed by the WHO Collaborating Centre for Pharmaceutical Pricing and Reimbursement Policies (WHO Collaborating Centre for Pharmaceutical Pricing and Reimbursement Policies 2013).

19.3 Health Care Systems in Europe

The European countries offer universal coverage and provide at least basic health care cost-free or against co-payments to the population. This is reflected in the comparably high shares of public health expenditure. Figure 19.1 provides an

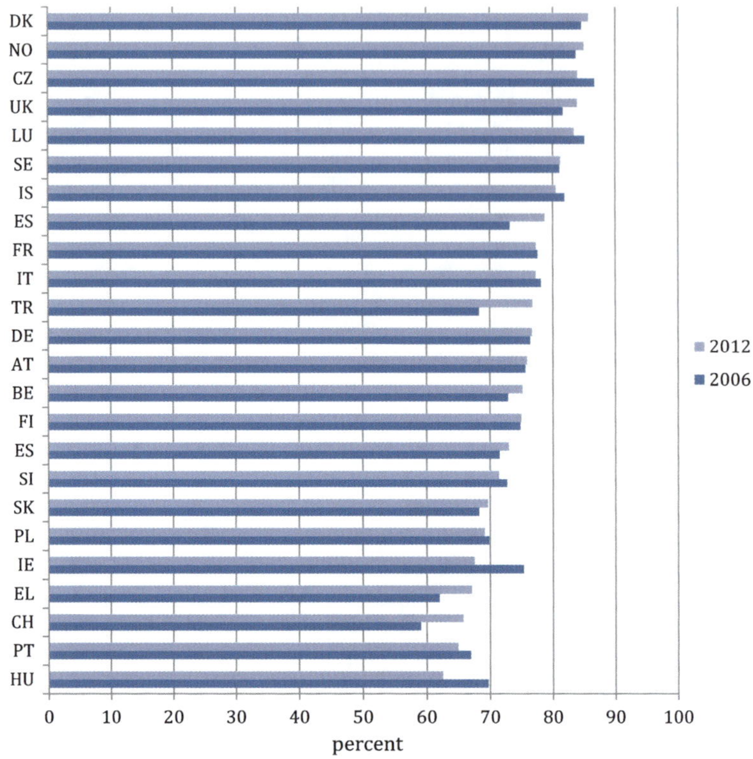

Fig. 19.1 Share of public expenditure in percentage of total health expenditure in the European countries in 2012, compared to 2006. Coverage: All European countries included in the OECD Health Data 2014. *CH* Switzerland, *IS* Iceland, *NO* Norway, *TR* Turkey; for the other country abbreviations see Table 19.1. No data on NL available; ES and PT = data as of 2011. Source: OECD Health Data 2014 (OECD 2014)

overview on the public funding of health expenditure in European countries. Most European countries have at least two thirds, maybe even three quarters of health expenditure publicly. However, the comparison to the year 2006 shows that, while the proportion has increased in several countries, it has reduced in some others, particularly countries (e.g. Ireland, Portugal, Hungary) which struggle with the global financial crisis.

Health care systems are either tax funded or financed from social insurance contributions, or a mix of both. In 19 European countries health care is organised based on a National Health Service (NHS)/'beverage system', whereas 11 countries have a social health insurance/'Bismark system' (Table 19.2). Central and Eastern European countries (e.g. Hungary, Poland, Slovakia) have a social health insurance which they implemented during the 1990-ties after their independence; before they had a Shemasko model-based health care system.

Table 19.2 Organisation of the health care system in Europe, 2014

Model	Countries
National Health Service (NHS)	CY, DK, ES, EL, FI, IE, IT, MT, NO, PT, SE, UK
Social Health Insurance (SHI)	AT, BE, BG, CH, CZ, DE, EE, FR, HR, HU, LT, LU, LV, NL, PL, RO, SI, SK

Source: Authors' compilation based on PPRI Pharma Profiles (PPRI Network Members 2007-2014a); updated and validated by PPRI network members

19.4 Pharmaceutical Systems in Europe

19.4.1 Competence at European and National Levels

Marketing authorization of medicines has been harmonized in the EU. The European Medicines Agency (EMA) plays a key role supplemented by national regulatory agencies in the Member States (see also Table 19.3). Pharmaceutical pricing and reimbursement, however, is a national competence of the EU Member States, although they have to comply with overall EU regulation. A major EU provision in this context is the EU Transparency Directive (The Council of the European Communities) that provides procedural rules (e.g. need of justification of reason for the pricing and reimbursement decision by the competent authority, possibility for appeal against the decision). A major requirement of the EU Transparency Directive concerns time-lines: Competent authorities have to take a pricing decision and a reimbursement decision within 90 days respectively, or in case of a joint pricing and reimbursement decision within 180 days. The Transparency Directive is currently under review.

19.4.2 Reimbursement and Funding

All European countries do a rational selection of medicines that are funded out of public sources. The common term 'essential medicine list' (EML) is, however, not generally used. European countries talk of a 'positive list', i.e. a list of medicines that may be prescribed at the expense of a third party payer, or a 'negative list', its opposite, for the out-patient sector. Positive lists are very common (applied, for instance, in Belgium, France, Lithuania, Portugal, Slovakia), whereas negative lists are only in place in Germany, Greece, Spain and UK (partially in addition to a positive list). The reimbursement authority (cf. Table 19.3) decides on the application of the marketing authorization holder whether a specific medicine is considered as reimbursable, i.e. eligible for public funding, or not. This decision is usually based on a medical, pharmacological and economic evaluation. The number of

Table 19.3 National competent authorities for marketing authorization, pricing and reimbursement of medicines in European countries in 2014

Country	Authorization	Pricing	Reimbursem.	Country	Authorization	Pricing	Reimbursem.
AT	MA	MoH	SHI	IE	MA	MoH	NHS
BE	MoH	MoE	MoSA	IT	MA	MA	MA
BG	MA	MoH	SHI	LT	MA	MoH	MoH
CH	MA	MoH	MoH	LU	MoH	MoE	SHI
CY	MA	MoH	MoH	LV	MA	NHS	NHS
CZ	MA	MA	MA	MT	MA	MoH	MoH
DE	MA	MoH/FJC	MoH/FJC/SHI	NL	MA	MoH	MoH/SHI
DK	MA	–	MA	NO	MA	MA	MA
EE	MA	MoSA	MoSA	PL	MA	MoH	MoH/SHI
EL	MA	MoH	MoH	PT	MA	MA	MA
ES	MA	MoH/FJC	MoH	RO	MA	MoH	MoH/SHI
FI	MA	MoH	MoH	SE	MA	PRA	PRA
FR	MA	FJC	SHI	SI	MA	MoH	SHI
HR	MA	SHI	SHI	SK	MA	MoH	MoH
HU	MA	MoH/SHI	SHI	UK	MA	MoH	MoH

Authorization Marketing Authorization, *FJC* Federal Joint Committee/Interministerial Committee, *MA* Medicines Agency, *MoSA* Ministry of Social Affairs, *MoE* Ministry of Economy/Economics, *MoH* Ministry of Health, *NHS* National Health Service, *PRA* Pricing and Reimbursement Agencies, *Reimbursem.* Reimbursement, *SHI* Social Health Insurance. Source: Authors' compilation based on PPRI Pharma Profiles (PPRI Network Members 2007-2014a), PPRI Posters (PPRI Network Members 2007-2014b), article on Croatia (Vogler et al. 2011a), ÖBIG FP report on Romania (Leopold and Vogler 2010), PPRI/PHIS database (PPRI Secretariat 2014a); updated and validated by PPRI network members medicines on the out-patient positive list varies between fewer than 1,000 medicines (Cyprus, Estonia) to up to more than 9,000 medicines (Italy) (Vogler et al. 2008). In some countries (e.g. Cyprus, Ireland, Malta) reimbursement eligibility is linked to the population group.

In the in-patient sector, these lists of medicines for use in the hospital are typically called Hospital Pharmaceutical Formularies (HPF). In many European countries HPFs are decentralized at the level of the single hospitals, and the hospital's Pharmaceutical and Therapeutics Committee decides about the inclusion of a medicine into this formulary.

In out-patient care, reimbursement eligibility of a medicine does not necessarily imply full cost coverage by the public payer but patients are charged co-payments. Austria, Croatia Denmark, Estonia, Finland, France, some regions in Italy, Poland, Slovakia and UK charge a fee, and Denmark, Ireland, Malta (private sector) and Sweden apply deductibles, i.e. an initial out-of pocket expense up to a fixed amount or over a defined period of time by an insured person before partial or full cost coverage by public or third party payer is reached. The most common co-payment for reimbursable medicines is, however, the percentage co-payment. Except for Austria, Germany, the Netherlands, Italy and UK, all other countries apply different reimbursement and co-payments rates. Medicines are typically classified according to the severity of the disease that they are intended to treat: Essential medicines, for instance, are reimbursed up to 100 %, whereas medicines for less severe illnesses are funded at lower percentage rates. Percentage co-payments may also be linked to population groups (e.g. lower co-payments for vulnerable groups, e.g. in France, Portugal). In Denmark and in Sweden the percentage co-payments are a kind of deductible, and their rates decrease with patients' increasing out-of-pocket expenditure within a calendar year.

In hospitals in European countries, patients do not co-pay for their medication.

In the European countries, pharmaceutical expenditure per capita in 2012 ranged from USD 295 (in constant prices and at PPP; corresponding to € 212) in Denmark and USD 311 (€ 223) in Estonia to USD 668 (€ 480) in Germany and USD 736 (€ 529) in Belgium. Since these data reflect the economic situation of a country, the share of total health expenditure spent on medicines is another relevant indicator in this respect. As Fig. 19.2 displays, there are again large variations: The share of pharmaceutical expenditure as percentage of total health care expenditure ranges from more than 30 % (Hungary) and around 25 % (Slovak Republic, Greece) to around 9 % (Switzerland, Luxemburg) and 6–7 % (Denmark, Norway). The shares tend to be higher in less affluent countries, in Central and Eastern European countries, for instance.

19.4.3 Pharmaceutical Industry and Distribution

Some of the 'big pharma countries' are located in Europe. Europe's 'big five' are Germany, France, Italy, Spain and UK. In 2012, Europe's research-oriented

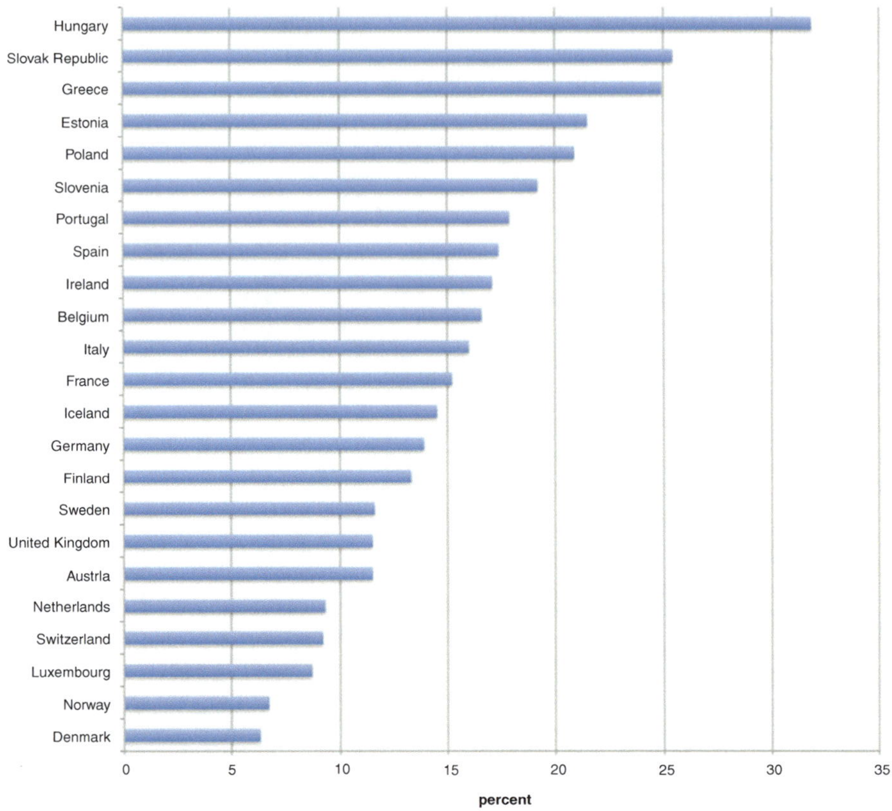

Fig. 19.2 Share of pharmaceutical expenditure in per cent of total health expenditure in the European countries in 2012, or latest available year. Coverage: All European countries included in the OECD Health Data 2014. No data on Turkey available; UK = data as of 2008; the Netherlands, Portugal and Spain = data as of 2011. Source: OECD Health Data 2014 (OECD 2014)

industry accounted for a total production of € 210 billion (leaders were Switzerland, Germany, Italy, UK, Ireland and France), corresponding to a pharmaceutical market value of € 163 billion (at ex-factory prices) and a total employment of 700,000 people (estimated data). In 2012, pharmaceutical industry invested € 30 billion in research & development (R&D) in Europe, which was higher than the investment in the USA and it shows an overall increasing trend (EFPIA 2013).

In the European countries, despite a high share of public pharmaceutical funding, pharmaceutical industry, wholesale and retail of medicines (with a few exceptions, e.g. a few community pharmacies owned by municipalities in Italy) is private. Pharmaceutical companies, wholesalers and pharmacies are private enterprises that conclude contracts with the public payers. Medicines are predominantly dispensed to patients by community pharmacies. Doctors are allowed to dispense prescription-only medicines to their patients in Austria, Cyprus, France, Hungary,

Ireland, the Netherlands, Poland and UK even though only in Austria and in Switzerland dispensing doctors are still relevant in quantitative terms (Vogler et al. 2008; Kanavos et al. 2011a). In Cyprus, the Czech Republic, France, Hungary, Lithuania, Malta, Norway, the Netherlands, Poland, Romania and in a few further countries (Austria, Belgium, Germany, Italy, Portugal, Slovenia, UK) under specific conditions hospital pharmacies may act as community pharmacies and dispense to out-patients (Vogler et al. 2010). In some countries (e.g. Ireland, Italy, Portugal, Sweden, UK) some or all Over-the-Counter (OTC) medicines, which are usually not reimbursed by public payers, may also be dispensed outside pharmacies, e.g. in parapharmacies, grocery stores and at petrol stations (Vogler et al. 2012a; Vogler 2014).

19.5 Competent Authorities

In some European countries, the responsibilities for marketing authorization, pricing and reimbursement are split between three institutions (e.g. Austria), whereas others countries (e.g. Italy) have one or two institutions that are in charge of these tasks.

Marketing authorization and pharmacovigilance are typically the competence of Medicines Agencies. Pricing is frequently the responsibility of the Ministry of Health or Ministry of Social Affairs. A decade ago, the Ministry of Economics or the Ministry of Finance used to be the pricing authority in some countries (e.g. Czech Republic, Portugal), then this competence was transferred to the Ministry of Health in some but not all countries. Reimbursement decisions tend to be taken by the Ministry of Health and/or the social health insurance institution (under the supervision of the Ministry of Health or Ministry of Social Affairs). Pricing and reimbursement is frequently linked, particularly in those countries where pricing and reimbursement decisions are taken in a joint process and/or by one institution. Table 19.3 provides an overview of the relevant competent authorities for pharmaceutical competence. Some of the listed institutions are also in charge of medical devices.

As a rule, pricing and reimbursement decisions are taken at national level and are, with few exceptions, valid for the whole country. However, while funding for medicines is decided at federal level, the actual payers of reimbursable medicines are often located at regional level: the sickness funds (e.g. France, Poland) or the regions (e.g. Italy, Sweden).

Health Technology Assessment (HTA) agencies, which assess (new) medicines and have increasingly become important, particularly if value-based pricing (VBP) is applied (see Sect. 19.5), are usually independent public institutions, not directly involved in pricing and reimbursement decisions. Well-known HTA agencies in Europe are NICE (National Institute for Health and Care Excellence) in England, HAS (Haute Autorité de Santé/High Health Authority) in France and IQWiG (Institut für Qualität und Wirtschaftlichkeit im Gesundheitswesen/Institute for Quality and Efficiency in Healthcare) in Germany.

19.6 Pricing in the Out-Patient Sector

19.6.1 Pricing at Ex-factory Price Level

Generally speaking, there is price control for reimbursable medicines in the European countries; this means that government authorities set the price of a medicine and/or indirectly influence it. For non-reimbursable medicines, which are frequently OTC medicines, free pricing is permitted so that pharmaceutical companies determine the price of the medicine they launch. In some European countries price control applies to all medicines, and in others to specific groups of medicines, e.g. to prescription-only medicines (see Table 19.4).

Prices are set at the ex-factory price level except for Cyprus, Denmark, Finland, the Netherlands, Norway, Sweden and UK because these countries determine the wholesale price.

In several European countries regulation provides for statutory pricing, i.e. setting the price on a regulatory, unilateral basis. Only few European countries (e.g. France, Italy) have price negotiations as the sole pricing procedure. In practice, in many European countries statutory pricing is accompanied by negotiations, particularly when it comes to reimbursement and (confidential) discounts may be granted (Sect. 19.8).

Policy-makers can apply different criteria to decide on the price of a medicine. In European countries, the key criterion in pricing decisions on new medicines is the

Table 19.4 Scope of price control for medicines at ex-factory price (or wholesale[a]) level in European countries in 2014

	Who decides on pharmaceutical prices?	
Countries	State/authority	Pharmaceutical company
CY, BE, EL, LV, LT, LU (6)	All medicines	–
AT, DE, DK, CH, CZ, EE, ES, FI, FR, HR, HU, IE, IT, PL, SE, SK, SI, UK[b] (18)	Reimbursable medicines	Non-reimbursable medicines
BG, NL, NO, PT, RO (5)	Prescription-only medicines	Over-the-counter medicines
MT (1)	Medicines in the public sector	Medicines in the private sector
DK[c] (1)	–	All medicines

Note: This refers to on-patent medicines. Additional provisions are relevant for off-patent medicines (cf. Sect. 19.9). Source: Authors' compilation based on PPRI Pharma Profiles (PPRI Network Members 2007-2014a), PPRI Posters (PPRI Network Members 2007-2014b), article on Croatia (Vogler et al. 2011a), OBIG FP report on Romania (Leopold and Vogler 2010), PPRI/PHIS database (PPRI Secretariat 2014a); updated and validated by PPRI network members

[a]Cyprus, Denmark, Finland, the Netherlands, Norway, Sweden and UK do not set the price at the ex-factory price level, but at the wholesale level

[b]UK has indirect price control via the Pharmaceutical Price Regulation Scheme (PPRS) that regulates the maximum allowed profits for companies

[c]Free pricing but reimbursement limits (reimbursement prices) are regulated

price of that medicine in other countries, or the 'value' of the medicines. The practice of using the price(s) of a medicine in one or several countries to derive a benchmark or reference price for the purposes of setting or negotiating the price of the product in a given country is called external price referencing (or international price benchmark), whereas pricing for new medicines based on the therapeutic value which the medicine offers, usually assessed through health technology assessment (HTA) or economic evaluation, is known under the concept of 'value based pricing' (WHO Collaborating Centre for Pharmaceutical Pricing and Reimbursement Policies 2013; Leopold et al. 2012; Paris and Belloni 2013).

External price referencing (EPR) is a very common pricing policy in Europe. As of 2014, 25 out of the 28 EU Member States (all but Denmark, Sweden and UK) apply external price referencing, at least as a supportive tool, for new medicines (see Fig. 19.3 for a map which also provides information on a few further European countries). Typically, European countries refer to medicine prices of around three to six countries, usually of similar or lower economic situation and sometimes neighbouring countries. A few countries (e.g. Czech Republic, Slovakia) refer to all other 27 countries of the European Union. While some countries (e.g. Austria, Portugal) take the average price of the reference countries, others (e.g. Hungary, Poland) take the lowest price in the basket as references or have some algorithm. For instance, Norway, with a basket of nine countries, calculates the average of the three lowest priced ones (Festöy et al. 2011). The change in the methodology of EPR, particularly of the variety of the reference countries, was a rather frequent

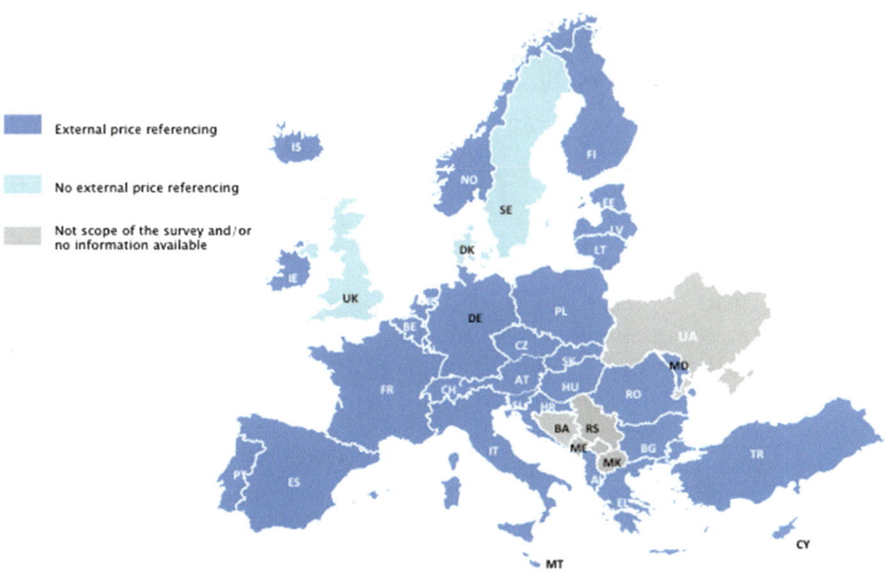

Fig. 19.3 External price referencing in the European countries in 2014. Source: Authors' compilation based on PPRI Pharma Profiles (PPRI Network Members 2007-2014a), PPRI Posters (PPRI Network Members 2007-2014b; Leopold et al. 2012), PPRI/PHIS database (PPRI Secretariat 2014a); updated and validated by PPRI network members

policy measure in recent years, probably in the response to the global financial crisis, when reference countries were substituted by countries of lower economic wealth to adjust for deteriorated economic situation in the country which applies EPR (PPRI Network Members 2007-2014b; WHO Collaborating Centre for Pharmaceutical Pricing and Reimbursement Policies 2014).

In addition, several European countries apply elements of value based pricing (VBP) for new medicines, particularly when it comes to new high-cost medicines with expected substantial therapeutic value. VBP for medicines means, broadly speaking, that in the price setting for new medicines the value the medicine offers is considered as assessed through health technology assessment (HTA) or economic evaluation (Husereau et al. 2011). However, there is no widely accepted definition as to what types of policies are in fact value based pricing systems. The OECD recently assessed the value based pricing elements in 10 European and 14 other OECD countries and concluded that all countries surveyed had a system in place that assesses the added value of medicines (Paris and Belloni 2013). A narrower understanding of VBP is that in addition to price setting of a medicine according to its value this takes place in a system in which pricing and reimbursement decisions are fully integrated. In such a case, VBP would be an alternative to EPR. According to this narrow definition of VBP, only very few countries use VBP. Sweden introduced VBP in 2002, and it applies three eligibility criteria in its pricing and reimbursement decision: the human value principle, the need and solidarity principle and the cost-effectiveness principle (Redman and Köping Höggärd 2007). England planned to implement VBP in 2014. While the new Pharmaceutical Pricing Regulation Scheme (PPRS) which entered in force at the beginning of 2014, embeds value assessment initiatives to be announced (Department of Health 2013), at the time of writing little is known about how the new pricing system will look like in practice (a public consultation on value-based assessment by NICE was closed end of June 2014).

19.6.2 Distribution and Taxes

In the European countries, regulation stipulates the maximum remuneration granted to the stakeholders involved in pharmaceutical distribution—in principle, regulation for pharmaceutical wholesalers and community pharmacies (in very few cases, also regulation for dispensing doctors).

As stated above, Cyprus, Denmark, Finland, the Netherlands, Norway, Sweden and UK set a medicine price at the wholesale level, and they do not have statutory wholesale mark-ups. Wholesale margins are negotiated between the manufacturer and the wholesaler, usually on a confidential basis. In these countries with no statutorily regulated wholesale remuneration, ex-factory prices can, at best, be calculated on the basis of an estimated average wholesale margin. Unlike wholesale remuneration, all European countries but the Netherlands regulate the maximum pharmacy remuneration. Wholesale and pharmacy remuneration regulation usually applies to all medicines, but is limited to reimbursable and prescription-only medicines in some countries (Kanavos et al. 2011a).

Distribution remuneration can take different forms. Several European countries, for example, opted for regressive wholesale and pharmacy mark-up or margin schemes, which gradually decrease the add-ons for high-cost medicines. The share of the price attributable to the distribution actors tends to be higher for low-price medicines in regressive schemes.

In addition to classical linear or regressive mark-ups (add-ons) or margins, pharmacy remuneration may also be designed independently from the price of the medicine in a way that they grant a fee for service, such as in the Netherlands or in the UK. Some European countries have combined a fixed fee per service (e.g. per prescription dispensed) and a price-dependent funding (see Fig. 19.4) (Vogler et al. 2014b).

Wholesale and pharmacy remuneration is typically regulated as maximum remuneration. However, in practice, the maximum allowed pharmacy remuneration corresponds to the actual remuneration. From a few Central and Eastern countries, it is known that the maximum remuneration is not fully used, e.g. in the OTC sector, which results in different prices of the same medicine across a country (Vogler et al. 2008). This is also the case for medicines in a sector without regulation for pharmacy remuneration. In France, for instance, prices of non-reimbursable medicines, with no regulated pharmacy remuneration, vary between pharmacies (personal communication).

Furthermore, the price of a medicine may be increased by duties and taxes, which are known to account for a considerable part of the medicine price in middle- and low-income countries (Cameron et al. 2009; Ball 2011; Levison and Laing 2003). In European countries, only the value-added tax is applied to medicines.

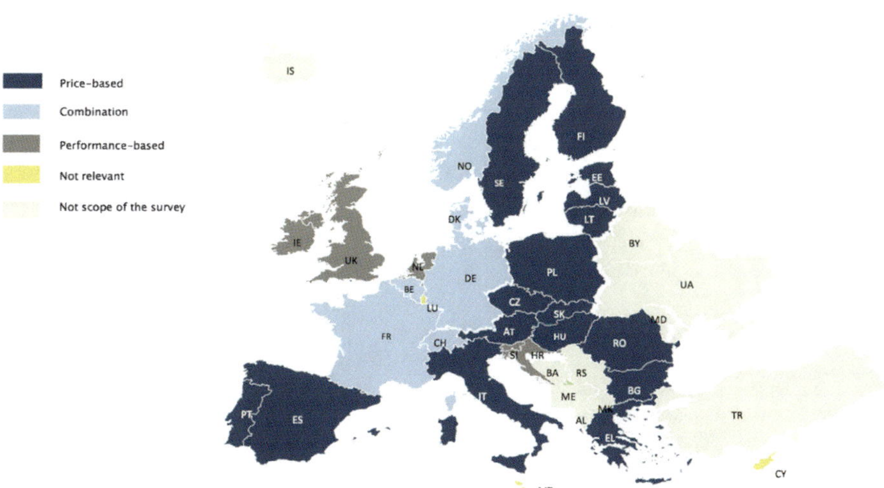

Fig. 19.4 Pharmacy remuneration in the European countries in 2014. Source: Vogler et al. (2014b)

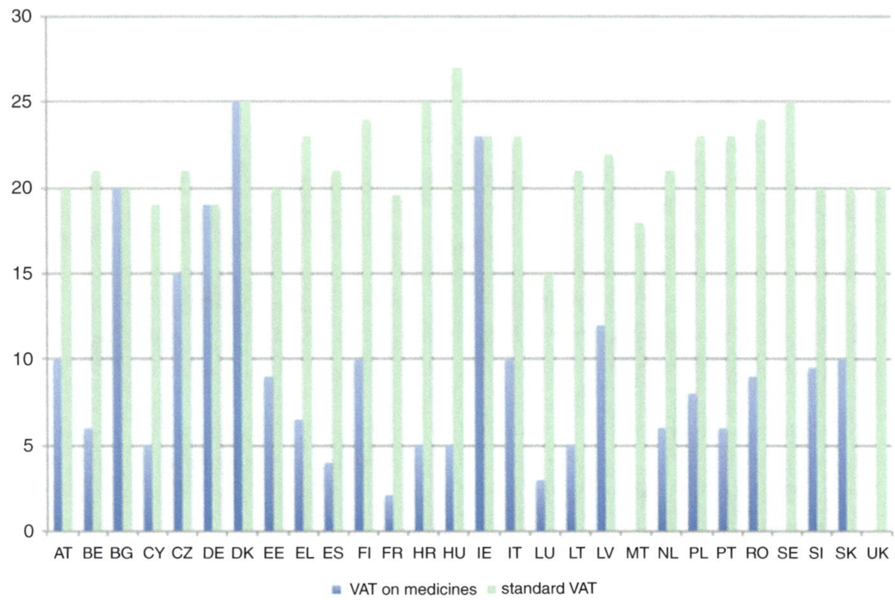

Fig. 19.5 Value-added tax (VAT) on medicines in the European countries in 2014. Please note that in FR, HR, LT and UK only the VAT rate for reimbursable medicines is displayed, in IE only the rate for oral medicines, and in SE for prescribed medicines. Specification on different VAT rates for different kind of medicines: FR: 2.1 % on reimbursable medicines, 10 % on non-reimbursable medicines. HR: 5 % on reimbursable medicines, 25 % on non-reimbursable medicines. IE: 0% on oral medicines, 23 % (external applications) and 13.5 % (low protein) on non-oral medicines. LT: 5 % on reimbursable medicines, 21 % on non-reimbursable medicines. SE: 0 % on prescribed medicines (prescription-only medicines and prescribed OTC medicines), 25 % on non-prescribed medicines. UK: 0 % on NHS medicines, 20 % on non-NHS medicines. Source: PPRI/PHIS database (PPRI Secretariat 2014a); updated and validated by PPRI network members

Most European countries apply a value-added tax rate on medicines that is lower than the standard rate. Some countries (e.g. France, Ireland, Sweden, UK) have different VAT rates for reimbursable/prescription-only medicines versus non-reimbursable/OTC medicines (Fig. 19.5).

19.6.3 Price Types

The usual price types for the out-patient sector are as follows:

- the ex-factory price (price set at the level of the manufacturer);
- the pharmacy purchasing price (price set at the level of the wholesaler); and
- the pharmacy retail price, also called ‘consumer price’ or ‘end price’ (set at the level of the pharmacy).

The pharmacy retail price is sometimes also referred to as 'public price', to indicate the price set for the public, i.e. consumers. We advise not using the term 'public price' because it could be misconstrued as a reference to the funding source of a 'public payer'.

In addition, the 'reimbursed price' or 'reimbursement price' refers to the maximum amount covered by public payers (usually social insurance or a national health service). In European countries, the term 'reimbursement price' is not explicitly indicated, except for Austria, which uses the term 'sickness fund price'. In other European countries, the reimbursement price can be derived from the medicine price, usually the pharmacy retail price, by deducting the percentage co-payments incurred by the consumers (all European Union Member States except Austria, Germany, Italy, the Netherlands and UK have a specific percentage co-payment, see above in Sect. 19.4). For instance, if the pharmacy retail price is € 100 and the reimbursement rate is 80 %, then the reimbursement price amounts to € 80. In this case, the patient is required to co-pay € 20, plus a prescription fee, if applicable.

The reference price is a particular reimbursement price. A reference price system is a reimbursement system in which identical or similar medicines (e.g. originator medicines and generics) are clustered to a reference group, and a public payer defines the maximum price (amount) that is reimbursed for all medicines clustered to this group (WHO Collaborating Centre for Pharmaceutical Pricing and Reimbursement Policies 2013; Habl et al. 2008). A reference group can be clustered for the molecule (Anatomical Therapeutic Chemical Classification level [ATC] 5), the class (ATC Level 4) or the therapeutic area (ATC Level 3) (WHO Collaborating Centre for Pharmaceutical Pricing and Reimbursement Policies 2013). The patient is required to pay the difference between the reference price and the pharmacy retail price, plus any further co-payments. For instance, in Portugal, the percentage co-payment is also applicable to the reference price (Habl et al. 2008). As of 2014, 24 of the 30 surveyed countries had a reference price system in place.

19.7 Pricing in the In-Patient Sector

Hospitals are usually directly supplied by the pharmaceutical industry and, in some cases, by wholesalers. Common procurement methods are tendering (usually done by the hospitals, in some countries also central tendering) and direct negotiations (Vogler et al. 2010, 2013b).

In contrast to the out-patient sector, only one official price type is applicable for the in-patient sector. This price, which can be called 'official hospital price' in international price comparisons (Vogler et al. 2010), generally corresponds to the ex-factory price or, in the case of delivery by a wholesaler, to the wholesale price, which includes the wholesale mark-up. Actual prices can be lower due to discounts and rebates (see below Sect. 19.8).

19.8 Role of Discounts and Similar Arrangements: Official Versus Actual Prices

Discounts and rebates can be arranged both in the out-patient and in the hospital sectors, and they are granted by the suppliers to the purchasers, which might be the public payers or private distribution actors in the supply chain.

Discounted prices are especially known from the hospital sector. Large discounts and rebates are offered on specific medicines to the hospitals. In some European countries, cost-free medicines are permitted, so hospitals can obtain medicines even at a price of zero Euro. Discounts and rebates, including a cost-free supply, have been observed, particularly for medicines, where competitors have come onto the market, and whose use might be required for long-term treatment (Vogler et al. 2010, 2013b). As a result, the actual hospital price is of greater relevance than official hospital prices, as the hospital's pharmaceutical bill is composed of what the hospital actually spends on medicines.

In general, particularly in the light of the global financial crisis, discounts and rebates granted to public payers have increasingly been gaining importance. According to a survey of European countries (Vogler et al. 2012b) as of 2011, discounts and rebates are granted to public payers by pharmaceutical companies in 25 of the 31 European countries surveyed (out-patient sector in 21 countries and in-patient sector in all 25 countries). The most common discounts and rebates are price reductions and refunds linked to sales volume, but types such as in-kind support, price-volume agreements (i.e. price is linked to the sales volume) and risk-sharing agreements (i.e. payments by industry or price cuts are foreseen if the expected therapeutic benefit cannot be achieved) are also in place. A mix of various types of discounts and rebates is common. Risk-sharing and further managed-entry agreements that attempt to manage uncertainty are on the rise in several European countries, such as UK (patient access schemes), Italy, the Netherlands, Poland and the Baltic States (Espín et al. 2011; Adamski et al. 2010).

With regard to discounts and rebates granted along the supply chain (e.g. from wholesaler to pharmacies, from pharmacies to consumers), legal provisions may either forbid them at all (e.g. Germany) or may stipulate specifications, e.g. the maximum amount of discounts and rebates granted (Kanavos et al. 2011a). In France, for example, pharmacies are permitted to obtain a maximum discount of 2.5 % on reimbursable medicines from wholesalers, whereas the limit is 17 % for reimbursable generics (Lopes et al. 2011).

In general, discounts and rebates tend to be agreed on a confidential basis. As a result, the actual prices are lower than the official list prices (at ex-factory or wholesale price level). This has an important policy implication because, as explained in Sect. 19.6, external price referencing is a major pricing policy in the European countries, but countries refer to higher list prices.

19.9 Generic Pricing Policies

Specific pricing policies as well demand-side measures apply related to generics and are used in European countries (Table 19.5).

Several European countries require generics—and other ‘follower products’—to be priced at a defined percentage lower than the originators—a policy called ‘generic price link’. This is a form in ‘internal price referencing’, i.e. the practice of using the price(s) of identical or similar products in a country for pricing and/or reimbursement decisions. The stipulated percentage at which generics have to be priced lower than the originator and further methodological specifications vary between the countries. Austria and Estonia, for example, specify that not only the first ‘follower’, but also all additional followers and the original products are required to lower their price. Since 2005, Norway has used the ‘stepped price model’ (‘Trinnprismodellen’) to incrementally reduce the price of a medicine according to pre-defined rates, depending on sales volumes. The first reduction occurs after a medicine has lost patent protection.

Countries that do not have a generic price link policy but rather rely on competition to reduce generic prices have been found to potentially have larger price differences among generics, compared to countries with generic price link policies (Vogler 2012a).

Generic pricing policies are supplemented by further, usually demand-side measures, to increase generics’ uptake. Most European countries either have generic substitution (i.e., the practice of substituting a medicine with a less expensive medicine, often containing the same active ingredient(s)), or INN prescribing (i.e., prescribing medicines by its active ingredient name instead of the brand name) in place, however, usually on a voluntary and not mandatory basis (Vogler 2012b; WHO Collaborating Centre for Pharmaceutical Pricing and Reimbursement Policies 2014).

19.10 Price Reviews and Changes

In addition to determining the market entry prices, prices may be reviewed and adjusted after the launch of a medicine. Price reviews can be undertaken together with a reimbursement review; or reimbursement reviews are done as stand-alone procedures. In France, for instance, any medicine included in the positive list will be re-assessed after 5 years to decide whether the reimbursement status and reimbursement level will be renewed. In addition, France had a few waves of reimbursement reviews related to specific therapeutic classes (Lopes et al. 2011).

Reviews might be necessary to check whether the provisions agreed in specific arrangements were met, e.g. in managed-entry agreements. In the stepped-price system in Norway (cf. Sect. 19.9), the maximum reimbursement price level is automatically reduced in stages (steps) following patent expiry, and prices are

Table 19.5 Generic pricing policies in European countries in 2014

Country	Generic price link	Generic substitution	INN prescribing	Country	Generic price link	Generic substitution	INN prescribing
AT	Yes	Not allowed	Not allowed	IS	Yes	Mandatory	Indicative
BE	Yes	Indicative[a]	Indicative	IC	Yes	Indicative	Indicative
BG	No	Not allowed	Indicative	LT	Yes	Indicative	Mandatory
CH	Yes	Not allowed	Indicative	LU	Yes	Not allowed	Indicative
CY	Yes	Mandatory	Mandatory	LV	Yes	Indicative	Indicative[b]
CZ	Yes	Indicative	Indicative	MT	No	Mandatory	Mandatory
DE	Yes	Mandatory	Indicative	NO	Yes	Indicative	Indicative
DK	No	Mandatory	Not allowed	PL	Yes	Indicative	Mandatory
EE	Yes	Indicative	Mandatory	PT	Yes	Indicative	Mandatory
EL	Yes	Indicative	Mandatory	RO	No	Indicative	Mandatory
ES	Yes	Indicative	Indicative	SE	No	Mandatory	Not allowed
FI	Yes	Mandatory	Indicative	SI	No	Indicative	Indicative
FR	Yes	Indicative	Indicative	SK	No	Mandatory	Indicative
HU	Yes	Indicative	Indicative	TR	Yes	Indicative	Not allowed
IE	Yes	Indicative	Indicative	UK	No	Not allowed	Mandatory

CH Switzerland, *IS* Iceland, *NO* Norway; for the other country abbreviations see Table 19.1. Source: Authors' compilation based on PPRI Pharma Profiles (PPRI Network Members 2007-2014a), PPRI Posters (PPRI Network Members 2007-2014b), PPRI/PHIS database (PPRI Secretariat 2014a); updated and validated by PPRI network members

[a]Indicative for antibiotics/antimycotics, but mandatory for acute diseases

[b]In general indicative, but mandatory for newly diagnosed patients

cut: the size of the price cuts depends on annual sales prior to the establishment of generic competition and the time since competition had been established (Festöy et al. 2011). Price reviews might be stipulated in external price referencing regulation because during the first price comparison prices might not be available in all reference countries but rather in high-price countries (particularly Germany) since for strategic reasons medicines tend to be launched in high-price countries (Danzon et al. 2005; Leopold et al. 2012; Kyle 2007; OECD 2008). In Austria, for instance, the regulation provides that the average EU price can be determined if price data from at least half of the Member States are available; otherwise an evaluation for updated information is required every 6 months (with a total to up to two evaluations) (Bundesministerium für Gesundheit 2008).

The legislation of some European countries requires to regularly review regulated medicine prices (e.g. Portugal—on a annual basis (Teixeira and Vieira 2008)). However, limited capacity may lead to authorities refraining from doing price reviews, or other arrangements (e.g. price cuts agreed with the industry) might be taken instead.

Limited capacity to monitor prices was suggested by an analysis on the impact of price cuts in Greece and Spain on other European countries which refer to these countries: It showed that the price reductions were not automatically translated into price decreases in referencing countries as expected. One of the possible explanations was that countries did not regularly monitor the medicines prices in the other countries (Vogler et al. 2011c; PPRI Secretariat 2014b).

In addition to these regular price revisions, ad-hoc price reviews can be performed, usually with the aim of price adjustments. This was observed in some countries in recent times, particularly in response to the global financial crisis. Price cuts were among the most common pharmaceutical interventions during the last years (Vogler et al. 2011b). Between January 2010 and February 2011, Greece applied quarterly price reviews followed by price cuts, and Lithuania imposed price cuts of between 10 and 11 % on non-reimbursable medicines. Similar price cuts were enforced in Portugal, Czech Republic and Iceland (Vogler et al. 2011b). In Spain, prices of original medicines and orphan medicinal products were cut by 7.5 % and 4 % respectively (Martinez et al. 2010). In Finland, for cost-containment reasons, prices of all reimbursed medicines not included in the reference price system were cut by 5 % in February 2013 (KELA 2013).

19.11 Medicine Price Data

Based on what has been said previously, data of medicine prices are presented as illustrative examples in this section. This is not intended as comprehensive information but should provide a snapshot of European pricing structure.

19.11.1 Medicine Price Comparison: An Example

Figure 19.6 highlights the differences in medicine prices in European countries: The ex-factory prices per unit (e.g. per tablet, vial) of three medicines are compared in 16 European countries. These are interferon beta 1a (with a median ex-factory price per unit of € 191.5, bosentan with a median price of € 39.5 and the combination product levodopa and decarboxylase inhibitor (DDCI) with a median price of € 0.10). In order to compare products of these different price levels, data are presented in an indexed way, with the median price taken as 100. In the case of interferon beta 1a Greece displays the lowest price in this comparison, and Germany the highest; the relevant countries are the Netherlands (lowest) and Denmark (highest) for bosentan, and Belgium (lowest) and Sweden (highest) for levodopa + DDCI. Overall, prices in Greece, Spain, Hungary and UK ranked rather low, whereas prices in Germany, Sweden, Denmark and Austria were rather high. This pattern of high-price and low-price countries was also shown in other price studies on European countries (Brekke et al. 2010; Kanavos et al. 2011b; Kanavos and Vandoros 2011; Leopold et al. 2013).

Data in Fig. 19.6 refers to on-patient medicines only, and to officially published list prices that do not take into account discounts and rebates. The impact of discounts and rebates as well as of patent expiry on medicine prices will be shown in the following.

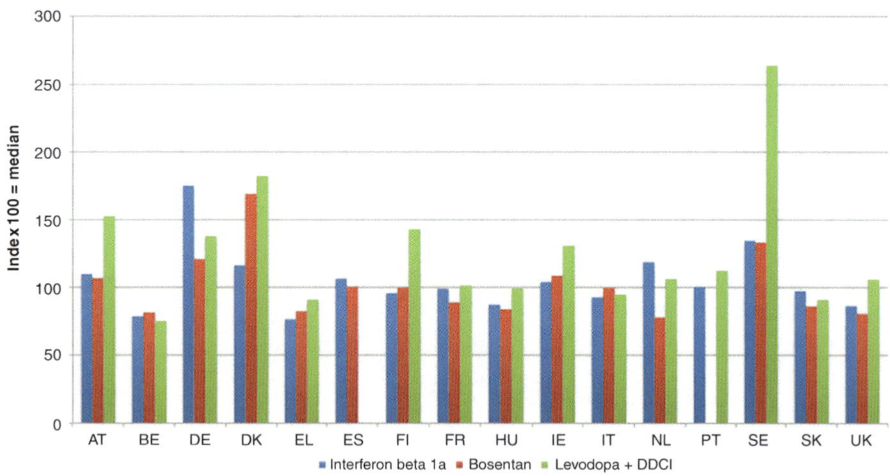

Fig. 19.6 Ex-factory prices per unit of 3 medicines in 16 European countries, as of April 2013 (median price indexed as 100). Interferon beta 1a: n = 16; bosentan: n = 15, no data on Portugal available, levodopa + DDCI (decarboxylase inhibitor): n = 15, no data on Spain available. Only data of on-patent medicines (levodopa + DDCI also had generics on the market in some countries at the time of the survey). In DK, FI, NL, SE and UK ex-factory prices are computed via average wholesale margins since they are not regulated. Calculation of € for non-Euro countries (DK, HU, SE and UK) with the exchange rate as of March 2013. Source: Pharma Price Information (PPI) service of Gesundheit Österreich GmbH; analysis and presentation: the authors

19.11.2 Discounts

As stated in Sect. 19.8, discounts and rebates granted by pharmaceutical industry to third party payers are common in European countries. However, discounts and rebates are usually not taken into consideration in price comparisons and price setting decisions based on external price referencing since they are usually kept confidential.

In Germany pharmaceutical industry is statutorily required to grant ‘manufacturer discounts’ to the sickness funds; these ‘manufacturer discounts’ are published. Figure 19.7 shows the differences when such discounts are taken into consideration. As example we chose ipilimumab, a high-cost medicine with a median ex-factory price of 17,000 € per unit. Without considering discounts, Germany was one of five countries that had the median price, and only UK had a slightly higher price per unit. If the German ‘manufacturer discounts’ were considered, the ranking changed, and the ex-factory price in Germany was the lowest one in comparison. We conclude that medicines prices are most likely to be, sometimes significantly, different if discounts and rebates granted to third party payers were revealed and could thus be considered.

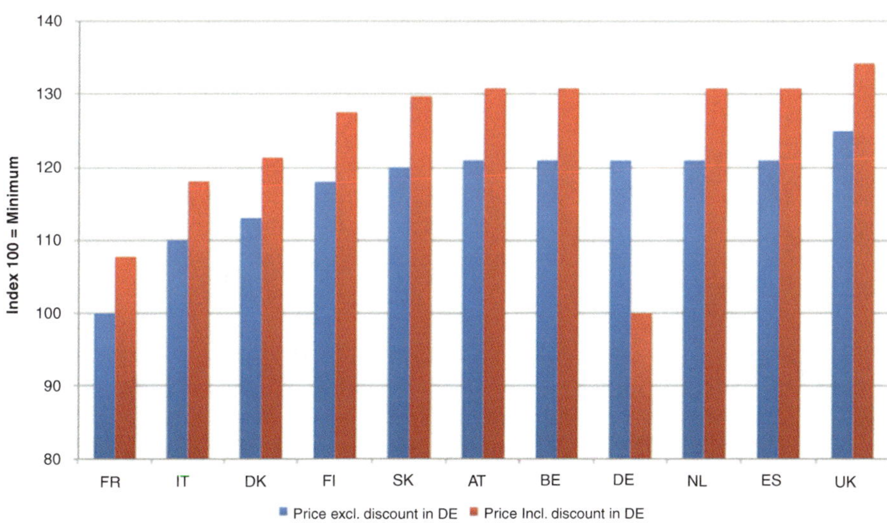

Fig. 19.7 Ex-factory prices per unit of ipilimumab (on-patent medicine) in 11 European countries, with and without the consideration of manufacturer discounts in Germany as of spring 2013 (lowest price indexed as 100). In DK, FI, NL and UK ex-factory prices are computed via average wholesale margins since they are not regulated. Calculation of € for non-Euro countries (DK and UK) with the exchange rate as of March 2013. Source: Pharma Price Information (PPI) service of Gesundheit Österreich GmbH; analysis and presentation: the authors

19.11.3 Generics: Price Dynamics After Patent Expiry

In European countries, the originator medicine tends to stay on the market when generics come to the market. Figure 19.8 displays the differences in originator and generic ex-factory prices for two medicines: the immunosuppressant mycophenolate mofetil and the antidepressant venlafaxine. We see comparably high price differences of, in some cases, more than 80–90 % in some European countries, particularly in the Netherlands and UK, but also in Denmark and Germany. For several years, these countries have been applying a range of measures to enhance generic uptake (see also Sect. 19.9), and these countries are also known to letting generic competition work (Vogler 2012a). In Spain there is no difference between the originator price and generic price for both selected medicines. It might be speculated that the originator company lowered its price before the market entry of competitors.

19.11.4 Further Price Levels

Figure 19.9 confirms that the add-ons (wholesale margin, pharmacy margin and value-added tax) make up a relevant part of the final medicine price (pharmacy retail price gross). Roughly speaking, the ex-factory price accounts for around 20 % of the price, wholesale remuneration for another 20 %, and the pharmacy

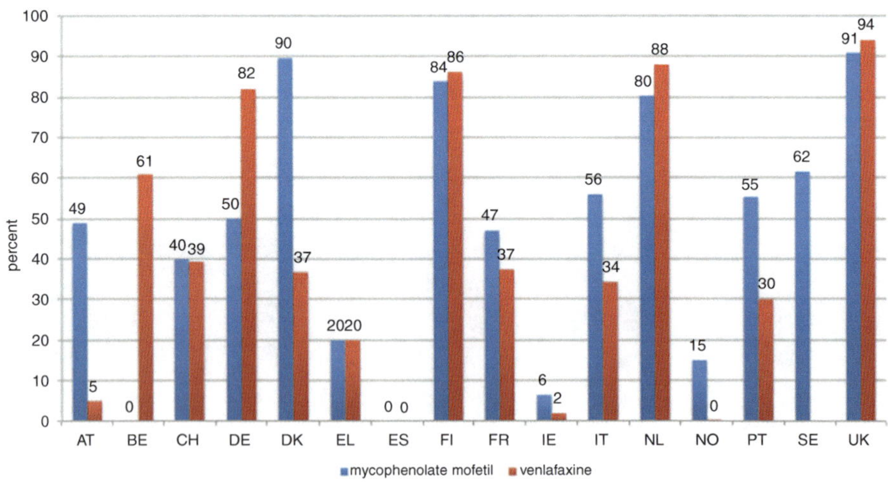

Fig. 19.8 Price differences between originator and comparable generics at ex-factory price level per unit of two medicines in 16 European countries, as of June 2013 (in per cent). mycophenolate mofetil: n = 16; venlafaxine: n = 15 (SE—only data for generics available, not for the originator). In DK, FI, NO, SE and UK ex-factory prices are computed via average wholesale margins since they are not regulated. Calculation of € for non-Euro countries (CH, DK, NO, SE and UK) with the exchange rate as of May 2013. Source: Pharma Price Information (PPI) service of Gesundheit Österreich GmbH; analysis and presentation: the authors

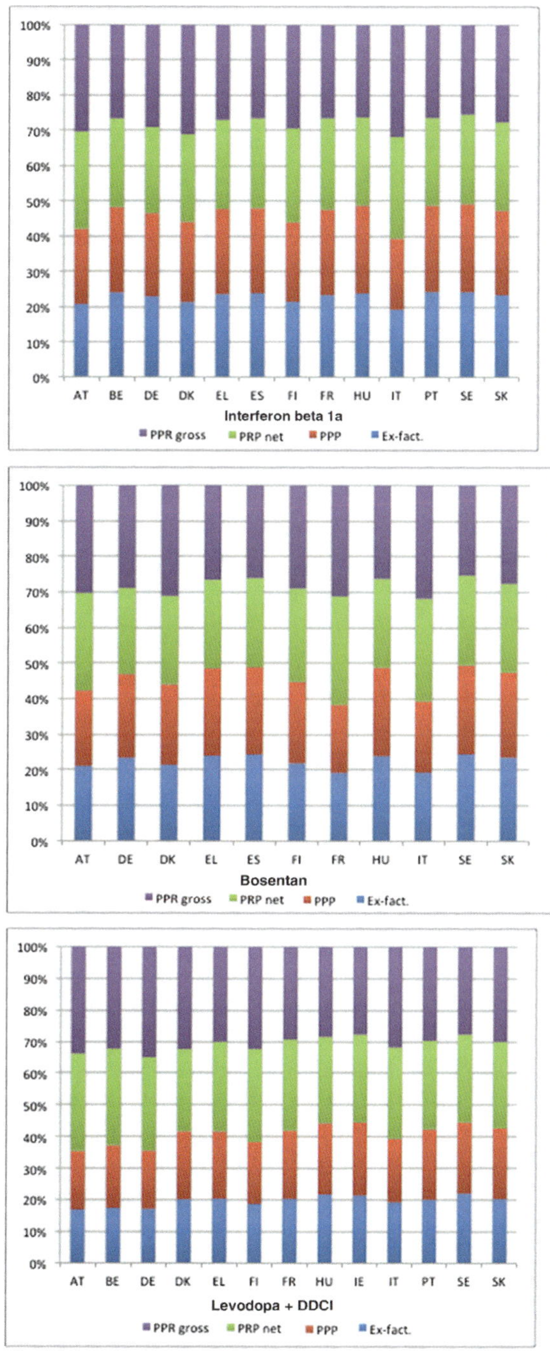

Fig. 19.9 Shares of ex-factory price (abbreviated: ex-fact), pharmacy purchasing price (PPP) and pharmacy retail price (PRP) net and gross of the total medicine price of three medicines in European countries, as of April 2013 (in per cent). Interferon beta 1a: n = 13; IE, NL and UK not included (no PRP in IE, NL and UK); bosentan: n = 11, BE, IE, NL, PT, UK not included (no PRP in BE, IE, NL and UK; no price data in PT), levodopa + DDCI (decarboxylase inhibitor): n = 13; ES, NL, UK not included (no PRP in NL and UK; no price data in ES). Only data of on-patent medicines (levodopa + DDCI also had generics on the market in some countries at the time of the survey). In DK, FI, NL, SE and UK ex-factory prices are computed via average wholesale margins since they are not regulated. Calculation of € for non-Euro countries (DK, HU and SE) with the exchange rate as of March 2013. Source: Pharma Price Information (PPI) service of Gesundheit Österreich GmbH; analysis and presentation: the authors

remuneration and the value-added tax for another 30 % respectively. However, there are variations among the countries and the products. Many European countries have regressive wholesale and pharmacy remuneration schemes, and, as a result, the relative shares of the ex-factory price are lower compared to other price components. This is reflected in the examples shown, with levodopa + DDCI as a low priced medicine (median = € 0.10 ex-factory price per unit) compared to bosentan (median = € 39.5) and interferon beta 1a (€ 191.5). The data show relatively high shares related to the pharmacy remuneration in Austria, France and Italy, whereas this price component is comparably low in Germany and Hungary, at least for higher priced medicines. The wholesale remuneration is comparatively high in Greece. Though these are single examples, price analyses for a larger basket of medicines, done by the PPI service, confirm this pattern.

19.12 Current Developments

Overall, European countries apply price control for medicines that are, at least partially, funded by public payers. All European countries struggle to provide equitable access to essential and, if possible, further medicines to their population despite tight budgets. In addition, the global financial crisis hit hard some of the European countries which had to impose austerity measures to comply with the provisions of funding institutions. The recent and expected launch of high-cost medicines, e.g. orphan medicines to treat rare diseases and oncology medicines, for instance, has become a major challenge for all European countries.

EU Member States have the competence to nationally decide on their pharmaceutical pricing and reimbursement policies. The methodological details of the selected practices differ but in general most European countries chose the same pricing policy options. External price referencing is the major pricing policy in the European countries. Even it was expected to come to an end soon (Seiter 2010), due to its limitations, it apparently will continue to play a major role in the future to come. At the same time, countries aims to achieve savings, which can be invested in rewarding innovation and financing high-cost medication, through generic promotion (generic pricing policies accompanied by demand-side measures) and the increased use of health technology assessments and pharmaco-economic evaluations to better assess the value, or added benefit, of new, particularly high-cost medicines. However, value based pricing as the sole pricing policy is an exception in European countries.

In order to have access to price information, pricing authorities have established departments involved in accessing medicine prices or checking price data submitted by the industry. In Austria, according to the General Social Insurance Law the national public health institute Gesundheit Österreich GmbH (GÖG) is responsible for checking at request the medicine price data submitted by industry to the Federal Ministry of Health (Bundesministerium für Gesundheit 2008). To do so, GÖG has established a Pharma Price Information (PPI) service (Gesundheit Österreich GmbH) which provides independent medicine price information in 30 European countries. Additionally, competent authorities of European countries have been involved in the development of a European price database, the so-called Euripid database: After 4 years of European Commission funding (2009–2013), Euripid is now maintained as joint effort of 24 EEA (European Economic Area) countries involved, under the lead of the Hungarian Social Health Insurance institution OEP and GÖG (Andert and Schröder 2011; Bouvy and Vogler 2013), updated information based on personal communication).

In recent years, confidential discounts and rebates have increasingly become an issue of debate. Pricing authorities are aware about distortionary effects on transparency due to the rising use of discounts, rebates and further arrangements (e.g. managed-entry agreements), and about the risk of overpaying when they reference to list prices. In 2011, the European Social Insurance Platform (ESIP) called for a transparent manner regarding 'real' prices, including price strategies of pharmaceutical industry and rebates negotiated by Member States (ESIP and AIM 2011). In spring 2014, Germany changed their procedure of external price referencing and reference to the 'real' discounted prices.

Another development with regard to pricing and procurement policies is an increased awareness for procurement in the in-patient sector and for an improved medicines management at the interface of the out-patient and in-patient sectors. Typically, pricing authorities are solely in charge of out-patient pricing policies. However, it has been increasingly acknowledged that the start of a therapy in hospitals impacts the further medication in the out-patient sector (Björkhem-Bergman et al. 2013; Gallini et al. 2012; Schröder-Bernhardi and Dietlein 2002; Stuffken 2011; Vogler et al. 2010, 2013a). To improve interface management, cooperation initiatives and new funding models are required. There are few good practice examples, e.g. joint reimbursement lists for the out-patient and the in-patient sectors in European countries; these include joint reimbursement lists and joint reimbursement committee in Stockholm County Council (Gustafsson et al. 2011) and in Scotland (Herms and Rutledge 2002).

Acknowledgements We thank the members of the Pharmaceutical Pricing and Reimbursement Information (PPRI) network for providing on a regular basis over several years information about pricing and reimbursement policies in their country. We appreciate that they validated the correctness and up-to-dateness of country-specific data and information used in this section.

Furthermore, we are grateful to the Pharma Price Information (PPI) team at Gesundheit Österreich GmbH for sharing medicine price data to allow for illustrative examples.

References

Adamski J, Godman B, Ofierska-Sujkowska G, Osinska B, Herholz H, Wendykowska K, Laius O, Jan S, Sermet C, Zara C, Kalaba M, Gustafsson R, Garuoliene K, Haycox A, Garattini S, Gustafsson LL (2010) Risk sharing arrangements for pharmaceuticals: potential considerations and recommendations for European payers. BMC Health Serv Res 10:153. doi:10.1186/1472-6963-10-153

Andert R, Schröder Y (2011) Local payers versus global players. Soziale Sicherheit 5:257–261

Ball D (2011) The regulation of mark-ups in the pharmaceutical supply chain. Working paper 3, WHO/HAI project on medicine prices and availability

Björkhem-Bergman L, Andersén-Karlsson E, Laing R, Diogene E, Melien O, Jirlow M, Malmström R, Vogler S, Godman B, Gustafsson L (2013) Interface management of pharmacotherapy. Joint hospital and primary care drug recommendations. Eur J Clin Pharmacol 69 (1):73–78. doi:10.1007/s00228-013-1497-5

Bouvy J, Vogler S (2013) Background paper 8.3 pricing and reimbursement policies: impacts on innovation. In: World Health Organization (ed) Priority medicines for Europe and the World. "A public health approach to innovation". Update on 2004 Background Paper

Brekke KR, Holmås TH, Straume OR (2010) Are pharmaceuticals still inexpensive in Norway? A comparison of prescription drug prices in ten European countries. SNF report no. 08/10

Bundesministerium für Gesundheit (2008) Regelung für die Vorgehensweise der Preiskommission bei der Ermittlung des EU-Durchschnittspreises gemäß § 351c Abs. 6 ASVG

Cameron A, Ewen M, Ross-Degnan D, Ball D, Laing R (2009) Medicine prices, availability, and affordability in 36 developing and middle-income countries: a secondary analysis. Lancet 373 (9659):240–249

Danzon PM, Wang YR, Wang L (2005) The impact of price regulation on the launch delay of new drugs—evidence from twenty-five major markets in the 1990s. Health Econ 14(3):269–292

Department of Health (2013) The pharmaceutical price regulation scheme 2014. Guidance

The Council of the European Communities Directive 89/105/EEC of 21 December 1988 relating to the transparency of measures regulating the pricing of medicinal products for human use and their inclusion in the scope of national health insurance systems

EFPIA (2013) The pharmaceutical industry in figures—edition 2013. European Federation of Pharmaceutical Industries and Associations, Brussels

ESIP, AIM (2011) Review of Council Directive 89/105/EEC of 21 December 1988 relating to the transparency of measures regulating the pricing of medicinal products for human use and their inclusion in the scope of national health insurance systems (Transparency Directive). Joint Position Paper. Submitted by European Social Insurance Platform (ESIP)/Association Internationale de la Mutualité (AIM) on 10 February 2011

Espín J, Rovira J, García L (2011) Experiences and impact of European risk-sharing schemes focusing on oncology medicines. EMINet, Vienna

Festöy H, Aanes T, Yu L-M, Ognøy AH, Gregersen T (2011) PHIS pharma profile Norway. Pharmaceutical Health Information System (PHIS), Vienna

Gallini A, Legal R, Taboulet F (2012) The influence of drug use in university hospitals on the pharmaceutical consumption in their surrounding communities. Br J Clin Pharmacol 7 (10):1365–2125

Gesundheit Österreich GmbH Pharma Price Information (PPI) service. Further information available from http://www.goeg.at/en/PPI. Vienna

Gustafsson LL, Wettermark B, Godman B, Andersén-Karlsson E, Bergman U, Hasselström J, Hensjö L-O, Hjemdahl P, Jägre I, Julander M, Ringertz B, Schmidt D, Sjöberg S, Sjöqvist F, Stiller C-O, Törnqvist E, Tryselius R, Vitols S, von Bahr C, Regional Drug Expert Consortium (2011) The 'Wise List'—a comprehensive concept to select, communicate and achieve adherence to recommendations of essential drugs in ambulatory care in Stockholm. Basic Clin Pharmacol Toxicol 108(4):224–233. doi:10.1111/j.1742-7843.2011.00682.x

Habl C, Vogler S, Leopold C, Schmickl B, Fröschl B (2008) Referenzpreissysteme in Europa. Analyse und Umsetzungsvoraussetzungen für Österreich [Reference price systems in Europe. Analysis and lessons learned for implementation in Austria]. ÖBIG Forschungs- und Planungsgesellschaft mbH, Vienna

Herms S, Rutledge P (2002) The Lothian Joint Formulary: overcoming the barriers to formulary success. Pharm Pract 12(6):279–285

Hoebert J, Mantel-Teuwisse A (2011) PHIS evaluation report. Pharmaceutical Health Information System (PHIS), Utrecht

Hogerzeil HV (2004) The concept of essential medicines: lessons for rich countries. BMJ 329 (7475):1169

Hogerzeil HV (2006) Essential medicines and human rights: what can they learn from each other? Bull World Health Organ 84(5):371–375

Hogerzeil HV, Samson M, Casanovas JV, Rahmani-Ocora L (2006) Is access to essential medicines as part of the fulfilment of the right to health enforceable through the courts? Lancet 368 (9532):305–311

Husereau DR, Cameron CG, Foundation CHSR (2011) Value-based pricing of pharmaceuticals in Canada: opportunities to expand the role of health technology assessment? Canadian Health Services Research Foundation, Ottawa

Kanavos PG, Vandoros S (2011) Determinants of branded prescription medicine prices in OECD countries. Health Econ Policy Law 6(3):337

Kanavos P, Schurer W, Vogler S (2011a) Pharmaceutical distribution chain in the European Union: structure and impact on pharmaceutical prices. EMINet, Vienna

Kanavos P, Vandoros S, Irwin R, Nicod E, Casson M (2011b) Differences in costs of and access to pharmaceutical products in the EU. European Parliament, Brussels

Karanikolos M, Mladovsky P, Cylus J, Thomson S, Basu S, Stuckler D, Mackenbach JP, McKee M (2013) Financial crisis, austerity, and health in Europe. Lancet 381(9874):1323–1331

KELA (2013) Finland. Recent changes in pharmaceutical policy measures and developments in pharmaceutical expenditure. Paper presented at the poster for the PPRI Network Meeting, London, March 2013

Kyle MK (2007) Pharmaceutical price controls and entry strategies. Rev Econ Stat 89(1):88–99

Leopold C, Vogler S (2010) Access to essential medicines in Romania Vienna

Leopold C, Vogler S, Mantel-Teeuwisse AK, de Joncheere K, Leufkens HG, Laing R (2012) Differences in external price referencing in Europe—a descriptive overview. Health Policy 104 (1):50–60. doi:10.1016/j.healthpol.2011.09.008

Leopold C, Mantel-Teeuwisse AK, Vogler S, de Joncheere K, Laing RO, Leufkens HGM (2013) Is Europe still heading to a common price level for on-patent medicines? An exploratory study among 15 Western European countries. Health Policy 112:209–216. doi:10.1016/j.healthpol.2013.08.012

Levison L, Laing R (2003) The hidden costs of essential medicines. Essent Drugs Monitor 33:20–21

Lopes S, Marty C, Berdai D (2011) PHIS pharma profile France. Pharmaceutical Health Information System (PHIS), Vienna

Martinez V, Ferré de la Peña P, Izquierdo G, Lens Cabrera C (2010) PHIS pharma profile Spain. Pharmaceutical Health Information System (PHIS), Vienna

Mladovsky P, Srivastava D, Cylus J, Karanikolos M, Evetovits T, Thomson S, McKee M (2012) Health policy responses to the financial crisis in Europe. Policy summary Dänemark

OECD (2008) Pharmaceutical pricing policies in a global market. OECD health policy studies. OECD, Paris

OECD (2014) OECD health data. OECD, Paris

Paris V, Belloni A (2013) Value in pharmaceutical pricing. OECD health working papers, no. 63. OECD Publishing, Paris

PPRI Network Members (2007-2014a) PPRI/PHIS pharma profiles—country specific reports on pharmaceutical systems and policies. http://whocc.goeg.at/Publications/CountryReports. Vienna

PPRI Network Members (2007-2014b) PPRI/PHIS posters—country specific information on different issues related to pharmaceutical systems and policies. Pharmaceutical Pricing and Reimbursement Information (PPRI)/Pharmaceutical Health Information System (PHIS), Vienna. http://whocc.goeg.at/Publications/CountryPosters

PPRI Network Members (2014) PPRI network query on generic price link (unpublished compilation). Pharmaceutical Pricing and Reimbursement Information (PPRI), Vienna

PPRI Secretariat (2014a) PPRI/PHIS database, update 2014. Pharmaceutical Pricing and Reimbursement Information (PPRI)/Pharmaceutical Health Information System (PHIS), Vienna

PPRI Secretariat (2014b) PPRI/PHIS database, update 2014. Pharmaceutical Pricing and Reimbursement Information (PPRI)/Pharmaceutical Health Information System (PHIS), Vienna

Redman T, Köping Höggärd M (2007) PPRI pharma profile Sweden. Pharmaceutical Pricing and Reimbursement Information (PPRI), Vienna

Schröder-Bernhardi D, Dietlein G (2002) Lipid-lowering therapy: do hospitals influence the prescribing behavior of general practitioners? Int J Clin Pharmacol Ther 40(7):317–321

Seiter A (2010) A practical approach to pharmaceutical policy. World Bank Publications, Washington, DC

Stuckler D, Basu S, Suhrcke M, Coutts A, McKee M (2011) Effects of the 2008 recession on health: a first look at European data. Lancet 378(9786):124–125

Stuffken R (2011) Medication changes in patients transitioning between health care settings. Utrecht University, Utrecht

Teixeira I, Vieira I (2008) PPRI pharma profile Portugal. Pharmaceutical Pricing and Reimbursement Information (PPRI), Vienna

The World Bank (2014) How we classify countries. http://data.worldbank.org/about/country-classifications/country-and-lending-groups. Accessed 20 May 2014

Vogler S (2012a) How large are the differences between originator and generic prices? Analysis of five molecules in 16 European countries. Farmeconomia Health Econ Ther Pathways 13(Suppl 3):29–41

Vogler S (2012b) The impact of pharmaceutical pricing and reimbursement policies on generics uptake: implementation of policy options on generics in 29 European countries—an overview. GaBI J 1(2):93–100. doi:10.5639/gabij.2012.0102.020

Vogler S (2012c) Preisbildung und Erstattung von Arzneimitteln in der EU—Gemeinsamkeiten, Unterschiede und Trends. Pharm Med 14(1):56

Vogler S (2014) Liberalization in the pharmacy sector. OECD global forum on distribution. OECD, Paris

Vogler S, Habl C, Leopold C, Rosian-Schikuta I, de Joncheere K, Lyager Thomsen T (2008) PPRI report. Pharmaceutical Pricing and Reimbursement Information, Vienna

Vogler S, Habl C, Leopold C, Mazag J, Morak S, Zimmermann N (2010) PHIS Hospital Pharma Report. Pharmaceutical Health Information System (PHIS); commissioned by the European Commission and the Austrian Federal Ministry of Health, Vienna

Vogler S, Habl C, Bogut M, Voncina L (2011a) Comparing pharmaceutical pricing and reimbursement policies in Croatia to the European Union Member States. Croat Med J 52(2):197

Vogler S, Zimmermann N, Leopold C, de Joncheere K (2011b) Pharmaceutical policies in European countries in response to the global financial crisis. South Med Review 4(2):32

Vogler S, Zimmermann N, Leopold C, Schmickl B, Windisch F (2011c) Impact of medicines price reductions in Greece and Spain on other European countries applying external price referencing. Poster. Paper presented at the drug utilisation and health policy meeting, Antwerp, 30 May 2012

Vogler S, Sandberger K, Arts D, Habl C (2012a) OTC medicines—distribution in Europe. EMINet, Vienna

Vogler S, Zimmermann N, Habl C, Piessnegger J, Bucsics A (2012b) Discounts and rebates granted to public payers for medicines in European countries. South Med Rev 5(1):38–46

Vogler S, Zimmermann N, Habl C, Leopold C, Dolinar E (2013a) Survey about interface management measures regarding medication. Poster at the EAHP (European Association of Hospital Pharmacists) Congress, Paris, 13–15 March 2013

Vogler S, Zimmermann N, Leopold C, Habl C, Mazag J (2013b) Discounts and rebates granted for medicines for hospital use in five European countries. Open Pharmacoecon Health Econ J 5:1–10. doi:10.2174/1876824520130426001

Vogler S, Leopold C, Zimmermann N, Habl C, de Joncheere K (2014a) The Pharmaceutical Pricing and Reimbursement Information (PPRI) initiative—experiences from engaging with pharmaceutical policy makers. Health Policy Technol 3(2):139–148. doi:10.1016/j.hlpt.2014.01.001

Vogler S, Pertl D, Schmickl B, Windisch F (2014b) Apothekenhonorierung in Europa [Pharmacy remuneration in Europe]. Gesundheit Österreich Forschungs- und Planungsgesellschaft mbH, Vienna

WHO Collaborating Centre for Pharmaceutical Pricing and Reimbursement Policies (2013) Glossary of pharmaceutical terms. Update 2014. Vienna

WHO Collaborating Centre for Pharmaceutical Pricing and Reimbursement Policies (2014) Pharmaceutical policy monitoring exercise with national competent authorities represented in the PPRI (Pharmaceutical Pricing and Reimbursement Information) network. Bi-annually, latest update: February 2014 (unpublished)

World Health Organization (2004) Equitable access to essential medicines: a framework for collective action. WHO policy perspectives on medicines

Chapter 20
UK Health Technology Assessment and Value Based Pricing

Emma E. Morrison and David J. Webb

Abstract All state funded healthcare providers have to ensure that they provide value for money and avoid wasting money on less cost-effective interventions. The National Health Service (NHS) is the largest public-funded healthcare service in the world, and as a consequence has developed an international reputation for Healthcare Technology Assessment (HTA). The challenge to provide safe, effective drugs on a budget has underpinned the development of cost-saving measures including cost-utility analysis, providing an assessment of cost-effectiveness that can successfully compare the societal value of disparate interventions and their effect on disease states.

In this chapter, we discuss the evolution of HTA in the UK and how financial pressures have driven a review of how we pay for drugs. Value Based Pricing (VBP), and latterly Value Based Assessment (VBA), have been proposed as novel approaches to updating drug pricing in the UK. These schemes aim to ascertain the perceived value of a drug with reference to societal utility and reimburse drug companies accordingly, with the aim of balancing affordability and innovation. We address VBP methodology, cost-effectiveness thresholds, pricing, the need for evidence and VBP experience beyond the UK. Rejuvenating our approach to drug pricing and replacing an outdated system is an invaluable opportunity, yet care must be taken not to inadvertently limit access to cost-effective drugs for those who need them.

20.1 Drug Pricing

Providing public-funded healthcare is complex. Pharmaceutical companies (sellers) need to price their products to cover the costs of drug discovery, development and manufacture, marketing and further R&D, while at the same time providing a sufficient return to investors. Healthcare providers (purchasers) want to provide a

E.E. Morrison • D.J. Webb (✉)
Clinical Pharmacology Unit, Queen's Medical Research Institute, University of Edinburgh, E3.22, 47 Little France Crescent, Edinburgh EH16 4TJ, UK
e-mail: d.j.webb@ed.ac.uk; cpu@ed.ac.uk

Z.-U.-D. Babar (ed.), *Pharmaceutical Prices in the 21st Century*,
DOI 10.1007/978-3-319-12169-7_20

range of treatments at a price that offers good value for money and is affordable. Patients (end-users) want access to safe and effective drugs, but are less concerned about what this might cost. These concerns are asymmetric, and create tension, mainly between healthcare services and patients.

Half the world's spending on patent-protected drugs is in the US and consequently the global pharmaceutical industry sets drug prices using the US as the main reference market. Referencing is used to maintain consistent drug prices and avoid parallel imports between countries. The US spends more money *per capita* on health than in any other country, with this expenditure increasing at a greater rate annually (Fig. 20.1). To avoid these financial challenges to effective healthcare provision, many countries use a variety of cost-saving measures, including: high generic use; employing formularies of preferred products; approval of cost-effective drugs using health technology assessment (HTA); and patient access schemes (PAS) to improve value for money. To this mix can now be added the broader scheme of value based pricing (VBP).

20.2 The UK National Health Service

The National Health Service (NHS) is the UK healthcare structure, originally created in 1948. Mainly funded by government through central taxation, the NHS provides a comprehensive range of healthcare services, free at the point of use for

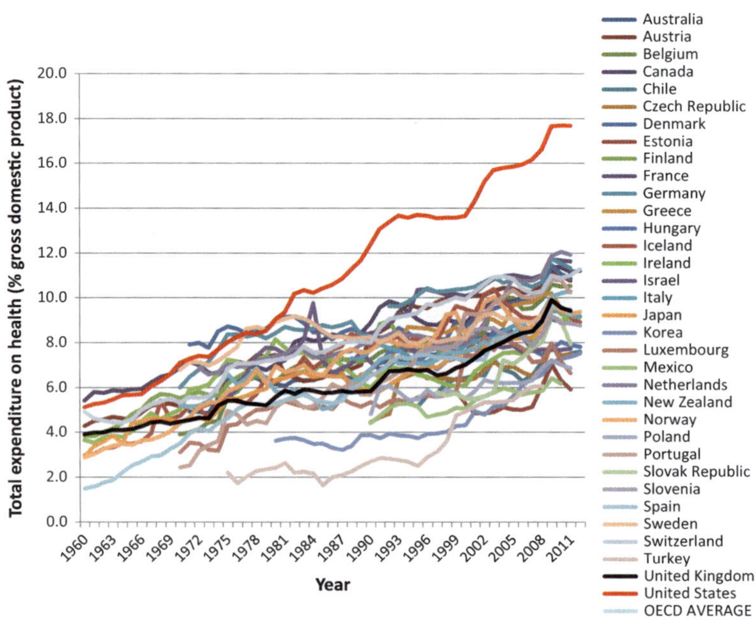

Fig. 20.1 Total annual expenditure on health by member country of OECD (Modelled on data from OECD 2013)

residents of the UK. This service is comprised of four systems: NHS (England), NHS Scotland, NHS Wales, and Health and Social Care in Northern Ireland.

The NHS is currently ranked as one of the best healthcare providers worldwide, demonstrating a strong performance in equity, efficiency, quality of care and access to services (Davis et al. 2014). Particularly of note is the delivery of effective, safe, and patient-centered care, despite spending a comparatively low percentage of the UK gross domestic product on health. After 60 years of operating as the largest public healthcare system in the world, the UK serves as a price referencing benchmark. The cost of a drug in the UK market has a far-reaching impact, beyond that of sales generated locally, on healthcare markets worldwide. Among the EU member states that use external reference pricing, the UK is the most frequently referenced (Leopold et al. 2012) and, as a result, UK patients have benefitted from early access to new drugs (Collier 2007).

20.3 Pharmaceutical Price Regulation Scheme

Although generic drugs make up almost 75 % of the prescriptions in the UK, they cost much less than branded drugs, so expenditure on generics is only 35 % of the total NHS spend on medicines (NHS Information Centre 2013). In 2012, spending in NHS (England) was around £100,000 million ($174 billion), with 8 % spent on drugs (NHS Information Centre 2013; HM Treasury 2012). Since 1957, expenditure on branded therapeutics has been controlled by the Pharmaceutical Price Regulation Scheme (PPRS) and the profit made by industry from patent-protected drugs is agreed between the Association of the British Pharmaceutical Industry (ABPI) and the Department of Health (DoH). This profit is renegotiated on a five-yearly cycle. The scheme has come under increasing scrutiny over recent years and a major report by the Office of Fair Trading (OFT) recommended reform, proposing the PPRS was inadequate in containing costs and encouraging innovation. The OFT backed a move away from price-control towards drug pricing on the value of the potential health benefits provided (OFT 2007; Collier 2007).

20.4 Healthcare Technology Assessment

Distributive justice describes the philosophical approaches to societal resource distribution. There are three contrasting approaches. Firstly, libertarianism describes the concept that it is the responsibility of an individual to provide healthcare for themselves and the responsibility of the state to ensure the means to do so. This is largely achieved through private healthcare systems funded by the individual, often through insurance schemes. Secondly, egalitarianism centres on provision of all possible healthcare interventions to society, a clearly unaffordable ideal. Lastly, utilitarianism is an approach focused on maximum efficiency of resource allocation. This approach provides the greatest benefit to the greatest number but does not distinguish the needs of an individual. Total utilitarianism overlooks areas of health inequality and does not allow resources to be channelled towards rare diseases or orphan drugs, due to their usually high cost and low contribution to population health. HTA uses a utilitarian approach but has the ability to modify distribution of resources to target areas of perceived need. This approach to HTA is the fairest at a societal level but does not address the rule of rescue '*the powerful human proclivity to rescue a single identified endangered life, regardless of cost, at the expense of any nameless faces who will therefore be denied health care*' (Osborne and Evans 1994).

HTA is most commonly undertaken using cost-utility analysis, although alternatives exist (Table 20.1). HTA is required to provide good value for money, and to avoid spending on less cost-effective technologies that reduce the opportunity to invest in those of greater value. Cost-utility analysis of a drug is most commonly

Table 20.1 Characteristics of different methods of HTA

Method	Unit of cost	Effect measured	Evaluation	Benefits	Limitations
Cost-utility analysis	Monetary	Cost per unit of utility i.e. QALYs/ DALYS	Cost of quality and quantity of life gained by an intervention	Allows comparison of disparate measures ('apples and pears') and combines more than one aspect of health	Complexity in assessing effect
Cost effectiveness analysis	Monetary	Natural units (Life years gained/disease or deaths prevented)	Relative effectiveness to achieve same outcome	Intuitive	Cannot be used to compare cost-effectiveness across different disease states. Only one outcome is measured
Cost-benefit analysis	Monetary	Monetary units	Resource consumption to achieve the same outcome	Allows comparison across interventions	Cannot ascertain quality of life in monetary value
Cost-minimisation analysis	Monetary	Not applicable, effect is presumed to be equivalent	Least cost comparison of programmes with the same effect	Straightforward	Few interventions achieve the same effect

Modified, with permission, from Polinder et al. (2011) (*DALYs* Disability Adjusted Life Years, *QALYs* Quality Adjusted Life Years)

calculated using Quality Adjusted Life Years (QALY); a measure of disease burden that includes both the quality and the quantity of life gained. The QALY is used to calculate the Incremental Cost Effectiveness Ratio (ICER)—the ratio of the change in costs to incremental QALY gained with a therapeutic intervention, compared to best existing therapy. Resources are limited in any public healthcare system and QALYs assign equal social value to an intervention, aiming to overcome subjectivity and allocate funds fairly. QALYs are ascribed to an intervention to facilitate fair comparison of competing programmes across different diseases and populations. They also enable comparison between new and established treatments. QALY are ascribed a numerical value, 1 year of full health is given a numerical value of 1, death a value of 0. Health state scoring systems (e.g. EQ-5D, HUI2, SK-6D) are used to generate an estimate of QALY impact if not in full health. EQ-5D, a self-reported questionnaire completed by patients using a choice-based elicitation technique, is the health state utility value most commonly used by NICE (Brazier and Rowen 2011). Concerns about validity exist in areas of healthcare in which patients may have difficulty in responding meaningfully e.g. dementia or extreme ill health (Brazier and Longworth 2011).

HTA can be additionally weighted to favour disease states or sub-populations. If efficiency were to be the single driver for weighted QALYs, those contributing to society through their higher productivity would be weighted higher than those who contribute less; i.e. using a utility-weighted QALY (Dolan and Tsuchiya 2006). Age is also a factor when considering utility: productivity of young adults would be ascribed a higher utility than children or the elderly. An alternative approach is equity-weighted QALYs, targeting healthcare towards defined subgroups, aiming to improve the health of a population by raising the minimum health rather than improving the average. Possible considerations include favouring low socioeconomic subgroups (where multi-morbidity is high) or children.

The use of QALYs as an economic tool in HTA has been the subject of high profile debates in both public and professional forums. QALYs cannot take into account multi-morbidity or overall distribution of illness at a societal level. One difficulty is ascertaining who can and should, fairly and independently, establish the value of health and illness (Whitehead and Ali 2010).

20.5 The National Institute for Health and Clinical Excellence and Associated UK Bodies

Evaluating economic evidence for a drug, and judging clinical and cost effectiveness, is central to any publicly funded healthcare system. In the UK, three bodies undertake HTA, providing clinical and cost effectiveness advice to their respective NHS system. The National Institute for Health and Clinical Excellence (NICE) was formed in 1999 to appraise the clinical use and cost-effectiveness of drugs and currently provides advice for NHS (England) and Health and Social Care in

Northern Ireland. NICE only appraises drugs, typically in the context of reviewing management of a single disease, referred by the UK government's Department of Health (DoH). In Scotland, since 2002, the appraisal of all new drugs, including all new formulations and indications, for which manufacturers seek a licence is undertaken by the Scottish Medicines Consortium (SMC). In Wales, the All Wales Medicines Strategy Group (AWMSG) appraises all newly licensed medicines, formulations and indications not on the NICE work programme. NICE decisions are mandated, whereas those of SMC are advisory. The SMC publishes decisions more quickly than NICE. This has led to the use of single technology assessment to hasten NICE's decision-making process, but is still far slower, especially for cancer drugs (Ford et al. 2012). In general, the outcomes of the reviews at NICE, SMC and AWMSG are remarkably, and reassuringly, similar. Where differences have occurred, these can generally be attributed to whether a subset of the indication has been approved for a submission that has been rejected by the other body, or in relation to variations in time to evaluation, because the evidence base for evaluation usually grows over time, providing more confidence in clinical effectiveness (Table 20.2) (Bennie et al. 2011; Cairns 2006). Since its formation, NICE has gained a worldwide reputation for independence and objectivity through application of rigorous analytical methodology to HTA, and SMC has developed an assessment process that is sufficiently cost-effective to make other countries consider adopting it. Decisions from both are widely 'noted' by

Table 20.2 Characteristics of the UK HTA agencies (AWMSG has a similar role to the SMC, appraising all newly licensed medicines, formulations and indications not reviewed by NICE)

	NICE	SMC
Established	1999	2002
NHS system	NHS (England) and NHS Wales	NHS Scotland
Referrals	Technologies referred by the Department of Health	All UK newly licensed medicines/formulations/indications
Meetings	Twice monthly (in public)	Monthly (closed meeting)
Number of technologies reviewed in 2009 (Ford et al. 2012)	21	66
Time to Decision (months) (Ford et al. 2012)	Mean 21.40 (range 2–77)	Mean 7.35 (range 1–44)
Budget in 2013/2014 (Wilsdon et al. 2014)	£12 million	£1 million
Approval rate (with or without restriction; Ford et al. (2012))	91.1 %	80.4 %
Resubmissions	Rare	Encouraged when new evidence emerges
Appraises Orphans	Yes (no specific policy)	Yes (uses 'modifiers')
Patient Access Schemes (2013)	42	46
Role of industry	HTA information independently assessed by NICE	HTA case from the manufacturer reviewed by SMC

health services outside the UK. In part due to the UK's application of HTA, UK pricing of the most commonly prescribed branded products is now lower than 12 comparator countries (DoH 2012).

When the ICER is too high to allow a positive recommendation, 'modifiers' can be used to allow greater flexibility in certain circumstances. In Scotland, these can be used to allow acceptance of a higher ICER and a similar system exists for NICE. SMC 'modifiers' include: substantial improvement in life expectancy; substantial improvement in quality of life; a sub-group of patients who may derive extra benefit, to which the drug can be targeted; absence of other therapeutic options; possible bridging to definitive therapy; and licensed medications that are alternatives to unlicensed products already established in clinical practice (SMC 2013). The SMC may also accept greater uncertainty in the health economic evaluation of orphan drugs, defined as a medicine '*licensed for treating or preventing life-threatening rare diseases affecting fewer than 5 in 10,000 people in the European Union*' (EMA 2014a).

The cost effectiveness threshold is not a cut off: those drugs above threshold are likely to be rejected and those below threshold are likely to be accepted; but the threshold cannot be absolute. Distributive justice and clinical judgement usually prevail, and the threshold should instead be considered a sigmoid shaped cost-acceptability curve (Rawlins 2013). NICE currently uses a threshold of £20,000 per QALY ($34,000), a limit that is considered by many to be too high. Estimations of the marginal cost of a 'life year' saved is quite low, at around £8,000 ($13,600) for circulatory disease and £13,100 ($22,270) for cancer (Martin et al. 2007); this discrepancy likely reflects palliative intervention in the latter situation. Using a higher cost per QALY benchmark causes a displacement of cost, with the funding ultimately having to be withdrawn from another area of healthcare. However, since the QALY threshold has remained unchanged since 1999, not reflecting changes in inflation over the same period, in relative terms the threshold has drifted down substantially.

20.6 Patient Access Schemes

Patient access schemes (PAS) enable price reductions for drugs otherwise refused by HTA agencies on grounds of poor cost-effectiveness. A PAS is proposed by a pharmaceutical company and agreed with the appropriate authority, with the aim of improving cost-effectiveness, and enabling a positive recommendation.

In 2002, NICE conducted an appraisal of acetate glatiramer and beta-interferon for multiple sclerosis, ultimately refusing the drugs on the basis that the cost per QALY was estimated at £380,000–780,000 ($646,000–1,326,000) (NICE 2002). This decision was overturned by government following media coverage, and much lobbying from pharma and patient organisations, with the resultant multiple sclerosis 'risk sharing scheme' costing £50–100 m ($85–170 million) per year (Raftery 2010). Bortezomib, in 2007, was similarly refused by NICE on the basis that it substantially exceeded the cost per QALY threshold. In response, Johnson and Johnson, its manufacturer, agreed to 'payment by result', with the cost reimbursed to the NHS if the patient did not have an adequate response to treatment (Garber and McClellan 2007). Treatment failure was defined by failure to achieve a 25 % drop in serum M protein by the fourth cycle (Breckenridge and Walley 2008). Technically at least, this enabled the drug to be stopped earlier in non-responders, improving the cost-effectiveness of the intervention.

These proposals heralded the advent of PAS in 2009, two different types of which are currently in use: finance-based schemes, where the NHS receives a discount, and performance-based schemes, where the reimbursement is based on agreed clinical outcomes. Companies can propose finance-based schemes involving price cuts, which may take the form of a simple discount through to more complex offers of free stock at various stages of patient treatment. Alternatively, patient targeting can be used, with refunds provided if a patient fail to respond to treatment, improving cost effectiveness by correlating price to clinical outcome. At present, NICE have 42 PAS, 29 of which are simple discounts (NICE 2014a). SMC has 46 PAS, 43 of which are simple discounts. Crucially, discounts due to PAS are confidential, so drug companies can maintain the higher 'list price' in other countries.

Performance-based schemes involve clinical criteria for a 'positive' outcome proposed by the manufacturer. These schemes are intended to address issues of inadequate clinical evidence of benefit at the time of approval (Towse 2010). Approaches include a risk-sharing scheme in which price adjustment occurs in response to evolving evidence of benefit in clinical practice, in a manner pre-approved by NICE; a rebate scheme in which the list price of a drug will revert to a pre-agreed lower range if it does not perform as expected in clinical practice (the company consequently also pays a rebate); and a discounted introductory price in which the discount is lost if the company delivers evidence to support the list price of the drug. Performance-based schemes are unlikely to be effective for the NHS because they are dependent on physicians reporting treatment failures (Webb 2011). Even IT-based systems using hospital coding and measurement of outcome have proven to be ineffective (Green and Wintfeld 1993), so reporting by medical staff seems unrealistic and unfair. Evidence from drug safety surveillance has already identified lethargy as a principal factor associated with spontaneous under-reporting (Lopez-Gonzalez et al. 2009).

In 2010, when the UK government established the Cancer Drugs Fund with the government bill *Equity and Excellence—Liberating the NHS* (DoH 2010a), £200 m ($340 m) per year of governmental funds were allocated to support use of cancer drugs rejected by NICE due to high cost per QALY, a move not supported by the views of the UK general public (Linley and Hughes 2013). Later, in 2011, NICE relaxed the cost-effectiveness criteria affecting end-of-life-drugs, raising the QALY threshold for patients with a short life expectancy, if the intervention would likely extend life by more than 3 months. This decision was based on the assumption that the UK public would favour HTA weighted towards patients receiving end-of-life care. However, this assumption is being increasingly challenged (Collins and

Latimer 2013; Shah et al. 2014). Whilst patient access to these medications is much improved, government intervention to amend the standard NICE process has evolved into an expensive experience. It is sobering to reflect that the Multiple Sclerosis Risk Sharing Scheme, the Cancer Drugs Fund and the end-of-life decision making scheme have together cost the NHS almost £1,000 million ($1.7 billion), equivalent to 10 % of the annual NHS spend on drugs (Raftery 2013).

20.7 Value Based Pricing (VBP)

In 2007, a VBP system for drugs was proposed (OFT 2007) to provide a broader definition of value, update the current model of NICE appraisal, replace PPRS and staunch the fierce criticism surrounding negative decisions by NICE affecting access to new medicines. New arrangements were made to address these issues and bring prices and benefits in line, prioritising a move away from a drugs budget and towards a health budget (Sussex 2012).

20.8 What Are the Principles of VBP?

When framing VBP, the UK Health Secretary, Andrew Lansley said '*we will move to an NHS where patients will be confident that, where their clinicians believe a particular drug is the right and most effective one for them, then the NHS will be able to provide it for them*' (Boseley 2010; Webb 2011). The value of a drug would be derived from the effect of expenditure for each drug on overall utility at a societal level. Pharmaceutical companies would then be reimbursed according to this perceived value of the drug. The VBP approach aimed to overhaul HTA by rewarding additional factors that offer added value to society. These included wider societal benefit (such as the ability to return to work and benefit to carers), unmet clinical need, innovation and burden of illness (defined as '*as the number of QALYs lost by a patient because of their condition*' (NICE 2014b)).

The original UK VBP scheme was to be spearheaded by a Commission on the Value of Medicines, comprising NICE, SMC, AWMSG and the MHRA, and for HTA to be done by NICE, SMC and AWMSG (OFT 2007). Once a drug price had been determined by the Commission, the DoH would approach the manufacturer and negotiate a price, although it was anticipated the Commission would eventually subsume this step. This approach was consistent with a single UK price for medicines (Webb 2011).

Conceptually, the VBP approach has merit; accounting for direct and indirect benefits of therapy that are not captured using more traditional assessments of cost-effectiveness. Such VBP is designed to avoid high costs for drugs that have only moderate benefits, to encourage innovation, to provide a stable environment, and give an incentive for the pharmaceutical industry to focus drug development in areas of unmet clinical need (Webb 2011).

20.9 Key Issues

The perceived benefits of VBP, though desirable, remain largely theoretical in clinical practice. What evidence we do have of advantages from VBP are largely limited to case studies and have to be interpreted accordingly. The risks of VBP, similarly limited by lack of evidence, pose a threat to its implementation. Concerns that a new VBP system might undermine the better-established cost-benefit framework could ultimately be its greatest weakness (Dixon et al. 2011).

20.9.1 VBP Methodology

Consideration of burden of illness, wider societal benefits, and a judgement of future productivity and resource consumption, are additions to the concept of value, yet concerns exist regarding the methodology underpinning VBP (Claxton et al. 2008). The 'wider societal benefit' criterion represents a constitutional problem for most state-funded healthcare systems (Raftery 2013). Firstly, the NHS constitution is clear that services are dictated by clinical need and not by an individual's ability to pay (DoH 2013). If social utility becomes a 'modifier' for value, inevitably public funds will be channelled towards those with the potential for employment, skewing the system to favouring an individual's future income. Secondly, cost implications of future employability are very different depending on the methodology used (Claxton et al. 2008). It seems inevitable that some diseases and treatments will be favoured. Drugs extending survival in highly dependant states will accrue a higher cost per QALY in comparison to treatment that enables employment or reduced care requirements (Raftery 2013). This is particularly relevant if survival, but not productivity, improves. For example, a patient with dementia requiring fewer carers due to treatment would be prioritised over a patient with cancer, who may survive longer but not experience a change in resource consumption.

Where VBP is deployed, care will have to be taken to ensure that treatments currently available to patients remain accessible (DoH 2010b). This is difficult if consistent value is to be ensured. Clearly these inequalities and their unintended consequences resulting in removal or denial of treatment would lead to painful and difficult discussions with any patient or family. This has been resolved in the UK by reviewing only new drugs with the new VBP system, enabling access to medications accessed on the old HTA analysis for an interim period (DoH 2010b).

20.9.2 Cost Effectiveness Threshold

The responsibility of assessment authorities like NICE is to reliably signal what is of value. At present, it is the responsibility of the manufacturer to present a body of evidence and a fixed price for their drug. NICE's decision-making is therefore limited to agreement, refusal or limiting use to a defined subgroup but notably these decisions must be at this fixed price. The VBP scheme centres on reimbursement of the drug company of the value perceived by the healthcare provider. The price is negotiable and, as a result, could result in more drugs being made available to more patients. Under the VBP system, manufacturers may price to the upper cost threshold, resulting in a higher ICER. Conversely, drugs currently refused due to above-threshold ICERs may become available due to price negotiation. The net resultant effect would be greater availability of drugs at the detriment of increasing average cost per QALY (Webb and Walker 2007). Pricing to threshold would therefore result in either fewer total QALYs available to the health service, or a higher total drugs spend.

The cost-effectiveness threshold has a pivotal role in any healthcare assessment system. This system has to be rigorous, transparent and based on independent scientific analysis (The Health Committee 2008; Raftery 2013), criteria not always seen in practice. Only if this is ensured, can any disputes between assessment authority and manufacturer be resolved through explicit scientific questioning and further investigation (Claxton et al. 2008). Although a VBP scheme would result in refusals and restricted use, the responsibility would be appropriately shared between industry (for not accepting the value of the drug ascribed by HTA), and the assessment authority (for not being able to afford the wider use of drugs).

20.9.3 Pricing and Need for Evidence

There is no clear consensus on the type of evidence required for the value of a drug to be derived, or whether it can be effectively derived after it has been is approved for use. If the information gathered might have a negative effect on perceived value, positive initial guidance would clearly influence a manufacturer's incentive to gather further information. A VBP scheme would need a dynamic approach to on-going evaluation, with mandatory participation. In this circumstance, cluster control groups within the national framework would be unethical, because they would result in variation of patient access to treatment. Use of placebo, and recruiting patients to large blinded trials, would be impractical on the scale required. The onus therefore should be on drug companies to collate information and, as evidence emerges, VBP decisions would be reviewed; so-called 'coverage with evidence development' (Hutton et al. 2007). If clinical effectiveness and value cannot be proven in practice, then the price of the drug ought to be reduced, reflecting the lack of certainty surrounding its cost-effectiveness (Claxton et al. 2008). Furthermore, the quality of the evidence should be taken into account when initial pricing decisions are made, favouring drug companies that invest in high-quality clinical trials over those that do not (Claxton 2007).

This issue of accessing new drugs in a timely manner under conditions of acknowledged uncertainty is addressed by adaptive licensing (AL). AL provides a flexible approach to drug regulation by ensuring evolving information of benefit and harms in clinical practice. This would involve prospectively planned, stepwise evaluation and licensing of a new drug to target areas of doubt and improve clinical knowledge (Eichler et al. 2012). The European Medicine Agency (EMA) is currently undertaking a pilot project to explore the AL approach in clinical practice (EMA 2014b). Caution must be exercised with this regard as early licensing and shortened review times have been associated with negative outcomes, including drug safety withdrawal from market (Darrow et al. 2014). Furthermore, previous experience in implementing drug withdrawals from clinical practice, due to lack of proven efficiency, resulted in public opposition and delay in implementation (FDA 2011).

20.9.4 Value of Innovation

In Canada, 80 % of the rise in drug expenditure between 1998 and 2003 was attributed to 'me-too' drugs, new medicines that 'didn't offer a substantial improvement over existing drug products' (Morgan et al. 2005). One of the principal drivers for changing to VBP is to encourage innovation whilst containing cost. The pharmaceutical industry is concerned that relinquishing price freedom to the reimbursement system of VBP would favour breakthrough drugs over more incremental innovation (ABPI 2011). Me-too drugs have arguably improved cost effectiveness over recent decades. As an example, the ICER for antihypertensive therapies has decreased to an extent that the initial breakthrough drug would not be available today using current HTA criteria (Refoios Camejo et al. 2012); the reduction of the ICER likely reflecting a combination of reduced rate of adverse drug reactions, improved clinical effectiveness and industry competition. The clinical potential of an innovative technology cannot be fully recognised at the outset and attempts to do so could result in paying twice, once for innovation and then again for the additional clinical benefit (judged by clinical effectiveness), and may encourage investments that are not worthwhile (Claxton et al. 2008). If a drug is innovative enough to change outcome for patients, this benefit should already by captured using HTA approaches without any additional reimbursement for innovation.

Engagement between drug companies and government is clearly pivotal to inward investment, allowing a drug company's host nation to benefit from this profitable industry. Of particular note in the UK, countries that play host to drug companies also need to balance the costs of healthcare against the revenue from national industry. Drug pricing in the UK is used as a reference range for Europe, with patients often benefitting from earlier access to novel therapies (Collier 2007).

Pricing reform in the UK may result in this reference price being driven down, consequently causing a delay in, or even avoidance of, companies seeking a UK licence. This would be particularly relevant if the incremental benefit afforded by the drug was felt to be small (Taylor and Craig 2009), and, ultimately, could adversely affect UK patients.

In the UK, the Department for Business, Innovation and Skills (BIS) supports the UK science and research industry to help economic growth. £4,600 million ($7,820 million) per annum funding for research, development and innovation is invested through funding for science, appropriated by BIS between different sectors (Department for Business, Innovation and Skills 2014). On this basis, and given the remit of the NHS, it is hard to see why it should be asked to fund innovation, beyond the benefit it brings to patients.

20.10 Value Based Assessment

Despite early enthusiasm about VBP from DoH and ABPI, the initial proposals have evolved into something very different: value based assessment (VBA). VBP would have been a radical departure from currently negotiated pricing whilst VBA consists of only two new factors (burden of illness and wider societal benefits) added to the existing mix. DoH has attempted to estimate burden of illness using patient surveys, but the results have been viewed as inconsistent (Raftery 2012). Of note, patient surveys have underpinned one of the principal constraints of QALYs: failure to capture aspects of health in some disease states. Wider societal benefits will be assessed from demographic estimates provided by the DoH (Raftery 2013).

VBA will only affect new drugs launched after 2014 and will include a 5-year pricing deal, including a initial 2-year price freeze agreed with the relevant pharmaceutical company. The pharmaceutical industry responded critically to these proposed changes, stating '*a critical opportunity has been missed to improve the health of the British public . . .* [*and*] *has failed to break down the barriers which are currently preventing patients from being treated with the most cutting edge and effective new medicines available*' (Kearney et al. 2013).

In June 2013, the UK Government handed control of VBA to NICE, whilst the DoH retained control of price negotiation, meaning little change to the current UK HTA scheme. This has followed the Health and Social Care Act 2012, evolving the responsibilities of NICE to incorporate social care, a change hallmarked by rebranding to the National Institute for Health and Care Excellence (still NICE). Standards and guidance for social care are provided using an evidence-based model. This move underlines the potential for NICE to oversee quality-standards outside healthcare and provide guidance on wider social issues.

The delay in implementation of a UK VBP scheme has led to speculation that it may never materialise (Fernando and Moss 2013). Certainly, it seems to have been less political support since the replacement of Andrew Lansley as Secretary of State for Health.

20.11 Experience Elsewhere

The Act for Reform of the Pharmaceutical Market for Medicinal Products (Arzneimittelmarkt-Neuordnungsgesetz; AMNOG) was introduced in Germany in 2011. This represented a move to VBP as a cost-saving measure, similar to a rebate PAS. Under the new system, Germany's branded drugs can be launched at a free market price for 1 year, time in which pharmaceutical companies have to prove the value of new pharmaceuticals in clinical practice when compared to existing offerings. If, at the end of a year, the threshold of value is achieved on this evidence, companies can charge a premium; if not, prices are set in line with drugs achieving a similar effect, which includes cheaper generics. Following implementation of VBP, the price of patent protected drugs in Germany dropped significantly, resulting in a knock-on effect on the rest of Europe as reference prices were driven down. This has been met with accusations of inequality from the pharmaceutical industry (The Economist 2013). As a consequence of the drop in patent-protected drug prices, some companies have refused to seek a German market licence (Cullen 2011).

The Swedish healthcare system was updated in 2002 and includes a reimbursement scheme. Following its introduction, an intrinsic problem with under-prescribing has emerged from the Swedish system, highlighting the difficulties in VBP implementation. Reimbursement decisions are taken at a national level, but decisions on indication are undertaken regionally. This has resulted in restricted prescribing, due to regional cost containment concerns, for indications in which the drug has proven value (Persson et al. 2012).

VBP remains largely theoretical, and pivotal conclusions have been drawn from a handful of case studies. One seminal study concluded that VBP allowed for effective risk-sharing of investment (between healthcare services and industry) and sufficient patient access to pharmaceuticals (Willis et al. 2010). The experience from Sweden would certainly suggest an overall cost saving following national implementation of VBP but, during this time, similar patterns of reduced drug expenditure were seen in European countries not using VBP (European Commission 2012). Reallocation of revenue will undoubtedly occur with VBP but this does not necessarily translate into saving in overall spend, especially if there is pricing to the threshold (Webb and Walker 2007).

Given diverse approaches to implementation, VBP in other countries has afforded little insight as to how a UK system could be shaped and the effects it could have. The pharmaceutical industry will certainly closely monitor the developing situation in Europe, alongside patient groups concerned about limiting access to health technologies and higher drug bills.

20.12 Future Focus

The opportunity to replace an out-dated pricing system with a newer, value based one still has attractions. Healthcare provision has already benefited from HTA and PAS, but improvements could be made. Significant benefits in reduced drug spend, enhanced innovation and diversion of development to areas of unmet clinical need, could result from a VBP scheme. Although the concerns surrounding VBP may be occasionally construed as scaremongering, the dangers of compromising the established healthcare system cannot be understated and concern about this risk may undermine future reform. The pharmaceutical industry is clearly concerned about adverse effects on profitability, and may obstruct such developments. Ultimately, the risk of such a scheme would be shouldered by the patient and could adversely affect public health.

References

ABPI (2011) Value-based pricing: key recommendations from ABPI. ABPI. http://www.abpi.org.uk/media-centre/newsreleases/2011/Pages/140311.aspx. Accessed 24 June 2014

Bennie M, Dear J, Hems S et al (2011) An investigation into the effect of advice from the Scottish Medicines Consortium on the use of medicines in Scotland's Health Service. Br J Clin Pharmacol 71:283–288

Boseley S (2010) NICE to lose powers to decide on new drugs. The Guardian, 29 Oct. http://www.guardian.co.uk/politics/2010/oct/29/nice-to-lose-new-drug-power. Accessed 24 June 2014

Brazier J, Longworth L (2011). NICE DSU technical support document 8: an introduction to the measurement and valuation of health for NICE submission. NICE Decision Support Unit. http://www.nicedsu.org.uk/Utilities-TSD-series(2391676).htm. Accessed 24 June 2014

Brazier J, Rowen D (2011). NICE DSU technical support document 11: alternatives to EQ-5D for generating health state utility values. NICE Decision Support Unit. http://www.nicedsu.org.uk/Utilities-TSD-series(2391676).htm. Accessed 24 June 2014

Breckenridge A, Walley T (2008) Risk sharing and payment by results. Clin Pharmacol Ther 83:666–667

Cairns J (2006) Providing guidance to the NHS: the Scottish Medicines Consortium and the National Institute for Clinical Excellence compared. Health Policy 76:134–143

Claxton K (2007) OFT, VBP: QED? Health Econ 16:545–558

Claxton K, Briggs A, Buxton MJ et al (2008) Value based pricing for NHS drugs: an opportunity not to be missed? BMJ 336:251

Collier J (2007) The pharmaceutical price regulation scheme. BMJ 334:435–436

Collins M, Latimer N (2013) NICE's end of life decision making scheme: impact on population health. BMJ 346:f1363

Cullen A (2011) Boehringer, Lilly won't introduce Trajenta in Germany on pricing. Bloomberg. http://www.bloomberg.com/news/2011-09-02/boehringer-lilly-won-t-introduce-trajenta-in-germany-on-pricing.html. Accessed 24 June 2014

Darrow JJ, Avorn J, Kesselheim AS (2014) New FDA breakthrough-drug category—implications for patients. N Engl J Med 370:1252–1258

Davis K, Stremikis K, Squires D et al (2014) Mirror, mirror on the wall: how the performance of the US healthcare system compares internationally. The Commonwealth Fund. http://www.

commonwealthfund.org/publications/fund-reports/2014/jun/mirror-mirror. Accessed 24 June 2014

Department for Business, Innovation and Skills (2014) Innovations report: innovation, research and skills. Department for Business, Innovation and Skills. https://www.gov.uk/government/uploads/system/uploads/attachment_data/file/293635/bis-14-p188-innovation-report-2014-revised.pdf. Accessed 24 June 2014

Dixon S, Tsuchiya A, Bazier J, et al (2011) Proceed with caution: an economic perspective on the UK's value based pricing proposals. The University of Sheffield. HEDS discussion paper (Unpublished). http://eprints.whiterose.ac.uk/42942/. Accessed 24 June 2014

DoH (2010a) Equality and excellence—liberating the NHS. Department of Health. https://www.gov.uk/government/uploads/system/uploads/attachment_data/file/213823/dh_117794.pdf. Accessed 23 June 2014

DoH (2010b) A new value based approach for the pricing of branded medicines—a consultation. Department of Health. http://webarchive.nationalarchives.gov.uk/20130107105354/http://www.dh.gov.uk/prod_consum_dh/groups/dh_digitalassets/@dh/@en/documents/digitalasset/dh_122793.pdf. Accessed 24 May 2014

DoH (2012) The pharmaceutical price regulation scheme: eleventh report to parliament. Department of Health. https://www.gov.uk/government/publications/pharmaceutical-price-regulation-scheme-11th-report-to-parliament. Accessed 24 June 2014

DoH (2013) NHS Constitution. Department of Health. https://www.gov.uk/government/publications/the-nhs-constitution-for-england. Accessed 23 June 2014

Dolan P, Tsuchiya A (2006) The elicitation of distributional judgements in the context of economic evaluation. In: Jones A (ed) Companion to health economics, 1st edn. Elgar, Northampton

Eichler HG, Oye K, Baird LG et al (2012) Adaptive licensing: taking the next step in the evolution of drug approval. Clin Pharmacol Ther 3:426–437

EMA (2014a) Orphan designation. European Medicines Agency. http://www.ema.europa.eu/ema/index.jsp?curl=pages/regulation/general/general_content_000029.jsp. Accessed 24 June 2014

EMA (2014b) Pilot project on adaptive licensing. European Medicines Agency. http://www.ema.europa.eu/ema/index.jsp?curl=pages/news_and_events/news/2014/03/news_detail_002046.jsp&mid=WC0b01ac058004d5c1. Accessed 24 June 2014

European Commission (2012). Cost-containment policies in public pharmaceutical spending in the EU. Directorate-General for Economic and Financial Affairs, European Commission. http://bookshop.europa.eu/en/cost-containment-policies-in-public-pharmaceutical-spending-in-the-eu-pbKCAI12461/. Accessed 24 June 2014

FDA (2011). Proposal to withdraw approval for the breast cancer indication for Avastin (bevacizumab): decision of the Commissioner. Department of Health and Human Services, Food and Drug Administration. http://www.fda.gov/downloads/NewsEvents/Newsroom/UCM280546.pdf. Accessed 24 June 2014

Fernando S, Moss A (2013) UK value-based pricing will struggle to materialise as year-end deadline approaches. The FT. http://www.ft.com/cms/s/2/db268c82-8be8-11e2-b001-00144feabdc0.html#axzz30wzZCRUu. Accessed 23 June 2014

Ford JA, Waugh N, Sharma P et al (2012) NICE guidance: a comparative study of the introduction of the single technology appraisal process and comparison with guidance from Scottish Medicines Consortium. BMJ Open 2:e000671

Garber AM, McClellan MB (2007) Satisfaction guaranteed—'payment by results' for biologic agents. N Engl J Med 357:1575–1577

Green J, Wintfeld N (1993) How accurate are hospital discharge data for evaluating effectiveness of care? Med Care 31:719–731

HM Treasury (2012) Public expenditure: statistical analyses 2012. HM Treasury. https://www.gov.uk/government/publications/public-expenditure-statistical-analyses-2012. Accessed 24 June 2014

Hutton J, Trueman P, Henshall C (2007) Coverage with evidence development: an examination of conceptual and policy issues. Int J Technol Assess Health Care 23:425–435

Kearney J, Pearce S, Burgin N et al (2013) The pharmaceutical giants' letter: in full. The Telegraph, 14 Nov 2013. http://www.telegraph.co.uk/finance/newsbysector/pharmaceuticalsandchemicals/10449540/The-pharmaceutical-giants-letter-in-full.html. Accessed 24 June 2014

Leopold C, Vogler S, Mantel-Teeuwisse A et al (2012) Differences in external price referencing in Europe: a descriptive overview. Health Policy 104:50–60

Linley WG, Hughes DA (2013) Societal views on NICE, Cancer Drugs Fund and value based pricing criteria for prioritizing medicines: a cross sectional survey of 4118 adults in Great Britain. Health Econ 22:948–964

Lopez-Gonzalez E, Herdeiro MT, Figueiras A (2009) Determinants of under-reporting of adverse drug reactions: a systematic review. Drug Saf 32:19–31

Martin S, Rice N, Smith PC (2007) The link between health care spending and health outcomes: evidence from English programme budgeting data. The Health Foundation. http://www.health.org.uk/publications/programme-budgeting-report/. Accessed 24 June 2014

Morgan SG, Bassett KL, Wright JM et al (2005) "Breakthrough" drugs and growth in expenditure on prescription drugs in Canada. BMJ 331:815

NHS Information Centre (2013) Prescriptions dispensed in the community: England, statistics for 2002–2012. NHS Information centre. http://www.hscic.gov.uk/catalogue/PUB06941. Accessed 24 June 2014

NICE (2002) Health Technology Assessment No 32—Beta interferon and glatiramer acetate for the treatment of multiple sclerosis. NICE. http://guidance.nice.org.uk/TA32/Guidance/pdf/English. Accessed 24 June 2014

NICE (2014a) List of technologies with approved patient access schemes, recommended by NICE for use in the NHS. NICE. http://www.nice.org.uk/aboutnice/howwework/paslu/ListOfPatientAccessSchemesApprovedAsPartOfANICEAppraisal.jsp. Accessed 24 June 2014

NICE (2014b) Methods of technology appraisal consultation: burden of illness briefing paper. NICE Decision support unit. http://www.nice.org.uk/getinvolved/currentniceconsultations/MethodsOfTechnologyAppraisalConsultation2014.jsp?domedia=1&mid=FE327531-EDE9-5747-133DB5A5F835A980. Accessed 24 June 2014

OECD (2013) OECD: health statistics 2013. OECD. http://www.oecd.org/els/health-systems/oecdhealthdata2013-frequentlyrequesteddata.htm. Accessed 24 June 2014

OFT (2007) The pharmaceutical price regulation scheme: an OFT market study. Office of Fair Trading. http://webarchive.nationalarchives.gov.uk/20140402142426/http://www.oft.gov.uk/OFTwork/markets-work/pprs. Accessed 24 June 2014

Osborne M, Evans TW (1994) Allocation of resources in intensive care: a transatlantic perspective. Lancet 343:778–780

Persson U, Svensson J, Pettersson B (2012) New reimbursement system for innovative pharmaceuticals combining value-based and free market pricing. Appl Health Econ Health Policy 10:217–225

Polinder S, Toet H, Pannemen M et al (2011) Methodological approaches for cost-effectiveness and cost-utility analysis of injury prevention measures. The World Health Organisation. http://www.euro.who.int/en/health-topics/disease-prevention/violence-and-injuries/publications/2011/methodological-approaches-for-costeffectiveness-and-costutility-analysis-of-injury-prevention-measures/. Accessed 24 June 2014

Raftery J (2010) Multiple sclerosis risk sharing scheme: a costly failure. BMJ 340:c1672

Raftery J (2012) Moving to value based pricing: adjusting costs. BMJ Group blogs. http://blogs.bmj.com/bmj/2012/11/20/james-raftery-moving-to-value-based-pricing-adjusting-costs/. Accessed 23 June 2014

Raftery J (2013) Value based pricing: can it work? BMJ 347:f5941

Rawlins M (2013) NICE, the first 14 years. Keynote lecture at EACPT Summer School, EACPT, Edinburgh, 5 July 2013

Refoios Camejo R, McGrath C, Herings R et al (2012) Antihypertensive drugs: a perspective on pharmaceutical price erosion and its impact on cost-effectiveness. Value Health 15:381–388

Shah K, Tsuchiya A, Risa Hole A et al (2014) Valuing health at the end of life: an empirical study of public preferences. J Health Econ 15:389–399

SMC (2013) Modifiers used in appraising new medicines. Scottish Medicines Consortium. http://www.scottishmedicines.org/About_SMC/Policy_Statements/SMC_Modifiers_used_in_Appraising_New_Medicines. Accessed 24 June 2013

Sussex (2012) The emerging picture of 'Value Based Pricing'. Office of Health Economics Kakushen Web based Conference. http://www.slideshare.net/OHENews/emerging-picutre-of-value-based-pricing. Accessed 24 June 2014

Taylor D, Craig T (2009) Value based pricing for NHS medicines: magic bullet, counterfeit treatment or the mixture as before? Health Econ Policy Law 4:515–526

The Economist (2013) UK/Germany: a question of value. The Economist. http://www.eiu.com/industry/article/41253588/ukgermany-a-question-of-value/2013-11-20. Accessed 24 June 2014

The Health Committee (2008) National Institute for Health and Clinical Excellence: first report of the health committee 2007–2008. House of Commons. Stationery Office, London

Towse A (2010) Value based pricing, research and development, and patient access schemes. Will the United Kingdom get it right or wrong? Br J Clin Pharmacol 70:360–366

Webb DJ (2011) Value-based medicine pricing: NICE work. Lancet 377:1552–1553

Webb DJ, Walker A (2007) Value-based pricing of drugs in the UK. Lancet 369:1415–1416

Whitehead SJ, Ali S (2010) Health outcomes in economic evaluation: the QALY and utilities. Br Med Bull 96:5–21

Willis M, Persson U, Zoellner Y et al (2010) Reducing uncertainty in value-based pricing using evidence development agreements: the case of continuous intraduodenal infusion of levodopa/carbidopa (Duodopa®) in Sweden. Appl Health Econ Health Policy 8:377–386

Wilsdon T, Fiz E, Haderi A (2014) A comparative analysis of the role and impact of Health Technology Assessment: 2013. PhRMA. http://www.crai.co.uk/ConsultingExpertise/listing.aspx?tID=900&subtID=0&tertID=0&fID=34. Accessed 27 June 2014

Chapter 21
Drug Prices and Incentives to Innovation by the Pharmaceutical Industry

Rosella Levaggi and Paolo Pertile

Abstract In the recent past, pharmaceutical expenditure has been steadily increasing, but the productivity of the sector—measured as the number of New Molecular Entities (NMEs)—has been decreasing. In this chapter we review and analyse the price regulation policies that are currently used by regulators worldwide and we will describe the salient features of these policies from a public health point of view. We will also discuss this in terms of their impact on innovation.

21.1 Introduction

Total expenditure for drugs across OECD countries in 2011 was estimated over USD800 billion, accounting for around 17 % of current health spending, with large variations across countries. Between 2000 and 2009, average spending on pharmaceuticals rose by around 50 % in real terms (OECD 2013), although it declined slightly in the following years because of the economic crisis.

Pharmaceutical price regulation is very heterogeneous across countries and includes, for example, direct price regulation through a negotiation process (e.g. France and Italy) and indirect price regulation through limits on reimbursement under social insurance programmes (e.g. Germany and Japan) (Danzon and Chao 2000; Capri and Levaggi 2007). The market is far from perfectly competitive even in systems where the role of the public sector is more limited. For instance, in the US pharmaceutical companies need to lobby big insurance companies to list their drugs among those that are reimbursable.

R. Levaggi (✉)
Department of Economics and Management, University of Brescia, Via San Faustino, 74b, Brescia 25122, Italy
e-mail: rosella.levaggi@unibs.it

P. Pertile
Department of Economics, University of Verona, Via dell'Artigliere, 19, Verona 37129, Italy
e-mail: paolo.pertile@univr.it

Z.-U.-D. Babar (ed.), *Pharmaceutical Prices in the 21st Century*,
DOI 10.1007/978-3-319-12169-7_21

Regulatory objectives are characterized by the trade-off between incentives to R&D investments for the industry and value for money for consumers. Regulatory solutions also seem to be changing over time; bargaining processes between the industry and the regulator, with uncertain outcomes, tend to be replaced by more transparent mechanisms with more predictable outcomes, such as reference pricing (Dickson and Redwood 1998), cost-effectiveness thresholds (Jena and Philipson 2008; Appleby et al. 2009), value based schemes and risk sharing agreements (De Pouvourville 2006; Cook et al. 2008; Adamski et al. 2010; Appleby et al. 2009).

The use of regulation, whatever the form it takes, is the subject of some controversy. Opponents argue that strict regulation may adversely affect incentives to develop new and better products because producers are not adequately reimbursed for the investments needed to bring new drugs to the market (Danzon and Chao 2000). The sharp decrease in the productivity of R&D spending from the industry is often referred to as evidence. In 2003, pharmaceutical companies invested more than US$33 billion in R&D worldwide compared to about US$13 billion just a decade before, but the number of new molecular entities (NMEs) approved by the Food and Drug Administration (FDA) in the US declined from 53 in 1996 to only 26 in 2010 (PhRMA 2011). DiMasi et al. (2003) report evidence of an increasing trend in the average R&D cost of new drugs. More recently, Pammolli et al. (2011) have empirically investigated the decline in productivity of the pharmaceutical industry since 1990 and argued that pricing mechanisms may be responsible for this decline.

On the other hand, public health care expenditure growth is a major concern for policy makers across industrialised countries. In Europe, where about 75 % of pharmaceutical expenditure is public, Governments are responding to the budgetary pressure resulting from the price dynamics with more stringent price regulation (Carone et al. 2012; Panos et al. 2010; OECD 2011).

The trade-off between access to new health care technologies and expenditure affordability has been extensively investigated by the literature. In most of these contributions the availability of innovations is taken as a fact. However, the body of empirical literature referred to above suggests that this should not be taken as granted.

In this chapter, we are taking a closer look at regulation by comparing several approaches to price regulation. In particular, we will study price setting through listing and we will compare it with other instruments such as the use of cost effectiveness thresholds, value based pricing and risk sharing arrangements. Our analysis aims to highlight the properties of alternative regulatory policies with respect to the balance between short-run objectives such as expenditure control and long-run incentives to investment in R&D.

21.2 The Problem Faced by the Regulator

The market for new drugs is not perfectly competitive for several well-known reasons.[1] The demand side is characterized by uncertainty on the effectiveness of the drug and patients' inability to translate their need for improved health into the demand for a specific treatment. The ensuing agency relationship between the patient and the physician[2] means that choice of the drug is largely entrusted to the latter, with a possible distortion of the market. Finally, the presence of a form of insurance (either private or public) means that patients do not pay for drugs directly. On the supply side, the market competition is limited by patents and severe restrictions and controls in the production and marketing process. The combination of all these market failures makes it closer to the monopoly-monopsony model than to perfect competition.

Regulation takes place in a highly uncertain environment, and involves several agents with different levels of information. The distinction between *efficacy* and *effectiveness* is fundamental for a better understanding of the problem. Efficacy is the theoretical improvement in health that can be obtained through health care. For drugs, efficacy corresponds to the impact on relevant patient outcomes, as observed in a clinical trial. Effectiveness is the actual impact that will be experienced by patients receiving the treatment through the real medical practice. Ideally, the effectiveness of a new drug should be very close to its efficacy. What is observed in practice is that effectiveness is often lower than efficacy. In some cases, the difference is unexpectedly large.[3] This complicates the task for the regulator, because pricing is usually decided on the basis of efficacy, but the actual benefit for patients depends on effectiveness. This source of uncertainty can well be asymmetric: in fact the industry may have better information than the regulator on the likely gap between efficacy and effectiveness. The reported efficacy of the drug increases the probability of being listed and, possibly, of obtaining a high price.

The number of patients to consider eligible for the use of the new drug is, at least to some extent, an additional choice that the pharmaceutical company has to make. A larger number of patients may reduce the probability of approval, due to the increased impact on the insurer's budget. However, conditional on adoption, it also increases profits.

Let's consider the case of a new drug that is about to be launched on the market and should be made available to n patients. To keep the example simple we assume that the efficacy of the drug is the same for all patients eligible for the treatment and that it does not depend on the number of patients actually treated. Due to

[1] Zweifel et al. (2009), Chap. 12.

[2] See Barigozzi and Levaggi (2008) and references therein.

[3] There may be several reasons for this, including patient compliance, interactions among different drugs in patients with co-morbidities and the behaviour of physicians that may prescribe drugs also to patients that will not fully benefit from the drug.

uncertainty on effectiveness, the benefit of the drug may vary in the range (0,B) with an expected value equal to b. The monetary value of one unit of the health benefit is equal to λ, so that λbn is the total expected health gain, in money terms. Since we assume, without loss of generality, that there are no other drugs that can treat these patients, this is also the monetary value of the incremental benefit. Let's also assume that the marginal cost to produce the drug is c. Before this, the company has paid I, which is the cost of developing the new product.

The price level defines how the gains—monetary and related to better health outcomes—are split between consumers and the industry. The first component is defined as consumer surplus and can be written as:

$$S = (\lambda b - p)n,$$

while the second (producer surplus) is the profit for the pharmaceutical company:

$$\Pi = (p - c)n - I.$$

A price close to λb means that there is hardly any gain for patients, whereas the company profits are comparatively large.[4] On the other hand, a price very close to c means that the industry will make a limited profit and may not be able to cover the sunk investment I. This raises the issue of whether a sufficient incentive is provided to the industry to make further investments in R&D.

The regulatory framework is complicated by additional considerations:

- the potential gap between efficacy and effectiveness that was discussed above, on which the company could be better informed;
- the asymmetry of information between the regulator and the industry. The willingness to pay for health gains may be private information to the regulator, while c and I can be observed only by the industry.

In this framework, defining an optimal policy for adoption and pricing of new products is very difficult. Below we present some of the solutions that are currently used by regulators in different countries, and discuss the main implications of the choice.

21.3 Pricing Through Listing

The schemes used to list new drugs are country-specific mechanisms whose essential features are the following:

[4] Of course, patients are often insured. In this case the argument remains valid, although the cost will be borne by the insurer.

- the pharmaceutical company faces uncertainty on the decision made by the regulator
- a lower Incremental Cost-Effectiveness Ratio (ICER) and a lower expected impact on budget positively affect the probability of success (Zaric and O'Brien 2005)

The industry applies for listing and proposes a price; the regulator may accept it or not. The decision depends on the value of the ICER. Assuming that no alternative treatment exists for the patient, the ICER can be written as

$$ICER = \frac{p}{b}$$

As mentioned in Levaggi (2014), we assume the existence of a range of values of the ICER such that the probability of the drug being approved is positive, but the regulator could still decide not to list it. If the drug is too costly, the regulator has no interest in reimbursing it because consumer surplus goes to zero. The upper limit of the range is:

$$T = \frac{\lambda b}{b} = \lambda$$

Let the lower limit of the range be denoted by the parameter β, which is set by the regulator. If the ICER is less than β the regulator always lists it. For prices in the range $p_\lambda < p < p_\beta$ the regulator may agree to list the drug or not, and the probability is directly related to the distance between the ICER proposed and λ. Let's assume that the probability of being listed can be described by the following function

$$Pr = \frac{\lambda - c_E}{\lambda - \beta},$$

where $c_E = \frac{p}{A/2}$. The probability is equal to zero for $ICER = \lambda$. In this case the price of the new drug is so high that society would not have any benefit, and the drug is not listed. For $ICER = \beta$ the drug is such good value for money that the regulator always list*s* it. In this environment the industry will ask for the price that maximises its expected profit.

Barros and Levaggi (2011) and Levaggi (2014) showed that this system is not welfare maximizing, although it allows a price to be set such that the benefits from innovation are equally split between patients and the industry. The reason is that the regulator, in the quest to avoid the industry tasking for the maximum price, ends up not listing some drugs which are good value for money. This second best strategy has been referred to in the literature[5]; in some contexts it may be the only second

[5] See Dulleck and Kerschbamer (2006). For applications to health care see Barigozzi and Levaggi (2008).

best option for the regulator, but in the market for drugs there may be better alternatives.

This system has several drawbacks: it lacks transparency, its outcome depends on the bargaining abilities of the actors, it may lead to relevant differences in the payment for unit of effectiveness across drugs, and it may not guarantee good value for money. This may lead regulators to delay listing in order to reduce uncertainty and get better value for money (Griffin et al. 2011).

21.4 Value Based Pricing

Value-based pricing is a strategy which sets prices primarily on the value, perceived or estimated, to the customer rather than on the cost of the product or historical prices. These schemes are far from new; Loeb and Magat (1979) have suggested their use for public utility while Gravelle (1998) has presented possible application to drug pricing. In this section we will present different ways that have been used by regulators to implement these schemes.

21.4.1 True Value Based Schemes

In this case, the price is set according to a "pure" value based scheme and the price of the new drug strictly depends on the (incremental) cost-effectiveness of the new drug. The price of the new drug will then be

$$p = v\lambda b$$

where $v\lambda$ is the maximum price the regulator is willing to pay for a unit of effectiveness and $v < 1$. Danzon et al. (2013) show how value based schemes can be used to determine the price of new drugs at international level. In particular, $v\lambda$ depends on the income of each country and the level of insurance. The price will be higher the higher the income and the lower the elasticity of demand, which in this model is related to the level of insurance protection (either private or public).

21.4.2 C/E Threshold

The idea behind C/E threshold schemes is to reduce the uncertainty and the welfare loss deriving from listing processes (see Sect. 21.3). As we noted in the previous section, listing has some important drawbacks: it forces the regulator to deny listing to some drugs even if they are good value for money; the price may be significantly affected by the bargaining power of the parties negotiating. In this case, the regulator only sets a level of the ICER beyond which it will not grant listing, thus eliminating the uncertainty which is typical of the listing process. If we use the notation of the previous section, the maximum ICER is equal to λ; hence the maximum price will be

$$p_{max} = \lambda b$$

Any price below this level will grant the industry listing, i.e. the reimbursement of the new drug. The industry can then set the price of the new drug as in the listing process, but in this case it knows that if it asks $p < p_{max}$ listing will be granted.

However, if the industry was granted this price, all the benefit from introducing the new drug would be turned into profit for the industry. For this reason, the regulator may set a lower threshold level, $\rho\lambda$ (with $0 \leq \rho \leq 1$). The scheme reduces the uncertainty with respect to the listing process, as long as $\rho\lambda$ can be observed by the industry. R&D costs do not play any explicit role in this framework (Jena and Philipson 2008, 2009). This means that different drugs with the same effectiveness, but potentially very different production/research costs, would be paid the same price. This may provide an incentive for the industry to invest in R&D only in the most profitable areas. One way to tackle this problem would be to tailor thresholds to the type of drugs. In other words, the regulator may decide a specific ρ for each sub-market, but this process is highly discretionary.

21.5 Risk Sharing

Once the drug has been introduced, almost all regulatory systems require greater effort in the post-marketing monitoring of drugs, not only from a purely medical perspective (De Pouvourville 2006). Public authorities, in fact, schedule procedures to control the drug for possible side effects. Until recently only few regulators had verified the real ex post value for money of the drug. This failure to verify efficacy and volume ex post creates perverse effects on the regulatory system. The industry, in fact, may have an interest in overestimating the efficacy and underestimating the number of people that will benefit from the drug in the listing process, as long as these parameters are not monitored ex-post by the regulator.

In general, verifying the discrepancy between efficacy and effectiveness may be very costly because of the number of patients involved and the tests needed to determine the drug's effectiveness. In areas where the patient's response to a drug can be objectively measured, such as oncology, monitoring may be less complicated than in others. In Italy, for instance, a specific registry for expensive cancer drugs has been created and for some of these drugs a variety of risk-sharing schemes are applied.[6] The patient is registered in the website and treatment is

[6] See http://antineoplastici.agenziafarmaco.it/

initially paid for by the Italian NHS (Servizio Saniario Nazionale). If treatment fails (disease progression or unacceptable toxicity at or before the agreed time), the pharmaceutical company reimburses (money or corresponding amount of drug) the whole delivered treatment or a set percent of it. An example for the UK is Janssen-Cilag's Velcade (bortezomib, see NICE 2007) in which patients who demonstrate a 50 % response rate at first relapse are eligible to continue treatment on the NHS, otherwise the manufacturer refunds the NHS. Adamski et al. (2010) review the principal agreements in this area and argue that there are two types of risk sharing: performance-based and financial-based contracts.

Performance-based contracts focus on the effectiveness of the new drug, whereas risk-sharing financial-based agreements involve expenditure considerations.

A performance-based risk-sharing agreement can be illustrated in the following way. The industry proposes to sell the new drug at a price p, but ex post, if the level of effectiveness e falls below a threshold d, a rebate on the price is applied and the firm has to pay back pk so that the price is

$$\begin{cases} p(1-k) & e < d, \\ p & e \geq d, \end{cases}$$

where d is the benefit on which the price is determined, e is the ex post benefit of the drug, which lies in the interval [0,B], p is the price asked by the industry and k is the rebate on the price asked by the regulator if the effectiveness falls below d. Assuming a uniform distribution for e in the range [0,B], the expected price under this scheme is defined by:

$$p^R = p - kp\int_0^d \frac{1}{B} de = p\left(1 - k\frac{d}{B}\right)$$

The formula is asymmetric since the industry pays a penalty if the ex post effectiveness falls short of the declared level, but it will not be rewarded if the drug is more effective than declared. The reason for this asymmetry mainly depends on the consideration that the industry may have better information than the regulator on the likely effects of the drug, hence it has a strong advantage in setting this parameter.

Towse and Garrison (2010) show that, from a purely economic point of view, most of these schemes should in fact be classified as risk shifting agreements since they are in fact designed to reduce the price paid for the drug. The industry may prefer this scheme to a straightforward price reduction for several reasons. In some markets the pharmaceutical company has a high incentive to show similar ex-factory prices across countries in order to assure an homogeneous pricing policy. Therefore, they are willing to accept the imposition of "undisclosed" discounts/ rebates which are part of the non-transparent risk-sharing agreement. The final result of the scheme (i.e. whether it is risk sharing or risk shifting) is mainly determined by the negotiation rules the regulator foresees. If, as seems to happen in several countries, risk sharing is used to increase the probability of listing new drugs, the effect of risk sharing agreements are less clear-cut than the present literature seems to suggest.

In order to evaluate the impact of risk sharing it is necessary to study its effect on price (Barros 2011) and on the expected profits of the industry and it is also necessary to distinguish between an uncertain listing process and value-based schemes where the uncertainty on the listing basically disappears.

Barros and Levaggi (2011) shows the effects of risk sharing on an uncertain listing process. In general, the expected price paid under risk sharing is lower than without this scheme, hence supporting Towse and Garrison (2010) argument. However, the expected profit may be larger under risk sharing. In particular, if the rebate for not hitting the target level of efficacy is sufficiently small and the listing process takes account of the rebate, the expected profit for the industry may be larger under this scheme.

Levaggi (2014) analyses the effects of a switch from an uncertain listing process to a value-based pricing scheme with risk sharing. In this case, risk sharing may be necessary in order to grant value for money to consumers. The interesting result of this paper is that if the rebate on the price is chosen appropriately, both consumer surplus and expected profit may be greater than under listing, i.e. value-based with risk sharing may be considered a Pareto improvement. In general, risk sharing should be inversely related to the price of the new drug, i.e. the schemes for drugs whose marginal production cost is relatively high should involve lower rebates.

21.6 Effects on Innovation

As discussed in Sect. 21.2 overall efficiency requires the price of the innovation to be neither too high, in which case patients who could benefit from a treatment might have no access to it, nor too low, because this would weaken the incentive to invest in R&D by the industry. The search for a balance between these competing objectives is sometimes referred to as the trade-off between static efficiency—ensuring access to the innovation—and dynamic efficiency—creating the conditions for innovation in the future. Although social insurance systems like those operating in most developed countries allow mitigation of this trade-off by allowing the patient not to face the full cost of the treatment Lakdawalla and Sood (2009), the complexity of the framework is such that an efficient regulatory policy is hard to characterize. Most of the literature on pharmaceutical regulation has focused on static efficiency, thus neglecting the implications for dynamic efficiency.

Among those contributions that have tried to explore the relationship between the two efficiency dimensions, Filson (2012) studies the welfare impact of pharmaceutical price controls by contrasting the US, where non-regulated market prices prevail, with most of the other countries that control prices. Price controls have mainly three types of impacts: they have short-term (positive) effects on consumer (patient) welfare; they tend to reduce the market value of pharmaceutical companies; they reduce the incentive to invest in new R&D projects. Filson (2012) concludes that in his baseline scenario consumers in the United States tend to be better-off without price regulation: long-term losses in static efficiency due to regulation outweigh short-term gains in static efficiency. One interesting consideration emerging from this analysis is that different countries may find different positions with respect to price regulation more or less convenient, depending on how important the pharmaceutical industry is in that country. Long-term benefits from one country abandoning price controls accrue to consumers in other countries, because they will benefit from the future flow of new products, without bearing the short-term costs of abandoning price regulation. This may induce some countries to free-ride on others.

Other contributions in the literature have focused more specifically on the impact of the specific regulatory regimes that were previously discussed. Jena and Philipson (2008) highlight the central role of the threshold value of (λ) in determining the allocation of surplus between consumers and producers and hence the incentive to invest in R&D. Danzon et al. (2013) show that with universal insurance, value-based prices can be second-best static and dynamic efficient within and across countries. In their model the price of the drug is different across countries and it reflects the different willingness/ability to pay of each nation. If the price*s* are set correctly, their method allows drugs to be introduced at the appropriate time (when their marginal benefit is equal to the marginal cost) and the price differentials are proportional to the different level of benefit each country receives through the adoption of a new drug.

One of the main concerns arising from the spreading of risk-sharing agreements like those described in Sect. 21.5 is related to their impact on the incentive to invest in R&D. In particular, some authors have observed that these agreements should rather be seen as forms of risk-shifting, because the price can only be adjusted downward (Towse and Garrison 2010). They have also been interpreted as warranties provided by the firm on the true effectiveness of the new product (Cook et al. 2008). Cook et al. conclude that risk-sharing agreements may reduce the attractiveness for the firm to invest in the development of new products, and lead to under-supply of innovation for consumers. Levaggi et al. (2013) use a dynamic stochastic model to compare the impacts of regulating through cost-effectiveness thresholds versus risk-sharing agreements on four policy objectives: making effective products quickly available to patients; ensuring that innovations adopted are good value for money; providing incentives to R&D investment by the industry; reducing the risk of true effectiveness of the new drug in clinical use falling below the level reported at the time of adoption. While risk-sharing agreements, by their very nature, cope better with the last objective, it has been shown that either scheme can do better with respect to the other policy goals, depending on the parameters that define how tight regulation is under the two schemes. Risk-sharing agreements can grant earlier access to innovation for patients without weakening the incentive to invest in R&D if regulators agree to reimburse new products whose cost-effectiveness ratio is above the threshold value of the cost-effectiveness ratio they set for reimbursement.

To summarize, although some recent contributions in the literature have extended the analysis to long-term impacts of pharmaceutical regulation on R&D investments, the area still looks under-explored with respect to its relevance. One reason for this might also be the challenges set by empirical analysis of the link between regulation and R&D investments. Therefore, better data availability would be another important step to take with a view to improve understanding of the mechanisms at work in this area.

21.7 Conclusions

In the recent past several attempts have been made to study the relationship between pricing policies and innovation. The empirical literature seems to conclude that stricter regulatory rules (such as the use of internal reference prices) may have an adverse impact on innovation. From a theoretical point of view the literature on this subject is rather scant and while the general link between price and incentive to innovation is well understood (a higher price will lead to greater innovation), the effects that specific regulatory setting have on innovation are less clear. Our contribution has reviewed and interpreted some of the most recent regulatory schemes in the light of their effects on the listing process, price setting and incentives to R&D. One of the principal features of the market for new drugs that is often overlooked is that having a drug approved is only the first step towards having a market. Only after third payers agree to reimburse, then only the drug will be profitable. In this respect, it should be noted that the listing process has changed considerably in the recent past and it has become more transparent. In this new environment, uncertainty on the listing process and the price is considerably reduced. This is per se a positive factor which may increase expected profits. The model proposed in this paper shows that firms react to changes in the regulation system; from an empirical point of view it should however be noted that due to the presence of sunk investment costs and to the lengthy process of research and development of new drugs, the impact is only visible after a number of years. For this reason any change involving drug pricing policies should be carefully studied before being enforced.

References

Adamski J, Godman B, Ofierska-Sujkowska G, Osinska B, Herholz H, Wendykowska K, Laius O, Jan S, Sermet C, Zara C, Kalaba M, Gustafsson R, Garuoliene K, Haycox A, Garattini S, Gustafsson L (2010) Risk sharing arrangements for pharmaceuticals: potential considerations and recommendations for European payers. BMC Health Serv Res 10(1):153, ISSN 1472-6963. doi:10.1186/1472-6963-10-153. http://www.biomedcentral.com/1472-6963/10/153

Appleby J, Devlin N, Parkin D, Buxton M, Chalkidou K (2009) Searching for cost effectiveness thresholds in the NHS. Health Policy 91(3):239–245, ISSN 0168-8510. doi:http://dx.doi.org/10.1016/j.healthpol.2008.12.010. http://www.sciencedirect.com/science/article/pii/S0168851008002911

Barigozzi F, Levaggi R (2008) Emotions in physician agency. Health Policy 88(1):1–14

Barros PP (2011) The simple economics of risk sharing agreements between the NHS and the pharmaceutical industry. Health Econ 20(4):461–470

Barros PP, Levaggi R (2011) Searching for approval: risk sharing as price discount? Mimeo

Capri S, Levaggi R (2007) International price regulations in the pharmaceutical sector: a common model to sharing cost and benefits. J Pharmaceut Finance Econ Pol 15(2):21–40

Carone G, Schwierz C, Xavier A (2012) Cost-containment policies in public pharmaceutical spending in the EU. Technical report, European Commission-Economic and Financial Affairs

Cook J, Vernon J, Mannin R (2008) Pharmaceutical risk-sharing agreements. Pharmacoeconomics 26:551–556. doi:10.2165/00019053-200826070-00002

Danzon PM, Chao L-W (2000) Does regulation drive out competition in pharmaceutical markets? J Law Econ 43(2):311–357

Danzon P, Towse A, Mestre-Ferrandiz J (2013) Value-based differential pricing: efficient prices for drugs in a global context. Health Econ. doi:10.1002/hec.3021

De Pouvourville G (2006) Risk-sharing agreements for innovative drugs. Eur J Health Econ 7:155–157, ISSN 1618-7598. http://dx.doi.org/10.1007/s10198-006-0386-6.10.1007/s10198-006-0386-6

Dickson M, Redwood H (1998) Pharmaceutical reference prices: how do they work in practice? Pharmacoeconomics 14(5):471–479, http://www.ingentaconnect.com/content/adis/pec/1998/00000014/00000005/art00002

DiMasi JA, Hansen RW, Grabowski HG (2003) The price of innovation: new estimates of drug development costs. J Health Econ 22(2):151–185, http://ideas.repec.org/a/eee/jhecon/v22y2003i2p151-185.html

Dulleck U, Kerschbamer R (2006) On doctors, mechanics, and computer specialists: the economics of credence goods. J Econ Lit 44(1):5–42

Filson D (2012) A Markov-perfect equilibrium model of the impacts of price controls on the performance of the pharmaceutical industry. RAND J Econ 43(1):110–138

Gravelle HSE (1998) Ex post value reimbursement for pharmaceuticals. Med Decis Making 18(2): S27–S38. doi:10.1177/0272989X9801800206. http://mdm.sagepub.com/content/18/2/S27.abstract

Griffin SC, Claxton KP, Palmer SJ, Sculpher MJ (2011) Dangerous omissions: the consequences of ignoring decision uncertainty. Health Econ 20(2):212–224, ISSN 1099-1050. doi:10.1002/hec.1586

Jena AB, Philipson T (2008) Cost-effectiveness analysis and innovation. J Health Econ 27 (5):1224–1236

Jena A, Philipson T (2009) Endogenous cost-effectiveness analysis in health care technology adoption. Working paper 15032, National Bureau of Economic Research, June 2009

Lakdawalla D, Sood N (2009) Innovation and the welfare effects of public drug insurance. J Public Econ 93(3–4):541–548

Levaggi R (2014) Pricing schemes for new drugs: a welfare analysis. Soc Sci Med 102:69–73, ISSN 0277-9536. doi:http://dx.doi.org/10.1016/j.socscimed.2013.11.048. http://www.sciencedirect.com/science/article/pii/S0277953613006606

Levaggi R, Moretto M, Pertile P (2013) The dynamics of pharmaceutical regulation and R&D investments. Working papers 13/2013, Department of Economics, University of Verona, Aug 2013. http://ideas.repec.org/p/ver/wpaper/13-2013.html

Loeb M, Magat WA (1979) A decentralized method for utility regulation. J Law Econ 22(2):399–404, ISSN 00222186. http://www.jstor.org/stable/725125

NICE (2007) Final appraisal determination bortezomib monotherapy for relapsed multiple myeloma. Accessed 3 Mar 2010

OECD (2011) Health at a glance 2011: OECD indicators. Technical report, OECD

OECD (2013) Health at a glance 2013: OECD indicators. OECD. http://dx.doi.org/10.1787/health_glance-2013-en

Pammolli F, Magazzini L, Riccaboni M (2011) The productivity crisis in pharmaceutical R&D. Nat Rev Drug Discov 10(6):428–438, ISSN 1474–1776

Panos K, Taylor D, Manning J, Carr M (2010) Implementing value-based pricing for pharmaceuticals in the UK. http://www.2020Health.org

PhRMA (2011) Annual report 2011. Technical report, PhRMA. http://www.phrma.org/sites/default/files/159/phrma_2011_annual_report.pdf

Towse A, Garrison L (2010) Can't get no satisfaction? Will pay for performance help? Toward an economic framework for understanding performance-based risk sharing agreements for innovative medical products. Pharmacoeconomics 28:93–102. doi:10.2165/11314080-000000000-00000

Zaric GS, O'Brien BJ (2005) Analysis of a pharmaceutical risk sharing agreement based on the purchaser's total budget. Health Econ 14(8):793–803, ISSN 1099-1050. doi:10.1002/hec.976. http://dx.doi.org/10.1002/hec.976

Zweifel P, Breyer F, Kifmann M (2009) Health economics, 2nd edn. Springer, Berlin. ISBN 978-3-540-27804-7

Chapter 22
The Pharmaceutical Policy Environment and Pharmaceutical Pricing Policies

Christine Y. Lu

Abstract Pharmaceutical pricing policies are an important component of the pharmaceutical policy environment given their role in the financial sustainability of the health system. This chapter outlines several key domains of the pharmaceutical policy environment within which pharmaceutical pricing policies exist. Every country has its unique mix of laws, regulations, policies, management strategies and support systems for pharmaceutical products. These guide provisions relating to the manufacturing, importing, marketing, labeling, distribution, prescribing, dispensing, and pricing of pharmaceutical products.

22.1 Introduction

When medicines are available, affordable, safe, efficacious, and appropriately used, they can save lives, prevent and cure diseases, reduce debilitation from chronic diseases, enhance quality of life for patients and caretakers, increase independence, and reduce the overall costs of treatment (World Health Organization 2004). Access to essential medicines is part of the fundamental right to health (World Health Organization 2011). Fundamental human rights guide public policies and national judicial systems (World Health Organization 2011), including those pertaining to the pharmaceutical sector.

Pharmaceutical policy making serves multiple, often competing, objectives that must be balanced with one another to arrive at the policy mix that best reflects the priorities of each country (Schweitzer 1997). Many countries face increasing pharmaceutical expenditure growth, which has exceeded both economic growth and growth in the health sector as a whole (World Health Organization 2011; Organisation for Economic Cooperation and Development 2008). Given this, there is often a tension between the objective of ensuring affordable access to effective medicines and strong pressures for cost-containment. A major challenge

C.Y. Lu (✉)
Department of Population Medicine, Harvard Medical School and Harvard Pilgrim Health Care Institute, 133 Brookline Avenue, 6th Floor, Boston, MA 02215, USA
e-mail: christine_lu@harvardpilgrim.org

Z.-U.-D. Babar (ed.), *Pharmaceutical Prices in the 21st Century*,
DOI 10.1007/978-3-319-12169-7_22

in the pharmaceutical policy environment is the inherent trade-off between *static efficiency* (that is, consumer welfare is maximized by getting the most health value from today's expenditures) and *dynamic efficiency* (that is, the R&D incentives serve to generate innovative alternatives in the future) (Schweitzer 1997; Organisation for Economic Cooperation and Development 2008). Adding to the complexity is the fact that pharmaceutical policies in one country stand to affect not only innovation, but also the prices and availability of medicines in other countries (Organisation for Economic Cooperation and Development 2008). Inevitably, pharmaceutical policy making is, to a certain degree, influenced by political and economic environment within a particular country as well as political and economic relations between countries. Considering the impact of policies in terms of only one objective would therefore be unsatisfactory and biased.

Globally, over 100 countries have established a national medicines policy (World Health Organization 2011; Hoebert et al. 2013). The overarching goal of a national medicines policy is to promote equity (fairness in access), efficiency (delivery of the maximum level of service given a certain level of resources), and sustainability (the ability to provide continued benefits without depending upon external support) of the pharmaceutical system (World Health Organization 2001). The national medicines policy is a political commitment to good governance practices, demonstrating how the government will ensure that efficacious and safe medicines of good quality are affordable, accessible and rationally used. It also aims to ensure transparency and accountability (World Health Organization 2001; Management Sciences for Health 2012). Transparency is essential to minimize the influence of political pressures and personal favors in the decision-making process and to make the government accountable for its actions. Transparency also adds credibility and authority to communications and actions from the government. The national medicines policy also provides a framework for coordinating communication and activities of all parties involved: the government, manufacturers, importers, distributors, health professionals, and consumers (World Health Organization 2001; Management Sciences for Health 2012).

Each country has a unique mix of laws, regulations, policies, management strategies and support systems pertaining to pharmaceutical products (World Health Organization 2011; Management Sciences for Health 2012). These guide provisions relating to the manufacturing, importing, marketing, labeling (including language), distribution, prescribing, dispensing, and pricing of pharmaceutical products, as well as the licensing, inspection, and control of personnel and facilities. Laws, regulations, and policies can have important impact on the availability of products in the market, and the diffusion and volume of use in practice (World Health Organization 2011; Management Sciences for Health 2012). Below discusses several key domains of the pharmaceutical policy environment within which pharmaceutical pricing policies exist.

22.2 Intellectual Property Laws

Intellectual property laws have important influence on the availability and affordability of medicines in an era of increasingly globalized trade (Management Sciences for Health 2012; Smith et al. 2009). The Agreement on Trade-Related Aspects of Intellectual Property Rights (TRIPS) is a set of global trade rules to monitor and enforce the protection of intellectual property rights among member countries of the World Trade Organization (Management Sciences for Health 2012; Smith et al. 2009).

Intellectual property rights guarantee the inventor both a period of market exclusivity and a monopoly price through patent rights, which aim to foster innovation that benefits the society (Management Sciences for Health 2012; Smith et al. 2009). These allow inventors the rights to exclude unauthorized production and sale of a product for a defined period of time. Intellectual property rights also play a very influential role in manufacturers' strategic decisions, including applications for marketing and for coverage and reimbursement under insurance programs. Market exclusivity rights provided by a patent allow high prices, which generate profits that fund the R&D necessary to bring new pharmaceutical products to the market (Smith et al. 2009). Because of higher prices during the patent term, patent rights and the market exclusivity period have important impacts on pharmaceutical expenditures (Management Sciences for Health 2012; Smith et al. 2009). When a patent expires, generic products enter the market and force prices down through competition.

22.3 Market Authorization

The use of ineffective, poor-quality, or harmful medicines can have negative consequences such as therapeutic failure, exacerbation of disease, resistance to medicines, and even death. To protect public health, most governments have established laws and regulations and national regulatory authorities to ensure that the manufacture, trade, and use of medicines are regulated appropriately and that the public has access to accurate information on medicines. This includes assessment of individual pharmaceutical products for quality, safety, and efficacy before they are registered (World Health Organization 2011; Organisation for Economic Cooperation and Development 2008; Management Sciences for Health 2012).

Registration (also known as licensing or marketing authorization) is the mandatory approval by a government agency before a drug can be sold, offered for sale, distributed or possessed for the purposes of sales, distribution or use. These policies may affect the registration of new products, deregistration, restrictions on registered drugs (e.g., clinical indication), and changes in classification (e.g., over-the-counter, behind-the-counter, prescription drugs) (World Health Organization 2011; Organisation for Economic Cooperation and Development 2008; Management Sciences for Health 2012).

Marketing authorization policies affect the timeliness of availability of new pharmaceutical products. Such policies are important determinants of manufacturers' strategic decisions with respect to the national market, and of national pharmaceutical expenditures. The time from application for market authorization to approval varies between countries. Countries invest in market authorization reviews differently, which result in differences in the thoroughness and the length of time for reviews. These all influence how soon new products would be launched on the market. A well-designed fast-track procedure can ensure priority medicines are reviewed in a timely fashion. In European Union countries, market access for some original drugs is less dependent on the capacity of the national authority through enhanced collective activity. However, because many generic drugs are produced for local markets, they heavily rely on prompt decisions regarding bioequivalence and substitutability from national regulatory authorities (World Health Organization 2011; Organisation for Economic Cooperation and Development 2008; Management Sciences for Health 2012).

22.4 Pharmaceutical Financing Strategies

Pharmaceutical financing is crucial to ensure access to essential medicines for all segments of the population. Financial sustainability of a health system is achieved only when resources are in balance with costs and that resources are sufficient to support a basic quality of care for a given level of demand for health care services. When demand surpasses available resources, stakeholders may need to accept a decline in quality of care, or policies must be implemented to improve efficiency, control demand, and/or increase financial resources. Pharmaceutical financing should focus on ways to improve efficiency and to ensure that demand is appropriate rather than emphasize methods to increase financial resources (Management Sciences for Health 2012; World Health Organization 2012).

Because of the scarcity of resources, payers, sellers, and consumers make choices about how resources will be used to maximize efficiency; these choices mean that using a resource in one way makes it no longer available for alternative uses. Health care demand may be virtually unlimited. Health systems often control demand through combinations of several approaches: increase cost to the patient, impose rationing or other administrative controls, provide alternatives, increase waiting time, decrease quality of services, and provide education (Management Sciences for Health 2012; World Health Organization 2012).

Pharmaceutical financing is not different from health financing. Funding options for pharmaceuticals in general include: public sources (local and national government revenues), user fees (e.g., direct payment by patients, that is, fee for service), health insurance (social insurance, private insurance), voluntary financing (e.g., employer provided health care), donor financing (e.g., bilateral and multilateral grants), and development loans (Management Sciences for Health 2012).

22.5 Pharmaceutical Pricing Policies

The interaction of manufacturers (supply) and consumers (demand) determines the price of goods and services, including pharmaceutical products, and how responsive (elastic) both supply and demand are to changes in price (Organisation for Economic Cooperation and Development 2008; Management Sciences for Health 2012). For instance, buyers will be less sensitive to higher prices for medicines that are considered essential and that the buyer must obtain, whereas medicines that are not considered essential will likely have more elastic prices. The pharmaceutical market is complex. Beyond manufacturers and consumers, there are often third party intermediaries such as insurers who act on behalf of consumers to obtain better prices. Also, medicines have certain traits that set them apart from other consumer products; for example, consumers need expert advice from prescribers to make appropriate choices between using and not using medicines and which product to use.

Pharmaceutical pricing policies are an important component of the pharmaceutical policy environment given their role in the financial sustainability of the health system. They are one of the tools by which policy makers affect the price, volume and mix of products used in a country. These are policies that determine the price that is paid for drugs such as price control and negotiations, rebates, generic substitution policies, reference pricing, international benchmarking, volume-based pricing, procurement policies, and pharmacoeconomic analyses (Organisation for Economic Cooperation and Development 2008; Management Sciences for Health 2012; Aaserud et al. 2006). Governments can intervene drug prices by regulating taxes and the different markups along the pharmaceutical supply chain (e.g., manufacturer price, wholesale price, retail price, dispensed price), which can substantially affect the costs to consumers (World Health Organization 2011; Organisation for Economic Cooperation and Development 2008; Management Sciences for Health 2012).

22.6 Coverage Schemes

Almost all countries have established mechanisms to subsidize the purchase of pharmaceuticals for some or all of their populations. The overall goal is to enable affordable access to pharmaceuticals to allow consumption by reducing out-of-pocket costs paid by the consumer (Organisation for Economic Cooperation and Development 2008; Management Sciences for Health 2012).

Coverage schemes by insurers and public institutions play an important role in influencing pharmaceutical expenditure, price levels and consumption patterns (World Health Organization 2011; Organisation for Economic Cooperation and Development 2008; Management Sciences for Health 2012). Many countries have a single, universal scheme that serves as the primary form of prescription drug coverage for the country's residents. In some of these countries, a share of the population purchases private health insurance that top up existing coverage by subsidizing pharmaceuticals not included in the basic coverage scheme and covering some or all of the cost-sharing that would otherwise be paid out-of-pocket (e.g., Australia) (Organisation for Economic Cooperation and Development 2008). Instead of a single, universal scheme, some countries have multiple forms of basic prescription drug coverage; for example, the United States and Canada, both of which have competing private health insurance plans and publicly financed coverage for eligible population groups (Organisation for Economic Cooperation and Development 2008). There is substantial variation between countries in the extent to which private health insurance finances medicines.

Following are some key differences between coverage schemes in countries (World Health Organization 2011; Organisation for Economic Cooperation and Development 2008; Management Sciences for Health 2012).

- *The market power of payers through coverage schemes*. Countries may choose to adopt a single, universal scheme for pharmaceutical coverage that maximizes equity and the prospects for cost control, or a pluralistic system of pharmaceutical coverage that maximizes consumer choice. This distinction is important because it influences the market power of payers. A single payer have greater power to obtain lower prices from pharmaceutical sellers, as compared to a system in which the national market features multiple, independent schemes. However, competing insurers may be able to be more or less active in their purchasing to meet the demands of their members.
- *The scope of drug coverage*. Countries differ in the extent to which they provide coverage for pharmaceuticals available on the market. The most comprehensive schemes ("open formulary") cover any drug approved for marketing in the country when it is prescribed by an authorized practitioner (Organisation for Economic Cooperation and Development 2008; Management Sciences for Health 2012). Sometimes, certain categories of products will be explicitly excluded. A variant of this approach is the "negative list" that indicates which products are not covered. Most third-party payers commonly define a list ("positive-list" or formulary) of pharmaceuticals that are subsidized in part or in full (Organisation for Economic Cooperation and Development 2008; Management Sciences for Health 2012). Many have established processes for health technology assessment to appraise and make decisions on which drugs are to be covered. In some cases, virtually all medicines that are proposed for coverage are subsidized once a decision on price has been made. In other cases, payers formally select products based on criteria such as effectiveness and cost-effectiveness ('value-for-money') and evaluate whether expected additional health benefits of a new drug justify its additional cost compared to therapies already covered. For most countries, the scope of coverage usually differs for medicines dispensed in hospitals and medicines prescribed by a physician in the outpatient setting (Organisation for Economic Cooperation and Development 2008; Management Sciences for Health 2012).

- *Restrictions on reimbursed drugs*. There are often administrative controls on the prescribing of reimbursed drugs to promote rational use of medicines and/or to control costs (Green et al. 2010). Prior authorization requirements are commonly used, for example, based on medical specialty, diagnostic requirements, and prior use of alternative treatments. Reimbursements for patients are reduced or denied if the restrictions are not followed.
- *Cost-sharing mechanisms*. Many coverage schemes have established the level of cost-sharing for pharmaceuticals, through which patients are required to contribute to the costs of the medicines they use. Cost-sharing requirements are commonly used to moderate demand for services (by increasing consumer price sensitivity) and shift the burden of financing to patients. Cost-sharing may take the form of fixed or variable copayment amounts, co-insurance rates, or fixed user charges (Organisation for Economic Cooperation and Development 2008; Management Sciences for Health 2012; Austvoll-Dahlgren et al. 2008). Exemptions from cost-sharing requirements are sometimes accorded to vulnerable population groups, particularly for beneficiaries of social assistance, disabled people and those with serious and/or chronic diseases (Organisation for Economic Cooperation and Development 2008; Management Sciences for Health 2012).
- *Financial protection against high costs*. Schemes also differ in the extent to which they offer protection against the risk of excessive out-of-pocket expenditure associated with the treatment of catastrophic or chronic illnesses through a defined patient expenditure limit. Differences between schemes in levels of cost-sharing and financial protection policies influence the total out-of-pocket spending and whether and how out-of-pocket expenditures may be limited (World Health Organization 2011; Organisation for Economic Cooperation and Development 2008; Management Sciences for Health 2012).

22.7 Policies Targeting Medication Use

Medicines can endanger health and waste resources when used incorrectly or unnecessarily (World Health Organization 2011). Rational use of medicines, as defined by the World Health Organization, requires that "patients receive medications appropriate to their clinical needs, in doses that meet their own individual requirements, for an adequate period of time, and at the lowest cost to them and their community" (World Health Organization 2012). To optimize use of medicines and quality of care and to control costs, governments and insurers may seek to influence the volume and mix of pharmaceuticals used. Policies may target physicians, pharmacists, and/or patients (Lu et al. 2008).

Many policies have been implemented to influence prescribing behavior in order to improve care, such as clinical practice guidelines, prescriber feedback, quality improvement initiatives, restrictions on reimbursement, and guidelines on education and promotional activities. There are also policies that influence prescribing by means of financial incentives and disincentives such as pay-for-performance programs (Organisation for Economic Cooperation and Development 2008; Green et al. 2010; Lu et al. 2008; Sturm et al. 2007).

Countries have attempted to increase the use of generic drugs through generic dispensing policies that allow pharmacists to substitute a generic drug for the prescribed medicine, when the patient agrees and the physician does not object. Varying by countries, laws and policies also regulate who can sell medicines, and regulate ownership, location and numbers of pharmacies (Organisation for Economic Cooperation and Development 2008; Management Sciences for Health 2012; Aaserud et al. 2006).

The most common approach targeting patients is policies that regulate out-of-pocket payments for medicines to influence patient demand. These include fixed or relative copayments, prescription caps, and deductibles (Austvoll-Dahlgren et al. 2008). Many schemes use differential copayments to steer use towards products that are less costly for the payer. Prohibition of direct-to-consumer advertising by law in some countries also influences consumer demand for medicines. Provision of drug information or patient education may also be used to influence medication use (Organisation for Economic Cooperation and Development 2008; Management Sciences for Health 2012).

The pharmaceutical policy environment is inherently complex. This is no surprise given its multiple, often competing, objectives that must be carefully balanced with one another as well as the local and external political and economic influences. This chapter does not attempt to summarize them all here, nor cite a complete list. It is important to recognize that pharmaceutical pricing policies sit within multiple domains of the pharmaceutical policy environment and their contribution to the pharmaceutical sector.

References

Aaserud M, Dahlgren AT, Kosters JP, Oxman AD, Ramsay C, Sturm H (2006) Pharmaceutical policies: effects of reference pricing, other pricing, and purchasing policies. Cochrane Database Syst Rev 2, CD005979

Austvoll-Dahlgren A, Aaserud M, Vist G et al (2008) Pharmaceutical policies: effects of cap and co-payment on rational drug use. Cochrane Database Syst Rev 1, CD007017

Green CJ, Maclure M, Fortin PM, Ramsay CR, Aaserud M, Bardal S (2010) Pharmaceutical policies: effects of restrictions on reimbursement. Cochrane Database Syst Rev 8, CD008654

Hoebert JM, van Dijk L, Mantel-Teeuwisse AK, Leufkens HG, Laing RO (2013) National medicines policies—a review of the evolution and development processes. J Pharm Policy Pract 6:5

Lu CY, Ross-Degnan D, Soumerai SB, Pearson SA (2008) Interventions designed to improve the quality and efficiency of medication use in managed care: a critical review of the literature—2001–2007. BMC Health Serv Res 8:75

Management Sciences for Health (2012) MDS-3: managing access to medicines and health technologies. Management Sciences for Health, Arlington

Organisation for Economic Cooperation and Development (2008) Pharmaceutical pricing policies in a global market. Organisation for Economic Cooperation and Development, Paris
Schweitzer S (1997) Pharmaceutical economics and policy. Oxford University Press, New York
Smith RD, Correa C, Oh C (2009) Trade, TRIPS, and pharmaceuticals. Lancet 373(9664):684–691
Sturm H, Austvoll-Dahlgren A, Aaserud M et al (2007) Pharmaceutical policies: effects of financial incentives for prescribers. Cochrane Database Syst Rev 3, CD006731
World Health Organization (2001) How to develop and implement a national drug policy, 2nd edn. WHO, Geneva
World Health Organization (2004) WHO policy perspectives on medicines: equitable access to essential medicines: a framework for collective action. WHO, Geneva
World Health Organization (2011) The world medicines situation, 3rd edn. WHO, Geneva
World Health Organization (2012) The pursuit of responsible use of medicines: sharing and learning from country experiences. WHO, Geneva

Printed by Printforce, the Netherlands